D1557902

Polo in Britain

Polo in Britain

A History

HORACE A. LAFFAYE

Foreword by
NICHOLAS J.A. COLQUHOUN-DENVERS

McFarland & Company, Inc., Publishers
Jefferson, North Carolina, and London

Except as noted, all the illustrations are courtesy of and with permission by the National Museum of Polo and Hall of Fame, Lake Worth, Florida.

LIBRARY OF CONGRESS CATALOGUING-IN-PUBLICATION DATA

Laffaye, Horace A., 1935–
Polo in Britain : a history / Horace A. Laffaye ;
foreword by Nicholas J.A. Colquhoun-Denvers.
p.   cm.
Includes bibliographical references and index.

ISBN 978-0-7864-6511-8
illustrated case binding : 50# and 70# acid free papers ∞

1. Polo—Great Britain—History.   I. Title.
GV1011.6.G7L34 2012   796.35'30941—dc23   2012008867

BRITISH LIBRARY CATALOGUING DATA ARE AVAILABLE

Front cover image: HM Queen Elizabeth II presenting to Henry Brett
the prize for Best Playing Pony in the 2004 Coronation Cup at Guards
Polo Club in Windsor Park (photograph by Alice Gipps, courtesy of Mrs. Hugh Brett);
British flag © 2012 Shutterstock

Manufactured in the United States of America

McFarland & Company, Inc., Publishers
Box 611, Jefferson, North Carolina 28640
www.mcfarlandpub.com

Table of Contents

Acknowledgments   vii

Foreword by Nicholas J. A. Colquhoun-Denvers   1

Preface   3

Part I. Pioneering Soldiers, 1860–1914   5

  1. The Beginning of Polo in Britain   7

  2. The Expansion of Provincial Polo   15

  3. Testing the Waters: The Early Internationals   32

  4. Initial Tournaments: The Hurlingham Champion Cup,
     the Inter-Regimental Tournament and the County Cup   39

  5. The Great Clubs and Polo Clubs Near London   47

  6. Polo in Ireland   59

  7. Spreading the Gospel Round the World   64

  8. The Climb to the Summit: The Westchester Cup   81

    Interlude I: 1914–1918   93

Part II. Gifted Amateurs, 1919–1939   95

  9. A Time for Recovery   97

10. The Olympic Games   107

11. Struggles for the Internationals   116

12. The Lean Years of the Depression   126

13. British Polo Sculptors and Painters   145

    Interlude II: 1939–1945   156

        **Between pages 156 and 157 are 8 color plates
        containing 20 photographs**

Part III. Gentlemen and Players, 1947–1985   157

14. Lord Cowdray Saves the Day for England   159

15. The Royal Family Lends a Hand   180

16. Colonials and Foreigners Change the Landscape   185

17. Renewal of the Coronation Cup   190

18. The Game Grows Unabated   194

19. Polo Tours Overseas   204

Part IV. Patrons and Professionals, 1986–2011   211

20. The Growth of the Professional Player   213

21. Women in Polo   225

22. An Uneasy Alliance: HPA and FIP   232

23. Literature of British Polo   241

24. Polo in Britain in the Twenty-First Century   250

25. Some Current Issues in British Polo   274

Appendix 1: Letter to The Field, *20 March 1869*   285

Appendix 2: Polo Player Recipients of the Victoria Cross   287

Appendix 3: Results of Major Championships   289

Chapter Notes   323

Bibliography   337

Index   341

Acknowledgments

The writer of a book that encompasses a century and a half of polo on the British Isles gathers information from so many sources and individuals that it is hard to recognize everyone who assisted, sometimes perhaps unwittingly. To all the unthanked, allow me to express my gratitude and my apologies.

A word of thanks to Nigel à Brassard, Esq., who read part of the manuscript and made countless comments and suggestions of great help, including solving the puzzle of the Coronation Cup in the year 1951. Nigel also put me in touch with Messrs. Philip Magor and Nigel Warr, who in turn provided information about contemporary polo in England.

Mr. Dennis J. Amato allowed me to research his extensive private library and offered information about the County Cup. I am particularly indebted to Dennis for bringing to my attention several obscure points of polo history and the publication of rare polo magazines.

Mr. Chris Ashton, the Australian journalist and author of *Geebung: The History of Polo in Australia*, regaled me with his recollections of the Oxford-Cambridge fixture, when he marked Prince Charles and scored the winning goal in extra time.

The list of the Cowdray Park Challenge Cup winners was supplied by Ms. Cheryl Bickett.

I wish to thank Mr. Thomas J. Biddle, Sr., the chairman of the U.S. Polo Association, for communicating his views on the current differences in the rules of the game.

Mrs. Hugh Brett, founder and erstwhile editor of *Polo Times*, saw fit to publish several of my writings on English polo. Hugh and Margie Brett were marvelous hosts during our visit to East End Farm in Oxfordshire.

Ms. Lisa Campbell, head librarian at the National Sporting Library, provided ample support during my stay in Middleburg as a John Daniels Fellow.

Dr. Alejandro Castro Almeyra, a friend since our long-ago schoolboy days, offered information on early British players in Argentina.

Through many years, Roger Chatterton-Newman, author of *Polo at Cowdray* and editor of *PQ International*, has been a great source of information on polo in the British Isles.

I am most grateful to Nicholas Colquhoun-Denvers, Esq., chairman of the Hurlingham Polo Association, for taking the time and trouble in writing such a thoughtful foreword. Nicholas also provided information about Ham Polo Club and the Roehampton Cup. My wife and I had the opportunity of watching him play polo at Ham in 1998; regrettably, eleven years went by before we met in Florida, when he was the leader of the English delegation for the Westchester Cup challenge.

J.W.M. Crisp, Esq., allowed me to browse through the holdings of the Hurlingham

Polo Association's book collection when he was the HPA's secretary. "Buff" Crisp, as he is known in polo circles, and his wife, Liza, were most gracious hosts during our visits to Winterlake.

Brigadier Arthur Douglas-Nugent, a former officer in that famous polo regiment the 17th/21st Lancers, provided data on the winners of the Inter-Regimental Tournament, reviewed parts of the manuscript and suggested several changes and additions. His column "Umpire's Corner" in *Polo Times* is a reflection of his deep understanding of important issues in contemporary polo and a font of knowledge and common sense.

Mr. George DuPont, director of the Polo Museum and Hall of Fame in Lake Worth, Florida, kindly permitted me the free run of the museum's extensive library and videotape holdings.

New information provided by Janice Farrell and Kelvin Johnson allowed the entire results of the Junior County Cup to be included in the appendix.

Michael Hanna shared his recollections of polo during my stay in the West Country, when my wife and I became frequent visitors to Cirencester Park.

Mrs. Margaret Hickey once more provided her editorial skills in perfecting this book. Marge started editing my scientific papers many years ago, and upon my retirement from teaching and surgical practice, she made an effortless transition to polo matters.

Julian Hipwood, Esq., who is a mine of information about contemporary polo, talked at length about his extraordinary career and the status of polo in England.

Mrs. Milly Hodges, née Scott, at the Hurlingham Polo Association, provided photographs and results of the Inter-Regimental Tournament and the Junior County Cup.

Edward Horswell, Esq., spent considerable time educating me about sporting art, polo bronzes in particular.

Eduardo Huergo, the president of the Federation of International Polo, shared his thoughts on the future of the game and the federation's position in several critical issues in current international polo.

Mrs. Zoë Innes, née Williams, gave data on the Williams family and polo at Cirencester and Inglesham.

Tony and Jean Lacey offered wonderful hospitality during our visit to Chester, including a tour of Eaton Hall and the Cheshire and Chester polo grounds.

Mrs. Sue Landis, née Hodgson, kindly loaned photographs of women's polo in England.

A word of thanks to Roy Law, Esq., whose gift of an HPA yearbook allowed me to complete that particular book collection.

Mrs. Lucy Lewis at the Hurlingham Polo Association office was a fountain of resources along the course of my research through the years.

Ms. Brenda Lynn, director of development at the Museum of Polo in Florida, provided incalculable help with research, selection and printing of photographs for inclusion in this work.

Philip Magor, Esq., provided data that filled some gaps in the County Cup.

Mrs. Sophie McPherson, née West, at the HPA office, obtained some of the photographs.

Another old friend, David Miles, gave much information about early British players in Argentina, the 1922 polo tour to England and America, and the 1924 Olympic Games in Paris, where his father John Miles was on the gold medal team.

Nigel Miskin was a marvelous guide during our visit to the Hurlingham Club and graciously gave my wife Martha a signed copy of his history of the club.

Thanks to Sir Jeremy and Lady Belinda Morse for their kindness during our London stay and for the gift of her marvelous book, *Calamity and Courage*.

In Buenos Aires, John P. Nelson, Esq., provided additional information on the tour of Media Luna to England and his fortuitous appearance in the Cowdray Park Gold Cup.

Mr. Peter Orthwein, my old teammate at Fairfield County Hunt Club, recounted his recollections of the Plainsmen team tour of England.

A word of thanks to Mr. Stephen Orthwein, chairman of the Museum of Polo and Hall of Fame, for his unswerving commitment to quality publications and support of research at that institution.

Mr. F. Turner Reuter, Jr., the noted sporting art authority and head of the Curatorial Department at the National Sporting Library in Virginia, shared his vast knowledge of that fascinating subject, besides being a wonderful host, together with his wife Dana.

Michael Roberts, the Guards Polo Club's official photographer, provided several photographic prints.

David Rollinson, Esq., our host at the Cheshire Polo Club, gave me new information about post–World War II tournaments in England.

In California, Mr. Charles R. "Bob" Skene reminisced at length about his participation in the 1939 Westchester Cup and the English International team appearance at Palermo ten years later.

My wife Martha and I wish to thank Mrs. Claire Tomlinson for her gracious hospitality at Down Farm and at Cirencester during my sabbatical academic year at the Bristol Royal Infirmary and for the loan of photographs.

I had the pleasure of access to the vast intellect of Marcos Uranga, whose friendship and companionship go back to our school and rugby football days. Marcos shared firsthand information on the founding of the Federation of International Polo, his polo travels around the world and his participation in the English polo season, as well as his assessment of several issues in contemporary polo.

Jack Williams shared his recollections of polo during my stay in Gloucestershire.

Other Windsor-Clive, Esq., provided information on the life and works of the artist Major Edward Longueville, MFH.

Through the years, art historian Mrs. David Wingfield enlightened me with her extensive knowledge of sporting art. No visit to England is complete without sharing a meal with David and Mary Ann.

Paul Withers, Esq., provided new information about his own and his father's polo careers, the participation of the Commonwealth team in Buenos Aires and polo at Cowdray, as well as his views on the game from a top player and umpire's point of view.

Colonel David Woodd allowed me to research data at the Hurlingham Polo Association's library in Little Coxwell.

I wish to thank the helpful staff at the British Library in London, where I consulted page by page available issues of the *Polo Monthly*. The staff went out of their way with help in searching material related to the game.

The librarians at the Pequot Library in Southport, Connecticut; the National Sporting Library in Middleburg, Virginia; and at the Wellington Branch of the Palm Beach County Library System were most helpful in obtaining additional published information for this work. I also wish to thank those institutions and individuals who allowed their works of art to be shown in this book.

Last, but most certainly not least, I wish to record the help given by our children,

Gisèle and Patrick, in several issues mainly related to computer matters and searches for documentation. The unswerving support of my wife, Martha, in all my polo endeavors from my polo-playing days to my current passion for documenting the game's development and historical heritage, has been an indispensable adjunct to my later career as an author.

Foreword by
Nicholas J. A. Colquhoun-Denvers

It was whilst attending the Westchester Cup challenge in Palm Beach 2009 that I first met Horace Laffaye, although his reputation as a polo author and historian long preceded our meeting. Both he and Martha were the most excellent and gracious of hosts and I was privileged to be shown a small part of his impressive collection of polo history that he kept in Florida, and from that time on he has become my oracle on polo history.

It has now been close to a century since anyone has had the temerity to attempt to write a treatise on the history of British polo. Yes, there have been many pictorial portraits of the UK and International polo scene such as Herbert Spencer's *Chakkar* and *A Century of Polo*, as well as many other useful books on the technical aspects of how to play our sport from the most learned of authors such as Lord Mountbatten, Brigadier General Ricketts, General Beauvoir de Lisle, John Board, Hugh Dawnay and Peter Grace, but until now no one has endeavored to update the modern history of polo in Britain and how it relates to polo overseas.

Even in the 1920s and 1930s, which were often referred to as the Golden Age of Polo, most of the books on the sport were merely compilations of essays penned by various authors and gathered together to create a book on the sport. Now at last we have an author whose painstaking and careful research has created a fascinating book to rival James Moray Brown's *Polo* published in the 1890s and the Reverend T.F. Dale's great *Polo at Home and Abroad* first published in 1915.

Horace Laffaye's extraordinary dedication to the history of the sport and his incredible attention to detail is an absolute inspiration. His *Polo Encyclopaedia*, *The Evolution of Polo*, *Profiles in Polo*, *Polo in the United States* and now *Polo in Britain* finally give us an historian that brings us into the twenty-first century. These titles, especially with the inclusion of the fascinating section on British polo sculptors and artists, will firmly establish these books for years to come as the foremost reference works for all who have an interest in the history of the sport.

I would like to commend Horace for his refreshing views in the section entitled "The Rise of Commercialism and Decline of Civility," a shrewd analysis of how the increase in professionalism and the win-at-all-costs attitude has adversely affected our sport. I had the opportunity to discuss this with Rege Ludwig, the renowned American coach, who felt that, with well over 95 percent of the world's players being amateurs, the sport's governing bodies should be concentrating more on "the sport" as opposed to "the Game," that maybe it is time for us to encourage a greater knowledge of horsemanship and certainly better sportsmanship. As Horace so aptly stated,

The concept of sportsmanship goes back a long time; however, it is now under siege by the twin forces of winning at all costs and the lack of graciousness in defeat. Several years ago, Thomas Glynn, a Harvard graduate known as "Mr. Polo" in America, quoted Tommy Hitchcock, a fierce competitor if ever there was one, as saying, "Win as if it is not important, and lose as if you were enjoying it." Those remarks, expressed in the times of the golden era of polo in the United States, sound totally out of date in today's sporting world. It has been suggested that the idea of sportsmanship was inspired by the myths from the age of chivalry, which also included the inspiration for teams' jerseys. Nevertheless, the ideal of sportsmanship is ageless. It was an unwritten law, tacitly understood by all and enforced by the dire prospect of ostracism.

Possibly we are in "King Canute" territory here, but it would gladden the heart to think that those who read Horace's book and really appreciate the rich panoply of British polo history would realize that all could be lost if we fail to address this unfortunate trend. This is a sport that Britain should be truly proud of. Having adopted this ancient sport from Asia, nurtured it, written the rules of the modern game and then exported it to over seventy-seven countries around the world, it has to be one of the great British sporting success stories, and we should take great pride in upholding its traditions.

Finally may I recommend this book to all those who love polo. It is an absolute treasure trove of information, and with it Horace has confidently written himself into the annals of our sport. As is so often the case, the study of the past often provides great service to the future.

Nicholas J. A. Colquhoun-Denvers has served as the chairman of the Hurlingham Polo Association since 2009. The son of a senior Australian diplomat, he learned his polo while an officer in the British Army. Mr. Colquhoun-Denvers is also the chairman of Ham Polo Club, the last surviving polo club in London.

Preface

This book was inspired by a conversation with Nigel à Brassard, who suggested I should write a history of polo in England, since in his opinion it presented a subject of sufficient scope to merit a volume of its own. Nigel cheerfully dismissed my objections when I pointed out that my firsthand knowledge of the game in Britain was limited to my frequent visits as a tourist and one longer stay for postgraduate medical education. For some unfathomable reason, I was asked on several instances to act as referee.

Nevertheless, it is amazing that no attempt dedicated exclusively to a history of polo in Britain has been undertaken since the Reverend Thomas Francis Dale wrote his monumental *Polo at Home and Abroad* in 1915. This handsome book set the bar for future historians extraordinarily high. However, it was written almost one hundred years ago, and the inexorable passage of time leaves space for an account that takes the story up to the present day.

Such a narrative should concentrate on what happened in the field of play but remain mindful that those who play, watch, referee, or administer the game have never existed in a cocoon but are the products of their time and place, acting within a wide sociological environment. At the same time, a work such as this should range widely in space as well as time, departing from the game's well-beaten track to acknowledge many lesser-known practitioners of this ancient game, alongside English international players and Gold Cup winners.

Therefore, in this book I have tried to provide a panorama of polo in Britain from the 1860s to the summer of 2011. The story includes the endeavors of those who were merely enthusiastic as well as those who achieved celebrity status. Thus, this history covers not only well-known players and events but also mentions some of the less famous, yet to me equally fascinating competitions and individuals, all part and parcel of the game of polo in Britain.

No history of any field is error free. But if historical knowledge seems less perfect than other forms of knowledge, it is the result of two human factors: the historian's personal approach to an event and his dependence upon the veracity of the data available to him. To that effect, some passages in the book point out the inconsistencies in the various sources.

Then again, writing a book about polo in Britain from the other shore of the pond is a very personal thing: I have tried to take this magnificent subject with proper seriousness but, as one Oxonian said to another a long time ago, cheerfulness keeps breaking through, in spite of my appreciation of English reserve.

It has been said that the English are not given easily to whimsy, that they are in fact a resolutely practical people. There may be some truth in this, but nonetheless the likes of

Winnie the Pooh and the Cheshire Cat have never been far from the English imagination. To wit, in the literature of the game, Rudyard Kipling's engaging story of *The Maltese Cat*, that jewel of polo fiction, brings up a wonderful sense of humor coupled with a keen observation of the game's nuances and social environment.

Searching out nostalgia and obscure bits of polo lore from long ago and far away has been a marvelous experience. One can only dream what it would have felt like to be in Hounslow Heath when the 9th Lancers and the 10th Hussars went to battle there, when polo was enchantingly naive yet dearly serious; when men were gentlemen but unpampered, and their mounts were true ponies; when spectators were sophisticated but unacquainted with the game, and umpires were of little account, yet respected without question; in two little words, when polo was both heroic and homely. We shall never see the likes of those days again.

Nowadays we have to cope with several serious issues affecting the game of polo. The increased commercialization and the astronomical rise of costs of an already expensive pastime has brought undesirable companions, most notably a decline in sportsmanship and an unhealthy lack of respect toward the umpires. The ruling bodies of the game must take action to stop and then prevent a recurrence of such trends. The survival of polo as the most elegant of games is at stake.

PART I

Pioneering Soldiers, 1860–1914

CHAPTER 1

The Beginning of Polo in Britain

The ancient game of polo might have been started in Ireland sometime between 1861 and 1865. So states the Spanish player from the Real Polo Club de Barcelona Norman James Cinnamond in his book *El Polo*, published in 1929. According to his narrative, Valentine Irwin, a Stonyhurst College graduate and an Indian Civil Service commissioner, had played polo in Manipur.[1] When home on holiday, Irwin introduced polo in county Roscommon. There were many casualties in the course of those early contests, and either due to the size of the horses or an excessive display of *furor Hibernicus*, the new pastime did not prosper.[2] Just recently, polo player Father James O'Mahony, from the All Ireland Polo Club, dryly mentioned to the author that he was not surprised at all by the apparent roughness of the Roscommon players.

Be that as it may, there is both written and oral documentation supporting the Irish connection. In its December 1927 issue, *Stonyhurst Magazine* carries a notice indicating that a polo stick from Tibet and a ball had been presented to the college museum. This gift reminded the author of the article that the game of polo had been introduced to the British Isles by a Stonyhurst alumnus, Valentine Irwin.[3] Norman Cinnamond himself goes on to write that by a happy coincidence his tutor at Stonyhurst was a nephew of Valentine Irwin, Father Francis Joseph Irwin, SJ, who confirmed the story. Cinnamond's conclusion is that polo in Britain was started on the Emerald Isle.[4]

There is more documentation that the game was played in Ireland prior to its appearance in England. In a letter to the *Polo Monthly*, Colonel Henry Russell, Royal Field Artillery, states that in the summer of 1868 there was a game in Limerick between local players and officers of a detachment of 10th Hussars that had been diverted to county Limerick.[5] A pasture in Rathbane Farm, near the city of Limerick, is the traditional venue for this game. The Limerick Polo Club website enthusiastically takes the issue further: "This first game was played by a detachment of the 10th Hussars who were being shipped back from India to England in 1868 and were temporarily stationed in Limerick on their way. They had seen the game being played in India and decided to have a go at it themselves. With local ponies and modified broom handles as mallets they played Rathbane into the history books of polo." The problem with this statement is that the 10th Hussars could not possibly have witnessed polo in India because the regiment had been deployed to Crimea in 1854, while the game was brought to Calcutta only in 1863. The 10th was brought home from Crimea in 1856.[6] Nevertheless, an early game in Rathbane remains part and parcel of polo lore in Ireland. It is quite probable that the game took place; Lionel Dawson mentions the Rathbane clash in his work *Sport in War*.[7]

The 10th Hussars arrived in Dublin from York in April 1863 and in July of the following year were ordered to the south of Ireland. Squadrons were posted in Cahir, Cork and Fermoy. In his detailed history of the regiment, Colonel Robert Liddell mentions sports, mainly fox-hunting, but there is no mention of either Limerick or the game of polo during the regiment's stay in Ireland. The point is that the 10th Hussars were stationed in the vicinity of Rathbane in the mid–1860s. In May 1868, the 10th Hussars returned to England, to be stationed in Brighton and Shorncliff.

All this precedes by years the well-documented game in Gormanstown Strand held in 1870, in which a local county Meath team captained by no other than the redoubtable Edward Hartopp defeated a 9th Lancers team. There is some confusion about the year, because at the time the 9th Lancers were deployed in Ireland.[8]

The well-known polo writer James Moray Brown throws another wrench in the equation in his *Polo*, published in 1891. His citation of "the first regular match ever played in Ireland" indicates that a county Carlow team of Horace Rochfort, Robert Watson, MFH, his son John, Mr. Steuart Duckett and James Butler defeated an 8th Hussars team, with Charles Gould, Edward Green, Charles Gregg, Edward Paley and John Baldock. Unfortunately, Moray Brown does not provide the date on which this game was held.[9] It could have taken place as early as 1869, when Lieutenant Paley transferred to the 8th Hussars from the 3rd Dragoon Guards.[10]

The Aldershot Tussle

There is ample documentation of the first polo endeavor in England. Two main sources are usually referred to when describing what happened in that celebrated afternoon in Aldershot Garrison during the summer of 1869. The primary source is the letter to the editor of *The Field* dated 20 March 1869 and signed N.S.S.[11] The second one is the recollection of Colonel Thomas Astell St. Quintin, at the time a subaltern in the 10th Hussars, who wrote his memoirs some forty years later.[12]

The story has been told many times. The bare facts are that Cornet Edward "Chicken" Hartopp read the letter to the editor of *The Field* and promptly enlisted some of his comrades-in-arms to give a go to the game. Mounted on cavalry chargers, using walking sticks as polo mallets and a cricket ball, armed with only a rudimentary knowledge of the infant rules, they tried to play a game near a parcel of land known as Cesar's Camp.

A somewhat different version is offered by Colonel Robert Lidell in his *Memoirs of the Tenth Royal Hussars*. Colonel Lidell, who eventually would be in command of the regiment, names as the originators Lt. Lord Arthur Valentia, Cornet Edward Hartopp and Lt. George Cheape, the latter from the 11th Hussars and temporarily attached to the 10th, who were joined by Cornet the Hon. Thomas Fitzwilliam, Lt. Edward Watson and other unnamed officers. According to this version, golf clubs and a billiard ball were the utensils. Colonel Liddell writes that the event took place in 1870.[13]

Nevertheless, it quickly became obvious that cavalry horses were totally unsuitable as polo mounts and Captain William Chaine was sent to Ireland, charged with purchasing suitable ponies. Captain Chaine returned with some seventeen mounts; the Hussars went back to Hounslow having completed the summer drills, rolled and marked a ground on the heath, and in due time they challenged the 9th Lancers, quartered in Aldershot after service in Ireland, to a polo match. The challenge was promptly accepted and the first organized polo game in England took place on Hounslow Heath on 28 June 1870.[14]

The 10th Hussars under canvas in 1875. Captain Hartopp, standing fifth from left, towers over his fellow officers. Edward, Prince of Wales, the regiment's colonel, sits fourth from left, next to Colonel Thomas St. Quintin.

One of the participants, Colonel St. Quintin, relates that some kind of lineup resembling football was tried: four forwards in the bully, a pair of halfbacks, one back and a lonely goalkeeper. In spite of their best intentions, quite soon everyone except the goalkeepers were jammed together, pushing into each other in fashion reminiscent of a rugby scrimmage, with very little idea of where the ball was. A contemporary report indicated that the game was more notable for the strength of the language than anything else; nevertheless, everyone seemed to enjoy the experience, and the game of polo took off.

This match attracted considerable attention: HRH the Prince of Wales and Princess Alexandra attended the proceedings, joined by Prince Arthur and the Duke of Cambridge, Queen Victoria's cousin and commander in chief of the British army. Royal patronage was evident from the earliest days of polo in England and remains vibrant into our days.

There is some discrepancy in who the players were. *The Field* states that the 9th Lancers were captains William Clayton, Frank Grissell and Charles Pailaret and lieutenants Lord William Beresford, William Fife, Philip Green, Francis Herbert and Robert St. Leger Moore. In his history of the 10th Hussars, Colonel Lidell indicates that the Hon. Ernest Willoughby played instead of "Tip" Herbert for the red and blue–clad 9th Lancers.

There is also a discrepancy regarding the 10th Hussars team: the news report indicates that captains Arthur Barthorp, Arthur Bulkeley, Uvedale Parry-Okeden and Thomas St. Quintin wore the blue and yellow colors, together with subalterns Edward Hartopp, Thomas Smith-Dorrien, Viscount Arthur Valentia and Henry Woods. Colonel Lidell lists William Chaine, Hon. Thomas Fitzwilliam, Hugh Gough and Edward Watson instead of Barthorp,

"Donjy" Bulkeley, Parry-Okeden and Woods. Furthermore, Lidell writes that the final score was 3–1 in favor of the Hussars, rather than the commonly quoted 3–2.

The protagonists of this seminal game went on to different ways. Lord William Beresford achieved fame and glory when he was awarded the Victoria Cross for heroism in rescuing a wounded sergeant that had been thrown from his horse in front of attacking Zulus. "Bill" Beresford as he was widely known, an outstanding sportsman, was military secretary to three viceroys of India.

Captain Philip Green married the dowager Lady Camden and founded the Sussex County Polo Club in Bayham Abbey, the site of the Marquis Camden, then a minor. The Sussex County polo team went on to achieve utmost dominance in British polo under the guidance of the celebrated Peat brothers.

Francis "Tip" Herbert, a multitalented sportsman, was one of the founders of the Monmouthshire Polo Club, the first provincial polo club, and a winner of Hurlingham's Champion Cup, as well as one of the earliest members of the Ranelagh Club and the Polo Pony Society.

The Irishman Robert St. Leger Moore transferred to the 5th Lancers and was on the team that took the Inter-Regimental Tournament.

Some went to their reward quite young; Capt. William "Dick" Clayton-Clayton was killed on Christmas Day, 1876, while playing polo at Delhi.[15]

On the Hussars' side, Viscount Valentia in due time became chairman of the Hurlingham Club Committee and of the National Polo Pony Society, while Colonel St. Quintin commanded both his original regiment and later the 8th Hussars. He is also credited with being one of the pioneers of polo in Australia. Edward "Chicken" Hartopp drafted the first written rules of the game in England and died at an early age in Dublin, alone but not forgotten.[16]

These two regiments played again in the same year at Woolwich. On this event, the 9th Lancers emerged the victors. Neither the players' names nor the final score is mentioned in the pertinent reference.[17]

Tentative Steps: The Early Matches

Following the qualified success achieved by the encounter at Hounslow Heath, the 9th Lancers and the 10th Hussars joined forces to present a combined effort in order to face a team formed by Heavy Cavalry officers from the Household Cavalry, the Royal Horse Guards (the Blues) and the Life Guards. Richmond Park was the venue, and the Heavies won the game by four goals. Playing for the Heavy Cavalry were Hon. Thomas Fitzwilliam (RHG), Hon. William Wentworth-Fitzwilliam (RHG), Lord Henry Rossmore (LG), Hon. Hugh Boscawen (LG) and Captain Edward Dansey (RHG), while Captain Hon. Ernest Willoughby, Captain William Chaine, Lt. Lord Valentia, Lt. Thomas Smith-Dorrien and Lt. Edward Hartopp represented the Light Cavalry.

The matches were mostly a dribbling contest, with only an occasional long shot at goal. Excerpts from a report of a game at Windsor Park in July 1872 are worth mentioning:

> Their Royal Highnesses the Prince and Princess of Wales went down to Windsor yesterday and witnessed a game at polo between the officers of the Royal Horse Guards and the 9th Lancers. This must have caused some bewilderment as to what polo was, and the explanation that it was hockey on horseback was perhaps hardly explanatory enough, but with that, for the present they must, in common with ourselves, be contented. It is an Indian game, and to Mr. Hartopp, of the 10th Hussars, and Lord Valentia, of the same regiment, belongs the credit of having introduced

it into the country. The gathering was a brilliant one, the Paddington officials being much astonished at the influx of a lot of pretty, well-dressed women, attended by equally well-dressed men, who all wanted to go to Windsor by the two o'clock train. For the Blues gave a luncheon to Royalty, and the pretty women and their attendant swells were bidden to assist thereat. Spital Barracks was the venue, and the important ceremony of feeding well got through, an adjournment took place to the open space in the Home Park, used by the cavalry quartered there as their exercise ground. When the trumpeter gave the signal, and the ball was flung into the centre of the ground, then began an exciting scene. Such dashing charges, such confused *mêlées*, a waving of hockey sticks in the air, a clever struggle between three or four of the combatants for a stroke at the white ball that lay under their ponies' feet, a struggle out of which one horseman emerges triumphantly, his hockey stick, it is true, broken, but with the ball flying before him to the goal, another charge and rally, and dense mingling of ponies' heads and a coming to grief of some human ones, another outcome of the ball, and a goal has been won.[18]

From the above, it is obvious that some three years after its rediscovery in Europe, the game was still known as hockey on horseback, played on small ponies mostly at the walk, with a long hockey stick and any kind of ball, a cricket ball painted white being the most popular. Soon enough it was found that eight players a side were far too many, and a gradual reduction in numbers resulted on one goalkeeper and four players roaming through the ground. Nevertheless, in no small way due to the royal interest as spectators, the game thrived in the metropolitan area and also in the provinces, as well as in Ireland. More about this development anon.

The formation in 1872 of a polo club in Lillie Bridge, simply known as the Royal Polo Club, added momentum to the development of the game. Edward, Prince of Wales, consented to be patron; Earl Spencer was president and Lord Valentia the vice president. The Committee of Selection admitted one hundred members, and the first match was held on 2 June 1873 in front of London's fashionable society. Lords versus Commons were the teams, the weather was beautiful and the field was in good shape. The Commons prevailed by four games (i.e., goals) to two.

Those early players at Lillie Bridge included Sir Bache Cunard, who soon left the game following the death of his brother, Edward, a 10th Hussars officer, while playing polo; another Hussar, "Chicken" Hartopp; the brothers Adrián and Cristóbal de Murrieta; Charles, Sixth Marquess of Londonderry; and the Earl of Mayo.

On 9 June 1874, a six-a-side match was held against the Monmouthshire Club. The Royal Polo Club was represented by Lord Kilmarnock, Hon. Charles Fitzwilliam, the Murrieta brothers, Sir Bache Cunard and Lord Castlereagh. For Monmouthshire, the players were Francis "Tip" Herbert, Sir Charles Wolseley, Captain Burchall Helme, James Mellor, Captain William Wheeley and Captain Ferdinand Hanbury-Williams.[19] The Royal Polo Club won the game by three goals to nil.

However, Lillie Bridge was a rather small ground, about two hundred yards in length, and the shift toward polo at the Hurlingham Club, to the detriment of the pigeon shooters, meant that after a couple of years the new club in Fulham became the epicenter of polo in England.

Polo in Wales

The game was started in the principality by the brothers Reginald and Francis Herbert, who founded Monmouthshire Polo Club, the first provincial club on the British Isles.[20]

Captain "Tip" Herbert resigned his commission in the 9th Lancers and with his older brother started the club with a ground in Clytha, near Usk, the chosen colors being red and white. The opening match was held on 23 September 1872, followed by a dinner at the Angel Hotel in Abergavenny.

Initially there was minimal competition for the simple reason that there were no other provincial clubs. As previously mentioned, in 1874, the Monmouthshire Club sent a team to the Polo Club at Lillie Bridge.

Following this initial defeat, the Monmouthshire quickly became one of the top teams in the United Kingdom, with quality players such as the founding Herbert brothers; Sir Edward Curre; the Hon. Charles Fitzwilliam; Captain Hanbury-Williams; Captain Burchall Helme, 89th Foot; James Mellor; Hugh Owen; Captain William Wheeley; and Sir Charles Wolseley. Sir Edward Curre was a first-class shot, a good fisherman and could hold his own at cricket. Captain "Ferdy" Hanbury-Williams painted a polo match in progress at the ground on the old Llanfoist racecourse, which is one of the earliest polo paintings depicting a game in Britain. Hugh Owen was a starter for the Jockey Club.

With different players in the lineup, the Monmouthshire team achieved success in two Hurlingham Champion Cup tournaments—one in 1878 and another in 1877 shared with the Tyros team — as well as a pair of runner-up finishes against the Royal Horse Guards in the first-ever championship, and against a Hurlingham Club team.

The annual polo tournament at Monmouthshire was played until 1896, but when the Herbert brothers took over the management of the Ranelagh Club in Barnes, their interest in the Monmouthshire Club began to decline and the members started to play at other clubs. By 1897, the Monmouthshire Polo Club had faded into the sunset.

Llantarnam Park was the site of Sir Clifford Cory's private ground at Llantarnam Abbey, near Newport in Wales. It was inaugurated in 1903. Initially a Cistercian monastery, the property was purchased in 1895 by Sir Clifford, a colliery owner, shipping entrepreneur and Liberal politician, who lived there until his death in 1921, when the baronetcy became extinct. After World War II, Llantarnam Abbey once more became a monastic retreat, now under the Sisters of St. Joseph of Annecy.

The Cardiff and County Polo Club was founded in 1905, with a ground at Whitechurch, near Cardiff. The Mackintosh of Mackintosh, at the time master of the Glamorgan Hounds, who owned the polo grounds, sold the parcel of land to the club. Some unusual developments followed with the formation of a lawn tennis club and no less than five hockey teams that played on the polo ground in winter. Players included Sir John Benyon; Hugh Bramwell; Joseph Hillier; Colonel A.P. James, Welch Regiment; Evan Lewis; Captain Lionel Lindsay; Sir Leonard Llewellyn; Captain Godfrey Masters, RHA; and W. Hastings Watson. Archibald Shirey, who played for Oxford University, was Cardiff's captain. The support of the polo-playing soldiers from the Newport Barracks was substantial for the well-being of the club. Then the war came and the grounds were plowed up.

There was also polo in Pembrokeshire, "the little England beyond Wales," so called because following the conquering policy of the Plantagenets, it was settled and protected by a chain of castles. The Tenby Polo Club was established in that seaside town. Not much is known about the club itself and the players. One of the players was the Hon. Colwyn Phillips, Royal Horse Guards, educated at Eton and Sandhurst, who was interested in all outdoor sports and was particularly fond of polo. Another player was David Harrison, Rugby School and Magdalene College, Cambridge, who played twice in the Inter-university matches. Later Mr. Harrison became a prominent gentleman rider who owned many steeplechasers and had large stables at Tenby. David Evans, buyer and seller, trainer and exhibitor of hunters and polo ponies, was a keen player at the Tenby club. Like so many other polo clubs, Tenby did not survive the Great War. Another club was Pembrokeshire, also active in 1910, whose honorary secretary was Captain Charles Hunter, 4th Dragoon Guards.[21] Could it be the same polo club as Tenby?

When the Tredegar Park Polo Club was established in 1920 at Tredegar House in Ruperra, polo interest in South Wales took a new lease on life. Former members of the Cardiff Club readily joined the new venture. Lord Tredegar placed at the club's disposal a ground next to his residence, and officers from the Newport Barracks joined as well. Among the latter were Colonel B.J. Brock, Colonel N.H. Johnston, Captain H.W. Barnard and Lt. H.V. Luckton.

The Game in Scotland

Polo in Scotland started about 1874 when the 7th Hussars, in which HRH the Duke of Connaught was serving with the rank of major, joined the 79th Cameron Highlanders in starting the game in a field near Duddingstone Cottage Park.[22] Those were the days of charging for the ball to start the match, and twenty years on, James Moray Brown, who played on the 79th team, remembered with a shudder a collision between himself and Queen Victoria's son. Both players went heels over head but were unhurt.

Play continued in a rather desultory way until 1880 when the Edinburgh Polo Club was formally established by Andrew, Jack and Tom Drybrough, George and John Younger, of the Edinburgh brewing family; and T. Binnie, John Craig, Frank Ogilvie and John Taylor. Play was on a ground in Gullane, near the racecourse. The following year saw a move to Coltbridge Park. Then the club was in abeyance for seven years, the civilian players turning out to play with the cavalry officers garrisoned at Piershill Barracks.

In 1889, some seventeen acres at Murrayfield were leased, and a regulation, boarded, polo ground was laid out. Eventually the Scottish Rugby Union purchased the land and the Murrayfield Stadium was inaugurated in 1925, with a match against England for the Calcutta Cup. The Calcutta Cup is the oldest international rugby fixture, played alternately at Murrayfield and Twickenham.

There is a polo link here. Due to the increasing popularity of polo in India, the Calcutta Rugby Football Club was disbanded in 1878 and the club's funds were used to purchase a trophy to be presented for matches between England and Scotland. The cup is made from silver melted down from rupees withdrawn from the bank when the Calcutta RFC closed its account.[23]

The relative isolation of a polo club in the northern reaches meant that games could only be played against cavalry regiments garrisoned there, such as the 4th Hussars, the 12th Lancers and the 13th Hussars. Home and away matches were also played against Liverpool and Wirral. In spite of this lack of competition, Edinburgh teams took the County Cup in 1893 and 1894. William "Snooks" Younger, Captain Cortlandt Gordon Mackenzie, Captain Francis Egerton Green and the brothers Thomas and Jack Drybrough carried the day for Scotland.

Polo was a rough game in those days. Lt. Col. Gerald Hobson reminisced of his days stationed in Edinburgh: "We seldom had an umpire and of course such things as polo helmets, knee pads, etc. were not only unheard of but would not for a moment have been countenanced, if they had been; as they would have been considered soft. There was quite a certain amount of foul play."[24]

There was no other polo club north of the border until the Ayrshire Polo Club was started in Troon, more noted as a golfing destination, in 1908. The polo ground was located near Fullarton House. There is also mention of a fixture with Aberdeen; however, no corroboration has been found regarding this particular event.[25] Some of the members were John Bell from Kilmarnock; Henry Cayzer; Captain Oswald Croshaw, 19th Hussars; Glen Cunningham; Duncan Hoyle Gibb, who played in Argentina; Major John Hoison-Craufurd; William Houldsworth; Colonel Aylmer Hunter-Weston, Royal Engineers; Richard Kidston from Troon, who helped start the club; Captain Frederick McConnel; Lord Montgomerie; and Captain Foster Swetenham, Royal Scots Greys, who was one of the founders. Commander the Viscount Kelburn, RN, who was involved in the beginnings of polo in New Zealand, was also an early member.

CHAPTER 2

The Expansion of Provincial Polo

The story of the provincial clubs merits much recognition, either briefly or at length, describing their trajectory in British polo; some flourished into our days while many others faded into oblivion.

Monmouthshire Polo Club, established in 1872 by Reginald Herbert and his brother Francis, is considered the first provincial club in the United Kingdom, as previously described in the section about polo in Wales. The polo field was on Reginald Herbert's property in Clytha, near Usk.

Bedfordshire

Bedford County Polo Club was started in 1900 by William Baker and Harry Boileau. The club had two grounds within the Old Race Meadow, Bedford's racetrack and also another between Bedford and Sharbrook. Polo awakened quite a bit of interest; *Baily's Magazine* reported, "Thus in the first match at Bedford between the Oakley and Cambridgeshire hunts, both sides of the ground on the Ampthill road were lined with carriages, foot people, and even a few motor cars. The Cambridgeshire side won the match, but both sides played well."[1] The Oakley Hunt side was P.A. Whitaker, MFH; Thomas Barnard; W. Barnett; and John Porter-Porter. The Cambridgeshire Hunt team aligned George Evans, MFH; Wolverley Fordham; H.W. Montgomery; and G. Baldwin.

Among the initial players at Bedford County were William Addington, William Balding, John Drage, Montague Lamb, Lt. Col. Brownlow Mathew-Lannowe, Colonel William Selby-Lowndes and Gordon Withers. Mr. Thomas Barnard was the captain. Regrettably, by 1911, the Bedford County Polo Club was in abeyance.

Berkshire

The Berkshire Polo Club was established around 1890, Ernest Targett being one of the enthusiasts. A team with Captain Victor Ferguson, Henry T. Fenwick, the Hon. William Lambton and Captain Julian Spicer took the County Cup in 1890.

The Wellington Polo Club was started in 1894 as a direct consequence of the military authorities prohibiting polo at the Royal Military Academy in Sandhurst.[2] Mr. A.C. Kenyon-Fuller was the prime mover. A polo club had been established by officer-cadets in 1884, which evolved into the Staff College Polo Club. The new club's ground was located close to the Wellington College Station. The original members were Captain Jeaves, the Hons. Osbert and Richard Molineux and the Hon. Reginald Ward. Later players included Major Eustace Abadie, Lt. Edward Beddington, Captain G. Percival Heywood, Hugh Noel Scott Robson and the Hon. Maurice Wingfield.

Cambridgeshire

The St. Neot's Polo Club was established in 1900 and had its ground in Little End, a hamlet at the southern end of Eaton Socon. A Challenge Cup was presented by Major Shuttleworth and was taken by Handley Cross, a team that included Harry Rich, Jay Mackey, Leonard Bucknell and Frank Ellison. Alfred Jordan and Aubrey Towgood have been identified as players in this small club. Alfred Jordan, H.W. Montgomery, Wolverley Fordham and George Evans, MFH of the Cambridgeshire Hunt, took the Cambridge University Open Cup in 1904.

Cheshire

The little-known Bowdon Club in Cheshire presents a claim to be the oldest polo club in the kingdom because it was formed in the 1860s by Messrs. Gaddum and Symonds, recently arrived from India, where they had been smitten by the game.[3] Ponies were obtained from Exmoor and a ground was secured at Cheadle, a Manchester suburb. Things did not go well; many of the ponies died, Mr. Gaddum's health took a turn for the worse, and there is a record of only one game being played. However, in 1891 the membership, including Harry Gaddum, a nephew of one of the founders, amalgamated with the Manchester Polo Club, and the game continued on its merry way.

A Chester County Club was started in 1881 by Lord Arthur Grosvenor; Alfred Ashton; Major Arthur Chambers, RA; Alfred Hasall; J. Henry Stock, MP; and William Hall Walker. Lord Harrington, who was out with his Yeomanry in Cheshire, became a mentor. The first match was played against a team brought by Sydney Platt from Llanfairfechan and started rather disastrously. In those days, it was common practice to begin the game charging for the ball, and as happened many times, Mr. C. Lane collided with the visiting captain, who remained unconscious for a period of time.

The club also played matches against Manchester, and at Vale Royal, Lord Hugh Delamer's seat. Chester County Club led a parlous existence, and polo expired at Chester, with the exception of Yeomanry Week, when the Earl of Harrington kept the game going. The club was eventually revived thanks to the efforts of Alfred Tyrer, who through the town council of Chester secured a ground within the Rodee, the local racecourse.

Close to Birkenhead, the Wirral Polo Club was founded in 1885 by F.W. Blain and G.K. Catto. Grounds were in Clatterbridge, near to Spital and its military barracks. Initial players, in addition to the founders, included William Ball, Roland Haig, Alfred Hassall, Colonel Hugh Melly, John Ravenscroft — who would go on to an illustrious polo career in Argentina — and F. Tinsley. The players were known as "The Wasps" on account of their yellow and black jerseys.

In 1889 the polo field was moved to Hooton Park. Wirral took the County Cup in 1908 with the team of Thomas Royden, George Lockett, Stanley Watson and Frederick Wignall.

The Wirral Ladies Cup, given by the club's ladies, is one of the largest polo trophies in England. It is still played for at the Cheshire Polo Club, a successor of the old Wirral Polo Club.

The four Lockett brothers, George, Robert, Vyvyan and William, were nephews of George A. Lockett, one of the founders of the Liverpool Polo Club. Other players were Major Noel Campbell; A.F. Crewdson, Jr.; H. Douglas Crewdson; F. Crewdson; Alfred Hassall; Edward Kearsley; and W. Hope Nelson.

Devon

There was a North Devon Polo Club in the 1880s, but a club with that name only affiliated in 1904.[4] Reputed to possess one of the better provincial grounds, it was located near Fremington. The Misses Houldsworth from Westward Ho! donated a trophy which was taken by the Tiverton team of the brothers de Las Casas, Alfredo, Juan and Luis, along with Pelham Puckle. They were the sons of the Spanish general consul in Liverpool. The four brothers, which also included Manuel de Las Casas, had started polo while undergraduates at Cambridge University. Other players were Captain Prideaux Brune, Lyons Clark, Arundell Clarke, Captain Ewing Paterson and Major Francis Penn-Curzon. Mr. James Pearce, from Rugby, presented in 1906 a Handicap Challenge Cup that was taken by Staddon House, with Richard Weatherby, Edward Weatherby, Major Jackson and Robert Eden. The finals of these two competitions attracted more than 2,000 spectators. The Houldsworth Cup is now played for under the auspices of the Taunton Vale Polo Club.

The Polo Club in Devon was established in 1891, and like many polo clubs of its vintage, the early days are sketchy. It was reorganized by Lionel Lambart in 1897; other players included John Bayly; Captain Loftus Bryant; Lt. Charles Burnard; Lt. Godfrey Faussett, RN; Lt. Lionel Lambart, RN; Major Harry McMicking; and Captain Richard Seddon. The ground was conveniently located opposite the George Inn, Roborough. The principal tournament was the Mount Edgecumbe Cup, presented by Lord Edgecumbe, the club's president.

The Otter Vale Polo Club started in 1904, playing on two grounds at Spence Cross, near Sidmouth Junction. The two main tournaments were the Otter Vale Challenge Cup, presented by the club, and the Tracey Cup, presented by the 8th Hussars. The initial winners of the Otter Vale Cup were Major H.E. Lambe, Luis de Las Casas, Jack Holford and Robert Eden, playing for Blackmore Vale. Aldershot took the inaugural Tracey Cup with a team formed by Lt. Edric Weldon, Lt. William Armitage, Captain Humphrey Clegg and Lt. Edgar Broadbent.

The club offered playing time to the officers garrisoned in Exeter. However, in 1912, the club's honorary secretary wrote a languid note: "I fear that this club will come to an end. We have been quite dependent on soldiers quartered at Exeter, but the present Brigade do not play."[5]

The Exeter Polo Club in Devon was started in 1905 and was in abeyance by 1911. After the war, it rejoined the County Polo Association in 1922, with grounds at Woolway's Farm, near Countess Wear. The major tournament was the Mardon Cup, the Mardon family being great supporters of the club. Many members were officers of the field artillery stationed at Topsham; when the unit was mechanized in 1938, the Exeter Polo Club became dormant.

The Taunton Vale Polo Club began in 1911 by John Clement de Las Casas and officers of the Somerset Light Infantry stationed in Taunton. They had a good field and a pavilion at Orchard Portman, in Mr. T. Chapman's farm. Players included Frederick Bradshaw, Captain Edward Troyte-Bullock, Dr. Richard Burgess, C. Leslie Fowler, Captain Cecil Samuda, Herman Tiarks, William Villar and Captain Arthur Yatman. When the Quantock Vale Polo Club closed down, the Taunton Vale club obtained its thatched pavilion, with its many memories and artifacts.

Dorset

The Blackmore Vale Polo Club dates back to 1899 with grounds at Spurles and at Purse Caundle, Milborne Port, in Dorset. In 1913 the club moved to a ground close to Sherborne. Initial enthusiasts were Dr. William Alexander, Henry Boden, Robert Eden, John Hargreaves, Jack Holford, Vivian Kennard—who had learned polo in Argentina at the Media Luna Club—Major H.E. Lambe and Captain Geoffrey Stanley Phipps-Hornby, Rifle Brigade. His son, Geoffrey Hardinge Phipps-Hornby, 9th Lancers, would be an international player in the 1920s. A prominent player was Frederick J.B. Wingfield Digby of Sherborne Castle, educated at Harrow and Trinity Hall, Cambridge. He played for Cambridge in the Inter-university match and hunted with the Blackmore Vale, the Cattistock and the Fitzwilliam. Hunting, polo, shooting and fishing, in that order, were his favorite sports. A capable player was Arthur Drake, who in consequence of a marriage assumed the prefix Tyrwhitt. Major Claude Ward-Jackson was another well-known player.

Members A.P. Wills Sandford and his cousin Horace Vachell went to America and were the pioneers of polo on the Pacific Coast near Los Angeles. Vachell returned to England after the demise of his American wife and became a novelist. Another member was Chamberlain "Jumbo" Hinchcliff who returned to England after years of ranching in Argentina. During his sojourn overseas, Jumbo, so called because of his corpulence, took the Polo Association of the River Plate Championship, nowadays the Argentine Open. Two prominent members of the Blackmore Vale Polo Club fell during the Great War: Captain Noel Edwards, the English international, and Captain Nigel Livingstone-Learmonth, from the well-known polo family. Later players included Captain Frederick Gray, H.G. Wyndham Gray, Oliver Hoare, Jack Holford, Lestock Livingstone-Learmonth and Major Philip Magor, owner of estancia La Estrella in Venado Tuerto, Argentina, who was a neighbor of Jumbo Hinchcliff.

Essex

The West Essex Polo Club traces its origins to 1878, when Messrs. B. Dickinson, George Dawson, Arthur Waters—polo captain for many years—and Harry Yerburgh started playing on "the Plain," a common located between Epping and the Lower Forest. Matches were played against Bishop's Stortford and Cambridge University. Four years after the inception of the club, Atherton Chisenhale-March came to live at Gaynes Park and at great expense enlarged his cricket ground into a polo field. The number of players increased significantly, including Mr. Chisenhale-March, Walter Buckmaster—destined to a brilliant career in English polo—Robert Ball, Alfred and Sydney Kemp, Sheffield Neave and Alfred Suart. The club entered the County Cup with little success.

The Priory Polo Club was formed in 1887, the ground being located near Shenfield. Years later, in 1895, the club changed its name to Hutton, where the last game was played in August 1914, just as war began. Players included T. Blundell Brown, A. Gordon Dickson, Captain Richard Neave, Charles Pilkington, Malcolm Pilkington, Captain John Tyson Wigan and Richard Stretton de Winton. The club had its moment of glory when a team — Malcolm Pilkington, L.R. and C.K. Carr, and Raymond Courage — took the County Cup in 1907. The Priory Polo Club was revived in 1923 under the name Mid-Essex.

The Stansted Polo Club was started by Tresham Gilbey in the autumn of 1892. Play was on a rough pitch, on a slope and full of rabbit holes.[6] This did not deter the players, who soon moved to a good ground in Bishop's Stortford. Walter Buckmaster, who had played his university polo at nearby Cambridge, was the stalwart player. Other players included Ormond and Rupert Blyth; Captain Richard Breeks, RA; George Game; and Arthur Lobb. A few members were some of the band of rowers that have distinguished themselves at polo: Harcourt Gold, stroke for the Eton boat, and William F.C. Holland, Brasenose College, who was president of the Oxford University Rowing Club and rowed on the varsity boat. As an aside, the well-known American players Devereux Milburn and Forrester Clark were excellent rowers: "Dev" Milburn for Oxford and "Tim" Clark for Harvard.

Twice the County Cup fell to teams from Stansted: Guy Gilbey, Gerald Gold, Arthur Gold and Walter Buckmaster in 1896, and Philip Gold, Captain George Gosling, Tresham Gilbey and Gerald Gold in 1899. Mr. Tresham Gilbey was a prominent breeder of polo ponies at the Grange, Bishop's Stortford, and was elected president of the Polo Pony Society. He left the ground in trust to the town of Bishop's Stortford, and when polo was resurrected in 1947 by Alfie Boyd-Gibbins with Silver Leys Polo Club, it took its name from the old polo ground.

Gloucestershire

Sometime around 1872, the Beaufort Polo Club was established by Captain Frank Henry, a former officer in the 9th Lancers and then in the Royal Gloucestershire Yeomanry. The grounds were in Norton, between Malmesbury and Hullavington. All the original members hunted with the Duke of Beaufort Hunt. There is no mention of the Beaufort Polo Club in the 1895 edition of Moray Brown's *Polo*; most likely it was in abeyance. The Beaufort Polo Club was revived in 1929 by Herbert Cox, a Canadian, who had a total of seven playing fields. The club fell into abeyance in 1939, and in 1977 the Tomlinsons purchased Down Farm and had the grounds rebuilt. A new Beaufort Polo Club was formally affiliated with the Hurlingham Polo Association in 1989.

The story of the Cirencester Polo Club, started in 1894, is described in a subsequent chapter.

The Cheltenham Polo Club was formed in that charming spa town by Major Thomas Longworth and Mr. H. Sidney Smith in 1898. Major Longworth, Royal Gloucestershire Hussars, leased the land and built the grounds at Prestbury Park. The main tournaments were the Senior and Junior Challenge Cups. Teams from the Cheltenham Club took both the County Cup and the Junior County Cup.

Players included Sir John Hume-Campbell; Captain Henry Bell; Arthur Cresswell; F. ffrench Davis; Captain George Farran; Sir Ralph Gore, later president of the Royal Yachting Association; RHA Gresson, who also was a member of the Calcutta Polo Club; Colonel Cecil

Heyworth-Savage; G. Lloyd Johnson; G. Lees Milne; Lt. Bolton Eyres Monsell, RN, later Viscount Monsell; Edward Munby; Lt. Col. Henry Porter of Birlingham; Henry Prior-Wandesforde; J. McClymont Reid; John Rogers; and R. Manners Wood, while Lt. Col. John Watkins Yardley was the polo captain.

Upon his return from Argentina, where he was the guiding light of the Polo Association of the River Plate and a six-time winner of the Open Championship, Frank Balfour took up residence in town and eventually became the club's president and also president of the Polo Pony Society.

West Gloucester was a club active in 1912. John S. Bakewell was one of the players.

Hampshire

The Winchester Polo Club affiliated with the County Polo Association in 1909; however, play on a small ground in Winchester had been carried on by officers of the Hampshire Carabineers Yeomanry. A new ground was secured on Flower Down, Harestock, close to the Winchester railway station. The club changed its name to Hampshire County in 1911.[7] The Invitation Tournament was established in 1907 for a challenge cup presented by Sir George Hurley, MFH. The 16th Lancers team, Lt. Edward Beddington, Colonel Hubert Gough, Captain George Bellville and Captain Charles Campbell, were the winners.

Hantfordshire

Brockenhurst Polo Club in Hantfordshire was started in 1898. The grounds and stables were at the back of the Rose and Crown Hotel. In 1912, the honorary secretary, Mr. James Bradford, sadly wrote, "No Polo here now, and I cannot say when we shall ever get any."[8]

South Hants Polo Club in Gosport was started in 1907, with an unboarded ground at Privett. Players included M.H.N. House and Philip House. By 1913, polo at the club was a doubtful proposition. It was revived in the 1920s with a boarded ground near Fort Grange Aerodrome at Gosport and became the main ground for the Royal Navy Polo Association.

Hereford

The Leominster Polo Club in Herefordshire was formed in 1907; the polo ground was adjacent to the railway station. Players were Captain John Cawley, 20th Hussars; Captain Robert Collis; Hugh Courage; H. Kevill Davies; Robert Evans, of Eyton Hall; Francis Greswolde-Williams; Captain Edward Heygate, West Kent Regiment; Captain Richard Heygate, RA; Hugh Kevill-Davies; and Captain Ralph Umfreville.

The Hatfield Polo Club was formed by Gerald Wilbraham Taylor. Little is known about this club.

Kent

Another polo club that appeared spontaneously was the Woldingham. While traveling on a train in 1891, Messrs. F.S. Bristow, Edward de Clermont, F.A. Edwards, Charles Taylor and H. Wilton, all businessmen residing in Kent, decided to start a polo club. With no grounds and no ponies, it was an uphill endeavor. A rough meadow was obtained at Godstone and ponies were hired from Mr. E. Woodland. The next year they moved the facilities to a better ground at Couldon, and then to an even better one at Woldingham. A pavilion was erected, the players purchased ponies and stabling was provided by Walpole Greenwell at Marden Park. Matches were played against Stansted, Woolwich Garrison and other clubs.

Lancashire

The path started by the Monmouthshire Club was soon followed by several early polo clubs. In the autumn of 1872, Hugh Gladstone started polo in Liverpool.[9] The Heywood Jones brothers, Llewellyn, Oliver and Richard, better known by their nicknames, "Wengy," "the Boss," and "Bengey," were the most prominent members. Other early players included R.E. "Tannar" Graves, Roland Haig, Henry Stocks and George Warren. These pioneers played mounted on their hunters, using long sticks, on a ground in Childwall. Soon enough, the members realized it did not pay to play on horses, so they purchased ponies and sent a team to play at Lillie Bridge, at the time the main center of polo in England.

The Liverpool Polo Club experienced some lean years until 1885, although the Heywood Jones brothers kept the game going at Childwall. At a dinner held at the Liverpool Racket Club, William Lee Pilkington and George Lockett — the latter would introduce polo in Peru and was one of the founders of the Lima Polo Club — suggested that the polo club should be reformed. Mr. W.L. Gladstone took the names of those interested, and the club soon had some fifty playing members wearing the chocolate and pink jerseys. These included J. and D. Irvine, A.T. and H.C. Neilson, F. Tinsley, Munro Walker and Sir Peter Walker. The ground at Childwall was boarded and had the advantage that the turf near the boards was elevated, so the ball would roll back. In a way, it was a precursor of the arris rail used on some polo grounds to avoid the ball leaning against the sideboards.

Liverpool's fixture with the Edinburgh Club was an annual event, and the club participated in the County Cup, emerging as winners in 1891 with a foursome that included Herbert Pilkington, C.E. Mason, Alfred Tyrer and William Hall Walker. Later players included Captain Charles Blackburne, Thomas Cookson, J. Watson Hughes, and H. and Milner Stewart Brown.

The Cheshire Champion Cup was given by the lady members of the Liverpool Polo Club in 1911 and was taken by the Old Childwallians, of which three players— J. Crewdson, W. Paul and Stanley Watson — were all Wirral Polo Club members. The trophy is nowadays played for at the Cheshire Polo Club.

The Manchester Polo Club traces its origins to 1872, when it was founded by James Ashton Radcliff, Colin Ross, Bailey Worthington and other like-minded men. The club flourished for some five years and then was in abeyance. In 1881 it was reformed by James Platt, Walter Roberts, Septimus Lambert and Colonel Hugh Melly. The help provided by the Queen's Bays, at the time stationed in Manchester, was instrumental in securing the club's well-being. The ground was at Old Trafford, nowadays home of the celebrated Manchester United Football Club. The club colors were chocolate and yellow. Eventually, Sir Humphrey de Trafford, proprietor of one of the best polo pony strings in England, became the club's president. Later members included Assheton Clegg; Sir Kenneth Crossley, high sheriff of Cheshire; William Dunkerley; Major Sidney Goldschmidt, the author of *Bridle*

Wise; Arthur Midwood; Oswald Grange Moseley; Clifford Schwabe; Captain Peter Winser; and Colin Ziegler.

Clitheroe Polo Club in Lancashire was founded in 1910 with grounds on Eddisford Bridge. Tournaments were played for the Jaucourt Cup and the Yerburgh Cup, both instituted in 1912. Players included Captain Thomas McG. Bridges, North Lancashire Regiment; the Frenchman Marquis Pierre de Jaucourt; J.G. Mellor; and Lt. Leslie Ormrod, 13th Hussars.

There is notice of the East Lancashire Polo Club being established in 1911 in Starling, near Bury.

Leicestershire

Market Harborough Polo Club was started in 1901 under the presidency of Sir Humphrey de Trafford, and closed in 1908. Philip Beatty; A. Bellville; a Mr. Dixon, of Great Stretton; William Payne Cowley; and J. Hornsby were some of the enthusiasts. Grounds were at Farndon, Market Harborough. The club was revived in 1924 by Lord Hugh Stalbridge and Major Sir Harold Wernher, the diamond magnate heir to the largest fortune in South Africa, £11,000,000 in 1912. At the time of his wedding to Lady Zia, daughter of Grand Duke Mikhail of Russia, he was the wealthiest bachelor in England.

The Melton Mowbray Polo Club was established in 1907 in the heartland of foxhunting in Leicestershire. In 1909 it started the Melton Mowbray Tournament, which was taken by the Kilworth Sticks. Captain St. John Douglas Loftus, William Balding, Leonard Tate and Asa Balding won the event. The club was not revived after the Great War.

Lincolnshire

Burghley Park was a small club established in 1892 at Burghley Deer Park at Stamford Town in Lincolnshire. The death knell was sounded in 1912, when an unknown correspondent wrote, "Very little polo here last season. The ground remains, but the club is almost extinct."[10]

A little-known club, Lafford, was active in Lincolnshire in 1912. Dr. Thomson, a player from Rushington, Sleaford, was the club's honorary secretary.

Norfolk

Norwich Polo Club was formed by Ivor Buxton, John Cooke, R.E. Parker and Robert Read, Jr., in 1908. A ground at Eaton was built, where the Eaton Golf Club is now located; a year later they moved to Sprowston. Other players included Geoffrey, John and Richard Buxton, Francis Crossley, Captain Forster, Quintin Gurney, Captain W.B. Long, Joseph Paul, William Thorold and Captain Humphrey Willett. A banner year for the club was 1913, when the County Cup and the Junior County Cup were taken by Norwich teams. Edward Leatham, Captain Reginald Badger, Basil Nicholas and Frederick Wormald took the County Cup, while Major Cecil Fane, Captain Badger, Edward Leatham and John Eden won the Junior County Cup.

The war put an end to polo at this club.

Northamptonshire

The Northampton County Polo Club was formed in 1905; the ground was at St. James's, Northampton. No other information was found about this club.

Northumberland

Northumberland Polo Club in Newcastle-on-Tyne was established in 1904. The ground was located in High Gosforth Park, some four miles from Newcastle. William Wharton Burdon, from Hartford Hall, was one of the players, as were D.E. Campbell and H.S. Bell, the latter being honorary secretary.

Oxfordshire

Just a few miles south of Little Faringdon, the current location of the Hurlingham Polo Association, there was polo in the 1910s. Perhaps the HPA staff is not aware that an enthusiastic foxhunter, Mr. Elliot R.F. Brunskill, started a polo club at Lechdale which ran for a few years.[11] Needless to say, they should not be blamed because there is no other information about this club.

Shropshire

Started in 1892, the Ludlow Polo Club was led by W. Howard and T. McMicking who secured a ground inside the Ludlow Racecourse in Bromfield. The players were a Mr. Boyd, H. Cunninghame, J.H. James-Moore, Hugo Martin and E. Tredenick. The club's colors were light blue, black and yellow.

Somerset

In the unofficial table of current active polo clubs' antiquity, West Somerset Polo Club ranks in fifth place, because it was established in 1904 at the Parks, Minehead; play was at Porlock Vale. The main competition was the West Somerset Challenge Cup, established in 1905 and first taken by Alva Cottage, with Major H.E. Lambe, Alfredo de Las Casas, H.S. Harrison and Robert Eden. Players included Frank D'Arcy Blofeld, who had learned the game in Argentina under the tutelage of Frank Balfour and was killed in the Great War; J. Vere Foster; and Dr. Thomas Ollerhead. It was in 1938 when it settled in the scenic surroundings of Dunster Downs, with the castle towering in the background and magnificent views of Exmoor and the Bristol Channel.

The Quantock Vale Polo Club was in activity from 1906 until 1910. The ground was located between Holford and Sturgston, in Somerset. A fox covert adjacent to one of the ground's corners was known as "the Polo Grounds Covert." The club enjoyed a brief revival in 1926, but it only lasted for three years. Another attempt was staged in 1931; however, it also was a failure.

Staffordshire

The North Staffordshire Polo Club was founded in 1909. The ground was located at Aston, near Stone. The North Stafford Tournament was played on handicap for trophies presented by Mr. J.G. Knight and Mr. A. Sidebottom. Players included W.A. Bowles; Sir Henry Fairfax-Lucy; the brothers A.D. and Spencer Flower, from the brewery family; Sir Hill Child; and Alfred Jordan. The club rejoined the County Polo Association in 1936; the new polo fields were in Willoughbridge, Pipe Gate, in Market Drayton.

Suffolk

The West Suffolk Polo Club was formed mainly by officers of the Suffolk Yeomanry in 1909, with a full-size, boarded ground at the Grange, in Beyton, some five miles from Bury St. Edmunds. Among the enthusiasts were Major John Agnew; Sir William Burton; C.F. Cattle, of Bury St. Edmunds; Hugh Dawson; Captain Geoffrey Horne; Bramwell Jackson; Captain Herbert Musker; Colonel J.W. Royce Tomkin; Edward Warner; Eugene Wells; and Reeve Wentworth. The club's membership suffered heavy losses during the war, and although some games were played in 1919, hopes of revival flickered the next year.

Sussex

An interesting entity was the International Gun and Polo Club started by George Marshall in 1874. A proprietary club, it was formed with the purpose of holding meetings involving polo, pigeon shooting, tent pegging, archery and other rural amusements. The club, which had a significant membership of foreigners, was based at the Bedford Hotel in Brighton. As to the polo grounds, they were located at Preston in Sussex. The game of polo played an important role in this club, which catered to the European nobility. Well-known players, such as the Marquis of Queensberry, Sir Charles Wolseley, the Peat brothers, Edward Baldock, Captain Grissell of the 9th Lancers, the Herbert brothers and Hugh Owen from the Monmouthshire Club, Adrián de Murrieta from Wadhurst Park in Kent, John Scott-Chisholme[12] and James Mellor, were active members. In addition to local games, the club participated in matches at Richmond Park and in Cheltenham.

The Brighton and County Polo Club was started by Lt. Col. Robert McKergow, of Twineham Grange, in 1906. The polo grounds were at Preston Park; perhaps it was the old location of the International Gun and Polo Club.

The West Sussex Polo Club was founded in 1908. It had a ground near the Pulborough railway station, on the Stopham estate. The West Sussex Open Tournament was played for four cups presented by the club. A team named Brixworth, formed by officers from the 7th Hussars, took the inaugural competition; Dermot McCalmont, George Meyrick, Edwin Brassey and Captain Allan Pollock were on the team. Some of the players were H.M. Harris, who also was honorary secretary; G.B. Horne; and C.B.A. Jackson.

Warwickshire

Much senior in antiquity to its neighbor Rugby Club, the Warwickshire Polo Club in Leamington was started in 1884 by Major Green, Albert Jones and J.F. Shaw. Play was at

Warwick Park and on a ground inside the local racecourse. The formative meeting at the Tennis Court Club was also attended by Charles Bell, Benjamin Bond-Cabbell, Hugh Charrington, a Mr. Kingsley, the Hon. Dudley Leigh, W.M. Low, Captain Prior and Ernest Trepplin. About three years later, a permanent ground was secured on the Sydenham Farm. The club thrived, and in 1894 some of the townspeople of Leamington offered for competition the Warwickshire Cup, which currently is one of the most coveted prizes in British polo. Later players included Eric Crossley; Oliver Haig; Henry, Michael and Richard Lakin; Captain Walter Pepys; Frederick Polehampton; Pelham Puckle; Sir Grey Skipwith; Captain Rudolph Valintine; Sir Francis Waller; and Donald Watson. Regrettably, the club disbanded in 1914 and most of the members joined the Moreton Morrell Polo Club.

The Stratford-on-Avon Polo Club was started in 1900, with a ground on Evesham Road. It promoted an annual tournament held in July for a challenge cup presented by Miss Marie Corell. Handley Cross, with Harry Rich, Jay Mackey, Frank Ellison and Leonard Bucknell, won the trophy in 1900.

The history of polo at Edgbaston Polo Club in Birmingham started in 1903 when a few players, having been to Leamington to watch a game, had the idea of purchasing sticks and knocked a ball around, mounted on their hunters or anything else found on the horse line. The first game, played on a field which had no previous preparation, counted C.J. Byner, S. Hollingsworth, H. Howes, C.H. Palethorpe and N. Thornicroft, under the leadership of Hubert Nicholas, later captain of polo. All were members of the Tally Ho!, which was a club of hunting men who rented a ground and had jumping competitions and a horse show. Eventually play was carried out on Mr. Thornicroft's property and the club was formally established. C.J. Byncr, a local veterinarian, was named honorary secretary and polo captain. Later on, Arthur Balding came over from Rugby and was a great help to the players, who previously had to get all their polo experience by personal practice.

A suitable ground was secured on Edgbaston Road, opposite the Warwickshire County Cricket Ground, and matches were played versus Stourbridge, a new club formed some twelve miles away. The main tournament was the Birmingham Polo Challenge Cup, a trophy presented by Count René de Montaigu.

Moreton Morrell Polo Club was established in 1906. Play was on a field loaned by the American player Charles Garland, a resident in England. The Moreton Morrell Tournament, for a cup presented by Mrs. C.T. Garland, always drew a large number of entries. Beauchamp Hall were the first winners in 1905; Major Thomas Pitman, Jay Mackey, Major Neil Haig and Michael Lakin were on the winning team.

Some of the members were William Beatty; Icky Bell, of foxhunting fame; Percy Bullivant; Robert Emmet; Sir Henry Fairfax-Lucy; George Game; Keats Gwyer; Henry, Michael and Richard Lakin; Frederick Polehampton; Pelham Puckle; Captain Rudolph Valintine; and Major Harvey Welman.

Wiltshire

Another interesting little polo club was the Swindon Club, which was started by unknown enthusiasts about 1891. They benefited from the support given by Major Thomas Calley, 1st Life Guards, who lent them a ground at Burderop Park and brought over a regimental team. The club then secured a field on the Wiltshire County Ground, which had a beautiful old turf that allowed the ball to run true. Among the ten to fifteen members were a Mr. Deacon, Dr. John Campbell McLean, Mr. Lawrence and Dr. Toomer.

The North Wiltshire Polo Club was established in 1896, near the Plough Inn, in Kington, St. Michael.

Wiltshire had another polo club, the Vale of the White Horse, founded in 1912. The ground was at Broome Manor on Coate Road, near Swindon. The Hon. Osmond Hastings was the polo captain. Surprisingly for a novice club, the Vale of the White Horse took the County Cup in the year of its foundation with a team essentially made up of Cirencester players: Maurice Kingscote, Hon. Aubrey Hastings, Noel Edwards and Jesse Gouldsmith. Some of the other players were Thomas Bennett, Colonel Colin Campbell, Captain Robert Ogilby — who purchased Moreton Hall from Charles Garland — Archibald Stuart and Thomas Sutton.

Worcestershire

Worcestershire Polo Club in Whittington was active from 1895 until 1905. Little is known about this entity. Anthony Hungerford Lechmere managed the club for many years.

Yorkshire

There is notice of Leeds Polo Club being established at Kirkstall in 1877. The club lapsed in 1880; it was revived at Allwoodley in 1888, only to become dormant in 1896. The entity was then revived as Allwoodley Polo Club in 1903, and completing the circle was renamed Leeds in 1905. The grounds, however, remained in Allwoodley. Edward Lane Fox was president and G. Constable Hayes, Herbert Sutton, Edward Tempest and Lt. John Wordsworth, 5th Lancers, were some of the players.

The Middlewood Polo Club in Yorkshire was started by Charles Howard Taylor and his brother in 1894, with a field near Highfield Farm in Darfield. Other members were Captain Albert North, Oxfordshire Light Infantry and Master of the Earl Fitzwilliam's Hounds; Charles Ellison; the Earl Fitzwilliam; J.E. Mitchell; T.W.H. Mitchell; Joseph Pickersgill, Jr., who had represented Cambridge; Harry Whithworth, MFH; Richard Wilkinson; and John and P.H. Wormald.

A remarkable club in many ways was Holderness Polo Club, established in East Yorkshire in 1894. Space adequate for two grounds was secured on Westbourne Avenue, Hull. Those players associated with the pioneering efforts were Nicholas Dobrée; Edward and Philip Hodgson; Thomas Holtby; George Houlton; Edward, Fred and Joseph Hurtley; Joseph Stephenson; and Clive Wilson. The members were enthusiastic but inexperienced and it was difficult to find players willing to coach the neophytes. The 17th Lancers, then stationed in York, gave some much needed help. The club never had more than a dozen players; however, the crowds were numerous, sometimes reaching 15,000 spectators. For such a small number of players, Holderness' fixture was all encompassing. Northward to Edinburgh; westward to Liverpool, Manchester and Wirral, and southward to Derbyshire, players and their ponies traveled far in the summer months. The nearer clubs such as Catterick Bridge faced their own problems, and eventually the Holderness Polo Club had to give up in 1907. It was a brave venture indeed, in an area were polo faced tough times.

The York County Polo Club was organized in 1896 and lapsed later that year. It depended heavily on the cavalry regiments stationed in York. It was revived in 1902 and took the Junior County Cup in 1912. The ground was at the Knavesmire, York.

Started in 1898, Catteridge Bridge Polo Club had a nice ground by the side of the River Swale, in Catteridge Bridge, Yorkshire. In the inaugural match, Walter Harrild, at the time an undergraduate at Cambridge, was mounted on a pony; the future Rear Admiral Christopher Craddock, a member of the Polo Pony Society who met his fate in the battle of Coronel, rode one of his father's carriage horses; and William Hardcastle was on a Shetland pony. Unabated enthusiasm counted for much. Catterick Bridge struggled until 1912, when the club closed. Players included Sir Henry Havelock-Allan; Alexander Dalgety; Captain Walter Neilson, 74th Highland Regiment; and William Edwin Pease.

The Cleveland Polo Club came into existence in 1899, with a ground near Nunthorpe, and later at the Redcar Racecourse in Redcar, Yorkshire. Some of the original members were Charles and George Dorman, Hubert Dorrington, Lord Richard Gisborough, Claud and Joseph Pease, and Colonel Alexander Watt. The club had a short life span, and when dissolved, some of the members moved on to the Catterick Bridge Club.

Darlington Polo Club affiliated with the County Polo Association in 1903, and another club in the northeast was Hurworth, in Darlington, which was active from 1907 until 1912.

Durham North was a club at Snipery Hall, Durham. It was active in 1912. John Ridley Ritson was one of the founders and most enthusiastic supporters of this little-known polo club, together with William Blackett.

Garrison Clubs

The polo club at Aldershot Garrison was one of the oldest in the United Kingdom, for it was established in 1885. There were five grounds in places like Queen's Parade, Ball Hill, and Cove. Teams from the garrison took the County Cup and the Junior County Cup on several occasions.

The Cavalry School Polo Club was founded in 1905. The grounds were in Netheravon, Wiltshire, which was the Army Riding School's location.

The Colchester Polo Club was started in 1912. Its two grounds were located in Middlewick and at Reed Hall.

The Fleet Polo Club began in 1887. It had three grounds adjacent to the Fleet railway station. Teams from the Fleet Polo Club were winners of the County Cup and the Junior County Cup. Their names are mentioned in appendix 3.

The Mounted Infantry Polo Club at Longmoor Camp in Hantfordshire was established in 1903. The polo grounds were in Blackmore Park, Selborne.

Salisbury Plain was founded in 1904 and had military and civilian members living in the vicinity of Salisbury Plain. A team from this club was the winner of the 1910 County Cup.

Shorncliffe Polo Club in Kent had grounds at Hawkinge and another in Paddlesworth. Later on, the club shared a ground with the Canterbury Polo Club.

Tidworth Polo Club came into being in 1908 but only joined the County Polo Association in 1920. The club had three grounds: two at Tidworth and one at Perham. Teams from Tidworth took the County Cup in 1938 and the Junior County Cup several times, the last occasion in 1968, with a team formed by Captain Ian McConnel, Peter Gifford, Timothy Harding and Major Charles Lockhart.

The Equitation School had a club in Weedon, which started activities in 1913. A team —

William Carr, Captain Arthur Moubray, Thomas Meyrick and William Brough Scott —
took the Junior County Cup in 1925.

The York Polo Club at the Barracks had a full-size ground at the Knavesmire. The Hon.
Alexander Leslie-Melville, Hugh Noel Scott Robson, Captain Douglas Duguid-McCombie
and Ralph Whitehead took the Junior County Cup in 1912. Another player of repute in this
club was Guy St. Maur Palmes.

Private Service Clubs

The Brigade of Guards Polo Club was established in 1903, with membership limited
to officers of the foot guards. The club made use of the polo grounds at Wimbledon Park,
near Southfields.

Canterbury Polo Club, based at the Cavalry Barracks, had two polo grounds near St.
Martin's Hill on Sandwich Road.

The Household Cavalry Polo Club was founded in 1897 by officers of the three mounted
regiments, the 1st and 2nd Life Guards and the Royal Horse Guards (the Blues). There was
a single ground at Datchet, utilized by each regiment when it was their turn to be stationed
at Combermere Barracks in Windsor.

The Royal Artillery Polo Club, also known as Woolwich, began in 1920. Play was at
Eltham, and later at Danson Park on Bexley Heath.

Polo in the Royal Navy

The Royal Naval Polo Association (RNPA) was started in 1929 by Admiral Sir Roger
Keyes, its first president. King George V was patron, and Lt. Commander Lord Louis Mountbatten, honorary secretary and treasurer. Admiral of the Fleet Lord Keyes of Zeebrugge and
Dover was the best friend the Navy polo ever had. A large proportion of the officers who
took up polo owed to him their introduction to the game.

The first match between Royal Navy and Royal Air Force teams in 1928 created such
great interest in polo circles that King George VI, then Duke of York and Ranelagh Club's
chairman, gave a trophy, the Duke of York Cup. The Navy won the first competition, and
although the trophy was not then in actual existence, HRH wished that match to count as
the inaugural one and had the winners' names engraved on the cup. The RAF took the trophy
the following year.

Lord Mountbatten organized a team, the Bluejackets, which participated in the London
season in 1930. Lt. Commander C.R.W. Gairdner, Lt. Edward Heywood-Lonsdale and Lt.
Commander Charles Lambe completed the team. Capt. Robert Neville, Royal Marines, was
the spare man. This team took the Military Handicap Tournament at Roehampton.

The scope of the RNPA was worldwide. The Home Station included Portsmouth in the
Southern Counties, Plymouth in the Western Counties, Ireland and Scotland. The Mediterranean Station included Gibraltar, where polo was played on a ground at the base of the
Rock; Egypt, with grounds in Alexandria and Cairo; and the Marsa grounds in Malta, the
main center of Navy polo. The Rundle Cup, still played for between Army and Navy teams,
was started in Malta in 1910 by Maj. Gen. Sir Leslie Rundle, the Governor of Malta.

Polo in the Far East Station was played in Hong Kong, Shanghai, Singapore and Hankow. In addition there were naval stations in New Zealand, Australia, Ceylon, South Africa, Canada and the West Indies.

Navy officers had the opportunity to play in Chile, Peru, Brazil, Uruguay and Argentina. The RNPA representative in Buenos Aires was Commander Leslie Farmer, RN (Retd.), a Hurlingham Club member and also an avid golfer.

Private Grounds

A private club was Derbyshire, started in 1880 by the Earl of Harrington at Elvaston Castle. Many top players participated, including the Peat brothers, Francis Mildmay, Thomas Kennedy and Henry Boden. A team — Edward Kenyon Stow, Lord Harrington, Gerald Hardy and Francis Herbert — won the County Cup in 1887. The club then went into a decline, but by 1906 it resumed operations and was quite active until the onset of the Great War. The Derbyshire Open Tournament was started in 1907. The team Handley Cross, Harry Rich, Freddy Freake, Herbert Rich and Frank Ellison were the winners.

That great sportsman, Lord Harrington, died in 1917. His rotund figure and flowing beard were a feature on English grounds for a long time. Charles Augustus Stanhope, Earl of Harrington, started his polo in Malta, took the County Cup with Gloucestershire and his own Derbyshire, the Hurlingham Champion Cup with Sussex County, and the Rugby Open Cup with Cheshire. He was president of the County Polo Association and the first president of the Polo Pony Society, being responsible for the establishment of the Polo Pony Stud Book. Lord Harrington also invented the goalposts made of papier-maché. His was a full life, punctuated with enormous contributions to the game of polo.

The Earl of Shrewsbury, who played at number one for the Rugby team, started his own private club with grounds at Lichfield and Stafford about 1893. However, there is notice of a match between the 7th Hussars and a Staffordshire side at Manchester in 1875.[13] It was won by the 7th Hussars, the players being Captain John Hunt, Captain Robert Roper, Captain Frank Shuttleworth, Thomas Graham Smith and Evelyn Atherley. Staffordshire had Lord Charles Castlereagh, Lord Charles Ingestre — the Earl of Shrewbury's heir — Captain Hyde Sergison-Smith of the Staffordshire Yeomanry Cavalry, Sir Charles Wolseley and Mr. Barrett. Thomas Pinchard Kempson, a Hurlingham member, played for Staffordshire for many years starting in 1877.

Only years later, in 1895, the club was formally organized as the Staffordshire Polo Club, at his residence, Ingestre Hall. The polo grounds were located near the River Trent, from which Lord Shrewsbury laid iron pipes connected with hydrants. These provided excellent irrigation, which could be complemented by his private steam fire engine. It was a club for friends; among the twenty-five members were the Earl of Harrington, Algernon Burnaby, Captain Daly Fergusson, Captain the Hon. Robert Greville, Gerald Hardy, Albert Jones, Captain "Wengy" Jones, Edward and George Miller, Norman Nickalls, Bertram Portal, Captain Gordon Renton, Jasper Selwyn and John Reid Walker. A team from his band of brothers took the Paris International Tournament in 1896.

Charles Chetwynd Talbot, Twentieth Earl of Shrewsbury, had long cherished an ambition to produce a motorcar of the highest class. Meanwhile, in Paris, M. Gustave-Adolph Clément had built a car that fitted well with the earl's plans. A meeting was arranged at which a company was formed to manufacture the Clément car in England under the Talbot name; the car's badge was a Talbot hound surmounted by a coronet. Both entrepreneurs suffered family losses that eventually led to the closure of the factory in England. Young Albert Clément was the Stirling Moss of his day; however, his motor racing career came to a tragic end during a practice run for the 1907 Grand Prix. The loss in the Western Front in 1915 of Viscount Ingestre, the only son of the Earl of Shrewsbury, was to bring Clement Talbot Ltd. to extinction as the earl lost interest in the enterprise.[14]

The Spanish family de Las Casas had their own club, Dulverton, in Tiverton, Devon. This private club had been established in 1902. The polo grounds were located at Holland Farm. Polo was played in earnest until 1930, when the Depression claimed the club as one of its many victims.

The Duke of Westminster had two polo grounds at his estate near Cheshire, Eaton Hall. The Eaton Tournament, established in 1904, was open to invited teams. The "C" Team, Charles Garland, the American expatriate; Winchester Clowes; Captain Gerald Hobson; and Cecil Nickalls, were the winners.

The King of Spain, Alfonso XIII, colonel of the 16th Lancers, was one of the regular players, as were the Marqués de Viana and the Earl of Rocksavage. A team wearing the Eaton colors, Cecil Nickalls, George Miller, Patteson Nickalls and Charles Miller, took Hurlingham's Champion Cup in 1911.

Surrenden was the private ground of Mr. Walter Winans at Surrenden Park in Pluckle, Kent. It opened for play in 1904. Walter Winans was born in St. Petersburg and was a world champion in revolver shot, and twelve-time champion of England. As a painter and artist, he won silver medals at the Paris Exhibition.

Toulston Polo Club was a private club with grounds on William Riley-Smith's estate near Tadcaster. It was started in 1913 by the former president and captain of the Cambridge University Polo Club. The club is still in existence, albeit as a registered club. The vintage years were in the 1930s, with several wins in the County Cup and the Junior County Cup.

Gunnersbury was the private club of Evelyn Achille de Rothschild in Acton, Middlesex. Polo was started in 1910. Major Rothschild, Buckinghamshire Yeomanry, was killed in France during the war in 1917. The place is now an open public park.

The Marquess of Stafford's (later Duke of Sutherland) polo ground was located at Lilleshall House, near Newport in Shropshire. It was inaugurated in 1910. It is now one of the National Sports Centres.

Polo at the Universities

The Cambridge University Polo Club was started by the Hon. John Fitzwilliam in 1873. The players managed to practice year round, but it was not until 1878 that the game was played seriously, rules framed and a match against Oxford decided upon. The club's colors were maroon and yellow, and after some discussion, and with the sanction of the C.U. Boat Club, the following resolutions was passed: "That the Polo Five (i.e., the five who ever have or shall play against Oxford) be allowed to Wear a light blue polo shirt, white forage cap, and belt."[15] To this there was the following addendum: "N.B. Anyone playing for the team may wear the blue shirt for that game, but that game *only*, since he *must* play against Oxford to be entitled to his blue."

The first Inter-university match was held on the Bullingdon Cricket Ground in Cowley, on 27 November 1878, in soaking wet weather. The teams were as follows:

Scenes from the 1879 Oxford-Cambridge Varsity match as depicted by Frank Dadd (private collection).

Oxford	*Cambridge*
Audley Charles Miles, Brasenose (Capt.)	William Chute Ellis, Trinity Hall (Capt.)
James Henry Stock, Christ Church	R.A. Bayley
Herbert Green-Price, Brasenose	Henry Cumberland Bentley, Trinity Hall
Walter McM. Kavanagh, Christ Church	S.C. Mitchell
John Blundell Leigh, Christ Church[16]	Henry Robert Jameson, Jesus[17]

The game lasted one and a half hours, Oxford winning by five goals to nil.

In 1892 Cambridge put together a very strong team: Godfrey Heseltine (Trinity Hall), Walter Carless Harrild (Trinity), Walter Buckmaster (Trinity) and Lawrence McCreery (Magdalene). Played at Hurlingham, the dark blues were overwhelmed by twelve goals to one. That same Cambridge University team entered the County Cup, being defeated in the semifinals by a single tally by the eventual champions, the Edinburgh Polo Club.

Polo at Oxford University began in 1874. It was Walter Hume Long (Christ Church), later First Viscount Long, who brought some friends from Wiltshire and started playing on a cut hayfield.[18] Apparently, no records were kept of those early years. The ground was in Port Meadow, but being near the river, it was subject to flooding, which forced some matches to be played on the Bullingdon Cricket Club field.

The Oxford-Cambridge match was played yearly — with hiccups in 1894 and 1900 — until the onset of World War I, with honors fairly evenly divided: eighteen wins for the dark blues, seventeen for the light blues.

CHAPTER 3

Testing the Waters:
The Early Internationals

A match between English and French teams held in 1880 in Dieppe can be considered the first international game involving a British team. Regrettably, there is scant reference about this contest in the literature.[1] The English fivesome was a most powerful one. Reginald Herbert, Francis' older brother, usually played at goalkeeper. He had two Hurlingham Club Champion Cups to his credit. Two of the Sussex County team Peat brothers, Arthur and Johnnie, were among the best players of their generation. Captain William Ince-Anderton, Grenadier Guards, also had two Hurlingham crowns in his polo resume. The fifth player, Edward Baldock, took three championship trophies. Therefore, the English team was a strong representation of the game as played in the 1880s.

The French team saw fit to include a pair of American players in its lineup. Marion Story played at the Country Club of Westchester, the home base of the famous Waterbury brothers, Larry and Monte. Henry Ridgeway was an American in Paris, whose polo took place at the Bagatelle Club. Raoul de Brinquant was a Frenchman who had played with James Gordon Bennett. The Vicomte León de Janze was a player of enough recognition to merit a cartoon by Charles-Fernand de Condamy.[2] The team captain was le Duc Armande de Guiche, a strong supporter of French polo in Paris, Laversine and Cannes.

Writing a decade after the event, Moray Brown wrote: "There was an enormous crowd present. The ground was kept by a regiment of infantry and enthusiasm ran high. Occasionally some gallant Gaul would rush in and pick up a ball when the game was going against his countrymen, while *sacres*! *Parbleus*! and other French expletives flew about thickly, accompanied by much shouting and gesticulation. In spite of all, however, the English team won by the crushing majority of eleven goals to none."[3]

The Westchester Cup, 1886

The next international contest took place in Newport, Rhode Island, the last week of August 1886, between teams officially representing the Hurlingham Club and the Westchester Polo Club. This is the oldest international competition and none other than the American ten-goaler John Elliott Cowdin called this series the most important games in the history of polo in the United States.[4]

The impetus for the starting point of a competition between American and English representative teams began in the spring of 1886, at a dinner in the Hurlingham Club in

This is the Hurlingham team that took the first Westchester Cup in 1886. The Hon. Charles Lambton, Thomas Hone, Hon. Richard Lawley, reserve Thomas Shaw, and John Watson. Seated, Captain Malcolm Little.

Fulham, attended by the American player Nathaniel Griswold Lorillard, an heir to the tobacco fortune. Mr. Lorillard's comment that polo was played in the United States aroused interest among his hosts, and the possibility of a challenge series was raised. Griswold Lorillard sent a cable to Frank Gray Griswold, secretary of the Westchester Polo Club, stating that the Hurlingham Club would send a representative team if the players' expenses and the freight for the ponies were taken care of by the Americans. This was promptly agreed to, and the show was on.[5]

The members of the Hurlingham team crossed the North Atlantic onboard the Cunard Line *Servia* in early August and endured rough weather. On the other hand, their fifteen ponies, embarked on the National Line *Erin*, had a clear sail earlier. Upon arriving in Newport, the team was lodged at the Ocean House Hotel, reputed to be the best in the summer resort. They quickly became the season's sensation, and hostesses vied with each other to invite the members of the British team to parties and dinners.

The Hurlingham team was led by Irishman John Henry Watson, the dominant figure in British polo in the late 19th century. With him came Captain Thomas Hone, 7th Hussars; Captain the Hon. Richard Lawley, later Lord Wenlock, also an officer in the 7th Hussars; and Malcolm Little, 9th Lancers. Mr. Thomas Shaw Safe, an Englishman who spent the summers in Newport, was the spare man, and the Hon. Charles Lambton, 5th Fusiliers, accompanied the delegation as umpire.

The Westchester Polo Club players elected to resort to holding an election among its members as the mechanism to select the best players. The chosen ones were Foxhall Keene;

Raymond Belmont, Jr.; Thomas Hitchcock; and Edwin Morgan. An undisclosed illness in the Morgan family prevented Edwin from taking his place on the team; therefore, William Thorn, Jr., who had played polo in France, took his place.[6]

The first game was played on Wednesday, August 24, at 4 P.M. By 3 o'clock, the three main roads to Izzard's Field—a parcel of land now next to Morton Park—were jammed with all manner of conveyance: four-in-hand coaches, phaetons, barouches, buggies, curricles, carryalls, jumpers of every style, men and women on horseback and even mobs on foot. Most of the last were off for Dead Head Hill, which overlooked Izzard's Field. The matches were played on the old Westchester Polo Club's ground. Pomp and circumstance permeated the ambience. The British and American flags were flying, alongside the club flags, yellow for Westchester, light blue for Hurlingham. Mullaly's Orchestra was playing, the clubhouse was overflowing and the spectators' coaches were drawn up to five and six rows deep. Newport had never seen anything like it.

The Hon. Charles Lambton was umpire for the British team and Mr. Egerton Winthrop, Jr., for the Americans. Mr. S. Howland Robbins, Jr., was the referee in the first match; then he resigned and Mr. Frederick Beach took his place for the second match on Saturday. Mr. Samuel Stevens Sands, Jr., acted as timekeeper.

Before the match had even started, team captain John Watson showed his mettle. Watson insisted that the referee, Howland Robbins, should not be mounted, as was the custom, but should stand on a platform at the edge of the ground. To the Americans, it seemed a small point; however, Watson informed the committee that his team would refuse to play if the change was not made.[7] The *New York Times* reported, "The referee was perched on a stand, as the visitors refused to play with him mounted."[8] This small unpleasantness was dealt with by erecting a small stand and placing Mr. Robbins therein. This argument was probably the motive for his refusal to referee the second match.

The shorter-than-regulation ground on Halidon Hill was on a slope, and the American team was hitting downhill. The ball was put in the center of the field, and the two designated hitters dashed out from behind the backlines and headed face to face. Up the gentle slope galloped Captain Little (the *New York Times* says "Lawley"); down galloped Foxie Keene, whose mount was a little faster, and got the ball first; he hit it and missed demolishing Captain Little by inches; he followed up his first shot with another, and the ball went through the British goalposts. First blood went to the American team.

After such a propitious beginning, the match became one sided in favor of the Hurlingham squad. As the unequal contest developed, it became a learning experience for the Americans. The folly of banning the backhander stroke became apparent rather quickly; for John Watson's powerful defensive shots—always on the offside of the pony—quickly convinced the Americans that it was a most powerful offensive tactic as well. While pony power was about equal, and so it was dash by the players, the visitors proved that combination play would always beat individual prowess, no matter how brilliant it might be. The final result, ten goals to four, tells the story. The second game was more of the same, with Hurlingham jolly cantering to a 14–2 win.

For the second game on Saturday the crowd far surpassed that of Wednesday's, with carriages twice as numerous. Dead Head Hill was more crowded, pressing against the wire fence. At game time, a light fog hung on the field and, as play progressed, became denser, until at the end it interfered with both view and comfort and caused many to leave before the finish.

Gracious in victory, John Watson remarked, "I have played polo in all parts of the world, and I have never met fairer or better intending opponents that those of to-day."[9]

After the series was over, the British players, following the practice started by the Manipuri players in Calcutta, sold their ponies at advantageous prices.

With the exception of the *New York Times* reports, the Westchester Cup matches received little attention in the American press. Lt. Col. Edward Miller, who was in the United States with a cricket team — the "Gentlemen of England"— was not even aware that there was an international polo series offered for competition.[10]

The Westchester Cup Trophy

Shortly after the competition's terms had been agreed to by the Hurlingham and Westchester clubs— the organization of the Polo Association was still in the future — the issue of an appropriate trophy came up. There are two versions regarding who paid for the trophy. James Calvin Cooley states that "the kindly Mr. William Waldorf Astor presented a challenge cup."[11] The second version is that Frederick Gebhard put $1,000 toward the trophy, whereupon other enthusiasts insisted they should be counted in.[12]

F. Gray Griswold, secretary of the Westchester Polo Club, was charged with obtaining an appropriate prize. This he accomplished with some difficulty, because Mr. Griswold wished the cup to be emblematic of the game of polo, and the designer responsible for the trophy had never seen a match and there was no opportunity for him to witness one.[13] Tiffany & Co. was commissioned to manufacture the trophy. A London silversmith described the cup as

comprising a base of series of twelve shields, interlaced with a design of laurel leaves. Above this, some boldly chased scrollwork, with six figures of polo players, mounted, springing there from, the whole being surmounted by a massive three-handled egg-shaped cup, with three panels on it. The first panel contains the inscription, *International Polo Cup USA*; the second bears the arms of England and America; while the third is a representation of a couple of players passing each other in opposite directions.[14]

Mr. Nigel à Brassard is of the opinion that the origins of the stylized representations of the players are clearly open to debate. Gray Griswold believed that the polo player with the forage cap was himself, while the one with the peaked cap was Lord Leesthorp, and that the ponies' heads were from sketches of Griswold's celebrated pony, Tommy.[15]

It appears that the players are Captain John Fielden Brocklehurst and Captain Francis "Tip" Herbert, as depicted in George Earl's monumental picture of a polo match between the Royal Horse Guards and the Monmouthshire Club that was decided at Hurlingham on 7 July 1877.[16]

The cup is said to have cost $1,200; the Tiffany archives show the cup was made from 396.3 ounces of sterling and the manufacturing cost was $840.[17] Although considered by many to be the most impressive international polo trophy, like in many art objects, there is room for a difference of opinion. James Calvin Cooley called the ornate cup "that dreadful example of the silversmith's art."[18]

Nevertheless, the Westchester Cup, last played for in 2009 at International Polo Club Palm Beach, remains the most coveted trophy in international competition.

Australia versus England, 1899

The first international match between Australia and England took place in Melbourne as part of the festivities associated with Thoroughbred Racing Week. Captain Neil Haig,

England v. Australia at Melbourne, 1899. Colonel St. Quintin, who officiated as umpire, stands next to Bertie Hill. George Bryant, Neil Haig and Thomas Brand are seated in front.

6th Inniskilling Dragoons, who was attached to the governor's staff in Western Australia, put together a team. The Hon. Thomas Brand, a former officer in the 10th Hussars, was on his father's, Viscount Hampden's, staff in New South Wales. Another former officer in the 10th Hussars, the Hon. George Bryant, was staying with Tom Brand, and they recruited Bertie Hill to complete the team.

The only one who had his own ponies was Captain Haig; the others purchased and borrowed mounts as best they could. They all met in Melbourne and played a couple of practice games before facing a strong Australian team in two matches. The Australians were three Manifold brothers from the Camperdown Polo Club and Ernest De Little, who on his return journey from an education at Cambridge University had honed his polo skills in India.

Because of their superior ponies, the Australians were considered the favorites. In his memoirs, Col. St. Quintin, who officiated as one of the umpires, wrote, "The Australians were undoubtedly as fine players as you could see, but, fortunately for us, they did not understand the science of the game and playing together, and each man played his own game. They were also a very rough lot in their play, and as they became more and more excited the element of danger was strong and the whistle more and more in demand."[19]

The Australian team ended up winning the match by seven goals to six. Only three days later, the second match was held. In another stern struggle, the English team defeated the host team by six goals to five. This contest between England and Australia was the last one until 1928 when a team representing Army-in-India visited New South Wales for six weeks.

As to the players, Maj. Gen. Neil Haig played at back for his regimental team, reaching a nine-goal handicap. His teams took the Irish Open Cup, the Inter-Regimental Tournament and the Moreton Morrell Tournament. He also reached the finals of the Hurlingham Champion Cup and was one of the few polo players that merited a caricature in *Vanity Fair*.

The Hon. Thomas Brand inherited the title of Viscount Hampden, was Colonel of the 10th Hussars and rose to the rank of brigadier general. Major George Bryan, 10th Hussars, was high sheriff of county Lough and in 1911 succeeded to the title of Baron Bellew of Barmeath.

Argentina versus England at Hurlingham (Argentina), 1908

A polo game between British Army officers and Argentine Army officers held on 30 November 1908 is considered the first international game between the two countries. Four officers traveled to Buenos Aires in connection with the International Horse Show and Sports in Buenos Aires. They were Lt. Geoffry Brooke, 16th Lancers; Major the Hon. John Beresford, 7th Hussars; Captain Edmund Bayford, 18th Hussars; and Colonel Alexander Godley, from the Aldershot staff. The visitors were mounted by members of the Hurlingham Club, on whose polo grounds the match took place. The final score was 4–1 in favor of the British Army team, on a heavy ground due to rain.[20]

Maj. Gen. Geoffry Brooke became a prolific writer on military and equestrian subjects, including polo. His *Horse Sense and Horsemanship of Today* is a classic and went through several editions. He took the 15th Hussars Cup in India and was painted by Sir Alfred Munnings when attached to the Canadian Cavalry Brigade in the Western Front. Brooke was a member of the 1924 British equestrian team at the Paris Olympic Games.

John Graham de la Poer Beresford, later Lord Decies, was on teams that took the 1900 Westchester Cup and the gold medal at the Paris Olympic Games. He took the Ranelagh Open, the Irish Open and the Inter-Regimental Tournament in both England and India. The then Captain Beresford presented the trophy that now bears his name, emblematic of the South African Polo Championship.

Not much is known about the life of Major Bayford, who was awarded the Distinguished Service Order.

General Godley was instrumental in training the New Zealand Army prior to World War I. His performance as commander of the New Zealand and Australian Division in Gallipoli has been severely criticized. Nevertheless, after the war was over, he was appointed commander in chief of the British Army of the Rhine, and later governor of Gibraltar.

The venue, Hurlingham's polo field, now officially named Lewis Lacey Field in memory of the English and Argentine international, is the oldest polo ground in activity in South America. It was laid in 1889 by Mr. William Lacey, Lewis' father.

The local team was Lt. Alberto de Oliveira Cézar, Lt. Samuel Casares, Lt. Alfredo Quiroga and Colonel Isaac de Oliveira Cézar. The match was umpired by Harold Schwind, a seven-goal handicap player who was born in Edinburgh and was the proprietor of a 30,000-acre estancia named El Bagual ("The Wild Horse"). Schwind took a team to play in the 1912 London season, where they took the Social Clubs Cup as the Argentine Club, and the Whitney Cup as the Wild Horse. Colonel Oliveira Cézar was the "father of military polo" in Argentina and was vice president of the Argentine Polo Association. In the 1920s, Colonel Casares was a military attaché in London, where he played for many years on a team named La Pampa.

There would be no international matches between Argentina and England until the 1924 Olympic Games in Paris.

CHAPTER 4

Initial Tournaments:
The Hurlingham Champion Cup,
the Inter-Regimental Tournament
and the County Cup

Hurlingham Champion Cup

The Hurlingham Champion Cup was offered for competition in 1876. The records are incomplete regarding this event. The Royal Horse Guards, also known as "the Blues," took this tournament from the Monmouthshire Polo Club. Regrettably, there is no record of who played for Monmouthshire. The Blues were led by the Hon. Charles FitzWilliam; Lord Charles Kilmarnock, Frederick Trench-Gascoigne, John Brocklehurst and Evelyn Atherley completed the team. The final score is also unknown.

Seven teams answered the call in 1877; once more, Monmouthshire reached the finals. The provincial team was Captain Francis "Tip" Herbert, James Mellor, Hugh Owen, Edward Curre and, at goalkeeper, Tip's older brother, Reginald Herbert. They faced a scratch team, captained by Sir Bache Cunard, completed by the Spanish brothers Adrián and Cristóbal de Murrieta, the Hon. Charles Cavendish and Edward Baldock. This match, umpired by Sir Charles Wolseley and Colonel George Gosling, was an extraordinary one, for not a single goal was scored after one hour and fifteen minutes of play. An extra time of half-hour was played, still with no goals. It was then decided to give each team a cup. This game was witnessed by the Prince and Princess of Wales, and the French, Danish and Chinese ambassadors to the Court of St. James.

Monmouthshire took the cup next year, with a team that included the Herbert brothers, Sir Charles Wolseley, Edward Curre and James Mellor. They defeated the 5th Lancers in a close match, three goals to two.

In 1879, the table was turned on Monmouthshire. The holders made one change: Windham Wyndham-Quin replaced Sir Charles Wolseley. It was the host team, Hurlingham, with Edward Baldock as captain that defeated Monmouthshire by three goals to nil. It was a sweet victory, because the previous year Monmouthshire had defeated Hurlingham in the semifinals game. The three Peat brothers and William Ince-Anderton completed the Hurlingham team. Baldock, Alfred and Johnnie Peat had been on the previous year's Hurlingham team.

Winners and losers mixed in the winning team for 1880. With the foundation of the

Ranelagh Club the Herberts allowed Monmouthshire to wither on the vine; it was a Ranelagh team formed by the two Herbert brothers, Edward Baldock, William Ince-Anderton and T. Stuart Kennedy that took the honors, defeating a Sussex County team that included the Peat brothers.

There were no other entries in 1881; therefore Sussex County walked over. It was the beginning of Sussex's dominance in the Champion Cup, fully described in the next section. Only John Watson's Freebooters were able to score wins, in 1884, 1886 and 1887. Otherwise, it was all Sussex County from 1881 to 1893.

The Sussex County Team of the Peat Brothers

Very few polo teams have surpassed the record posted between 1880 and 1893 by the Sussex County Polo Club. Along those years, Sussex posted ten championship titles—three by walkover—and two losses, to Ranelagh and the Freebooters. The record speaks for itself:

1877: Three Peats, with Henry Howard and their brother-in-law Edward Kenyon-Stow, who broke his leg in the first period, played for the International Gun and Polo Club, but being a man short, they were beaten in the first round by the Herberts' Monmouthshire Club.

1878: Alfred and Johnnie Peat played for Hurlingham with Edward Baldock, Henry Case and Thomas Kempson; they were beaten by Monmouthshire in the semifinal round.

1879: Three Peats, with Edward Baldock and William Ince-Anderton, played for Hurlingham and won, beating Monmouthshire in the finals.

1880: Playing for Sussex, three Peats, the Earl of Lewes and Geoffrey Phipps-Hornby, who retired injured in the first period, lost to Ranelagh.

1881: Sussex won by walkover. Algernon Peyton, the Earl of Lewes, and three Peats.

1882: Sussex won. Johnnie Peat, Arthur Peat, Edward Kenyon-Stow, Algernon Peyton and James Babington were on the team.

1883: Sussex won by walkover. Geoffrey Phipps-Hornby and three Peats

1884: Sussex lost to John Watson's Freebooters. Johnnie Peat, Thomas Kennedy, Edward Kenyon-Stow and Geoffrey Phipps-Hornby, who retired halfway in the match.

1885: Sussex won. Three Peats and Francis Mildmay.

1886: The Peats did not play due to a family bereavement. Francis Mildmay played for Gloucestershire, beaten in semifinal.

1887: Johnnie Peat and Arthur Peat played for Derbyshire with Lord Harrington and Gerald Hardy. Beaten in the final by John Watson's Freebooters.

1888–1891: Sussex won. Three Peats and Francis Mildmay.

1892: Sussex won: Alfred Peat, Johnnie Peat, Francis Mildmay and Lord Harrington.

1893: Sussex won: Three Peats and Francis Mildmay

1894: Sussex lost in the final to the Freebooters, Gerald Hardy, Lord Southampton, Capt. Jules Le Gallais and Capt. Dennis Daly, after three minutes and seventeen seconds of overtime. Three Peats and Lord Harrington played for Sussex County.[1]

Gerald Hardy, who had previously been on the Sussex team, scored the winning tally. Educated at Eton and Christ Church, Oxford, Gerald Hardy was called to the Bar and became MFH of the Meynell.

This last year (1894), the rule allowing a one-minute stoppage every time the ball went

The famous Sussex County polo team, winners of ten Hurlingham Champion Cups. Alfred Peat, Arthur Peat, Francis Mildmay and Johnnie Peat.

out of play was discontinued. The Sussex County ponies had been trained to be changed every time play stopped and were not able to keep up the pace throughout the match. In a huff, the Peat brothers sold their ponies and did not appear ever again on a polo ground.

Contemporary reports point out that the success of the Sussex County team was based upon two factors. The first one was that the three brothers were endowed with a strong physique that allowed them to become heavy and accurate hitters, using mallets longer than average. The second was that they spent a considerable time training their ponies. Each one having four or five ponies, they also kept fit by constant practice.

The fourth player, Francis Mildmay, an Eton and Cambridge man and later MP for South Devon, was described by Moray Brown as "a most beautiful and finished player, and for neatness and style unsurpassed. Though slight of built, he yet could hit tremendously hard."[2] Mildmay served in both the South African and European wars, displaying unusual bravery at Ypres. When he retired from Parliament, he was created Baron Mildmay of Flete, his ancestral home. His son, Anthony, was a skilled steeplechase rider, who in 1949 convinced HM Queen Elizabeth to purchase a horse, Monaveen, which he rode to victory on its first outing. This contributed to the Queen Mother's lifelong interest in National Hunt racing.

The Rugby Polo Club Team

In the game of polo it is not unusual at all that one or two teams tend to be the dominant power in each decade. When the Peat brothers abandoned the arena, the Rugby team of the

Miller brothers, Captain Renton, Walter Jones, the Earl of Shrewsbury and Jack Drybrough at back began their years of supremacy. Their performance in the Hurlingham Champion Cup and the Ranelagh Open Cup left no doubt whatsoever as to which was the premier team in the waning years of the nineteenth century and the dawn of the twentieth. A total of five Champion Cups, three Ranelagh Open Cups and three All Ireland Open Cups are proof enough of their mastery.

The heart of the Rugby team was Edward Miller, who served his apprenticeship in the 17th Lancers. Eventually, Lt. Col. Miller would become one of the most respected figures in the world of polo, as a player, horseman, organizer and prolific writer. His mentor was another officer, William Gordon Renton, who while stationed in India developed a regimental style of play that emphasized combination play between the backs and the forwards. As number 3, Ted Miller was the first to freely change positions with back, and he also encouraged his number 2 to change places with number 1 and number 3. Captain Renton's teaching paid handsome dividends when four subalterns from the 17th Lancers took the Indian Inter-Regimental Tournament in 1888 and 1889.

There is a polo link from Sussex to Rugby. Before going to India, Gordon Renton had played with the Peat brothers at Hurlingham and there he learned the beauty of combination play. This he passed on to the 17th Lancers, including Ted Miller, who in turn coached the Rugby team on the importance of short, accurate passing, because they were not heavy hitters. Edward Miller was of the opinion that the strongest Rugby team was Walter Jones at number 1 because he had the best polo pony string in England at the time. George Miller at number 2 was an accurate goal getter, and Charles Miller was perhaps the best back in England. Under the leadership of Ted Miller, Rugby was the team to beat for a long time.

Alumni Cantabrigienses

The big challenge to Rugby's hegemony came from the Old Cantabs, a team of former Cambridge University undergraduates assembled under the leadership of Walter Selby Buckmaster, the first ten-goal player in England. His initial teammates were the brothers Walter and Lawrence McCreery, whose father was Andrew B. McCreery from San Francisco, an American living in England, and F.C.M. Freake, later Sir Frederick. "Freddie" Freake was a quiet man who schooled his own ponies and reached international status and a nine-goal rating.

Later players included Godfrey Heseltine, MFH, who was once described by Walter Buckmaster as "a fine striker and a good goal-hitter. His strong point is dribbling up the ball when coming to the opposing back, and at this we can safely say he has no equal."[3] Another member of the squad was Captain George Bellville, 16th Lancers, an eight-goal player who played at number 1 on the Old Cantabs teams that took the Champion Cup on four occasions between 1908 and 1914. Captain Bellville was wounded in both the South African War and in the Western Front in France, so severely that he had to give up polo. Lord John Wodehouse, later Earl of Kimberley, who also served in the 16th Lancers, was a ten-goal international player and usually played at back. He became a civilian casualty in World War II when his home in London was bombed during the blitz in 1941.

The Old Cantabs won the Champion Cup six times, the last one in 1914 when England was basking in the sun of the last summer of peace.

The Hurlingham Champion Cup Before the War

The third prominent team in the era before the war was Roehampton. Cecil and Pat Nickalls joined Captains Herbert Wilson and John Hardress Lloyd to win back-to-back Champion Cups in 1905–6. Roehampton took the tournament again in 1909, with Rivy Grenfell and Lt. Noel Edwards in place of the Nickall brothers. The Nickalls were not out of the picture by any means, because in 1911 they joined with veterans Charles and George Miller to take Hurlingham Club's Champion Cup.

The three brothers teamed up with Captain Henry de Lisle on a team named the Students. They surprised everyone when they reached the finals of the 1899 Hurlingham Champion Cup, only to be defeated by the Rugby team. Cecil Nickalls— the Millers' brother-in-law — was a complete sportsman: when a schoolboy at Rugby he excelled at football and cricket. At Oxford most likely he would have been a double blue; however, he concentrated on polo and hunting. Ted Miller thought he was the best number 1 in England,[4] in which position he played in the Westchester Cup in 1902. During the war he was blown up and gassed and never recovered his health.

Patteson Nickalls, the older brother, learned polo at their home in Chislehurst, Kent, where all the siblings, including five girls, played on ponies on a rough pasture. "Pat" Nickalls developed into a powerful back and the best all-round player in the family. The youngest sibling, Morres, better known as "Bobby," was a clever number 2 and a good horseman. Both Bobby and Pat represented Oxford University, and all three played for England in different Westchester Cup teams.

An interesting team, Quidnuncs, took the tournament in 1913. It was made up by the Duque de Peñaranda, a Spanish Grandee, the younger brother of the Duke of Berwick and Alba, a direct descendant of King James II; the ten-goaler Captain William Palmes who achieved fame as the number 3 on the formidable 10th Hussars team that was unbeatable in the Indian Inter-Regimental Tournament; Captain Henry Tomkinson, who carried the reputation of being able to play on ponies no other horseman could handle; and the Irishman Captain Frederick Barrett, 15th Hussars, another ten-goal handicap player. Edward, Prince of Wales, frequently played on Quidnuncs teams in the 1920s.

The Inter-Regimental Tournament

The oldest continuous polo competition — save for interruptions due to armed conflicts — is the Inter-Regimental Tournament, started in 1878. Next in order of antiquity is the Oxford versus Cambridge varsity fixture, also launched in 1878. The Oxford v. Cambridge match was held in November of that year; it is safe to assume that the Inter-Regimental took place during the summer months. No records appear to have been kept of the inaugural event. However, it is known that three teams entered the competition. The final match was played between the 5th Lancers, Julian Spicer, George Tufton, Cosmo Little, Llewellyn Heywood Jones and Captain Richard St. Leger Moore, and the 16th Lancers, Captain the Hon. Charles Cavendish, Captain Thomas Davison, Frederick Blair, Eustace Maudsley and Henry Lloyd Howard. The Royal Irish Lancers won by three goals to one.

The 5th Lancers held on to the title in 1879, again defeating the 16th Lancers by one goal to nil, on a ground heavy from rain. Captain Edward Paley hit the only tally after fifty minutes of play. Paley and Captain Joseph Benyon had replaced Cosmo Little and Captain Moore.

In 1880, the 16th Lancers took revenge over the 5th, with a team that included Henry Lloyd Howard, James Babington, Frederick Blair, John Baird and Windham Wyndham-Quin. Then in 1881, the 16th retained the championship, Byron Browne being the fourth man in the year that teams were reduced to four players; Blair and Howard stepped down. Captain Babington hit all three goals for the 16th Lancers, while their opponents, the 4th Hussars, were blanked out.

The 5th Lancers remained the team to beat; winners in 1882 and semifinalists the following year, when they fell in overtime to the 7th Hussars, recently arrived from their tour of duty in South Africa. The latter regiment went on to take the championship with the help of two novelties: the "flying man," or number 1, and the use of the backhander. Up to that time, teams had played with one back and the other three players anywhere. The 7th Hussars placed the Hon. Richard Lawley, later to play in the 1886 Westchester Cup, continuously up in front. It was not a surprise at all that the 7th retained the title in 1884 defeating the 5th Lancers 4–3 after half-hour overtime had been played. The great left-handed player Captain Francis Wise gave the 7th Hussars a clear advantage over its adversaries.

The 7th Hussars went on to win four tournaments in a row before the 5th Lancers, with the help of Captain Julian Spicer, one of the best players of his generation, regained the title in 1887. The 9th Lancers, one of the originators of polo in England, took the tournament four times; the 13th Hussars thrice; the Inniskillings twice; the 10th Hussars, another pioneer regiment, once; and the 7th Hussars added one more title to their harvest.

The Inter-Regimental Tournament was interrupted by the outbreak of the Boer War. However, the soldiers' thirst for polo could not be quenched in the veldt. Lt. Col. Edward Miller, at the time attached to the Imperial Yeomanry, tells that while passing through Heilbron, Simon Lovat was there with his Scouts and asked him to have a game of polo. Ted Miller believes that the game took place, but his superior officer, Lord Charles Chesham, would not let him play.[5]

A tournament took place at Kroonstad on 22 September 1900. In the first round, the Yeomanry defeated the Garrison, and the 17th Lancers' first team beat the 9th Lancers. Captain Henry Fiennes, Lt. Lord Frederick Blackwood, Lt. F. William Cavendish[6] and Lt. John Duckett were on the 9th's team. The 17th Lancers' second team beat the Yeomanry, only to fall when they faced their own regiment's first team.[7]

Nevertheless, the Anglo-Boer war inflicted a deep wound into the ranks of British polo-playing officers. Foremost among the casualties was Lt. Col. P.W. Jules Le Gallais, 8th Hussars, from an old Jersey family, a winner of the Champion Cup at Hurlingham and the Inter-Regimental Tournament in India, who was considered one of the best at number 3 in his time. He was also the designer of the stick head that carries his name, probably the most popular among players well into the twentieth century. Lt. Col. Le Gallais died of his wounds near Bothaville in 1900.

David Ogilvy, 10th Earl of Airlie, was killed while in command of the 12th Lancers leading a charge that saved the guns during the action at Diamond Hill, near Pretoria. The Boers had concentrated their fire on the colonel and his white horse.[8] A great supporter of the game, he presented the trophy for the Infantry Tournament in India. A generous man, previous to the departure from Lucknow of his regiment, the 10th Hussars, the Earl of Airlie had a well sunk next to the Divisional Polo Ground, for the benefit of future players. It was named David's Well after his lordship.

These are just two of the many players that lost their lives in South Africa. A list of players, their regiments and the actions is given in note 9 of this chapter.

When the hostilities in South Africa ended, the 17th Lancers, the "Glory or Death Boys," took the Inter-Regimental twice, in 1903 and 1904, a feat only equaled by the 20th Hussars, the 11th Hussars and the Royal Horse Guards. Other winning teams included the Inniskillings, the 4th Dragoon Guards, the 15th Hussars and the 12th Lancers. (For a complete list of teams and players, see appendix 3.)

Then came about the madness of the Great War, which changed the fabric of military polo in England forever. The list of polo players killed in that conflict is far too long to publish. Mons, Ypres, the Somme, Gallipoli, Passchendaele and Palestine are just a few places where the flower of British youth was mowed down during the War to End All Wars.

The County Cup

The implementation of the County Cup precedes the foundation of the County Polo Association (CPA) by several years. While the County Cup was first played for in 1885, the County Polo Association only saw the light of day in 1898. Mr. Tresham Gilbey was the first president. The healthy tradition of nominating polo players to that office has remained throughout the passage of time.

The tournament was instituted by the Hurlingham Club; however, control of the competition was passed on to the County Polo Association in 1898, when the CPA offered a challenge cup, now the National Sixteen-Goal Championship held at Cirencester Park. Some of the membership at Hurlingham had complained that hosting the final stages of the County Cup cluttered the grounds to an extent that members' matches had to be canceled. The County Polo Association then reached an agreement with the Eden Park Polo Club — an entity that always welcomed players from overseas — to hold the semifinals on its ground. Eventually, the preliminary ties were played regionally in the Northern, Midland, Southeastern and Southwestern divisions and the semifinals and the finals were played at Ranelagh Club during County Polo Week, a most popular event. A new trophy, the Dewar Cup, was given to the winner of the division that had the most entrants. Full results of the County Cup are enumerated in appendix 3.

The roster of County Cup winners is replete with names famous in the annals of British polo. It bears some resemblance to the Copa República Argentina, where any player and club can participate, from seasoned ten-goalers to tyros whose main achievement in the game has been reaching the final rounds at Palermo. Superstars and barely known players share, for once in a lifetime, a moment of glory.

Lord Harrington was on teams that took the first three County Cups, from 1885 to 1887. The first winner, the Gloucestershire team, also had Edward Kenyon-Stow, the Peats' brother-in-law, who later went to America to continue his polo career in Philadelphia; Francis Matthews, from St. Fagans, near Cardiff and an original member of the Polo Pony Society; and T.S. Baxter, of whose further polo achievements nothing is known. The next year, 1888, Mr. Baxter's place on the team was taken by Malcolm Little, who that same year would travel to America on John Watson's Westchester Cup team. Captain Little would eventually be in command of the 9th Lancers during the Boer War, a regiment that had been commanded by his father, Sir Archibald Little, during the Indian Mutiny. Another of his sons, Cosmo, was a polo player of repute, winner of the first Inter-Regimental Tournament with the 5th Lancers team. Little was a Scottish Border family, of which a saying was, "If you see a Little, a horse won't be far away." Sportsmen and warriors, Sir Archibald's brother "Josey" Little, King's Dragoon Guards, won the Grand National on Chandler in 1848, and his grandson, Lt. Col. Malcolm A.A. Little, Royal Horse Guards, was killed in action in Italy in October 1944.

The Kent team, winner in 1888, had Robert Stewart-Savile, who when ADC to the Earl of Onslow, governor general of New Zealand, presented the Savile Cup, emblematic of polo supremacy on the New Zealand islands. East Kent had a man of the cloth, the Reverend Frank Timins, among the enthusiasts.

Barton Polo Club, winners in 1889, had once more Lord Harrington, and the Walker brothers, the club's founders. William Hall Walker, a winner of the Paris International Tournament, was later created Lord Wavertree of Delamere. Lord Wavertree presented to the nation his thoroughbred breeding operation in Ireland; it is now the Irish National Stud in Tully, Kildare. His older brother John was also a winner of the Paris Tournament and an original member of the Polo Pony Society.

Berkshire had Captain Victor Ferguson, Major Ronald Ferguson's grandfather; Sir William Lambton; Colonel Thomas Fenwick, a winner of the Irish Open Cup; and Captain Julian Spicer, the 5th Lancers' star player.

In the 1890s, teams from Ireland and Scotland added spice to the competition, county Meath, led by the great John Watson, and Edinburgh Polo Club, with the Drybrough brothers, twice carried the laurels.

The time spent at Chislehurst hitting a ball while mounted on small ponies paid off for the Nickalls brothers, Bobby, Cecil and Pat, ably supported by Henry Savill. Like so many other players, this is the only instance in which a single name appears on a major tournament.

The first military team to take the County Cup was Salisbury Plain in 1910, with Capt. Walter "Toby" Long, Malcolm Borwick, John Readman and Major Charles Bulkeley-Johnson, all Royal Scots Greys officers. Brig. Gen. Long was killed in France while in command of the 56th Infantry Brigade. Lt. Malcolm Borwick rose to the rank of lieutenant colonel. His descendant Malcolm Peter Borwick is currently one of Britain's top players, with a seven-goal handicap. Lt. Col. John Jeffrey Readman, DSO, retired from the service in 1928. Brig. Gen. Bulkeley-Johnston was killed in France near Arras; at the time he was in command of the 8th Cavalry Brigade. The names of brigadiers C.B. Bulkeley-Johnston and W. Long are at the top of the list on the bronze plaque at the Royal Scots Greys Memorial on Princes Street, Edinburgh.

Chapter 5

The Great Clubs and Polo Clubs Near London

Hurlingham Club

The Hurlingham mystique is as old as the club itself. Aristocratic and autocratic, the Hurlingham Club Committee ruled the game of polo as if it was a Roman province; dissent was neither expected nor tolerated. The club's beginnings were far from polo, because it was established as a pigeon-shooting endeavor in 1869. The Hurlingham Club's badge still carries a pigeon as the emblem, even though the practice at the club ended more than a century ago, when the majority of its members decided it was a barbaric pastime.

The club membership purchased the estate from Mr. Richard Naylor for £27,500, and a polo ground was laid out with the expenditure of a large sum for felling and uprooting the trees in the orchard and leveling the ground. The first polo game was held between the 1st Life Guards and the Royal Horse Guards (the Blues) on 6 June 1874, with Prince Edward and Princess Alexandra of Wales, and the Duke and Duchess of Edinburgh among the spectators.[1]

Among the earliest players were Sir Bache Cunard, the Hon. Charles FitzWilliam, Lord Kilmarnock and the brothers Adrián and Cristóbal de Murrieta. They were all veterans of the matches at Lillie Bridge, a club that closed in 1875.

When the Hurlingham rules of polo were published in 1873, they were intended for the guidance of the polo-playing members; however, such was their influence that the club became de facto the governing body of the game, not only in the United Kingdom, but with the spread of polo around the world, as the only authority regarding the administration of the rules and their interpretation. Although some other polo associations, such as in Australia and India, made some changes to conform to local conditions, only the Polo Association in America produced a different code of rules. The Argentine Polo Association implemented its own rules only in 1939, after a four-year study. The initial draft had been conveyed to Lord Louis Mountbatten, chairman of the international committee, who made several suggestions. These were adopted in toto, and thus Lord Mountbatten added to his impressive polo résumé this contribution to the game in Argentina.[2] The Hurlingham Polo Committee became the Marylebone Cricket Club of polo because most of the world followed its rules, a situation that remains as of today. In 1949, those powers became the province of the Hurlingham Polo Association.

The Hurlingham Club also offered other sports and games: lawn tennis, polo pony races, pony and hack shows, croquet, skittles, archery on a few occasions, and even the

The opening polo game at Hurlingham Club, June 1874, as seen by the *Illustrated London News* (private collection).

royal and ancient game of golf. A nine-hole course was constructed, but very few members played and it was discontinued in 1899. Then, as well as many years later in many clubs around the globe, polo players bitterly complained to club committees about using polo grounds for driving ranges. On the other hand, golfers complained to the same committees reporting desecration of greens by runaway polo ponies.

A second polo ground was constructed and was ready for play in May 1895, but it was a small ground. This deficiency was solved when the Broom House property of fifty-two acres became available for purchase. However, there was never enough space to accommodate all the players who wished to play, a situation which was a constant headache for successive polo managers. In part, this congestion led to the creation of the Ranelagh and Roehampton clubs.

The number One Polo Ground at Hurlingham was the site of the international contests for the Westchester Cup in 1900, 1902, 1909, 1921 and 1936, with honors equally divided. From a financial point of view these matches were a bonanza to the club's coffers. The number of tournaments organized by Hurlingham explains the logjam at the two polo grounds: the Hurlingham Champion Cup, the Inter-Regimental Tournament, for a while the County Cup, the Social Clubs' Cup, the Patriotic Challenge Cup against Ireland, the Oxford versus Cambridge Inter-varsity Match, the Whitney Cup in conjunction with Roehampton Club, several handicap tournaments and scheduled matches between excellent teams such as Old Cantabs and Woodpeckers. With the addition of members' matches at the end of the day, it is astonishing that the two polo grounds could remain playable through a polo season that began in April and lasted until the end of July.

The Social Clubs' Cup was of significance in the years up to the beginning of the war. No team with an aggregate of more than twenty-six goals was allowed to enter; it was open to members of recognized social clubs in London or country. Among the early champions were Bath, the Cavalry Club, Nimrod, Orleans, Raleigh, RAC, the newcomer Argentine, and White's, the initial winners.

The Whitney Cup was another high-goal competition played simultaneously at Hurlingham and Roehampton; the finals to be decided alternatively at each club. It was presented by Harry Payne Whitney, the American team's captain, in 1909.

As related elsewhere, the polo competition in the 1908 Olympic Games took place at Hurlingham Club.

Oddly enough, the Number One Ground barely conformed to the Hurlingham Polo Committee's own specifications. It has always been customary that a polo field is to be rectangular in shape, occasionally with the boards curving toward the goalposts near the backline. The Hurlingham Club's ground was egg shaped; for some time even the backlines were curved, which anomaly made play near the goals rather tricky.[3] In addition, there was a considerable incline toward the north end, commonly known as the chestnuts end. However, the luscious turf, Hurlingham's glory, made up handsomely for those technical deviations.

During the Great War, Mounted Yeomanry squadrons occupied the grounds. Considerable damage was done to the Number One Ground by trench mortar rounds; whether they went astray or it was routine training is not recorded. The Royal Flying Corps used the grounds as a balloon site and constructed a hangar. In World War II, the Royal Air Force placed a balloon barrage on the Number One field and put to use the Number Two field as a site for an antiaircraft battery. For some unknown reason, Hurlingham received a dose of one land mine and twenty-seven bombs, most likely due to random bombing by the Luftwaffe, or perhaps just poor aiming. It is certain that the stiff upper lip remained immobile.

The London County Council and the Fulham Borough Council proved more lethal to the club than the German bombers. In October 1946, a Compulsory Purchase Order was served for the entire property with the exception of the Number Two Ground as a public open space. Not that Number Two field was to be spared; the Fulham Borough Council also served an order for a housing project. Typically, the Hurlingham Club fought the compulsory purchases in the courts of law and also used its considerable clout with certain personalities to defend its case. The final outcome was that the Number Two field became Sullivan Court, a housing development, and the hallowed Number One Ground became Hurlingham Park, a sporting facility with a football pitch and a running track. So the club survived the worst crisis in its long history.[4]

Nevertheless, the optimistic view expressed by the committee when the Broom House was purchased, that "the rural amenities of our Club are now secured in perpetuity," was not fulfilled.[5]

The dilapidated grandstand built for the 1936 Westchester Cup matches was demolished in 2003. Something akin to the ancient game of polo took place on that ground in 2009. It was no more than a charade, with rules that had stood for a long time significantly changed to make the game more attractive to an audience that most likely had no idea whatsoever of polo's traditions, whys and wherefores.

A portion of Mr. Nigel Miskin's last paragraph in his book *History of Hurlingham* is most appropriate to end this section:

The future is unknowable but we may reasonably assume that in a thousand years time Father Thames will still be rolling along between these banks and trust that, somehow, in Hurlingham Field, there will still be standing a beautiful old house with its trees and its gardens and its flowers, for the ease and enjoyment of all who resort there.[6]

Ranelagh Club

The success of polo at Hurlingham was so extraordinary that soon enough the requirement for more polo grounds became a dire necessity. In 1878, a property near the Hurlingham Club which had belonged to Lord Ranelagh was available for lease. The brothers Reginald and Francis Herbert joined Edward Kenyon Stow in securing a short-term lease. The club offered, in addition to polo, lawn tennis, pony shows, and dear to the Herberts, pony racing.

The first significant polo game was a novelty because it took place under electric lights. The teams were Hurlingham, with Lord Petersham, later Earl of Harrington; Johnny Peat; Windham Wyndham-Quin; and Alfred Peat against Ranelagh, with Arthur Peat, Lord William Lewes, William Ince-Anderton and Edward Baldock. The Prince of Wales was present, which ensured the approval of the event by the world of fashion. There is no record of the result, which is not of much consequence because it was most likely the equivalent of an exhibition game.

At the time, Ranelagh was not a competitor for Hurlingham; it was more of a complement. Soon that relationship changed, when a beautiful parcel of land, Barn Elms, encompassing over one hundred acres across the River Thames, became available in 1883. The site belonged to the Ecclesiastical Chapter of St. Paul's; it was a significant change since the days where many questions of honor were settled by the sword. The most notorious duel involved the ancestor of a prominent polo player, the Earl of Shrewsbury, a Rugby team stalwart.[7]

The club had modest beginnings, but when the Herbert brothers decided to quit, a strong committee was formed, chaired by Lord Dudley, but the prime force was Dr. (later Sir George) Hastings. Nothing but perfection would satisfy him, and very soon the Ranelagh Club surpassed Hurlingham in polo membership. Three full-size grounds were constructed, with ample stabling and practice area. Golf became part and parcel of the club, and good relationships were maintained between polo players and golfers. The latter group offered for competition the Ranelagh Open Cup, second only to the Hurlingham Champion Cup in prestige. There was also a golf tournament for polo players only.

The polo pavilion overlooking the Old Field was considered the best in the land to watch a polo game. Another innovation by Ranelagh was the formation of a club team, rare in London in those early days of polo. Captain Leopold Jenner, Alfred "Toby" Rawlinson, Frederick Gill and Hugh Scott Robson, the ambidextrous back from Argentina, upheld the red and white quartered colors.

Ranelagh Club was a strong supporter of polo in the military. The Aldershot Cup was open to regiments stationed in the Aldershot Command, the Eastern Command and the London District. It was an unusual tournament, played on a single day with four twenty-minute games going on simultaneously. The practice ground was pressed into service to accommodate all the matches. The Aldershot Infantry Cup conditions were the same, but it was restricted to infantry regiments. The Army Cup was held at Ranelagh for a trophy presented by Lt. Col. Roland Forestier-Walker. It was open to regular army officers, past and present. Finally, the Subalterns' Gold Cup was open to teams of subalterns in the regular or auxiliary forces. The trophy was donated by Sydney Sidney-Humphries. This tournament was revived in 1958.

The House of Lords versus the House of Commons polo fixture was started in 1906, for a challenge cup presented by the Earl of Harrington. It was resumed in 1922 with a match that included the Prince of Wales, the Duke of Westminster, Earl Fitzwilliam and Viscount Wimborne for the Lords. They beat the Commons, which had Sir Philip Sassoon, Lt. Col. Hon. Frederick Vernon, Captain Hon. Frederick Guest and Winston Churchill, by five goals to three. Due to an injury sustained during his days in India with the 4th Hussars, the future prime minister had to play with his right shoulder protected by a cumbersome contraption.

Provincial polo was not forgotten. Besides hosting some of the semifinals and finals of the County Cup and the Junior County Cup, the club organized a popular event, the Hunt Cup, for a trophy presented by the club. The competition was open to any member or subscriber of any recognized pack of Foxhounds or Staghounds in the United Kingdom or from abroad. There was a handicap limit of twenty-four goals.

A well-subscribed tournament was the Novices' Cup. The conditions were rather restrictive because it was limited to members of Ranelagh, teams belonging to the County Polo Association and teams quartered in the London District.

The story of the Coronation Cup, started at the Ranelagh Club, is described elsewhere in this book.

Although many polo players belonged to both Ranelagh and Hurlingham, the respective committees did not always see eye to eye. The foremost issue was that of adequate representation in the Hurlingham Polo Committee, the game's ruling body. When formed, obviously all members were from the Hurlingham Club. In 1903, three members of the County Polo Association, two from the Army Polo Committee and one from Roehampton Club were added to the committee; however, the Hurlingham Club still held the majority of votes. The Ranelagh Club refused the offer of one seat, on the grounds that it was the largest polo club in the world in terms of playing members.

Ranelagh continued to thrive into the late 1930s, when insurmountable financial problems forced its closure in 1939. The beautiful property was taken over by the London County Council at the beginning of the war for use as the Barn Elms sports ground. The bells tolled for the once proud citadel of polo. Let it rest.

Rugby Polo Club

Sometime in 1891, the brothers Edward and George Miller decided to combine pleasure with business by training polo ponies and then dealing in them. They found a suitable spot in Spring Hill, the farm of the well-known horse dealer John Darby of Rugby, 180 acres of good grassland, with boxes and stalls capable of accommodating more than fifty horses.[8] The location was near Hillmorton Gorse, a place famous in foxhunting as the point where the Atherstone, the North Warwickshire and the Pytchley converge. Alfred Brocas-Clay was one of those who helped the Miller brothers start the club.

There were some difficulties at first. Some of the local residents looked askance at the new game in town, and there were few polo players in the vicinity. Nevertheless, a polo ground was built and boarded, and a pavilion was constructed to provide refreshments and a comfortable view of the proceedings. However, the new line laid by the Great Central Railway cut through one of the ends of the polo ground, and it had to be rebuilt.

The first match was against Leamington, and the three Miller brothers with Bertram Portal at back defeated the visiting Leamington squad with ease. But the great career of the Rugby team began in 1897, when the club took the Champion Cup at Hurlingham, the Ranelagh Open Cup and the Irish Open Cup, without suffering a single defeat in the entire season. A mighty back, Jack Drybrough; Charles, Edward and George Miller; and Captain Gordon Renton were the players. Lt. Col. Edward Miller states that the full Rugby team did not lose a match until 1903.[9] Frank Hargreaves, Walter Jones and Lord Shrewsbury also played at Number One. Regrettably, the Scot Jack Drybrough, who used to play bareheaded, was killed in 1899 in a collision involving three players. As a result of this tragedy, helmets became mandatory.

The Rugby Polo remained the premier provincial club until the Second World War. The main tournaments were the Rugby Challenge Cup, instituted in 1893 by the Miller brothers; the Junior Challenge Cup; the Summer Tournament, for a trophy donated by Mr. James Mason of the Cirencester Club; the Autumn Cup; the Montaigu Cup, presented by Count Réné de Montaigu; and the Autumn Handicap. It was a full schedule in a season, beginning in April and ending in September, which congregated most of the best players in England and a significant number of foreign visitors.

The Rugby Polo Club successes were not limited to high-goal tournaments because different teams took a record ten County Cups and the Junior County Cup on two occasions.

Cirencester Polo Club

The Cirencester Polo Club stands a monument to the earlier days of the game. The club came into being on 9 June 1894, after a meeting in the Deer Park within the Earl of Bathurst's estate. The 4th Gloucester Militia was encamped for training. Those present were Earl Bathurst; John Adamthwaite; Gardner Bazley; W. Blunson, V.S.; E. Denby; James Farmer; W.F. Felton; Jesse Gouldsmith; Captain M. Dew Keating; Colonel Chester Master; Digby Master; A.E. Morris; Major Arthur Paget; and F.J. Townsend. The seventh Earl of Bathurst was elected chairman and gave permission to use land on his property for use as a polo ground. The support of the Bathurst family has not wavered ever since.

That same afternoon a match consisting of three games was played between a team of civilians and the Gloucesters. The Civilians were Digby Master, John Adamthwaite, W.F. Felton and James Farmer. The Gloucestershire Militia aligned Colonel Chester Master, Major the Lord Bathurst, Major Arthur Paget and Captain Jesse Gouldsmith. The Civilians took the first game 2–0; the second was a draw and the third was won by the Civilians 1–0. The second teams then played a three-a-side match, in which the Civilians, F.J. Townsend, W. Blumson and A.E. Morris beat by eight goals to nil the 4th Gloucester Militia, Captain Henry Goodlake, Captain Digby and Captain Gardner Bazley.[10]

Among the players in 1894 were Major Francis Butler, 18th Hussars; Frederick Freake, the future international; G. Lees Milne; Henry Talbot Rice; and Harry Rich.

The Cirencester Challenge Cup was established in 1895 for a trophy presented by Colonel Henry Talbot Rice. It was first won by the Royal Scots Greys, Captain Charles Maxwell, Captain Pringle, Lt. John Harrison and Captain Arthur Richards. Another competition was the Cirencester Spring Tournament, instituted in 1907 and taken by the Potchefstroom Pilgrims, Walter Neilson, Captain Antony Stokes, Noel Edwards and Captain Richard Brocklebank.

The club prospered and during the period prior to the Great War took the County Cup in 1904, with the team of James Mason, the Hon. Aubrey Hastings, Reginald Barker and John Adamthwaite. Further successes followed in 1911 when Walter Burdon, the Hon. Aubrey Hastings, Hugh Baker and James Mason took the trophy back to Gloucestershire. Fifty-two years would pass before the County Cup was retaken by the club, now renamed Cirencester Park. Major John Mayne and Jack Williams, with the aid of two Argentinians, the veteran Eduardo Rojas Lanusse and the up-and-coming Eduardo "Gordo" Moore, gathered the spoils of victory in 1963. The feat was repeated in 1968, when Lord Samuel Vestey, Eduardo Moore, Peter Perkins and Captain Frederick Barker took the County Cup once more.

The Junior County Cup was taken in 1911 by Hugh Baker, Stanley Barton, Jesse Gouldsmith and James Mason; in 1957 by Col. Raymond Barrow, Brian Bethell, Lt. Col. Anthony McConnel and the Hon. George Bathurst; and in 1961 with Dirk Sellschopp, the Hon. George Bathurst, Lt. Col. Anthony McConnel and Andrew Summers.

Another important trophy taken by Cirencester was the Roehampton Cup, which was taken back to back in 1922 and 1923 by the team of Captain Maurice Kingscote, the Hon. Aubrey Hasting, Captain Rex Smart and Captain Lindsay Shedden.

Other players were Captain Nugent Allfrey, 2nd Dragoon Guards; Reginald Barker; Heywood Farmer; Charles Devenish, Jesse's brother; Captain A.G. James, RN; A. Lawson Johnston; Lt. Col. Cyril Martyr, Duke of Cornwall L.I.; Captain Geoffrey Metcalfe, 8th Hussars; John C. Metcalfe; Captain George Rennie; and Percy Woolcott.

The worldwide depression hit the Cirencester Club hard, and the members decided it was not possible to carry on. Another factor was the success of the nearby Beaufort Polo Club with its assortment of grounds at Norton and Westonbirt.[11] The assets were put up for auction and some of the trophies were given to neighboring polo clubs, such as Beaufort and Cheltenham. The Cirencester Polo Club was in abeyance from 1932 until 1953.[12]

Roehampton Club

The failure of the Wimbledon Park Polo Club and the success of the Ranelagh Club contributed to the overcrowding of polo grounds in London. In the meantime, Charles Miller had found a suitable parcel of land in Roehampton, quite close to both Hurlingham and Ranelagh. The enterprising Miller brothers came to the fore and established a limited liability company, unlike Ranelagh Club which had selected a syndicate to form the club. The Earl of Shrewsbury, one of their teammates in the Rugby team, was elected chairman. Most of the initial shareholders were aristocrats and military officers. The first 400 members paid no initial fees. Three polo grounds were laid out, as well as a pony racing track, a horse show ground, stables, and a ground reserved for women to practice jumping and driving. Other attractions were archery and croquet, and later a nine-hole golf course, which was expanded to eighteen holes when additional land was leased.

The Roehampton Cup was instituted in 1903 for a trophy presented by Mrs. John (Alison) Cuningham of Craigends (see results in appendix 3). It was the club's most important competition until the Roehampton Open Cup was established in 1913. The winner of the

Roehampton Open competed for the Coronation Cup against the winning teams of the Inter-Regimental Tournament, the Hurlingham Champion Cup and the Ranelagh Open. Another trophy of significance was the Roehampton Junior Championship, a trophy donated by William Hazard, long-time secretary of the Polo Association in the United States and its chairman in 1921. The Ladies' Nomination Cup was a tournament in which every player on a team was nominated by a woman. The individual cups awarded to the members of the winning team were given to the nominating lady, presumably as a reward for their prescience in selecting the best players.

The Public Schools Cup was instituted in 1901 and played at Ranelagh, Old Malburians—Captain Leopold Jenner, Edward Sheppard and two Miller brothers, George and Charles—being the first winners. The following year the venue was moved to Roehampton, but the same team won again, and also in 1904. The elder Miller sibling, Edward, took matters into hand and led his Old Harrovians to victory. Walter Jones, Captain Renton and the Hon. Dudley Marjoribanks completed the team. This tournament was always well subscribed. The Madrid Cup, open to battalions of the Guard, was presented by the members of the Marqués de Villavieja's Madrid team in 1908. The Irish Guards took the initial tournament with a team that had Lt. John Guthrie, Major Hubert Crichton, Lt. (later Brig. Gen.) Sir Smith Hill Child and Lt. John Harvey.

Polo at Roehampton recovered after the Great War under a new manager, Major Charles Lister, 21st Lancers, who was one of the original shareholders. Major Lister helped newcomers to the game as well as children to learn the basic of polo. In this endeavor he was joined by the Miller brothers and Johnny Traill, whose property La Esterlina was located across the street from the club. The wooden horse had plenty of use in the years between the two world wars.

Roehampton played a significant role in the polo boom that occurred in England during the 1920s, about which more anon.[13]

Cowdray Polo Club

Polo at Cowdray was started in 1910 by the Hon. Harold Pearson, who was captain of the Oxford University team in 1905.[14] The year before, he was on the team that beat Cambridge; also on that team was Devereux Milburn, the American who is considered one of the best ever at back. Harold Pearson called his team Capron House, after his home located close to the Cowdray ruins, and laid out the first polo ground in front of the renovated Cowdray House. Two more grounds were to follow: the celebrated Lawns, in front of Cowdray's ruins, the distant background provided by the South Downs, and the River Ground, named after the Rother, a river that is known to defy the gods of polo by flooding the field.

The first players were Colonel George Ansell, Iniskilling Dragoons; Lt. Col. Hugh Ashton, Life Guards; Roland Burn, Lord Dalmeny; Lt. Col. Robert McKergow, Sussex Yeomanry; Lt. Col. Eustace Morrison-Bell, Westminster Dragoons; and Lt. Col. Hon. Edward Wyndham, Life Guards. Since most of the members played in the London season, play at Cowdray was confined to the months of April and August. The main social occasion was Goodwood Week, during the thoroughbred racing at Goodwood Park, the Earl of Richmond's estate.

The Cowdray Park Challenge Cup, presented by the 1st Viscount Cowdray, was started in 1911 and was taken by the host team: Norman Loder; the Hon. Clive Pearson, Harold's younger brother; Captain Hugh Ashton; and Captain Eustace Morrison-Bell. A Cowdray team was successful in the 1922 Ranelagh Open Cup with the Hon. Harold Pearson, Lord Albert Dalmeny, Walter Buckmaster and Lord George Cholmondeley. Other successes for the orange-clad teams were the Junior Championship at Roehampton, the Bordon Challenge Cup, and the Novices' Cup at Ranelagh.

Up to the onset of World War II, polo at Cowdray was mostly a family affair, where the game was played for the benefit of the Pearson family and friends. The game at Cowdray Park became emblematic of polo by invitation, a place where the game was played by ladies and gentlemen, with unwritten but well-understood patterns of behavior.

There was no polo in the 1927 season as a mark of mourning for the death of the First Viscount Cowdray. Harold Pearson, the Second Viscount, was chairman of the Hurlingham Polo Committee during difficult times. On his premature passing in 1932 his only son — there were five daughters — inherited the title. John Pearson, Third Viscount Cowdray, led the English expedition to America in quest of the Westchester Cup. After the war, Lord Cowdray was the main force in reviving polo in England and took a team to Argentina in 1949. He became chairman of the Hurlingham Polo Association for twenty years, after which he retired of his own accord.

Polo Clubs Near London

The London Polo Club, also known as the Crystal Palace because play was on that oval pitch used for football, lasted from 1889 to 1905. Captain Francis Herbert was in charge of management, and he arranged that players could hire ponies for a fee per period. Many beginners, officers on home leave and visitors from the colonies, found the club a great convenience in spite of the ground's heavy usage. Among the leading players were the Earl of Huntingdon, Sir Charles Wolseley, Mr. Brammall and Dr. MacArthur.

Middlesex

The Kingsbury (Middlesex) Polo Club was started in 1896 by Mr. W. Walton, on two grounds at Roe Green, Kingsbury. The better teams competed in the Tattersall Challenge Cup, presented by Mr. Rupert Tattersall, while the tyros did battle for the Winans Cup, presented by Mr. Walter Winans. A club team — Julian Winans, Harry Rich, Gordon Withers and Paul Winans— took the County Cup in 1909, defeating the Cavalry School from Netheravon in the finals. Some of the club members were Percy Bullivant, Frederick Egan, Dr. Alexander Findlater, William Fuller, J. Colin Newman, and St. Leger G. Stephen. That same year the club hosted practice games for the visiting American international team.

The Wembley Park Polo Club, started in 1905, was a close neighbor to Kingsbury, and its two pitches saw more play than any other club. The vast majority of players hired ponies from the club. Games would start at eight o'clock in the morning, usually featuring busy men in the civil service and others that had to get back to town in good time. Then they retired making room for the House of Commons players, where many celebrated names were found on the play sheets. Another group from the Foreign Office also played. In the afternoon matches, members from Kingsbury also participated. On Saturdays there were matches at both clubs.

After the Great War, the Wembley Park Polo Club had to drop out because their lease expired and the grounds were earmarked for an aerodrome. Eventually, it became Wembley Stadium, the venue for, among other sports, the Football Association Cup finals and the 1948 Olympic Games.

Kent

An important polo club near London was Eden Park in Beckenham, Kent. Founded in 1897, it had a single polo ground; however, it was a large one, quite first class, where the going was always good. Play could take place after a heavy rain that would make all other fields unsuitable for matches. Players such as Edward de Clermont; Frank Kinchant, multiple-time winner of the Polo Association of the River Plate Championship; and Norman Noakes, were among the top practitioners.

Eden Park took the County Cup in 1901 and 1902, with players such as Leonard Bucknell, Percy Bullivant, Hugh Cardwell, Hubert Marsham, John Clement de Las Casas, Alfredo de Las Casas and Harry Rich.

Surrey

The Ashtead Polo Club was started in 1887 by Walter Peake on a small ground lent by his father. The club prospered, reaching the finals of the County Cup in 1890, when they were defeated 2–1 at Hurlingham by the Berkshire County team. Two years later, Walter Peake left Ashtead, and the club removed to Fetcham, where J. Barnard Hankey put a ground in his park at their disposal. Then the club assumed the name Fetcham Park. The major players were Ernest Courage, William Fraser-Tytler, Arthur Moon and Lewis Paine. Wearing their colorful red-and-gray-striped jerseys, the club took the Abergavenny Tournament in 1892.

Stoke D'Abernon Polo Club, founded in 1905, was located in Cobham, Surrey; play was at Mrs. Bowen Buscarlet's park. Early members were Sir Clinton Dawkins, Frederick Phillips, Captain Noel Phillips, Aubrey Price, and the Reverend William Vincent. Stoke D'Abernon's teams took the Junior County Cup on four occasions between 1909 and 1913. Roland Burn, Clifford Trollope, Edmund Bennett, Noel Price, Aubrey Price, the Hon. Robert Douglas-Scott-Montagu, the Hon. Charles Douglas-Pennant and Arthur Hankey were on the winning teams.

After the war, play was only resumed in 1929, but W. Payne, William Withycombe, James Withycombe and Noel Docker revived old glories when, once more, a Stoke D'Abernon team took the Junior County Cup in 1931.

The Worcester Park Polo Club, with grounds at Motspur Park, Malden, came into being in 1902 by the efforts of Sir Thomas Bucknill, with A. Auriol-Baker and Dunbar Kelley as the main movers. The grounds were close to the Hurlingham Club which occasionally leased them to alleviate the congestion brought about by the large number of players looking to play chukkers. Other players were D. Auriol-Baker, Roland Burn, Edward de Clermont, J. Collyer-Bristow, Frank and Fred Houlder, and Captain A.D. Sloane. One of the competitions was for the Cicero Cup, presented by the Earl of Rosebery, then club president, to commemorate the victory of his thoroughbred in the 1905 Derby at Epsom. The first winners of the Cicero Cup were James Pearce, William Balding, Alfredo de Las Casas and John Drage.

There was also another polo club at Wimbledon Park, of which very little is known. Its grounds, near Southfields Station, were well laid out, and the quality of play was good.[15] Wimbledon Park also had a golf course, cricket fields, and a lake used for boating. The grounds were held by a speculative syndicate that held an option to purchase the entire park. The syndicate was unable to take up its option, so the land reverted to the landlord. After a couple of seasons the club ceased to exist, and the two grounds were used by the Household Cavalry as a private venue.[16]

The Recent Form List

The recent form list, quickly nicknamed the "blacklist" by the irreverent players, was implemented by the Hurlingham Committee at the request of the County Polo Association in 1903.[17] The first list contained the names of thirty-one players considered to be the best exponents of the game in England. It was an attempt at individual player handicaps that had been established in America in 1888 by Henry Lloyd Herbert.

In some tournaments, no more than two players on the blacklist were allowed to play on the same team. In reality it was a partial solution to a thorny problem, because it made no allowances for different abilities among the top players. It only separated all the players into two groups: the blessed and those in limbo.

The Reverend Thomas Dale, a keen observer of the polo scene, suggested a numerical handicap system in 1905, similar to the one active in America. It is interesting to read his list of top players with the proposed handicaps:

Walter Buckmaster	10	Pat Nickalls	6
Alfred Rawlinson	8	Morres Nickalls	6
George Miller	8	Neil Haig	6
Frederick Freake	7	Godfrey Heseltine	6
Edward Miller	7	Frederick Gill	6
Hardress Lloyd	6	Leopold Jenner	6

The rest of the players were handicapped at five or less. Numbers, not goals, was the measurement proposed by Thomas Dale.[18]

The Reverend Dale also suggested other considerations to be taken into account. For example, three players from the Rugby Club rated at five — Lord Shrewsbury, Charles Miller and Walter Jones— would be rated at four when playing on other teams. He also suggested that ponies should be part of the equation, as well as the time spent practicing together, because he felt that the opportunities of family teams to practice together should be taken into account.

Nothing came out of the Rev. Thomas Dale's suggestions.

The Long Debate Over the Offside Rule

The offside rule, a relic derived from the ancient game of football, both Association and Rugby codes, simply mandated that an attacking player was "offside" when at the time of the ball being hit, there was no opponent between him and the backline. This rule gave a tremendous advantage to the defending back, which in those early days was usually the strongest player on the team. The end result was that there was a paucity of goals scored in most matches.

Old-timers, mostly personified by the Rugby Club, favored the offside rule because they felt it improved combination play in order to defeat a stubborn defense. As late as 1923, Lt. Col. Edward Miller felt that the abolition of the offside-rule had resulted in a lack of combination play and contributed to the decline of polo in England.[19]

The demise of the offside came about at the hands of the American Big Four team in the 1909 Westchester Cup. Endowed with fast ponies, long hitters and Devereux Milburn, a back that was not averse to moving up to the number 1 territory, the American style of play overwhelmed the British defenders, unaccustomed to such an onslaught.

Eventually, the Hurlingham Polo Committee was forced to abolish the offside rule in order to compete for the Westchester Cup in America. The deed of gift specifically stated that the matches must be played under the rules of the host country. Therefore, in 1911, the offside rule was confined to the history books.

Measuring the Polo Ponies

It has been said of the height limit for polo ponies that the measurement rule was more often broken than complied with. The main argument put forward by the proponents of the limitation in height was that if abolished, the price of polo horseflesh would go sky-high. Those who felt that there should be no limits pointed out that the aim of high-class polo was to play a better and faster sport. Furthermore, it would legalize an almost universal practice of disregarding the measurement.

The most vociferous advocate of limiting the height of polo ponies to 14.2 hands was the Reverend Thomas Dale. In his magnificent *Polo at Home and Abroad*, he devotes an entire chapter, "The Height and Measurement of Polo Ponies," to this issue.[20] His main argument is that increasing the height of the ponies would make the game far more dangerous, because collision between larger ponies would be more serious, and the players would have to handle longer sticks, more difficult to control, which would add to the perils of the game. The Reverend Dale stated that is was clearly to the benefit of polo that ponies should be as small as possible. He also proposed that there should be a limit to the stick's length. The Reverend Dale admitted that there was no provision for enforcing the rules of measurement and that they were, in fact, not observed. His final point was that "the present standard of height is found very useful by secretaries of county polo clubs, whose grounds are apt to be invaded by animals which are unsuited and unsafe for polo."[21]

This measurement rule, which was in the book in both the United States and Argentina, was in fact totally ignored in both polo-playing countries. The periodical extension of the height limit by the Hurlingham Committee pointed to ultimate abolition, which came about in 1919.

CHAPTER 6

Polo in Ireland

Following the game's first tentative steps, Colonel Horace Rochford was the principal mover in the foundation of the All Ireland Polo Club.[1] This event took place in 1873. The first committee consisted of Horace Rochford as honorary secretary and treasurer, John Brooks, Matt D'Arcy and W.T. Stewart. The All Ireland Polo Club drew up a set of rules, which governed polo in Ireland until 1886 when the Hurlingham rules were adopted.

The City of Dublin Board of Works gave permission to build a small pavilion and to place a wooden railing along the polo field's sides on a parcel of land known as Nine Acres in Phoenix Park. This ground still holds polo games in our day; it is the oldest polo ground in the British Isles. An accident on that field resulted in a significant change in the laws of the game. Lord Harrington was on Cyclops, an excellent bay gelding who was blind in one eye. Unfortunately, Cyclops came to grief when he collided with another pony on his blind side. This was the direct cause for implementing the rule that prohibited playing on one-eyed ponies.[2]

It was in 1878 that John Watson, having left his regiment, the 13th Hussars, returned to Ireland and by the force of his personality changed the game as it was played in his day.[3] What Watson saw was a game played five-a-side that started with a wild charge from behind the backline, leading to frequent collisions. There was no combination among the team players; it was each player on his own, running around the field until he got close to the goalposts. The backhander stroke was unknown.

John Henry Watson, MFH, changed all that. A man who never suffered fools gladly, by persistence and example he soon improved the game. It is of interest that although he brought the backhander into general play, he was an opponent of the soon practiced nearside backhander. The reason was probably that being a big man and a consummate horseman, Watson was always able to keep the opposing number 1 on his near-side, which allowed him to hit booming backhanders on his right side. Those were the days of the offside rule, which gave the back a considerable advantage over the opposing number 1 in defensive plays.

The All Ireland Open Challenge Cup was offered for competition in 1878. The first winners were the 7th Royal Fusiliers; all the players were subalterns: Henry Mandel-Pleydell, Lord Percy St. Maur, Robert Saunders, George Hayhurst and Francis Sartoris. One of the conditions was that any team taking the cup two years running would gain permanent possession of the trophy. Not surprisingly, John Watson's Freebooters took the trophy in 1885 and 1886. The Freebooters team then presented a new cup, to be kept by the winning team if won three years in succession.

Many English teams crossed the Irish Sea to participate in the Open Championship.

Among the winners were military teams such as the 7th Hussars, the Scots Greys, the 5th Lancers, the 15th Hussars, the 9th Lancers, the Inniskilling Dragoons and the 13th Hussars—John Watson's old regiment. Civilian teams included Eaton, Rugby, another squad from Warwickshire called Hillmorton; Old Cantabs and scratch sides with names like Nomads, Wanderers and Woodpeckers. All were invariably strong teams that counted among their numbers celebrated players such as the three Miller brothers, Edward, George and Charles; Jack Drybrough; Walter Buckmaster; Major George Ansell; Freddie Freake; Rivy Grenfell; John Beresford; Cecil and Pat Nickalls; Lord Wodehouse; Noel Edwards and Captain Bertie Wilson.

Winning Irish teams were Carlow, All Ireland, several versions of Freebooters and a team representing the Irish County Polo Union. The players were the cream of Irish polo, starting with Thomas Hone, who played in the first Westchester Cup, John Watson, James Jameson, Frederick Fetherstonhaugh, William Gore Lambarde, Charles O'Hara, Percy O'Reilly, Auston Rotheram, Samuel Watt and ending with John Hardress Lloyd, a ten-goal handicap player who came so close to recovering the 1911 Westchester Cup at Meadow Brook. General Hardress Lloyd was described as a man of much practical common sense, not easily perturbed.

The Irish Clubs

County Carlow Polo Club, started in 1873, had its grounds at Purser's Forge, Carlow. Players were Dr. Francis Colgan, Steuart Duckett, Major John Eustace, William Grogan, Thomas Roark, D.J. Ross of Burrin House, and Benjamin, Samuel and Walter Slocock of Hanover House. The latter had a successful professional career in America after the war.

The All Ireland Polo Club came into being in 1873 and became the ruling body of polo in Ireland. The members used as a polo ground the Nine Acres, in Phoenix Park. The All Ireland team took the Open Championship three times in four years in the 1887–1890 time span. J.D. Calley; Captain James Babington; James Locke; Colonel James Reilly, who had played in India; Captain George Middleton; James Jameson; Captain Hone; and the infallible John Watson were on the champion teams. There was a large membership at the All Ireland Polo Club because many players also carried membership in other clubs.

Among the most prominent were Maxwell Arnott; Frank Barbour; Captain Bernard Daly, 6th Royal Irish Rifles; Wilfred Fitzgerald—also a keen yachtsman; John Leonard; Arthur and John McCann; Captain Reginald Murphy; Vere Brudenell Murphy; Baron Henry de Robeck; George Rotheram; and John Trench. One player, American-born Isaac "Icky" Bell, MFH, spent most of his life in Britain, although he had a "cottage" in plush Newport, Rhode Island. Bell received his education at Harrow and Trinity Hall, Cambridge; there is a polo link here, because his mother was James Gordon Bennett's sister.

Polo at county Westmeath was started in 1880 by Arthur Joyce, James Harvey Locke and Marshall Murray; play was on a ground at Liddeston, Mullingar. The club had so many players that a second club, North Westmeath, was formed by Hugh Wilson, with a ground near Castlepollard. Both went on to achieve success in the County Cup several times. Two of the finest polo players were Major Auston Rotheram and Captain Percy O'Reilly. Rotheram at number 1 was described as extraordinarily clever in picking up the ball and galloping clear of the whole field.[4] Captain O'Reilly was a brilliant striker of the ball and a sound back. These two gentlemen represented Ireland in the Olympic Games and also in the Patriotic Cup. Players in later years included Edward Bayley, Jasper Grant, Major Thomas Smyth Odell, Edward Rotheram, Jr., and C.P. Vivian. Another player, John Dunville, who had played for Cambridge University, was a balloonist of repute. Dunville came in second in the 1908 Gordon Bennett race that started in Berlin.

County Meath, which is connected with one of the first — if not the first — game on Irish soil, formed a Polo Club in 1885. A team — Gore Lambarde, Frederick Fetherstonhaugh, James Jameson, Thomas Hone and John Watson — took the English County Cup at Ranelagh in 1893. Later players included Captain Geoffrey Baynes, the Marquis Victor Conyngham, P. Dunne Cullinan, Captain Alexander Napper and Andrew Watt — the chairman of United Distilleries — and his son Samuel. An iconic figure was John Hanly, who had witnessed the first game in Ireland at Gormanstown.

County Dublin was formed in 1889 and had a ground at Ashtown. In 1902 this ground was taken over by the Phoenix Park Racecourse management. A ground was then secured at Cabra, near the All Ireland polo ground. An arrangement was made between the two clubs, and polo was played five days a week to the benefit of the citizens of Dublin, who were able to watch the games free of charge. Major Albert Clerke, M.M. King French, John Leonard, Thomas Levins Moore, Major Robert Mayne and Leonard Morrogh Ryan were among the prominent players.

King's County in central Ireland was formed in 1895, with grounds at Sharavogue Park. A club team, A. Stoney, Hon. Aubrey Hastings, the then Captain John Hardress Lloyd and Hubert Gairdner, took the County Cup. Other players were Major Sinclair Butson, his son Henry, Christopher Cradock, Major Charles Head, the Earl of Huntingdon, J.W. Nolans and Colonel W. Wickham.

The County Wexford Polo Club was formed 1895, with grounds one mile northwest of Enniscorthy railway station. The main tournament was the County Wexford Challenge Cup, presented by the County Wexford Agricultural Society. The final game was held on the last day of the Annual Agricultural Show — the last winners in 1911, being John Cowlard, Gilbert Sanford, Seymour Barne and Thomas Harman, all subalterns in the 20th Hussars. Captain Loftus Bryan was the club's main engine. Other members included Joseph Casson, one of the first to play in Wexford; Philip Vandeleur Beatty; and Captain Crosbie Harvey, who served in the Lancashire Horse during the Boer War.

County Antrim's ground was on Castlereagh Road, Belfast. The club had a large membership but failed to win any major tournaments. Frank Barbour; Arthur Charley; Samuel Barbour Combe; Robert Grimshaw Dunville and his son John; Edward, John and Richard Blakiston-Houston; Captain Anthony Maude; William Mitchell, who had played in South Africa; the Hon. Arthur O'Neill; Charles Slacke; and Captain Holt Waring, North Irish Horse, were some of the polo-playing members.

County Sligo, located far away from most other clubs, had a ground at Hazlewood Demesne. Such remoteness did not prevent the club from obtaining remarkable success in the County Cup — no less than seven times between 1894 and 1902. W. Campbell, P.W. Connolly, Major G.M. Eccles, J. FitzGerald, Henry G. L'Estrange and Major Charles O'Hara were all in the winning teams. Mr. FitzGerald and Major O'Hara were on the team on every occasion.

County Kildare had its original grounds near Naas and then moved to Celbridge where Major Edward Conolly provided a field in his Castletown Demesne. Ernest Bellemy; John Bobbet; Douglas Cox; William Dease, who built the Castledown ground; Captain D.B. Mcculloch and Henry Montgomery, 17th Lancers; and F. Morgan Mooney were among the players. The stars were Major Andrew H. Watt and Samuel Watt. Together with Captain Arnold Wills, Asa Balding and Captain Morley Dennis, they took the County Cup on two occasions.

There were also a few smaller clubs. Sir Vere Foster was the power behind county Louth, which was formed in 1897. The grounds were at the Dundalk Demesne. Among the members were Francis Charles Osborne who had participated with "Chicken" Hartopp in the famous tussle between the 9th Lancers and county Meath in 1872, and Richard A.B. Henry.[5]

South Westmeath started in 1903 with Cuthbert J. "Bertie" Clibborn, H.R. Davis and Captain A.V.C. Holmes as the enthusiasts.

Ian Bullough, MFH, and S.T. Groome kept the game going on in county Cork. The polo ground was located along the Cork and Blarney tramway lines.

John F. Cooke, from Glengollan Fahan, and Captain Whyte from Lough Gate Castle, kept the flame alive in county Donegal.

County Derry, which dates back to 1887, had a fine ground at Granshaw, Londonderry. The Watt and Montgomery families were great supporters of this club. Finally, county Kilkenny, formed in 1888, had its grounds in Prospect. Captain Walter Lindsay and George Smithwick were the stalwarts in this club.[6]

A relic of Irish polo was James Davidson, one of the founders of the Silchar Polo Club in 1859, while a tea planter in Soubong. Mr. Davidson contributed to the expansion of the game by collecting subscriptions in the Cachar district to defray the expenses of sending a team of Manipuris to Calcutta in charge of Captain Joseph Sherer, the "Father of English Polo." The novel game took well with the Calcutta merchants, who purchased all the Manipuri ponies. After practicing for about one year they challenged the Manipuris to a return match. However, the Calcutta players still had a lot to learn, because the Manipuris, on their home ground, did not allow the visitors to score a single goal. In 1909, Mr. Davidson was reported to be the oldest hunting man in Ulster.[7]

Some Other Tournaments

The Irish County Cup was established in 1890 for a challenge trophy to be awarded outright after three wins. County Fermanagh accomplished such requisite in the historic three years of competition. The winning team then presented a second cup, which was taken by county Sligo in 1900. The Irish County Polo Union then presented a third trophy, which could not be won outright. The venue was Phoenix Park, which the All Ireland Polo Club turned over to the County Polo Union for the week of competition; the time was the week preceding the Dublin Horse Show.

The first winners, county Fermanagh, presented a team of Anthony Maude, Charles D'Arcy Irvine, Edward Archdale and John Porter-Porter, who was born John Porter Archdale. This same team won in 1891 and 1892; however, county Fermanagh Polo Club soon after went into abeyance. County Meath took the cup in the following year, with Arthur Shirley-Ball, Captain William Hollwey Steeds, James Jameson and Captain Thomas Hone. Mr. Shirley-Ball had a bad fall during the 1899 Dublin Horse Show and died the following morning, without regaining consciousness.

The County Cup became an important tournament in Ireland because it was an occasion in which all the provincial clubs met at the Dublin grounds. In order to facilitate attendance, the Irish County Polo Union developed a scheme to subsidize the transportation of ponies by railway, thus helping the smaller clubs in their endeavor to bring home the cup.

Several other cups were offered for competition during this period. The All-Ireland Military Challenge Cup was instituted in 1886 and was taken by that grand old polo regiment, the 10th Hussars. The All-Ireland Subalterns' Tournament began in 1896 and was also taken by the 10th Hussars. The All-Ireland Novices' Tournament was started in 1898 and in 1910 was reserved for teams whose total handicap did not exceed twenty goals. The Pirates were the winner that year: Thomas Roark's team, progenitor of the famous players Captain Charles T.I. "Pat" and Aidan Roark. Edward Wienholt, John McCann and D.J. Ross joined Mr. Roark in that successful endeavor.

There was even an All-Ireland Social Club's Cup, modeled after the London version. There is a record of only one event, in 1913, when the St. Stephen's Club took the honors with John Leonard, Arthur McCann, John McCann and Leonard Morrogh-Ryan.

The Patriotic Cup

There was also an international competition between Ireland and England: the Patriotic Cup given jointly by the Hurlingham Club and some Irish subscribers in 1903.

It was to be played in alternate years at Phoenix Park and at Hurlingham Club in Fulham. The players were chosen by Hurlingham and the All Ireland Polo Club. The English team was the first winner, at a match that took place in Dublin.

Through the years until 1914, England took most of the games; Ireland was only able to post victories in 1905 and 1913, both within the friendly confines of Phoenix Park. J. Morrogh-Ryan, Captain the Hon. Denis Bingham, Captain Hardress Lloyd and Captain Frederick "Rattle" Barrett were on the winning team in Ireland's last victory.[8]

Nineteen fourteen and all that stopped polo in Ireland for years to come, county Meath being the only polo club to resume operations in 1919. The All Ireland Open Cup was also resumed that year, but play was stopped after three competitions, in 1921.

CHAPTER 7

Spreading the Gospel Round the World

The very same article in *The Field* that inspired "Chicken" Hartopp to organize an impromptu game of hockey on horseback at Aldershot Garrison found a reader in faraway Argentina. A British resident who chose to hide his identity behind the pseudonym "a Gaucho" wrote a letter to *The Field* requesting more information about the game and its accoutrements:

> Hockey on horseback: Could any of your readers oblige me by informing me, through the columns of The Field, the rules of hockey as played on horse in India? Also as to what kind of sticks and balls are employed. I saw an account in The Field about a twelve-month ago, and then thought it a very suitable game to introduce into this country.
> A Gaucho. Buenos Ayres, Jan. 12 [1870][1]

The letter from "a Gaucho" evoked several responses. In the 16 April 1870 edition, *The Field* published two letters on the matter. "Bhal" writes about how the game is played in Hazaribagh in the state of Bihar and attaches a diagram of the field of play showing the positions of the players, including the place of that essentially Biharian figure, the goalkeeper. The second letter, signed "Musafir," mentions that the game has Persian origins and describes how it is played. This correspondence provoked a missive from Mr. F. D'Acosta — it is nice to record a name at last — who played at Barrackpore, north of Calcutta. Mr. D'Acosta, probably a member of the Calcutta Polo Club, informs the reader with a lengthy description of the game, including an explanation of the "charge" or bumping. D'Acosta mentions that such practice, although dangerous at times, is inevitable. If charge you must, do not do so at a ninety-degree angle. Mr. D'Acosta states that the previous writers will confuse "a Gaucho" because "Bhal" mentions the grounds dimensions as 120 yards in length by 50 yards in width, while the other, "Musafir," calls for a field measuring 400 yards by 120 yards. It is likely that local topography dictated such discrepancy. His letter ends conveying to "a Gaucho" his best wishes for a successful launch of the game in Buenos Aires and the practical admonition to have an ample supply of brandy and soda for the players.

There is no more information regarding polo in the local press until a notice in the 19 September 1872 edition of *The Standard* announcing that a polo game would be held at Cañada de Gómez in Santa Fe Province in conjunction with a racing festival organized by the Rosario English Race Club on 3 November 1872. Even though the match was scheduled to take place six weeks later, both teams and umpire were announced.[2] Perversely, when the results of the races were published on 9 November and 14 November, there was no mention of the polo game.

Did this match ever take place? If so, it predates by three years documented games at Estancia La Buena Suerte in January 1875 and later matches at Estancia Negrete held in August, 1875. The latter matches are traditionally regarded as the first in Argentina, one of the polo myths. Nevertheless, it is most likely that the first games in Argentina took place in Caballito, a Buenos Aires neighborhood, perhaps as early as 1871.[3]

British influence upon polo in Argentina was overwhelmingly powerful until the Great War. The Buenos Aires Polo Club was started in 1882 by John Ravenscroft, originally from Cheshire. The second was the Belgrano Polo Club, promoted by Frank Balfour, who years later would become a forceful personality at the Cheltenham Polo Club and as president of the Polo Pony Society in England.

Venado Tuerto Athletic & Polo Club is the oldest polo club in activity, founded in 1888 by Irish and English settlers and followed shortly after by the Hurlingham Club. The Polo Association of the River Plate was established on 4 March 1892 incorporating clubs on both margins of the River Plate, with the Montevideo Polo Club in Uruguay, joined later by the Camp Polo Club of Uruguay, the Bellaco Polo Club and the San Jorge Polo Club, all on the eastern shore of the river.

The first Polo Championship of the River Plate, forerunner of the Argentine Open Championship, was held at the Hurlingham Club in April 1893. For the first three years of its inception two annual championships were held, one at Hurlingham and the other at Cañada de Gómez, reflecting the importance of polo in the provinces. Oddly enough, the Argentine Polo Association mistakenly recognizes only one champion team in each of those years— another myth, this one with official sanction in spite of overwhelming evidence to the contrary.[4]

The railways in Argentina were constructed with English capital and had enormous influence on the rural development which made the country one of the richest in the world until 1930. It is of interest that the Buenos Aires & Rosario Railway had its own polo club in 1892. The only other railroad with its own polo club was the Bengal-Nagpur Railway in India, active in the 1920s.[5]

An examination of the teams that took the Polo Association of the River Plate Championship, from 1893 until 1922, reveals that out of sixty-one players, all but eleven were of British origin. The first natives to be in championship teams were peons and foremen working on estancias owned by Englishmen. Frank Kinchant, an Irishman that participated in the London polo season, was the administrator at estancia Las Petacas, owned by Charles and Ernest Jewell. Kinchant explained the game's rudiments to the estancia's foreman Sixto Martínez, his brother José and Francisco Benítez, another peon. They proved to be quick learners because the team took the championship in 1895 and 1896. How good a polo player was Sixto Martínez? Frank Balfour, a good judge of ponies and players, thought Sixto was as good as Johnny Traill and Lewis Lacey, both ten-goal handicap players.

It could have been thought that the presence of hired hands in the championship might have raised some eyebrows. A letter to the editor of *River Plate Sport and Pastime* reads, "Do you know Mr. Kinchant? He is the sort of man that makes one proud of being English. When his biography comes to be written, not the least creditable effort and success of his life will be having trained his native team to play polo, not only well but according to the rules; they were sometimes even too considerate of their opponents."[6]

The practice of including estancia workers on polo teams persisted until 1909. On this subject, Frank Balfour, longtime honorary secretary of the Polo Association of the River Plate, wrote: "The champion team in 1901, San Carlos, included two native players, and the Western team were helped to victory by another brilliant native player, but the inclusion of native servants by their masters in a team competing for the Championship has now been discouraged, as the practice savoured too much of professionalism."[7]

The Western Camps team was captained by John Argentine Campbell, who was a frequent visitor during the London season, taking, among other tournaments, the Whitney Cup and the Social Clubs Cup. Eduardo Lucero was a gifted player and the foreman at Campbell's estancia El Jabalí. Mr. Campbell was a nine-goal handicap player, always beautifully mounted. He received his education at Fettes College in Edinburgh, where he was school captain; he went on to Cambridge University where he was a Blue in athletics, cricket and rugby. Campbell represented Scotland in rugby football and Argentina in cricket against Lord Hawke's Marylebone Cricket Club XI in 1912. Lt. John Campbell, a forty-one-year-old officer in the Inniskilling Dragoons, was killed near Honnechy, France, in 1917. His grandson, also named John Argentine, still lives at estancia El Jabalí (wild boar), part of which is now a model dairy farm. John Campbell was one of 528 volunteers from Argentina, many of them polo players, who died during the Great War.

Besides individual players, teams from Argentina participated in the London polo season. In 1896 a team named Buenos Aires that included the brothers Frank and Stanley Furber, Hugh Scott Robson, Dr. Newman Smith and Robert McC. "Johnny" Smyth took the International Tournament at Ranelagh. Teams from America, England and France entered the competition.[8] A quality American team was the other finalist: Walter McCreery, Jay Mackey, William Wright and Charles Wheeler, the latter a player from Philadelphia. The other three members would participate in the 1900 Olympic Games in Paris.

The following year Frank Balfour, John Ravenscroft, the Hon. Francis White and Maj. John Porteous, with Henry Bedford and Edgar Jacobs as reserves, traveled to England with their own ponies, which gave a favorable impression for their stamina. This started a profitable market for Argentine ponies in England and also on the Continent. The team played twenty-three matches; they won seventeen and three ended in a tie.

The Hon. Francis William White was the youngest son of Sir Luke White, baron Annaly of Annaly and Rathcline. White farmed in Cañada de Gómez; later he removed to South Africa and then returned to England, where he played at the Rugby Club. During the Great War he was attached to the Remount Service. Maj. John James Porteous, Royal Artillery, bred polo ponies at estancia "Las Tres Lagunas" in Santa Fe Province. He was seriously wounded in Afghanistan; however, because of his experience with horses he was recalled as remount officer in both the Boer War and World War I.

The next polo expedition to England from Argentina was in 1912 when Harold Schwind, a wealthy estanciero from San Luis Province took his team Wild Horse to participate in the London season. Joseph and John Traill, Leonard Lynch-Staunton and John Campbell completed the delegation. The *Polo Monthly* described the Wild Horse team as the sensation of the London season, referring to the team as brilliant Argentine players.[9] Actually, only John Campbell was born in Argentina, of Scottish parentage. The Traill cousins, Joe and Johnny, were Irish, as well as Lynch-Staunton. They were examples of what Professor Eduardo Archetti has called the "hybridization of Argentine polo."[10] While the British considered themselves English, Scots or Irish in Argentina were always referred to as "Ingleses" by the locals. On the other hand, they were called "Argentines" in London. Nevertheless, for all of them, "home" was always Britain.

The team — Lynch-Staunton, Joe Traill, Schwind and Johnny Traill — playing as the Argentine Club, defeated Sir Charles Lowther's Cavalry Club 11–4 in the first match. The final game was against the Bath Club, with Evelyn de Rothschild, Hon. Weetman Pearson, Walter Buckmaster and Lord Dalmeny the favorites to take the trophy. However, by the end of the first chukker those who had backed the Bath Club team saw that there was very little chance of winning their money. The final score after a good, fast game was ten to five in favor of Wild Horse.

There were fifteen entrants for the tournament for the Whitney Cup, with aggregate handicaps varying from twenty-two to thirty-two. The Wild Horse team faced the 1st Life Guards; the former won 7–3. In the second round they faced the Wasps and won again 7–3, receiving one goal by handicap. For the semifinal game John Campbell replaced Lynch-Staunton who had injured his leg. Receiving ten goals by handicap, The Wild Horse beat Old Cantabs 15–9. The final match was against Eaton, a thirty-two-goal team that included Cecil Nickalls, Charles Miller, Captain Gerald Ritson and the Earl of Rocksavage. The Argentines received eleven goals and scored ten, five by John Campbell, for a final tally of twenty-one to eleven. It was a brilliant victory.

The Wild Horse team did not enter the Hurlingham Champion Cup and the Ranelagh Open Cup because their aggregate total of twenty-two goals did not reach the minimum requirement of twenty-six goals. This was the last visit to England of a team from Argentina until 1922.

Australia

Colonel Thomas St. Quintin, a participant in the first organized polo game in Britain, is credited with bringing polo to Australia.[11] In 1874, St. Quintin was serving in India and was seconded to accompany the Indian Government Remount Agent, Colonel James Tacker, on a journey to Australia to purchase horses, which were found to adapt to the climate in the subcontinent much better than the English breeds. With him, St. Quintin brought along mallets, polo balls and an engaging personality and enthusiasm for spreading the word. As a guest of the different governors, he was in a position to influence the development of the game. After arriving at Sydney, the first match in New South Wales took place on 23 July 1874 at Moore Park, where Colonel St. Quintin had marked a polo ground.

The teams, identified by red and white scarves, included the governor, Sir Hercules Robinson; his ADC, Captain Edward St. John; and other officers, of whom W. Maxwell, Morisset and G.P. Want are known.

In their report of the game *The Town and Country Journal* mentioned that "it was found that there had been great destruction to the sticks, though no horse accidents."[12]

Colonel St. Quintin moved on to Victoria where his brothers Henry and John were prosperous farmers at Dwarroon Station in the Western District. A polo game took place on 20 August 1874 at Jerry Flats; the players were Tom Brown, A. Mackenzie, Oliver Palmer, A. Urquhart, C. Woodward and the three St. Quintin brothers. While polo thrived in the Western District, St. Quintin wrote about his frustration in trying to obtain support from the governor, Sir George Bowden: "I went there [Melbourne] myself and stayed with the Governor of Victoria and tried hard to get him to support it, without avail."[13]

Polo began in Western Australia in 1892 when members of the Fremantle Hunt took up the game, in which Capt. Cairnes-Derrick Candy, ADC to the Governor Sir William Robinson, was prominent in starting polo. The games took place at Orgy's Field, a racecourse close to Preston Point Road and in Richmond Park, then known as Pearse's Paddock.[14]

Organized polo on the island state of Tasmania was started by the governor's private secretary, Mr. W.H.B. Robinson, who founded the Hobart Polo Club in 1899. The polo field was located within the Risdon Racecourse. However, it is certain that polo was played years before. In his memoirs, the Earl of Glasgow, then Lt. Viscount Kelburn serving onboard HMS *Curacoa*, recalls playing polo against Tasmanian farmers in 1892.

> With eyes like hawks they seldom missed the ball but their knowledge of the rules was rudimentary! Wherever the ball went they made for it and crosses were frequent. I don't want to exaggerate but certainly one arm was broken as a result of a collision between two ponies. I remember seeing, as the result of another collision between ponies, the pony of Lieut. Vivian de Crespigny going round in circles with de Crespigny dismounted, being dragged over the ground, holding on to the bridle. It was the most dangerous game I have ever seen.[15]

South Africa

Usually the cavalry regiments were in the forefront of polo. However, in South Africa, an infantry regiment played in the first game on record. The 75th Infantry of the Line Regiment, also known as the Gordon Highlanders, was deployed to the Cape Province following service in Hong Kong and Singapore. About the same time the Cape Mounted Rifles, a South African unit, was garrisoned in King William's Town, sharing quarters with the Gordons. The first game in South Africa took place between these units in October 1874 at the Parade Grounds.[16]

There is another version that indicates that three regiments pooled their resources to constitute two teams. The third unit was the Duke of Cornwall Light Infantry, also stationed in King William's Town. In a visit to King William's Town, Dianne Grinstead consulted with the curator of the town's museum, Mr. D. Comins, who confirmed that the game was between the Mounted Rifles and the Gordon Highlanders. In their comprehensive *Polo in South Africa*, Donald and John McKenzie are of the opinion that the curator's version is the one to be taken as authentic.[17]

Polo in South Africa at the top level was dominated by British cavalry regiments until the onset of World War I. The Beresford Cup, presented initially in 1897 to the Rand Polo Club by John Beresford, later Lord Decies, became emblematic of South Africa's polo championship. The team from the 5th Lancers took the first edition of the Beresford Cup, with Lt. William Tucker Hill, Captain James Jardine, Major Robert Brown-Clayton and Lt. Harold Hulse. They defeated the 18th Hussars by five goals to nil in the final match. From its inception in 1899 until 1912 the Beresford Cup winners were all British officers. Only in 1913 the civilian team from Mooi River took the honors. Bill Drysdale, Rob Hall, Harry Hall and Johnny Gibson accomplished that feat.[18]

America

James Gordon Bennett and Hermann Oelrichs were responsible for the introduction of polo in the United States. The newspaper magnate and the shipping entrepreneur shared the initiative; however, all the credit has been given to Gordon Bennett. Oelrichs, the American agent for the North German Lloyd shipping line, was one of the richest men in the country. He was also a multitalented sportsman, excelling in swimming, baseball, athletics and boxing. Oelrichs was the first president of the U.S. Lacrosse Association.

An article in the *San Francisco Call* states, "James Gordon Bennett and friends concluded that polo ought to be introduced to America. As Mr. Herman [*sic*] Oelrichs was going to Europe, he was commissioned to bring back from England the necessary paraphernalia. When Mr. Oelrichs returned with the outfit necessary the practicing began at Dickel's. Mr. Bennett and Mr. Oelrichs were the main movers."[19]

Nevertheless, there was English presence in the early polo matches in America. The Westchester Polo Club was founded in March 1876; among the members was Lord George Mandeville, later Duke of Manchester, who also played in the first match in Newport, Rhode Island, when the Westchester Polo Club moved lock, stock and barrel from Jerome Park in the Bronx borough of New York City to the friendly confines of Newport. Sir Bache Cunard was also one of the early players in America.

In those balmy days Newport was the summer retreat for some of the wealthiest families in America. Large readership newspapers such as the *New York Times* felt obliged to send reporters to inform the public about the comings and goings of the American elite. There were balls and dinner parties at the so-called cottages on Bellevue Avenue, sailing races on the waters of Narragansett Bay, polo games on the Westchester field and lawn tennis at the Casino.

There was a touch of naughty behavior as well. A bizarre incident involving James Gordon Bennett and Captain Henry "Sugar" Candy, an officer and a gentleman in the 9th Lancers, resulted in a vote of censure from the Reading Room authorities. For a wager, probably quite substantial, Captain Candy rode his horse into the sacred confines of the Reading Room, the most exclusive social club in Newport. There are three versions of the escapade, but whether Captain Candy guided his mount onto the club's porch, into the salon, or up the stairs was totally immaterial to the powers that be at the club. Thus came about a vote of censure against Gordon Bennett, who had introduced Captain Candy to the Reading Room membership.

English Army Officers in Boerne, Texas

There is a strong oral tradition that polo in America was started by British Army officers in Texas. However, there is no written evidence indicating that polo in the Lone Star State was played before the practice games at Dickel's Riding Academy in New York City in the winter of 1876. The *Galveston Daily News* reported in its 6 April 1876 issue, "Mr. Harry Blasson from New York has been in the region [Bexar County, Texas] as agent of *The New York Herald* Mr. James Gordon Bennett, to purchase twenty small ponies for a Polo Club of which he is president. This institution requires particularly small and active nags.... The New York Club is first to introduce it into this country."

Something is known about the pioneers: they were retired British Army officers. Captain Glynn Turquand bought the Balcones Ranch in Boerne, near San Antonio, in 1878.[20] Apparently, the original polo ground is still visible.[21]

Another pioneer polo player was Captain Egremont Shearburn, 9th Lancers, who carried the dubious reputation on being a most extravagant officer.[22] From Texas, Shearburn moved to Wyoming and his story turns ugly. Captain Shearburn had asked the brothers Moreton, Richard and Stephen Frewell, prominent Englishmen, one of whom, Moreton, was manager of the vast Powder River Cattle Co., to introduce him at the elite Cheyenne Club and also at the Stebbins & Post Bank, to endorse his notes. Shearburn then proceeded to gamble away the cash and default the payment. His name is mentioned in criminal warrants, indictments and complaints by the state of Wyoming in 1882.[23] By 1891, he was back in England, married and living in Hammersmith.

The English Colony in Iowa

In Iowa, Englishman Frederick Brooke Close thought of himself as the first polo player in America. Fred Close came to America passing up the opportunity of a Cambridge education that his brothers John, James and William had pursued. Their father was a well-connected banker and financial advisor to King Ferdinand II of Naples. While in Virginia, Fred Close met Daniel Paullin and — with the financial support of the family — they formed the Iowa Land Company. By 1882, the company was offering half a million acres for sale.

Many young Englishmen, the "remittance men," came to Iowa to learn the basics of ranching and then to manage their large families' holdings in the Mid- and Far West, as well as in Western Canada and Argentina. Known locally as "pups," many did not take kindly to the rough life of a rancher. Some of them were known to have unhitched plow horses and arranged races. Just like most British around the wide world, they brought with them the tools to engage in sports and games. Cricket and tennis became a common sight on Iowa's weekends, and horse racing developed very quickly. It is not surprising at all that polo became a popular game among the settlers in the Le Mars area. Frederick Close created the Northwestern Polo League in Le Mars, and soon enough there were clubs at Blair and Omaha in Nebraska, at Yankton and Sioux Falls in South Dakota, and in many towns in Iowa. The top teams were Sibley, Le Mars and Sioux City. In 1887, the Le Mars team traveled to St. Louis to play an exhibition polo match. In 1893, at the St. Louis Exposition, a team from Le Mars played the inaugural match against the St. Louis Country Club, where polo is still played today.

The Le Mars polo team became a major attraction at county fairs, wearing their shirts made in England and showing skills handling their mallets that outgunned the opposition. Regrettably, the gods of polo were unkind to Frederick Close. In 1890, while playing a match at Crescent Park, the Sioux City team's home ground, there was a collision between Close's pony and his teammate Jack Watson.[24] Both ponies rolled over Mr. Close, and he became the first recorded casualty of polo in America.

Scots Bring Polo to Wyoming

The British also brought polo to Wyoming. The first polo grounds in the territory was a parcel of land used as a grazing area by the Powder River Cattle Company, a corporation established by British capitalists in 1882. Those were the days of the free range when hundreds of thousands of head of cattle grazed on federal lands, free of charge, but with no title to the land. The disastrous winter of 1886–1887 brought hard times to the cattlemen in Wyoming. Most of the British in the area cut their losses and left, seeking other venues to invest their money. Therefore, whatever polo was played in the Powder River basin was short-lived and probably was only an amusement for the British contingent.

Most likely one of the players was Moreton Frewell, manager of the Powder River Cattle Company. An ambitious young man with many interests, Frewell was an uncle of Winston Churchill by his marriage to Clara Jerome, Jenny's older sister. Moreton was a polo player, steeplechaser and friend of the "Jersey Lily," Mrs. Edward Langtry.

Nevertheless, the seeds had been planted in Wyoming, and the Sheridan Polo Club was started by Captain Frank Grissell and Captain G.G. "Pete" Stockwell, both British Army officers, in June 1893. Frank Grissell had participated in the first organized polo match played in England in June 1870 at Hounslow Heath, as a subaltern in the 9th Lancers. Captain Grissell, who exchanged into the 11th Hussars in 1875, then retired from the service and immigrated to America, joining the band of British cowboys who went out to the Far West, some on their own and others to look after their families' land and cattle investments. Their education at Eton, Harrow and other public schools had taught them to be leaders, not shopkeepers as Napoleon Bonaparte had wrongly thought. Some were "remittance men," others youngsters who were willing to risk life and limb in an unfamiliar environment. However, the financial rewards could be handsome. The huge Prairie Cattle Company, whose chairman was the Earl of Airlie—father of David, the tenth Earl, a polo player who met his fate in the action at Diamond Hill, South Africa—returned a 20.5 percent dividend in 1883.[25]

The formation of the polo club in Sheridan was followed shortly after by new clubs in Beckton, Big Horn, and Buffalo. All these polo clubs played the game by the Hurlingham Club rules.[26]

Captain Grissell initially purchased 156 acres of ranch land in the Powder River basin, near the Tongue River in Dayton, under a cash sale on 18 March 1891. Grissell named the ranch IXL, after his former regiment. A larger-than-life-size statute of a 9th Lancer greets the visitor near the homestead, in the middle of an impeccable garden, tended carefully— a bit of England in the Far West.[27] The ranch became the site of the Ellbogen Foundation and is now in private hands.

In 1898, Scotsman Malcolm Moncreiffe moved from the Powder River basin to Big Horn, built a polo field and started a cattle-breeding operation on his Polo Ranch, near Sheridan. Moncreiffe exported Wyoming-bred polo horses and hunters to England and organized local horsemen to play polo at Big Horn.

The Moncreiffe and Wallop surnames are intimately associated with polo in Wyoming. Malcolm Moncreiffe was the fifteenth of sixteen children born to Sir Thomas Moncreiffe and his wife, Lady Louisa. Malcolm went to America, first to Miles City, Montana, where William Lindsay had started polo, and then settled in the area north of Gillette, beginning a cattle operation. Malcolm purchased the land that was known for many years by the name of the Polo Ranch. His older brother William, a Cambridge University graduate, stopped in Wyoming along a round-the-world journey. He liked the area and purchased the Charles Becker Ranch. The brothers formed a partnership; their properties are now the Gallatin and Brinton ranches.[28]

Oliver Henry Wallop, the other polo pioneer in the Big Horn country, was the second son of the Earl of Portsmouth. After graduating from Oxford University, he immigrated to the United States, and after the mandatory stop in Miles City, he purchased land on Otter Creek in southeast Montana. Oliver Wallop sold some horses to a settler in Wyoming, and the Big Horn area's beautiful scenery caught his eye; in 1891 he purchased the Oliver Hanna homestead. The Wallop and Oliver families became not only business partners providing thousands of horses to the British Army but also developed family ties: Oliver Wallop married Marguerite Walker, and Malcolm Moncreiffe, the son of a Scottish baronet, in turn married her sister Amy.[29]

Their descendants still live in the area and a few achieved distinctions in the New World. Oliver Wallop was on the Inter-collegiate championship polo team playing for Yale University, and Malcolm Wallop represented Wyoming in the U.S. Senate from 1976 to 1994.

The game still thrives in that area, with S.K. Johnston's Flying H Polo Club being a destination for twenty-goal summer polo, while its neighbor, Big Horn Polo Club, caters to lower-handicap players in a friendly, congenial atmosphere.

"Little London": The Game in Colorado Springs

In 1920, Charles Phelps Cushing wrote in the social magazine *Country Life*,

> The sobriquet of Colorado Springs has long been "Little London" because so many settlers from England took up residence there in pioneer days. Colorado Springs is still Anglified, for The Cheyenne Mountain Country Club lives up to the best traditions of "Little London." It is written in local history that Scotch and English members of this venerable Club knocked golf balls around the meadows of Broadmoor a year before the game was ever played in New England. Twenty-nine years ago, too, they were playing polo in the suburbs of Colorado Springs, when the club was not more than a month old, and they even made futile attempts to popularize cricket.[30]

Indeed, polo was played at the Cheyenne Mountain Country Club in 1891, but the British involvement with the game in Colorado had started in the mid–1880s in Glenwood Springs, at the time a frontier town. Walter Devereux, Sr., was the manager of a smelter and went on to amass a considerable fortune with a gold mine. Mr. Devereux had the Irishman Hervey Lyle, who had learned the game in India, coach his brother Horace and his sons Walter and William, both future polo players at Princeton University. There is another polo link, because John G. Milburn named his son Devereux after his friend Walter Devereux, Sr.

Among the club members, president William Sanford headed the Polo Committee, Walter Douglas started cricket and rugby football as he had known them in England and Scotland, and Englishman Richard Hutton promoted golf. Dr. William Bell was a physician from England who eventually left Colorado to spend the rest of his life as a country gentleman at Pendell Court in England. Scotsman J. Arthur Connell was head of Colorado Title and Trust Co.; he later bought a mining company and gave it a Scot name, Glasgow. John Curr, another Scot, was a rancher, as was Lt. John Lees Armit, who had served with Kitchener in the Tower Hamlets Corps. Many were health seekers, attracted by the reputation of Colorado Springs as a cure for many illnesses, mainly the dreaded tuberculosis.

The Cripple Creek gold rush resulted in a lucrative boom for Colorado Springs. The Devereux brothers brought with them their polo mentor Hervey Lyle, who away from the polo grounds entranced the membership with his renditions of "Drink to Me Only with Thine Eyes." Years later, Lyle developed appendicitis and insisted on playing a polo game before treatment; regrettably, he died following an operation.

Englishman Dr. Gerald Webb was a top-notch cricket player, and he also excelled at polo, being captain of the team that took the Rocky Mountain Polo Championship. His teammates were Horace Devereux, Harold Bryant and Charles Baldwin, who built Claremont, an elegant home modeled after Louis XIV's Petit Trianon palace at Versailles. It is now the Colorado Springs School. Charles Baldwin, polo player and business executive, was educated in England at Harrow School and later at Harvard College.

Colorado Springs remained one of the largest polo centers in the West until the onset of World War I.

Hurlingham Rules in California

Polo in California started in 1976, the same year that practice games began at the indoor arena in New York City. Capt. Nell Mowry led the attempt that according to historian Dennis Amato "was at best a fad that lasted several months and then quickly died out."[31]

It was left for English residents to revive the game in Southern California, led by Mr. C.A. Summers and Captain Hutcheson. It is possible that A.P. Wills Sandford and his cousin Horace Vachell, later members of the Blackmore Vale Polo Club in Dorset, were involved in this short-lived endeavor. In 1891, Robert Lee Bettner joined a group of Englishmen to establish the Riverside Polo Club.

Many players from England spent the winter season in California. Mention can be made of Lord Alastair Innes-Ker, who played on the Royal Horse Guards team; Lord Tweed-mouth; the Earl of Pembroke; Viscount Gower; Lord Reginald Herbert, RHG; Captain John Isaac, Northumberland Fusiliers; and Hugh Drury, of Rugby. Maj. Gen. Gerald Cookson, Bangalore Cavalry Brigade, umpired most of the games. An interesting personage was the peripatetic James Campbell Besley, explorer, miner, secret agent, and geologist — in other words, the kind of man that occasionally dots the panorama of polo.[32]

The Pacific Coast Polo and Pony Racing Association was dissolved in 1909. Clubs were located in Burlingame, Coronado, Los Angeles, Riverside, San Mateo, Santa Barbara and Santa Monica. The Polo Association then took over as the ruling body of the game in the Golden State.

Canada

The first game in the Dominion was played in July 1878 by some officers of the 20th Regiment in Halifax, Nova Scotia, at Mr. G. Hoskins' property named Brucefield, on Quinpool Road. Other matches took place in Fort Needham, where some civilians from Halifax also participated. By 1893, polo in Halifax was dormant. Perhaps the deployment of the 20th Regiment to England in 1885 had something to do with the decline of the game in Nova Scotia.

Across the vast country that is Canada, the Royal Navy was instrumental in starting polo on the island of Victoria in the spring of 1889. Officers serving on HMS *Warspite* challenged a team of civilians, Mortimer Drummond, H.A. Barton, H.F. Newton and Cecil Ward. The naval officers were Captain the Hon. Hedworth Lambdon, who was in command of the *Warspite*; Lt. Thomas Thynne; Lt. George Warrenton; and Staff Surgeon Christopher Pearson. There is no record of which team won and by how much.

Of those officers, Sir Hedworth Lambton rose to the rank of admiral and was commander in chief of the naval base in Portsmouth. Vice Admiral Sir George Warrender commanded the 2nd Battle Squadron and later was commander in chief at Plymouth.

The next match on record was again between teams from Victoria and the *Warspite*, at Beacon Hill Park on Victoria's waterfront. Messrs. Barton, Newton and Ward were joined by a new player, Mr. B. Powell. The sailors were Lt. Robert Arbuthnot, who was also captain of the ship's cricket team; Lt. Alfred Ethelston; Lt. C. St. A. Pearse; and Dr. Pearson. The navy team took the match 7–5. It should be noted that Rear Admiral Sir Robert Arbuthnot was killed in action during the battle of Jutland in 1916.

These games became customary, and the Victoria Polo Club was formed in 1892. But when the warships at anchor in Esquimalt Station were ordered to sail, polo in Victoria came to a premature end.

The game in Alberta, which was to become the main polo center in Canada, was brought about by British settlers and remittance men. The other two main sources of polo abroad had no representation in landlocked Alberta because the Royal Navy was based on Victoria Island and there were no British regiments in Western Canada. Polo started to be played in earnest at ranches in Alberta in 1886 by managers, cowboys and the occasional Mountie; however, the remittance men were the prime movers. These young men, upon arrival from England, usually stopped at the Guelph Agricultural College in Ontario to be educated in the ways and mores of ranching. Many of the locals considered the new arrivals as "too lazy to plow and too shiftless to own cattle."[33] Some returned to England after the first hard winter; however, many settled and purchased land, and their descendants still live in Western Canada.

Captain Edmund "Teddy" Wilmot is considered to be the founder of the first polo club in Canada.[34] Born in the Midlands in 1860, Wilmot was educated at Rugby School and then went to Canada, making the almost obligatory stop at Guelph Agricultural College. Along with Sir Francis de Winton — Secretary to the governor general of Canada, the Marquis of Lorne — Wilmot's father was one of the principal investors in the Alberta Ranche Company. Some of the company's holdings were a 28,000-acre ranch near Pincher Creek, a hamlet near Crow's Nest Pass. Happy with his prospects in Alberta, the hardworking Wilmot went back to England, where he resigned his commission in the Derbyshire Rifles and returned to Alberta with a new wife and a large supply of polo equipment.

The Pincher Creek Polo Club was formed shortly after, and the game extended to High River, where English-born Colin Ross was having practice games on his ranch, and Fort Macleod, where another remittance man, Stanley Pinhorne, held sway over Oxley Ranche. Pinhorne, a good polo player, had been sent to Alberta by his uncle, Alexander Staveley Hill, MP, the ranch's principal investor. The best polo player on the Fort Macloud team was Herbert Samson, an Oxford-educated man from a family prominent in banking. Mr. Samson, one of the owners of the Bar XY Ranch, became an officer of the Alberta Stockgrowers Association and was one of the prime movers in the founding of the Ranchmen's Club in Calgary. At the onset of the war in South Africa, he volunteered into the Imperial Yeomanry, and at that conflict's end, he chose to remain in South Africa to farm.

Later on, the game spread to Pekisko, Millarville and Fish Creek in Alberta, to Brandon and Winnipeg in Manitoba; and to Indian Head in Saskatchewan. The Calgary Polo Club was formed by Henry Bruen Alexander in July 1890. A team — Inspector Duncan McPherson, North West Mounted Police; Thomas Lee, the first president of the Ranchmen's Club; H.R. Jamison, manager of the huge Quorn Ranch; and Herbert Samson — traveled to Victoria. It was actually a mixed team, including players from both Calgary and High River. At the last minute, Samson was replaced by Louis Cuppage from Calgary. They brought along their ponies, disparagingly referred to by a Victoria newspaper as "strong, close-knit little brutes."[35] The game was held on a field within the Willows racecourse against a mixed Civilians–Royal Navy team that included Lieutenants Pearse and Arbuthnot, Cecil Ward and Alfred Ethelston.

Polo in the rest of the provinces was developed by Canadians; however, there was a link to English polo. In 1910, an English team representing the Ranelagh Club that had taken the U.S. Open Championship at Narragansett Pier, visited Canada. The five players were Lord Hugh Grosvenor, the Earl of Rocksavage, Frederick Gill and the Grenfell twins, Francis and Riversdale Grenfell. Canada was represented by Marton Sexsmith, Major Hartland MacDougall, Harry Robertson and Captain McBrien. At the end of the game, a trophy was presented to the Canadians on behalf of Arthur Grenfell, who was in Western Canada with the purpose of investing capital. The trophy was to be played for annually and became the symbol of the Open Championship until the onset of World War II. The Grenfell Cup is now in the Canadian Sports Hall of Fame in Toronto.

New Zealand

Arthur Rhodes, recently returned from completing his studies at Jesus College, Cambridge University, and being called to the bar at the Inner Temple, founded the Christchurch Polo Club in 1885.[36] Most likely, Rhodes learned the game while at university; what is certain is that polo was played in Christchurch in the summer of 1885 and each summer thereafter.[37]

These events preceded by three years the inauguration of the graving dock Calliope at the Devonport Naval Base in Auckland's Waitemata Harbor in February 1888, which gathered several Royal Navy vessels that had polo players serving on board. Lt. the Hon. Reginald Tyrwhitt and Lt. William Storey were the players from HMS *Opal*; Lieutenants Seymour Erskine, Maurice Fenwick and Francis Garforth were on HMS *Orlando*.[38]

The party line is that some of the officers met Edward O'Rorke in Auckland and the game began in Auckland. In reality, Teddy O'Rorke had already been in Christchurch playing polo with his cousins Arthur and Heaton Rhodes. The dashing O'Rorke also had other interests in Christchurch because he wooed and won Amy, Heaton Rhodes' sister. Nevertheless, the Auckland Polo Club was started in 1888.

An important event in New Zealand polo was the institution of the Savile Cup in 1889. The competition for this trophy in Auckland in 1890 gave impulse to the formation of the New Zealand Polo Association the following year. Lt. Robert Stewart-Savile was for a brief period ADC to the governor general of New Zealand, William Hillier, Earl of Onslow. He was raised in Kent, the son of a clergyman, and attended Harrow School and Jesus College at Cambridge University. Savile then joined the West Kent Yeomanry Cavalry and was on the Kent team that took the County Cup in 1888. Following his return from the Antipodes, Savile became MFH of the West Kent. During the Great War he was in command of the armed yacht *Sea Fay* with the rank of lt. commander and later was appointed major in the Remount Service. The Savile Cup is the oldest sporting trophy in New Zealand.

The conditions Lt. Savile attached to the trophy that bears his name were simple. The cup should be played for under the Hurlingham rules. Second, it should be competed annually at one center, and third, entry was allowed to teams from the Imperial Services. In the course of the first competition, a Royal Navy team — Lieutenants Trywhitt, Storey, George Cumings and Edward Garland — the last two from HMS *Orlando*, was defeated by the Christchurch team of Arthur Rhodes, A.W. Bennetts, Heaton Rhodes and Joseph Palmer.

The Royal Navy contributed further to the expansion of the game on the islands when HMS *Curacoa* docked in Wellington in 1894. The same band of sailor-players that had participated in a rough game in Tasmania brought their nine ponies to New Zealand's capital city. There is no record of the games played; however the playing officers were Lt. Commander Arthur Harford; Lt. Vivian Champion de Crespigny; Lt. A.C. Warren; Lt. Arthur

Cole; Midshipman John Crawley; Viscount Patrick Kelburn, later Earl of Glasgow; and Chaplain Hugh Moore.

Although some individual players, such as Jack and Walter Strang who participated in some tournaments at Crystal Palace, undertook the long sea voyage to England to play polo, no team from New Zealand visited England until the Aotea team made the journey in 1956.

The Rest of the World

The influence of the British people extended throughout the world, and polo was included in the baggage carried by settlers and Navy officers, diplomats and soldiers. The list of countries where polo was developed by Britons is extensive and exhaustive.

Africa

The first polo game in Southern Rhodesia, now Zimbabwe, was held in Bulawayo in November 1895. Whatever progress the game made, it was rudely interrupted by the Matabele Rebellion the following year and the Boer War of 1899–1902. The Salisbury Polo Club was inaugurated in December 1896, and the Carnival Cup was presented in 1897 during Queen Victoria's Jubilee.[39] Fixtures between Mashonaland and Matabele were regularly played until 1914. When Southern Rhodesia affiliated with the South African Polo Association in 1927, Salisbury was the only polo club extant. Teams from South Africa played in Rhodesia in 1933 and 1936.

The game was revived after the war in 1947, with the foundation of the Rhodesian Polo Association. The founding member clubs were Banket, Bindura, Chakari, Marandellas and Salisbury, with Nkana being the only one in Northern Rhodesia. In 1957, the Rhodesian Polo Association affiliated with the Hurlingham Polo Association.

Polo in the Gold Coast, now Ghana, started in 1902 with the establishment of the Accra Polo Club. The game enjoyed the patronage of the governor, Sir Matthew Nathan, who played in the first recorded match. The game thrived until the Great War and was resumed in 1922 by Brig. Gen. Sir Frederick Gordon Guggisberg, governor and commander in chief of the Gold Coast. A polo enthusiast, the governor was known as "good chukkas."[40]

In British East Africa, later Kenya, the game began in 1903 when play was carried out on a twenty-acre parcel of land near the King's African Rifles' barracks on Nairobi Hill. During the Duke of Connaught's 1909 visit to Kenya, he presented the Connaught Cup, to be played for in an open championship. At the same time, the Cavalry Cup was played on handicap.

The game started in Nigeria in 1904 in Lagos and took wings when army officers played in Northern Nigeria after the war. The Nigerian Polo Association was founded in 1924 with the object of bringing Nigeria into line with other colonies where the game was played and also of having a central organization responsible for arranging and supervising the various annual tournaments.[41] The initial clubs were Ibadan, Ilorin, Kaduna, Kano, Katsina, Lagos, Maidugari, Sokoto and Zaria, all of which were busy polo centers.

The principal tournaments were the Georgian Cup, an interclub open tournament played on the flat; the Nigerian Cup, played on handicap; and the Commandant's Cup, also played on handicap, for teams belonging to any unit of the Nigerian Regiment. Each team was limited to ten ponies in all those tournaments.

Asia

The Aden Polo Club was founded in 1884. A full-size polo ground without boards was located at Khor Maksar, on the isthmus that joins the port to the mainland.

The infantry branch started polo in Singapore in 1886, when officers of the Buffs (East Kent Regiment) decided to start a polo club. The Singapore Sporting Club, founded in 1842, gave permission for a polo ground to be constructed in the center of the racecourse. The first committee elected Sir Frederick Weld, the governor of Singapore, as president, and H.H. the Sultan of Johore, a keen anglophile sportsman, as vice president. Other members were Captain Craig of the Royal Artillery, Major Allsopp, Captain Hughes, Lt. Philips and a civilian member, Mr. A. Currie. The committee issued a set of rules that included the establishment of a thirteen-hand maximum height for ponies. This item aroused some discussion, one of the members pointing out, "Ponies, except for matches, are never measured for polo and no pony would ever be objected to unless a member was to play a big pony that was so fast that he spoilt the game for the others."[42]

In March 1886, the *Singapore Free Press* reported that "a Polo Club has just started with every prospect of success." Then an intriguing item appeared in the *Free Press* on 17 July: "Oh, what about the polo ground, the polo play, the polo ponies, and last but not least, the polo rules? Smashed up, I guess."[43] What happened was that the Buffs were to be transferred from Singapore and could be replaced by a non-polo-playing regiment. Nothing more appeared about the game, not even in 1890, when there was another attempt to restart the game.

The new regiment was the 5th Fusiliers, a polo-playing unit endowed with wealthy officers who could easily afford good ponies. However, they ran afoul of the golfers, who coveted the center of the racecourse for a nine-hole venue. In the battle of the polo sticks versus the golf clubs, the latter emerged victors. However, the warfare was not over. The Singapore polo community received unexpected support when the Royal Lancasters were transferred from Hong Kong, where they played plenty of polo. To the indignation of the golfers, the Singapore Sporting Club beat a retreat, allowing polo to be played on Mondays and Thursdays.

While the new polo ground was put into shape under the glowing eyes of the golf crowd, the players had to be content by knocking a ball about at the Raffles Reclamation ground, which was being used for football by the police. This parcel of land, opposite the Raffles Hotel and bounded by the sea wall, Bras Basah and Nicholl Highway, was used by polo players until the new ground was ready for use in 1895. There is no evidence that it was used by the Buffs in 1886.

Burma

Polo in Burma — nowadays Myanmar — was started in the early 1890s by civil service administrators playing for the Commission Cup on 12.3-hand Burmese "tats." Henry Todd-Naylor, ICS, deputy commissioner in Magwe, Upper Burma, and doyen of polo in Burma, presented the Todd-Naylor Challenge Trophy. This was followed by the Burma Polo Association Cup in 1904. These were the only two tournaments until the war. Teams from the commission, graduates from Cooper's Hill — the Royal Indian Engineer's College — the police, and several outstations battled for those cups on the local 12.3 ponies.

Then the Royal Welch Fusiliers arrived on the scene, purchased Australian Walers, and ran away with the trophies. No one in the outstations could compete with the stronger Walers. When the Fusiliers ended their tour of duty, the police teams took over as the dominant force in Burmese polo.

Individual handicaps were adopted in 1916, and five new tournaments were started. The first one was the Lim Ching Tsong, a handicap tournament to be played in Rangoon. In 1920 Sir Vere Bonamy Fane, commanding Burma Division, donated the Fane Senior Cup to be played at Maymo, and the Fane Junior Cup, a handicap tournament under local rules to encourage newcomers to the game. The Frontier Cup was created to be played between the two frontier stations, Mytikyina and Bhamo. The governor of Burma, Sir Spencer Harcourt Butler, presented the trophy bearing his name to be played in Mandalay during Christmas.

Central and South America

The West India Regiment introduced polo to the island of Jamaica in 1882, and civilian players took up the game soon after.

A polo club was organized in Barbados in 1884. A local tournament was the Grant Cup, and there was also an annual fixture with Trinidad for the Inter-Colonial Challenge Cup.

There was polo at the Belize Colony and Athletic Club in 1901. Little is known about the game in British Honduras. The *Polo Monthly* mentions that polo in British Honduras flourished despite the scarcities of players and ponies in comparison to other countries. A photograph of the winning team in the annual polo tournament in Belize is included in the article.[44] The players are H.R. Furness, the Hon. Secretary; J.J. Franco; H. Malhado; and E. Hofius.

POLO IN CHILE

The Royal Navy introduced polo in Chile in 1888. HMS *Triumph* anchored in Valparaiso Bay and some of the officers at once went ashore and asked about arranging a game of polo. They had polo sticks and balls; the locals had ponies, but no knowledge of the game. Nevertheless, a friendly game was got up amid great excitement in the local British colony.

Mr. R. Percy Wilson gathered some ponies, and a fast and furious game followed, which ended with a surprise victory for Valparaiso. Wilson borrowed a pony from a good sportsman, who told him, "He will turn on a three-penny bit, and charge and knock over any horse you ride him at." Perhaps that attitude led to success, because none of the Valparaiso players knew the rules; however, no one was seriously hurt, and everyone enjoyed themselves, to the delight of the huge crowd. In his reminiscences, Mr. Wilson stated, "The sailors knew more of the game but less of the saddle."[45]

The teams were: HMS *Triumph*, Lt. Ulric Thynne, Lt. S.H. Gray, Lt. H. Carmichael and Midshipman W.B. Macdonald. Meanwhile, Valparaiso had Percy Wilson, C.R. Giles, William Ancrum and Edward Edmondson. Mr. Edward Wilson Edmonson, from the shippers Edmonson & Co. in Valparaiso, was on the team that played against Argentina in 1893 and was playing in England in 1897.

An international match against Argentina was played at nearby Viña de Mar in November 1893. In reality, it was a match played between British residents on both sides of the Andes Mountains. The occasion was the tour of a cricket team from Buenos Aires to Valparaiso. When some polo players on the cricket team found out that polo was played in Chile, a game was arranged. The team representing Chile won what is considered the first international polo contest in South America. Victor Raby, Andrew Scott, Horace Lyon and Edward Edmonson played on the home team. The visitors aligned Tom Preston, Frank Clunie, Percy Clarke and Richard "Harry" Anderson. A scheduled return match in Argentina was not played. Although a few teams from Argentina toured Chile, no team from that country played in Buenos Aires until 1931.

Later on, British nationals, including George Alexander Lockett, running a mining operation, formed the Tarapacá Polo Club in Iquique, in northern Chile, which was active in the 1910s.

POLO IN URUGUAY

British settlers started polo in Uruguay sometime before 1892. When the Polo Association of the River Plate was founded in 1892, two polo clubs from Uruguay, Colonia and Montevideo were among the founders of the new organization. Dr. H.J. Walker represented the Colonia Polo Club and Mr. Harry H. Jefferies the Montevideo Polo Club.

THE GAME IN PERU

George Lockett, a nitrates merchant from the well-known Liverpool polo family, introduced the game to Peru in 1898. Several other Englishmen joined Lockett, a left-handed player, in his pioneer efforts: John Bayly, John Coward, Frank Cook, Ian MacIver and Alexander Milne. The first ponies were brought over from Chile, and matches were played in the open country some two miles from Plaza San Martín. Even in those long-ago days, urban development from Lima soon engulfed the polo grounds.

The Lima Polo and Hunt Club was started around the turn of the century, two polo fields being built, one on the club's grounds and the other a few minutes away in the center of the Santa Beatriz hippodrome. Years later, members of the British community in Lima were instrumental in keeping the Lima Polo Club alive when difficult circumstances arose.

There was also polo at Talara, the site of the headquarters of the International Petroleum Co. The polo ground, close to the Pacific Ocean, was sandy, bumpy, and salty. After every other chukker, a motor lorry with a trailing brush had to sweep the bumps level. In spite of many vicissitudes and the relative isolation, the members kept the club running. The highlight of the club's existence occurred when HMS *Exeter* presented a ship's bell to the Talara Polo Club as a mark of appreciation of their kindness to visiting Royal Navy Polo Association members. Both Commodore Henry Harwood and HMS *Exeter* covered themselves with glory during the battle of the River Plate in 1939, when together with HMS *Ajax* and HMS *Achilles* they defeated the pocket battleship *Graf Spee*.

POLO IN BRAZIL

English engineers involved in the construction of the São Paulo Railway were the first to introduce polo in Brazil. Most regrettably, none of the pioneers' names have been recorded. The same people started the game in Rio de Janeiro.[46] Walter Pretyman, an English foxhunter, arrived in Brazil in 1923 and while riding in the Quinta de Boa Vista Park met an American Navy officer, Commander Bryan Hamilton, a polo player frustrated because he could not find anyone with whom to play polo. After searching for a suitable ground, they found a parcel in Petrópolis, where they began to play polo. The first recruits included Pretyman's brother Herbert, a retired Royal Navy officer; Raymundo Castro Maya; Alfredo

Santos; Mr. Millard from the American embassy; a Captain McNeill; Major José Pessoa, just arrived from London; and a player named Daniel, whose surname is unknown. Later on, the group moved to the Parade Ground of the 1st Cavalry Regiment, commanded by Major Pessoa. Sir John Tilley, the British ambassador, presented a trophy that was taken by the 1st Cavalry two years running.

Also in the early 1920s, Major Wilfred Warwick Parker, who had played in India and fine-tuned his game in Argentina while working at Harold Schwind's estancia El Bagual, immigrated to Brazil and started polo in Analandia, north of São Paulo.[47] Those polo-playing ranchers eventually formed the Sociedade Hípica Paulista, where the game is played to this day.

Oceania

The game of polo was brought to the remote island of Samoa by Mr. T.B. (later Sir Thomas) Cusack-Smith, the British consul at Apia. It was a tremendous pioneering effort, considering the horse was an unknown animal on the island a few years back.[48] The exact date when polo started is not recorded; however it can be certainly dated between 1890, when Cusack-Smith was appointed HM's consul in the Navigator's Islands, and 1897, when he was named consul in Valparaíso, Chile.[49]

CHAPTER 8

The Climb to the Summit: The Westchester Cup

Several years went by before the Americans felt they had progressed enough in their skills in order to challenge the English for the Westchester Cup.

In *Full Tilt*, his memoirs written with Alden Hatch, Foxhall Keene states that as far back as 1892 he traveled to England to arrange another visit by an English team. The *New York Herald* published an article stating, "Mr. Foxhall Keene, when he went abroad, was to carry a certain authority granted him by the Polo Association to induce an English team to come over here and try conclusions with our crack teams."[1] Keene goes on to say that the enterprise failed because of disagreements regarding the rules of the game. At the time England had in effect the offside rule, similar to football; on the other hand, the American rules did not allow the hooking of mallets.[2] A search through the Polo Association's Executive Committee minutes failed to find any mention of a proposed renewal of the international series, or the granting of any kind of authority to Mr. Keene to negotiate on behalf of the Polo Association.[3]

1900 at Hurlingham

The persistent Mr. Keene did not falter in his quest to return the International Cup to America. While foxhunting in England, he was instrumental in assembling a team of American players to contest the trophy. They were Walter McCreery, his brother Lawrence, and Frank Jay Mackey, a globetrotting Chicagoan who spent much of his time in Europe and also in Southern California.

Walter Adolph McCreery was born in Zurich to an American father and was educated at Cambridge University. Walter took the silver medal in the 1900 Olympic Games as a member on the Rugby team, and the Hurlingham Champion Cup in 1900 and 1904 with the Old Cantabs team, all former students at Cambridge. His brother Richard, who also received his graduate education at Cambridge, took the 1900 Hurlingham Champion Cup.

Jay Mackey was a winner of the gold medal at the Paris Games with the Anglo-American Foxhunters team. Mr. Mackey was the donor of trophies bearing his name in Paris, Warwickshire and California. He made his considerable fortune when he started Household International, the forerunner of Mastercard/Visa. Moving to Chicago from Wisconsin, Mackey found that his business' reputation prevented him and his wife, the former Florence May from Minneapolis, from being admitted to the circles of prominent society; therefore they moved first to New York and then overseas. The Mackeys were among the wealthiest Americans living in Europe. They owned a town house in Mayfair and a noted country site, Beauchamp Hall, in Leamington Spa, Warwickshire. They also became part of the Prince of Wales' social circle. Meanwhile, at home, the *Chicago Tribune* labeled Jay Mackey — a five-goal handicap player in America — "the king of usurers."[4]

The report in *Baily's* indicates that "the good form shown by American players this season certainly justified their challenge and attempt to take the Cup across the Atlantic. They made a good fight, and might have done better had they not been a little over-anxious."[5]

Played at Hurlingham, the match was rather one sided, the holders winning easily by eight goals to only two by the American team. The British team scored six goals straight off the reel and then cruised on to the finish. *Baily's Magazine* also made the comment that the umpires, Lord Harrington and Colonel Richard Lawley, "had an easy time, for a fairer game has never been seen."[6]

Captain the Hon. John Beresford, Frederick Freake, Walter Buckmaster and the old warrior John Watson were selected to represent the Union Jack.

Captain Beresford, a scion of that famous sporting family, took the gold medal in the Olympic Games held in Paris as a member of the mixed team Foxhunters. He also was on the winning British Army team in Argentina in 1908 and presented the Beresford Cup in South Africa, still played for as emblematic of the South African Polo Championship. Later on, he was created Lord Decies.

Frederick Charles Maitland Freake, later Sir Frederick, was a quiet man who schooled his own ponies. Born in 1876, he was admitted to Magdalene College in Cambridge University and was on the winning team against Oxford in 1895. A brilliant number 2, Freake was considered alongside Charles Miller as the best in that position. His partnership on different teams with Walter Buckmaster lasted from 1898 until 1914, when he left the game to go to France with the Royal Artillery. He never took polo again after the war.

Walter Selby Buckmaster is rightly considered one of the all-time greats in English polo. Born in 1872, he was brought up in the country and was sent to Repton, where he excelled at association football. During the summer, he was a habitué at the West Essex Polo Club, where he served his apprenticeship with good players such as Arthur Waters and Robert Ball. Buckmaster then went to Trinity College, Cambridge, and played in the fixtures against Oxford. After leaving Cambridge University, he went to London to start a successful career as a stockbroker in the city. His polo was at Hurlingham, Ranelagh and Stansted. Rather quickly, Buckmaster rose to the top rank among polo players, winning just about every cup offered for competition. It was not much of a surprise that when individual handicaps were established in England his name was listed at ten goals, a distinction he shared with the four members of the "Big Four," which were rated at nine goals in America.

His best ponies were the celebrated Bendigo, imported from Canada; Sunshine, his first top pony; The Cat, Rufus, Early Dawn, Mainspring, Fusilier and Patricia. Playing at number 3 or at back, his game was faultless. Walter Buckmaster's record in the Hurlingham Champion Cup is impressive: with the Old Cantabs team he took the Champion Cup on six occasions, and four times with the Freebooters, the last one in 1921, at age forty-seven. Shortly after, Walter Buckmaster retired from high-handicap polo to concentrate on his other sporting passion, riding to hounds.

It was unfortunate that he only played against the Americans in 1900 and 1902, the reason being that he was prone to injury. Besides being a superb rider, Edward Miller thought of him, "There can be no two opinions about his being one of the very best, and certainly the most graceful horseman ever seen on a polo ground."[7]

On the polo field, Buckmaster was absolutely scrupulous about the rules of the game. Lt. Col. Edward Miller once more: "During all those years I do not believe 'Buck' ever committed a foul against us, and, since I gave up first-class polo about a dozen years ago, I have umpired scores of matches in which he was playing, and I do not believe that I have ever given a foul against him."[8]

During the war, he was considered too old for active service, so he volunteered to work with the French Ambulance Service, for which he was awarded the Croix de Guerre.

There is some controversy regarding this 1900 contest. *The Hurlingham Polo Association Year Book* lists the event as part and parcel of the history of the Westchester Cup.[9] It is, however, cautiously ignored in the *U.S. Polo Association Year Book*. Anyway, this 1900 event deserves more recognition than the 1988 competition between the United States and a team from Australasia that was played in contravention of the deed of gift, which clearly specifies that the Westchester Cup is the exclusive domain of America and Britain.

1902 at Hurlingham Club

There is much more documentation regarding the 1902 competition. A formal challenge was sent from the Polo Association to the Hurlingham Polo Committee. A team was selected, comprising the best American players: Rodolphe Agassiz, John Cowdin, Foxhall Keene as captain, and the Waterbury siblings, Lawrence and his younger brother, James Montgomery, Jr., known as Monte.

The pony string left early, accompanied by Foxie Keene, en route to England for the foxhunting season. This proved to be a mixed blessing, because Keene had a bad spill while hunting with the Quorn, injuring his neck and raising doubts as to his availability to anchor the American team.

The American squad played six matches against strong opposition, winning four and being at the wrong end of the score in the other two. Both ponies and players made a favorable impression on their hosts. *The Field* noticed that their hitting was clean, everyone used his stick with equal facility on each side, and the ponies ridden by the challengers, although not fast, were handy and responsive to their riders' directions.[10]

On Saturday morning of the first match, John Cowdin, the reserve player, was placed at the number 2 position, previously occupied by Monte Waterbury. Agassiz played forward, and Keene and Larry Waterbury in defense. The English team was Cecil Nickalls, Patteson Nickalls, Walter Buckmaster and Charles Miller. Umpires were William Corcoran Eustis for America and Captain Gordon Renton for England; Captain Denis St. G. Daly was the referee.

The start was good for the American team, because Larry Waterbury scored a goal less than three minutes after the throw-in. The second period opened tamely until a breakaway headed by Dolph Agassiz resulted in a goal by Keene. In the third period, Cowdin came a cropper, without suffering bodily injury, only perhaps to his ego. While Cowdin was down, Cecil Nickalls—the Millers' brother-in-law—scored a goal. *The Field* correspondent's commentary is of interest: "While he was down, Mr. C. Nickalls hit a goal, but, of course, the point was disallowed on appeal to the umpire."[11] Therefore, at halftime the Americans led 2–0.

The American team was outplayed in the 1902 Westchester Cup and they resorted to the legal tactic of hitting behind their own line when pressed by the English squad. John Cowdin is shown hitting in from between the goal posts.

Dryly, *The Field* reports that the second half was by no means interesting, the fourth period being a stumbling one. England kept on pressing, Miller scoring, but the goal was nullified for offside. Toward the end of the match, Cecil Nickalls hit a goal for England, the game thus ending 2–1 in favor of the American team, their first win against England.

Why was the second half so uninspiring? The reason is that, being two goals ahead in a tight game, the Americans resorted to a legal tactic allowed by the Hurlingham rules: if a team hit the ball behind his own backline, play was resumed by a hit-in by the defending team. There is no mention of this tactic in *The Field*'s detailed coverage of the game; however, it was considered an unfair maneuver in England. The American team, under heavy pressure by their opponents, resorted time and time again to hitting behind their own line. As an aside, the Hurlingham Polo Committee quickly changed this rule after the polo season had ended, allowing the attacking team a free hit from sixty yards, opposite where the ball crossed the backline. This was the modern origin of the safety penalty, called corner in Argentina.[12]

The first game's negative results brought changes to the British team. Frederick Freake replaced Pat Nickalls at number 2; Charles Miller was dropped from the team, his replacement being his older brother George. The American team was unchanged. The game was a runaway victory for England, the final score being 6–1.

For the third and decisive match, postponed because of bad weather, England again made changes: Pat Nickalls returned to the team at number 3, and George Miller moved to the number 2 position instead of Freake. The American team made one change, Monte Waterbury played at number 1 because John Cowdin had returned to America to attend to some business commitments.

At the beginning, the match was fairly even, as the first period ended in a one-all tie and the second was a scoreless one. However, in the third period Walter Buckmaster started hitting long shots at goal in an attempt to break the stubborn American defense. In these attempts he was successful, and the score started to mount; at halftime it was 4–1.[13] In the second half, the American ponies began to show signs of being tired. As the numbers on the scoreboard deteriorated from the American point of view, Larry Waterbury, Dolph Agassiz and Keene played at times in the back's position. They were unable to stop the British onslaught. The final score was 7–1, the hosts winning both game and series.

Thus England retained the cup first won in 1886. It is of interest that the magazine *Baily's* correspondent made the observation that one result of the matches might be the adoption on uniform rules, "so that it will be one of the simplest, as well as the grandest of games."[14]

Regrettably, more than one hundred years later, the world's leading polo nations seem to be unable to reach an agreement regarding uniformity in the rules of polo.

1909 at Hurlingham Club

No other challenge for the Westchester Cup has matched the degree of advanced planning enjoyed by the American effort to conquer the silver trophy. Once the decision to challenge for the cup was made, the Polo Association placed the organization of the entire project in Harry Payne Whitney's capable hands. Mr. Whitney's first task was to identify and recruit the best American players, then to collect the best polo pony string ever seen on a polo grounds, and thirdly, to assemble the parts into a congenial whole.[15]

Whitney almost always played at number 3, the most important position on a polo team. A born leader, he felt strongly that the pivot slot was the place for the team captain to be. This was against customary dogma. Since the early days of modern polo, best exemplified by John Watson's towering personality, back was considered the proper place for the team's leader. The gospel according to Watson also mandated that back must be basically a defensive player, never venturing near the opponent's goalpost and being content with feeding the halfback and the forwards with booming shots.

In young Devereux Milburn, the Buffalonian now on Long Island by way of Oxford University and Harvard Law School, Harry Whitney found a player possessed of considerable brawn, complemented with a healthy dose of brains. It was a magnificent amalgam that resulted in a player that exemplified number 4 play at its best: rock solid in defense, formidable in attack.

As to the forward contingent, two brothers who had been blooded by their father in the old Country Club of Westchester in Pelham were picked not only for their individual talents, but also for their exquisite combination play. Larry and Monte Waterbury had developed combination play in polo at a time in which individual prowess and effort counted for more than its share on the polo ground. Tried, tested and proven in countless matches, Larry's versatility — he is the only player in the history of international polo to have played in all four positions — nicely complemented his younger brother's keen positional play.

At the time, Foxhall Keene was considered to be the top individual player in America, for no other was ever rated higher than he was on the handicap list. Nevertheless, there were two obstacles, one positional, the other philosophical. Keene, like Whitney, always played number 3. Harry Payne Whitney, the anointed captain, wanted to assemble a team, each player in the correct slot. Simply put, there was no room for a pair of number 3s. The second hurdle was the different thoughts about polo exhibited by Keene and Whitney. In his memoirs, Foxhall Keene reminisced:

> He [Dev Milburn] and Harry Whitney made a great combination in the back field. But in a way their style was bad for polo. As Harry could only hit on the offside of his pony, he played everything to pass to Dev and let him go to the side of the field with the ball. Everyone imitated this method of attack, but few could get away with it. It depended on the brilliance of one man.[16]

Two years later, while both were foxhunting in England, Keene asked Whitney about the American team, "Are you going to leave it open to all, or keep it in the family?" When Whitney answered that, as they had taken the Cup, they should have the first chance at defending it, Keene agreed while saying, "I'll come back and give you all the practice you want, but nothing will ever make me go on the team."[17] Thus the "Big Four," one of the most influential teams in the modern development of the game of polo, was born.

In assembling the polo pony string, Harry Whitney sent his purchasing agents in search of the best horseflesh available. California, England, Ireland and Texas were the primary hunting grounds. Endowed with more than his share of the world's goods, Whitney spared nothing in procuring the best polo ponies.

Herbert Wilson, a nine-goal international player, on the pony Alice. Captain "Bertie" Wilson was killed in France in 1917.

Ponies bred on the British Isles were an important addition to the American string, and several English players were surprised to see some of their erstwhile better mounts on the American team.

From Ireland came the brown mare Solitaire, a winner of the Best Polo Pony prize in Dublin. Another Irish-bred mare bought from Frederick Freake was Ballin a Hone, Whitney's favorite mount after the incomparable Cottontail. Ballin a Hone was a superb chestnut mare with a big blaze, exuding quality and substance. Also from Ireland came the bay mare Balada, which was played in Hurlingham's Champion Cup by Walter Buckmaster. Another of Buckmaster's ponies, Cinders, a gray mare, was also a top performer. Summer Lightning was purchased by Robert Beeckman, polo player and sometime governor of Rhode Island, who loaned it to the American team.

The beautiful chestnut mare Cobnut, who had a perfect conformation, was purchased in England by Mr. Whitney's agents, as was the chestnut gelding Greyling, bred in Cheshire. Little Mary, a bay mare, was considered by the Americans to be second only to Cottontail. There was nothing diminutive about Little Mary, because she was a big pony. Another English pony was Cinderella, a black mare that had been played by Rivy Grenfell. Ralla, a big chestnut mare bred in Ireland, had a past history of being ridden to hounds and carried the reputation of being a temperamental horse. Nevertheless, Ralla was unsurpassed in the hands of a good horseman and yielded in looks only to Cobnut.

Herbert Haseltine immortalized in bronze five of those superb polo ponies: Cobnut, Cottontail, Little Mary and the Roan Mare, the "Big Four" in the Meadow Brook Team, of which an example was presented by Mr. Whitney to the Hurlingham Club. Ralla merited a bronze of her own; a quarter-life cast is at the Whitney Museum of American Art in New York City.

The American team won all the friendly games with one exception, when a Hurlingham team won a practice game by eight goals to four.

As part of the preparations for the big event, the team, under the name of Meadow Brook, entered the competition for the Ranelagh Open Cup, the second in importance in England after the Hurlingham Champion Cup. They took the tournament with ease, on a slow ground, beating the Tigers team of the Frenchman Comte Jean de Madré, Ulric Thynne, Colonel Chunga Singh and Captain Brownlow Mathew-Lannowe, by fourteen goals to one.

In the semifinals, they faced and defeated Beauchamp Hall — which had Foxie Keene and Louis Stoddard on its lineup — by seven goals to four. This was the game mentioned by Keene in his *Full Tilt* when he collided with two other players, being knocked out for a while.[18]

The final game was against Roehampton, in which game Meadow Brook gave another sterling performance, taking both match and the Ranelagh Open Cup by six goals to one. This impressive victory gave the team some comfort in facing the might of British polo in the forthcoming Westchester Cup matches scheduled to begin only four days later.

Early on, the British realized the supreme qualities of the American team's ponies, and a public appeal was issued for the loan of quality ponies, led by Captain the Hon. Frederick Guest and Major Francis Egerton-Green. Out of the many ponies offered for loan, eleven were selected to play. The remaining eight ponies were the property of the players riding them.

The English selectors had some difficulties in picking their team, which finally presented Captain Herbert Wilson, Frederick Freake, Pat Nickalls and Lord Wodehouse. The latter was pressed into service just twenty-four hours before the match because of Charles Miller's illness and Walter Buckmaster's dislocated shoulder in the last practice match for the English squad.

The Irishman John Hardress Lloyd was a ten-goal handicap player and captain of the 1911 international team. Here he is on the celebrated pony Energy.

In fact, the series was rather lopsided, the Americans taking both matches by scores of 9–5 and 8–2. For the second game, postponed because of inclement weather, the British selection committee made two changes: Harry Rich replaced Captain Wilson, and Captain John Hardress Lloyd took Lord Wodehouse's position at back. It made no difference. The disparity between the pony strings and the combination play exhibited by the American foursome was even more overwhelming in the return match.

After the contest was over, the Westchester Cup was presented to Harry Payne Whitney by Lord Frederick Roberts, who when commander in chief of India had the foresight to make compulsory the use of polo helmets. The trophy returned to America after an absence of twenty-three years.

To the English public, as well as the players, the new American style of play was both a revelation and a revolution. In spite of slow grounds and the constraint imposed upon the visitors by the offside rule, the combination of speed, long hitting, and smooth interchange of places among the American players left the hosts in a trance. It was an onslaught of constant attack, with even the back finding himself at times in the number 1 position. Pace, accurate hitting, superb ponies at the peak of fitness, and strong leadership, were the successful ingredients of the Big Four.

Lt. Noel Edwards on Darling. Rated at nine goals, Edwards died from the effects of chlorine gas in Flanders.

1911 at Meadow Brook Club

On the American side of the pond there was no question of what team would defend the Westchester Cup following the impressive performance of H.P. Whitney and company on Hurlingham's number-one ground.

The British team arrived in America toward the end of April, the first match having been scheduled for the end of May. Capt. John Hardress Lloyd was joined by four Army captains, Frederick Barrett, Leslie Cheape and Eustace "Bill" Palmes, all ten-goalers in India, and Herbert Wilson, a nine-goal handicap player. Lt. Arthur Noel Edwards was the designated spare man.

The team trained intensely, first at the Gould's Lakewood Polo Club in New Jersey, and then at the Rockaway Club in Cedarhurst on Long Island. On 22 May, the English team played a practice game on the International Field at Meadow Brook against a strong local squad, Louis Stoddard, René La Montagne, Foxhall Keéne and Malcolm Stevenson. The result was a shocker: 11¼ goals were scored by the local team to 1¼ goals for the English team.

An explanation is due for the fractions of a goal in the score. The regulations of the

Westchester Cup provided that the games must be played under the rules of the host country. In America, a hit by a team behind its goal line was punished by deleting one quarter of a goal from its tally; the penalty for a foul was half a goal.

Several explanations were offered to justify the one-sided result of the practice match. The ponies were overtrained and got tired toward the end of each period; the team had been practicing on grounds smaller than International Field; the club team was trying very hard, perhaps with an eye on a place for some of its members on the international team. In view of the excellent showing later by the British team in the international matches, the most logical explanation is twofold. The visiting team had a limited supply of top ponies, and to obtain a further supply would be difficult, if not impossible. It was a question of getting used to their ponies and to the fast American grounds, without tiring the pony string.

Nevertheless, Captain Hardress Lloyd changed the lineup, inserting Bertie Wilson at back, himself at number 3 and Edwards and Cheape at forwards. In the event, the visitors acquitted themselves nobly, scoring three goals— all from Lt. Edwards' mallet — against 4½ for the Big Four. The American ponies performed better than their English counterparts— a scribe noted that Leslie Cheape was certainly the worst mounted man on the field — not surprising since the nucleus of the American string was still the fantastic core of the 1909 ponies.[19]

The second match was described as "the finest game of polo ever seen, being full of accurate hitting, hard riding, and brilliant tactics. Either side would have been unlucky to have lost the day. Every man on the field played up to the top of his form, not a weak link on either side."[20]

To place the second game into perspective, it was the closest result in international play for the unbeaten Big Four. However, grand teams somehow have a knack for winning close matches, just as the Argentine champion team Coronel Suárez would do, time and time again, in its heyday sixty years later.

1913 at Meadow Brook Club

Encouraged by the performance demonstrated by the 1911 team, the Hurlingham Polo Committee issued another challenge for the 1913 season. The Big Four was ready and able to face the challenge; however, it proved to be the occasion for its swansong.

The British felt that the quality of their pony string, compared to the American lot, had let them down. Accordingly, the Duke of Westminster, reputed to be one of the wealthiest men in England, took up the daunting task of assembling their pony string. At the end of the day, forty-two ponies were available to the British squad. Walter Buckmaster, the stockbroker who was England's first ten-goal player was selected as team captain. However, a bad fall, one of many that marred the polo career of this brilliant player, prevented him from taking his place on the team, and Captain Ralph Gerald Ritson was chosen to be the team leader. Lt. Col. Edward Miller, the guru of British polo, accompanied the team as manager. The players practiced at the Piping Rock Club, close to Meadow Brook. It was a strong squad, with Leslie Cheape at the top of his form; Noel Edwards, now a captain in the 9th Lancers, playing well; a steady leader in ten-goaler Jerry Ritson; and, at back, another ten-goaler, Captain Vivian Lockett.

For all their past glories, the Big Four gave the selection committee some headaches.

The team played badly in the practice games, incurring some criticism that Harry Whitney took to heart, thus resigning his captaincy of the national team. Foxhall Keene, who had for a long time been waiting in the wings, was appointed captain. With Mr. Whitney gone, so were the Waterbury brothers. The selection committee then announced the anointed team: Louis Stoddard, Devereux Milburn — a top back in the number 2 position — Foxie Keene and Malcolm "Mike" Stevenson. It will never be known what this team would have achieved against the fast-improving challengers. Fate intervened when four days before the first match, Keene had a fall, breaking his collarbone. The committee beat a hasty retreat; the new team was discarded, and the Big Four was back into the picture.

As was its wont, the American team started with a tremendous rush, gaining a lead that was held to the end. In the sixth chukker, Monte Waterbury sustained a broken finger, making it impossible for him to hold a mallet. He was ably replaced by Louis Stoddard. The final score was America 5½ goals, England 3 goals.

With Monte Waterbury out of the lineup, Stoddard started at number 1, and Lawrence Waterbury moved to the number 2 position. On the British side, the old warrior, Sir Frederick Freake, replaced Noel Edwards. The second match was a desperate struggle, both teams scoring five goals each. It came down to penalties; both England and America were penalized half a goal for crossing. The difference was a quarter goal for a safety against England, when Captain Ritson was forced to hit behind his own line to prevent an American goal. Once more, the British team came so very close, only to be bitterly disappointed at the final bell.

The final match was played in a wave of oppressive heat. James Cooley described the situation:

> The second game in 1913 was played on a day when the mercury was trying to break through the top of the glass. Freddie Freake, who played in Capt. Edwards' place, almost succumbed at half-time, and when the game was over neither players nor spectators cared whether school kept or not. All they wanted to do was to rush north or south to the seas and therein dive.[21]

1914 at Meadow Brook Club

Ivor Guest, Lord Wimborne, was in charge of the British challenge and with tremendous energy was able to secure an exceptional number of ponies, including the outstanding chestnut mare Energy. The selected team included at number 1 Captain Henry Tomkinson, a fine horseman who carried the reputation of being able to handle ponies no other player could manage. Captains Cheape and Barrett were at the height of their powers, and at back it was Johnny Traill, the Irishman from Argentina who was rated at ten goals. Regrettably, at the last minute Traill was taken ill and was replaced by Vivian Lockett. Major Frederick Barrett was the field captain.

The year the First World War started in Europe was a watershed mark in American polo. That great leader, Harry Payne Whitney, retired from international polo, and the Big Four was no more. However, the other three members were still there, and the selection committee felt certain that the surging tide of British polo would be, once more, contained. As substitutes, Foxhall Keene, Harold C. Phipps, Charles Cary Rumsey and Malcolm Stevenson were ready.

The American squad lined up with René La Montagne, Jr., Monte Waterbury, Devereux Milburn and Lawrence Waterbury. This time around it was the British who scored the first goal, and the mistake of taking away Dev Milburn from his accustomed position at the last line of defense was quickly uncovered. Soon after, Milburn and Larry Waterbury exchanges places; however, the damage had been done. At the game's end the scoreboard displayed 8½ goals for the English team against only 3 for the disappointed Americans.

The second game was closer. The American team started with Devereux Milburn in his usual back position and played a great game. But so did Captain Leslie Cheape, one of the top British players in the period before the war. Penalties wrecked the American effort, because the final score was 4 goals for England and a meager 2¾ goals for the United States. And so the Westchester Cup went across the pond once more.

Thus ended the first era of international competition between the United States and Great Britain for the Westchester Cup. It was a time during which sportsmanship was at a high point; there were several instances in which both sides refused to take advantage of what appeared to be a situation within the written laws of the game. In his chairman's report, Mr. Henry Lloyd Herbert put it as well as it can be expressed:

> The ruling spirit of polo the world over is one of absolute fairness no matter how important the match or how bitter the contest — not one infinitesimal unfair advantage of one team or player over another has been known to occur.
>
> Beautiful illustrations of that spirit of honest sport have been shown in all important events and notably in the international matches. In the contest of 1911 the English team was lined up and ready for the ball; the time bell sounded and the ball was thrown in while two of the American team were off the field on account of some small mishap. Captain John Hardress Lloyd of the English team, according to the rule, could have dashed off with his full team of four against only two opponents; instead he gallantly tapped the ball to the side line and awaited the full American team. It was an example of true sportsmanship at a moment when the score was within a fraction of a goal from being a tie, and when the people of England were anxiously awaiting news of an expected victory; also it was in the presence of 30,000 spectators, the larger proportion of who were rooting for the American team. Later in the day the ball was on the end line with the American team all in position for the hit-in; the time bell sounded when the English team was not quite ready but Mr. Milburn withheld his stroke until the Englishmen were in their places. It is this very spirit in all polo and particularly international events which helps to cement the feeling of friendship between neighbors as well as nations.[22]

Interlude I: 1914–1918

In spite of the guns of war, some English officers went out of their way to have a game of polo. Of necessity, most of the games took place out of firing range, but there are well-documented matches that took place near the trenches in France and in Salonika.

Lt. Col. George Railston, DSO, later Playdell-Railston, was in command of the Scottish Horse facing the Bulgarian forces. An improvised field was prepared, horses were borrowed, Indian pugaree martingales were used and the Sussex Yeomanry on duty nearby was invited to partake of a four-chukker polo game. The game, duly won by the Scottish Horse, ended, and the officers were getting ready to sip some tea which had arrived on a pack mule in charge of Colonel Railston's pipe major. The tea party broke up in disorder when the Bulgarians sent some shrapnel that landed on the polo ground. Nevertheless, polo took hold and games were played by the 28th Division in more sheltered places.[1]

On the Western Front, the 1st King Edward's Horse somehow managed to put together a team in spite of the miserable conditions associated with warfare in the trenches. In his *History of the King Edward's Horse*, Lt. Col. Lionel James writes,

> Gen. Sir A.E.A. Holland who commanded the 1st Corps was a keen polo player. He had a quite serviceable team in his H.Q. and it played several games against the "C" Squadron, King Edward's Horse, billeted near. With Lieutenant Lacy [sic] as No. 4 and lieutenants Fannin, Murray and McCulloch playing forward the unit had quite a creditable team, but the regiment could not produce much in the way of ponies, and there was little time or opportunity to train them.[2]

Lt. Gen. Sir Arthur Holland, Royal Artillery, was commandant, Royal Military Academy. Lt. Col. Edward Miller knew him from South Africa, where Holland, who acquired the reputation of always being ready to go anywhere or do anything, managed to keep his horses in wonderful condition, and taught the Yeomanry — where Miller was serving — much in the way to procure extra forage. In France, Lt. Col. Miller asked him if he was as good at looting in the Western Front as he had been in South Africa. General Holland's reply was "Oh, no; it is now my job to see that no one does that sort of thing."[3]

Lewis Lacey, at the time a subaltern in the King Edward's Horse, became a ten-goal player and was an international for both England and Argentina. No trace has been found of the subsequent polo careers, if any, of lieutenants V.G. Fannin, William McCulloch and E.M. Murray. Lt. McCulloch was awarded the Military Cross for valor during an action on 9 November 1918, two days before the end of the war.

The Welsh Guards also engaged in polo in France. Charles Dudley Ward in his regimental history writes,

> At this time polo was played practically in sight of the enemy. On a clear day one could see the hill of Monchy from the polo-ground, and maybe the German artillery observer, when he

Leslie Cheape was one of the best players in England and played on the Westchester Cup winning team in 1914. He was killed in Palestine on Easter Sunday, 1916.

turned his telescope that way, sometimes wondered what was happening. Col. Vickery who commanded the 74th Artillery Brigade was responsible for the ground, and the Commanding Officer and Keith Menzies were the chief players from the battalion — the brigadier played also.[4]

The list of polo players killed in the Great War is interminable. Among the ten-goalers, Captain Leslie St. Clair Cheape, King's Dragoon Guards, was killed on Easter Sunday, 1916, in Ogleratina, Palestine. Two other internationals rated at nine goals were also lost: Captain Herbert Wilson died near Mochy-le-Preux, where gunnners and Welsh guardsmen managed to play some polo; Captain Arthur Noel Edwards, 9th Lancers, died near Ypres in May 1915 from the effects of chlorine gas during the German attack on Bellewaarde Ridge.

Promising and accomplished players that surely would have been candidates for international honors after the war, such as the twins Francis and Rivy Grenfell, Lt. Edward Leatham and Lt. Brian Osborne, also lost their lives in the war to end all wars.

PART II

Gifted Amateurs, 1919–1939

CHAPTER 9

A Time for Recovery

When the guns fell silent on the Western Front at eleven o'clock in the morning of the eleventh day of the eleventh month of the year 1918, the entire world enjoyed a sigh of relief. Not that all calamities were out of the way; a terrible epidemic of typhus broke out in the Balkans, and the worldwide influenza took the lives of an estimated 3 percent of the population. In Great Britain alone there were about 250,000 deaths.

In America, a ditty became common:

> *I had a little bird*
> *And its name was Enza.*
> *I opened the window*
> *And in-flew-Enza.*

The Coronation Cup

Somehow, in the aftermath of this mixture of relief and desperation, the game of polo in Britain began to recover. Hurlingham and Ranelagh resumed their respective open championships; the Freebooters, victorious in Hurlingham's Champion Cup, and Thornby, winners of the Ranelagh Open Cup, battled for the Coronation Cup, which was taken by the Freebooters with Sir John Ramsden, Captain Ivor Buxton, Lord George Rocksavage and Major John Harrison.

The King's Coronation Cup was presented by the Ranelagh Club to commemorate the coronation of King George V. The conditions specified that it was to be played for by the winners of the Hurlingham Champion Cup, the Ranelagh Open Cup and the Inter-Regimental Tournament. When the Roehampton Club established its own Open Cup, it was added to the roster. There was also a provision that allowed visiting teams from India, the colonies and dominions to participate in this competition, by invitation only. It was precisely a team representing the Indian Polo Association that took the inaugural Coronation Cup in 1911.

The 4th Dragoon Guards had surprisingly defeated the Blues (RHG) in the finals of the Inter-Regimental Tournament. The Royal Horse Guards had taken the Ranelagh Open Cup and met Eaton, in the finals of the Hurlingham Champion Cup. It was a hard game, won by Eaton, which took much out of the ponies' stamina. Due to an inexplicable schedule, Eaton was to face a well-rested Indian Polo Association team on the next afternoon. Reluctantly, Eaton had to scratch the contest for the ponies' safety. How the Ranelagh Polo Committee allowed such a situation to happen defies reason.

The Indian Polo Association, lacking sufficient funds to send ponies on the long sea voyage, dictated that the team should be selected from players already in England. Three army captains were picked to represent the IPA: Leslie Cheape, King's Dragoon Guards; Gerald Ritson, Inniskilling Dragoons; and Vivian Lockett, 17th Lancers. They were joined by Major Shah Mizra Beg, of the Nizam of Hyderabad's army, who was considered one of the top players in India. On 15 July, they took on the 4th Dragoon Guards, Captain Adrian Carton de Wiart, Captain Charles Hornby, Major "Bunny" Mathew-Lannowe and Captain Charles Hunter. An unknown correspondent wrote, "Capt. Shah Mizra Beg gave a beautiful display of artistic hitting. His command over the ball was the admiration of the crowd, and he scored six of the goals. The Dragoon Guards were clearly overmatched, and their plucky fight was worthy of all praise."[1]

One of the 4th Dragoon Guards merits a sketch. Adrian Carton de Wiart was born in Brussels to a Belgian father and an Irish mother. He was admitted to Balliol College in Oxford but left to join the army in the Boer War. Shortly after, he was shot through the chest, the first one of his many injuries. Sent home on leave, he returned to South Africa to join the 4th Dragoon Guards. When the Great War started, de Wiart was on his way to Somalia where the Madhi's War was on. He was badly shot and wore a black patch over his left eye for the rest of his life. Carton de Wiart was awarded the Victoria Cross for heroism at the beginning of the battle of the Somme, after he had lost his left hand in 1915. He was wounded several more times, always repairing at the Sir Douglas Shield's Nursing Home to recuperate, and became a regular customer. It was said that there was always a room ready for him at this nursing home on Park Lane. At the war's end, he was in command of a brigade. Then he was sent to Poland with the British Military Mission and in spite of his diplomatic status was involved in minor skirmishes with Russians and Ukrainians. At the end of the conflict he was placed on retired pay and spent the interwar years living in Poland. Carton de Wiart was recalled to active service in World War II, being in command of an Anglo-French expeditionary force to Norway. Left with no supplies, the force was evacuated by a flotilla under Lord Mountbatten. An appointment to the military mission in Yugoslavia followed. The engines in the aircraft carrying the mission failed, and it crashed in the Mediterranean Sea about one mile from Libya. Somehow he managed to swim to the coast, where he was captured by the Italians and sent to a special prison for high-ranking officers. He made several attempts to escape, including tunneling, and was finally successful, but he was recaptured a few days later. He was repatriated when Italy changed sides in the war. Within a month, Winston Churchill sent him to China as his personal representative. Finally, the old warrior retired as a lieutenant general, with a chain of letters after his name. The most important win during the polo career of this indomitable man was the Inter-Regimental Tournament at Hurlingham.

There was no Inter-Regimental Tournament in 1919; it was substituted by the Military Cup. The winner was the team from the Northamptonshire Yeomanry: Lord Hugh Stalbridge, Lt. Col. Sir Charles Lowther, Major Patteson Nickalls and Captain John Lowther.

Many other trophies were taken off the shelves and offered for competition in 1919. The County Cup was taken by a soldiers' "A" team from the Wellington Club; the Royal Automobile Club won the Social Clubs' Cup, and the Roehampton Freebooters took the Whitney Cup. Ranelagh Club resumed the Subalterns' Cup, won by the 8th Hussars, and the Novices' Cup, which was taken by a team named Wanderers, made up by Army officers.

At Roehampton, the Old Etonians took the Public Schools Cup with a strong team: Sir John Ramsden, Ivor Buxton, Lord Rocksavage and Major Jack Harrison. The Junior

Championship was taken by Cowdray, Clive Pearson, Harold Pearson, Lord Stalbridge and Captain John Lowther.

The Rugby Tournament, dating back to 1893, was taken by the Foxhunters, with Eric Forwood, Harry Rich, Lt. Col. Gerald Hobson and Major Philip Magor.

New Polo Clubs in the 1920s

The Bordon Officers' Polo Club was formed in 1920 by Maj. Gen. Arthur Crawford Daly and Major Adam. The players were in the main officers of the 5th Fusiliers, the Dublin Fusiliers, the Royal Scots and the Garrison Gunners, all stationed at Bordon, and the Mountain Batteries and the 17th Lancers from Longmoor. A few civilian members also joined the club. Among the players were Mr. Laird of Ropley, Colonel Guy Mort, Major William Bakewell and Major Richard Grenside Hooper.

Captain Sir Thomas Marden presented a Fortnightly Challenge Cup, which added to the Bordon Silver Cup and the Daly Cup, the main competitions. A team from the 19th Field Brigade, Royal Artillery, represented Bordon in the 1934 County Cup and returned from London covered with glory; John Evatt, Captain Charles Rugge-Price, William Holman and Major Charles Allfrey were the heroes of the day.

A new club, known as the Occasional Polo Club, opened the season early in May 1921, at the London Country Club in Hendon. The ground was in excellent condition, and the ball traveled fast and truly in the opening practice game. William, Earl FitzWilliam; Major Digle; Captain Rose; and Major Williams on the one side opposed Viscount Carlton, Captain Conway Fisher-Rowe, Colonel Herbert Braine and Captain Humphrey de Trafford on the other.[2]

The West Gloucester and Bristol Polo Club was formed in 1922. It had two grounds in Filton, opposite the airport and near the Bristol Aeroplane Company works. Some of the players were Major Alexander Mitchell, Major George Pinney, Mr. T.P. Rogers and Major E.M. Watts. The Bethell and Greenslade families were great supporters of the club, which catered to professional and business men in Bristol. Play was on Monday and Wednesday, at six o'clock in the afternoon for their benefit. When World War II started, the grounds were requisitioned to expand both factory and aerodrome.

The Mid-Essex Polo Club was started in 1923 as a revival of the old Hutton Polo Club. Players were Oliver Bury, the president; Ernest Barraclough; F.H. Buckenham; Peter Dalziel; A.E. Heatley; Colonel Frank Hilder; Major Pierre Inchbald; L.C. Lyster and Sheffield Neave, among others. Play was at Rookwood Field in Margaretting, near Ingatestone.

The Arthingworth Polo Club was started in 1924 by Mr. Norman Perkins at his property in Oxendon, near Market Harborough. Two competitions were organized, the Nimrod Vase and the Arthingworth Hall Cup. It was a family club, where members on the Market Harborough Club played mostly friendly matches. The latter was revived in that same year as successor to the old Market Harborough Polo Club of 1902–1908. The new polo grounds were at East Farndon.

Eastbourne Polo Club was formed in April 1926. The inaugural match at Black Robin Farm, one mile from Beachy Head, was between the Colours, Reginald Summerhays, the equine expert; C.B. Wylde; A.E. Hanlon; and Sir Peter Grant-Lawson, and the Whites, R.M. Cardwell, F. Conway, T.N. Davidson and Sir Kenneth Beatty. Other players were G. Birley; Captain Lionel Liddell, RA; and J.C. Eden, the club's honorary secretary.

Kirtlington Park Polo Club was formed in 1926 and inaugurated in May 1927. It was established by Mr. Hugh Budgett, master of the Bicester hounds, in his park in Oxfordshire. Soon after, his sons Alan and Arthur started playing polo, and his grandsons Charlie Budgett and Sam Tylor continue the family polo-playing tradition. Local tournaments included the Kirtlington Cup; the Rousham Cup, presented by the Dutch player Adriaan "Mossy" Mosselmans; an American Handicap Tournament; and the annual match between the Bicester and the Heythrop Hunts.

Ham Common Polo Club was started in 1926; play was on a field next to Brown Gates House, near Ham Gate in Richmond Park, on the property of Loftus Storey, a guiding light in the County Polo Association and author of *The Training of Mount and Man for Polo*. Later on, a second ground was built next to Latchmere House, the Dysart family property. Ham Common soldiered on until the onset of World War II put an end to many good things, including polo.

The Eridge Polo Club was started in 1929 under the presidency of the Marquess of Abergavenny. Captain Alexander Drummond was the polo captain, who offered a Challenge Cup to be played for by the members. The ground was located at the Chase Farm in Frant Hill, near Tunbridge Wells.

Finally, the RAF Halton Polo Club was established near Aylesbury in Buckinghamshire. This meant that all three services had polo clubs within the military establishment.

Trophies Old and New

There was a plethora of tournaments offered for competition, not only by the London clubs, but across the land as well. Some astute observers of the game noticed that with so many cups being played for, there was little time left for bringing up new players and

The RAF team taking a halftime break during the 1927 match versus the Royal Navy.

training the ponies. The wastage of turf on the polo grounds was enormous, some fields holding six games in any given day. The polo grounds became cut up and bumpy; even the best players had difficulty striking the ball with confidence. The constant rolling need to maintain a hard surface made the ground hard and slippery, especially at season's end. Nevertheless, this frenzy of competitions did not ease up until the 1930s.

In 1930 there were forty tournaments scheduled at the three London clubs, Hurlingham, Ranelagh and Roehampton. The polo season in the capital was a short one, from the first week in May to the end of July; then provincial polo began in earnest.

An interesting match for the Villavieja Cup was played at Hurlingham on 4 July 1921. The Villavieja Cup had been presented by the Marqués de Villavieja, an old supporter of Continental polo, for teams named Juniors and Seniors. The Juniors had to be an aggregate age of less than one hundred and the Seniors must be over two hundred. HRH the Prince of Wales expressed to the Marqués his desire to play in the game; therefore, Villavieja arranged the following two teams:

Juniors	*age*	*Seniors*	*age*
The Prince of Wales	27	Maj. Godfrey Heseltine	48
Marqués de Villabrágima	26	Duque de Peñaranda	38
Tommy Hitchcock	21	Walter Buckmaster	51
Rodman Wanamaker	19	Marqués de Villavieja	64
Total: 93		Total: 201	

The game produced great expectations because it was the first time that the Prince of Wales had played in an open match, and it was not entirely approved of.[3] Villavieja wrote in his memoirs, "I myself was quite nervous about it, knowing how dashing and fearless the Prince was. Suppose he should have a fall and get hurt! But luckily all went well, and the Prince threw himself and his ponies into the game whole-heartedly, and gave a wonderful show of his sporting spirit. He won the game by 12 goals to 6, and was delighted."[4]

Rugby remained the most important polo club in the countryside, until the advent of a revived Beaufort with its multiple polo grounds and new facilities put a dent in Rugby's hitherto supremacy. However, in the balmy days of the late twenties there was enough room for everything and everybody.

Top Teams and Players in the 1920s

The main tournaments remained the same: Hurlingham, Ranelagh and Roehampton with their respective Open Championship Cups, the Inter-Regimental Tournament and the Coronation Cup. The civilian teams came to the fore because the wastage of army players during the war could not possibly restore to the services its former glories. This was the era of the gifted amateurs.

For a while, the old-timers held their own. Walter Buckmaster continued to show his mastery at striking the ball, superb horsemanship and tactical genius with assorted Freebooters teams and his vintage concoction, the Old Cantabs. However, the leaves of the calendar and the siren call of foxhunting proved just too much, and after an illustrious career, "Buck" hung up his polo stick and took over the mastership of the Warwickshire hounds. With his departure from the polo grounds, an era came to an end.

Three teams dominated polo in England in the 1920s. The 17th Lancers and then the amalgamated 17th/21st Lancers took the Inter-Regimental Tournament with only one defeat, by the Royal Artillery in 1927. In addition, the 17th Lancers won the coveted Coronation Cup in 1922; this tournament was held before amalgamation, which took place in August 1922. This team got going with Lt. Col. Teignmouth Melvill, Captain Herbert Turnor, Major Vivian Lockett and Captain Dennis Boles. In successive years, Captain Charles Lister and subalterns Desmond Miller, Edward Miller's son; Ronald Cooke; Hugh Walford; and Henry Forester were added to the team. It was a marvelous run that ended in 1931, when the Lancers were posted to India.

The other two teams were the Duke of Peñaranda's El Gordo— the Fat One, after his property in Spain — and Stephen "Laddie" Sanford's Hurricanes from America. During that decade El Gordo took eight major championships, including the Coronation Cup on three consecutive years. The Duke of Peñaranda counted upon the services of ten-goalers Lewis Lacey and Johnny Traill, plus another ten-goal handicap player in the person of Earle Hopping the elder, and the Marqués of Villabrágima, rated at eight goals.

The Hurricanes' main strength was their pony power. John Sanford, Laddie's father, was not averse to paying top prices for good ponies that came for sale on the market. Polo

Robots: Lord Dalmeny, Earle W. Hopping, Lord Cholmondeley and Jack Harrison. The winners of the 1923 Hurlingham Champion Cup.

ponies such as Fairy Story, the property of Lord Cholmondeley; Jupiter, owned by Lewis Lacey; My Girl; and many others were the envy of connoisseurs.

Stephen Sanford, a good player but not an exceptional one, also secured players of the quality of Pat Roark, an Irishman who had served on the Poona Horse in India and is widely considered the best British player of his times. Other stalwarts wearing the violet jersey were Wing Commander Percival Wise, rated at nine goals; Major Jack Harrison, also a nine-goaler; Gerald Balding from Rugby, who had not yet reached the maturity that made him an international ten-goal player; and on a single occasion the promising young Desmond Miller.

Both teams shared even honors between 1926 and 1930, with eight major tournaments each. Only the Harlequins— Captain Richard McCreery, Lt. Walter McCreery, Percival Wise and Lord Wodehouse — were able to break their hegemony when they took the Hurlingham Champion Cup in 1926; otherwise, it was either El Gordo or Hurricanes, with no room whatsoever for interlopers.

Visitors from Overseas

The visit to London in 1922 of a team sent by the Argentine Polo Federation rang a bell in the world of polo.[5] Although the touring party professed their intention to learn, at the end of the day they had taught as much as they had learned. John Miles, Jack Nelson, David Miles and Lewis Lacey went on to take the U.S. Open Championship following the tour to England. The second team was Louis Nelson, Jack's older brother; Grahame "Toby" Paul; Alfredo Peña Unzué; and Carlos Uranga, father of the founder of the Federation of International Polo, Marcos Uranga. Mixed teams took the Junior Championship at Roehampton, the Whitney Cup and the Ladies Nomination Cup. The senior team won the Hurlingham Champion Cup and the Roehampton Open Cup.

In the first tie of the Hurlingham Champion Cup, the visitors got through by the skins of their teeth. The Quidnuncs—Billy Kirkwood, Geoffrey Phipps-Hornby, Alfred Tate and the Viscount Wimborne—gave them a tremendous fight. The Argentines won 8–7 after five minutes of extra time. The match, played in a heavy rain, was worthy of the best tradition of the tournament.

In the semifinals, the federation team won 12–5 over the Freebooters: the Spaniard Duque de Peñaranda, Lord Wodehouse, Philip Magor and Frank Rich. On to the finals, where the federation's team won match and championship with a 12–8 victory over Eastcott, which had on its lineup Stephen Sanford, Alfred Grisar, Earle Hopping and Vivian Lockett.

Three teams qualified to enter the Coronation Cup. In the initial tie the 17th Lancers won in extra time 7–6 over the Argentine Polo Federation. It should be noted that Jack Nelson was unable to play because of a bad cold contracted during the final game for the Champion Cup; he was replaced by Alfredo Peña. In the finals, the 17th Lancers won 6–3 over Cowdray, which had Major the Hon. Harold Pearson, the Hon. Clive Pearson, the evergreen Walter Buckmaster and Major Jack Harrison. This Lancers team, Lt. Col. Teignmouth Melvill, Captain Herbert Turnor, Major Vivian Lockett and Captain Dennis Boles, went on to be practically invincible in the Inter-Regimental Tournament in the Roaring Twenties.

The Comte Jean de Madré was a well-known polo personality in Rugby and in London. His team, named the Tigers, competed in India, the Continent and also in America. A fussy man, the good Count Jean insisted that the players should be mounted on ponies of identical colors in each chukker, a practice that was more likely than not detrimental to the final outcome of a match. Another peculiarity was that the team's members sported pure silk jerseys, with an embossed tiger on the chest. In the 1920s the stalwart players were two Indian players, Jaswant Singh and Jagindar Singh, both handicapped at ten goals. Major Eric Atkinson, an excellent back with a sterling reputation in India, joined the team that took the Coronation Cup in 1923.

In 1925, Jodhpur, a team from India, made its appearance on the London grounds. Thakur Prithi Singh, Captain Austin Williams, Rao Rajah Hanut Singh and Thakur Ram Singh made a formidable quartet. It marked the presentation of Hanut Singh, who did so much for polo in England in years to come. How the handicap committees in both England and India failed to reward his outstanding characteristics as a team player, horse master and sheer individual artistry with a ten-goal rating is an unanswered question.

Austin Henry "Bill" Williams, Central India Horse, was also a scratch in golf, a fine tennis player and represented England in cricket. Brigadier Wilmot Vickers wrote about him, "It was a joy to play in front of him at polo. The ball always came up to you exactly in the right place."

This Jodhpur team took both the Hurlingham Champion Cup and the Roehampton Open Cup.

Polo Returns to Ireland

Slowly, very slowly, the game of polo started is journey toward recovery in Ireland. The game had not been played in earnest since the summer of 1914, with the exception of a few matches for the Patriotic Cup in 1920 and 1921. A team representing the All Ireland Polo Club visited America in 1922, playing at the Rumson Country Club in the Herbert Memorial Trophy and the U.S. Open Championship in a special series of matches at the Philadelphia Country Club and the Bryn Mawr Polo Club in Pennsylvania, and in the Monty Waterbury Cup at Meadow Brook on Long Island. The team members were Captain W.L.A. Goulding, later Sir William; John Trench; Lt. George Scott-Douglas; and Captain Federick Gill, a twenty-seven-goal combination.

No cups were taken during the tour, and the comment was made that the team was beset from the start by lack of practice together as a team and, more fatally, by the fact that their mounts were young, comparatively inexperienced and not properly conditioned.[6]

That the game survived during the "troubles" was nothing short of a miracle. Polo stopped altogether on the grounds in the county towns, and the country clubs went out of existence. Some of the players remained in the country, but when the game began its recovery, many were rather old. The surnames Barbour, Daly, Hastings, O'Hara, Roark, Slocock, Smithwick and Watson had mostly left center stage during the years of strife and turmoil.

The All Ireland Polo Club, where more than 20,000 thousand spectators had lined the rails in the golden days, soldiered on, and about 5,000 people watched the first revival game in 1928.[7]

After a lapse of ten years, the Patriotic Cup was revived in 1932 at Phoenix Park, in front of a crowd of 25,000. Ireland overwhelmed the English team, scoring twelve goals against a single tally by the visitors. The Irish team was Captain Joshua Chaytor, 14th/20th Hussars; the veteran John McCann; Major Charles Gairdner; and Maj. William Kirkwood. In its disappointing performance, England was represented by Thomas Hilder, Major Evelyn Fanshawe, Major Eric Atkinson and W.T. Hunter.[8]

The Cochrane Cup, taken by the Quidnuncs; The Polo Monthly Cup, won by county Tipperary; and the Ladies' Cup tournament, taken by Simmposcourt, were also played for in 1932 at Phoenix Park.

The British Army–American Army Series

Two significant events in military polo were the matches for the International Military Title Cups held in 1923 and 1925. The idea originated in America and General John "Black Jack" Pershing, commander in chief of the American Army, wrote to the Earl of Cavan, chief of the Imperial General Staff, with an invitation for a series of international matches between two representative army teams.

In his reply, Lord Frederick Cavan wrote, in part,

The British Army squad arrives at New York harbor. Lt. James Leaf, Lt. Walter McCreery, Maj. Frank Hurndall, Maj. Vivian Lockett and Lt. Col. T.P. Melvill are greeted by Maj. Gen. Robert Bullard, U.S. Army.

I am anxious that this matter should set an example to all the world for clear sportsmanship. I, therefore, strongly advocate (1) that the teams be strictly confined to officers on the active list of our regular forces and (2) that the ponies shall be the bona-fide property of the officers on the active list of the regular army or the actual property of the War Department. This, I think, should preclude any borrowing or temporary acquiring of international ponies by either side. What we both want, I am sure, is a fair and square match between our respective army officers with their own resources.[9]

The U.S. Polo Association supported the series and arranged that they should be held at the Meadow Brook Club International Field on Long Island. The Meadow Brook Club gave the trophies. The first match was played on 12 September 1923, the teams being as follows:

U.S. Army	*British Army*
Maj. Arthur Wilson	Lt. Col. Teingmouth Melvill, 17th/21st Lancers
Maj. John Herr	Lt. Walter McCreery, 12th Lancers
Lt. Col. Lewis Brown	Maj. Frank Hurndall, 20th Hussars
Maj. Louis Beard	Maj. Eric Atkinson, 15th Lancers

The American Army took the first match 11–7. On Saturday, 15 September, the same teams competed; this time the British Army won by twelve goals to ten. The final game was played on Tuesday, 18 September. The American side was unchanged; the British placed

Maj. Vivian Lockett at back, moving Major Atkinson to the number 2 position. The American Army team won the contest, scoring ten goals against only three by the British team. Lt. Thomas McCreery was in charge of the American pony string, and his meticulous preparation of the ponies was the determining factor in the decisive third game, when it appeared that the English ponies had not recovered from the exertions of two hard games in seventy-two hours.

A return series took place at Hurlingham in June 1925. King George V and Queen Mary were present, the weather was kind, and the visitors were not, taking the game by eight goals to four. The American team lined up with Major Wilson, Captain Charles Gerhardt, Captain Peter Rodes and Major Louis Beard.

The British Army was represented by Captain Richard McCreery, 12th Lancers; his younger brother Lt. Walter McCreery; the monocled Captain John Dening, 11th Cavalry; and Major Dennis Boles, 17th/21st Lancers.

The same teams played the second match four days later under a slight rain, but in front of a large crowd. It was an even game; however, in the fifth chukker Major Dening sustained a concussion and had to be replaced by Major Lockett. This accident, the result of a collision between two English players, disrupted the British Army teamwork, and the American Army squeezed a 6–4 win.

This international army contest was scheduled to be resumed in 1929; however, it was not to be.

CHAPTER 10

The Olympic Games

The earliest recorded date in Western civilization is 776 B.C., the year of the first Olympic Games held in Greece. Therefore, it can be safely stated that sporting endeavors have been part of human culture since the dawn of the ancient world.

England had much to do with the revival of the Olympic Games in the nineteenth century. The most significant endeavor happened in the small town of Much Wenlock in Shropshire, when games described as "Olympian" took place on 22 October 1850.[1] The festival was the creation of a physician and sports enthusiast, Dr William Brookes, a family practitioner in Much Wenlock.[2] The initial events were cricket, fourteen-a-side football, high and long jumping, a hopping race, quoits and a running race. Several events were added through the years, including tilting at the ring, with the competitors wearing medieval costumes. Later venues were Wellington and Shrewsbury. These were followed by "Olympian Games" under the aegis of the National Olympic Association in London, Birmingham, Wellington, Much Wenlock, Shrewsbury and Hadley.

The Much Wenlock games are important in the development of the Olympic Games revival because Pierre de Coubertin was aware of Dr. Brookes' accomplishments and visited the games in 1890 and 1891.[3]

Nevertheless, Pierre de Fredí, Baron de Coubertin, is the man credited with the renewal of the Olympic Games. It was not an easy path. At the Sorbonne Congress in 1894 it was proposed that the games take place in Paris; however, the majority of the delegates decided that Greece, as the ancient site of the games, should be the host nation. Thus, Athens became the site of the first Olympic Games of the modern era.

The success of those games went to the Greek authorities' head, and they promptly proposed that Athens should be the permanent venue. The King of the Hellenes put pressure on Coubertin and the International Olympic Committee to declare the city the next host. Coubertin's resistance annoyed the Greeks, who called him "a thief, trying to strip Greece of one of the historic jewels of her raiment."[4] Coubertin stood firm. He addressed an open letter to King Georgios thanking him and his subjects for the energy and enthusiasm organizing the 1896 games, but confirmed that the 1900 games would be held in Paris. Anyway, Greece's military intervention against Turkey in Crete precluded the chance to host the games.

More and serious trouble awaited Pierre de Coubertin in his home country. An Olympic Congress was organized in Le Havre in 1897, but no discussion of the games took place. There were fifty-nine delegates, of which thirty-seven were French. A large world fair was in the offing for 1900 in Paris, l'Exposition Universelle Internationale. The director was M. Alfred Picard, an official who thought sport was a useless and absurd activity.[5] Coubertin appointed the Vicomte Charles de La Rochefoucauld as president of the organizing committee of the Games. It was a wise choice because the viscount had an impeccable reputation as a sportsman, and his social stature made him a man that could command support in this endeavor. Robert Fournier-Sarloveze, polo player and army officer, was placed in the all-important position of secretary general.

All seemed to be on track until the Union des Sociétés Françaises Sports Athlétiques claimed its exclusive right to anything and everything related to sports and games. Rochefoucauld did not wish to be involved in a political in-fight and resigned his post. Without his support, Coubertin stepped out, and his name did not appear again in the preparations.

From then on, almost everything went wrong. The new organizing committee discarded the term "Olympic Games," and the competitions were variously referred to as "International Championships," "International Games," "Paris Championships" and "World Championships." This has led to different interpretations of what polo tournaments played in the early summer of 1900 were truly the Olympic Games.

Reduced to a mere accompaniment to the Universal Exposition, the Paris Games—spread out through five months from May to October—turned out to be an unmitigated disaster, beset by poor attendance and worse organization.[6] Some participants were not even aware that they had participated in an Olympic competition.

Paris 1900: The Olympics That Weren't

Olympic Games historian Dr. Bill Mallon has stated, "It is difficult to make sense of what was and was not the 'Olympic' polo tournament in 1900. Many different match scores, tournaments results, and team rosters have been seen in the varying sources."[7]

Nevertheless, most authorities consider the Grand Prix International d'Exposition as the Olympic competition. All the matches took place at the Bagatelle Polo Club in the Bois de Boulogne. Five teams entered the competition:

Compiègne	Mexico	Foxhunters	Bagatelle	Rugby
Duc de Bissacia	Guillermo H.	Alfred Rawlinson	Baron Edouard	Walter McCreery
Auguste Fauquet-	Wright	Frank Mackay	de Rothschild	Frederick Freake
Lemaître	Eustaquio de	Foxhall Keene	Robert Fournier-	Walter Buckmas-
Jean Boussoud	Escandón	Dennis Daly	Sarlovèze	ter
Maurice Raoul-	Pablo de Escan-		Frederick Gill	Comte Jean de
Duval	dón		Maurice Raoul-	Madré
	Marqués de		Duval	
	Villaveja			

In a straight elimination contest, the preliminary round saw the Foxhunters overwhelm Compiègne by ten goals to nil. In the semifinals, Foxhunters beat Bagatelle 6–4, with John Beresford taking Foxie Keene's place. Rugby defeated Mexico 8–0 in the second semifinal game. In the final match Foxhunters defeated Rugby 3–1. The other three teams were jointly awarded third place.

With the exception of the Mexican and Compiègne teams, none of the other participants can be remotely considered national teams. The winning team, Foxhunters, had two Americans, Foxhall Keene and Jay Mackay. Rugby, the runners-up, had a Frenchman on its lineup, the good Count Jean de Madré, patron of the Tigers team. And the host team,

Bagatalle, had an Englishman, Captain Gill. Perhaps his position as Bagatelle's polo manager qualified him as a Frenchman. There is also no explanation of the fact that Maurice Raoul-Duval, the best French player before the war, played for both Bagatelle and Compiègne.

It is not surprising at all that two historians from Australia wrote, "These Games were certainly not worthy to be considered an Olympic games, and with the lack of involvement of Coubertin and the IOC, it can successfully be argued that no Olympics were held in Paris in 1900."[8]

London 1908: The Battle of Shepherd's Bush

Rome was selected to be the site for the 1908 Olympiad; however, the eruption of Mount Vesuvius and a critical financial situation engendered by large amounts of spending on public works by the government resulted in the withdrawal of Italy as a host nation.

On short notice, England was asked to organize the Games. Luckily, there was a man ready and able to accept the enormous challenge. Lord William Desborough was the prototype of the Victorian gentleman and a phenomenal sportsman. As an undergraduate he was a Blue at Oxford, in rowing and athletics; stroked an eight across the Channel; and swam twice across the Niagara. Lord Desborough also had a reputation as a big-game hunter, an ardent deep-sea fisherman and a finished whip. While at university, he was master of the Oxford Drag and later of the Bucks and Berks Harriers. A mountain climber, he reached the summit of the Matterhorn by three different routes. Lord Desborough was also chairman of the Thames Conservancy Board.[9] Under such an energetic chairman, the London Olympic Games were on schedule and well organized.

These games were also known as "the Battle of Shepherd's Bush" because of the bickering between Americans and organizers in several events, which led to a serious rift between British and American sporting authorities. Sheperd's Bush eventually became White City Stadium and at the time of the games was a multi-purpose facility that included a cycle tract, a football pitch, a running track, a swimming pool and platforms for gymnastics and wrestling.

The polo competition was held at the Hurlingham Club and consisted of only two matches. The teams were as follows:

Hurlingham	*All Ireland*	*Roehampton*
Walter Jones	Auston Rotheram	Herbert Wilson
Frederick Freake	John Paul McCann	George Miller
Walter Buckmaster	John Hardress Lloyd	Patteson Nickalls
Lord Wodehouse	Percy O'Reilly	Charles Miller

The umpires were Captain — later Sir Edward — Fagan and Major Kenneth MacLaren. On 18 June, Roehampton beat Hurlingham by four goals to one, and on 21 June, Roehampton defeated All Ireland by eight goals to one. All Ireland and Hurlingham were declared joint silver medalists.

At the closing ceremonies on 28 July, HM Queen Alexandra presented the Hurlingham Trophy amid much pomp and circumstance. It is reported that the trophy is now at the International Olympic Committee headquarters in Lausanne, Switzerland.

John Jacob Astor, a six-goal handicap player and an officer in the Life Guards, participated in the rackets competition, in which he won the gold medal in doubles with Vane Pennell, and the bronze medal in singles. A member of the Polo Pony Society, Lt. Col. Astor won the Indian Open Championship in 1913. In England, Astor took the Whitney Cup and the Ranelagh Subalterns' Tournament. He then entered the political arena, became the proprietor of *The Times* and was created Lord Astor of Hever in 1956.

Another polo player took a gold medal. The American player Jay Gould from Lakewood, New Jersey, the site of Georgian Court, the baronial site of his father the multimillionaire George Gould, took first place in Jeu de Paune, or Real Tennis. Jay Gould took both the American and British Championships several times and, oddly enough for a wealthy man, the world professional title in 1914 and 1916.

Another future polo player also made his mark in the games. Reginald Leslie "Snowy" Baker, Australia's most versatile sportsman, represented his country in boxing and swimming. In boxing, after winning three bouts, two by knockouts, he was defeated in the finals of the middleweight division on points, earning the silver medal. All four bouts were held in only one day. John Douglas, the gold medalist, was actually better known as a cricketer, who later captained Essex and England.

In the event for Fancy High Diving (springboard), Baker failed to qualify for the final round. In swimming, the Australian team, with Snowy in the third slot, won the heat and finished fourth in the 4 × 200 meter freestyle relay.

Antwerp 1920: Polo at Ostende

The city of Antwerp was chosen to be the host of the 1920 games as a gesture to recognize the devastation suffered by the Belgians during the Great War through no fault of their own. Time was short and Antwerp had to prepare for the Olympic Games in a shorter period than any other host city.

Austria, Bulgaria, Germany, Hungary and Turkey were not invited because they were considered the aggressors in the war. Baron de Coubertin had reservations on the matter: "Common sense suggested that it would hardly be wise for a German team to appear in the Olympic stadium before 1924. On the other hand, to ostracize any member country, even right after the conflict that had torn Europe asunder, would create a rift in the Olympic constitution which had been so strong until then; and it might become a dangerous precedent."[10]

The polo competition was held on a ground within the Wellington Hippodrome in the town of Ostende, on the shores of the North Sea. The well-known Belgian player Alfred Grisar was the president of the executive committee; all the other members were British: Major Frederick Barrett, Major Vivian Lockett and Herbert T. Rich. Four teams took part in the competition:

Belgium	Great Britain	Spain	United States
Alfred Grisar	Lt. Col. Teignmouth Melvill	Marqués de Villabrágima	Maj. Arthur Harris
Maurice Lysen	Maj. Frederick Barrett	Duque de Peñaranda	Maj. Terry Allen
Clément van der Straaten	Lord Wodehouse	Conde de La Maza	Col. John Montgomery
Gastón Peers	Maj. Vivian Lockett	Duque de Alba	Col. Nelson Margetts

As to the players, Alfred Grisar, a registered left-hander, was a multiple sportsman, for he started playing polo at the Hurlingham Club in Argentina, represented his country in football, and participated in national competitions in cycling and tennis. Baron Gastón Peers de Niewburgh took the Polo Association of the River Plate Championship — later the

Argentine Open Championship — in 1900 with his own team, San Carlos. Baron Peers administered the Belgian Colony La Barrancosa and during his sojourn in Argentina married a society lady, Ernestina Costa Oliveira Cézar. Maurice Lysen was a player at the Antwerp Polo Club, and not much is known about Clément van der Straaten, except as a winner of the Novices' Cup at Ostende.

The United States sent a team formed by officers in the Army of the Occupation of the Rhine. Prior to their participation in the Olympic Games, the American squad entered and won the Novices' Tournament at Ranelagh. Major Arthur Ringland Harris was a Field Artillery officer. Brig. Gen. Terry de la Mesa Allen, U.S. Cavalry, was wounded at St. Mihiel in World War I and commanded the 1st Infantry Division — the "Big Red One" — in the Second World War. Brigadier Allen was once described as having the bowed stride of a horseman saddle hardened as a child. He was one of the few players to appear on *Time* magazine's cover.[11] Colonel John Carter Montgomery, U.S. Cavalry, had already won a bronze medal at the 1912 Olympic Games in Stockholm, with his horse Deceive. Colonel Nelson Emery Margetts, Field Artillery, later had a long career in America and the Far East, playing polo in the Philippines, Hong Kong and China.

The Spanish team had two brothers, the Duke of Peñaranda and his older sibling, "Jimmy" Duke of Alba and Berwick. Both went on to distinguish themselves during the London season with the team El Gordo. The Duke Hernando of Peñaranda was executed by the Nationalists in the course of the Spanish Civil War. Alvaro Figueroa, Marqués de Villabrágima, went on to be the best Spanish polo player ever. Conde Leopoldo de La Maza reached a nine-goal handicap in England.

Lt. Col. Teignmouth Philip Melvill was the posthumous son of Lt. Teignmouth Melvill, 24th Regiment, who was awarded the Victoria Cross for saving the Queen's Colours — together with Lt. Nevill Coghill — during the battle of Isandhlwana at the beginning of the Zulu War. The Colours were found some days later in the Buffalo River and restored; they hang now in Brecon Cathedral in Wales. Lt. Col. Melvill played in the 1924 Westchester Cup and took the Inter-Regimental Tournament in both England and India; he also took the Coronation Cup and the Junior Championship at Roehampton, among a host of other tournaments. Lt. Col. T.P. Melvill reached an eight-goal handicap.

Born in Ireland near Cork, Frederick Whitfield "Rattle" Barrett, 15th Hussars, was a ten-goal handicap player who was the team captain in the successful 1914 Westchester Cup contest at Meadow Brook. Barrett was a winner of the Inter-Regimental Tournament, the Hurlingham Champion Cup, and the Coronation, Warwickshire, Whitney, Social Clubs, Roehampton Open and the Patriotic Cup, the latter representing Ireland. In India he took the Indian Open Championship and the Inter-Regimental Tournament.

Lord John Wodehouse, later Earl of Kimberley, was another ten-goal handicap player, who won fame as a member of that most successful team, the Old Cantabs. "Jack" Wodehouse was educated at Eton and Trinity Hall, Cambridge. He started playing polo at university, being captain of the successful Light Blue team in the inter-varsity matches of 1904 and 1905. His prowess at back caught Walter Buckmaster's attention, and Lord Wodehouse joined the Old Cantabs. In the 1909 Westchester Cup, he played at the last minute on strange ponies and failed to do himself justice. His performance in the 1921 contest was faultless, but surprisingly, he did not play at Meadow Brook three years later. The Earl of Kimberley edited the volume on polo in the Lonsdale Library. He was killed in 1941 during the London blitz, age fifty-seven.

Lt. Col. Vyvyan Noverre Lockett, better known as Vivian, was gazetted into the Royal

Artillery and transferred to the 17th Lancers in 1907.[12] He began play at Hooton Park, Cheshire, and reached a ten-goal handicap rating in 1913. His tournament wins include the Coronation Cup, a run of nine Inter-Regimental tournaments from 1920 until 1930 with the 17th/21st Lancers, the Ranelagh and Roehampton Open Cups, and the Whitney, Cicero and Public Schools Cups. In India he won the Indian P.A. Open Championship. His nearside shots were among the best seen on London grounds.

The Olympic polo tournament began on Sunday, 25 July, with Spain easily beating the American team by 13–3. It should be noted that the Spaniards had an aggregate of twenty-two goals, while the American team added up to nine goals.

The next day, Monday, there was rain and wind from the North Sea, which made conditions unpleasant. The team from Great Britain, Lt. Col. Melvill at eight goals, Barrett and Lockett at nine goals each and Lord Wodehouse at ten goals, defeated Belgium with ease, playing well within their capability. Only six periods were played in this match because of rain and wind, which became a storm.[13] The Belgians were simply outmatched, and the British pulled up somehow. Otherwise, the game's result would have been a massacre.

Two days later, the host team had another loss, when the United States team won by eleven goals to three. The championship game between Spain and Great Britain was played on 29 July, on a heavy ground, with local stalwart Alfred Grisar acting as sole umpire. It was "the nearest run thing you ever saw," to borrow a quote from the Duke of Wellington about his victory at not too far Waterloo. The British team accumulated a 7–2 lead after three chukkers. However, there was a letup in the fourth period, and the Spaniards closed the gap to a two-goal differential. The equalizing factor was the pony string, as always. The Spaniards were beautifully mounted, having brought their best ponies from Spain. The British team had left its ponies in England and was essentially mounted on regimental ponies, not on ponies of international caliber. The Spaniards ran around in circles from the British team and twice came within two goals of equalizing the match; however, the more experienced team kept its cool and maintained its advantage. The final score was England thirteen, Spain eleven.

Paris 1924: Bagatelle and St. Cloud

The games held in Paris attracted teams from five nations. Argentina sent their best players and mounts, while the United States had only one player of international stand, Tommy Hitchcock. Britain was represented by a team that did not include some of the best players in the country, the reason being that at the time the London season was in full bloom and several top players elected to compete in the local tournaments. Spain, in an effort to improve on their silver medal gained at Ostende, selected no less than seven players in the delegation. The host country went even further, having eight players on the roster.

The teams aligned as follows:

Argentina	France	Great Britain	Spain	United States
Arturo Kenny	Comte Pierre de	Capt. Hon. Fred-	Marqués Luis de	Elmer Boeseke,
Juan Nelson	Jumilhac	erick Guest	San Miguel	Jr.
Capt. Enrique	Jules Macaire	Lt. Col. Hon.	Duque Hernando	Thomas Hitch-
Padilla	Comte Charles de	Denis Bing-	de Peñaranda	cock, Jr.
Juan Miles	Polignac	ham	Marqués Alvaro	Frederick Roe

Argentina	*France*	*Great Britain*	*Spain*	*United States*
	Hubert de Monbrison	Wing Cmdr. P.K. Wise	de Villabrágima Conde Leopoldo	Rodman Wanamaker II
		Maj. Frederick Barrett	de La Maza	

Games were played at Garches-Sainte Cloud and Bagatelle on a daily basis, with the following results:

June 28	America	13	France	1	
July 1	America	15	Spain	2	
July 2	Argentina	15	France	2	at Bagatelle
July 3	America	10	Great Britain	2	
July 4	Argentina	16	Spain	1	
July 5	Great Britain	15	France	2	at Bagatelle
July 6	Argentina	6	America	5	
July 7	Great Britain	10	Spain	3	
July 9	Argentina	9	Great Britain	5	
July 10	Spain	15	France	1	

The final scores speak for themselves regarding the huge difference among the teams. The local press mentioned that France and Spain had been completely *surclasés* when facing the other three teams.[14]

Capt. the Hon. Frederick Edward Guest, a five-goal player, was the chairman of the Hurlingham Polo Committee. He was the father of Winston Guest, a ten-goal handicap player who, although born in England, chose to play for America in international contests; he was, indeed, captain of the American team in the 1936 Westchester Cup played at Hurlingham. Perhaps his mother, Ann Phipps, who was an American, had something to do with Winston's choice.

The Hon. John Denis Yelverton Bingham reached a handicap of eight goals. He took the Inter-Regimental Tournament in India with the 15th Hussars and the Warwickshire Cup in England.

Wing Commander Percival Kinnear Wise, a nine-goal player, took the Hurlingham Champion Cup thrice as a member of the Hurricanes team. He also won the Roehampton Open Cup, the Ranelagh Open Cup and the Coronation Cup. He was gazetted in 1903 into the Seaforth Highlanders, and then transferred to the Wiltshire Regiment, then to the 33rd Queen's Own Light Cavalry in the Indian Army, finally joining the Royal Flying Corps, ending the war with a Companion of the Order of St. Michael and St. George Medal (CMG) and a Distinguished Service Order (DSO). In 1930, Wing Commander Wise was at the top of the Hurlingham handicap list.

Another polo player achieved distinction in the Paris Olympic Games. Major Geoffry Heremon Brooke, 16th Lancers, was on the British team that entered the jumping competition for the Prix des Nations. The team, which also included Philip Bowden-Smith, Capel Brunker and Keith Hervey, finished seventh overall.

Berlin 1936: Jesse Owens and Adolf Hitler

The last time that polo has been an Olympic competition was in 1936 at the Maifeld in Berlin. This polo ground was located next to the Olympic Stadium. Five nations answered the call: the defending gold medalists Argentina, Great Britain, Hungary, Mexico and the hosts, represented by members of the Hamburg Polo Club.

Argentina	Germany	Great Britain	Hungary	Mexico
Luis Duggan	Heinrich Amsink	Capt. Bryan	Lt. Tivadar	Maj. Juan Gracia
Roberto Cava-	Walter Bartram	Fowler	Dienes-ohem	Zazueta
nagh	Miles Reincke	Capt. Robert	Capt. Imre	Capt. Antonio
Andrés Gazzotti	Arthur Köser	Hinde	Szentpály	Nava Castillo
Manuel Andrada		Capt. David	Kálmán von Bar-	Julio Muller
		Dawnay	talis	Luján
		Capt. Humphrey	Graf István	Capt. Alberto
		Guinness	Bethlen	Ramos Sesma

Just as in the two previous Olympic Games, there was a significant discrepancy among the teams. Brigadier Jack Gannon, who had been called by the organizers for advice in the running of the event, suggested that the teams be divided into two groups: Argentina, Britain and Mexico in one, and Germany and Hungary in the other. The winner of the second group would play for the bronze medal with the last team on the other group.[15] This formula was adopted by the organizing committee.

Great Britain was represented by four serving Army officers. The players that had done so well against the American team at Hurlingham in the Westchester Cup had been invited, and all agreed to go. Regrettably, quite late, three of them found it impossible to make the journey and only Captain Humphrey Guinness was able to travel. Lt. Col. Evelyn Fanshawe went along as fifth man and umpire. At such short notice it was not possible to assemble even a moderate pony string, so the team was mounted on regimental ponies. This situation had dire consequences for the British team.

The organizing committee had insisted that there should be a game every day; the results follow:

August 3	Great Britain	11	Mexico	9	
August 4	Germany	8	Hungary	8	
August 5	Argentina	15	Mexico	5	
August 6	Hungary	16	Germany	6	
August 7	Argentina	11	Great Britain	0	for the Gold Medal
August 8	Mexico	16	Hungary	2	for the Bronze Medal

The British team had a hard game in the opening round; Brigadier Gannon again:

> I thought we should have an easy win, as we were hitting a much longer ball. Humphrey Guinness was playing beautifully, and Friz Fowler at No. 1 was hitting goals with great accuracy. We got 6 or 7 goals ahead, and it looked easy sailing, but our ponies began going badly and I am afraid they had not got over the journey. In the last two chukkas we went worse and finally we only won by 13 goals to 11.[16]

On Wednesday, Argentina played Mexico. While watching the game, Brigadier Gannon thought the Argentines were so superbly mounted that it made him tremble to contemplate what would happen when Britain met them. His misgivings were correct. The Argentines just cantered past the tired British ponies, and the players themselves hardly were able to hit the ball twice in succession. Captain Guinness played very well indeed, but he was overwhelmed by the relentless offensive play of the Argentines. Three shots by British players hit the goalpost and bounced out.

That kind of result will happen in polo when thoroughbreds are matched against regimental ponies. To place the result in perspective, when the identical Argentine team went

Humphrey Guinness in hot pursuit of Luis Duggan, the speedy number 1 from Argentina. The decisive game for the Olympic gold medal at Maifeld Stadium in Berlin, 1936 (private collection).

to Meadow Brook to challenge for the Cup of the Americas, they defeated a well-mounted American team by twenty-one goals to nine, a twelve-goal differential. In the last four chukkers, the United States team was only able to score a single goal.

The Argentine team was made up by two scions of wealthy Irish landowners. Luis Duggan's grandfather left county Longford and accumulated vast properties in Argentina, as did Roberto Cavangh's grandfather, from county Westmeath, although on a lesser scale.[17] There is a polo link here, because the current president of the FIP, Eduardo Huergo, is Roberto Cavanagh's nephew once-removed, through his mother Cora Cavanagh.[18] Of the other two members, Manuel Andrada was married to the daughter of an English settler, and Andrés Gazzotti was a farmer of Italian origins.

CHAPTER 11

Struggles for the Internationals

Following the cessation of the hostilities in Europe, the Americans were anxious to recover the Westchester Cup as soon as possible. However, the terrible losses inflicted upon British young men during the Great War made a delay imperative to allow England to recover and be able to mount a meaningful contest.

When the Polo Association made overtures to challenge for the cup in 1920, the Hurlingham Polo Committee, the ruling body of the game in the United Kingdom, requested that the contest be postponed for one year. This was agreed to by the Americans. Nevertheless, preparations across the pond began in earnest. The players were selected, and a formidable string of polo ponies was assembled and sent to England under the care of Mr. Henry Colt in December of 1920, well ahead of the scheduled matches for the month of June.

At the end of the 1920 polo season, the Hurlingham Committee nominated Lt. Col. Hugh Ashton, Major Frederick "Rattle" Barrett, Walter Buckmaster, Lord Dalmeny, Major John Harrison, Lt. Col. Charles Hunter, Major Frank Hurndall, Lord Rocksavage, Lt. Col. Henry "Mouse" Tomkinson, Johnny Traill and Lord Wodehouse as possible members of the international team. Furthermore, the committee appointed Major Vivian Lockett as team captain. Three trial matches were conducted before inclement weather made it impossible to allow further play until spring arrived.

In April, test matches started in earnest at Tidworth, and Lt. Col. Brown, Lt. Col. Teingmouth Melvill, Colonel Thomas Tait, Captain Herbert Turnor, Captain Austin Williams and Lord Wimborne were added to the roster. Such proliferation of candidates only two months before the matches were to be held did not bode well for the team's future endeavors. However, Major Lockett decided to experiment with different players in different positions. Some keen observers of the game showed some concern over the delay in selecting a final team, while the Americans were practicing assiduously with only four players, Rumsey, Hitchcock, Webb and Milburn.

Finally, in early May the team was announced with Tomkinson, Dalmeny, Lockett and Hunter. Later in the month, Lord Dalmeny was replaced by Major Barrett, and Charles Hunter by Lord Wodehouse. T.P. Melvill and John Harrison were the spare men.

On the American side, Devereux Milburn was appointed team captain, and the rest of the squad consisted of Tommy Hitchcock, at the time an undergraduate at Brasenose College in Oxford; James Watson Webb; Louis Stoddard; and Charles "Pad" Rumsey. Upon arrival in England, the American team was lavishly entertained by their hosts, most notably by Buck's Club members.[1] The visitors were also invited to a luncheon with King George V. Regrettably, Devereux Milburn was unable to attend because of an attack of lumbago. Most sportingly, the English team requested from Hurlingham Polo Committee (HPC) their wish that the first game be postponed. The good sportsmanship reflected in the British players' request was not echoed by the committee. The HPC indicated that the request had been forwarded late and also pointed out that the American team had not asked for a postponement. At any rate, Milburn recovered and took his place on the team.

Under a bright sun on Saturday 18 June at Hurlingham's number-one ground, both teams were presented to HM King George V and the Prince of Wales. The Royal Box attendance included Queen Alexandra, Princess Victoria, and Alfonso XIII, king of Spain, a dedicated polo player. England, in dark blue jerseys, lined up with Lt. Col. Henry Tomkinson, handicap eight; Major Frederick Barrett, handicap nine; Lord Wodehouse; and Major Vivian Lockett, both ten-goal handicap players. The United States of America, wearing white shirts, were represented by Louis Stoddard, Thomas Hitchcock, Jr., Watson Webb and Devereux Milburn. All were ten-goalers, with the exception of Tommy Hitchcock at nine goals. Pad Rumsey and Earle W. Hopping were the spare men for America. The umpires were Walter Buckmaster and Lt. Col. Edward Miller.

In typical American fashion the visitors took off in the first chukker on goals by Webb and Hitchcock and were never behind in the scoreboard during the match. The score's progression tells the story: 2–0, 3–1, 5–3, 5–4, 7–4, 9–4 and 11–4 at the end of the seventh and final period. Watson Webb was high scorer with five tallies; Hitchcock scored four goals, and Milburn and Stoddard one each. For England, Tomkinson scored three goals and Barrett one.

The teams remained the same for the second match. Umpire Walter Buckmaster was indisposed, and Colonel Carlyle Dunbar took his place. Once more, the American team pressed hard from the first throw-in and finished the period three to nil ahead on two goals by Webb and one by Stoddard. This three-goal cushion obtained early in the game by the Americans proved fatal for the British team, because the final tally was 10–6 in favor of the challengers. Essentially, the British played even with the Americans for the game's last six chukkers. Louis Stoddard scored four goals, Watson Webb three, Hitchcock two and Dev Milburn closed the proceedings with a penalty shot. On the British team, Barrett, Tomkinson and Lord Wodehouse scored two goals each.

Thus the Westchester Cup returned to America, in whose hands it would remain until 1997. The large American contingent that had traveled to England to witness the series celebrated the victory with unabashed joy. The English supporters watched with a mixture of surprise and bewilderment when a long conga line was formed by American men and women spectators in an impromptu celebration of their team's success.

1924: The Westchester Cup at Meadow Brook

The 1924 challenge by the Hurlingham Club's Polo Committee resulted in what was the weakest series for the Westchester Cup. The main reason was the disparity in quality of play between the two teams. America's colors were, once more, worn by four men who were eventually tagged with the sobriquet "the second Big Four." James Watson Webb, the left-hander now playing at number 1; the incomparable Tommy Hitchcock; Malcolm Stevenson; and Devereux Milburn, mounted on the best ponies money could buy, constituted an unbeatable combination.

In a repeat of the successful 1914 challenge, the Hurlingham Polo Committee placed everything in Lord Ivor Wimborne's hands.

Britain was represented in the main by serving army officers. Major Thomas "Billy" Kirkwood and Lt. Col. Teignmouth Melvill alternated at number 1, while Major Frank Hurndall and Major Geoffrey Phipps-Hornby did the same in the number 2 slot. Major Eric Atkinson played in the pivot position. Canada-born Lewis Lacey, one of the world's top players, was at back. However, it was an ailing Lewis Lacey. During a practice match, he sustained a shoulder injury that required a mechanical contraption in order to protect the shoulder's socket. To this injury, an acute attack of shingles was added, a benign but painful viral condition on his chest that presented itself just before the start of the series.

The presence of the Prince of Wales in the stands did much to assure substantial gate receipts and was a source of great moral support for the embattled British team. Nevertheless, no amount of royal encouragement could alter the imbalance on the field of play. In spite of Lacey's superhuman efforts, ably supported by Eric Atkinson, the disparity between the two teams was enormous. The final scores, 16–5 and 14–5, are indicative of what transpired on the polo grounds.

Wringing of the Hands

The adverse result of the 1924 games shocked the polo establishment in England, not so much because of the failure to regain the Westchester Cup, but for the magnitude of the two defeats. Unlike the poet Joachim Miller,[2] who was ready to extend "great honor and glory and tears" to those who tried and failed, the English polo establishment's reaction to failure was less than kind. The repercussions reached the highest level of the polo authorities in Fulham.

Lord Wimborne had been given total control of the enterprise aimed at recovering the trophy. Following the common pattern that success has many parents and defeat is an orphan, at the end of the day there was much recrimination and finger-pointing.

Lord John Wodehouse, who thought that Lord Wimborne had been a polo dictator, fired the opening salvo with an article in the *Daily Express*:

> I consider that the way the British international polo team has been handled during the last year and a half put back polo in England for at least two years. In my opinion Hurlingham made a great mistake in handling over the whole control to Lord Wimborne in January, 1923. They ought to have kept control in their own hands. I consider the best have been Traill, Lacey, Wise and Harrison, a 38-goal handicap team.[3]

Lord Dalmeny was reported to have said, "I have no personal feeling against Lord Wimborne and the other two selectors, bur their methods have proven to be an abject failure."[4]

An opposite view was taken by Lt. Col. Edward Miller, who was interviewed in America on the subject of Lord Wodehouse's criticisms and stated that his comments were uncalled for:

> The American team is the finest I ever have seen. I used to think that the Big Four that consisted of Harry Payne Whitney, Devereux Milburn and the two Waterbury brothers, Larry and Monty, would never be equaled but the team that the Americans put on the field this year, in my opinion, was superior even to the combination of fifteen years ago.[5]

With the benefit of hindsight, it is difficult to argue with the validity of Lord Wodehouse's comments. The prime example of the woes of the selection committees in England in the 1920s is the fact that Johnny Traill, a ten-goal handicap player for many years, was persistently passed over by the selectors, although he was one of the few players in the London season that played up to international standards.

Nevertheless, there were several factors beyond the questionable selection of lower-handicapped players. The paramount reason for the failure of British players was the high quality of the opposition, as cogently pointed out by Colonel Miller. The 1920s was the golden era of American polo, with central worthies such as Tommy Hitchcock and Devereux Milburn, who were ably supported by ten-goalers Louis Stoddard, Watson Webb and Malcolm Stevenson; nine-goalers Eric Pedley, Winston Guest and Bobby Strawbridge, and Earle Hopping the younger at eight goals. It was an embarrassment of riches.

The issue of home-field advantage was also in favor of the Americans. This was proven time and time again in both the contests for the Westchester Cup and the Cup of the Americas. Beyond that, the British players were accustomed to the lush turf of the best polo grounds in England; the pace of play was much slower that in the United States. No English team had the chance to practice at length on the lightning-fast American polo fields. Only in 1939 was this deficiency corrected. Playing occasional games in Spain against weak teams was no substitute for the real thing.

The final straw was that polo in England took time to recuperate from the carnage of polo players in the war. The question of the perceived decline of English polo provoked extensive coverage in the *Polo Monthly*, with several worthies expressing their candid opinion. The respected Walter Buckmaster voiced the thought that the main culprit was the lack of good grounds. "London's three clubs have two small practice grounds always crowded and after the first fortnight cut to ribbons."[6]

General Hardress Lloyd felt that the main cause of the decline of English polo was the lack of young players and trained ponies. Major Philip Magor, who had ample experience of the game in Argentina, said,

> We have men and ponies equal to the Americans. But we have not the perfect grounds to practice. At the tournament at Minehead there were 46 players and one ground. We played three matches nearly every afternoon, and even played in the morning. The polo to start with was very good, but as the ground became cut up it became slower and slower, and ultimately impossible for high handicap players to play up to their handicaps. All the grounds in London became bumpy and difficult to hit the ball on.[7]

Col. James Richardson had a mouthful to say:

> Chief culprit is the neglect, even among our front rank players, of the sound principles of the game. Individual selfishness, the bane of all team games, is seen in even the best matches and is rampant in tournaments of secondary significance. Other is the decline of horsemanship. The effect of this is in seeing players unable to place their ponies and themselves in positions from which they can make accurate strokes, and being able to stop and turn their ponies quickly—in short, in not having their ponies handy and in hand.[8]

Lt. Col. Edward Miller added his bit of wisdom in three articles published in the *Morning Post*. An old-timer, Ted Miller felt that the abolition of the offside rule had resulted in a lack of combination play. He added, "The troubles in Ireland have stopped both polo and the breeding of ponies in that country. The chief difficulty is that the young players have not the money, and so cannot mount themselves properly. Another very bad fault is 'hitting behind the line' instead of making an approach shot first."[9]

Colonel Miller was of the opinion that turning on the ball was an unpardonable mistake in nine cases out of ten, for it is done instead of a backhander. Many excellent chances of scoring were thrown away in the 1921 international matches, and he suggested that the weakest point in most good English players was their goal hitting.

Change of the Guard in England

A negative impression was created in America when Lord Wimborne, who was in charge of the English enterprise, left New York City en route to Paris on the morning of the first match. The aftermath was that at a meeting at the Cavalry Club, the chairman of the Hurlingham Club, Sir Harold Snagge,[10] proposed, "This Committee shall be a Committee of the Hurlingham Club and known in future as The Hurlingham Club Polo Committee."[11]

The resolution, properly seconded, was carried by an overwhelming majority. It should be noted that only twenty-one members were present at the meeting, out of thirty-five. Several committee members did not vote, because they did not recognize the power of the committee to abolish themselves. Be that as it may, the Hurlingham Club regained control of the destinies of polo in the United Kingdom.

1927: The Westchester Cup at Meadow Brook

Three years later, once more at Meadow Brook's International Field, it was a different story, although when all was said and done the final result was identical: America retained the Westchester Cup.

In a surprising move after regaining control of the game of polo in England, the Hurlingham Polo Committee asked the Army in India to attempt the recovery of the Westchester Cup. The Army in India selectors followed a winning formula. The team was chosen well in advance. The players knew each other well. A superb string of horses was obtained. Finally, the squad did not practice on the slow English polo fields but went directly from the fast Indian grounds to the fast American fields.

Seven officers were selected to make the journey to America. Major Eric "Joey" Atkinson, 15th Lancers and Captain Charles "Pat" Roark, late Poona Horse, were nine-goal handicap players. Rated at eight goals were Captain John Dening, Prince Albert Victor's Own, Captain Richard George, Central India Horse, and Major Austin "Bill" Williams, also from the CIH. A young subaltern of great promise, Humphrey Guinness, Royal Scots Greys, and Captain Claude Pert, 15th Lancers, both rated at seven goals, completed the squad.

Lt. Col. George de la Poer Beresford was responsible for the vital issue of the polo ponies. Col. Commandant Henry Tomkinson, a veteran of the 1914 and 1921 Westchester Cup teams, was in overall charge. The selectors also offered the following communiqué: "The Selection Committee of the Army-in-India Polo Association wishes to make it quite clear that the ultimate composition of the team must depend on the form shown in America in the preliminary practice games."[12]

This time around, everyone knew what was going on.

America placed on the field, once more and for the last time, the Second Big Four: the left-hander James Watson Webb, MFH; Tommy Hitchcock; Malcolm "Mike" Stevenson; and, as back and team captain, one of the game's immortals, Devereux Milburn. It was one of the best ever international teams.

Pert, Williams, Roark and Atkinson played in the first match. From the first throw-in, the American team put on a display of virtuosity seldom seen on a polo ground. The final score, 13–3, tells the story. Following an unsatisfactory performance from the British point of view, Captains George and Dening replaced Captains Pert and Williams. This new lineup played very well; the three unanswered goals scored by Tommy Hitchcock in the first chukker was the difference at match's end. In this game the Army-in-India team had much to be proud of. Facing the best team in the world, only days after a crushing defeat, they gave the Americans a stern battle.

The matches were ably described by polo player Frank S. Butterworth in *The Sportsman*:

> The long trail, the high hopes, the tremendous preparations for lifting the highly prized international sport trophy, The Westchester Cup, ended for the British in defeat in two straight games on September 10 and 14, after magnificent polo. No more inspiring or more perfectly played game has been seen in any match between England and America than the first one played by the American four, each of whom equaled or surpassed the best game he had ever shown.
>
> Four men that day played unbeatable polo, and England was overwhelmed, scoring only three goals. While America scored from one to three goals in every period excepting the second. And because England was outpaced and outplayed by super polo, the game was not a great contest; the joy came in seeing such fine individual and team play, at a speed that few of us will see again on any field.
>
> From the first throw-in America seized the ball, assumed the mastery, and began scoring, piling up 13 goals. Team captain Milburn played his best game. It was quickly evident that Stevenson was in rare form, and that Milburn could play with confidence that his Number 3 was not only in harmony but effective, and the great back proceeded to open up all his longest and best shots in defending his goal and turning to offense.
>
> It was Hitchcock, the incomparable, who set the standard of play. His influence on the team is almost as remarkable as his individual skill — so remarkable, indeed, that it can almost be said that as Hitchcock plays, and so will the team play. His own scoring ability, out of 13 goals he scored six, his feeding to others, his talent for coming back on occasions and getting the ball and sending or carrying it to the antagonist's goal, his booming drives, and his ability to hit all sorts of shots and score from difficult angles. His knowledge of polo and team play were all shown from the start.
>
> At Number 1, the most difficult position in polo, Webb played his elevated game. Well-mounted, true and at times uncanny in his hitting, always in his place for scoring or riding-off, and showing skill in handling Atkinson, he, too, played at top speed and form.
>
> The two British defensive players, Atkinson and Roark, played better than the forwards, and there were flashes of team play. The hitting of the British four was not accurate, and it was not improved by the hurrying that they were subjected.
>
> The second game, however, was not a runaway. In fact, barring the first period, in which Hitchcock scored three times, it was a hard fought game. Those three tallies were the difference at day's end, the score being 8–5. For this second game, captains Dening and George replaced Williams and Pert. Dening particularly, made a difference in the match. On the other hand, the American team could not possibly duplicate their form of the first day.[13]

Peter Vischer, *Polo* magazine's editor, felt that both teams were equal with one exception: the Americans were better with their shots at goal.[14] This deficiency in high-goal polo had previously been noted by astute observers of the game in England.

Prelude to Yet Another Defeat: The Chaos of Selection in 1930

England tried, once more, to recover the Westchester Cup in 1930. The Hurlingham Club Polo Committee adopted a different tack this time around. Captain Charles Tremayne, 19th Hussars, was appointed team captain and instructed to select three players to compose a team. Captain Tremayne was also asked to collect half a dozen other players to serve as spare men to step into the team as such necessity arose. At an address to members of the polo community at the Savoy Hotel, Lord Cowdray expressed that after due consideration the committee felt that the advantages of putting the responsibility on the shoulders of one man rather than a committee of selection was the more likely way to ensure that those selected would be a team in every sense of the word, rather than a collection of four individual players.[15] Capt. Maurice Kingscote, of the Cirencester Polo Club, was placed in charge of selecting the ponies and their entire management.

The English side as originally selected was Major Geoffrey Phipps-Hornby, Captain Pat Roark, Captain Tremayne and Lt. Humphrey Guinness, a twenty-nine-goal combination.[16] The choice of Captain Tremayne as playing captain remained an open question because he lacked any international experience at all. A brave man and a veteran seven-goal player, he had gone to France in 1914 and returned in 1918 with a bullet inside his chest and two Military Crosses on the outside. The team went through a large number of practice matches, some said far too many, trying to figure out what would be the best combination to face the formidable American team.

The initial trial matches at Beaufort Polo Club in Gloucestershire did not bode well for the team. It became clear to observers that both Major Phipps-Hornby, a member of the 1924 team, and Captain Tremayne, were not up to the international standards required to offer battle to the Americans. Most sportingly, Captain Tremayne stepped aside to give room for younger blood.

The first practice game took place at Beaufort on April 20 and the last one also at Beaufort on July 23. Along the course of those three months, at no time were four players put together as a team for an extended period of time to develop team cohesion and understanding among the teammates. Continuous changes after each trial game was the order of the day at Beaufort, Hurlingham and Roehampton. Lewis Lacey, the world's best back at the time, was inserted at number 1; although his opponent was his friend Johnny Traill, another ten-goaler, Lacey played remarkably well. Then Lacey was switched to back, and later on to number 2. Johnny Traill was once more taken out of consideration. Gerald Balding; Pat Roark; his younger brother Aidan; Captain Richard George from India; Humphrey Guinness; Hugh "Chicken" Walford, a promising youngster in the 17th/21st Lancers; Major Eric Atkinson; Colonel Percival Wise; and the Australian Geoffrey Ashton, a member of the visiting Goulburn team, played in the selection matches. Even foreigners, such as Laddie Sanford and the Spanish Marqués de Villagrágima, where inserted in these trial matches. There was neither rhyme nor rhythm in the selection process. In the last trial game, Captain George, Gerald Balding, Pat Roark and Lewis Lacey, a thirty-two-goal combination, barely squeezed by six goals to four by the 17th/21st Lancers, the veteran Lt. Col. Vivian Lockett and three subalterns, Ronald Cooke, Desmond Miller and "Chicken" Walford.

For its part, the USPA announced the names of sixteen players invited to participate in the official test matches. Thomas Hitchcock, Jr., was appointed captain and chairman of the defense committee and was also given the power to select its members. In other words, Tommy Hitchcock was allowed to have absolute control. For his committee, Hitchcock chose the savvy Carleton Burke; his father Thomas Hitchcock, who had played in the 1886 contest; David Iglehart; George Mead; Charles Schwartz; and John Hay Whitney. The trial matches began in July, at a rate of two a week on the grounds of Piping Rock and Sands Point. The final selection fell upon Eric Pedley, who Tommy Hitchcock thought was the best American number 1 ever; the young Earle A.S. Hopping, proven as an asset in the 1928 final match against Argentina; and, at back, Winston Guest.

The final English team was Gerald Balding, Lewis Lacey, Pat Roark and Aidan Roark.

The 1930 Westchester Cup team at Meadow Brook: Gerald Balding, Lewis Lacey, Pat Roark and Humphrey Guinness.

A last-minute change became necessary because Aidan Roark developed an infection in his throat; his replacement at back was Humphrey Guinness. Gerald Balding played number 1, Lacey at number 2, and Pat Roark at number 3. The big problem was that the team, throughout practices and during the Westchester Cup games, did not possess a true number 1.

The American team retained the Westchester Cup in two games, although the general opinion was that this had been the most serious challenge to the Americans since the international series was resumed after the war.[17] The games were far closer than the five-goal differential in both games. The first match was quite even, 7–5, until the seventh chukker, when the American team went into high gear on its way to a 10–5 win. In the second game the English team started ahead; however, in a critical sixth chukker, the British ponies appeared to be "cooked," and the United States team pulled away for a 14–9 victory.[18]

Horse power, as usual, made the difference. Eric Pedley made the most of his many chances at goal, while Gerald Balding, playing in an unaccustomed position, had fewer shots at goal during the entire series than Pedley had in a few chukkers. The offensive spirit advocated by Thomas Hitchcock in his pregame instructions — still being quoted in print — paid handsome dividends.

But perhaps the last word belongs to Brigadier Robert Ricketts, an outstanding thinker in matters of polo:

In England the system of succession of tournaments, with little or no interval for pony train-ing, was very detrimental to the production of any thought-out, tactical development. Teams were thrown together for short periods, the men often finding themselves in one position in one team and in another position in another team. A notable exception was the team of the 17th Lancers already mentioned, which was a combined side. It gave further evidence of its worth when at Beaufort, just before the British went to America to compete for the Westchester Cup, it held that collection of players to the extent of leading by 4 goals to 3 in the fourth chukker.

The absence of any sound system of tactics in the trial matches for the selection of the British team to go to America in 1933 [*sic*, 1930] was most marked, almost every polo crime being com-mitted repeatedly. It seems astonishing that a collection of such experienced and excellent ball-hitters and horsemen should have played such bad polo, if polo can be defined as the combined efforts of four players to defeat their opponents.[19]

Brigadier Ricketts on Polo in England

Robert Lumsden Ricketts possessed one of the most fertile and innovative brains in the game of polo. In 1931, he wrote a two-page article about the game on English grounds that was published in the American magazine *Polo*.[20] Subtitled "A Discussion of the Reasons that Have Brought England Sporting Defeats," it is an incisive assessment of British sports in general and polo in particular.

According to Ricketts, proficiency in international sporting contests depends upon at least six considerations: physique, intellect, mental attitude, temperament, climate and money.

Regarding the physical aspect, Brigadier Ricketts felt that there was no difference among the British and other peoples, except perhaps a less elastic type best exemplified by the marked agility of the big men that toured the British Isles from New Zealand and South Africa on their rugby football teams.

The mental attitude toward games appears to be the deciding factor. In order to achieve the best results, the best brains must be combined with the best bodies. In Ricketts' own words:

> But though the British, as a nation, are very fond of ball games, these games, in England at any rate, are looked upon by the great majority merely as being good for bodily development and good fun, to be played for amusement only, to which a certain amount of competition adds some zest. They are not looked upon as subjects for deep thought. Partly as a result of this atti-tude of mind, International competitions do not appeal strongly to most people. Local and tra-ditional sporting events, such as the Henley regatta, Ascot races, and Lords, which carry with them a large element of social jollification, and in which the onlookers have a personal and inti-mal connection with the performers, attract more real sympathy than International events with their highly competitive and comparatively serious atmosphere.[21]

Another aspect of the British mind, says Ricketts, is its attitude toward theoretical and logical thought, any expression of which is more likely to be boring than to encourage fur-ther thought and action. "A pound of practice is worth a ton of theory" or "Give me the practical man" is the direction most British minds turn. This leads to the inability to have any really definite idea of the aim in view.

As regards polo in particular, the social aspect must be considered. The game is expen-sive and high class is usually confined to moneyed young men, and they have marked char-acteristics. Among these are an intense independence of spirit and a determination to enjoy themselves in the way, to which is added courage both physical and of their own opinion.

Neither the capacity nor the wish for deep thought is present, nor is there much high-class knowledge. Theoretical study is most unwelcome.

Brigadier Ricketts goes on to state that this atmosphere is most inimical to the highest level of games tactics and performance. Discipline becomes almost impossible, and a real disciplinarian would never be tolerated as a leader. It is only such a man, however, who incidentally must be a thinker as well, who can train a team to its highest pitch.

As to the English climate, it certainly is against those players who cannot travel abroad to play. The season is short and uncertain; the polo grounds are slow and encourage a heavy, slow type of play which soon develops into a habit. Continuous practice on a slow ground will lead to a kind of polo totally unsuited to international standards.

The issue of temperament is incalculable. It both gives and takes away victory. Brigadier Ricketts gives the example of many French international rugby teams that after forcing themselves into a winning position, lose the match through lack of finish caused by excitement. Temperament assists a will to win if the team is well trained; it precipitates collapse in the reverse case.

Finally, there must be present the will to win, in the shape of determination as distinguished from mere wish. It depends upon the spirit in which the undertaking has been approached. The morale of the players in this respect is largely a matter of training and the attitude of mind engendered by that training. Some leaders inspire, others do not. "High morale can be consciously cultivated. If control has been loose, the will to win is likely to be weak, or at least to show itself merely in desperate personal efforts. In a well-disciplined and well-taught side it shows itself in a spirit of offense, which never degenerates lower than a tight defensive combination at moments when things go badly."[22]

Thus, the gospel of international polo according to Ricketts.

CHAPTER 12

The Lean Years of the Depression

The economic situation prevalent in the early 1930s affected polo in England in a significant way. Especially in 1931, the polo season was wrecked by "the terrible twins," bad weather and bad times, as the *Polo Monthly* quaintly put it.[1]

The Hurlingham Club Polo Committee thought it advisable to cut the number of chukkers for the most important tournaments to only six, and to just four chukkers for club matches. The committee felt that during those difficult times this temporary measure was important in effecting savings in the matter of mounts.

Among the several clubs that curtailed or stopped operations, the Cirencester Polo Club went into abeyance, and Wirrall suspended its polo season in 1932. Later on, Dulverton and Melton Mowbray closed in 1934.

The Rhinefield Polo Club — nowadays the New Forest — was founded in 1935 by Major Ronald Walker-Munro with the purpose of providing inexpensive polo. By and large, New Forest ponies were used. An interesting rule was that no pony purchased or valued over fifty pounds could be played. When a sixty-eight-guinea pony was found out, an explanation was requested from the owner. Subsequently, the pony was warned off the premises.

Harrogate Polo Club was started in 1935, play being conducted at the Stray, a two-hundred-acre public park in the center of town. The onset of war placed this club in abeyance.

An unusual polo club arose in Suffolk when the Hon. Alastair Watson, who had learned polo at Oxford, built the Chillesford Polo Ground at Sudbourne, near Woodbridge. The technology used was ahead of the times. An underground main was laid, and water was supplied from a duck decoy half a mile away to hydrants situated alongside the boards. No other polo ground in England possessed such a modern system for irrigation. Further advancements were in place when Alastair Watson returned from America with a cargo of traveling sprinklers he had seen operating at the Santa Barbara Polo Club in California.

It was country polo at its best, because Chillesford was a private club where the game was played only for enjoyment of family and friends. No trophies were awarded, and teams and players came to Chillesford by invitation. However, the Hon. Alastair Watson was keen to encourage spectators, who were admitted free of charge. The printed programs had color covers, another innovation for a small polo club in the 1930s.

The war put a stop to this fine example of country polo at Chillesford; however, it was resumed in 1948.

One of the longest spells in English polo occurred in the tie for the Cicero Cup between the Hornets and the Chinchillas. At the end of six chukkers, the score was even at four-all. It was only after two minutes of play in the tenth chukker that Lt. Col. Graham Rees-Mogg hit the winning goal for the Hornets. This team made it all the way to the finals, being defeated by the Royal Guards "B" team.[2]

Beaufort Polo Club

There was, however, an important addition to polo in England. The Beaufort Polo Club was established in 1929 by the Duke of Beaufort, Herbert Cox, a Canadian player; Captain George Scott-Douglas; and Major Thomas Longworth. Eventually the club would have twelve polo grounds and five practice fields. Available stabling was also on a lavish scale; there were forty boxes at the club and a further forty at Home Farm in Westonbirt.

In a short period of time the Beaufort became the premier location for provincial polo in England. A new club with the same name and on the same grounds was established when the Tomlinsons purchased Down Farm in 1976. The Beaufort Polo Club was formally affiliated with the Hurlingham Polo Association in 1989, the third club with the Beaufort name in Gloucestershire.[3]

Stoke d'Abernon

Stoke d'Abernon Polo Club in Cobham, Surrey, was also revived in 1929 carrying a full schedule during the summer months on its two full-size grounds. A scheme by which members could have ponies for hire helped in bringing in new recruits to the game.

Ranelagh

The Ranelagh Club adjusted its polo season to the strains of the economic downturn; nevertheless, eleven tournaments were played for challenge cups plus the matches for the Harrington and Verdun trophies, and a few nonchallenge tournaments. Ranelagh also hosted the County Polo Association tournaments during one week in July. In an effort to obtain more teams competing for the Colts Cup — a fine trophy presented by the American Olympic player Rodman Wanamaker II — the conditions for entry were modified from the requirement that all team members must be under thirty to only two members in each team be of that age.

The entry requirements for the Junior Colts Cup were also amended. Formerly, only players under twenty-five years of age were eligible, and no one with a handicap above seven goals. The new requirements were that the aggregate handicap could not exceed eleven points, and no player was to have a handicap over five. The club also hosted the Duke of York Cup, played between Royal Air Force and Royal Navy teams.

In spite of all those cost-cutting measures, the membership dropped from 107 members in 1930 to 80 in 1931. However, the total number of games played remained stable, 105 in 1930 and 101 in the following year.[4]

Australia's Goulburn Team Tours England

In early March 1930, the MS *Port Huon* docked in Hull after a long sea voyage — six weeks and four days — with its cargo of polo ponies, their grooms and some of the Ashton

Australians at the Hurlingham Champion Cup, 1930. Bob Ashton shakes hands with Alfonso XIII, King of Spain. In the background, Jim Ashton, Geoff Ashton, Phil Ashton, Mrs. Helen Ashton, and on the far right, James Ashton, Sr.

brothers from New South Wales. It was a most sporting venture. The Hurlingham Club Committee rated Geoffrey and Robert Ashton at seven goals, James at six goals and Philip at four goals, for an aggregate handicap of twenty-four. Overall, the Goulburn team flattered to deceive.

Following conditioning at Westonbirt in Wiltshire, the young Australians took the Whitney Cup and the Ranelagh Invitation Cup. In the finals of the Whitney Cup played at Hurlingham, Goulburn defeated the Hurricanes 13–8, after receiving six goals by handicap. The Hurricanes proved to be a little better than Goulburn in the finals of the Hurlingham Champion Cup. In reaching the final tie, Goulburn defeated the Knaves— Hanut Singh, Aidan Roark, Major Eric Atkinson and Major Jack Harrison — a twenty-nine-goal combine, by the odd goal in seven, Geoff Ashton scoring the winning goal in the last minute of play. Then Goulburn defeated the Old Etonians, a twenty-six-goal team which had in its lineup Arthur Pilkington, Walter McCrecry, Charles Tremayne and Hugh Noel Scott Robson, all four Army captains, scoring eight goals against six by the Old Etonians.

The Hurricanes were a thirty-one-goal team, superbly mounted on Laddie Sanford's ponies. Gerald Balding, Pat Roark and Percival Wise completed the squad. Trailing 6–2 after four chukkers, Goulburn drew level at six-all in the fifth. No goals were scored in the final chukker, the Hurricanes eking out a 9–7 win. The real winners were the Australian ponies. Matched against what was considered the best string in the world and giving away in both size and weight, the Australian ponies put up a remarkable good show, staying even with a team that would have been called to give seven goals had the match been played on the handicap. It was a noble defeat.

Goulburn returned to England in 1937. In a rare occasion for the Ashton brothers' team, a family member was dropped from the team to make room for another player, in this case the up-and-coming Bob Skene, who had accompanied the four brothers as a reserve player.[5] The brilliant young Australian played at number 1 alongside Geoffrey, Jim and Robert Ashton. The change paid a handsome result when Goulburn took Hurlingham's Champion Cup, where Skene accounted for six of the nine goals obtained by the Australians in the final game against Keith Rous' Jaguars.

Hurlingham Champion Cup

Only five teams answered the bell in 1931, when the Panthers scratched to Merchiston. The latter team, assembled by Godfrey Madlener, who had played extensively in Argentina, defeated Ubique in the first tie. As their name implies, Ubique was a Royal Artillery team rated at seventeen goals. Captain Bryan Fowler, Lt. Horace Elton, Captain Jock Campbell and Lt. Roy Mews put up a tremendous fight against the twenty-nine-goal Merchiston in a losing effort. The final tally was 9–4 in favor of Merchiston.

The Hurricanes, the holders of the trophy, defeated Someries House 12–8, and the Spaniard Marquis de Portago's Los Piratas 12–4 in the semifinals. Stephen Sanford, Pat Roark, Wing Commander Percival Wise and Captain Dudley Norton were fancied to retain the Champion Cup. They faced Merchiston, with Johnny Traill at number 1, Captain John Sanderson, Captain Noel Scott Robson and Lt. Humphrey Guinness.

Things started badly for Merchiston when the Hurricanes jumped to a 3–1 early lead. For all of his skill, John Traill was out of his element in the forward position. Before the start of the sixth chukker, the Merchiston players held a council of war and Traill was moved back to number 3. This move changed the entire course of the game, and Merchiston emerged the winners by six goals to four after a marvelous game.

Abominable weather during the month of May 1932 wrecked the start of the polo season. Old-timers felt it had been the worst rainfall in recent memory. The pouring rained meant cancellation of all matches at Roehampton; one game was played at Hurlingham and four at Ranelagh. There was polo for only three days during the entire month.

The Whitney Cup, whose final game was played alternately at Hurlingham and Roehampton, was the first tournament played in England under a numerical handicap allowance. Someries House, with Sir Harold Wernher, Captain "Chicken" Walford, Desmond Miller and Humphrey Guinness, defeated Merchiston by 11 goals to 7½ after giving 5½ by handicap.

The postponed Champion Cup saw Sir Ian Walker's Osmaston team walk away with the trophy after a close game against Someries House, the score being 6–5. The Hurlingham Champion Cup, which was not a challenge trophy, a new one being given each year, then took the journey northward to Osmaston Manor in Derbyshire.

The year 1933 was Jaipur's time to take the Hurlingham Champion Cup, described in the pertinent section in this chapter, as is Aurora's win at Hurlingham the following year.

The dominance by foreign teams continued in 1935 when a team from Kashmir, Maj. Gen. Nawab Khusru Jung, Captain Charles Roark, Percival Sanger and the Maharajah of Kashmir took the Champion Cup. The Maharajah of Kashmir was no passenger on his own team, for he was one of the few players in the world rated at nine goals. In typical Indian fashion, no expenses were spared. The forty-four ponies were taken care of by thirty-three grooms during the acclimatization period at Beaufort. During their stay, they took the Holford Cup in Gloucestershire.

On the occasion of the 1936 Westchester Cup, the American team Templeton, with Mike Phipps, Jimmy Mills, team captain Winston Guest and Bobby Strawbridge were the winners.

The trend continued the next two years with Goulburn first doing the honors: Bob Skene, Geoffrey, Jim and Robert Ashton took the cup to the Antipodes in 1937. In the same year, the Nawab of Bhopal brought over his own team, with no luck at Hurlingham. Then the Texas Rangers with patron Charles Wrightsman, Cecil Smith, Aidan Roark and Englishman Eric Tyrrell-Martin, who was a frequent sight in California polo, took the Champion Cup in 1938.

Gerald Balding, playing for the Jaguars, attempts to ride off Jim Ashton. Final game of the 1937 Hurlingham Champion Cup, taken by Goulburn.

The spell was finally broken in 1939 when the Jaguars with the spectacled Captain Nigel Dugdale, the Hon. Keith Rous, the Hon. John Hamilton-Russell and Captain Humphrey Guinness, a most successful team that season, retained the Hurlingham Champion Cup on English soil.

Ranelagh Open Challenge Cup

The first tie for the 1931 Ranelagh Open Cup was between Philip Magor's Panthers and Jack Harrison's Knaves, the Panthers winning easily, 10–4. The Panthers went on to defeat the Marqués de Portago's Los Piratas and qualified for the finals, where they faced Merchiston, a surprise winner over the Hurricanes, a thirty-two-goal team. Godfrey Madlener sustained a shoulder injury and was unable to continue play;

he was replaced by Geoffrey Phipps-Hornby, who was enjoying the game as a spectator. Major Phipps-Hornby went on the field in leather chaps over flannel trousers and immediately made his mark on the game.[6] Merchiston, out-handicapped by ten points, went on to win the match, 4–3. John Sanderson, Hugh Noel Robson and Humphrey Guinness completed the squad. They went on to take the final game, defeating the Panthers 8–6 in a good match.

In 1932, the Panthers, which the previous week had taken the Roehampton Open Cup, were defeated in the first tie by Ubique, the Royal Artillery's team. The Gunners faced Someries House in the final. With the score tied at six-all at the end of the sixth and final chukker, the surprising Ubique team elected to scratch without playing, because even if they had won they could not have played in the finals, having on that date a match against the Royal Horse Guards in the Inter-Regimental Tournament. Thus, Sir Harold Wernher's team qualified for the final tie. Someries House faced the Cavaliers, Captain Arthur Pilkington, Henry Scott, Colonel Vivian Lockett and Johnny Traill. In a good match, the Cavaliers prevailed by seven goals to five.

On their journey to the Coronation Cup, Major Jack Harrison's team, the Knaves, took the Ranelagh Open in 1934. Arthur Pilkington, Charles "Pat" Roark and Captain Errol Prior-Palmer were the other Knaves.

A team named the Optimists, Geoffrey Phipps-Hornby, the American international Michael Phipps, Hesketh Hughes and Tom Guy, another American player, was the winner in 1935.

The 1936 Ranelagh Open Cup was not finished, owing to the international matches and wet weather crowding the London season calendar. Those two factors contributed to the failure to draw to a conclusion several other tournaments, such as the Roehampton Cup, the Frank Hargreaves (Warwickshire) Cup, the Shaw Cup, the Military Handicap, the Ladies Nomination Cup and the Junior Tournament, all at Roehampton. The Hurlingham Club canceled the Visitors Handicap Tournament and portions of the Weekly Cup.[7]

In 1937, the visiting Bhopal from India, with Prithi Singh, Major Claude Pert, an English international player, Hanut Singh and the 17th Lancers' Hugh Walford were the winners.

The Texas Rangers continued their domination of polo in London with their usual characters: patron Charles Wrightsman, Cecil Smith, Aidan Roark and Eric Tyrrell-Martin.

Finally, the last Ranelagh Open Cup ever, the 1939 contest, was won by the Giant Pandas, a team assembled by Lt. the Hon. Keith Rous, RN, and completed with Captain Nigel Dugdale, 17th/21st Lancers; the Hon. John Hamilton-Russell, 1st Royal Dragoons Guards; and Captain Humphrey Guinness, Royal Scots Greys.

Roehampton Open Challenge Cup

In 1931, the Roehampton Open Cup was limited to eight teams, and the matches' duration was decreased from seven to six chukkers, a change dictated by the economic downturn.

Osmaston, Sir Ian Walker's team, defeated Ubique in the first tie, and the Cavaliers took the measure of Merchiston. The Panthers and Someries House found their way to the finals, where the Panthers, Philip Magor's team, defeated Someries House 9–5. Humphrey Guinness, Someries House's best player, was unable to play for the team because he had an Inter-Regimental Tournament tie that same afternoon. That was one of the vagaries of the crowded London polo season.

Panthers, the winners of the 1931 Roehampton Open Cup: Philip Magor, Johnny Traill, Geoffrey Phipps-Hornby and Eric Tyrrell-Martin.

The Panthers team was Geoffrey Phipps-Hornby, Eric Tyrrell-Martin, Philip Magor and Johnny Traill. This same team, with the Marqués Antonio de Portago in Major Phipps-Hornby's place, repeated the victory in 1932.

London's high-goal season's initial competition was usually the Whitney Cup presented by Mr. Harry Payne Whitney on the occasion of the American international team's visit in 1909. A scratch side, the Optimists, with William Horbury, Hesketh Hughes, Major A. Leonard Tate and Johnny Traill, took the trophy from Wykham in the 1934 finals.

The Whitney Cup was followed by the Roehampton Open Cup, which was taken by the Aurora team: Harold Talbott, team captain Seymour "Shorty" Knox, the ten-goaler Elmer Boeseke and Billy Post. The American visitors had an easy path to the finals, by defeating Wykham 8–2 in the initial tie and Someries House, with Lewis Lacey on this lineup in the semifinals. At time's end the scoreboard showed nine goals for Aurora and only three for Someries House, all from Mr. Lacey's mallet. The final tie was another story. Major Philip Magor was unable to play due to illness and was replaced by Hugo Backhouse, another player whose polo skills had been honed in Argentina. Dudley Frost, who also played in Argentina, Hesketh Hughes and Eric Tyrrell-Martin completed the Panthers team. As the bell sounded the termination of the fifth chukker, the Panthers were down by a single goal, 6–5. They should have equalized at the start of the last chukker, but the ball rebounded off a goalpost and Aurora availed itself of the missed chance to score two quick goals in succession. Then both sides exchanged goals, and Aurora took match and championship by nine goals to six.

The Panthers regained the Roehampton Open trophy in 1935. It was a mixed-bag team: Philip Magor played at back, with two Americans, Laddie Sanford and Mike Phipps as forwards and Eric Tyrrell-Martin in the pivot position.

Templeton took the trophy in 1936. There were plenty of American players in London that summer because of the series for the Westchester Cup, and Michael Phipps, James Mills, Winston Guest and Robert Strawbridge, Jr., took the honors.

The Jaguars, a successful team in the late 1930s, took the Roehampton Open Cup in 1937. The Hon. W. Keith Rous, Stephen Sanford, Gerald Balding and Winston Guest were the team members. They faced in the finals a team called the Four Winds. The program for Thursday, 3 June 1937, reads,

The Four Winds	*v.*	*Jaguars*
Capt. B.J. Fowler (South)	1	Hon. W. Keith Rous
H. Hughes (West)	2	S. Sanford
Capt. G.E. Prior-Palmer (East)	3	G. Balding
Capt. H.P. Guinness (North)	Bk.	Winston Guest

No mention is made of any distinctive markers for the players, save for the colors: green and yellow for the Four Winds, red and gray for the Jaguars. The players' handicaps are not listed; however, a notice reads, "The Management will much appreciate the assistance of spectators in replacing the turf between Chukkers." The referee was Lt. Col. C.D. Miller, the umpires Lt. Col. Sydney Kennedy and Major M. Cox. Mrs. Charles Miller was to present the cup to the winners immediately after the match.

Postponements due to foul weather pushed the finals of the 1938 Roehampton Open Cup to the end of the high-goal season. Mid-July saw the last of the several struggles between the Jaguars and the Texas Rangers. Once more, Cecil Smith did great things and took the chestnuts out of the fire for a narrow 7–6 victory. The match was marred by a bumpy ground and, more importantly, by mishaps to two ponies. Charles Wrightsman's Beauty Spot broke a pastern bone, and Keith Rous' Midtoi was knocked unconscious by a blow over the eye from a player's stick. Motion pictures mogul Darryl Zanuck, Cecil Smith, Aidan Roark and Eric Tyrrell-Martin made up the Texas Rangers team.

The last Roehampton Open Cup was taken by Someries House, with patron Sir Harold Wernher; Captain Andrew Horsburgh-Porter, 12th Lancers, later Sir Andrew; Captain Errol Prior-Palmer, 9th Lancers; and Capt. David Dawnay, 10th Hussars. Thus, two players from the regiments that started polo in England were participants in one of the last high-goal polo tournaments before the war.

The Inter-Regimental Tournament

Eleven teams participated in the 1931 Inter-Regimental Tournament, including a team representing the Royal Navy. The largest crowd of the season gathered at Hurlingham Club to watch the finals between the Queen's Bays and the Royal Artillery teams. In a close game, the Queen's Bays—captains George Draffen, Alexander Barclay and the brothers George and Evelyn Fanshawe — ended up winners by five goals to two.

No fewer than thirteen teams started the 1932 Inter-Regimental Tournament. The holders, Queen's Bays, were defeated in the semifinals by the Royal Scots Greys in extra time, after a terrific struggle. In the other semifinal, the Royal Artillery team overwhelmed the 7th Hussars by six goals to one. This display made the Gunners the team to be fancied in the finals. The pundits were correct, and the Royal Artillery obtained its second Inter-Regimental Tournament after defeating a good Scots Greys team. Bryan Fowler, Horace Elton, Humphrey Morrison and Jock Campbell were on the Gunners team. Captains Fowler, Morrison and Campbell were members of the 1927 championship team.

Not everything was lost for the Scots Greys because other regimental teams took the Junior Colts' Cup and the Subalterns' Cup at Ranelagh, as well as the Blakiston-Houston Cup at Tidworth.

The following year saw the Royal Scots Greys take the coveted Inter-Regimental trophy with a team that included three subalterns, Massey Lopes— later Lord Roborough — Roland Findlay and Humphrey Guinness. The team was captained by Major Cyril Gaisford–St. Lawrence, a commanding officer described as "a very military and warlike grizzled individual,"[8] who "never thought of himself at all."[9]

The 1934 final game was witnessed by the visiting Aurora team from upstate New York. Seymour Knox recorded, "The Final of the Inter-Regimental which was supposed to be one of the high points of the polo season produced mediocre but exciting polo full of danger."[10]

Some other observers voiced similar comments about the at times wild nature of play in the Inter-Regimental Tournament in the 1970s and 1980s.

The tournament was taken by the 7th Hussars, which was considered an upset. In the best soldiers' polo tradition, the 7th Hussars were led by Lt. Col. Gabriel Breitmeyer, the commanding officer. Captain Frederick Bass, Captain Richard Sheppard and Captain Geoffrey Fielden were the other team members.

The 3rd Brigade of the Royal Horse Artillery, with Captain Bryan Fowler, Lt. Guy Gregson, Lt. Hugh Cowan and Major John "Jock" Campbell took the cup in 1935.

Then it was the turn of the 12th Lancers, who had been denied the spoils of victory since 1914. George Kidston, Lt. Col. Richard L. McCreery, Richard W. Hobson and Andrew Horsbrugh-Porter were the championship team members. Colonel McCreery was the son of Walter McCreery, who was on winning squads in the Paris Olympic Games and winner of the Champion Cup on Old Cantabs teams. McCreery himself took the Champion Cup with the Harlequins in 1925. He ended the war as Sir Richard McCreery, commander in chief, British Army of the Rhine.

The year 1937 belonged to that famous polo regiment, the 10th Hussars. Four captains, Michael Macmullen, Charles Harvey, David Dawnay and John Archer-Shee, formed the winning team

The Royal Scots Greys once more took the Inter-Regimental in 1938 with a strong team that included Lord Roborough, Harry Mackenson, Roland Findlay and Humphrey Guinness. All but Captain Mackenson had been on the 1933 winning team.

The last Inter-Regimental competition played before World War II was taken by the 10th Hussars. Captain Macmullen, Captain Dawnay and Captain Archer-Shee were joined by Lt. John Malet in this successful endeavor.

The Coronation Cup

The Coronation Cup was not played in 1930 because of conflict with the selection matches for the Westchester Cup held at Meadow Brook.

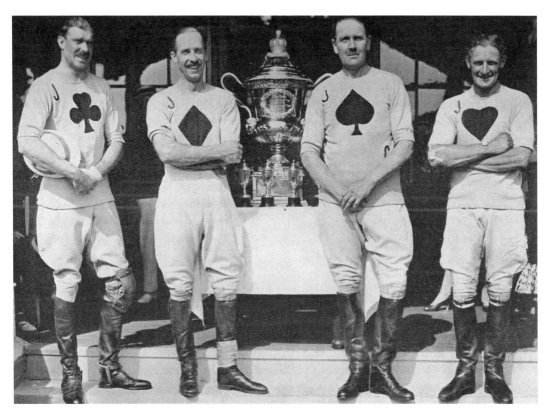

The Knaves took the Coronation Cup in 1934: Arthur Pilkington, Pat Roark, Jack Harrison and Errol Prior-Palmer.

A team assembled by Philip Magor, named the Panthers, took the trophy in 1931, having qualified by virtue of their win in the Roehampton Open Cup. The team was Eric Tyrrell-Martin, Pat Roark, Major Magor and Johnny Traill. The Panthers won the Coronation once more in 1935, with the American Laddie Sanford and Captain Prior-Palmer replacing Roark and Traill.

Four teams qualified to enter the 1932 King's Coronation Cup: Osmaston, the Panthers, Royal Artillery and the Cavaliers. The latter team scratched; therefore, Osmaston and the RA team battled out in the single semifinal. The Gunners acquitted themselves well. They were defeated 7–3 by a team that had an aggregate handicap six goals higher. Osmaston went on to beat the Panthers by five goals in the final game. Sir Ian Walker, Pat Roark, Capt. G. Errol Prior-Palmer and Jack Harrison thus completed a magnificent double, the Champion Cup and the Coronation Cup.

Jaipur monopolized the major tournaments in 1933, and the Knaves won the Coronation Cup the following year, defeating the American team Aurora.

Templeton, Winston Guest's team named after his ancestral home in England, was the winner in the year of the Westchester Cup. His cousin Michael Phipps, James Mills and Robert Strawbridge, Jr., the U.S. Polo Association chairman, completed the powerful American squad.

The Jaguars, with the Hon. Keith Rous, Captain Pat Roark, Gerald Balding and Stephen Sanford, were the winners in 1937. Goulburn, Bhopal and the Royal Scots Greys also qualified.

In 1938, only two matches were played in the competition held for the next-to-last Coronation Cup. The Texas Rangers had been successful in both the Hurlingham Champion Cup and the Ranelagh Open Cup, while the Roehampton Open Cup had not reached its conclusion. The Royal Scots Greys, winners of the Inter-Regimental Tournament, did not wish to participate in the Coronation Cup, so the committee invited the Jaguars and the Gauchos to take part in the tournament. These two teams played for the right to face Charles Wrightsman's Texas Rangers, the Jaguars easily defeating the visitors from Argentina by nine goals to four. In the finals, the Jaguars— a team assembled by Lt. W.K. Rous, a serving Royal Navy officer — once more gave the Texas Rangers a hard tussle, only to remain again as bridesmaids by the score of eight to six goals.

The Hon. Keith Rous finally obtained the Coronation Cup when his team, now named the Giant Pandas, took the trophy in 1939. Nigel Dugdale, the Hon. John Hamilton-Russell and Capt. Humphrey Guinness completed the Giant Pandas team. Captain Hamilton-Russell was killed in Sicily during World War II, one of many polo players who fell in that conflict.

Take No Prisoners: The Jaipur Team Invasion

A full side composed of Indian players visited England in 1933. Takur Prithi Singh, Rao Rajah Abhey Singh, Rao Rajah Hanut Singh, and the Maharajah of Jaipur formed the team in that order.[11] Soon after its debut, the Jaipur squad became the sensation of the London season with their colorful turbans, impeccable blazers and, above all, their quality combination play.

This Indian polo team led by the Maharajah of Jaipur took all the major trophies in the 1933 London polo season, winning every one of its tournament matches. Only Osmaston scored a win over Jaipur in the first practice match at Hurlingham, by 8½ goals to 6, after receiving 4½ goals by handicap. Osmaston was the best team England could offer, with Sir Ian Walker, Pat Roark, Captain Prior-Palmer and Major Harrison. They were defeated by Jaipur in all of the tournament finals.

The Jaipur pony string consisted of thirty-nine horses, each one with a syce looking after them. It was a cosmopolitan lot: there were sixteen Australian ponies, ten English, six from Argentina, one from France, and one was Spanish. Only five were from India, most likely a reflection of the difficulty assembling a high-quality string from the homebred pony population.

The superiority of the Jaipur team was never seriously challenged. *The Times* polo correspondent wrote, "Their hitting, their ball control, their combination and sense of anticipation left one wondering if there had ever been a team in the past who could have stood up to them. I doubt it, with all due respect to the Meadow Brook 'Big Four' of the years preceding the war."[12]

Sometimes exuberance gets in the way of objective comparisons. At the time of their expedition to England in 1909, the Big Four members were rated at nine goals each; when the Hurlingham Polo Association produced its first handicap list for the 1911 season, all were rated at ten goals. The Jaipur team, for all its brilliancy, was a thirty-goal side; furthermore, the quality of high-goal polo in England in 1933 was at a lower level than in 1909.

Be that as it may, the Jaipur team took the open tournaments at Roehampton, Ranelagh and Hurlingham, the Indian Princes' Shield and the Coronation Cup, a record not to be surpassed.

Aurora in England

In 1934, Seymour Knox, Jr., took his team Aurora, based at the Ess Kay Farm in East Aurora, close to Buffalo in upstate New York, to England in order to participate in the London season.[13] This was a well-mounted, powerful team, with Harold Talbott from Ohio, a seven-goal player; "Shorty" Knox; the Californian Elmer Boeseke, Jr., riding the crest of his newly anointed ten-goal rating; and, at back, William Post II, a Princeton University man, who was a superb horseman rated at eight goals. Billy Post had been the star of the American international team that took both the Argentine Open Championship and the Cup of the Americas at Palermo in 1932. The spare man was Howard Howell, a four-goal handicap player from Dayton, who was not called to play on the team during the entire tour, with the exception of some practice games.

The Anglo-Argentine Thomas Nelson was engaged to look after the ponies. Tommy Nelson had been in charge of the Argentine ponies in the 1928 Cup of the Americas at Meadow Brook. Such was his reputation that one of the conditions imposed by the Americans in their expedition to Palermo in 1932 was that Nelson must be in charge of the American pony string. Tommy was also responsible for the conditioning and management of the Argentine ponies in the 1936 Olympic Games in Berlin and at Meadow Brook for the Cup of the Americas.

The American squad gathered at Beaufort for practice and conditioning for both mounts and players. It is interesting the opinion of the visiting American players in regard to umpiring in England. In his detailed account of the tour, Shorty Knox wrote:

"After playing with American referees, one couldn't help but notice the difference strict umpiring means to a game of polo. We found it difficult to get used to having the ball whisked from under our noses with no penalty imposed and were convinced that strict umpiring would speed up English polo besides making it safer."[14]

Aurora went on to take Hurlingham's Champion Cup, defeating a team assembled by Vivian Lockett called Resurrection Pie. Major Frank Hurndall, Major Geoffrey Phipps-Hornby, both veterans from the 1924 Westchester Cup team, and Captain Robert Bingley, 11th Hussars, completed the squad. Following a loss in the semifinals at the hands of Someries House, which team included Lewis Lacey, Aurora took the Roehampton Open Cup. The finals of the Coronation Cup pitted Jack Harrison's Knaves versus Aurora. The Knaves, wearing their distinctive yellow jerseys with playing card motifs (jokers), won match and cup by six goals to three. "Shorty" Knox, once more:"Post knocked-in four times against 13 by the Knaves seemed to indicate that the game was closer than the score showed."[15]

It seems to be a case of inaccuracy in front of the goalposts that was the main factor in Aurora's defeat. The Americans offered no excuses after the game, which was deservedly won by the Knaves. Captain Arthur Milborne-Swinnerton-Pilkington, the Irishman Pat Roark and Capt. Errol Prior-Palmer joined Jack Harrison in their successful quest for the massive silver trophy.

"English Team in Paris — A Bad Beating"

That was the title of an article in the *Polo Monthly* describing a match between Hurlingham and a French team at Bagatelle. The occasion was a cup offered by the journal *Paris Soir*. Hurlingham sent a team that was described as a side good enough to win. Apparently,

Paris and polo did not mix well for the English players, because they were soundly defeated by the crushing score of thirteen goals to one.

The Hurlingham team was Sir Ian Walker; Major Noel Leaf, 15th/19th Hussars; John Morrison; and Major Evelyn Fanshawe, Queen's Bays. The winning French team was formed by J. "Teddy" Rasson, Henri Couturié, Hubert de Monbrison, and Robert Gautier.

Rather dryly, the commentary ended with the sentence "Hurlingham must certainly contrive to do better if the invitation is extended again next year."[16]

The previous year the French team had defeated the Queen's Bays 4–3, with a team that included Messrs. Rasson, Monbrison, Couturié and Jules Macaire.

The Hurlingham Club and Polo Spectators

The Hurlingham Club was never known to be overly friendly with the general public, which was more tolerated than welcomed. In 1932, the club decided to stop general admission to Saturday polo games. Such an arbitrary decision provoked some disbelief on the part of polo correspondents and a degree of outrage among spectators. Miss Hilda Harrison, from far away Penzance, wrote the following letter:

> I am distressed to hear that the Hurlingham Polo Committee have decided not to allow the public on Saturday to their ground. This is a terrible blow to lovers of the game. It always seemed to me that the public was most enthusiastic, and it certainly meant a great deal of pleasure to me and my friends. Indeed, the summer without Hurlingham polo is hardly a summer at all. We can't all afford Hurlingham Club fees, and yet may have some claim on consideration, and we are no real offence to the members. I am hoping still for the best.[17]

There is no record of a response to Miss Harrison's letter. Nevertheless, after a period of time, spectators were, once more, admitted to the sacred confines of the number-one polo ground.

Visitors from South America

Sayago, a club in Uruguay, sent a team to England in the summer of 1936. Henry Hugh Grindley, the club's founder and president of the Polo Association of Uruguay; Mrs. Marjorie Lancaster, the first woman player registered in Uruguay; her husband Oliver; and Frank Rauer were the team members.[18] They participated in low-goal tournaments, and Mr. Grindley was on the winning Kirtlington Park team that took the Kirtlington Cup. Arthur Budgett, Air Vice Marshal J.E.A. (later Sir John) Baldwin, and Alan Budgett completed the team.

The Gauchos, a team composed of Robert Loewenstein from Belgium, Hesketh Hughes, Jaime and Jorge O'Farrell, Roberto Cavanagh and Ricardo Santamarina, played some tournaments in the West Country in 1938, based at the West Somerset Polo Club in Dunster Downs, and also at Stoke d'Aberon in Cobham.[19]

Polo in Ireland

A rather unusual situation occurred at Phoenix Park when the All Ireland Polo Club, W. Magee, J. Johnson, J. Martin and Major T.W. Kirkwood, drew five-all with the Freebooters, a British military team composed by Captain Frederick Byass, Colonel Willoughby Norrie, Captain Joshua Chaytor and Captain K. Alexander. An extra seventh chukker was played, with no goals scored. Lady Lingard Goulding presented the trophy to the Freebooters, who held the cup for half a year, then passing the silver to the All Ireland team for the rest of the year. Most likely, lack of pony power was the reason for not drawing the match to a definition. As an aside, the longest official match on record took place in South Africa between the Harrismith and Kokstad clubs in the semifinals of the 1923 Kokstad Tournament. At the end of the regulation seventh chukker, the game was tied at four-all. After the end of the fourteenth chukker darkness fell and the match continued the following day. Gordon Campbell scored the winning goal for Harrismith in the last minute of the twenty-first chukker.[20]

An interesting game took place in the summer of 1938 when a team from Dublin traveled north to play against a side representing the newly formed Ulster Polo Club. The Eire team, a four-goal squad, was: G.V. Malcolmson, zero; H.T. Tyrrell, zero; John A. Leonard, Jr., three; and A. Levins Moore, one, at back. The Northern Ireland team was formed by Captain John Blakiston-Houston, Lt. Col. Samuel McVicker, Major W.J. Arnold and, at back, J.W. Molloy. It was an uneven struggle at the polo ground in Dundonald, the team from Dublin winning the match 13–1.[21]

Polo at the old Nine Acres ground in Phoenix Park saw the Blackbirds, D. McGillycuddy, P. McCann, Maj. Thomas W. "Billy" Kirkwood and H. Tyrrell, take the Irish Fortnightly Cup from the Kestrels, H.J. Irwin, D. Harvey, R. Gill and J. Martin, by four goals to three, with Mr. McCann hitting the winning goal with the last stroke of the game.[22]

The Westchester Cup at Hurlingham, 1936

The usual schedule for the Westchester Cup was for every series to be played after a three-year interval at the holders' home country. However, the economic situation prevalent in England made it impossible for the Hurlingham Polo Committee to launch a challenge in 1933. The next challenge was wired to the U.S. Polo Association to take place in the Olympic year of 1936. Most sportingly, the Americans consented to hold the matches in England. The Hurlingham Club in Fulham, a London suburb, was once more the venue. It had been a lapse of fifteen years since the Westchester Cup had been competed for in England.

The Hurlingham Polo Committee faced some problems in selecting a representative team. A year before the Westchester Cup was held, a Hurlingham team was sent to Long Island to compete in the U.S. Open Championship. The team, composed of Hugh Walford, Percival "Tony" Sanger, Eric Tyrrell-Martin and Humphrey Guinness, was beaten 9–8 in the first tie by Laddie Sanford's Hurricanes.

Captain Michael Ansell replaced Captain "Chicken" Walford in the Monty Waterbury Cup, played on handicaps among the teams participating in the U.S. Open Championship. Things did not go well either in this tournament. A scratch team, Long Island, defeated the Hurlingham squad 16–10, after receiving one goal by handicap from Hurlingham.

In 1936, following a revamping of the squad, the British team that took the field had the benefit of only one practice game playing together. Hesketh Hughes, Gerald Balding, Eric Tyrrell-Martin and Humphrey Guinness, a thirty-one-goal side that matched the American team as far as total handicap. Captain Bryan Fowler and Captain Errol Prior-

Palmer were selected as alternates. Rao Rajah Hanut Singh, the brilliant nine-goaler from India, was unable to play because of a shoulder injury sustained during one of the practice matches.

It was a good team, perhaps the best that could be assembled, with the sterling absence of Captain Pat Roark, the Irishman who is considered the best British player of the interwar period. The Welshman Hesketh Hughes had acquired valuable experience in high-goal polo during a prolonged sojourn in Argentina. Gerald Balding was in the upswing of a successful polo career that would see him reach the pinnacle of a ten-goal handicap rating. Cambridge man Eric Tyrrell-Martin, the team captain, was a nine-goaler, and Captain Humphrey Guinness, the Royal Scots Greys' star back, was in his prime.

Nevertheless, the selected foursome did not enjoy the confidence of the London press corps. Peter Vischer, *Horse & Horseman*'s editor who had traveled to England to report on the series, wrote that the announcement was greeted with catcalls and boos of the London newspapers, which were particularly cruel to Hesketh Hughes, being told in no uncertain terms that he was no polo player.[23]

The Americans planned the journey to England with utmost care. Tommy Hitchcock excused himself from duty because of pressure to remain in his job at Lehman Brothers, the Wall Street brokerage firm. More likely, it was his aversion to playing competitive polo overseas. Four years before, Hitchcock, the undisputed leader of the American international polo team, had declined an invitation to travel to Buenos Aires in order to play in the Argentine Open and in the Cup of the Americas. The International Polo Field at Meadow Brook was his own turf, and that was it.

English-born Winston Guest, by now a seasoned international player, was trusted with the team's captaincy, playing at back. Stewart Iglehart, about to reach a ten-goal handicap, ably filled the number 3 position. The forward slot presented a bit of a problem, because both Michael Phipps and Eric Pedley excelled in that critical position. The decision was made to place there Eric Pedley, while Mike Phipps, a much better number 1 than a number 2, went to the second forward position. In the event, Phipps was far from his best, particularly in the first game. The reserves were Elbridge Gerry and Robert Strawbridge, Jr. Perhaps politics played some role in the selection. All the selected players, with the exception of Californian Eric Pedley, belonged to the Eastern establishment. Of note is that Texan Cecil Smith, already having achieved a 10-goal handicap, and who was playing the London season on Charles Wrightsman's Texas Rangers team with his own ponies, was not invited to be part of the American squad. No reason was given for this notorious omission.

The white-clad American team took the first match 10–9, with a little bit of luck on their side. It was such a close match that either side could easily have been the winner. The American weakness at number 2 turned out not to be a factor of major importance on Hurlingham's number-one ground, because it was considerably shorter than Meadow Brook's International Field. Therefore, Iglehart and Guest, both long hitters, were able to place the ball within Pedley's range. The American number 1 took twenty-four shots at goal in the games, scoring a total of eleven goals, the highest of any player on the field. Mike Phipps had a total of four shots in both games, scoring only once.

Stewart Iglehart was the outstanding player on the American side. He had to do plenty of work because of the sag at number 2, and he also had to protect his own goal to cover Winston Guest's frequent forays upfield. In his international debut, Iglehart rose to the challenge in rare form and showed his admirable style and positional play.

Winston Guest was an important factor in America's victory. His hitting was excellent, long and accurate. However, he paid little attention to the British attacks and was frequently out of position, adding considerably to Iglehart's worries.

The second game was played ten days after the first because of intermittent rains, which made the luscious turf at Hurlingham virtually unplayable. It was another grand match, won by the Americans 8–6 after a terrific battle.

As to the British players, they surprised their supporters and confounded their critics. The players proved beyond any doubt how wrong the critics had been in their pregames dire predictions. Hesketh Hughes, the hardy Welshman rider who had received his polo education in Argentina, amply justified his selection, scoring a total of nine goals, by far the highest of his team. In the first game, Hughes accomplished perfect accuracy in his strikes at the American goal: six shots, six goals. It is sad to record that Hugh Hesketh Hughes, a lieutenant in the Welsh Guards, was killed near Dunkirk in the early stages of World War II.

Both Gerald Balding and Eric Tyrrell-Martin played high-class polo in the middle of the field, where most games are won and lost. Humphrey Guinness was once more the star of the British team, showing his development as a great back since the 1930 contest. His knock-ins were of great length, as good as Winston Guest's, and he also made a great number of saves near his goal. His weakness, if any, was that he allowed himself to ride inferior mounts, in comparison to the rest of the players.

The Americans were quite satisfied with the standard of umpiring offered by Australian Robert Ashton and Captain Hugh Walford as well as the refereeing by Jack Nelson, president of the Argentine Polo Association. Some members of the press objected to a penalty 1—a rarity in international contests—awarded against the English teams. The two umpires consulted with Mr. Nelson who agreed with the call. To his credit the Captain of England, Eric Tyrrell-Martin, agreed with the decision after the game ended. It is with regret that the record shows that Lt. Col. Walford, 17th/21st Lancers, was killed in an airplane crash in Norfolk during World War II.

Although the issue for the Westchester Cup had been decided in only two games, a third match was staged on the Hurlingham ground on June 4. It was intended to be an opportunity for the reserves to show their skill; however, Capt. Bryan Fowler broke a finger two days before the scheduled match and was unable to participate. Ebby Gerry, Pedley, Iglehart and Bobby Strawbridge played for America, and Captain Errol Prior-Palmer was joined by Hughes, Balding and Tyrrell-Martin in a losing effort, 15–9.

Thus, a Westchester Cup series that most observers thought would end in a comfortable success for the American team, turned out to be one of the best ever, and by far the closest and most competitive during the interwar period. It was a noble effort by the British team, worthy of a better result.

The Westchester Cup at Meadow Brook, 1939

Encouraged by the good showing of British players against the American team at Hurlingham, when they were beaten by only very narrow margins, England once more challenged the United States for the Westchester Cup, a trophy that Peter Vischer described as "the most hideous old trophy offered in any sport."[24]

Britain mounted the best possible organization ever. The Hurlingham Polo Committee had a budget of 35,000 sterling to cover the costs, and successfully raised that amount, making it a patriotic duty for British sportsmen to subscribe to the recovery fund. Lord Cowdray was appointed nonplaying captain of the team. The players were sent to California early in the year, with plenty of time to weld themselves together as a unit on the fast American polo grounds at the traditionally fast American pace. In October 1938, approximately eighteen ponies were sent by ship to Long Island, and then by train to California, to acclimatize and get ready for the trial matches at Del Monte.

Major Noel Leaf was sent to Argentina to buy a string of horses, with Hesketh Hughes as an advisor, because of his experience living and playing polo in Argentina. Gerald Balding went to India to borrow all the good ones he could from the stables of the Indian princes. They asked Bob Skene to bring the best he could find in Australia. They combed England's best pony stables.

It did not work out as expected. At the end of the series, out of all ponies played, the Hurlingham Polo Committee had provided eight, Indian princes seven, the Viscount Cowdray had sent out four from his own string, the Duke of Roxburghe three, Gerald Balding and Major Leaf had furnished two each, Bob Skene two, and Ricardo Santamarina, Eric Tyrrell-Martin, and a sporting English lady, Mrs. Marjorie Whitefoord, one pony each.[25] When the critical time came, the British team, short of good mounts, had to buy ponies from the well-known Long Island dealer, Godfrey Preece.

For some unexplained reasons, some of their best players were left out of the final team. The great Irishman Pat Roark, widely thought of as the best British player in the interwar era, and a former ten-goal handicap, was left out. A lack of form was offered as the reason, but his play during the California season was reminiscent of his former glory and raised questions among the polo community. Those questions were never answered because Pat Roark sustained a fatal head injury during a match at Del Monte. Captain Roark had recently married an American socialite, Patsy Hostetter Smith; their son was born a month before Pat Roark died two days after his accident.

Eric Tyrrell-Martin, a nine-goal player, had won high praise for both his leadership and individual play on the 1936 British team; however, he was relieved of his captaincy and acted as an alternate. The accomplished Indian player Hanut Singh, another nine-goaler, was not selected to be on the squad. Nor were any of the great Indian stars persuaded to join the British squad, even though the spectacular Rao Rajah Hanut Singh would have played in 1936 had he not, a few days before the opening match, been injured. Captain Humphrey Guinness, who had played so well at back in 1936, was on military duty in Palestine and could not be spared.

Additionally, the ponies were in two railroad accidents going from California to the East, and two of them died, one being killed outright, the other succumbing to pneumonia. Major Noel Leaf, in charge of the pony string, developed a serious infection, was taken to hospital, and died there. Truly, it seemed a doomed expedition for the British.

For the United States, it was an embarrassment of riches. If the team originally selected, Michael Phipps, Cecil Smith, Stewart Iglehart and Tommy Hitchcock, could not beat any team in the world, there was something very wrong in the handicap ratings. These four superstars were thought to be a perfect team; moreover, there were plenty of players almost as good to take their places. Pete Bostwick, Ebby Gerry, Winston Guest, James Mills, Eric Pedley, Billy Post — the list is interminable. They had reserves of top ponies, all experienced in international contests. They were playing at home, in front of supporting crowds, under conditions they liked. And, they had a tradition of winning, broken but once in the past thirty-five years.

England in America, 1939. Lord Cowdray, his future wife Lady Bridgeman and John Lakin at Del Monte in California, where the English squad prepared for the Westchester Cup series (private collection).

The American team was well mounted, under a formula that required each player to mount himself and have his string ready for action. It is of interest that Tommy Hitchcock had no mounts of his own; Sonny Whitney lent him four ponies, Jock Whitney three, and Raymond Guest and Seymour Knox one pony each.

When the time came to put the American team on the field, it was found that Iglehart, not fully recovered from a gastric malaise, was playing below his best form. It was personally unfortunate for him, but not really serious for the United States' chances, because his announced replacement, Winston Guest, was performing so well in the trial matches that the side was still considered unbeatable. Nevertheless, in the last practice game, Cecil Smith suffered a nasty spill. The great Texan was concussed, and it was felt that he could not play without danger to himself. At the fifty-ninth minute of the eleventh hour, the American team had to be revamped. Michael Phipps stayed at number 1; Tommy Hitchcock, who had not played the demanding and traditionally strong number 2 position in an American team for ten years, moved up to fill the breach. Stewart Iglehart, whose form was improving rapidly, was called back into the lineup, and Winston Guest was inserted at back, a position that he had successfully filled against Argentina in 1928, and in the Westchester matches of 1930 and 1936. It was a formidable combination.

After much debate and argument, the British side was Bob Skene at number 1, Aidan Roark at number 2, team captain Gerald Balding at number 3, and at back, Eric Tyrrell-Martin, again in the good graces of the selection committee.

The day of the scheduled first game, June 4, dawned with rain and bad weather forecast. Members from both teams met and debated for some time before deciding to go ahead with the game. With the heavy ground, it was the polo that failed to live up to international standards. The field's condition did not favor fast play and long hitting. The Americans got out in front, but by the fourth chukker the British came within one goal. In the second half, the American team scored five goals against only two by the visitors, both in the last chukker when the issue was already decided. Hitchcock and Phipps were the high scorers, with four goals each; Guest had two and Iglehart one tally. For Great Britain, Balding and Skene had three goals each, and Roark one.

Neither team made changes for the second match, which was held one week after the initial contest. It was more of the same story as in the first game. Britain stayed close during the first five periods; however, they were able to score only one more goal, again in the last chukker. The final score, 9–4, reflected the American superiority. Tommy Hitchcock closed his outstanding international polo career being the high scorer, with four goals. Mike Phipps scored three goals, Iglehart and Guest, one each. For Britain, Bob Skene had two goals, and Roark and Tyrrell-Martin, one each. Many years later, Bob Skene made the observation that before the start of the series, he was hitting all the penalty shots with great accuracy. When the day of the matches came, Gerald Balding took the penalties, scoring three in the first game and none in the second. Bob Skene commented that had he been allowed to hit the penalties, the matches might have had a different outcome.[26]

Nevertheless, the young Australian's play caught the eyes of spectators and critics alike, who discerned in his performance the sterling qualities that would take him to the top of the game and a place among polo's immortals.

Since the outcome of the Westchester Cup was decided in only two games, an interesting special match was arranged. The visiting officials put up some prizes for a game on handicap against the highest team the United States could assemble. Therefore, Mike Phipps, Cecil Smith, Tommy Hitchcock and Stewart Iglehart, a forty-goal combination, faced Bob Skene, John Lakin, Gerald Balding and Eric Tyrell-Martin. The American team gave ten goals on handicap and was defeated by sixteen goals to fourteen goals. At the end of the fifth chukker the score was 14–13 in favor of the British team, and the crowd expected an American victory. In the last three chukkers the visitors outscored the U.S. team 2–1, displaying the best polo they showed in this country, of which the *USPA Yearbook* said, "The last three periods of this match were as great as polo has seen anywhere."[27]

This historic game was the first one to show a forty-goal team in competitive action since the special match between Meadow Brook — Stoddard, Hitchcock, Webb and Milburn — and Flamingo, held in October 1922.

CHAPTER 13

British Polo Sculptors and Painters

The game of polo has been a rich source of inspiration for many sporting artists. England in particular has been the beneficiary of works produced by gifted sculptors and painters. This chapter will only address the lives and works of British artists—and the occasional foreigner—who depicted scenes and personalities within the polo panorama in the United Kingdom and international contests in America. A detailed list of artists and works would take a whole book to describe.

Cecil Charles Windsor Aldin (1870–1935) was a distinguished English artist best known for his dog subjects, who included polo scenes among his works. His most important polo work is a pastel and watercolor of Velocity, a gray pony ridden by Captain Vivian Lockett in the Westchester Cup.[1] Prints were published by Welbeck under the title *Activity—A Polo Pony* as one of a series of four. The others were *Brains*, showing a bay hunter and foxhounds; *Strength*; *Squire Benyon's Shire Horse*; and *Quality*, a show jumper.

Dull Polo! depicts impressions of a match between British and American Army teams in 1925. It is illustrated in Roy Heron's *The Sporting Art of Cecil Aldin.*[2] Two other of his works are also shown in the book *The Duke of Windsor When Prince of Wales*[3] and two beautiful colored chalks, *A Polo Match in Progress at Dunster Lawns, 1924* and *Polo at Dunster*, with the castle in the background.[4] Finally, *The Colonel* is a watercolor that shows to great advantage Aldin's masterful economy of line and color.

Cecil Alden's economy of line is shown to advantage in *The Colonel*, a nice watercolor (private collection).

George Denholm Armour (1864–1949) was a Scot sporting artist whose horse portraiture could seldom be faulted. Armour was one of the outstanding British artists of his time, together with Lionel Edwards, Gilbert Holiday and Sir Alfred Munnings. In 1913, Armour went to America with the Westchester Cup team and was made an honorary member of the Meadow Brook Club. During his stay on Long Island, Armour painted several scenes with the Westchester Cup as the main subject, including *D. Milburn (U.S. back)*, *A Near-Side Shot by Leslie Cheape*, *Larry Waterbury Scoring*, *Capt. Ritson Making a Run*, *Saving a Goal*, and *Mounted Polo Player*, thought to be the Duke of Westminster, who was the team's sponsor.[5] His best painting from that year is *A Polo Match*, a watercolor and gouache showing the second match of the 1913 International Series. It was offered for sale at Christie's, New York, in 1988.

Wright Barker (1864–1941) was a talented painter of hunting scenes. One of his polo paintings shows Monkey, a gray pony purchased in South Africa by Lt. Col. Reginald Badger; it is shown in his book *A Record of Horses*.[6] Another is the chestnut polo pony Dagmar in an open landscape, illustrated in Sally Mitchell's *Dictionary of British Sporting Artists*.[7]

Carl Ferdinand Bauer (1879–1954) was an Austrian caricaturist of considerable repute who visited England and produced many illustrations for magazines as well as in *Polosport*, the official publication of the Central European Polo Association in Vienna. Among his work depicting English personalities are *Col. H.G.M. Playdell-Railston*; *The Champion of the Much-Feared Snakes*, Major John Dening; *Hurry Up*, Captain James Pierce wearing Baron de Rothschild's Chamois colors; and *Pat*, depicting Captain Charles Roark. All these appeared, along with many other polo caricatures, in the magazine *Polo*, published in Vienna in 1930.

John Alexander Harington Bird (1846–1936) worked in both oil and watercolor, particularly depicting horses. One of his works illustrates the article on polo written by Francis Herbert in *The Encyclopaedia of* Sports.[8]

John Arthur Board (1895–1965) wrote for the *Times* for thirty years about polo, horse shows, real tennis and even golf, when the legendary Bernard Darwin was unavailable. Major Board also illustrated his own books. He not only wrote and painted with grace and style, but he also was a proficient sportsman, reaching the quarterfinals of the golf Amateur Championship, and a keen cricketer. John Board had a natural ability for painting the polo pony at speed and catching the fine points of the game.

Cuthbert Bradley (1861–1943) was an English painter of numerous polo subjects, among them a watercolor titled *County Cup Final Game, July 9 1891*.[9] Other paintings by Bradley are *Ranelagh — Mr. Milburn on Teddy Roosevelt*; *Roehampton Open Challenge Cup*; *Lewis Lacey on Marie Sol*, a mare played in the 1930 Westchester Cup; and the famous *Jupiter*, also owned by Lacey. A prolific painter, his work does not compare with the masters of equestrian art.

W. Smithson Broadhead (1888–1960) painted a portrait of Captain Charles Tremayne, 19th Hussars, in polo gear.[10] Captain Tremayne was the leader of the British team that competed for the 1930 Westchester Cup at Meadow Brook.

Henry Jamyn Brooks (born c. 1865; active 1884–1909) painted the monumental *The Hurlingham Polo Team in Front of the Pavilion, 1890* with a key identifying all but one of the players and spectators.[11] The original work hangs at the Hurlingham Club; several prints were made of this major work.

Cecil Brown's (1868–1929) paintings and bronzes are barely known; however, his work is of the highest quality. Major Brown painted *A Game of Polo* on silk laid on board[12] and *Riding-Off*.[13]

Paul Desmond Brown (1893–1858) and American polo art go together hand in hand. His production of polo drawings and watercolors is immense. His style emphasizes hard-edge lines, with color a secondary adjunct. Paul Brown worked primarily on paper in pencil, pen or ink, crayon, and gouache, although he produced some work in oil. After some tentative beginnings in the late 1920s, mostly in pen and ink, Brown's work reached full maturity with his watercolors in the 1930s. His extensive opus covers most of the main polo events on the East Coast, prominently showing the international competitions for the Westchester Cup and the U.S. Open Championship.

Peter Ronald Buchanan "the Tout" (1870–1950) was a well-known illustrator and caricaturist. *The Ashton Brothers* is reproduced in Major J.N.P. Watson's *The World of Polo.*[14] Other polo players painted by the Tout include Sir Walter Gilbey, Brig. Gen. Henry Tomkinson and Sir Humphrey de Trafford, all as *Racing Characters.*

Heather Budgett (Mrs. John Tylor) is the daughter of Alan Budgett, MFH, polo player and breeder of thoroughbreds. She studied in England with Nigel Harcourt Lees and in Italy with Signorina Nerina Sime, in Florence, one of the most outstanding teachers in Europe. Her works include paintings of horses, dogs and sporting scenes, especially polo, since her husband played at Cowdray Park and Kirtlington and is a past chairman of the Hurlingham Polo Association. Mrs. Tylor works in Conté pencil, watercolor and oil.

George A. Cattley (1896–1978) was a staff instructor at the School of Equitation at Weedon. Cattley painted while in the Army and became a professional painter upon retirement from active duty. He was a competent artist but not in the top rank. His *Polo Lines* is illustrated in Mary Ann Wingfield's *Sport and the Artist.*[15]

Neil Cawthorne (b. 1936) did his sporting works mostly on commission. *The Last Chukka* is reproduced in Watson's *The World of Polo.*[16]

Jean Clagett sculpted a bronze of Julian Hipwood, captain of the English international team for twenty years.[17]

Imogen Collier (op. 1896–1904) was an early member of the National Polo Pony Society who exhibited at the Royal Academy. She bred polo ponies at Foxhams, in Horrabridge, Devon. A painting of a polo pony hangs at the Player's Club in Wellington, Florida. *Fitz,* signed and dated 1896, the property of Edward Sheppard and later of Captain Thomas Fenwick, Royal Horse Guards, is reproduced on plate 31 of *Polo at Home and Abroad.*

Nina Colmore (1889–1973), born Nina Murray, was the wife of Lt. Col. Horace Colmore, Inniskilling Dragoons, an eight-goal handicap player. Travel and painting were her two great interests. A portrait of her husband hangs at Buck's Club in London. Her polo paintings include *Blandford Meg,* a liver chestnut polo pony, the property of Windsor "Mike" Holden White, an American expatriate sponsor of the Polo Cottage team. The painting *At Cowdray Park during Polo Week, 1927* is reproduced in Roger Chatterton-Newman's *Polo at Cowdray.* The picture shows Stringer, the groundsman; Major Vivian Lockett, umpiring on Heave Ho; Willie Quinnell, a stable boy; scoring clerks at a table; a player in Cowdray Park's colors; Bullen, the stud groom; May Queen, a polo pony; and Star Shoot, a hunter. Nina Colmore is considered one of the outstanding woman sporting painters of all time.

George Couper (op. late 19th–early 20th cent.) was a lieutenant in the Royal Navy and a talented amateur artist who painted sporting scenes wherever he was around the world. Couper covered polo in Argentina and Vancouver, bull fighting in Peru, and horse races in Montevideo, Hong Kong and Sydney. Most of his sketches were in grisaille, pen and ink, with colored washes.

Susan Crawford was raised at a farm in Haddington, near the Firth of Forth. Her father was a racehorse trainer in Scotland. Her commissions include several by members of the Royal Family. Her polo watercolors include *Two Bays Riding-Off, The Winning Hit, Good Swing,* and *The Sultan of Brunei.*

Joseph E. Crawhall (1861–1913) was the son of the Lord Mayor of Newcastle. During a journey to Tangier, he met George Armour and the two became good friends; for two years they had a racing stud in England. He was an outstanding horseman who rode to hounds with the York and Ainsty, the Sinnington and the Middleton's. Crawhall is one of the most important painters of the twentieth century. His polo works in include *The Polo Player*, *Polo Pony* and *Polo Ball on Toast*.

Terence Tenison Cuneo (1907–1996) achieved early fame painting automobile races, such as the Twenty-Four Hours of Le Mans, and the Coupe de L'Auto. His work covered a wide range of sporting subjects, such as "The F.A. Challenge Cup Final" between Burnley and Tottenham Hotspurs at Wembley, aeroplanes, equestrian sports, wild animals and ceremonial pictures. The famous mouse that appears inconspicuously placed in many of his paintings gave Cuneo the sobriquet of "the Mouseman."[18]

Terence Cuneo's polo paintings include *Polo Lines, Cirencester 1972*, of which many prints have been made; *Polo*; and the spectacular *The Centenary of the First Polo Match, June 28, 1970*.[19]

Juliet Cursham sculpted several polo bronzes, among them *Near-side Backhand*, *Goal Shot*, *Off-side Backhand*, *Quick Change*, *Strong Ride-off*, and *Spoiling the Backhand*.[20] A polo player and rider to hounds, Juliet Cursham brings to her bronzes a notable quality of motion.

Henry Cotterill Deykin (1905–1989), a portrait and landscape artist, painted *Polo at Cowdray Park, Sussex. Cowdray Park Defeat Henley 6.5 to 9, 27th August 1951*.[21] The Henley team included Major Archie David, Edmund Roark, Squadron Leader Alan Roberts and the Maharajah of Jaipur. Cowdray had Commander P. Howes, RN; Lord Cowdray; Charles Smith-Ryland; and Lt. Col. Peter Dollar. This work is one of the few paintings of English polo in the 1950s.

H.B. Dickinson painted *Lord Wavertree (Formerly Colonel William Hall-Walker) on First, a Polo Pony*. Lord Wavertree of Delamere was one of the founders of the Barton Polo Club in 1889. This painting hangs in the Walker Art Gallery in Liverpool.

George Earl (op. 1864–1943) was a painter of sporting and Highland scenes; however in 1880 he exhibited at the Royal Academy his monumental work *Polo Match at Hurlingham between the Royal Horse Guards (The Blues) and the Monmouthshire Team, July 7th, 1877*. Many prints have been published of this outstanding picture.[22]

Lionel Dalhousie Robertson Edwards (1878–1966) was a sporting English artist of the first rank. Watercolor was his favorite medium, although later in life he used oils frequently. His work was very sensitive, showing a superb understanding of horses and a great ability to paint fine landscapes and skies. Edwards painted *The Westchester Cup: America v. England, Hurlingham 1909*, a depiction of the Big Four in England. Other works include *Polo — An Ounce of Blood Is Worth a Pound of Bone*, *A Run Down the Boards*, *The Winning Goal* and *Riding-Off*.

A watercolor depicting the Duke of Edinburgh playing at Guards Polo Club and a similar work showing Lord Cowdray at his own Cowdray Park are two of the best polo paintings by the hand of Lionel Edwards. Another high-quality painting is *The Polo Match, Ivy Lodge, Cirencester Park*, oil on canvas commissioned in 1957 by Ian Hunt to commemorate a three-season unbeaten run. The players wearing blue shirts were members of the Fernham team: Michael Eveleigh on Garza; in the center, Ian Hunt on Joanina; and the third player depicts Brian Bethell on Cola.

Wilson Ellsworth (op. 1930s) painted a scene of the 1930 Westchester Cup at Meadow Brook, showing Winston Guest for America and Lewis Lacey for England. It appeared on the cover of the September 1933 edition of *Polo* magazine.

A polo game in the early twentieth century depicted by Lionel Edwards, signed and dated 1904. Although helmets had become mandatory, many players eschewed their use (private collection).

George Algernon Fothergill (b. 1868) signed many of his works GAF. A multitalented individual, Fothergill was an Uppingham and Edinburgh University man, a physician, writer, amateur archeologist, tennis player and foxhunter. Two of his polo caricatures for *Vanity Fair* included officers in the Inniskilling Dragoons: *I Say* depicts Lt. Neil Haig and *Descended from Edward Longshanks* represents Major Michael Rimington. Both officers would reach general rank.

Another drawing is *A Polo Back — Jack Drybrough on Magic Spell*.[23] Magic Spell was described as a remarkable performer under the punishing weight it had to carry.

Terence Gilbert (b. 1946) painted an oil of the 1987 Coronation Cup, offered for sale at Sotheby's, New York, in 1980, and a charcoal of Howard Hipwood.

Godfrey Douglas Giles (1857–1941), a retired major in the Indian Army, painted *Polo at Hurlingham*, of which many prints have been published.[24]

Ernest-Gustave Girardot (1860–1903) was a French portraitist who lived in London. Girardot painted an oil of Walter Jones, the Rugby team's number 1, signed and dated 1902. Among his sitters was William Gladstone, the Liberal Party prime minister.

Vincent Haddelsey (b. 1929) is a naive painter with a large opus of English countryside scenes. A polo player himself, his pictures of the game include *Polo Match* on the cover of the American magazine *Polo*; *Country Polo*; *Polo at Dunster*, that favorite target of polo artists; *Taunton Vale Polo Club*; *Polo at Bagatelle*; and *Polo*, set in Canada where Haddelsey lived for many years. The latter work depicts players at his own Southlands Polo Club.

Alfred Grenfell Haigh (1870–1963) painted several polo ponies, among them *Dainty and Girton Girl*, two of Lt. Col. Reginald Badger best ponies; *Silvery II, Silver Queen and Her Foal*, and *Silverdale Aquatint*, all ponies the property of Mr. Herbert Bright.[25]

Priscilla Hann (b. 1943), painter and sculptor, cast a series of nine bronzes of excellent quality simply titled *Polo*.[26]

Herbert Haseltine (1877–1962) is considered the best animalier of the twentieth century. Herbert Haseltine was one of the first polo players in Italy. Then he moved to Paris, where his mentor Aimé Morot encouraged him to send one of his works to the Paris Salon. The result was that his first attempt at sculpture, *Riding-Off*, received an honorable mention. Seven casts were made; there is one at Hurlingham Club in Fulham. Another similar bronze is *Polo*, of which examples were cast in 1907 and 1908.

The Meadow Brook Team was commissioned by Harry Payne Whitney and cast in 1911. This, the most important bronze in polo, shows Devereux Milburn on the Roan Mare, followed by Harry Payne Whitney on Cottontail, Larry Waterbury on Little Mary and Monte Waterbury on Cobnut. An example was presented to the Hurlingham Club, and it is in the entrance hall.

In 1921, the Royal Agricultural Show inspired a series of British Champion Animals. The polo pony selected by Haseltine as a model was Perfection, a heavyweight pony bred in Ireland, owned by Major John Harrison, a superb polo pony that carried Captain Henry Tomkinson in the Westchester Cup.

Herbert Haseltine also modeled the individual prizes for the 1921 and 1924 Westchester Cup contests, and an individual bronze of the magnificent mare Ralla, bred in Ireland like so many outstanding polo ponies.

Michael Heseltine (b. 1961) painted a watercolor signed and dated 1988, titled *Guards Polo, Smith's Lawn, Windsor*.[27]

Charles Gilbert Joseph Holiday (1879–1937) was one of the outstanding sporting artists of the twentieth century. His contemporary Lionel Edwards said of him, "No one can, or ever could, paint a horse in action better than Gilbert could."[28]

His polo masterpiece is *The 1936 Westchester Cup*, which hangs at the Hurlingham Club. The draftsmanship is perfect; the ponies are magnificent. A goal has just been scored, emphatically signaled by the flag person, wearing a silk long coat. It is likely the Americans have scored the goal: the British players are near the goalposts, and an American player is raising his mallet in jubilation. The old Hurlingham grandstand appears in the background, with three flags on top of the roof. Six of the eight players can be identified with certainty. The British back, Lt. Col. Humphrey Guinness, is to the right, wearing his blue pith helmet. Gerald Balding, the number 2, is returning to the center of the field, while Eric Tyrrell-Martin is next to Guinness; both can be identified by their respective helmets, a blue polo cap and a number 2 on Balding's shirt and a white pith helmet worn by Tyrrell-Martin. Further back, Hesketh Hughes is side by side with Winston Guest; the latter wears his trademark blue polo cap. Stewart Iglehart is between Humphrey Guinness and the American player who has scored a goal. Iglehart was the only American to wear long sleeves. The two other American players, Eric Pedley and Mike Phipps, cannot be identified with certainty.[29]

Other polo paintings by Gilbert Holiday include *The Polo Meet*, an outstanding work which depicts a scene of a polo game about to begin. The central figure is an elegant woman in a colorful dress, escorted by an older man with the appearance of a typical military gentleman. They are greeting a polo player holding a gray pony. The background shows the preparatives before a game: players chatting, grooms holding ponies and impeccably dressed spectators in a mixed crowd.

Polo at Hurlingham, *After the Ball*, *A Game of Polo*, *Roehampton* and an interesting cartoon, *Polo at Eltham*, showing a practice match at the Royal Artillery ground in Avery Hill, Eltham, between the 1921 American international team and the Gunners, are others of Gilbert Holiday's polo paintings.[30]

Thomas Ivester-Lloyd (1873–1942) was a self-taught painter celebrated for his high-quality pictures of horse, hounds and beagles. Ivester-Lloyd did not exhibit his work, most of which is in private collections. One of his few polo paintings is *Polo*, a nice watercolor showing plenty of action.

Adrian Jones (1845–1938) painted some fine horse portraits but is better known as a gifted sculptor. *Hurlingham: Nimble, Cicely, Dynamite and Lady Jane* is at the Walker Art Gallery in Liverpool. In 1894, Jones sculpted *Polo Player*, a unique bronze in the artist's family's possession.[31]

George Goodwin Kilburne, Jr. (1863–1938), produced work of high quality and his horses are faithful representations of the real thing. His only known polo painting is *The Hunt Cup at Ranelagh*.[32] That tournament was taken by the Pytchley, with Graham McIvor, Captain Gordon Renton, Walter Buckmaster and the Comte Jean de Madré.

John Gregory King (b. 1929) is an English painter who studied with Lionel Edwards and was one of the founders of the Society of Equestrian Artists. John King is on the forefront of British sporting artists. He painted *Smith's Lawn* depicting the match of Young England versus Young America at Guards Polo Club in Windsor on 5 August 1972. The central figure is Prince Charles, followed closely by Benjy Toda. As an aside, the game was won 5–4 by the Young America team, on a goal by Red Armour in overtime. Other works by this artist include *Polo Tidworth 1966* and *The Warwickshire Cup 1986 at Cirencester Polo Club*.

Thomas Sherwood La Fontaine (1915–2007) painted subjects mostly on commission, and his works are in private collections all over the world. La Fontaine spent much time in Gloucestershire and made Cirencester Park his favorite place for polo paintings. His portraiture of humans, dogs and horses is of the highest quality and much sought after. One of his works depicts Harry Cushing IV in front of the goalposts while playing in Rome, where he was an American expatriate.

Edward Longueville (1877–1965) had an interesting life as a painter, soldier and sportsman. He was commissioned into the Coldstream Guards from Sandhurst and learned to play polo and drive a coach from horse dealer John Heatherington, on a ground in Cricklewood. At the same time, he was taking painting lessons from Charles Lutyens, the celebrated architect Edwin Lutyens' father. During the Boer War, Longueville formed a polo club at Naauport and found time to hunt a pack after stein buck. Back in England, he was manager of the Brigade of Guards Polo Club, where he played for his regiment, usually at number 1. Invalided during the Great War, Longueville retired from the service because of wounds. However, he commanded Home Guard Units in World War II and was MFH of the Radnorshire and West Hereford for more than thirty years. A son, John, was killed in action in 1944. Major Longueville privately wrote his memoirs, but the manuscript was never published.

A very good portrait of Czar, a polo pony owned by the 7th Hussars regimental team, was auctioned at Sotheby's in 1988.

Henry Frederick Lucas-Lucas (1848–1943) was a prolific English painter based in Rugby. Many ponies that played in the Westchester Cup matches were painted by Lucas-

Lucas. Among them are Charmer, a bay mare the property of Walter Jones, My Girl, a brown mare played by Charles Miller; Luna, a bay mare played by George Miller; and Blue Sleeve, a gray mare owned and played by Pat Nickalls in the 1909 contest. Lucas-Lucas was one of the artists who tried his hand in the Westchester Cup; his painting *England versus America at Hurlingham* is dated 1921 and was offered for sale by Sotheby's.[33] Lucas-Lucas also painted Sir Humphrey de Trafford's polo ponies with the Old Ground Pavilion at Ranelagh as the backdrop; the ponies are Rugby, Sister Grey, Peter, Grey Legs and Rasper. Another painting of Sir Henry's ponies shows Piper, Miss Edge, Redskin, Gold and Dainty, all famous in their day.

A monumental picture is *A Game of Polo at Rugby*, of which many prints have been made. It shows Sir Humphrey de Trafford on The General, Comte de Madré on Taffy, Charles Miller (umpire) on My Girl, Morres Nickalls on Lucilla, George Miller on Billy, Keith Marsham on Tom Tiddler, Walter Jones on Luna, Lord Shrewsbury on Conceit and Pat Nickalls on Blue Sleeve.

Polo at Rugby depicts the 1893 August Open Tournament, won by Rugby 8–2 over the 14th Hussars. The Rugby team players are George Miller, Ronald Chaplin, Ted Miller and John Reid Walker; the Hussars are Robert Stephens, William Eley, Captain Cyril Stacey and Captain James Richardson.

Charles Edward Michael Lyne (1912–1989), a talented painter of sporting scenes, reminiscent of Lionel Edwards, illustrated *Polo Demands Co-ordination of Hand and Leg*, a full-page drawing in Lt. Col. Sidney Goldschmidt's *Skilled Horsemanship*.

Kenneth Stevens MacIntire (1891–1979) moved from Wiscasset, Maine, to California, eventually to Sonoma County. His production of polo paintings, totaling 38 in all, was purchased by a California collector who in turn sold the works to two brothers in Rhode Island. The collection was then dispersed. The famous Irishman Pat Roark was one of his sitters.

Lorne McKean, a contemporary artist, sculpted bronzes of HRH the Duke of Edinburgh on one his favorite ponies, Porteño, which was commissioned by HM the Queen; *Three Polo Players*; *Riding-Off*, a polo group; and a set of polo players, numbered one to three.

Phyllida Meacham was born in Kenya. Among her works are *Polo* in an edition of ten bronzes; *Polo Group*, of which there are nine casts; and *The Long Ball*.[34]

Sir Alfred Munnings (1878–1959) is one of the great masters of equestrian art. He worked mostly in oils but also produced watercolors. Munnings was a controversial president of the Royal Academy because of his strong dislike of modern art. His polo paintings include *Brigade-Major Geoffrey Brooke*, a polo player well known for his *Horse-Sense and Horsemanship of To-Day*. *Making a Polo Ground* shows Frederick Prince's polo grounds at Pride's Crossing in Massachusetts under construction. The celebrated *Devereux Milburn, the American Polo Player, Changing Ponies* is one of the outstanding paintings in the world of polo. Several prints were made of this painting, which originally was in the Milburn home and is now in a private collection. Two U.S. Polo Association chairmen sat for Munnings: Louis Stoddard and Robert Strawbridge, Jr.

Another painting is *W. Riley-Smith Changing Ponies*. Mr. Riley Smith, founder of the Toulston Polo Club in Yorkshire, is portrayed seated on a polo pony while his groom stands by holding another pony.

Stella Mynors (op. 1920–1945) was a painter of equestrian subjects, specially hunting. She also painted *The Earl of Londesborough on the Polo Field*, in mixed media. The work of art was offered for sale by Bonhams in 1988.

Basil Nightingale (1864–1940) achieved quite a reputation as a horseman and produced paintings of considerable quality, mainly depicting foxhunting scenes. There is a beautiful watercolor titled *C.C. Ellison on Snowstorm*, dated 1913. Charles Chetwynd Ellison was a four-goal handicap player at the Middlewood Polo Club in Yorkshire, whose colors, dark blue and light blue quartered, he is wearing in this painting. There is no information about this polo pony; however, there is a photograph of Mr. Ellison on Snowstorm in *Polo and Coaching*.[35]

M.F. Nuttall (fl. c. 1900) painted "Between Chukkers," oil on canvas, signed and dated 1899. The setting is the number-one ground at Hurlingham Club, near the chestnuts' goal. There is a print of this work at the Hurlingham Club; the original painting is in a private collection.

John Oldfield (b. 1918) was commissioned from Sandhurst into the Green Howards and retired as a brigadier. Among his polo painting are three watercolors, *Pony Lines — Rhinefield*, *Polo Sketch — Smith's Lawn* and *Rhinefield — Polo*, all from the 1980s.

Amy Oxenbould (b. 1921) sculpted some famous horses such as Mill Reef, Tyro and Sea Pigeon. Her polo bronzes are of superb quality and include *Off-side Forehand* and *Near-side Backhander*. Both rider and mount showed perfect form and balance. Her bronzes were produced in limited editions only.

Amy Oxenbould sculpted this bronze that shows a perfect near-side backhander at the top of the swing (private collection).

George Paice (1854–1925) was a sporting artist who exhibited at the Royal Academy. His many polo paintings include *Marsh Mallow*, a bay polo pony by a polo ground, at the Walker Art Gallery, Liverpool; *Helen*, a polo pony the property of Lt. Col. Leopold Jenner; Sir Alfred Rawlinson on Surf Beauty; and *Bath Bun*, a polo pony in front of the sideboards of a polo field.

Henry Powell Palfrey (1830–1902) was a Welsh painter who became a full-time equestrian artist. A painting of Sandiway, the famous polo pony stallion owned by Sir Walter Gilbey, Palfrey's patron, is illustrated in T.F. Dale's *Riding and Polo Ponies*.[36]

James Lynwood Palmer (1868–1941) painted a portrait of Mary Morrison and Snow, two of General Beauvoir de Lisle's polo ponies, illustrated in his *Reminiscences of Sport and War*.[37] It is said that Rudyard Kipling got his idea for *The Maltese Cat* after watching Mary Morrison perform on the Lucknow polo ground. Snow was De Lisle's second-best pony and went to stud in Australia.

Gill Parker, a contemporary artist, is an experienced horsewoman who has had solo exhibitions at Sladmore Gallery in London. Her polo bronzes, all limited editions of nine, are numbered *Polo I* to *Polo VII*. A bronze of *Polo I* was selected as the prize for the Tattersall Trophy.[38]

Charlie Johnson Payne "Snaffles" (1894–1967) produced a large number of sporting and hunting prints. His works on polo include *Sport in the Shiny* and *Carpet Beaters v. Bob-*

bery Wallahs, two of the most famous polo prints. *The 5th Lancers, 1907*, watercolor and gouache, depicts Capt. James Jardine, Captain McTaggart, Mr. Montefiore, Major Browne-Clayton and Captain Chance, plus Sandy, a little black terrier carrying a polo ball. *The Westchester Cup, England versus America, 1921*, is a pencil and watercolor depicting the action at the Hurlingham Club.[39] *Corner Boy*, shows Captain Alexander's polo pony in his old age dreaming of glories past. Two other works by Snaffles are *Polo at Aldershot — Impressions of the First Cavalry Brigade* and *Polo at Hurlingham — Some Impressions at the Inter-Regimental Final*.

Walter Roche (op. 1881–1911) is thought to be Irish and was based in London, where he submitted bronzes to the Royal Academy, the Walker Art Gallery and the London Salon. His bronzes are quite scarce and of surprising quality from someone about whom so little is known. His *Polo Player*, signed W. Roche, inscribed Coalbrookdale — the foundry — and dated 1882, was exhibited that year at the Royal Academy. There is a contemporary casting of nine examples, a half inch taller than the original.

George Derville Rowlandson's (1861–1930) artistic productions consist mostly of equestrian or military themes. His polo paintings include a pair of *Games of Polo, Red v. Whites and Light Blue v. Dark Blue*, at the Museum of Polo in Lake Worth, Florida; *Breaking Through*, the Westchester Cup final game in 1902; *A Try at Goal*, on the Ranelagh field; and *The Game*, oil on canvas, in a private collection.

Heather St. Clair-Davis (1937–1999) grew up in the Cotswolds and became a proficient horsewoman. She immigrated to America and settled at a farm in Vermont, where she painted high-quality equestrian paintings. Her polo subjects are not identified; some of the titles are *The Referee*, *Full Tilt*, *Waiting Their Turn* and *The Players*.

Marcia de Savory, a contemporary artist, sculpted a bronze of Lord Patrick Beresford on Amberjack. This horse was twice Best Polo Pony at the Windsor Show.

Charles Walter Simpson (1885–1971) was destined for the Army; however, a riding accident while young prevented him from starting a military career and he became an artist. His works include *HRH the Duke of Windsor, When Prince of Wales, Playing Polo at Cowdray*. This painting, reproduced in *Sport and the Artist*, actually depicts Hurlingham Club's number-one ground, showing in the background the unmistakable stand with its large clock.[40] Other works are *The Final of the Buenos Aires Cup, 1928* in which Templeton defeated Scopwick 11–6½. The brothers Raymond and Winston Guest, their father the Hon. Frederick Guest, and Lewis Lacey were on the winning team. There is also a nice oil painting of a polo game, untitled and dating back to circa 1930, of which copies were made in China. The original was sold at auction in New York and now resides in a private collection.

Geoffrey Snell, a contemporary artist, sculpted a bronze titled *After the Game* depicting Bagorita, a polo pony the property of the international player Paul Withers. Charles Heidsieck commissioned this piece as the trophy for the Warwickshire Cup in 1976. Bagorita was Best Playing Pony in the 1975 Warwickshire Cup.

Maurice Tulloch (1894–1974) was a talented artist who took up serious painting after retiring from the Army. Tulloch illustrated J.K. Stanford's *Last Chukker*, an enthralling tale of a polo-playing police officer in Burma, and some of his drawings have appeared in several HPA Yearbooks. Sally Mitchell wrote of Maurice Tulloch, "Although his work is quite rare, he is to be ranked amongst the best artists of his period."[41] Perhaps his best polo painting is a depiction of a game at Guards Polo Club.

Joan Wankyln, a contemporary artist who was raised in Cheltenham, painted *Smith's Lawn, 1967, Windsor No. 2 Ground — Windsor v. Cholmondeley*, and a large watercolor, *Polo* *at Windsor, 1967*. This work shows all eight players and the two umpires. From left to right, the Prince of Wales on a gray pony; Hanut Singh, one of the umpires; Micky Moseley; the Duke of Edinburgh; the Earl of Brecknock; Sebastian de Ferrante; James Withycombe; the Marquess of Waterford; John Macdonald-Buchanan; and Mathwin Maunder, the umpire. Many prints have been made of this painting, which illustrates the dust jacket of Major J.N.P. Watson's *The World of Polo*.

Other works include *The Chairman's Cup — 1967*, depicting HRH Prince Philip playing for Windsor Park versus Cholmondeley, a view from the pony lines.

Susan Anne Clare Whitcombe (b. 1957) has shown natural talent as an equestrian artist. She is also a competent horsewoman, having played polo and ridden show jumping, hunting, dressage, and has an amateur jockey license. Her polo works include *Lagos Polo Ground, Pony Lines, The Coronation Cup, 1979* and *Pony Lines, Epsikopi*.

William Woodhouse (1857–1939) painted animals, particularly dogs and game, and occasionally sporting subjects. *A Saddled Polo Pony with Stables Beyond*, was in the Pilkington Collection. It depicts a polo pony circa 1900, fully saddled, with no martingale and an old polo stick on the ground.

Richard Caton Woodville (1856–1927) worked in black and white for *The Illustrated London News* but turned to oil painting in the 1890s. His often reproduced work *Under Spotlight at Ranelagh* illustrates the famous night game at the Ranelagh Club.

George Wright (1856–1942) exhibited at the Royal Academy. His polo paintings dated from 1901 on, when he moved to Rugby, the main provincial center of polo. His works include *Washing Down Polo Ponies, Port Meadow, Oxford*,[42] *At the Stables, Before the Start of the Match*, *A Hard Chukka* and *Polo Match*, showing two players and their mounts falling on the ground.

Washing Down Polo Ponies, Port Meadow, Oxfordshire. Oil on canvas, George Wright, exhibited at the Royal Academy in 1922. Port Meadow was one of the grounds for the Oxford University team (private collection).

Gilbert Scott Wright (1880–1958), the younger brother of George Wright, painted *A Head Study of a Polo Pony and a Pony with Rider Up Coming onto the Field*, auctioned at Christie's New York in 1985.

Interlude II: 1939–1945

There was no polo in England during the Second World War. The celebrated Ivy Lodge ground at Cirencester was plowed up for crops, and so was part of the Hurlingham Club grounds. Horses and players were gone, engaged in a struggle for survival.

Three polo players were awarded the Victoria Cross, two of them posthumously.

Captain Bernard Warburton-Lee was a six-goal player while stationed in Malta and played on the Royal Navy team against the Army. In April 1940, he led the 2nd Destroyer Flotilla into the Narvik Fjord in Northern Norway, encountering larger German destroyers. Warburton-Lee's force was outgunned and outnumbered. During the ensuing battle, his flagship, HMS *Hardy*, was heavily damaged and was beached. Capt. B.A.W. Warburton-Lee, RN, died of his wounds. A few days later, Winston Churchill, First Lord of the Admiralty, sent the battleship HMS *Warspite* to Narvik, and all the German destroyers were sunk or scuttled by their crews.[1]

Lt. Col. Geoffrey Keyes, Royal Scots Greys, was awarded the Victoria Cross after the "Rommel Raid" in North Africa, in November 1941. A party of Commandos was sent in two submarines two hundred miles behind the front line to capture or eliminate General Erwin Rommel. During the skirmish, Keyes, reputed to be the youngest colonel in the British Army, and four Germans, were killed. When Admiral Roger Keyes mentioned to Winston Churchill that he hoped that Rommel had been killed, the prime minister answered, "I would far rather have Geoffrey alive than Rommel dead."[2]

Brig. Gen. John Charles Campbell, Royal Horse Artillery, won the Victoria Cross in the battle of Sidi Rezegh in November 1941. The Australian writer Alan Moorehead penned these lines: "They say that Campbell won the V.C. half a dozen times that day. The men loved this Elizabethan figure. He was the reality of all the pirate yarns and tales of high adventure, and in the extremes of fear and courage of the battle he had only courage. He went laughing into the fighting."[3]

"Jock" Campbell was a six-goal handicap player, and a three-time winner of the Inter-Regimental Tournament. While a major general in command of the 7th Armoured Division, he was killed in February 1942 when his vehicle skidded and overturned on a tarmac road near Halfaya.

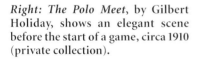

Sir Humphrey de Trafford owned one of the best polo pony strings. Piper, Miss Edge, Redskin, Gold, and Dainty, painted by Henry Lucas-Lucas (private collection).

Right: The Polo Meet, by Gilbert Holiday, shows an elegant scene before the start of a game, circa 1910 (private collection).

C1

Top: George Armour painted the 1913 Westchester Cup. The American player in white (foreground) is Lawrence Waterbury, identified by his moustache. The British player hitting a backhander is their number 3, Captain Jerry Ritson. The British player (background left) is Frederick Freake. This can be identified as the second game of the series because Freake played instead of Noel Edwards and was the only British player to wear a polo cap. The British player on the white pony (center background) is probably Leslie Cheape (private collection). *Above: C.C. Ellison on Snowstorm*, watercolor heightened with body color, dated 1913, by Basil Nightingale. Charles Chetwyn Ellison was a well-known player, shown wearing the colors of the Middlewood Polo Club in Yorkshire (private collection).

Thomas La Fontaine found the Cirencester Park Polo Club a perfect setting for his polo paintings (private collection).

Left: Blandford Meg, a liver chestnut pony, the property of Mike Holden White, considered one of the top ponies in England. Signed and dated, "N. Colmore '63" (private collection). *Right:* George Milford Haven offers a sip to Kinta in celebration of the Queen's Cup victory in 1988 (courtesy Mike Roberts).

Left: Claire Tomlinson at the top of an offside swing. Her contributions to English polo as a player, coach, mentor and reformer are immense.

Below: Team captains Cameron Walton Masters for Oxford, and Emma Tomlinson for Cambridge, shown here in the 1995 Varsity match, continued the tradition started in 1878 by Audley Miles, Brasenose, and William Ellis, Trinity Hall (courtesy Mike Roberts).

Bottom: Peter Grace, at right, immigrated from New Zealand and started the Rangitiki Polo Club that evolved into the Ascot Park Polo Club and training center. The four daughters of Peter and Elisabeth play polo. Janey, Pippa, Tor and Katie became known as "the Four Graces." Victoria (Tor) is one of England's top female players and Pippa is the main force in the International Women's Polo Association (courtesy Peter Grace).

Left: From Argentina to Rutland: La Ema, with Tony Emerson, Gus Prentice, Mark Emerson and Will Emerson, took the Assam Cup, a trophy that dates back to 1897 (courtesy G.D.A. Emerson, Esq.). *Right:* Nicholas Colquhoun-Denvers, the guiding light at Ham Polo Club and dedicated polo memorabilia collector, is chairman of the Hurlingham Polo Association.

Left: HM Queen Elizabeth II, flanked by players Lord Charles Beresford (left) and Adrian Wade (right), directs traffic during the trophy presentation of the Coronation Cup in 1994. M. Arnaud Bamberger (dark suit) is at center (courtesy Mike Roberts).

Left to right, Major Christopher Hanbury, Douglas Brown and Nigel à Brassard, three personalities in British polo, at Cirencester Park. Courtenay is a team sponsored by Mr. à Brassard.

Two Continental patrons of polo in England, Hubert Perrodo for Labegorce and Urs Schwarzenbach for Black Bears, playing in the 1997 Prince Philip Trophy (courtesy Mike Roberts).

Above: The winners of the Women's World Cup at Ascot Park: Claire Tomlinson, Milly Scott, Sue Hodgson and Emma Tomlinson (Nicky Randall photograph, courtesy Mrs. Sue Hodgson Landis). *Left:* Eight-goaler Henry Brett is one of the long line of captains of England dating back to John Watson (courtesy Mrs. Hugh Brett). *Below:* Max Gottschalk, Mariano González, Ignacio Novillo Astrada and Ignatius du Plessis took the Warwickshire Cup in 2008 for Les Lions.

Emlor was the winner of the 2009 Warwickshire Cup: Spencer McCarthy, Joaquín Pittaluga, Luke Tomlinson and Ignacio Gonzalez were the team's members.

Queen Elizabeth II presents a trophy to Facundo Pieres. Colonel Paul Belcher, Guards Polo Club's chairman, is bareheaded in the center (courtesy Mike Roberts).

PART III

Gentlemen and Players, 1947–1985

CHAPTER 14

Lord Cowdray Saves the Day for England

The Hurlingham Polo Association came into being as the result of the merger of the County Polo Association and the Hurlingham Club Polo Committee in 1949. Lord John Cowdray was elected chairman, a position he would hold with great distinction until his voluntary retirement in 1967.

The war was over; nevertheless, polo in London became a casualty. The two polo grounds at Hurlingham fell victims to compulsory purchasing by the London City Council and the Fulham Borough Council. The Roehampton Club lost one ground to make room for the golfers, and polo was restricted to a fortnight in the month of July. This brief respite lasted until 1956. The third London big polo club, Ranelagh, had gone under in 1939.

Ham Polo Club

Not everything polo was lost in London, because one, if not the first, club to resume polo in England — perhaps as early as 1946 — was Ham Polo Club, the same club that had been founded in 1926 as Ham Common. Major John Board wrote,

> The first club to begin playing again when the war ended was Ham and for that reason alone its fame should not be allowed to dim. Since 1946 it has had vicissitudes, not the least of which has been constant changes of ground. Two were taken for building, that down toward the river near Ham House, where it played last year, was not very satisfactory, but better than nothing.[1]

William "Billy" Walsh was the prime mover in the revival of the game in London, being able to assemble some thirty ponies at the Equestrian Centre. Permission was secured to use a field in Richmond Park, between Ham Gate and Sudbrook Park, and play has been carried on without interruptions ever since.

Nicholas Colquhoun-Denvers, chairman of the Ham Polo Club, writes,

> In 1936 Capt. Tom Brigg, owner of the Equestrian Centre at Ham Gate and a member of the Swaine Adeney Brigg family, invited Billy (Walsh) to run his stables and teach polo there. Three years later he joined the cavalry and, after his Army service, returned to Ham to find that Capt. Brigg had died and that the Equestrian Centre was on the market. Using his gratuity, he bought the stables and revived Ham Polo Club under HPA rules. Indeed, he may be ranked — together with the late Lord Cowdray and Arthur Lucas — as being one of a trio to whom English polo will forever be indebted. The first post-war English tournament was held at Roehampton in 1947 and, appropriately, Ham carried off the premier trophy, the Roehampton Cup which, after many vicissitudes, has now found a permanent home at Ham. Three years later a field adjoining

Ham House, the magnificent Jacobean "sleeping beauty" seat of the Dysarts, now in National Trust keeping, was used for matches.[2]

Before the war, Captain Brigg had played on Johnny Traill's team the Traillers, with Jimmy and Jack Traill. Flight Lieutenant James Robert Traill, RAFVR, a winner of the National Handicap Tournament in Argentina, was shot down by friendly fire while escorting a convoy in the North Atlantic in 1942. Jack Traill went on to play for England at Palermo in 1949.

In 1954, a Ham team took the Harrison Cup at Cowdray Park, defeating Barton Abbey by 4 goals to 2½. Another significant event was the Archie David Cup, which was taken by another Ham team led by Jack Williams.

Polo at Cowdray Park

The provincial clubs also moved on to pick up the pieces and resuscitate the game in England. It was thought that the Rugby Polo Club in Warwickshire would recover the pre-eminence it had acquired from earlier days; however, it was not to be. Rugby enjoyed but one brief season in 1947.

According to an article in *Polo Quarterly International*, in May of 1946 a polo game was held at New Park Farm in Brockenhurst.[3]

Contemporary reports indicate that polo at Cowdray Park was restarted by Lord Cowdray in the summer of 1947. The *Southern Weekly News* published the renewal of polo in Sussex: "For the first time since the war, polo is being played at Cowdray Park. Teams competing in an American tournament are Cowdray, Henley, Friar Park and Cotswold. On Tuesday night an exciting match between Cowdray and Friar Park resulted in a narrow win for the latter by 6 goals to 5."[4]

Never mind that it had started as three-a-side practice games, with the addition of Lord Cowdray's sisters, Angela, Daphne and Yoskyl, who had entered in tournament play in the 1930s. It was real polo, played on ponies collected by John Cowdray before the war. Although the Cowdray Park Challenge Cup, dating back to the club's origins in 1911, was not played for in 1947, a tournament for the Harrison Cup, named for Major Jack Harrison, the great Royal Horse Guards player and owner of the celebrated polo pony Perfection, took place in 1947, making it one of the first postwar polo tournaments. A Cowdray Park team took the trophy, now a regular feature in Cowdray Park's fixture.

Perfection, a heavyweight pony bred in Ireland and owned by Major Jack Harrison, was selected by Herbert Haseltine for his series of British Champion Animals. The entire collection is at the Virginia Museum of Fine Art in Richmond (private collection).

The Cowdray Park Challenge Cup, traditionally played during Goodwood Week, was revived in 1948, with seven entrants. Most appropriately, the trophy was taken by a Cowdray Park team: Major Colin Davenport, Daphne Lakin, Lord Cowdray and his brother-in-law John Lakin.

This was a momentous occasion, because among the spectators there were two gentlemen from Argentina, Lewis Lacey and Jack Nelson. Lewis Lacey was one of the world's top players, rated at ten goals, and Jack Nelson, an Olympic gold medalist and eight-goal player, was the president of the Argentine Polo Association. Based upon their assessment of the quality of polo in England, Mr. Nelson invited Lord Cowdray to assemble a team to participate in the Argentine polo season. That endeavor is described further anon.

A Sussex team from Cowdray, Alastair Gibb, Lt. Col. Geoffrey Phipps-Hornby, Lt. Col. Peter Dollar and John Lakin, took the Roehampton Cup in 1950, a feat repeated in 1954 by the orange-clad Cowdray team of Peter Cruden, Colonel Dollar, Hanut Singh and John Lakin.

Peter Dollar was one of the characters at Cowdray. Commissioned into the 19th Lancers after the Kaiser War, he transferred to the 4th Hussars, achieving a six-goal handicap. Captain Dollar was taken prisoner in Greece and was an unwilling guest at various POW camps, culminating with confinement in Colditz Castle, the place reserved for troublesome officers. There he shared a double bunk with Wing Commander Douglas Bader, the famous legless RAF ace. Lt. Col. Peter Dollar played at number 1 on several Cowdray Park teams, including an appearance at the Argentine Open in 1949.

Throughout these times, he was a weekend player at Cowdray and a devoted attendee at the many parties in polo's social scene. The Dollar Cup was presented for competition by Colonel Dollar and his family after his retirement from the game at age seventy-two.

Polo Cottage Team

An interesting personality at Cowdray Park was Windsor "Mike" Holden White, a scion of the celebrated White polo family from the Chagrin Valley Hunt Club, near Cleveland, Ohio. Mike Holden White removed to England after the war and for many years was the patron of the Polo Cottage team — named after his home in nearby Eastbourne — which became a regular competitor on English polo grounds for a long time. When Lord Cowdray restarted polo in 1947, Holden White was one of the original guarantors of the club. The team was quite successful in the 1950s and 1960s, and also served as a springboard for promising young players, thanks to the patron's generosity. Upon Mr. White's passing in 1975, the Polo Cottage team was dissolved.

Mike Holden White had an eye for a horse; among his famous polo ponies were Pampero, a champion at Wembley; Pulpero, who lived to the ripe old age of twenty-eight, purchased from Wyndham Lacey, and Blandford Meg, a favorite of Paul Withers, a thoroughbred liver chestnut painted by Nina Colmore in 1963.

The Holden White Challenge Cup is played for every summer on the Cowdray Park grounds.

Fernhurst Team

Major Jack Robinson formed his own polo team, Fernhurst, which took the Harrison Cup in 1951. A prewar five-goal handicap player, Maj. John P.B. Robinson, Dublin Fusiliers

Lord Louis and Lady Edwina Mountbatten with Major Jack Robinson and the Whitney Cup. The players wear the Asdean team jerseys.

and Berkshire Regiment, was a winner of the Coronation Cup with the Someries House team in 1939, in addition to several other trophies, such as the Whitney Cup on Lord Mountbatten's Asdean team, the Warwickshire, Bluejackets and the Cowdray Park Challenge Cups. During his military service in India, he was on the winning team for the Sir Patrap Singh Cup. Major Robinson also managed Eric Moller's Jersey Lilies team and for many years was a familiar figure at Cowdray Park. The Farewell Cup, traditionally the closing tournament at Cowdray, was given by Major Jack Robinson.

Henley Polo Club

Polo at Henley was also played in 1947. Major Archie David, a former tea planter that played polo at Cowdray Park in the 1930s, was the founder and mover. Play was on two grounds leased by Colonel Henry Micklem east of the town of Henley, by the London Road. The club members moved to the Household Brigade Club when established in 1955, the grounds at Henley being kept as reserve if the need arose.

The Hon. Daphne Pearson, by then Mrs. John Lakin, played at Henley on a team with her sister Yoskyl, Mrs. Alistair Gibbs. She reminisced, "It was a case of Lakins 1 and 3, and Gibbs 2 and back at the Henley polo tournaments in 1947. I remembered that we met the Jaipur side in 1948. I played to 1 [handicap] in those days— they wanted to put my handicap up to 2, but I resisted: I knew that nobody would want me in their team!"[5]

A Henley team, Mrs. Philip (Celia) Fleming, Billy Walsh from Ham Polo Club, Squadron Leader Alan Roberts and Capt. Patrick Butler, took the Cowdray Park Challenge Cup in 1949. Thus, two ladies were on teams that took the most important tournament in England at the time.

Henley was also the home base for Major Archie David's maroon-clad Friar Park team, which was quite successful in medium and low-goal polo.

A notable personality was General Sir Richard McCreery, the son of Walter McCreery of Bilton Park, Rugby, and a winner of the silver medal in the 1900 Olympic Games.

Richard Loudon McCreery misstated his age in order to join in the 1914 war and obtained a commission into the 12th Lancers; he was wounded in action, remaining with a limp for the rest of his days. This disability did not prevent him from riding, playing polo and enjoying a most successful military career. McCreery was in command of his regiment, was chief of staff to Sir Harold Alexander in North Africa, became the last commander of the famous 8th Army and ended his career as commander in chief, British Army of the Rhine, with a string of letters after his name. Together with his younger brother Walter, also a 12th Lancer, they represented the British Army in the international series against the American Army. Sir Richard was an accomplished rider, winning twice the Grand Military Gold Cup at Sandown Park, and was also master of the Blackmore Valley Hunt. His name appears on polo teams in the late 1950s, playing the game at an age when most people watch the game from the sidelines.

Silver Leys Polo Club

The Silver Leys Polo Club was established by Arthur Grant "Alfie" Boyd Gibbins in 1947. The polo ground was located about one mile from the center of the town of Bishops Stortford in Essex, which had been given in trust to the town by Tresham Gilbey. Thus, the game of polo returned after some forty years in abeyance. Jim Butter, Percy Ryan and Nessie Streeter played regularly along with Alfie Boyd Gibbins. Later on, Brian Bethell, Peter Buckenham, Miss J. Blackbourn and Percy Rhimes joined the fray. A club team took the County Cup in 1960, with Alfie Boyd Gibbins, Richard Harding, Brian Bethell and Kishen Singh, the latter being replaced by Gaje Singh. Another team, Boyd Gibbins, Captain Hugh Pitman, Maharajah Prem Singh and Risaldar Gaje Singh, took the Queen's Cup at Windsor Park in 1961.

Indifferent health forced Alfie Boyd Gibbins to give up the game, and the club was in abeyance until 1976, when one of the original starters, Jim Butter, was joined by George Knowles and Martin State in reviving the club.

Chillesford Polo Ground and the Orford Polo Club

The game at the Hon. Alastair Watson's Chillesford Lodge in Suffolk was resumed in 1948, on a polo ground reputed to be the best in England, with a new irrigation system that replaced the one installed before the war. The original polo ground had been plowed for crops to aid the war effort; a new one was laid out with the help of several East Anglia companies. Suffolk Seed Stores provided rye grass from New Zealand; the world-known Ransomes donated five gang lawn mowers, and Warners gave and installed the new irrigation system.

Polo at Chillesford remained a game of invitation. Alastair Watson purchased thirty-five Arab ponies in Baghdad and had them transported by air to England. Apparently, the newly formed Hurlingham Polo Association did not entirely approved of Arab ponies for polo, even though there were not too many polo mounts available in England during the immediate postwar period.[6] Under the name Orford Polo Club, the Chillesford ground is listed in the 1951 HPA yearbook.

Most regrettably, the Hon. Alastair Watson passed away in 1955 at the age of fifty-four. The game of polo in its purest form was gone in the county of Suffolk.

Hertfordshire Polo Club

The Hertfordshire Polo Club was founded in 1949 by Lascelles Arthur Lucas, one of the main supporters of the game during the difficult times following the war's end. His home, Woolmers Park, is located between Hatfield and Hertford, where a second ground was added in 1955. It was a family endeavor: Mrs. Ethel Lucas played, as did their children Patricia and John; later on, the youngster Claire — who would become England's best woman player — joined the fray. Most generously, Mr. Lucas allowed the Cambridge University team to play at Woolmers Park, providing both ponies and expert instruction.

An early game at Woolmers saw the local team — John Lucas, then an undergraduate at Cambridge; his father Arthur; James Withycombe; and George Strakosh — lose by the odd goal in seven to the Surrey team of C.J. Busby, the Italian player A. Carrara, Lt. Col. Rodolph de Salis and Billy Walsh.

The County Cup was taken in 1952 by Edmund Roark, John Lucas, James Withycombe and Arthur Lucas, while the Cowdray Park Challenge Cup was won in 1953 with the team of Francisco Astaburuaga from Chile, Carlos de la Serna, Colonel Prem Singh and John Lucas.

Teams from Woolmers Park crossed the Channel to play at Deauville, winning the Gold Cup in 1953 with a team that included Francisco Astaburuaga; Carlos de la Serna, a grand Argentine player; Maharajah Prem Singh from India; and, at back, Arthur Lucas. Dublin, Madrid, Rome and Biarritz were also points of destination for Woolmers Park's squads. A team representing the club participated in the 1953 Coronation Cup tournament, the first one held after the war. Woolmers Park was the venue for the initial match, in which Argentina, the eventual winner, defeated the host team.

1949 England at Palermo

The Argentine Polo Association organized in the spring of 1949 an eight-week festival of polo. Invited teams from Chile, England, Mexico and the United States participated in several tournaments ranging from twenty goals aggregate to forty goals for the first — and so far the only one — world championship with no handicap limit.

Lord Cowdray selected a team that included Lt. Col. Humphrey Guinness, the Royal Scots Grey redoubtable back; John Lakin, Cowdray Park's best player; Australian Bob Skene, who had played for England in the 1939 Westchester Cup at Meadow Brook, at the time employed as a steward in the Malayan Racing Association; and Eric Tyrrell-Martin, the captain of the 1936 Westchester Cup team, then in Egypt working for BOAC. All were veteran players and each was given arbitrarily a six-goal handicap. Lt. Col. Peter Dollar was selected as the spare man.

Misfortune hit the selected squad before travel started, when Tyrrell-Martin broke an ankle just before his departure from Cairo to join the team in England. His place on the team was taken by John Basil "Jack" Traill, the son of the legendary J.A.E. "Johnny" Traill, the first ten-goal handicap player in Argentina and a familiar presence on London's polo grounds, especially Roehampton.

On 12 October 1949, on Palermo's number-one polo field, England presented Traill, Lakin, Skene and Guinness. It was the first international appearance for England since the 1939 Westchester Cup matches at Meadow Brook. A large crowd saw the English team defeat Chile by twelve goals to nine. Chile had Alfonso Chadwick, Francisco Astaburuaga, Pablo Moreno and Jorge Lyon. Four days later the Argentine military team — Mario Laprida, Rubén Fernández Sarraua, Julio Grosse, Manuel Laprida — defeated England 11–9 in a very close match. Penalties in the closing two chukkers sealed the English team's fate. The last game was against the Argentine Civilians team, the brothers Ernesto, Alfredo and Luis Lalor, and at back, Juan Carlos Harriott, Sr. The Lalor family had eight polo-playing brothers, of which Alfredo and Luis became presidents of the Argentine Polo Association. The incumbent in 2011 is Luis Eduardo Lalor, a former nine-goaler, the son of Luis A. Lalor. In the event, the Civilians defeated England 10–7 in a good game, also played at Palermo.

A team representing Cowdray Park entered the Argentine Open Championship, Peter Dollar taking Jack Traill's place at number 1. They faced the local team Los Indios — Luis Heguy, Juan Carlos Landry, Rodolfo Taylor, Nicolás Cazón — in the first round and lost 7–5, without displaying the good form they had shown in the international twenty-four-goal tournament.

This tour to Argentina led by Viscount Cowdray was a noble effort. It should be noted that none of the players on the England squad had experienced the kind of polo played in Argentina in 1949 since before the war. They were mounted on good but unfamiliar ponies, pitted against international teams representing countries that had been untouched by the ravages of a six-year world war.

John Lakin was on an ascending career that culminated with him being considered the best English player until his retirement due to medical reasons. Humphrey Patrick Guinness soldiered on, always solid in defense, a welcome presence anywhere polo was played. Eventually, Colonel Guinness retired to a cottage in Gloucestershire near Cirencester Park, an iconic figure in British polo. Charles Robertson "Bob" Skene moved on to California, playing first at Beverly Hills and then at Santa Barbara, on his way to three U.S. Open crowns, two Argentine Open Championships, a ten-goal rating and a place among polo's immortals.

Sutton Park

The Duke of Sutherland had a polo ground built on Sutton Place, his seat in the vicinity of Guilford. Besides Cowdray polo grounds, it was the only regulation field in Southern England. The inaugural match was held in July 1950, when a Sussex team from Cowdray Park beat an Oxfordshire team by four goals to one. The Hon. Angela Campbell-Preston, her twin brother Lord John Cowdray, Colonel Robert Campbell-Preston and Alastair Gibbs played for Sussex.

Other Polo Clubs in England

The Canford Magna Polo Club was started in 1948 by Major Robin Harding and his sons Richard and Tim at Moortown Farm, near Canford Village in Hantfordshire.[7]

In 1950, just three years after the resumption of polo in England, there were twelve clubs affiliated with the Hurlingham Polo Association. The Roehampton Club maintained its three representatives at the HPA council, although polo at the old club was limited to a fortnight in July. To the already mentioned Cowdray Park, Ham, Henley, Hertfordshire, Orford, Silver Leys and Sutton Park, were added the reaffiliated Rhinefield in Hampshire, Taunton Vale in Dorset, and Toulston in Yorkshire.

Taunton Vale was revived by Colonel Sir Henry Farrington, Lt. Col. David Worrall, Major John Power, C.H. "Tish" Tilley and some other officers.

Toulston had been kept as a private club by its founder William Riley-Smith and resumed play after the war. When Captain Riley-Smith passed away in 1954, the Toulston Polo Club became a registered club.

New polo clubs were Billericay and Jericho Priory in Essex. The latter was established in 1952 by Mr. E.B. "Ted" Marriage at his Jericho Priory estate in Blackmore.

Soldiers' Polo

Upon the renewal of military polo in Germany after the war, playing regiments in the British Army of the Rhine (BAOR) were the Queen's Bays, 3rd Hussars, 4th/7th Dragoon Guards, 7th Hussars, 11th Hussars, Royal Scots Greys, the Rifle Brigade, the Border Regiment, Scot Fusiliers, plus detachments from the Royal Artillery, the Royal Engineers and the Horse Artillery. Military polo in Germany thrived thanks to the support and experience given by the veteran hands that had gained their polo laurels in India. When independence came along with the almost simultaneous partition of Pakistan in 1948, many British officers returned to Europe to continue their polo endeavors, albeit in a reduced scale. But it was polo, nevertheless, and the old guard became mentors for a new generation of polo-playing soldiers.

Regimental polo clubs were started in Bad Lippspringe, Düsseldorf, Hohne, Munster and Wesendorf. The Inter-Regimental Tournament of the BAOR was started in 1951, when the 3rd Hussars took the honors. This regimental team retained the championship the next two years; then it was the 17th/21st Lancers team that took the title five years in a row, a string of victories reminiscent of those obtained by the regiment in the 1920s.

This row of triumphs began in 1954 with a team that included Lt. Arthur Douglas-Nugent, Major Ronald Coaker, Lt. Col. David Barbour and Lt. Anthony Bateman. The following year Captain Gordon Hedley and Lt. Simon Walford played instead of Major Croaker and Lt. Bateman. Simon Walford was the son of "Chicken" Walford, a member of the successful 17th/21st Lancers team in the 1920s. In 1956, Captain Anthony Dacres-Dixon replaced Gordon Hedley. The next two years saw the new commanding officer, Colonel Coaker, lead the regimental team; Montagu Berryman, Douglas-Nugent and Walford completed the team.[8]

Finally, in 1959, the Queen's Dragoon Guards took the title, defeating the Royals in the decisive match. The 17th/21st Lancers also were the winner of the United Services Cup, a competition between the winners of the Inter-Regimental Tournaments at home and in

The 7th Hussars took thee first Inter-Regimental tournament in England after the war: Maj. Hilary Hook, Capt. William Richardson, Capt. Michael Fraser, and Lt. Col. Charles T. Llewellen Palmer.

Germany. Captain Arthur Douglas-Nugent, Captain Montagu Berryman, Major Ronald Coaker and Simon Walford were on the winning teams.

Military polo in England was revived at Tidworth, the Army's facility in Wiltshire, in 1955 at the Tattoo Ground and later at the Perham Down Ground. There has been polo at Tidworth since 1908. General Sir Bertie Drew Burdett-Fisher was the man responsible for its prominence among military polo clubs. The Fisher polo ground is located in front of Tedworth House near the village of Tidworth, an incongruous spelling. The club is the venue for the Rundle Cup, competed for by Army and Navy teams. Originally played for in Malta, the trophy was given by Maj. Gen. Sir Leslie Rundle in 1910, when governor of the island.[9] Other tournaments include the Captains and Subalterns Gold Cup, dating to 1896, and the Hartopp Cup, in memory of the officer who started polo in England. The original Subalterns' Gold Cup was played for at Ranelagh Club; regrettably it has disappeared from sight. The current trophy is a cup won by the Queen's Bays and presented to the reorganized tournament committee in the 1950s.

Play at Catterick Garrison was resumed in 1957 on a ground located in the RAF airfield. Some civilian players were allowed to play at the club. The game was revived at its cradle, Aldershot Garrison, in 1958. Two fields were used, one being the old number-one field.

The Inter-Regimental and the Subalterns' tournaments in England were resumed in 1958, mainly through the enthusiasm of Lt. Col. Charles T. Llewellen Palmer. Nine entries made the competition a successful one. The 7th Hussars won the final game from the 3rd Royal Horse Artillery. Most appropriately, the winning team was led by Lt. Col. Tim Llewellen Palmer. Captain Hilary Hook, later a television personality; Captain William Richardson; and Captain Michael Fraser completed the winning squad. The 10th Hussars took the Subalterns' Tournament.

In the Inter-Regimental Tournament, the 3rd RHA took its revenge in 1960, when the team of Major William Mangham, a young subaltern named Paul Withers, Lt. Col. Philip Tower and Captain Jeremy Hemming defeated the Queen's Own Hussars by the odd goal in five. This victory entitled the 3rd RHA to face the Queen's Dragoon Guards, the winners of the British Army of the Rhine's Inter-Regimental, to play for the Army Championship Cup. In a good game at Tidworth, regulation time ended with a tie. Then the 3rd Royal Horse Artillery obtained the winning goal in extra time.

Other Early Tournaments

The Junior County Cup was first played after the war in 1948, when the Birkdale team — Mrs. Dorothy Kitson, Arthur Lucas, Captain Patrick Butler and Major Thomas Hilder — won the trophy at Roehampton. At this stage the Junior County Cup was played for by the teams defeated in the quarterfinal round of the County Cup; however, in 1959 it reverted to its original status as an independent competition.

The Oxford versus Cambridge fixture was resumed in 1951, the Dark Blues being the winners. In that same year, the County Cup was revived, and Beechwood, with William Wallace, sometime escort to Princess Margaret; Harold Freeborn, master of the horse to Lord Cowdray; Brigadier Henry Young; and the Argentine Juan Reynal, a member of La Espadaña team, were the winners at the Roehampton Club.

Harrogate Polo Club, where play had started in 1935 and become dormant because of the world conflict, was revived in 1957, when a tournament was held to test the waters for a possible full revival.

1951— The Year of the Festival Cup

The highlight of the 1951 summer season was a series of three test matches for the Festival Cup between a squad selected by the Hurlingham Polo Association and La Espadaña, a team sent by the Argentine Polo Association in retribution of Cowdray Park's visit to Buenos Aires in 1949. The selection committee paid the visitors the compliment of picking the best possible team, at an aggregate of a twenty-four-goal handicap. Gerald Balding, a ten-goal handicap player in 1939, played at number 2. Humphrey Guinness, another seasoned international, was at number 3, while John Lakin, at the top of his form, played at back. At number 1, the Achilles' heel of many teams, Lt. Col. Alexander Forrest Harper was a most fortunate choice. This was his first season on English grounds, although he had gained a well-earned reputation as a player on the Deccan Horse polo team just before the war. A good horseman, Alec Harper showed great anticipation in slipping away while chasing the long passes hit by the heavy hitters behind him.

This team represented England in the 1951 Festival Cup and in the 1953 Coronation Cup. John Lakin, Humphrey Guinness, Gerald Balding and Alec Harper.

La Espadaña — named after the Garrahan family polo team — made Cowdray Park their home base. Juan Reynal was number 1; Carlos Buchanan played number 2; Juan "Buddy" Ross, at seven goals, played number 3; and Luis Garrahan was back. Julio Gómez Thwaites was the spare man. La Espadaña was a twenty-one-goal combination.

The first test was played on the River Ground at Cowdray Park on July 7. It had been scheduled to be played at Sutton Place, the Duke of Sutherland's seat, but winter flooding had damaged the polo ground. The Hurlingham team got off to a good start, three goals to nil at halftime. Brothers-in-law Buchanan and Garrahan exchanged places, and the game went better for them, but it was a case of too little, too late. Hurlingham won with ease, four goals to one.

The second game was held at Roehampton on July 25, following the competitions for the County Cup and the Roehampton Cup. The ground was not in good condition, some twenty games having taken place during the previous fortnight. La Espadaña was full of confidence, having previously taken the Roehampton Cup. Nevertheless, Hurlingham once more started brilliantly, the score at halftime being four–nil in their favor, eventually winning by six goals to three. Princess Elizabeth presented the Festival Cup to a beaming Hurlingham team.[10] Oddly enough, the trophy itself was the old Ranelagh Club's Coronation Cup.[11] Nevertheless, the Hurlingham Polo Association decided to engrave the winning England team on the Coronation Cup. There is, however, no mention of the Coronation Cup in contemporary reports.

The series already decided, the third test match was played on August Bank Holiday at Cowdray's River Ground, under continuous rain. La Espadaña was without Reynal and Ross, and on the Hurlingham side Lt. Col. Andrew Horsburgh-Porter took Gerald Balding's place. In spite of the heavy rain, there were nearly a thousand carloads of spectators, plus many on foot. Hurlingham won the game by a five-goal margin, nine goals to four.

The visit of La Espadaña was an unqualified success. Besides the pleasure they gave the thousands of spectators that witnessed the test matches, the visitors gave encouragement and help to many players, by splitting up the team and playing in tournaments with three English players on each team.

Other events of note were the restart of the annual Oxford versus Cambridge match, which dates back to 1878. The Cambridge side was helped enormously by Mr. Arthur Lucas, who lent ponies to the team and allowed the use of his ground at Woolmers Park for practice games. Henley Polo Club helped the Oxford team, which won the match by some five goals.

During Goodwood Week, Cowdray Park took their own Challenge Cup, beating La Espadaña in the final game. Lord Cowdray, Lt. Col. Alec Harper, Lt. Col. Peter Dollar and John Lakin were on the winning team.

Cheshire Polo Club

The Cheshire Polo Club presents a strong claim to being the oldest polo club in England by way of mergers and succession. It is the descendant of an amalgamation among three polo clubs, Bowdon (1860s), Manchester (1872) and Wirral (1885). Bowdon merged with Manchester in 1908; the Bowdon named disappeared, and Manchester and Wirral joined forces in 1939. In the late 1940s it was revived as the Mid-Cheshire, taking its present name, Cheshire Polo Club, in 1951.

Oswald Grange Moseley kept the Manchester Club going, and his son Pat and Francis Spielberger were instrumental in merging Wirral and Manchester into what evolved as Mid-Cheshire Polo Club, together with Pat's brother Michael. The younger Moseley, Micky, had played in Argentina in the late 1930s, and after the war he invited players from that country to play in England. Among the first to play the season in England were young Miguel Indart, from El Rincón Polo Club, and the veteran Eduardo Rojas Lanusse, a winner of the 1937 Argentine Open Championship. The Indart Cup is still played for at Cheshire, while the Eduardo Rojas Lanusse Cup is a fixture at Beaufort Polo Club.

The Cheshire Polo Club grew in numbers; by 1956 it had twenty-five playing members and organized two club tournaments, the Russell Allan Cup and the Demetriade Cup.[12]

All this resulted in a fifteen-goal match in 1959 between Cheshire, with Jonty Ramsden, Micky Moseley, Juan José Diaz Alberdi and Alex Mihanovich, versus the South, the Hon. George Bathurst, Lt. Col. Alec Harper, Alan Budgett and Charles Smith-Ryland. The contest ended in a Solomon draw.

Cirencester Park

The Ivy Lodge field — reputed to be the best all-weather polo ground in England — was plowed up during the war; however, in 1951, Earl Bathurst had it reseeded with a view to reviving polo in the near future. Play was resumed in 1953, and soon enough the Harrison Cup was taken at Cowdray Park by a team from Cirencester. The two initial tournaments after the war were the Cheltenham Cup, presented by former members of the club following dissolution, and the Kingscote Cup, named after Maurice Kingscote, an old Gloucestershire player.

Other successes followed. A team of Major John Mayne and Jack Williams, with the aid of two Argentineans, the veteran Eduardo Rojas Lanusse and the up-and-coming Eduardo "Gordo" Moore, gathered the spoils of victory in the 1963 County Cup. The feat was repeated in 1968, when Lord Samuel Vestey, Eduardo Moore, Peter Perkins and Captain Frederick Barker took the County Cup once more.

The Junior County Cup was taken in 1957 by Colonel Raymond Barrow, Brian Bethell, Lt. Col. Anthony McConnel and the Hon. George Bathurst, and in 1961 with Dirk Sell-schopp, George Bathurst, Lt. Col. McConnel and Andrew Summers.

Cirencester Park's teams achieved enormous success in the 1970s. Stowell Park, Los Locos and Foxcote dominated the English polo scene during those glory years.

The Social Clubs' Cup, instituted in 1897 by the Hurlingham Club, was revived at Cirencester Park in 1957 and taken by the Cavalry Club, who won it again in 1958, 1959 and 1961. It was not played in 1960, and by then it was held at Windsor. This ancient trophy returned to Cirencester in 1997, when it was taken by Buck's Club.

In spite of being one of the "Big Three" polo clubs in England, Cirencester still maintains a bucolic country feeling, even during the finals of the Warwickshire Cup, one of the oldest and most prestigious trophies in the world of polo. The Sweethills ground is endowed with old and lush turf, having escaped the wartime plow. The main polo field, the magnificent Ivy Lodge, is located next to the no-less-magnificent Broad Ride, the center of the Bathurst estate's parkland. On the Meadow ground, the trail of an ancient pathway is still visible, and the scenery from the Peddington ground overviews some of Gloucestershire's finest hunting landscape. Country polo at Cirencester Park remains at its best, just as it was when the club was formed in the waning years of the nineteenth century.

Jersey Lilies Polo Team

The chocolate jersey with a gold hoop was a familiar sight on English polo grounds for many years. This team was the creation of Eric Moller, a Swedish-born player. The Moller brothers, Eric the younger and Ralph, made their fortune as maritime shippers and builders in Shanghai — their historic Moller villa is currently a prime tourist attraction — and stayed unwillingly during the Japanese invasion, leaving in 1949 because of the Communist threat in mainland China.

Mr. Eric Moller became a player and a patron of low-, mid- and high-goal teams, achieving a great deal of success. Jersey Lilies teams took Cowdray Park's Gold Cup in 1964 and 1965 under the guidance of Rao Rajah Hanut Singh, the team's high watermark. Other successes included the Royal Windsor Cup and the Smith's Lawn Cup at Windsor Park; the Cheltenham Cup at Cirencester, the Argentine Ambassador's Cup and the County Cup, the latter on four occasions.

1953 — The Coronation Year

The coronation of HM Queen Elizabeth II at Westminster Abbey became the symbol of Britain's recovery following the hardships endured during the long years of the war and the austerity measures imposed by the Labour government following the conflict's end. Appropriately enough, the Hurlingham Polo Association organized an international twenty-four-goal tournament for the Coronation Cup, now in the custody of the HPA after the demise of the Ranelagh Club in 1939. Seven teams answered the call: America, Argentina, Chile and Spain joined local clubs Cowdray Park and Woolmers Park, plus a team representing England in a contest played during the month of June.

Argentina, with Eduardo Braun Cantilo, Ernesto Lalor, Alejandro Mihanovich and Juan Carlos Alberdi, faced Woolmers Park on the home ground, winning by ten goals to four. Jack Nelson from Argentina, Maharajah Jabar Singh, Colonel Prem Singh and Carlos de la Serna, another Argentinean, wore the red and green of Mr. Arthur Lucas' team.

On the same day at Midhurst, Cowdray Park won their match against Meadow Brook, which was representing America, by ten goals to seven. The Cowdray team was Lt. Col. Peter Dollar, Enrique Alberdi, Hanut Singh and Teófilo Bordeu. Both "Quito" Alberdi and "Toti" Bordeu hailed from Argentina.

Also on that same date at Cirencester Park, the veteran English team consisting of Lt. Col. Alec Harper, Gerald Balding, Lt. Col. Humphrey Guinness and John Lakin defeated Spain, composed of Francisco López de Carrizosa, Pedro Domecq de la Riva, Heriberto Duggan — an Argentine nine-goal player — and José Ignacio Domecq González. The final score was England, thirteen goals; Spain, four goals.

That same English team beat Chile 10–4 in the first semifinal at Cowdray Park. Chile, which had drawn a bye in the first round, had Pablo Moreno, Francisco Astaburuaga, Julio Zegers and Gustavo Larrain. Argentina defeated Cowdray Park in the other semifinal match.

The final game took place on 21 June on the Lawns Ground at Cowdray Park. In a very close match, Argentina won by seven goals to six. Queen Elizabeth II presented the Coronation Cup to an elated Juan Carlos Alberdi, Argentina's captain. It was a hard-fought game, which could have gone either way.

Alan Budgett, chairman of the Hurlingham Polo Association from 1967 until 1974.

Kirtlington Polo Club

This club, first started in 1926 by Mr. Hugh Budgett, was revived in 1954 by Richard Alan Budgett, master of the Bicester, and future chairman of the Hurlingham Polo Association. Another ground was added in Kirtlington Park to complement the initial polo field. The annual tournament for the Kirtlington Cup was also revived at this time.

The club had an unusual number of female players for those times. Among them were Mrs. Alan Budgett, Mrs. A. Beloe, Mrs. Celia (later Lady) Fleming, Mrs. Betty Pacey and Mrs. V. Walsh.

Among the tournaments taken by the club were the Junior County Cup in 1958 with Lt. Col. Anthony Taylor, Miss Judy Forwood, Clem Barton and Alan Budgett; in 1984 with Christopher Courage, Roderick Matthews, John Tylor and Crispin Matthews; and in 1991 with Andrew Barlow, Christopher Whiteley, John Tylor and Crispin Matthews.

Other national titles include the Royal Windsor Cup in 1970, with a team of Richard Clifford, Mark Barlow, the Mexican player Antonio Herrera and Martin Trotter, and the Friar Park Cup with Jeremy Taylor, Mark Barlow, Martin Trotter and Simon Loder.

Currently Kirtlington offers seven polo grounds and a polo school in a gorgeous setting in Oxfordshire. Mr. Budgett's son-in-law, John Tylor, long the club's chairman, also served as chairman of the Hurlingham Polo Association from 1991 to 1995, in addition to being one of the top amateur players in his polo-playing days.

Hurlingham at Deauville

The seaside resort of Deauville has a long history of hosting teams from across the English Channel. Two teams representing Hurlingham took the Coupe d'Or. In 1955, Wing Commander Huntly Sinclair, RCAF; Lt. Col. Alec Harper; Rao Rajah Hanut Singh; and Lt. Col. Humphrey Guinness were the members of the winning team. The following year Hurlingham repeated the feat, with Hari Singh, Hanut's youngest son, and C.M.T. (later Sir Charles) Smith-Ryland in place of Wing Commander Sinclair and Lt. Col. Alec Harper.

The Household Brigade Polo Club

The original Household Cavalry Club was founded in 1897 and remained a garrison club for the three Household Cavalry regiments. The 1st and 2nd Life Guards were amalgamated into one unit after World War I, while the Royal Horse Guards, also known as the Blues, remained untouched by the wave of amalgamation that swept through the cavalry regiments. The polo ground was located in Datchet.

In 1955, a new Household Brigade Polo Club was formed through the efforts of HRH Prince Philip, Duke of Edinburgh; Colonel David Smiley, commanding officer of the Blues; Sir Eric Savill; Major the Marquess Douro; and Major Archie David, who had offered his polo ground at Henley for play by the officers at Combermere Barracks in Windsor.[13] Lt. Lord Patrick Beresford was given the task of getting the polo grounds in shape and organizing the initial chukkers. Lord Beresford went on to be the longest serving member of the committee.

The Royal Windsor Cup, a medium-goal tournament, was started in the year of the club's foundation. Ratanada, the Rao Rajah Hanut Singh's team, was the first winner.

Eventually, the Household Brigade Polo Club became the Guards Polo Club, about which more anon.

The Death Knell for Polo at Roehampton

By July 1947, polo had made a welcome return at Roehampton Club, although in a minor scale. By 1950, the club's board arrived to the conclusion that the number-two polo ground was unlikely to be utilized "this year or, indeed, ever again."[14] This was a somewhat erroneous assessment, because in the following year the sole surviving field was the site for more than twenty games in a fortnight. Nevertheless, the ground was sacrificed on the altar of the golfing membership. The *Times* deplored the fact that the polo ground had been used "to provide a few extra bunkers for the golf" and also commented rather sourly on the dissolution of the neighboring Ranelagh Club and the mutilation of the Hurlingham Club by compulsory purchase.[15]

The Roehampton Club finally decided to allow the general public entrance to the club grounds to watch polo— shades of Hurlingham —but only on the far side of the field.

Colonel Charles Miller, the last surviving of the three famous brothers, the Roehampton Club's founders, passed away in 1951. It was a grievous loss for polo and for the club. Although the Roehampton Cup, dating back to the club's beginnings in 1902, was still played for, as well as the more ancient County Cup, polo was only played in the month of July. The Roehampton Open Cup, established in 1913, was not reinstituted, while the Roehampton Cup became a golf trophy, until rescued by Ham Polo Club member Edward Taucher in 1967.

The last game of polo at the historic Roehampton Club took place in July 1956.

Aotea Sails from New Zealand

At the invitation of Lord Cowdray, who offered to purchase their ponies after the tour, a New Zealand team undertook the monthlong sea voyage to England via the Panama Canal. They called themselves Aotea, after the canoe that brought over the Polynesians to the islands.

The team was led by J.G. "Hame" (later Sir James) Wilson of the Rangitikei Club, Derrick Glazebrook and A.F. "Sandy" Mackenzie of the Hawke's Bay Club, and Tony Kay of the Kihikihi Club. Seventeen ponies were taken. Jack Masters, a Hawke's Bay player; T.C. Lowry, a junior; and Hame Wilson went with the ponies on board the SS *Persic*, while the rest of the players traveled by plane later on. The Aotea team was a twenty-two-goal aggregate.[16]

Playing their first match late in June, Glazebrook, Mackenzie, Wilson and Kay were defeated by a Hurlingham team at Windsor Park. Daphne Lakin, the Duke of Edinburgh, Peter Dollar and John Lakin were their opponents. After the game, the visitors were presented to Queen Elizabeth II.

The next game was against a Cowdray side; this ended in another defeat by eleven goals to two. In the match, the spectators included Lord Glasgow, who as Viscount Kelburn had helped to introduce polo in New Zealand. Jack Masters replaced Glazebrook at number 1, and Aotea took the Neil Haig Cup at Roehampton, defeating Friar Park 6–1 in the finals. The Neil Haig Cup, originally a point-to-point trophy, was presented by Maj. Gen. Haig's widow, Mrs. Ailward Wyndham, in 1951.

Reality came back with a vengeance in the first round of Cowdray Park's Gold Cup. The draw placed the Aotea team against Los Indios, the team from Argentina that eventually took the title. The scoreboard at game's end showed thirteen goals for Los Indios against a single tally by Aotea.

At this stage of the tour, Lord Cowdray reduced the Aotea team handicap to twelve goals. The visitors were able to hold their own in the last five matches, winning the last two encounters at Cirencester Park.

The New Zealanders had no experience of world polo at that time—except for tours from and to Australia—and conditions were not easy for the visitors. The ponies arrived with very little time to be appropriately conditioned after the long sea voyage; the players had not been playing together prior to the tour, and interpretation of the rules and the style of play were totally different from the game as played in New Zealand.

Nevertheless, it was a learning experience, and the Aotea players opened the way for later visits from New Zealand to the mother country, including matches for the Coronation Cup.

Cowdray Park's Gold Cup

The Cowdray Park Gold Cup was started as a twenty-goal tournament in 1956, eventually becoming symbolic of the English Polo Championship. The final game in this first edition was between the home team, Alec Harper, Charles Smith-Ryland, Hanut Singh and John Lakin, and the visiting team from Argentina Los Indios, Dr. Jorge Marín Moreno, Pablo Nagore, Antonio Heguy and Juan Echeverz. Both teams were rated at twenty goals. On a bright and sunny day, on a slow ground due to morning heavy rain, Los Indios defeated Cowdray Park 9–4.

Dr. Marín Moreno became a frequent visitor to England, while team captain Antonio Heguy was on the Coronel Suárez team that took the 1958 Argentine Open Championship. Two of his sons, Horacio and Alberto Pedro, were rated at ten goals; Horacio's four sons, Horacio, Gonzalo, Marcos and Bautista, and Alberto Pedro's sons, Eduardo "Ruso," Alberto "Pepe" and Ignacio "Nachi," also reached the pinnacle of a ten-goal rating. All eventually played in England, with the exception of Alberto Pedro, a veterinarian and polo-pony breeder of high repute.

The following year Windsor Park took the trophy with a team that included two Argentines, Juan Patricio Nelson, son of the legendary Jack Nelson, and Ernesto "Tito" Lalor. HRH Prince Philip played at back, and Colonel Humphrey Guinness showed his prewar form in the pivot number 3 position. They defeated Casarejo, which had vanquished Cowdray Park in the semifinals.

Cowdray Park, with Peter Dollar, Alec Harper, Hanut Singh and John Lakin won the cup in 1958, beating Arthur Lucas' Woolmers Park with a convincing 10–3 score. Dr. Marín Moreno, John Lucas, Pedro Llorente and Rafael Braun Cantilo played for Woolmers Park. John Lucas would get his Gold Cup later on, while "Rafi" Braun Cantilo was a product of Belgrano Day School in Buenos Aires and a most promising young polo player who would take holy orders and is now Monsignor Braun Cantilo.

In 1959, the Casarejo team—the Spaniard Pedro Domecq de la Riva, the Mexican brothers Rubén "Pato" and Alejandro "Cano" Gracida and Baron Elie de Rothschild, from the family's French branch—took the Gold Cup in a thrilling match against the Centaurs, Mr. Evelyn de Rothschild's, later Sir Evelyn, British team. Two other Gracida brothers, Gabriel "Chino" and Guillermo "Memo," were on the Centaurs team. The Gracida brothers four would have been a twenty-five-goal combine; it was a pity that no game was organized against a top English foursome. Most likely, it would have been a grand game.

The Whitbread Cup Tournament

In 1956, Colonel William Whitbread endowed a tournament to be played on the American system among clubs from five districts, Northern, Southern, Western, Central and Eastern. The rules were quite strict. Teams were to be of 8–2 goals handicap, and to include two young postwar players. Through the years, the rules underwent some alterations. The format was changed to a knockout competition, the postwar players had to be under thirty, and all players were British.

The idea remained the same: a low-goal handicap tournament intended to bring up young British players. The Whitbread Cup remains a most popular competition.

Media Luna Polo Team

The 1957 polo season was enlivened by the visit of an amateur team from Argentina representing the Media Luna Polo Club, currently the third in antiquity in that country, after the Venado Tuerto and Hurlingham Clubs. Media Luna, named after a fort of that name in Western Buenos Aires Province, located in the vicinity of two ponds shaped like half moons, had started their polo by British settlers in 1890.

Four young players, Juan Patricio Nelson, his cousin Luis Nelson, Jr., Arturo Reynal and Guillermo Goñi Durañona brought their own ponies to try their luck on English polo grounds. Typical of Argentine players, all four were descendants of polo families. Jack Nelson and his older brother Louis had been on the Argentine Polo Federation squad that visited England in 1922, and Arturo Reynal's father, José, was a nine-goal player, a winner of the U.S. Open Championship and the Argentine Open.

They had a most successful season, taking the Royal Windsor Cup and the County Cup. In addition, John Nelson was on the winning team of Cowdray Park's Gold Cup with Tito Lalor, Colonel Humphrey Guinness and HRH Prince Philip.

A Season of Polo

The year 1959 was a good one for polo in England, another significant step on the way to recovery. The season started with the Combermere Cup on Smith's Lawn at Windsor Park. Alfie Boyd Gibbins' Silver Leys defeated the Welsh Guards in the finals. The Welshmen took their revenge two weeks later, now with the Duke of Edinburgh — the Welsh Guards' colonel — recently returned from a world tour, inspiring his team to a winning effort in the Victoria Cup. Douglas Riley-Smith took his Brewhurst team to Windsor to take the Windsor Horse Show Club trophy. Windsor Park, with Lord Patrick Beresford, Ernesto Lalor, Colonel Guinness and HRH Prince Philip won the Smith-Ryland Cup at Cowdray. On the same afternoon at Cirencester, Barton Abbey, with Charles Smith-Ryland, Clem Barton, Mrs. Philip Fleming and her son Nicholas, won a match for the Gerald Balding Cup from Beechanger, the Worsley family's team.

The ancient County Cup was played for at Tidworth. Eric Moller's chocolate and yellow Jersey Lilies took the trophy, defeating a gallant Cheshire side in the finals. The Maharajah of Cooch Behar, John Lucas and Charles Smith-Ryland completed the Jersey Lilies team. Also at Tidworth, the Inter-Regimental Tournament was taken for the first time ever by a Territorial team, the Royal Wiltshire Yeomanry just beating the Queen's Own Hussars in the semifinals, and the Blues in the final game. The Royal Horse Guards were again runners-up in the Captains' and Subalterns' Cup. It was an exciting match, the Queen's Own Hussars in the lead throughout the game. With only half a minute to go, Lord Patrick Beresford called his number 1, S.T. Clarke, off the ball and lofted a magnificent shot ball between the goalposts to even the score. Only three seconds remained in extra time when Captain Michael Fraser scored the winning goal for the Hussars.

The Junior County Cup also fell to Jersey Lilies, putting the finishing touch to a nice double. Major Dennis Grehan, Captain Robert Baxter, Lt. Col. Alec Harper and Eric Moller took the honors.

The Oxford versus Cambridge match was held at Cowdray Park through the courtesy of Lord Cowdray, an Old Oxonian who had represented the Dark Blues in the 1930s. Cambridge University had a strong team: Geoffrey Ashton from Australia, Tom Barlow from South Africa, Jonathan Riley-Smith from Yorkshire, all three with impeccable polo pedigrees, and V. Lukshumeyesh from Malaya.[17] Peter Palumbo, the two Maltese players Drs. Anthony and Edward De Bono, and Edward Cazalet were on the Oxford University team.[18] The Light Blues won the match with some ease.

For the first time, a Cowdray Park team took the Royal Windsor Cup. Lord Brecknock, Paul Withers, Peter Dollar and the famous Argentine polo-pony breeder Ricardo Santamarina were on the Cowdray squad. In the subsidiary for the Smith's Lawn Cup, Silver Leys defeated Cheshire, and Jack Williams scored all three goals when Ham beat Beechanger 3–2 in the Friar Park Cup.

The season's main event, the Cowdray Park Gold Cup, drew six teams, and all the games took place in successive Sundays, to the discomfort of some other polo clubs.

Ratanada, Hanut Singh's team that was minus its guru, defeated Windsor Park, and then Cowdray Park sent Brewhurst back to Yorkshire. The semifinals saw the home team down 5–7 at the end of the fifth chukker, only to turn the game around and emerge the victors 8–7. Ratanada sorely missed Hanut in their contest with Casarejo, going down 12–4. The final was a good game. Cowdray was down 1–5 at the midway break. They altered their lineup, sending John Lakin up to number 2 and placing Santamarina at back. The prescription worked well, the score at the start of the last chukker being five-all. Then Cano Gracida scored, only for Lakin to even the issue with a lofted sixty-yard penalty. Only seconds to go, and Rubén Gracida scored the winning goal for Casarejo.

Baron Elie de Rothschild received the Gold Cup, and later that afternoon the baroness handed the Midhurst Town Cup to her cousin Evelyn de Rothschild, captain of the Centaurs team that took the subsidiary tournament. Not a bad day for the banking family.

Only three more trophies remained to be played. At Cowdray Park's Lawn Ground, two teams from Tidworth fought out the Holden White Cup. The 3rd Royal Horse Artillery took the best from the Queen's Own Hussars, who suffered what a polo correspondent described as "a self-imposed injury."[19]

In August at Smith's Lawn, Windsor took the Whitbread Cup, defeating Kirtlington. Colonel Whitbread once more donated ten pounds to the grooms of the winning team. Finally, in the Horse and Hound Cup, Windsor beat Silver Leys by 5½ to 3 goals.

Thus ended the 1959 polo season.

Polo in Scotland

After the Second World War, the game of polo was absent from Scotland until 1966, when Captain Mervyn Fox-Pitt went to Fifeshire to manage the estate of the Earl of Dundee, his step-father-in-law. With the enthusiastic support of the Earl of Dundee as president, the Dundee Polo Club was started on a recently cut silage field.[20]

The cooperation of the local authorities allowed polo to be played on some public parks in Dundee and Perth. The Army then appeared on the scene when the old Dreghorn polo ground in Edinburgh saw once more the polo ponies' galloping hooves.

Three years later, John Douglas, later Earl of Morton, resuscitated the old Edinburgh Polo Club at his Dalmahoy Park. With his polo-playing wife Sheila, daughter Mary and son James, the Earl of Morton was able to field an all-family team.

Then the Earl of Mansfield allowed the use of a ground inside the Scone racecourse, and the original polo club changed its denomination to Dundee and Perth Polo Club. This new venue near Scone Palace attracted spectators in large numbers, and teams from Ireland and Canada, as well as from south of Hadrian's Wall, came to play on Scottish fields.

The Canadian team, Jonty Parker, Charles Hetherington, Tony Yonge and Patrick Oswald, took the Perth Cup to Western Canada. The trophy was retrieved by the Hurlingham Rovers, which included Captain Fox-Pitt and David Drummond Moray from Scotland.

Other clubs followed suit. Near Edinburgh, Alan More-Nesbitt's The Drum provided a local rivalry to Dalmahoy Polo Club. William Drummond Moray started polo at Abercairny, near Crieff, together with his brother David. Mervyn Fox-Pitt based his Birkhill team at his home, The Grange.

Scottish teams also traveled overseas. The Edinburgh Polo Club visited Lagos and Ibadan in Nigeria in 1978. Bobby Stewart, Jake Scott, James Manclark and Declan Collins were victorious in only one game. This showing was attributed to several factors: the unstinted hospitality that went long into the African night, the quick transition from a Scottish cold February to a hot and humid Nigerian climate, unfamiliar horseflesh and, more likely, a dislocated finger and a broken collarbone suffered by two of the Scots.

The visiting Edinburgh team was accompanied by the talented artist Susan Whitcombe, who produced some paintings based upon her witnessing the games and the activity in the pony lines.

Polo in Ireland

The game of polo returned to Phoenix Park in 1951, although in a much limited scale. Teams from England resumed their visits to Ireland in the late 1950s.

The Patriotic Cup was resumed in 1999, All Ireland versus Hurlingham; played at Cirencester; and then taken by Cheshire. In 2003, a Ham team, with Chris Mathias, Chris Graham, Tim Healy and Nicholas Colquhoun-Denvers, lost to Ireland's John O'Driscoll, Ken O'Reilly, James O'Connell and Chris Murphy in the competition's centenary year.

Polo at the 1958 Commonwealth Games

A polo match was held at Cardiff's Llandaff Field on 23 July 1958 as part of the celebrations. Cowdray Park enlisted Lt. Col. Peter Dollar, John Lakin, Hanut Singh and Prince

Philip, Duke of Edinburgh. Their opponents were a Cirencester side, reinforced by Lt. Col. Alec Harper from Cowdray. Lt. Col. Anthony McConnel, Wyndham Lacey from Argentina and the Hon. George Bathurst completed the squad.

The four-chukker game was won by Cowdray, by four goals to three. The umpires were Colonels Richard Barrow and Sydney Kennedy; Brigadier Jack Gannon was referee. This is probably the only instance in which polo was played at the Commonwealth Games.

The State of the Art in 1958

Mike Holden White, the American expatriate patron of the Polo Cottage team, wrote a thoughtful essay on the polo situation in England one decade after its revival.[21] According to White, the question most asked was, "I know all the old pre-war players are still going, but who is coming on?"

His answer was four-fold:

1. The inability of most prospects to ride, and/or willingness to learn to ride. 2. Unwillingness of potential good players to work hard and learn their polo trade. 3. Too many tournaments and/or public games. 4. Clubs do not give youngsters opportunity of experience.

When young men get on a polo pony for the first time, the majority can sit on a horse but lack basic concepts such as proper use of the reins, how to stop a pony, what leg the pony is on, and proper use of the aids, have never been heard of. Riding a hack or a hunter is one thing; riding a polo pony is a more specialized endeavor.

Having good form in striking a ball is essential. With a handful of exceptions—and each of them have improved enormously—the young players to-day will not and do not work at their trade. They come to the club to practice chukkers, play six of them, then they hurry off. If they had spent more on the practice ground quietly formulating their strokes, they would be a thousand times better off.

A young player with a magnificent string of ponies came to us saying: "I don't seem to be able to hit goals—what do I do about it?" We suggested that he take a bucket full of balls, string them out forty yards from the goal, and then circle around hitting at goal. Came the reply: "Oh, but I never stick and ball."

The best example of a player working at his trade is the Duke of Edinburgh. In his limited time, and no one can claim to be busier than he, Prince Philip stick-and-balls any available moment. If he arrives to play at any given ground, he gets on a pony and practices. He likes his polo and knows the more practice he puts in, the better he will enjoy playing the game.

Too many tournaments, as well as clubs not giving youngsters the opportunity of experience, are part and parcel of the same thing. Polo neophytes who can manage to ride and hit a polo ball, then immediately want to appear in public. It is a good incentive and fun playing for silver, but at the same time is a terrible deterrent to giving experience to beginners.[22]

Half a century after the above words of wisdom were written, the problem persists. Nowadays, players old and young are still put on a polo ground before they are ready, on ponies they cannot ride well, and in medium- or high-goal tournaments, where they are more of a hindrance than meaningful help.

CHAPTER 15

The Royal Family Lends a Hand

The game of polo in Britain has benefited enormously from the support given by the royal family since the earlier days of eight-a-side matches. The Prince of Wales, later King Edward VII, was a frequent spectator at polo games, quite often accompanied by his consort, Queen Alexandra, and their children.

Prince George, the Prince of Wales' second son, and future King George V, played polo in Argentina in 1881. When Prince Albert Victor, Duke of Clarence, second in the line of succession to the throne, and his younger brother George, Duke of York, were midshipmen on HMS *Bacchante*, they were invited to estancia Negrete. The Reverend John Neale Dalton, the princes' tutor, kept a minute diary of the voyage. The pertinent entry reads,

> After lunch there was a game of polo; on one side were Mr. Shennan (*il Patrone*), George, Prince Louis, Mr. Cooper, while on the other side were Mr. St. John, the captain, Eddy and Osbourne. Six games were played; of those the first three were won by the latter (the Baccantees as they called themselves) and the last three by the other side. The ponies were well trained, and the game is often played there, and makes an agreeable variety in the "camp life" which is said to be monotonous, owing to the want of neighbours.[1]

"George" and "Eddy" refer to the princes. David Anderson Shennan, a Scot, owned the estancia; Prince Louis was Prince Louis of Battenberg, later Mountbatten, the father of Lord Louis Mountbatten, the celebrated "Marco." George St. John was one of the early polo players in Argentina, who had participated on the first matches played at Negrete on 30 August 1875. The "captain" was Lord Charles Scott, the *Bacchante*'s commanding officer. Cooper and Osbourne were probably naval officers. There is a Charles Ernest Osbourne listed in the *London Gazette* as an officer in the Royal Navy.

The princes left a tangible memento of their visit to Negrete; they ceremonially planted two specimens of *Cypress Lambertiana*, one of which still stands in front of the manor house. A faded plaque memorializes the royal occasion.

The Duke of York became attracted to polo through his friendship with Sir George Godfrey-Fawcett, which had started when they were on HMS *Britannia*.[2] Prince George kept on playing polo, mostly at Malta, during his naval career. The demise of the Duke of Clarence, which made Prince George next in line for the succession, ended both his naval career and his polo endeavors.

Most of the polo played by the Duke of York took place in Malta. There is a record of a match played in December 1887 between the Berkshire Regiment and a Royal Navy team. The latter was formed by Lt. James Startin, Lt. HRH Prince George of Wales, Lt. Colin Keppel and Lt. Thomas Troubridge. The final result was a draw at three-all.

Several of the Royal Navy's ships in the Mediterranean Fleet had polo teams, including

The Duke of York, later King George VI, preparing to play for Hillmorton against Templeton, 1922 (private collection).

the flagship HMS *Alexandra*, HMS *Dolphin* and HMS *Surprise*. Prince George played most of his matches on the Alexandra's Team. On 17 July 1888 this team played the Gordon Highlanders, winning 6–2, with four goals scored by the prince. The team was Lt. HRH Prince George, Lt. Hon. Stanley Colville, Lt. Startin and Lt. Hon. Seymour Fortescue. The following day another match took place against a scratch Army team. The sailors won 7–6, with Lt. Allenby playing at back. At this time, Prince George was twenty-three years old, and his favorite pony was named Real Jam.[3]

Three of George V's sons played polo: the Prince of Wales, later Edward VIII; the Duke

Prince Philip and a pensive Prince Charles on their way to the pony lines. Both made immense contributions to the expansion of polo in Britain (courtesy Mike Roberts).

of York, later George VI; and Prince Henry, Duke of Gloucester. The latter was considered the best polo player of the three. The Duke of York was a good enough tennis player, competing in doubles in the All England Championships at Wimbledon. His partner was Wing Commander Louis Grigg. A natural left-handed player, the Duke of York played polo as a right-hander.

King Edward VIII was introduced to polo during a royal visit to India in 1921, when still Prince of Wales. His cousin Lord Louis Mountbatten was on the Royal entourage, and he too was smitten. A young Indian Cavalry officer, Capt. Edward Metcalfe, was attached to the prince's staff and became his polo manager. Upon his return to England, the Prince of Wales became a familiar figure on the London polo grounds. Just as he was when following hounds, the Prince of Wales was fanatically keen and fearless on the polo field

The next generation of royals saw Prince Philip, Duke of Edinburgh, come to the fore. There is no doubt whatsoever that his polo-playing endeavors, closely followed by Queen Elizabeth II, gave a tremendous impetus to the revival of polo in England after the war.

Lt. Philip Mountbatten's skills in polo were nurtured by his uncle, Lord Louis Mountbatten. At the time, the young Lt. Mountbatten was serving aboard HMS *Chequers*, deployed to the Mediterranean Fleet based in Malta. When the Duke of Edinburgh returned to England, he became one of the founding members of a revived Household Brigade Polo Club, which had been founded in 1897 as the Household Cavalry Polo Club.

Prince Philip took up polo with a passion and an unquenchable thirst to succeed. In spite of his innumerable public duties, Prince Philip reached a five-goal handicap and was quite successful as a valued captain and back of the Windsor Park team. With different players, his team took Cowdray Park's Gold Cup, emblematic of the British Open Championship, the Warwickshire Cup and the Cowdray Park Challenge Cup, among many other tournaments.

Perhaps the finest hour of the Duke of Edinburgh's polo career was in Argentina during the final game of the Hurlingham Club Open Championship in 1966. The Windsor Park team enlisted the brothers Alberto and Horacio Heguy, Daniel González and HRH Prince Philip. They faced the Argentine thirty-goal team, Alfredo Harriott, Gastón Dorignac, Juan Carlos Harriott, Jr., and Gonzalo Tanoira, all of whom were or eventually would be ten-goal handicap players. The Argentine Selection barely squeezed an 11–10 win, in a tight match in which Prince Philip shined at back. To put the result into perspective, that same Argentine team had defeated the thirty-goal Commonwealth team by twenty-four goals to two.

It appears that the Duke of Edinburgh seemed to play his best when it was a close game, going a little against his team; it was the mark of a seasoned competitor. Prince Philip retired from active polo in 1971, to dedicate his tremendous energy to coaching.

HRH the Prince of Wales inherited his father's passion for polo. Prince Charles began playing polo at age fourteen, knocking a ball on one of his father's docile polo ponies. HRH the Princess Anne sometimes joined her older brother in that endeavor; however, she achieved fame and glory in eventing, taking the 1971 European individual three-day-event, encompassing dressage, steeplechase, and show jumping. Princess Anne also represented Great Britain in the Montreal Olympic Games in 1972.

HRH Prince Charles' first important tournament win was the 1967 Junior County Cup, on a Windsor Park team that included his father HRH Prince Philip; Lt. Col. Peter Thwaites, later chairman of the Hurlingham Polo Association; and George Routledge, from the Guards Polo Club.

HRH Princes William and Harry at a charity match in Cirencester.

The prince's game was fine-tuned by Sinclair Hill, the talented Australian ten-goaler. With his steady improvement as a polo player, Prince Charles was selected to play for Young England against France, with the match ending in a win for the novice English team. Then Prince Charles represented Young England against a powerful American team with future nine-goaler Lester "Red" Armour as pivot. The game ended in a one-goal difference favoring the Young America team; however, Prince Charles acquitted himself well in his customary place at back.

Sporting a well-deserved four-goal handicap, Prince Charles joined Frenchman Guy Wildenstein's Les Diables Bleus team. Unfortunately, Prince Charles had, just like so many other good players, the agony of defeat in the final matches for the top prize in English polo, the coveted Cowdray Park Gold Cup. Always a gracious gentleman after a losing effort, Prince Charles set the standard for sportsmanship on the polo grounds in Britain. Upon his retirement from the game, at the time when the Prince of Wales was the most recognized figure in world polo, the royal torch has been taken by his two sons, Prince William and Prince Harry.

The Royal tradition in polo goes on without interruption, now on its fifth continuous generation, probably the longest ever in the game, from 1880 to date.

CHAPTER 16

Colonials and Foreigners
Change the Landscape

The 1960s witnessed the slow but steady influx of visitors that brought their own ponies, most with a previous understanding that the polo string would be purchased at season's end. The majority came from Argentina; however, there were a significant number of Brazilian, Indian, Pakistani and Mexican players, and a few from South Africa and Australia as well.

Cowdray Park Gold Cup

A review of the winning teams of the Cowdray Park Gold Cup reveals that from its inception in 1956 to the time of writing (2011), every championship winner has had a foreign player on the team, with the single sterling exception of Windsor Park in 1969, when the foursome of Lord Patrick Beresford, his brother the Marquis of Waterford, HRH Prince Philip and Paul Withers carried the trophy.[1]

Cowdray Park started the decade by defeating Baron Elie de Rothschild's Laversine in 1961. Brigadier Hesky Baig, Paul Withers, Alec Harper and Charles Smith-Ryland carried the orange jerseys. Just before halftime Colonel Harper suffered an injury to his arm and was unable to continue. John Lakin ably took his place on the team. Cowdray Park kept the trophy at home the next year, with Brian Bethell in Lt. Col. Alec Harper's place.

The Italian team La Vulci met Cowdray Park in the finals of the 1963 Gold Cup. The local team was ahead 6–2 at halftime but then made the mistake of playing a more defensive game. In protecting their hard-earned lead, Cowdray allowed Carlos de la Serna and Daniel González, La Vulci's defenders, to come up in the game. The game turned around, and La Vulci took the trophy by one goal, on a forty-yard penalty shot by Daniel González in extra time. The Marchese Giacinto Guglielme di Vulci and José "Negro" Torres Zavaleta from Argentina were the other players on La Vulci's team.

Then came one of Rao Rajah Hanut Singh's finest hours. Along with three young players, Patrick Kemple from Rhodesia, and the Argentines Ricardo Díaz Dale and Eduardo Moore, although only a seventeen-goal team, they took the Gold Cup two years running. Hanut once more revealed his masterful judgment of ponies and players. Under his strict direction, and mounted on Eric Moller's fast ponies, the chocolate and yellow Jersey Lilies team was unbeatable.

A young Gonzalo Tanoira, on his way to a ten-goal handicap rating, anchored the

Windsor Park team that took the trophy in 1966. The Beresford brothers and the Duke of Edinburgh provided solid support in their win over, once more, Cowdray Park.

John Lucas' team, Woolmers Park, swept the high-goal tournaments in 1967. Having assembled an outstanding polo pony string in Argentina with the help of his sister Claire, John Lucas, Dr. Marín Moreno, Enrique Zorrilla and Celestino Garrós proceeded to beat Sir David Brown's Chequers Manor in the finals. Chequers Manor — Peter Palumbo, Roberto James, Juan J. Díaz Alberdi and Edward Bowlby — took a measure of consolation when they took the Warwickshire Cup for beaten teams. As an aside, Celestino Garrós is one of the few, perhaps the only polo player that kept a lion as a pet, in his case at his estancia in Coronel Suárez.

In 1968 Chequers Manor made it to the finals again, only to lose the game to Lord David Brecknok's Pimms, which also had Julian Hipwood, Daniel González and Alfredo Goti in the lineup. Sadly, the Gold Cup trophy was stolen during a burglary at the Brecknocks' home and was never recovered. A replica was then commissioned. The Earl of Brecknock would go on to take the Gold Cup again in 1971 and 1972.

John Oxley's visiting Boca Raton team from Florida took the Gold Cup in 1970. Joey Casey, Jack Oxley and Roy Barry were the other team members. This was the first win by an American team in a major English tournament since 1938, when Charles Wrightsman's Texas Rangers took all four open tournaments in the London season, thus duplicating the Maharajah of Jaipur's 1933 feat.

The Queen's Cup

The Queen's Cup, presented by HM Queen Elizabeth II, was first played at the 13–20 goal level on handicap at Windsor Park in 1960, just prior to the Ascot Week. The first winners were Sir Evelyn de Rothschild's Centaurs, with Dr. Jorge Marín Moreno, John Lucas and Gabriel "Chino" Gracida.

The Centaurs would go on to take the handsome silver trophy in 1964, with South African Dereck Goodman, one of the well-known twins, in the number 1 slot, replacing Chino Gracida. The handicap level had been raised to twenty-two goals, and Jersey Lilies with Juan José Díaz Alberdi in place of Eric Moller was defeated in the semifinals by the favorites, Windsor Park, which had an impressive team, the Marquess of Waterford, Gonzalo Tanoira, Juan Carlos Harriott, Jr., and the Duke of Edinburgh. This was described as the best game of the tournament.[2] The Centaurs beat Cowdray in the first round and Silver Leys in the semifinals. They received 3½ goals from Windsor Park in the decisive game and hung on by their teeth to take game and cup by 5½ to 5.

It was then the turn of Silver Leys, with patron Alfie Boyd Gibbins; Captain Hugh Pitman, Royal Horse Guards; and two Indians, Maharajah Prem Singh and Risaldar Gaje Singh. A mixed Brazilian-Argentine team, Sao Silvestre, sponsored by Wally Simonsen, João Adao, Juan José Díaz Alberdi and Alejandro Mihanovich, won the 1962 edition.

Cowdray Park took the Queen's Cup in 1963 with a team of Cowdray regulars, Colonel Harper, Paul Withers, Sinclair Hill and Brian Bethell. This combine defeated Sao Silvestre in the semifinals and the Centaurs in the final, by 9 goals to 4½. Cowdray won again in 1970, with the perennial Harper, the Hipwood brothers and the Hon. Michael Hare, Lord Cowdray's nephew.

Lord George Brecknock's Pimms, one of the strongest teams in the 1960s, took the cup three out of four years. Brian Bethell, Celestino Garrós, Dr. Jorge Marín Moreno, John Lucas, Daniel González and Alejandro Soldati were also on the winning teams. In 1965, Pimms defeated Cowdray 10–9 in extra time; the following year they victimized Friar Park 6½ to 6, and in 1969, Chequers Manor went down 10–6½.

Woolmers Park showed its mettle in 1967, when Dr. Jorge Marín Moreno, Enrique Zorrilla, John Lucas and Celestino Garrós gave Cowdray Park seven goals by handicap, only to run away to a twenty to eleven goals win. The Lucas entry held the Queen's Cup the following year by besting Chequers Manor by 5 goals to 2½, giving half a goal on handicap. Sir Evelyn de Rothschild and Hernán Valenzuela replaced the Coronel Suárez duo of brothers-in-law Zorrilla and Garrós.

The Argentine Invasion

The trickle of Argentine players in the 1950s became the start of an avalanche in the 1960s, ranging from high-goal players to low-goalers, almost always accompanied by expansive horseflesh and ubiquitous *petiseros*.

A pair of 10-goal players, Juan Carlos Harriott, Jr., and Carlos Menditeguy, played in England, Harriott for Windsor Park and Charlie for Sao Silvestre. Both failed to have their names engraved on big-time silver trophies. Future ten-goalers Horacio Heguy and Gonzalo Tanoira represented Sao Silvestre and Windsor Park, respectively. Tanoira was on the team that took Cowdray's Gold Cup. Daniel González, another ten-goaler who took the Argentine Open Championship with both Coronel Suárez and Santa Ana, had a successful career in England.

Among many others, Horacio Baibiene; Eduardo Huergo, the current president of the Federation of International Polo; and Bertil Grahn played for the Centaurs; Juan Cavanagh, a nine-goaler from the legendary Venado Tuerto team, winner of seven Argentine Open Championships, played for Windsor Park, winning Cowdray's Challenge Cup and the Warwickshire with the Buccaneers. Also with the Cirencester-based Buccaneers, Robin Willans from Media Luna — whose father was killed during the war flying in the RAF — took the Warwickshire Cup on a team with Eduardo Moore and the Vestey brothers.

Wyndham Lacey, polo captain of the Hurlingham Club in Argentina, was a frequent visitor to England and played for the English Hurlingham team in South Africa. Rodolfo Lagos Mármol, one of four polo-playing brothers from Pergamino, took the County Cup with Ronnie Driver's Todham and the Warwickshire Cup with Sebastian de Ferranti's Kerfield. Finally, Carlos Miguens, Gonzalo Tanoira's father-in-law, was a finalist in the Cowdray Park Gold Cup on the Laversine team, Baron Elie de Rothschild's team.

Some came along as a team, such as San Miguel, with Miguel Cárcano, Francisco "Pancho" Soldati, Gastón Dorignac and Jorge Conte McDonnell, a team that took the Gold Cup at Deauville but failed to show its true potential on British soil.

Players from America

A Meadow Brook team from Long Island led by Alan Corey, Jr., visited England and also played at Deauville after the conclusion of the British season. In addition to the team captain, Alan Corey, the American squad included his son Alan III; George Sherman, Jr., soon to be chairman of the U.S. Polo Association; Juan Rodriguez; and William Hudson. The Meadow Brook team took along twenty-two ponies and was based at the Park House and the Spread Eagle in Midhurst.[3]

In the first round of the Cowdray Gold Cup, Meadow Brook drew the Centaurs, Dr. Marín Moreno, John Lucas, Gabriel Gracida and Evelyn de Rothschild. Lord Cowdray was the umpire, and the Centaurs won 10–3. In the subsidiary Midhurst Town Cup, a drastic change in the lineup put Rodriguez at back, Corey senior at number 3 and Hudson at 2, Sherman remaining at number 1. The ponies went much better than in the opening game, and the robin's egg blue team decisively defeated Argentina's La Espadaña 18–9½. On to the semifinals, where Meadow Brook won again, this time 8–6. In the finals, Hanut Singh led the Silver Leys team — Brian Bethell, Kishen, Hanut and Gaje — to a convincing 12–5 win over Meadow Brook.

In the Cowdray Park Challenge Cup, Alan Corey III, Sherman, Corey the elder and Rodriguez lost 5–4 to the Cowdray team — Withers, Harper, Hanut Singh and John Lakin — the eventual winners.

The same Meadow Brook team took the Westbury Cup at Windsor Park from the local team, Captain Ronald Ferguson, Prem Singh, Colonel Guinness and the Maharajah of Jaipur. Meadow Brook's final appearance was in the Horse and Hound Cup, when another Windsor team, Kisha Singh, HRH Prince Philip, Humphrey Guinness and Maj. Gen. David Dawnay, took the trophy.

Among the individual players from America that competed in England during these years were Lewis Smith, a nine-goal player born in England who worked for the Knox family in Buffalo and Aiken, and eight-goaler Peter Perkins, the son of Englishman Arthur Perkins, a winner of the U.S. Open Championship, eight-goal player and a horseman and instructor of great repute. Peter Perkins was in the Philippines at the start of World War II and was a survivor of the infamous Bataan Death March. While languishing in a Japanese POW camp, he was rescued by a Rangers unit commanded by his friend Maj. George Oliver, a future American international and nine-goal player. On seeing an elated Oliver, Perkins' laconic question was, "What took you so long?"[4]

A team from Hawaii but playing under the Santa Barbara name and sponsored by businessman Ruddy Tongg visited England in 1964. Dr. William Linfoot (nine goals), Ray Harrington (eight goals), Ronnie Tongg (three goals) and Harold Merck (two goals), with spare man Tenney Tongg, made up the team. They did well in the first tournament, The Duke of Sutherland Cup, by defeating Cowdray Park 13–3.[5]

In the Gold Cup, Santa Barbara was beaten by the Centaurs by one goal; however, they recovered to take the Midhurst Town Cup. With Billy Linfoot, a veterinarian; the brothers Tongg; and Harold Merck, they took the Harrison Cup and went on to Deauville to win the Coupe d'Or, with Daniel González in place of Tenney Tongg.

The Plainsmen Team

Another team from America was the Plainsmen, with John Armstrong, his son Charles and the Orthwein twins, Stephen and Peter, just graduated from Yale and Cornell. They had faced each other in three consecutive finals of the Inter-Collegiate Championship, Cornell University winning twice. They brought their own well-trained ponies for the English polo season. Brigadier Jack Gannon wrote, "The run of the ball was unkind to them in close finishes, causing them to lose by a goal or half a goal against eventual winners throughout."[6]

There were twenty entries in the Royal Windsor Cup, which was played mostly in the evenings after the races at Ascot Park. The semifinals saw Cirencester-based Lushill defeat Windsor Park, and the Plainsmen won over Friar Park. In the final game, Lushill — Frederick Barker, Howard Hipwood, Peter Perkins and Peter Gifford — was trailing 3–1 in the last chukker. Lushill made it three-all and time came after the Plainsmen missed a thirty-yard penalty shot. In extra time with widened goals, Lushill won 4–3.

In the Gold Cup semifinals Windsor Park had a comfortable lead at halftime, only for the Plainsmen to recover and tie the game at seven-all. At the final bell, Windsor scored to win by the odd goal in fifteen. Windsor Park went on to take the Gold Cup from Pimms on a penalty shot by Paul Withers.

A Team from Kenya

The Army Polo Committee invited a team from Kenya to play in Britain, the players being mounted by the clubs they played against. The team was composed of Francis Erskine, Petre Barclay, Johnnie Nimmo and Robin Savage, their back and captain, with Peter Davis as reserve.

Kenya lost in extra time the first match played at Windsor for the Godley Memorial Tournament.[7] The second match was played at Tidworth and was abandoned due to heavy weather, with the score tied at seven-all.

Then at Cowdray Park the hosts were too strong for the Kenyans, even though they had to concede 2½ goals by handicap. After an American tournament at Windsor, the team crossed the Irish Sea to play at Phoenix Park in Dublin against Irish teams, winning one and losing the other.

Back to England and on to Cirencester Park, where they defeated an Army team by four goals. Thus ended this tour, which was much enjoyed by visitors and hosts.

New Clubs in the 1960s

During this decade several clubs became affiliated with the Hurlingham Polo Association. The short-lived Canterbury Polo Club was started in 1966 under the name Invicta, with grounds on New House Lane, some three miles south of Canterbury. It failed five years later because of lack of players.

The Stapleford Polo Club was started by John Lucas at Old Enton, near Goldaming in Surrey in 1960. Then it moved to Suttons, Stapleford Tawney, in Essex.

The Stourhead Polo Club was started by Lt. Col. Thomas M. Baring, 10th Hussars, at Stourhead House in Somerset. A small club, its main tournament was the Stourhead Invitational Cup, traditionally played in early September.

CHAPTER 17

Renewal of the Coronation Cup

The Coronation Cup had been in abeyance since 1953, when it had been revived after World War II. The presence on British soil of two American teams, Columbia and Green-hill Farm, facilitated the renewal of the competition in a single match. The year was 1971, and the American team was Ronnie Tongg, Dr. William Linfoot, Harold "Chico Barry" and his son Harold "Joe" Barry, a twenty-eight-goal combination. England presented the Hon. Mark Vestey, Howard and Julian Hipwood, and Paul Withers, totaling twenty-three goals.

Played at Cowdray Park in front of the largest crowd since the 1953 Coronation Cup at the same venue, for some unknown reason the game was contested on the level. England did well on a losing cause, 9–6. Had the match been played on handicap, England would have won by two goals (complete results appear in appendix 3).

The venue was moved to Smith's Lawn at Windsor Park, America once more being the winner by six goals to three. Paul Withers was playing on a rainy day with a cast due to a fractured thumb on his left hand. The wet conditions softened his cast, and Withers had to be replaced by Lord Patrick Beresford during the first chukker.[1]

The Young England team that included HRH Prince Charles at back played in the second game against a Young America team. It was touch and go throughout in a rainy day, on a rather cut-up ground, with the contest being locked in a tie in the last chukker. Lester "Red" Armour scored the winning goal for Young America on a penalty shot.

In 1973, again at Windsor, the American team took the Coronation Cup by the odd goal in thirteen, on a forty-yard penalty converted by Billy Linfoot with twenty seconds remaining on the clock.

Once more, England lost in 1974 by a single goal, 4–3. It was the same story: an even match through five chukkers, with Paul Withers scoring the equalizer at three-all in the final chukker. England kept on pressing, but a breakaway by Tommy Wayman resulted in the winning tally within seconds of the final bell.

Four years of frustration for England facing the United States were followed by another four years of defeat against teams of Argentine players labeled South America.

The 1978 contest had three first cousins on the South American team: Gonzalo Pieres Garrahan, Héctor Crotto Garrahan and Alex Garrahan. Abel "Negro" Aguero was the fourth member.

Only in 1979 England's John Horswell, Paul Withers, Julian Hipwood and Howard Hipwood were able to lift the massive Coronation Cup, after a twenty-six-year drought. They defeated Mexico by nine goals to seven.

England won again in 1981, when Alan Kent, the Hipwood brothers and Lord Charles

Above: Julian Hipwood, Captain of England for over twenty years, playing at Guards Polo Club for the Coronation Cup (courtesy Mike Roberts). *Right:* Howard Hipwood in the foreground, followed by Henry Brett, playing for England in the Coronation Cup.

Beresford beat New Zealand by six goals to four. The same players, albeit in different slots, defeated New Zealand 8–6 the following year.

Two successive wins by Mexico, with the Gracida brothers Carlos and Guillermo "Memo," were followed by a USA win. In 1988 England defeated America with Andrew Seavill, Julian Hipwood, John Horswell and Lord Charles Beresford, followed by wins over Australasia and France — the latter with some Argentine reinforcements, Santiago Gaztambide in this case — and a defeat at the hands of New Zealand in 1991.

There was no competition for the Coronation Cup in 1992 on account of the Westchester Cup being held at Windsor Park.

Upon resumption of the competition, Chile and South Africa went down, the latter by a somewhat embarrassing 11–1 score. The Hurlingham Polo Association then felt that the time had come to challenge Argentina once more, and they selected Will Lucas, Alan Kent, Howard Hipwood and Lord Beresford to carry the Rose of England. Alas, the Argentines proved just too strong and denied England by scoring fourteen goals against eight. England then beat Brazil 8–4 before another parenthesis for the Westchester Cup, taken by England for the first time since 1914. To paraphrase the musical Cats, a day of celebration was proclaimed in London town.

The last three Coronation Cups of the twentieth century were all decided by a single goal. Chile beat England 7–6, England defeated Australasia 11–10 and Argentina won 10–9 in extra time. Oh, so close and yet so far.

Long before the turn of the century the International Polo Day had become by far the most important single-day event in the polo season. The presence of HM Queen Elizabeth to give the trophy at the game's end assured that a huge crowd, surpassing 20,000, would witness the celebrations. In the rare case of her absence, some other royal personage would give away the trophy. As part of the show, a morning match for the Silver Jubilee Cup, and after 2002 for the Golden Jubilee Cup, provided good entertainment value for the spectators and also served as a trial game for younger players who had shown the possibilities of reaching full international status.

Close games became the norm for the Coronation Cup. In 2001, England — Julian Daniels, replaced during the match by Roddy Williams; Henry Brett; William Lucas; and Andrew Hine — beat Brazil 8–7. The next year, the Rest of the Commonwealth defeated England in the seventh chukker by eleven goals to ten. Fred Mannix, from Canada; Australians John Baillieu and Glen Gilmore; and Simon Keyte from New Zealand were on the winning team.

In 2003, England defeated Mexico, represented by four members of the Gracida family: the brothers Carlos and Memo, and cousins Rubén Gracida and Roberto González Gracida. The score was 8–7; England had Will Lucas, his cousin Luke Tomlinson, Henry Brett and Andrew Hine.

The Chileans proved to be a thorn in England's side. Alejandro Vial, brothers José and Gabriel Donoso, and Jaime García Huidobro won 10–8 in 2004 and repeated the performance three years later, with a 9–8 win. José Zegers, Martín Zegers, José Donoso and Jaime García Huidobro played for Chile on this occasion. Starting with a one-goal handicap, Chile played an emotional game because their star player Gabriel Donoso had died the previous December as the result of a polo accident in Argentina. The score was tied at four-all at halftime; then Chile went ahead, leading by three goals in the last chukker. Henry Brett and James Beim scored for England, to trail by a single tally, 9–8. Then Luke Tomlison went on a break away and hit the ball straight toward goal. Inexplicably, the ball veered away, wide of the goal. Chile was saved from going into extra time. After the match was over, José Donoso said, "I don't know what happened. It was as if Gabriel had leant down from heaven, stuck out a hand and pushed the ball away from the goal line."[2]

In 2005, Australia beat England in extra chukker, eight goals to seven. The next year, England came back to defeat New Zealand 9–7. Beim, Mark Tomlinson, Brett and Luke Tomlinson were on the team. England took revenge from Australia in 2008, when James Beim, Mark Tomlinson, Malcolm Borwick and team captain Luke Tomlinson beat the Aussies in a very close game by ten goals to nine.

The bogeyman, Argentina, once more proved too good for the same English team in 2009. The Argentines send two of the best players in the world, Adolfo Cambiaso and

Facundo Pieres, with Gustavo Usandizaga and Martín Valent completing the team, to do battle on Smith's Lawn. The South Americans asserted their superiority with a 12–5 win.

That same England team, Beim, the Tomlinsons and Borwick, defeated New Zealand in 2010, not without some anxious moments. England jumped to an apparently unassailable 6–1 lead at tread-in time. Borwick added one tally to make the scoreboard 7–1; somehow, New Zealand tied the game at seven-all with five minutes to go in the sixth and final chukker. The rattled English team regained its composure, Beim and Luke Tomlinson scoring one goal each in the waning minutes of a terrific game.

CHAPTER 18

The Game Grows Unabated

The 1970s were a period of great expansion in English polo. The decade was dominated by the Vestey brothers' organization, which had started in 1969. Their star player was the mercurial Eddie Moore, a scion of an Irish family in Argentina, who eventually would become the first ten-goal handicap player in England since Gerald Balding had achieved that rating in 1939.

Stowell Park and Foxcote teams were primordial in England based upon the financial support of Lord Samuel Vestey and the Hon. Mark Vestey. The bulky Héctor Barrantes' playing at back provided solid support to Eduardo "Gordo" Moore's at times idiosyncratic moves. Nevertheless, the image of Eddie Moore on the ponies Fabiola and Lass will remain forever in the minds of those lucky enough to have witnessed his play. Lass was an Australian pony, and Fabiola was bred in Argentina by Eduardo Rojas Lanusse.

The record of high-goal trophies taken by the Vestey's organization is most impressive: six Cowdray Park Gold Cups, seven Queen's Cups, five Warwickshire Cups and four Cowdray Challenge Cups. To all those, it might be added a pair of County Cups and innumerable other tournaments.

In addition to the four starters, David Gemmell, a Scot friend of the Vesteys; Nick Williams, a useful player from Gloucestershire; Peter Palumbo; and Philip Elliott were on those championship teams. It was mostly teamwork, because only Mark Vestey caught the selectors' eye to earn a place on the English international team. Add a superb pony string, masterfully managed by another "Gordo," Héctor Barrantes, good chemistry among the players, and you have a winning formula.

The Centenary Polo Match

In commemoration of the first organized polo game in England, a polo match was held at Smith's Lawn in June 1970. Players and umpires were attired in contemporary clothing: pillbox hats, regimental ties and long trousers. The match was witnessed by the Queen Mother and painted on canvas by the artist Terence Cuneo.[1] A reproduction of this painting is on the cover of Major J.P.N. Watson's book *Smith's Lawn — The History of Guards Polo Club*.[2]

The 10th Hussars were represented by serving and retired officers: Lord George Willoughby Norrie, General John Willis, Brigadier Jack Archer-Shee, Brigadier Roscoe Harvey, Colonel Sir Piers Bengough, Major Hugh Dawnay, Peter Derryhouse and Guy Malet de Carteret. Players on the 9th Lancers team included David Gemmell and Peter Swindells. The umpires were HRH the Duke of Edinburgh and Louis Mountbatten, Earl of Burma.

Chatting in the rain: HM the Queen with the Stowell Park team following one of their many victories, in this case the Queen's Cup. Lord Samuel Vestey, the dynamic duo of Barrantes and Moore, and Chris Bethell, who replaced Mark Vestey (courtesy Mike Roberts).

Rutland Polo Club

A new polo club was established in 1971 by Colonel A.P. "Tony" Gilks, Charles Humfrey, Major John Gillies Shields and I.M. "Mike" Seckington, among other enthusiasts. The original fields were at Luffenham Airfield and then were moved to Cream Gorse and the Oakham Showground. In 1984, the club moved to a ground at Langham owned by Ronnie Anker. There was also another field at Langham, and John Tinsley, sometime chairman of the HPA, allows the club members the use of his private ground. A team from the club made history by touring Kenya in 1976.

Colonel Sir Roland Findlay, Royal Scots Greys, was president, a post he held until his death in 1980. Colonel Gilks was chairman for a remarkable thirty years. He became president in 2001, when he handed the reins to Edwin De Lisle.

The club's trophies include the Assam Cup, which was originally presented in 1897 as the First Sibsagar Cup, played at the Decoy Club in Assam. The cup was taken to England by Ian Leetham in 1963, and later was given to the Rutland Polo Club by the HPA. The current trophy is a copy of the original, which was stolen in 1997. Mr. Leetham was unable to play due to an injury sustained during a game in India; however, Mrs. Leetham played occasionally in the 1970s.

The Rutland Cup was presented by Peter Harvey, a member in the 1970s. About this time, John Tinsley gave the Spring Cup. Colin Seavill joined the club and with his three sons played at Rutland before moving near Cowdray upon inheriting a family home. After he left Rutland, Mr. Seavill gave a silver bowl, which is the main Challenge Trophy and is known as the Seavill Bowl. As a memorial to Sir Roland Findlay, the club, with most generous help from Lady Findlay, acquired a fine bronze statue of a polo player in action. The Bronze Horse Trophy is played for annually. Lady Findlay also gave the club a small silver trophy, a miniature replica of the English Inter-Regimental Challenge Cup that Sir Roland won as a member of the Scots Greys team in 1937. The Findlay Cup is the main trophy for one of the club's internal competitions annually.

The Corinthian Trophy was commissioned by the club using a legacy left by Colonel Stephen Eve, the club's second president. The trophy itself is in the shape of a hussar's busby that commemorates Colonel Eve's long service in the Queen's Own Hussars. This is a challenge cup for an all-amateur competition.

The Rutland Club also hosts the Whitbread Cup, a national HPA competition presented by Colonel William Whitbread to encourage low-handicap players and beginners in the game.

The Queen's Cup

The presence of two teams from America added significant interest to the 1971 polo season. Oak Brook, led by Michael Butler, and Greenhill Farm from Oklahoma, owned by former Chaparral racing car driver James Sharp, competed in the high-handicap tournaments.

Lt. Col. Sean O'Dwyer, Paul Withers, Lord Patrick Beresford and Prince William of Gloucester enjoy the spoils of victory. A promising polo player, Prince William's life was cut short in an aircraft accident (courtesy Mike Roberts).

Top: Stowell Park, with Nicky Williams, Héctor Barrantes, Lord Vestey and Eduardo Moore, retained the 1978 Queen's Cup within Gloucestershire's friendly confines. *Bottom:* Los Locos was the dominant team in medium- and low-goal polo. Emma Tomlinson, David Stirling, Rosie Vestey presenting the trophies, Gastón Laulhé and Claire Tomlinson.

In the first round Oak Brook gave Pimms 4½ goals and sneaked a 9–8½ win. Greenhill Farm defeated Windsor Park 7½ to 4; Jersey Lilies beat Lavender Hill 6½–5, and in a crucial contest, powerhouses Cowdray and Stowell gave and took with gusto; a pair of last chukker penalties gave the Vestey team a 9–7½ win. The pundits favored a final between the two American entries; however, Jersey Lilies defeated Oak Brook in extra time, and Stowell Park ran by Greenhill Farm 7–3. So much for prognostications by the experts.

The final was a dandy. Peter Palumbo, with an injured hand, was replaced before the start by Robert Hodgkinson, a Cambridge man who played at Cowdray. This change made the teams even on handicap. Stowell Park entered the last chukker comfortably ahead by five goals to two. The Jersey Lilies battled hard and scored a pair of goals, and kept the pressure on. However, Stowell Park's defense stood firm, and the match ended 5–4.

Teams from Gloucestershire continued to get the lion's share of the Queen's Cup in the 1970s. Stowell Park took the cup in 1973, 1978 and 1980, while the other Vestey entry, Foxcote, won in 1975 and 1977, the Silver Jubilee year. And the up-and-coming Los Locos, venturing into the rarified atmosphere of high-goal polo after sweeping the board at lower levels, took the Queen's Cup in 1979. It was a personal victory for Claire Lucas Tomlinson, who finally was allowed to participate in high-goal tournaments after a protracted struggle to gain recognition for women's polo in general and her own individual ability in particular.[3]

Cowdray Park, and San Flamingo twice, were the other winning teams in this decade.[4] Full results are listed in appendix 3.

The Cowdray Park team, winners of the Warwickshire Cup and the 1977 Rothman Trophy. Standing, Patrick Churchward, John Cowdray and Paul Withers. In front, Gonzalo Pieres and the Hon. Michael Hare, Lord Cowdray's nephew (courtesy Mike Roberts).

The Warwickshire Cup

After spending some years out of the limelight, when it was competed for at the 15–20 goal level by teams beaten in the quarterfinals of the Gold Cup, the Warwickshire Cup was resumed as a tournament in its own right during County Cup Week at Cirencester Park. A modest number of teams, four, entered the competition. Ronnie Driver's San Flamingo had the Hipwood brothers and New Zealander Anthony Devcich. This team proved too strong for Stowell Park, which had Peter Perkins in Héctor Barrantes' place. Pimms had Lord Brecknock, Enrique Zorrilla, Daniel González and Major Ferguson. This combination disposed of Lavender Hill and faced San Flamingo in the championship game. In a good game at Ivy Lodge, San Flamingo took the cup 6½–5, holding on to the handicap they had received.

Once more, another trophy became an opportunity for Stowell Park to demonstrate its superiority, taking the Warwickshire on several occasions. However, Cowdray Park gave as good as it took, winning the cup four times in the decade. Sandy Harper, Colonel Harper's son; Paul Withers; Michael Hare; Celestino Garrós; Australian Richard Walker; Patrick Churchward; Gonzalo Pieres; Mexican Antonio Herrera; and Charles Pearson were on the Cowdray Park teams

The Golden Eagles and Galen Weston's Roundwood Park were the other winning teams of the old trophy, given by some of the townspeople of Leamington Spa in 1894.

The Gold Cup

The American team Columbia, named after Heath Manning's hometown in South Carolina, drew Cowdray Park in the first round of the 1971 competition. Columbia — Ronnie Tongg, Corky Linfoot, his father Billy and Heath Manning — defeated the hosts 11–10 in extra chukker. An identical situation happened in the game between Pimms and Jersey Lilies, won by Pimms by the odd goal in twenty-one. Lord Brecknock most appropriately scored the winning goal in extra time. Greenhill Farm disposed of Stowell Park, which was missing Barrantes, by eight goals to seven, and Windsor Park beat Lavender Hill 6–3. In the semifinals, Columbia won over Windsor Park, and Pimms beat Greenhill Farm in a close-run thing, nine goals to eight.

So on to the final, where Pimms took off scoring four goals in the first chukker. Undaunted, Columbia made it even at five goals before the ritual of treading-in. Three sixty-yard penalties converted by Doc Linfoot, against a single tally by Pimms meant an 8–6 lead for Columbia at the start of the last chukker. An exciting final chukker followed: Daniel González scored two goals and set up Zorrilla for another, only for Linfoot to tie the game at nine-all. Enrique Zorrilla scored, and Linfoot — always Linfoot — made it ten-all. With time running out, Ronald Ferguson took an angled shot that was flagged for the winning goal. It was a last chukker for the ages.

Pimms went on to take the Cowdray Park Challenge Cup, and Cowdray won the subsidiary Midhurst Town Cup for those teams defeated in the Gold Cup.

Persistent stormy weather marred most of the 1972 season, with the exception of a glorious August. The Cowdray Park team — William Cort Linfoot, Howard Hipwood, Dr. William Linfoot and the Hon. Michael Hare — which had looked as the top of the class in taking the Queen's Cup, lost to Guy Wildenstein's Les Diables Bleus in the first round of their own Gold Cup. Conversely, Pimms, beaten in the first round of the Queen's Cup, went off to win the tournament beating Stowell Park in the finals. Stowell Park then proceeded to take Cowdray's Challenge Cup.

Then began the glory years of Stowell Park, for they took the Gold Cup no less than five times in the next eight-year span. In addition to the four regular players, David Gemmell, Nick Williams and Philip Elliott were on the winning teams. The concomitant raise

Stowell Park's glory days: Héctor Barrantes and the Hon. Mark Vestey turning the play and looking for the ball (courtesy Mike Roberts).

in the players' handicaps meant that Mark Vestey entered the lids with his own Foxcote team. Peter Palumbo, Eduardo Moore and the hard-hitting Daniel Devrient won the Gold Cup in the Silver Jubilee year, beating perennial finalist Cowdray Park.

In 1975, the Greenhill Farm team from Tulsa, Oklahoma, sponsored by James "Hap" Sharp, with son-in-law Tommy Wayman, Red Armour and Major Ronald Ferguson, put a parenthesis in the Gloucestershire team's unbeaten run.

The only other winner in the course of this decade was Songhai, with Millfield School product Alan Kent, the brothers Alvaro and Gonzalo Pieres, and Oliver Ellis.

The Inter-Regimental Tournament

The Blues and Royals were the dominant team in this decade, with four wins. Major Brian Lockhart, Captain Andrew Parker Bowles, Major Hugh Pitman and Major William Boucher were the team members. In later years, Nigel Haddon-Paton, Dennis Darley and the irrepressible Captain Somerville Livingstone-Learmonth were on winning teams.

Then in 1972, it was the turn of the 17th/21st Lancers, a polo-playing regiment with a long and successful history dating back to 1903, when a 17th Lancers team took two consecutive tournaments under the captaincy of their commanding officer, Lt. Col. Bertram

The Welsh Guards team posted a most impressive string of wins in the Inter-Regimental Tournament. This is the 1991 squad: Capt. Oliver Richardson, Maj. Simon Stephenson, Maj. Anthony Ballard and Lt. Col. Reddy Watt, now General Sir Redmond Watt. The trophy is the United Services Cup, designed after the Warwick Vase (courtesy Mike Roberts).

Portal. This healthy tradition of the colonel leading the team was continued during the formidable run in the 1920s and 1930s, with T.P. Melvill and Vivian Lockett, following amalgamation with the 21st Lancers. After World War II, the commanding officers, David Barbour, Ronald Coaker and Arthur Douglas-Nugent, maintained the flame alive. The 1972 winning team, led by Lt. Col. Douglas-Nugent, was completed with a subaltern, Michael Amoore, later of the Royal Berkshire Club, Captain Fiennes Strang-Steele and Captain Christopher Churton.

The following year, the Queen's Own Hussars team, Harold Cunningham, Major Charles Lockhart, Ian Farquhar and Captain Hugh Boucher, revived the glory days of the previous decade, when three consecutive championships were obtained in 1965–1967. This regiment was the result of the amalgamation of the 3rd Hussars and the 7th Hussars in 1958.

The Welsh Guards, led on the polo field by the superior play of "Reddy" Watt, now General Sir Redmond Watt, KBC, KCVO, CBE, took the Inter-Regimental Tournament in 1976, the first one of seven titles won by this regiment.

The remaining two tournaments held during this decade were won by the Royal Military Academy at Sandhurst, and the Life Guards.

Polo at the Pony Club

Pony Club polo was started in 1959 by the Hon. Guy Cubitt, Major Claude Davenport and Brigadier Jack Gannon, at the time joint secretary of the HPA. Teams from five branches gathered at Aldershot Garrison on a Sunday afternoon to compete in an American tournament. The Hampshire Hunt branch took the honors, the teams playing one eight-minute chukker, extended to two minutes in the final game.

Eight teams entered the following year; the Staff College was the winner. In 1962 the Vale of the White Horse, with David Braund, Adam Smail, and Howard and Julian Hipwood, took the rosettes. In 1964, the venue was changed to Cirencester, and three years later it became a two-day tournament. By then, there were two competitions: the Gannon Trophy, reserved for twenty-one-year-old players, and the Handley Cross Cup, for under sixteen.

J.W.M. "Buff" Crisp took over the chairmanship in 1977, and he was to have the longest tenure, until 1988. Under his strong leadership, pony club polo took off. More divisions were added, entries skyrocketed and sponsorships were obtained. Furthermore, branches have organized their own tournaments, besides the championship proper.

Windsor, Cirencester and then Cowdray Park became the venues. When Mr. Crisp — who had succeeded Colonel Patrick Langford as chairman — moved on to be the Hurlingham Polo Association's secretary, his position was occupied by Brigadier John Wright, who in turn was succeeded by Luke Borwick.

J.W.M. Crisp, chairman of the Polo Pony Club and the long-term secretary of the Hurlingham Polo Association.

Then David Cowley took over, and during his eight-year tenure, pony club polo grew exponentially.[5]

The Hurlingham Polo Association

This decade was a time for change in the leadership of the HPA when R. Alan Budgett, who had succeeded Lord John Cowdray as chairman, decided he would not be able to give sufficient time to the association's activities and elected to step down after seven productive years at the helm.

Mr. Budgett was succeeded by Douglas Riley-Smith, TD, from the Toulston Polo Club in Yorkshire. Like his predecessor, Mr. Riley-Smith was a keen polo player, thus continuing the healthy and time-proven tradition that active players should be guiding the destiny of the Hurlingham Polo Association. Lord Cowdray remained in his position as vice chairman.

Brigadier Jack Gannon, CBE, MVO, and Lt. Col. Alexander Harper, DSO, continued in their roles as joint honorary secretaries.

The number of polo clubs in England remained stable; in 1970 there were nineteen affiliated clubs and in 1980 the number was twenty-one.[6] On the other hand, the number of players rose from 387 to 518 in the same time span.

The Buck's Club Dinner

"A minor landmark in the history of the game, was established a few weeks ago when 27 Englishmen on the polo scene entertained some of the visiting players to dinner in London. The party, which took place in Buck's on July 21, marked an old Club tradition. When Cap. Herbert Buckmaster and some of his brother-officers in the Royal Horse Guards were on leave from the trenches in the First World War they took exception to the numerous—and, as they thought, petty—rules of the Cavalry Club, and, as a result, Buckmaster promised them he would have his own club. He was a considerable athlete and a keen, though not brilliant, polo player, and he had a wonderful feeling for sportsmanship. Through his cousin, Walter Buckmaster, whose team won the Champion Cup 11 times between 1900 and 1921, he followed closely the fortunes of the English foursome and got to know and like their American Westchester opponents. To foster England's image as a host nation he organized annual polo dinners at his club, and these gave rise to the considerable American membership that still thrives. The idea of resurrecting these dinners came from two club members, W.E. Channing and a former Blues player, J.N.P. Watson, who is now polo correspondent to *Country Life*. A third member, Lord Vestey, who was to take the chair, sent out the invitations. Although, in the end, no Americans could be in England on July 21, and only three visiting players attended—Luis Sosa Basualdo (Argentina), Sinclair Hill (Australia) and Galen Weston (Canada)—the dinner was such a popular success that the organizers plan to make it an annual affair. Col. Humphrey Guinness, the prewar international; Lord Vestey; Douglas Riley-Smith, chairman of the Hurlingham Polo Association; Malcolm Lyell, the chairman of Buck's; and Sinclair Hill entertained those present with amusing speeches, and besides those already named, the following were at the table to hear them: Col. Alec Harper, the British team manager, and Messrs. David Bagnell, Colin Baillieu, Geoffrey Cross, Peter Cruden, the Hon. Michael Hare, John Hine, Harry Horswell, John Horswell, Victor Law, Major Willie Loyd, Peter Palumbo and Major Ronnie Scott."[7]

CHAPTER 19

Polo Tours Overseas

Polo in Colombia and Kenya

In the autumn of 1960, two tours were undertaken by young players. The first one was to Colombia, where the players, the Hon. George Bathurst, Clement Barton, the Marquis of Waterford and Paul Withers, total handicap eleven goals, were hospitably entertained. Five matches were played against mixed opposition. The British won the first three encounters; then the locals brought some heavy artillery to the field and won the last two matches.[1]

The Army Saddle Club organized the second tour, to Kenya. Captain Lord Patrick Beresford, Lt. Paul Withers, Lt. Col. Jakes W. Harman, Captain Ronald Ferguson, and Lt. Malcolm Sherwin as spare, went on the tour. Nine matches were played, all on handicap, and ended with the British Army team winning all nine.[2]

Hurlingham at Santa Barbara

A British team under the name Hurlingham visited the Santa Barbara Polo Club in California in 1962. Mounted by the local players, Lord Patrick Beresford, his brother Tyrone Waterford, Ronald Ferguson and Charles Smith-Ryland defeated their hosts in the most important match. In a close contest, Hurlingham ended on the right side of an 8–7 result.

Cowdray Park at Oak Brook and Milwaukee

Of major significance was the tour undertaken by a team wearing Cowdray Park's orange jerseys in 1963. Led by Australian ace Sinclair Hill, Paul Withers, Major Ferguson and the Beresford brothers started the proceedings at the Milwaukee Polo Club's home ground, with a two-game series for the Robert A. Uihlein International Cup. The two games were split; Cowdray took the first 11–3 and lost the second 8–7, thus taking the trophy on aggregate goals.

Unfortunately, an equine viral epidemic affected the fourteen ponies brought from England and over one hundred local mounts. Practice games were shortened to five chukkers in order to save the mounts for the Butler National Handicap, an important USPA tournament held annually at Paul Butler's Oak Brook complex located in the outskirts of Chicago.

In this competition's semifinals, Oak Brook most sportingly defaulted to Cowdray Park, so they could loan the ponies to the visitors. In the other semifinal game, Tulsa beat Milwaukee, to earn the right to face Cowdray in the finals. Tulsa was a twenty-five-goal team formed by Jules Romfh, Ray Harrington, Harold "Chico" Barry and John Oxley the elder. Tulsa gave Cowdray two goals by handicap, and that pair of goals was all Cowdray Park needed to carry the cup 12–10.

It was a most significant victory. Chris Ashton wrote,

> The London Times waxed lyrical: Let the flags fly high at Midhurst tonight and bells ring out at Willow Tree, N.S.W., for this week Australian Sinclair Hill and his team have written the name Cowdray Park into American polo history. They have played and defeated two of the best 25-goal teams in the U.S. and in the manner of their victory have earned a new respect for British polo overseas.[3]

The British Army Attacks Washington

"The Red Coats came again, but this time it was a cheery four-man polo team made up of officers from crack British Cavalry regiments on an invitational polo tour arranged by Bob Beer of Potomac, Jack Shirley of the Woodland Polo Club and the instigation of Major David Nicholson, attached to the British Embassy here."[4]

The 1973 visitors were team captain Major Hugh Pitman, Household Cavalry; Major Roland Notley, Scots Dragoon Guards; Captain Bristow Bovill, Inniskilling Dragoons and Captain Michael Strang-Steel, 17th/21st Lancers, a ten-goal team.

Upon arrival on a RAF flight, the team was almost immediately taken to the polo arena for socializing, dining and a polo match against a local team of Frank Wilson, Rennie Eisinger and Peter Rizzo. Everyone was prepared to make allowances for the English team because of the new time zone, strange ponies, and the fact that they had not played an arena game. Nevertheless, the British Army team played very well, barely losing to an experienced arena polo team and being able to party afterward. Their fearless leader, Major Pitman, said, "Headquarters would never consider sending a cavalry team over that couldn't drink, stay up late, and still play better than ever."[5]

It was the beginning of the hunting season in the beautiful Virginia countryside, and the officers were treated to a hunt breakfast, morning cubbing, hunting and other pastimes, including sailing, a cruise along the Potomac River and a visit to Chesapeake Bay.

Polo at Washington took place on Sunday at the Lincoln Mall, for the Chief of Protocol Tournament, given by Colonel Marion Smoak, a polo player. At an American system tournament, the British Army team defeated the American Colonels and lost to Potomac.

In Pennsylvania, the Army team defeated a Brandywine team led by Fred Fortugno, and then they played a four chukker match prior to the Harvard-Princeton American football game.

A trip to Charlottesville for more polo and a visit with Dr. and Mrs. Douglas Vere Nicoll followed, with more hunting and a tour of Monticello, Thomas Jefferson's home.

After hunting in Maryland, Pennsylvania and Virginia, playing polo in three different clubs, a delay in their flight back to Europe allowed the squad to attend the Fairfax Hunt meet, where Major Notley was conscripted to enter in the Mule Race. The results of that particular event are not available.

The British Commonwealth Team in Argentina, 1966

The 1966 edition of the Cup of the Americas was played in Buenos Aires in the South American spring of 1966. As part of the celebrations of the sesquicentennial of Argentina's independence from Spain, the Argentine Polo Association organized a thirty-goal tournament among teams from the United States, Argentina and England. A British Commonwealth squad was selected to travel to Buenos Aires under the guidance of Rao Rajah Hanut Singh.

The selected players were HRH Prince Philip (five goals), Sinclair Hill (nine goals) from Australia, Patrick Kemple (seven goals) from Rhodesia, Lord Patrick Beresford (four goals), Major Ronald Ferguson (five goals), Lord Waterford (four goals) and Paul Withers (six goals). At first, the team lined up Beresford 1, Kemple 2, Hill 3 and Withers, back. This was changed later to Kemple, Hill, Ferguson and Withers.[6]

The team entered the Hurlingham Open Championship, defeating in the first round a twenty-four-goal Tortugas side by nine goals to seven. In the semifinals, Windsor Park, with Alberto Heguy, Horacio Heguy, Daniel González and the Duke of Edinburgh, won the match 15–5. This unfavorable result was the reason for the team's lineup change.

In the Argentine Open, the first round matched England versus another Tortugas team, this one a twenty-seven-goal team. England prevailed 11–10, only to lose in the semifinals to perennial champion Coronel Suárez by nineteen goals to six.

The International thirty-goal series started with the Commonwealth facing the Americans, Northrup Knox, Robert Beveridge, Harold Barry and Jackie Murphy, at Palermo's number-one field. It was a most satisfactory win for the British team. The scoring by chukker was: 2/1, 5/2, 8/3, 10/4, 12/5, 13/6 and 13/8. Seven chukkers were played as a compromise between the six periods common in America and the United Kingdom, and the customary eight chukkers in Argentina high-goal competitions.

This encouraging result gave high hopes for the match against the Argentine thirty-goal side, Alfredo Harriott, Gastón Dorignac, Juan Carlos Harriott and Gonzalo Tanoira. Due to rain, there was a two-week delay that made it practically impossible to play practice games. When the day came about at Palermo, everything went Argentina's way. The final score, 24–2, tells the story without further words.

The Argentine team went on to beat the Americans by thirteen goals to six. All four players on the local team went on to achieve a ten-goal rating. Seasoned observers felt that the thirty-goal team was better than the Cup of the Americas team, at thirty-five goals. When the handicap committee modified the individual handicaps at season's end, the international thirty-goal squad became a thirty-four-goal team.

UK Tours of South Africa

A team named Hurlingham Rovers, comprised of the Marquis of Waterford; Lord Patrick Beresford; Wyndham Lacey, an Anglo-Argentine that served during World War II; and Major Ronald Ferguson — an eighteen-goal side — landed in Johannesburg in August 1965 for a series of matches played without handicap over six chukkers.

The first one was held on a sunbaked field at Inanda Country Club against Orange Free State, Hurlingham winning 5–4. Next, the visitors defeated Transvaal by eight goals to five. Robin Wilson, who had spent time in England under Hanut Singh's tuition, was on the Transvaal side.

A Combined Northern Provinces was the next adversary, which inflicted the first defeat for the Rovers, 9–4. Lacey injured a riding muscle and was unable to play in the next game against Rhodesia. His place was taken by Donald Buchanan, an Irish-Argentine two-goaler. Hurlingham Rovers won the contest 5–4.

The visitors then moved on to Natal, where they played the first match at Richmond, on a ground that Lord Beresford described as "a polo field that bears comparison with any ground I have ever seen."[7] An exhibition game against a composite Richmond team ended in a comfortable 11–2 win; however, Wyndham Lacey had to retire after four chukkers, his place taken by South African Julian "Buddy" Chaplin. A match against East Griqualand resulted in another win for the Rovers, 6–5.

Next on to the South African Championship for the Beresford Cup, presented in 1899 by then Captain John Beresford, later Lord Decies. Hurlingham Rovers, with Rhodesian Patrick Kemple playing number 2, defeated in succession Maseru 12–2, Underberg 9–2 and Rhodesia 7–2.

Lord Waterford had to return home due to a family bereavement, and Wyndham Lacey returned to the lineup, well strapped and with plenty of liniment. The finals against Zwartberg had a little bit of drama. The hard South African grounds had taken its toll of men and mounts, and the match was no exception. In the third chukker, Wyndham Lacey came a cropper, his riding muscle torn beyond repair. Donald Buchanan entered the fray, and Hurlingham Rovers saved a 5–3 championship win.

That same afternoon, a test match was played between Hurlingham and the Springboks after a three-hour break. Donald Buchanan sportingly stood down to make room for Robin Wilson, who because of having had an HPA handicap was qualified to play for Hurlingham. The green and yellow Springboks were Mike Miller, Davis Culverwell, Alastair Gordon and Doug McDonald, a total of twenty-four goals. Hurlingham lined up with Wilson, Kemple, Beresford and Ferguson, which added up to nineteen goals.

A hard-fought battle ensued, for a battle it was. At the end of regulation time the scoreboard read 4–4. The match went into a third extra-time chukker, Peter Wilson's sixteenth of the day, because he had played for the Junior Springboks in the curtain raiser versus Rhodesia. Hurlingham had two chances with sixty-yard penalties; however, both failed. With the shadows rapidly obscuring vision, Alastair Gordon scored the winning goal after almost seven minutes of the third extra chukker.

John Horswell, Howard Hipwood, Julian Hipwood and Paul Withers, a twenty-six-goal combination, embarked on a tour in September 1975, playing their first match at Noodsberg, which was described as "the traditional touring team pipe opener's game."[8]

The next game was at Lion's River against the Junior Springboks. In a one-sided affair the British team galloped to an 18–2 win.

The first International was held at Shongweni against Jim Watson, Mike Miller, Dougie McDonald and Terence Craig. The UK team won 14–8 after eight chukkers of play, a real international match.

The visitors moved on to the Orange Free State, were they romped over the OFS team 19–4, at the old Roderick Park, the Bloemfontein Polo Club grounds. The second and final International took place at the same venue. The visitors were relentless in their attacking game and ended up winning the game by eighteen goals to eight. Both teams presented the same players as in the first International; however, one of the South African players, after a heavy fall in the sixth chukker, left the field midway through the seventh. His replacement was Kit Watson, another of the four polo-playing brothers.

Another team from England toured South Africa in 1983. David Yeoman; Lord Charles Beresford; Kiwi John Walker, who was playing in England; and Robert Graham made up the team. The first International was played at Shongweni; however, only six chukkers were played this time around. Murray Heaton-Nicholls, Steve Erskine, Richard Kimber and Gavin Chaplin played for the Springboks. The final score was 7–5 in favor of the visitors.

The second test between the same teams, also played at Shongweni, had an identical result. The third test match, played at Inanda, had the same score, but this time in favor of the Boks.

In 1990, three tests were played. David Jamison, the patron of the Southfields team; Robert Graham; Hector Galindo, who was playing at Cowdray; and Patrick Churchward, also from Cowdray Park, played for the UK. Stephen Erskine, Russell Watson, George Morgan and Simon Armstrong represented South Africa.

The first test held at Shongweni was won by the UK 8–7, in very close game as the score suggests. The second test at the same venue saw a change in the visitors' team; Robert Graham, laid low by a flu virus, was replaced by Gavin Chaplin from the Karkloof club. This time around the Springboks dominated the flow of play, winning with ease eleven goals to five.

On to the third and decisive test at Inanda in the high veldt. Hector Galindo played an outstanding game, and the UK team took match and series with a 7–5 victory.

Stowell Park in New Zealand

Early in 1975 a Stowell Park team played fourteen games in New Zealand. It turned out to be too much polo in too little time. The original plan was to stage eleven games; however, many of the New Zealand clubs wished to host matches at their grounds, and the New Zealand Polo Association relented. The Stowell Park team was Lord Samuel Vestey, Eddie Moore, Héctor Barrantes and Paul Withers, a twenty-six-goal combine. Not since an Army-in-India squad had played in New Zealand in 1928 had a team from outside the Pacific basin competed on the islands.

Shortly after the tour started, both Barrantes and Moore contracted a virulent flu that kept them off the polo grounds for ten days. Stowell had to recur to Nicky Jacinto from the Philippines and Jaime Mackay from Australia to present a team on the field. Nevertheless, Stowell Park won ten matches and lost four, including the only test match at the end of the tour.

The tour gave rise to some controversy. The visitors thought that the New Zealand ponies were not properly trained because they were not able to turn on their haunches. The criticism was meant to be constructive; the lessons learned by the Aotea team in England had either not been adopted or had been forgotten. There was nothing wrong with the New Zealand ponies' breeding; Eddie Moore, who knew a thing or two about polo ponies, took with him a New Zealand pony he considered among the best he had ever ridden. It was the question of training and bitting that had the visitors by the ears.

The second issue was the quality of umpiring. Paul Withers, a respected umpire in both England and America, was critical of both the style of play and the permissiveness allowed by the umpires. In an article published in *Chukka Round*, Withers stated,

Frankly, I have been appalled at the standard of umpiring. Apart from few exceptions, there is either no knowledge of the rules or there is a reluctance to use the whistle. Umpires can make or break a polo game; and I am afraid that in a majority of cases in New Zealand, they allow to be played a game that is a cross between rugby and hockey, but which has very little to do with polo.[9]

On their part, the New Zealanders were not shy in criticizing foreign umpires. When a New South Wales team led by Sinclair Hill toured the island, they brought along an Australian umpire, Ken Austin. He was found by the New Zealanders to be "excessively eager to find fault. It was also said that his control was unnecessarily rigorous."[10]

Sinclair Hill's assessment of umpiring in New Zealand was that generally of a four-goal standard in matches played by players rated at six- or seven-goals handicap.

Regarding the style of play, Mr. Withers wrote, "In my opinion there is, in New Zealand polo, far too much rough play, hitting behind the saddle, dangerous stick work and hitting in front of other ponies' legs."[11]

Windsor at Mexico City

A Windsor twenty-goal team led by Lord Patrick Beresford and completed with John Horswell, Paul Withers and David Gemmell competed in a four-team round-robin tournament in Mexico City in 1979. The rest of the teams were Tecamac, Pablo Rincón Gallardo's outfit; Portales, Francisco Olazábal's team; and a South America team from Peru, completed by Paco Camarena, a Mexican player.

The Windsor team defeated the Carlos and Memo Gracida's Portales combine 7–5 and South America 8–7. These results placed the English team in the finals of the competition against Tecamac. Played at Campo de Marte, the venue of FIP's World Cup in 2009, the sixth chukker ended in a ten-all tie. Widened goals became the order of the day, and Windsor emerged the winner, 11–10.[12]

PART IV

Patrons and Professionals, 1986–2011

The waning years of the twentieth century in England witnessed a rise in the number of polo clubs, an increase in the number of competitions and a large number of foreign professional players that sought work opportunities in the British Isles, and the concomitant competition among patrons of the game in search of professional players and their polo ponies.

During the 1950s, it became common usage in England to refer to the visiting players from overseas as "hired assassins." This derogatory term originated in Burma in the early 1920s.[1] This occurrence happened long before the onslaught of semiprofessionals from Argentina first went to England, perhaps in retribution of the British invasions of Buenos Aires in 1806 and 1807. Here, there is a thin link to polo, because the first British expedition to the River Plate was under the command of Sir William Beresford, arguably the Duke of Wellington's best general, from the celebrated sporting family from Ireland.

Regrettably, the term remains current in the twenty-first century, and a prestigious English magazine as recently as 2003 writes, "The day of the ubiquitous Latin American 'hired assassin' was still in the future."[2]

The free-spending patron was exemplified by Australian press magnate Kerry Packer, who had jolted international cricket with his new ideas of one-day internationals instead of five-day test matches, spreading uproar and turmoil across the white-flannelled land.

CHAPTER **20**

The Growth of the Professional Player

In 1990 there were eighteen polo clubs in England, two in Ireland and two in Scotland. The total number increased to forty-four in 2000: thirty-five in England, two in Scotland, six in Ireland, and one in Northern Ireland. Practically all employed one or more professional players.[1]

New Polo Clubs in the Late Twentieth Century

The Anglesey Polo Club was founded by Flight Lieutenant David Wildridge, RAF, in 1981. It was the first club in Wales since the Tredegar Park Polo Club was established in 1920. The first ground was on the Mona Airfield; then a new ground was built by Malcolm Innes at Henblas. The local tournament was for the curiously named Paget Boots. The Lady Louisa Paget was one of the initial players. Regrettably, the relative isolation and the departure of some members led the club to abeyance some seven years later.

Another club in Wales was the Monmouthshire Polo Club, which was formed in 2000 by Ashrak Barakat. Grounds were at Ruperra Castle in South Wales. The club claimed it as a reincarnation of the old Monmouthshire Polo Club founded by the Herbert brothers, but the link is very tenuous at best.

The Colchester Garrison Polo Club, which dated back to 1912 and had become dormant by 1936, when the old Cherry Tree ground was allowed to go fallow, was revived by Brig. John F. Rickett in 1984. The Ypres Road ground was also brought up to date, and play began in earnest the following year.

An important club started operations in 1986, the Royal County of Berkshire Polo Club, to give it the full name. Started by musical impresario Bryan Morrison, erstwhile patron of the Chopendoz team, and Norman Lobel, this club very quickly carved a niche in British polo. Located on a prime location in Winkfield, on the old Ascot Cottage race training ground, the RCBPC organized a seventy-goal polo game and created the Prince of Wales Trophy, a twenty-two-goal tournament that became part and parcel of the high-goal scene in England.

The Epsom Polo Club was founded in 1986 by David Anderson and Anthony Hackett-Jones. The ground was located in Horton Country Park, adjoining Epsom Common, and later another field, Priest Hill, was added.

Ascot Park Polo Club was started by New Zealand's Olympic rider Peter Grace at the

213

Westcroft Park Farm, near Sunningdale, in 1976. The land was previously the property of Sir Martin Brown. The intention was to provide a stepping-stone into the game to players from the Rangitiki Polo School who wanted to pursue further improvement in their polo skills. The club moved to its current location in the Surrey countryside in 1988. Ascot Park is also the home base for the International Women's Polo Association, started by Pippa Grace in 1997 and the venue for the UK National Women's Polo Tournament.

The revived Beaufort Polo Club affiliated with the HPA in 1989, but the game had been renewed in 1977 at Down Farm by the Tomlinsons.

Cressing Park Polo Club in Essex was founded by K.R. Lodge in 1988. The grounds were in Cressing Park in Cressing.

Offchurch Bury Polo Club was formed in 1989 by Lord Pritchard and the Hon. Diana Johnson, in Leamington Spa, Warwickshire. The club changed its name to Stoneleigh Park in 1992.

The Cambridge and Newmarket Polo Club was formed in 1989 by Christopher Walkin-shaw, Alison Schwabe and Laurance Le Ggatt. Grounds were at Lower Farm in Dillingham, near Newmarket. The club offered its facilities to the Cambridge University polo team.

Knepp Castle Polo Club was started by Kim Richardson in 1990, when some friends would play chukkers on a sheep paddock in the Sussex countryside. Richardson contacted two of his neighbors, Anthony Burrell from Bakers Farm and Charlie Burrell from Knepp Castle estate, and the Knepp Castle Polo Club came into being. It became affiliated with the HPA in 1994. The main idea was to enjoy country polo and encourage young players to start the game.

The West Somerset Polo Club, dating back to 1904, was re-formed in 1990.

Ashfields Polo Club started in 1993 at Ashfields Farm in Great Canfield, Essex. Later on, the name was changed to Pegasus Polo Centre, under the ownership of Mark Sinnott, VS.

Ham Polo Club purchased in 1997 another ground at Petersham near Richmond Park, in the orchard of Ham House, a beautiful Jacobean manor now under the aegis of the National Trust. The new ground was financed by a grant from the Hurlingham Polo Association, membership debentures, and a long-term bank loan. Thus, the survival of London's last polo club was ensured.[2] The club offers for competition the intermediate twelve-goal Dubai Trophy, the Roehampton Cup, played for since 1902, the Billy Walsh Cup and the Ham House Tournament.

Irishman William Francis Walsh was the driving spirit behind polo at Ham. Upon his retirement from the game, Billy remained as the club's polo manager. In 1982, he was appointed president, and his legacy is continued by his daughter, Mrs. Peggy Healey, and her sons William and Tim.

Hurtwood Park Polo Club was started in 1995 by musician Kenny Jones on his property in Ewhurst Green, county of Surrey. The site was purchased in 1987, and a practice ground was built. This feature attracted several local riders, and the club grew exponentially to its present six grounds, boasting a high-goal HPA certificate. Initially utilized for charity events, the club now hosts the Polo Masters, an eighteen-goal tournament.

Checkendon Polo Club was formed in 1992 by Lord Phillimore and Toby Greenbury and changed its name to Binfield Heath in 1994. The grounds are located on Lord Philli-more's estate.

In Gloucestershire, the Edgeworth Polo Club was started in 1993 by John P. Smail at Field Barn, near Cirencester.

The West Wycombe Polo Club was formed in 1992, at Pyatts Farm in High Wycombe, Buckinghamshire.

Ansty Polo Club was started in 1995 at New Barn Farm in Ansty, Wiltshire. It went into abeyance in 1999 and was revived in 2002 by David and Kristin Heaton-Ellis.

The Anningsdale Polo Club was founded by Paul Sweeney in 1996 in Ottershaw, Surrey.

The Hampstead Polo Club was formed in 1995 and originally played through the Silver Leys Club. With the assistance of the Lucas family, the club moved to Woolmers Park. It changed its name to Woolmers Park in 1998.

The Inglesham Polo Centre was started by Nick Williams at his Lynt Farm near Swinton, Wiltshire. It affiliated with the HPA in 1996.

FHM Polo Club was started by Francis Matthews in response to a need for low-cost polo in the area. The location is at West End Farm, in Goddards Green, West Sussex.

The Orchard Polo Club was formed by Dick Rowe in 2000 to fill the void left by the closure of the Ansty Polo Club. The club membership grew out of the Pony Club teachings given by Rowe and Jeremy Mains. Dick Rowe placed an advertisement in the local freebie stating, "I want to play polo in Dorset, does anybody want to play with me?"[3] The advertisement elicited a good response, and the show was on. The ground is at Vale Farm in West Orchard.

Polo Clubs in Ireland

The Kildare Polo Club located at the Baroda Stud in Newbridge was founded in 1991 by Malcolm Kidd. The club had two boarded grounds.

Northern Ireland Polo Club was formed in 1994, with five grounds on different locations.

The Moyne Polo Club was formed in 1996 in county Laois.

The Brannockstown Polo Club in county Kildare was founded to fill the void left when the Kildare Club closed. The grounds are in James Sheeran's farm.

Curraghmore Polo Club was founded by the Marquis of Waterford in the Curraghmore estate at Portlaw, near Waterford. The game has been played for many years, since the time when Lord Waterford build the first polo ground. It was formally affiliated with the HPA in 2000.

The High-Goal (Twenty-Two-Handicap) Tournaments

Cowdray Park took the Queen's Cup, the opening high-goal tournament of the 1980s, with the Hon. Charles Pearson, Carlos Jauregui from Argentina, Paul Withers and Alexander "Sandy" Harper. They defeated their auld adversaries Stowell Park in the finals; however, they never showed their top form during the rest of the season; poor pony management was mentioned as the main cause of failure.[4]

The Maple Leafs, beaten in the semifinals of the Queen's Cup by Cowdray Park, went on to take the Warwickshire Cup from Southfields in an extraordinary game in which Howard Hipwood and Stuart Mackenzie scored three goals in the last four minutes of play to take the cup by one goal. Galen Weston and Reddy Watt completed the team.

Some thirty matches were needed to complete the Gold Cup at Cowdray. The Falcons, Alex Ebeid, Gonzalo Pieres, Héctor Merlos and Luis Amaya, defeated Ipanema in the final game. Once more, good management of pony power yielded the best results. By the final game, Ipanema's ponies had "had it."[5]

Sladmore, the Horswell's entry, carefully saved their mounts and took Cowdray Park's Challenge Cup, the final high-goal competition of the season. Alfonso Pieres and Major Ferguson completed the Sladmore squad. Sladmore also made it to the finals of the Midhurst Town Cup, for teams beaten in the Gold Cup, where they yielded to Galen Weston's Maple Leafs.

For the first time in more than thirty years, there were no Argentine players in the polo season because the ripples of the conflict in the South Atlantic had reached the shores of the British Isles.

The big four tournaments were evenly divided between the Boehm's Team and Southfield. Boehm's, with Lord Patrick Beresford, Howard Hipwood, Stuart Mackenzie and Mark Vestey took the Queen's Cup and the Cowdray Park Challenge Cup; Philip Elliott replaced Howard Hipwood in the Cowdray Challenge Cup. Southfield was the winner of the Gold Cup and the Warwickshire Cup. The Southfield team had David Yeoman, Carlos Gracida, John Walker and Lord Charles Beresford.

The year 1983 was also bereft of players from Argentina; as a matter of fact, they were not welcomed until 1989. Cowdray Park once more took the Queen's Cup at Smith's Lawn, with the Hon. Charles Pearson — Lord Cowdray's younger son — Cody Forsyth, Paul Withers and Patrick Churchward. The Boehm Team, Lord Patrick Beresford; Graham Thomas, another Kiwi; Howard Hipwood; Philip Elliot; and the Hon. Mark Vestey, were the winners of the Warwickshire Cup at Cirencester.

Alexandre Ebeid's Falcons took the Cowdray Park Gold Cup. The two Mexican brothers Guillermo and Carlos Gracida, with Andrew Hine, completed the Falcons team. Then Maple Leafs, Galen Weston, Alan Kent, Tony Devcich and Cody Forsyth, both from New Zealand, won the Cowdray Park Challenge Cup from the home team.

The two medium-goal tournaments, the County Cup and the Royal Windsor Cup, went to Ingwenya, Nick Hahn's team, ably anchored by Howard Hipwood.

In 1984 the Queen's Cup was taken by Foxcote, the Hon. Mark Vestey's team. Regrettably, a hunting accident put an end to his brilliant polo career; however, Foxcote continues to be successful in today's polo, thanks to the support given by Mark and Rosie Vestey to their children Tamara, Nina and Ben. Lord Samuel Vestey came out of retirement to take his brother's place on the team. The other team members were Lord Charles Beresford,

The 14th/20th Hussars won the Inter-Regimental Tournament three consecutive years from 1985 to 1987. Majors Michael Vickery and David Woodd were on the team all three years.

Brazilian Silvio Novaes and Philip Elliott. The Hon. Mark Vestey received the trophy from HM the Queen.

The Cowdray Park Gold Cup and the Warwickshire Cup were both won by Southfield, David Yeoman, Alan Kent, the American Owen Rinehart and David Jamison.

David Jamison went to Argentina in the early 1970s under the tutelage of Juan Carlos "Bebé" Alberdi, a ten-goal handicap player who was the captain of the Argentine team in the 1953 Coronation Cup. Alberdi took away Jamison's mallets and put him on a horse practicing riding. The instructor was following the time-tested formula for learning the game of polo: first, learn how to ride; then, learn how to strike the ball; and finally, learn how to play the game.

The Cowdray Park Challenge Cup remained in the hands of the Maple Leafs.

The following year Southfield competed under the Centaurs name — no relation to Sir Evelyn de Rothschild's Centaurs of the 1950 and 1960s— and took both the Queen's and the Warwickshire cups. In the Gold Cup, the Centaurs survived a big scare against the unheralded Kouros, only to be defeated by Cowdray Park. This left Les Diables Bleus and Maple Leafs to fight it out in the finals. In a marvelous game, the Maple Leafs won in extra time. Galen Weston, Julian Hipwood, Martin Glue and Tony Devcich went on to take the Cowdray Park Challenge Cup as well.

The year 1986 marked the first of four consecutive victories in the Gold Cup by Tramontana. Anthony Embiricos, Jesús Baez, Carlos Gracida and Martin Brown were the winners; in later years, Mexicans Valerio Aguilar and Roberto González Gracida, and David Jamison contributed to that remarkable achievement.

Les Diables Bleus, with patron Guy Wildenstein, Rodrigo Vial from Chile, Guillermo Gracida and HRH the Prince of Wales, took the Queen's Cup. The Falcons, Martin Brown, Jesús Baez, Carlos Gracida and Alexandre Ebeid, won the Warwickshire Cup, while Los Locos won the Cowdray Park Challenge Cup.

In 1987, Southfield took the Queen's Cup, the newly established Prince of Wales Trophy at Royal County of Berkshire Polo Club, and the Warwickshire Cup; while Windsor Park joined Gold Cup winner Tramontana as a high-goal successful team when Prince Charles and three colonials, Geoffrey Kent from Kenya, Cody Forsyth and Stuart Mackenzie from New Zealand, took the Cowdray Park Challenge Cup.

The next year a new patron, the Marquis George Milford Haven, led the NPC Broncos to victory on the Queen's Cup. Cody Forsyth, Gabriel Donoso and Martin Glue were the other players on this team. They defeated pow-

HRH the Prince of Wales at Guards Polo Club. Prince Charles wears the red jersey of the Maple Leafs, Galen Weston's team from Canada.

Sladmore, the Horswells' family team, was very successful in medium-goal polo. This is the winning team of the 1987 County Cup played at Cirencester Park: Edward Horswell, John Horswell, Patrick McIldowie and Alex Brodie (courtesy Edward Horswell).

erhouse Tramontana in the finals. The Black Bears took the Warwickshire Cup, and the Maple Leafs were the winners of the Cowdray Park Challenge Cup.

The Horswell brothers' Sladmore took two of the medium-goal tournaments: the Harrison Cup and the Royal Windsor Cup. Major David Woodd, Alex Brodie and Patrick McIldowie from New Zealand completed the squad. Brent Walker, with George Milford Haven, Will Lucas, Alan Kent and William Roberts, won the third leg of the medium-goal, the Royal Windsor Cup.

In 1989, Hilditch and Key, in reality the Maple Leafs, took the Queen's Cup: Andrew Hine; Julian Hipwood; Robert D. Walton, the American player; and Galen Weston, Sr., were on that team. Tramontana added the Prince of Wales Trophy to their fourth consecutive Gold Cup. With a fifth tournament added to the high-goal schedule, plus the increase in the number of other competitions, horse management became a top priority, and some teams, notably Tramontana, elected to skip some tournaments.

Cirencester Park again hosted the Warwickshire Cup, the grand old lady of English high-goal competitions. Southfield — John Yeoman, Alan Kent, Owen Rinehart and Chris Bethell — took the old 1894 trophy. The last high-goal tournament of the season, Cowdray Park's Challenge Cup, was taken by a French team. Chateau Giscours, the Bordeaux wine vineyard owned by M. Pierre Tari, had Santiago Gaztambide, Lionel Macaire, Adrian Wade and Louis Tari, the owner's son.

The players from Argentina were at long last welcomed to participate in the English season, which also saw the first appearance of Ellerston, Kerry Packer's organization that was destined to change the economics of the game forever.

The last year of the decade saw the five major trophies evenly decided. Tramontana — Patrick Cowley, Roberto González Gracida, Carlos Gracida, and Anthony Embiricos — won the Prince of Wales Trophy at Berkshire. The Queen's Cup was taken by Santa Fe, with Andrew Hine, Cody Forsyth, Héctor "Juni" Crotto from Argentina and William Bond-Elliott. A portent of things to come, Ellerston White—Adrian Wade, Gonzalo Tanoira, Gonzalo Pieres and Kerry Packer—took the Warwickshire Cup, and Hildon House ended Tramontana's four-year reign at Cowdray Park. Captain Michael Amoore, Norman Lobel, Tomás Fernández Llorente and Howard Hipwood wore the light blue shirts of Hildon House.

A most popular win was that of Rosamundo in the Cowdray Park Challenge Cup. David Pearl, Antonio Herrera from Mexico, Argentinean Alejandro Díaz Alberdi, J.J.'s son, and Roderick Matthews were the winners

The Game's Administration

The 1980s decade started with the sad news of the passing of the Hurlingham Polo Association's chairman, Mr. Douglas Riley-Smith. Lord Cowdray acted as interim chairman until Brigadier Peter Thwaites took over the HPA's helm.

Lt. Col. Alec Harper, who had done so much for English polo since his return from India after the war, resigned his position as HPA's secretary after eighteen years of service. Colonel Harper played for England in the international contests of 1951, taking the Festival Cup versus an Argentine team, and in 1953 was runner-up to the Argentine national team for the Coronation Cup at Cowdray Park.

The much respected Brigadier Peter Thwaites passed away after ten years as chairman of the HPA. The winds of change were much in evidence during his watch. There was a tremendous growth of polo in both the United Kingdom and overseas; more professional players made it to England; the Federation of International Polo and its attendant World Championship became a reality; commercial sponsorship was established as a way of life; the Argentine players were temporarily banned as a consequence of the conflict in the icy waters and desolate islands in the South Atlantic; after a decent interlude, they were welcomed back into the fold; and there was the problem of umpiring and the decline in sportsmanship which remained a thorn in the HPA Council's side. All these issues were handled by Brigadier Thwaites with infallible charm and judicious restraint.

John Tylor, a player from the Kirtlington Polo Club, was then elected to the chairmanship of the Hurlingham Polo Association and served from 1991 until 1995. The Hon. Mark Vestey followed Mr. Tylor's path upon his election as chairman, and his mandate lasted until 2000. Mark Vestey was succeeded by John Tinsley, who played his polo at the Rutland Club.

John "Buff" Crisp succeeded Alec Harper as the HPA secretary, a post that he would fill with distinction for many years. In 2000, Colonel David Woodd took over as chief executive of the Hurlingham Polo Association, a new title.

The 1990s

The expansion of the game in both tournaments and players was preeminent in the 1990s. The winning teams of the five high-goal tournaments, the Warwickshire Cup, the Cowdray Park Challenge Cup, the Cowdray Park Gold Cup, the Queen's Cup and the Prince of Wales Trophy, are included in appendix 3 in order of antiquity.

Above: The Hon. Mark Vestey, sponsor of the Foxcote team, played for England and was chairman of the Hurlingham Polo Association from 1995 until 2000. *Right:* In his time, John Tylor was a very good amateur player and eventually became chairman of the HPA from 1991 to 1995.

David Woodd in a relaxed mood outside the HPA office in Oxfordshire. Colonel Woodd, a three-time winner of the Inter-Regimental Tournament with the 14th/20th Hussars team, is CEO of the Hurlingham Polo Association (courtesy Hurlingham Polo Association).

Furthermore, there were two competitions for the Westchester Cup, both held in England, with the participation of American players engaged in several teams entered in the polo season.

The Prince of Wales Trophy

With the advent of the Prince of Wales Cup at Berkshire in 1986, this competition became the first high-goal tournament in the calendar. The local team Munipore, Peter Scott, Bautista Heguy, his cousin Eduardo "Ruso" Heguy and Bryan Morrison, won the cup defeating Sladmore in the 1991 finals.

Then it was Ellerston's turn— Henry Brett, Bautista Heguy, Eduardo Heguy, Alasdair Archibald—to take the silver home. Ellerston would win again in 1999 with a totally different team: James Beim, Adolfo Cambiaso, Gonzalo Pieres and Tristan Wade. The only other double winner in this decade was John Manconi's Alcatel, with Gabriel Donoso and Alejandro "Piki" Díaz Alberdi. Antony Fanshawe and Tarquin Southwell were the lucky Britons chosen to comply with the official tournaments rule 7: "No team may have four foreign players."

Galen Weston's Maple Leafs, Cowdray Park, Australian Rick Stowe's Geebungs, Jefri

Bolkiah's Jerudong Park and Prince Rahman's Royal Pahang were the other winners.

The Queen's Cup

This, the second high-goal tournament of the season, became Ellerston's bailiwick, because they won the tournament five times out of ten. It was a show of stars: Adolfo Cambiaso, Javier Novillo Astrada, Alfonso and Gonzalo Pieres, Alberto "Pepe" and Bautista Heguy, all nine- or ten-goalers. The supporting cast was Alasdair Archibald, Henry Brett, Julian Daniels, James Beam, John Fisher, Tristan Wade, and the man who signed the checks, Kerry Packer.

Swiss patron Urs Schwarzenbach's Bears took the Queen's Cup on two instances, with the Merlos brothers, Sebastián and Juan Ignacio "Pite," with help from Oliver Hipwood, James Dixon and Tarquin Southwell.

The rest of the winners during this decade were Hubert Perrodo's Labegorce, John Goodman's Isla Carroll and Rick Stowe's Geebung.

Two of polo's superstars, Gonzalo Pieres and his son Gonzalito, in a relaxed mood before a game at Guards Polo Club. Gonzalo played on teams sponsored by Lord John Cowdray and Kerry Packer. His eldest son took Cowdray Park's Gold Cup with Jean-François Decaux (courtesy Mike Roberts).

The Warwickshire Cup

The usual cast of characters figured prominently in the engraving on the Warwickshire Cup. Black Bears took the trophy three times, and Ellerston White twice.

Other winning teams were Los Locos, Royal Pahang, Major Christopher Hanbury's Lovelocks, John Manconi's Pommery and Craig McKinney's Woodchester.

The British Open Championship for the Cowdray Park Gold Cup

Ellerston once more, with its White, the father's, and Black, his son Jamie's, versions, was the most prolific winner of the Gold Cup. The Australian powerful machine took the Gold Cup on three occasions and was finalist four times.

The decade started with Tramontana taking its fifth title, with the team of Adam Buchanan, Adolfo Cambiaso, Carlos Gracida and patron Anthony Embiricos. In 1992 the

Black Bears won the title defeating Santa Fe in the finals. Urs Schwarzenbach, Sebastián Merlos, Pite Merlos and Martin Brown took the gold in this event.

The next year, Alcatel, with Peter Webb in place of the injured John Manconi, Gabriel Donoso, Alejandro Díaz Alberdi and Ignacio González, defeated the holders, the Black Bears, by nine goals to eight in the eighth chukker, with widened goals.

The next two years were the time for Ellerston. The Ellerston Black team, Jamie Packer at back, with Oliver Taylor, Roberto González Gracida and Carlos Gracida, defeated the American team Pegasus. The following summer, Ellerston White had Oliver Hipwood, Carlos Gracida, Gonzalo Pieres and Kerry Packer. This team defeated the Black Bears by twelve goals to nine.

In 1996, C.S. Brooks, with the mandatory Englishman, in this case John Fisher, plus Ignacio Heguy, his older brother Eduardo and Brook Johnson, beat Ellerston by a single goal in the final game. Sebastian Dawnay replaced the team's patron after Johnson took a fall in the course of the game.

The French-sponsored team Labegorce was a popular winner in 1997. "Le Patron," M. Hubert Perrodo, Javier Novillo Astrada, Carlos Gracida and Jamie Le Hardy defeated the visiting American team Isla Carroll, which had Guillermo "Memo" Gracida on the lineup, by ten goals to eight. Labegorce also took the Prince Philip Trophy, completing a nice double.

Ellerston regained the Gold Cup in 1998. James Beim, Adolfo Cambiaso, Gonzalo Pieres and John Fisher took ample revenge from C.S. Brooks which had beaten them two years previously. The score was a categorical 13–7.

John Manconi added another Gold Cup to his trophy cabinet. Playing as Pommery, Henry Brett, Alejandro Díaz Alberdi and Juan Bollini carried the bubbly to victory. It was a wonderful addition to the win in the Warwickshire Cup by the same team.

The decade — and the century — ended with the Australian team Geebung, named after "Banjo" Paterson's celebrated polo poem, which had Rick Stowe, Bautista Heguy, Adolfo Cambiaso and David Allen.

Cowdray Park Challenge Cup

This tournament, played during Goodwood Week in August, traditionally signals the end of the English high-goal season. C.S. Brooks, sponsored by U.S. Senate hopeful "Brook" Johnson, had a good run from 1996 to 1998, thrice taking the trophy home. Actually, home was Drovers, as the team was based in Ambersham. Among the players on C.S. Brooks teams were Mike Rutherford, Lord Charles Beresford, Adam Buchanan, Andrew Seavill, Henry Brett, and the Johnsons, Brook the father and Senter the son. The team is named after Johnson's towel and bedding company. Mr. Johnson's name is Charles Senter; however, he prefers to be called "Brook," a childhood nickname.

During the time span covered in this section, Los Locos, Alcatel, Maple Leafs Black Bears, the Italian team Azzurra and Isabelle Hayen's Groeninghe had their names engraved on the silver trophy.

International Polo: The Westchester Cup

The renewal of the Westchester Cup series occurred in 1992 when several American players were participating in the British polo season. Played at the thirty-goal level, the

The Beresford family has been involved in sporting activities for a long time. Lord Richard Le Poer, his father the Earl of Tyrone, the Marquess and Marchioness of Waterford, Lord Charles Beresford and his uncle Lord Patrick Beresford (courtesy Mike Roberts).

English selectors picked William Lucas, New Zealander Cody Forsyth, Alan Kent and Howard Hipwood to wear the red rose of England. The American team was John Gobin, Adam Snow, Owen Rinehart and Robert Walton. Guillermo "Memo" Gracida was named coach of the English team, and his younger sibling Carlos had the same task on behalf of the American team.

The tricky issue of mounts, always the most difficult obstacle in staging international competitions, was solved thanks to the generosity of several patrons in England. David Jamison performed a yeoman's work trying to obtain the best possible mounts. Jamison was quoted, "It wasn't the national but the personal connections of patrons, and their sense of how particular players would ride their ponies that was determining."[6]

Off they went, both teams trading goals and the lead; at tread-in time it was England five goals, America four goals. Howard Hipwood played brilliantly, and his performance earned England's back the accolade of Man of the Match. Both coaches gathered with the teams and offered plenty of advice. Memo Gracida to Will Lucas: "You're going this way and that, William. You have to pick a line and drive for it and get some penetration." The coach praised Hipwood for his long backhanders and control of plays. "You're dominating the game, Howard, and if you can keep it up, we'll win."[7]

What worried Carlos Gracida most was Howard Hipwood's superiority over John Gobin. "You have to take the center of the field away from him on his knock-ins. And you have to avoid getting back into the game."[8]

The second half was different. The Americans were ahead by one goal in the sixth chukker when Howard Hipwood outsmarted his opponents while about to take a penalty from a wide angle, some ninety yards from the goalposts. When the whistle went, Forsyth and Gobin galloped to change horses; they were followed by Adam Snow, who assumed that with Forsyth off the field of play, Hipwood would take a wide circle and delay taking the penalty. Hipwood tapped the ball standing still for Alan Kent to score the equalizer goal.

The scoreboard was all sevens at the start of extra time. Both teams had penalties from midfield, with no consequences. The eighth chukker was tense and scoreless. On to the ninth chukker, the longest game in Westchester Cup history. Some four minutes later, Adam Snow picked a loose ball sixty yards from the American goal and sailed away, with Forsyth and Lucas giving chase. Snow was taken off the play, and Rinehart, left alone while following the play, took a shot that Gobin picked with a cut backhander toward goal. Alan Kent's desperate attempt to save at the goal line failed, and a game for the ages was over.

The 1997 Westchester Cup: England's Overdue Victory

The Isla Carroll team, John Goodman's own, successfully competed in the British summer season of 1997, taking the Queen's Cup and losing the finals of Cowdray Park's Gold by two goals to Hubert Perrodo's Labegorce. Guillermo "Memo" Gracida played alongside eighteen-year-old Mathew Pannell, Juan Ignacio "Pite" Merlos and John B. Goodman. With an American team fully mounted, it was relatively easy to stage another edition of the oldest international trophy in polo. Julio Arellano, Michael Azzaro, Gracida and Goodman formed the American team, coached by former nine-goaler Joe Barry.

England was represented by William Lucas, Cody Forsyth, Howard Hipwood and Andrew Hine. The Americans were considered to be heavy favorites; however, the punters failed to consider the discrepancy between the two pony strings. Before the event, a flood of borrowed ponies swelled the English lines with the happy result that each player could count on eight top ponies for the match. Conversely, the Isla Carroll ponies appeared to be tired after a long and exhausting campaign.

Nevertheless, off they went, and America jumped to an early two-goal lead. Penalty conversions by Cody Forsyth evened the score and at halftime England enjoyed a 9–3 advantage. Coach Joe Barry made changes: Mike Azzaro to the back position, John Goodman at number 1 and Julio Arellano at number 2. The fourth chukker was split, each side scoring one goal. In the fifth chukker that gap was narrowed to 11–4; however, it was too little, too late. The final tally was England twelve goals, America nine goals. After eighty-three long years, the Westchester Cup was returned to England.

CHAPTER 21

Women in Polo

The first documented game of women's polo in England was held at the Ranelagh Club in Barnes in 1905. It was witnessed by royal presence, HM Queen Alexandra. The teams were three-a-side. For the Whites, Miss N. Barrow, Mrs. Bampfield and Miss Lillian Ark-wrigth; the Rainbows presented Angela Hume Spry, Miss K.S. Young and Mrs. Webley. The *Bystander* reported the event.[1] An illustration from the article shows that at least some of the ladies rode sidesaddle. The pertinent caption mentions the fact that Miss Barrow scored most of the goals.

A later recollection of this protogame at Ranelagh was called by an eyewitness "farcical." The players rode sidesaddle, and nearly every movement of their polo sticks was hampered by their riding habits. The spectators grinned as the players bunched together and failed to smack the ball hard enough to get it away from the heels of their ponies.[2] Nevertheless, it was a beginning.

Nothing more is written about women's polo in Britain until 1920, when a short article appeared in the *Polo Monthly*.[3] The article was about Miss Noëla Whiting, the only woman player in England at the time. She played at Taunton Vale Polo Club in Somerset, being handicapped at two goals. Miss Whiting had learned the game in Burma during the war, where she had taken a pioneering role in bringing polo to the military post where her step-father, Major Claude Ward-Jackson, was stationed. Colonel Thomas Townley Macan, of the Cameronians, wrote,

> Until Miss Whiting arrived in Burma in October 1915 there had been no thought of a 2/5 Som-erset polo team. Miss Whiting for several years had ample opportunity of watching good polo and schooling with her stepfather's ponies. Within a month, slow chukkers were in full swing, and gradually as the fever developed, polo became the sole topic of conversation. The fact stands that had it not been for Miss Whiting's energy and organizing capacity there would have been no team.[4]

In another article, the *Polo Monthly* further expanded:

> There is in this country, for some reason or other, a prejudice against women playing polo, pos-sibly because it is thought that they are not equal to the strenuous happenings of the game — the riding-off, etc. But as Miss Whiting is concerned, no such prejudice can exist, as she is a strong horsewoman and can ride out as well as most men. She is very quick on the ball, hits well on both sides of the pony, is a very certain goal-hitter, and last, but certainly not least, not only knows the game thoroughly but plays it. She is well mounted on quick, handy ponies. To those who do not believe in a woman being able to play polo all I can say is: come and see her play.[5]

The West Somerset Polo Club was the host for a two-chukker game in 1921 against an all-male team, which was described as a sideshow. Mrs. Maurice (Violet) Kingscote, Lady

Margot Chesham, Miss Waters and Miss Lee were on the distaff side. Roland Corbett, Captain William Riley, Gandar Dower and A.L Wilson made the men's team. Miss Lee was the best player and led the ladies to a 2–1 win.[6]

The Beaufort Club had the first ladies' polo game on 22 July 1930. Even though the weather was cold there was a large attendance to watch the match. The Melton team was as follows: the Hon. Mrs. Edward (Josephine) Greenall, who shortly after would be killed foxhunting; the Hon. Mrs. Gilbert (Betty Isobel) Greenall; Miss Lexia Wilson — who eventually was prevented from playing by a family bereavement; and Mr. Gerald Balding. They played the West of England: Miss Wagge, Mrs. "Bobby" Watts, Miss Jackman and Mr. Aidan Roark.

The *Polo Monthly*'s report follows:

> The wind was at first in favor of Melton, but this did not altogether account for the splendid goal scored by Mrs. Greenall in the first chukker. Mrs. Watts and Miss Jackman played well in the second chukker. Mrs. Gilbert Greenall scored again in the third chukker, and the result was Melton two, West of England nil. Miss Balding took the place which was to have been filled by Miss Leslie Wilson. The game was umpired by Captain Maurice Kingscote and Major Leonard Avery. The Duchess of Beaufort presented the women players with silk scarves.[7]

This summer tournament was continued the following year. Melton Ladies was represented by Josephine and Betty Greenall, Leslie Wilson and Gerald Balding. Their opponents, the West Country team, were Mrs. George Philippi, Mrs. Watts, Yoskyl Pearson and Capt. Maurice Kingscote. Melton Ladies won the match by four goals to one.[8]

Foxbury and Invaders faced each other at Henry Tiarks Foxbury's home ground in 1930. The prize was a challenge cup to be played for annually. The local team was Lady Millicent Tiarks, team captain; Miss Cicely Nickalls; Miss Tinker Nickalls; and Miss K. Jackman from Oxfordshire. The host team defeated the Invaders, the Hon. Yoskill Pearson, Cowdray Park; the Misses M. and E. Jackman; and Mrs. Haley.

Then there was another game at Ranelagh, which was considered the best game seen so far in England between teams composed entirely of women. The date was 11 August 1933, and the sides were as follows:

National School of Equitation	*Southdown*
Lady Violet Pakenham	Mrs. Henry Merckel
Lady Catherine Willoughby	Miss Winnie Hilder
Miss Muriel Wright	Miss Denis Holt
Lady Priscilla Willoughby	Miss D'Arcy Defries

This was a return match, since the Southdown ladies had won the first match, played at Brighton, but on this occasion, thanks largely to the fine work of Lady Priscilla Willoughby, both in attack and defense, the School of Equitation won by four goals to one.[9]

As part of Kirtlington Park's Annual Summer Tournaments in July 1938, the attractions included a ladies' match for the Seven Springs Cup. The team from Rugby, Miss F. Phillips, Miss J. Nickalls, Mrs. Frost and Miss Judy Forwood, with seven goals, won against the four goals obtained by Barton Abbey, with Miss B. Rigden, Mrs. Philip Fleming, Miss Kitty Tatham-Warter and Mrs. Judith Bott.[10] It is of note that Mrs. Celia Fleming played on the Barton Abbey men's team that took the Visitors' Cup at the same meeting. Her husband, Major Peter Fleming, also played on that team, with the Hon. Henry Hermon-Hodge and Captain Geoffrey Webber, RAF.

Polo at Chillesford

An all-women team played a game against an all-men combine at Chillesford — the Hon. Alastair Watson's ground in Suffolk — on Sunday, 17 July 1938. The ladies' team, named Mannequins for the occasion, was Miss Binks Hawden, described as a "very young and decorative player"; Miss Muriel Wright; Miss Pamela Schreiber; and Lady Priscilla Willoughby, "Great Britain's best woman player."[11] The men's team was R.F. Watson, who flew from Kent every Sunday to play polo at Chillesford; R.N. Cobbold, director of the Ipswich Football Club; Captain William Bucknall, the Black Watch; and M.O. Springfield. The team was named Gigolos. The Mannequins received six goals by handicap in the three-chukker match. The final tally is not recorded.

The Women's Open Championship

The 1938 English Women's Open Championship was held on the Dunster Castle grounds near Minehead, the site of the West Somerset Polo Club. The final game was between Linborne, Miss P. Pacey, Miss Baby Balding, Miss Judy Balding and Miss B. Balding. In a game of four chukkers, they defeated Fontwell Magna by ten goals to two. Miss Lanyon, Miss P. Kelly, Miss Denison Pender and Miss Elizabeth Kelly, later Mrs. Trevor Smail, played for Fontwell Magna.[12]

The Clanbrassil Cup

An important milestone on the road to recognition for women's polo in England was the Clanbrassil Cup, presented by Mr. Hans Rowan-Hamilton and played on the hallowed grounds of the Hurlingham Club. Four teams competed. In the first semifinal, Grimsthorpe, with Miss S.M. Rolt, the Hon. Mrs. Yoskyl Gurdon, Lady Priscilla Willoughby and the Hon. Mrs. Angela Murray, defeated Rugby, with Miss F. Phillips, Miss Judy Forwood, Miss J. Nickalls and Miss Baby Balding. Lady Willoughby scored all five goals for Grimsthorpe.

The second semifinal was as lopsided as the first one, Oddments beating Cheetahs 11–1. Lady Margaret Drummond-Hay, the Hon. Mrs. Greenall, Mrs. Peter (Celia) Fleming and Mrs. Judith Bott played on the Oddments team. Miss J. Robertson, Miss Nell Campbell, Miss Kitty Tatham-Warter and Miss R. Giffard were the Cheetahs.

The final was a close-run affair, Grimsthorpe eking out a 5–4 win. Mrs. Gurdon scored three goals for the winners, and Lady Willoughby added two more. Mrs. Greenall hit through twice for the Oddments, Lady Drummond-Hay and Mrs. Fleming also scoring.

An invitation tournament for the Ladies Invitation Cup followed at the Ranelagh Club with the same teams. The Rugby team defeated both the Oddments and Grimsthorpe to take the honors. The Hon. Daphne Pearson took her sister Angela's place on the Grimsthorpe team.[13]

An interesting player at Rhinefield Polo Club was Shirley Faulkner-Horne, who achieved fame as a writer of children's books, including *Pat and Her Polo Pony*. After the war was over she married an RAF pilot and did not play polo, but she went on to successfully show jumpers and for many years was an active participant at her old polo club, now the New Forest Polo Club.[14]

The Ladies' Polo Association

The Ladies' Polo Association was founded on 9 November 1938 as a direct result of the enthusiasm generated by the Clanbrassil Championship Cup. The association started with three main objects. The first one was to obtain recognition by the Hurlingham Club, which was soon achieved. The second was to be recognized by the County Polo Association, and the third one was to arrange handicaps for women polo players. Regrettably, the invasion of Poland by Germany put a sudden stop to the proceedings.

The Struggle for Recognition

Before the start of the Second World War, English women polo players had started agitating the waters in their quest to obtain official handicaps. There was one alarmingly good player, Lady Priscilla Willoughby. In 1936, Lady Willoughby took two club tournaments at Harrogate, playing at number 2 on men's teams, Stray Lambs and Boston Spa. The team members were the same: N. Hardy, Michael Moseley and Captain Walter Griffiths. In spite of her achievements as a player, she was denied a handicap rating by both the Hurlingham Polo Committee and the County Polo Association.

The Hurlingham Polo Committee, at the time the ruling body of the game in England and most of the world, simply ignored the request. The County Polo Association modified its bylaws to read, "Ladies are not eligible to receive an official handicap or play in tournaments, but may receive a Local Handicap by the Committee of their Club to enable them to play in a Local Tournament."[15]

Postwar Women's Polo

The main factor in changing the negative attitude toward women playing was simply the scarcity of players in 1947, when polo in England began its recovery. The initial practice games at Cowdray Park were three-a-side, and the enthusiasm of Lord Cowdray's sisters was paramount in making a game of polo a practical endeavor.

It was of great significance that three ladies were on teams that took two of the principal polo tournaments. Mrs. Dorothy Kidston was on the team that took the 1948 Junior County Cup; in the same year Daphne Lakin won the Cowdray Park Challenge Cup. Mrs. Peter Fleming, better known as Celia Johnson, DBE, for her career in the theater and in motion pictures, took Cowdray Park's Challenge Cup in 1949 as a member of the Henley team, the Junior County Cup the following year and also the Roehampton Cup.

The 1951 Official Handicap List includes thirty-five women, none rated above zero. Rhinefield had eight women players; Canford Magna had six; Taunton Vale, Silver Leys and Cowdray Park five each; and Hertfordshire three.

That same year four members of the Lucas family took the Holden White Cup at Cowdray Park. Arthur Lucas, his wife Ethel, his daughter Pat and his son John were on the winning team. Certainly, little Claire was on the sidelines.

Not until 1958 did a woman take a major tournament; Miss Judy Forwood, daughter of the Rugby player Eric Forwood, won the Warwickshire Cup with a Kirtlington team.

Claire's Crusade

Claire Janet Lucas was born on Valentine's Day and from early age showed an independent spirit.[16] She was exposed to polo early in life and went to Somerville College in Oxford, where she was on the university fencing team and also in the national junior team. Claire also won a squash blue, and a half-blue for her captaincy of the polo team that vanquished Cambridge seven–nil.

Married to Capt. Simon Tomlinson, their Los Locos team swept through low- and medium-level polo in England. When she reached the three-goal handicap level, Claire indicated that she wished to play in high-goal polo. Her request was denied, even though her handicap was higher than many other male players that participated at that level. *Polo Magazine*, edited by Mr. Geoffrey Cross, had this to say:

> Lady Players and High-Goal polo. Of the numerous members on the HPA Council, presumably the ones upholding the no lady players rule, there are only 3 members who hold a higher handicap than Mrs. Tomlinson! The award of a 3 handicap must logically be as a result of ability and therefore the question of physique holds little water in any argument. So what is the reason for denying lady players the opportunity of high-goal?[17]

The absurdity of the situation is so obvious that, thirty-five years later, it is difficult to understand the HPA's position in that issue. The situation was even more difficult because her father was a steward and a member of the HPA council.

The crux of the matter was the infamous rule 10 of the Rules for Official Tournaments. It simply stated, "Women may not play in high goal tournaments."[18] High-goal tournaments were those with a minimum handicap of fifteen goals.

Unwilling to challenge the stewards, Claire consulted with Lord Cowdray. She pointed out that she had played at twenty-five-goal level in Argentina, and no one had complained. Claire also mentioned that she was safer on the field than some one-goal players competing at that rarified level. Lord Cowdray asked her to prove that players did not mind.

Then Claire got to work and collected signatures from most of the high-handicap players that had participated in the Gold Cup and Goodwood Week. Then she presented a petition to the Hurlingham Polo Association.

The 1978 HPA yearbook tells the story:

> The question of women playing in High Goal Polo has also been under discussion. The two women players who are of high enough handicap to qualify for this, would not be unwelcome to most high goal players, but in principle there has still been some doubt about the matter and to take "special cases" is usually an unsound expedient. Women and men do not play together in serious competition in any other team game in which rough contact is permitted. There are not enough women players for them to have their own Association as in Cricket or Hockey so it would be very drastic to ban them altogether. The Council of the Hurlingham Polo Association has finally decided to drop Rule 10 of Official Tournaments which bars women players from high goal tournaments, but clubs are still free to frame their own conditions.[19]

The HPA had fought hard in a losing battle. Vindication was not far away. In June 1979, at Smith's Lawn, HM Queen Elizabeth handed Claire Tomlinson the Queen's Cup.

Her teammates on the Los Locos red and green jerseys, the same colors worn by her father's Woolmers Park, were Simon Tomlinson, Hector "Juni" Crotto and David Gemmell.

The Road to the Gold Cup

Once the barrier was broken, the road to further achievements was uphill, but free of major obstacles. Lavinia Roberts, the daughter of Squadron-Leader Alan Roberts, of Maidensgrove fame, was the second-ranked English player and competed after a sojourn in Argentina. Isabelle Hayen, the Belgian sponsor of the Groeninghe team, took Cowdray's Park Challenge Cup, a feat also accomplished by Emma Tomlinson — Claire's daughter — and Katie Seabrook with her father's Lambourne team. Tamara Vestey won the Warwickshire Cup on her father's Foxcote team; however, the main prize went to her sister Carina who played on the 2003 Hildon team that took the Cowdray Park Gold Cup.

The Vestey siblings, Ben, Tamara and Nina, wearing Foxcote's colors. Mrs. Carina Clarkin is the top English woman player and the first female to take Cowdray Park's Gold Cup (courtesy Mike Roberts).

"The Four Graces," Janey, Katie, Pippa and Victoria, caught the public's attention when they formed the first all-sisters polo team. Her father Peter, the well-known player, accomplished instructor and author of a treatise on the game, had emigrated from New Zealand and started the Rangitiki Polo Club in Berkshire. Victoria "Tor" Grace became one of the top women players in England and manages the Ascot Park Polo Club, Rangitiki's successor in Surrey. Pippa Gillard, née Grace, became the torch carrier of the International Women's Polo Association. The other two sisters followed different paths. Janey was a Cordon Bleu chef with her own catering company and later embarked on a public relations and marketing career. Katie qualified as a surgeon, obtaining her FRCS certification and is now a cancer specialist in Southwest England.

Another four ladies, Lucy Taylor from Cheshire, Emma Tomlinson, Nina Vestey and Tamara Vestey, all three from Gloucestershire, made history when their team Coombe Farm took the Gerald Balding Cup at Cirencester Park, thus becoming the first all-woman team to win a tournament for all comers.

The International Women's Polo Association

The International Women's Polo Association was founded by Philippa "Pippa" Grace in April 1997, with the aim to assist with the development of women polo players through scholarships and the identification of international playing opportunities and to increase the level of sponsorship and financial support toward women's polo.

The organization sponsors tournaments worldwide. In England, the IWPA sponsors the UK National Tournament, as well as the UK National Arena Tournament at Ascot Park.

Women's polo has come a long way from the prototype game at Ranelagh Club over a century ago.

CHAPTER 22

An Uneasy Alliance: HPA and FIP

The need for creating a worldwide body in charge of supervising the game was recognized prior to the onset of World War II by Lord Louis Mountbatten, who was the chairman of a meeting of the International Rules Committee held in London in 1937. Lord Mountbatten drafted a set of rules that became known as the International Rules of Polo, which was adopted and followed by the Hurlingham Polo Association upon its creation in 1949.

The first rules of the game in England were those written in longhand by Captain Edward Hartopp on Tenth Hussars' Mess notepaper. The rules numbered nine and were quite simple. Then the Herbert's Monmouthshire Club published a set of rules in April 1873, probably by the hand of Francis "Tip" Herbert. The more formal rules of polo issued by the Hurlingham Club on 12 May 1874 became ipso facto the universal code of the game.

Following the organization of the former thirteen colonies into the United States of America, the Polo Association — as it was originally known — produced its own set of rules in 1890. The Indian Polo Association was established in 1892 and promptly published it own rules. With those two exceptions, America and India, the rest of the world, including Argentina, followed the Hurlingham code.

With the passage of time, national governing bodies made some modifications to the Hurlingham rules, mainly to adapt to local conditions, mostly in Australia. By 1938, the differences between American and English rules were quite significant. Thus, the need arose for a meeting to try to implement a single code of rules. Germany's attack on Poland on 1 September 1939 put an end to many good things, including the ratification of the international polo rules.

Furthermore, Argentina, which had strictly followed the Hurlingham rules— translation into Spanish did not happened until 1923 — decided that its own level of polo merited separate rules. Therefore, the Argentine Polo Association published its own set in 1939. The differences among the major polo playing countries remain unsolved more than seventy years later.

A most important open letter to the chairmen and presidents of the Federation of International Polo, the Argentine Polo Association, the Hurlingham Polo Association and the U.S. Polo Association was written by Chris Jones from New Zealand in 2001 and published in *Polo Times*.[1] Mr. Jones made a cogent appeal to the higher authorities of the four ruling bodies to meet at a negotiation table and iron out the differences in the rules, starting with the unification of the rules of play. Regarding other thorny issues, such as drug usage protocols, Mr. Jones felt that they could be decided later. The full text of the letter is reproduced in note 1.

In the spring of 2011, the author mailed a letter to the heads of the four major polo organizations, the alphabet soup of the FIP, AAP, HPA and USPA. Simply stated, the question asked was, if football, which is played by millions of people worldwide, can be conducted under a single set of rules, why cannot polo, which boasts fewer than 20,000 players, achieve uniformity in its rules?

The Hurlingham Polo Association promptly answered the query. In essence, the HPA felt that the issue of welfare was quite different in each country. Regarding the amount of detail in the rules, the feeling was that the Americans were keen on the fine print, while the Argentines did not worry too much about what was written in the rule book. According to the HPA, polo varies according to the level of play, and under patron polo there is no incentive to play four-man polo, for which the original rules were written. Each association prefers its own rules and is reluctant to give up their independence in the matter. Finally, there is not enough polo at the international level to drive the associations toward a single set of rules.[2]

The U.S. Polo Association's response arrived next. It only mentioned its concern about the inability or unwillingness of the high-goal patrons to play by the USPA rules. In fact, the main question was not addressed.[3]

The FIP sent a lengthy letter outlining their opinion. Basically the three national associations are happy with their own rules and show no interest in change. On the other hand, unification of the rules has been discussed since 1995, and the FIP has printed an International Rules of the Game, which is periodically modified, and in force in the World Championships. The USPA changes its rules very often; not so the AAP. The main differences are in how each chukker ends and which penalties may be defended.[4]

At the time of writing, no reply has been received from the Argentine Polo Association.

Federation of International Polo

The Federation of International Polo came into being at a meeting held at the palatial Jockey Club in Buenos Aires in December 1982. Delegates from America, Chile, Colombia, France, Germany, Italy, Mexico, Nigeria, Peru, Spain and Zimbabwe attended the meeting. Because of the lingering effects of the armed conflict in the South Atlantic, members of the Commonwealth did not send delegates. Another notable absentee was Brazil. Marcos Uranga was elected president of the new entity; Luis Valdés from Spain, vice president; Paul de Ganay from France, treasurer; and Carlos Palacios from Peru, secretary.[5]

The FIP organized a World Championship limited to fourteen goals aggregate, with no player over five goals handicap allowed to participate. The first tournament was held at Palermo in 1987. Argentina took the gold, Mexico the silver and Brazil the bronze. For results of all championships, see Note 5.[6]

England's Teams in the World Championship

The Hurlingham Polo Association had declined to join the FIP at the time of its formal organization. The HPA's secretary, Lt. Col. Alec Harper was quoted as saying, "partly because we were not in the best of terms with Argentina at the time and partly because we weren't sure what good it would do."[7]

Berlin, 1989

Even though England was not a member of the Federation of International Polo, an invitation was offered to a representative team to participate in the contest, which was held in Berlin. The rationale offered by the FIP was that Great Britain qualified as a cohost country, together with West Germany, because the venue was located on the British-controlled sector of West Berlin.[8]

The English team, James Lucas, William Lucas, Alex Brodie and Jason Dixon, did well in their bracket, defeating Switzerland, which had three Argentine players with dual nationality. Then they beat Australia, which put them in a virtual semifinal against the holders, Argentina. Regrettably, in some quarters there were efforts to bill this encounter as a "grudge" match.[9] However, nothing was further from the truth. Players from both teams had become good friends as the tournament developed and spent some evenings together exploring the bars on the Kurfurstendam, "training" as one member of the British squad put it.

In the event, England surprised Argentina 9–6 in the semifinals. It was a sweet victory for the English side, because on that same Maifeld the Argentines had vanquished England in the 1936 Olympic Games.

Some 26,000 spectators turned out to watch the final game against the American team, which was a dandy. The Americans changed their lineup at the last moment, although they kept the original numbers on their jerseys. At the end of five chukkers, England was ahead, six goals to five. Two goals by the American team reversed the scoreboard with two minutes to go. England had one last chance; however, the shot at goal hit a pony, and the ball rolled harmlessly toward the sidelines. The game, and along with it Britain's hope for a championship, went astray.

Santiago, 1992

England won the European Zone and qualified for the final round to be played at the San Cristóbal Club in Santiago de Chile. James Lucas, Andrew Hine, Jason Dixon and Henry Brett made the team. Julian Daniels was the reserve and substituted for Henry Brett, who was injured in the last game.

England drew Guatemala and Argentina in their zone. England beat Guatemala and played well in the first chukker against Argentina, eventually losing 10–5. The young Argentines, who had been playing together for some time, proved too strong for the British; as a matter of fact they were too strong for everybody else. An American supporter likened the experience to "taking a knife to a gun-fight."[10]

The match for third place was between the runners-up from each zone. England defeated the USA 10–9. The Americans were ahead by two goals halfway through the sixth chukker; however two penalty conversions made the contest a tie, and within seconds of the final bell, James Lucas scored the winning goal. Thus England took home the bronze medal.

St. Moritz, 1995

The 1995 World Cup was scheduled to be played in Switzerland; however a preliminary tie took place in Dusseldorf, Germany, among the zone winners. England had taken the

European Zone from Italy, Spain and France. In Germany, England and Brazil qualified from Group B for the final round in St. Moritz. England was represented by Tarquin Southwell, Antony Fanshawe, William Hine and Alasdair Archibald. Argentina advanced to the finals when they defeated England 15–6. The match for third place was a good one; both England and Mexico gave all they had. Mexico won in extra time 11–10.

Santa Barbara, 1998

The 1998 contest took place on the magnificent grounds of the Santa Barbara Polo Club in California, overlooking the Pacific Ocean. The English squad included James Beim, Malcolm Borwick, Jason Dixon, James Glasson, William Hine and Caspar West, with David Morley as coach. It was a rough road for the English team because in the European Zone, held in Spain at Club de Polo Soto Mozanaque, just north of Madrid, the team went down to defeat at the hands of the Italians, 10–9. Spain then beat Italy by nine goals to seven. In the third match England redeemed itself by a 10–6 score, thus winning the European Zone play-offs by virtue of a better net-goal differential.

In California, England drew Guatemala and the United States in their bracket, winning both games. Giving four goals on handicap, England beat Guatemala 12–7, allowing no goals from the field. Malcolm Borwick was deadly accurate with his penalty shots, scoring five goals. In a Sunday game, played in glorious weather in front of 7,000 spectators, England defeated the host country 10–5, after conceding two goals by handicap.

Borwick, Hine, Dixon (captain), and Beim faced Brazil in the semifinals. Comfortably leading 7–2 in the third chukker, the English team let up and allowed Brazil to come back into the game. Two Brazilian goals in the last chukker decided the issue in favor of the defending champions. Argentina beat the USA 10–3 in the semifinals and Brazil in the championship game by thirteen goals to eight, after receiving three goals on handicap! Mr. Luke Borwick, who accompanied the English delegation, was of the opinion that the Argentine team could hold its own in twenty-two-goal polo.[11]

There was a problem with some of the Brazilian players' handicap even before the tournament started because the Brazilian players had their handicaps lowered six months prior to the World Championship. The committee arbitrarily raised Brazil's team's handicap to seventeen goals aggregate.[12] Presciently, Buff Crisp commented, "Handicapping at that level internationally is an undeveloped art."[13]

The match for the bronze medal against America was played in San Diego, eight hours south by truck. In a lackadaisical game, in which the U.S. team changed starters and reserves at will, England took the third-place medal.

Melbourne, 2001

The 2001 World Cup at Werribee Park in Melbourne is still considered a model of efficient organization. Under the strong leadership of James Ashton, a scion of the celebrated Australian polo family, three hundred ponies were loaned by the Australian polo community. For the first time in the competition, the top two teams from each zone in the world were admitted to the final round. The issue of accurate handicapping again raised its head, with Brazil and England competing as sixteen-goal teams.

England prepared carefully for this event. The players were selected twelve months before the event, and Claire Tomlinson was appointed coach. The team qualified for Australia by virtue of winning the European Zone in Rome, with Italy finishing in second place, thereby also earning a journey to the Antipodes. England's Tom Rutherford, Alasdair Archibald, Luke Tomlinson and Malcolm Borwick defeated France 14–6, Germany 9–5½, Spain 10–4½ and Italy 10–6.

When the final decision was made, Malcolm Borwick, Jamie Le Hardy, Luke and Mark Tomlinson and Tristan Pemble were the chosen ones. The team arrived in Australia two weeks before the start of the World Cup and competed in Ellerston's eighteen-goal tournament, performing satisfactorily.

A setback occurred when team captain Luke Tomlinson suffered a broken thumb. His place was taken by Australian-born Jamie Le Hardie. England defeated India 19–10 and lost to the United States 11–10. These results made the game against Argentina a must win. Argentina would qualify for the semifinal round even if they lost by three goals. Full of confidence, the Argentines led 4–1 in the second chukker. Then they made the fatal mistake of easing up, and England crawled back into the game. Tied at the end of the fourth chukker, England went ahead 8–6 in the fifth and 11–7 in the last chukker. Ignacio Toccalino converted a penalty shot to keep Argentina's hope alive; however, Mark Tomlinson's goal with ten seconds remaining sealed the issue. America was in and Argentina was out of the semifinals. The Argentines took the defeat gamely, trudging across the field to congratulate the victors. In the meantime, bells rang out in Sao Paulo and Rio de Janeiro.

The exhilaration of defeating Argentina came to a sudden end when Australia defeated England 14–12 in the semifinal round. Australia proved to be a tough team, beating Italy — which had the Nero brothers from Argentine — drawn with Canada and losing to Brazil by a one-goal margin.

Malcolm Borwick was the top gun for England; out of sixty-five goals scored by the team, Borwick made forty-two, most of them from penalty shots.

Chantilly, 2004

England was the host country for the European Zone play-offs that were held at the RLS Polo Club in Warwickshire. Germany, Holland, Ireland, Italy and Spain sent their national teams to compete for only one slot, France already having qualified as the host country. The English team had an inauspicious start by losing to Italy; however, they recovered to defeat Italy in the final game and earn a trip across the English Channel.

The final match of the World Cup at Chantilly was a heartbreaking loss for the British team. The title on the report on the competition in *Polo Times* as "Brazil by a Whistle" could very well imply a double meaning.[14] The unsinkable Claire Tomlinson was, once more, appointed coach of the British squad. Andrew Blake-Thomas and Matt Loder, both at two goals, were backed up by five-goalers Tom Morley and James Harper. A tight defense and fast runners up front was the strategy. Jonny Good and Ed Hitchman were the reserves.

The opening game was against Brazil, the holders. The team played quite well, in control of the game's flow most of the time, only to lose by a single tally, nine goals to eight. Mexico was the next opponent, England running away to a 11–7 win. The last group game versus Pakistan was an easy one — if there is such a thing in international polo — England emerging winners by fourteen goals to four. In the semifinals, England defeated a strong team from Chile that had knocked out Argentina in the South American Zone, by a score of seven goals to six.

On to the championship match, which started with the scoreboard showing the handicap differential, 1–0 in Brazil's favor. England was down 5–2 in the second chukker, only to score five consecutive goals to edge ahead 7–5. Brazil equalized and went up 9–7 with a minute and a half remaining. Then James Harper scored from one hundred yards out. The ball was thrown in with twenty seconds left of the ticking clock. England won the ball, and Tom Morley tied the game with a cut shot. The scoreboard at the end of regulation time read 9–9.

Extra time was painful even before the start. FIP regulations allow a tie to be the game's final score. Each horse was allowed to play seven minutes per game, and several players complained that they did not have enough ponies to play another chukker. This time limitation presented a sticking point, but finally the game was resumed.

Once more, England won the key throw-in, and Tom Morley took a long shot. The flagman signaled a goal; however, he was judged to be flutter happy, to the dismay of the cheering English partisans. England kept on pressing, and what appeared to be an obvious foul in front of the Brazilian goalposts was not called by the umpires. Further along, two fouls from the spot were awarded to England, while Brazil missed one forty-yarder and two penalties from sixty yards.

Then the whistle went against England a few yards in front of the goal. The Brazilian players jumped off their ponies, and their supporters invaded the field. The penalty was not taken, and no goal was flagged. Attempts to ascertain what penalty was awarded were fruitless.[15]

The only positive result from this embarrassing extra-time mess was that the FIP ruled that in future World Cup finals, a tie should be broken by a penalty shoot-out, rather than an overtime chukker.

Mexico City, 2008

The European Zone matches were held in Spain at the Santa María Polo Club in Sotogrande. England, France, Italy, the Netherlands and the host country were the participants. Nina Vestey Clarkin — the first woman to participate in an FIP World Cup event — George Meyrick, Ed Hitchman and Tom Morley — faced France in their match, which they won by 9 to 5½ goals. Next came the Netherlands, the only all-amateur team, which was vanquished 18–6½. England then proceeded to lose against Italy by the odd goal in nineteen. The Italian team drew much criticism because it included three Argentine professionals sporting Italian passports. The final game was against Spain, which was won by the English squad by nine goals to six. Therefore, Spain, Italy and England finished with a 3–1 match record. Because of the better goal differential, England and Spain qualified for the journey to Mexico.

No fewer than nine players — John Fisher, Bobby Dundas, Henry Fisher, John Martin and Max Routledge were added to the four that had qualified in Sotogrande — were selected to travel to the high-altitude capital city of Mexico. Coach Claire Tomlinson opined that it was "the best prepared team that England had ever had."[16]

They had trained in Argentina for some time and arrived in Mexico City early to acclimatize for the relative lack of oxygen. The team had played well in the preliminaries and was a cohesive, well-coached squad. Yet they were winless and ended up in seventh place out of eight teams. How could that happen?

The luck of the draw placed England against the championship holders Brazil in the first game. Clarkin, Hitchman, Morley and Henry Fisher lost 7–5 after a tough match. The second game was against the host country, always a very challenging situation. The team played well, holding a three-goal lead in the final chukker. Mexico scored four unanswered goals to eliminate England from the semifinals.

In a meaningless match in which both teams had no chance of advancing, South Africa took the last game in the bracket by half a goal.

The World Cup Trophy

The World Cup trophy was donated by the Maharajah of Jaipur, son of the famous nine-goaler "Jai," whose team swept all the London tournaments in 1933. Following the foundation of the Federation of International Polo, Glen Holden and Marcos Uranga undertook a tour of many polo-playing nations to persuade them to join and support the newly created world entity. When they reached India, they suggested to the Maharajah of Jaipur, known throughout the polo world as "Bubbles" after the enormous amount of champagne consumed at his birth, that he consent to commission and donate an appropriate trophy to be emblematic of the World Cup. The Maharajah graciously gave his consent, and the handsome trophy was ready for presentation at the first World Cup in Buenos Aires in 1987. This was a way to recognize the important influence that the state of Jaipur has had in the game of polo.[17]

The HPA and the FIP

Because of the aftermath of the war in the South Atlantic, the Hurlingham Polo Association did not send representatives to the organizational meeting held in Buenos Aires that led to the establishment of the Federation of International Polo. For that matter, neither did any of the Commonwealth countries. Australia finally broke the ice, and a team led by future FIP President James Ashton participated in the first World Cup held at the Palermo polo grounds in 1987. England followed suit after entering the 1989 World Cup in Berlin.

The events in the championship game versus Brazil at Chantilly left a bitter taste in British mouths. Following the event, the English coach was quoted, "We were robbed," and an unnamed FIP official apologized for the quality of umpiring.[18]

Things did not improve following the Mexican debacle. Luke Tomlinson, Captain of England, wrote words to the effect that, in his opinion, the importance of the World Cup is not what it used to be.[19] The English coach in Mexico, Claire Tomlinson, felt that "unless FIP organizes its tournaments more professionally, the HPA could put their money to better use, perhaps playing tournaments in Argentina."[20]

The Hurlingham Polo Association rushed to mend fences. At an open forum at Guards Polo Club chaired by FIP president Patrick Guerrand-Hermès, the ruling body of English polo reaffirmed its commitment to support the World Cup. Furthermore, the Hurlingham Polo Association renewed its vows of friendship with the federation and agreement with its objectives. Peace on earth.

However, not all was well in the world of polo. The heads of the "Big Three" organizations, America, Argentina and Britain, were approached by senior members within the FIP, including past presidents, voicing their concern about M. Guerrand-Hermès' penchant for running the federation as his personal fiefdom, without consulting the executive committee regarding many important issues. The senior members asked if there was any way that the respective chairmen would be able to assist in resolving the situation.

Some of the concerns regarding the course chartered by M. Patrick Guerrand-Hermès as president of the Federation of International Polo were repeated at a special meeting of the FIP Council of Administration in London in July 2009. Thomas Biddle, chairman of the U.S. Polo Association; Nicholas Colquhoun-Denvers, the Hurlingham Polo Association's chairman; and Luis Lalor, recently elected president of the Asociación Argentina de Polo, agreed about the functions of the FIP; however, they expressed serious reserva-

Luke Tomlinson was the captain of the English team that took the 2009 Westchester Cup at International Polo Club Palm Beach.

tions about the ways and means by which the FIP was conducted. Briefly, the three officers felt that all the elected and appointed FIP officials should be approved by the three associations.

Secondly, they felt that the current bylaws allowed almost unlimited power to the president. The third concern voiced was that the FIP was soliciting sponsorship from commercial companies already committed to each association, the most egregious example being the so-called "return match" of the Argentine Open, played at Deauville by eight Argentine ten-goal players.

Patrick Guerrand-Hermès disagreed with the objections raised at this meeting. In an interview published by *Polo Times*, M. Guerrand-Hermès pointed out that since his election to the presidency of the FIP he had tried to develop the game of polo globally and to bring it out of media obscurity.[21] He mentioned the official recognition by the International Equestrian Federation, with a view to include polo in the World Equestrian Games, as another step toward restoring the game of polo as an Olympic event. Patrick Guerrand-Hermès also mentioned his efforts in giving increased exposure in front of international sporting institutions, major corporations and television channels.

The chairmen of the Big Three associations put in writing the aforementioned concerns in August 2010. According to the chairmen, no response was received from M. Patrick Guerrand-Hermès. In the words of one of the protagonists, "We tried to talk to him and failed spectacularly, we tried to get him to resign and failed spectacularly and were left with our ultimate sanction of resigning knowing FIP without the strength of the Argentine, America and United Kingdom players would be pretty toothless."[22]

The next, irrevocable step occurred in October, when the AA de Polo, the Hurlingham PA and the USPA, each counting over 3,000 members out of a total FIP membership of 16,726, threatened to resign if their demands were not met. The three associations burned the bridges when Argentina resigned from the FIP on 26 October, followed by the Hurlingham Polo Association and the U.S. Polo Association on the following day.

The annual meeting of the FIP was scheduled for late November in Buenos Aires. Diplomacy took over in the persons of Marcos Uranga and Glen Holden, two respected statesmen and the first two presidents of the Federation of International Polo. Diplomacy failed, and as a direct result of the intervention of Nicholas Colquhoun-Denvers, Luis Eduardo Lalor and Stephen Orthwein the evening before the General Assembly, M. Patrick Guerrand-Hermès graciously resigned his post. James Ashton from Australia was elected interim president, pending confirmation at the April meeting in Florida, hopefully getting the Federation of International Polo on the right track.

America, Argentina and the United Kingdom returned to the fold, and a new, brilliant era was seen on the horizon. Mr. James Ashton was a highly respected worldwide administrator with impeccable credentials. His organization of the World Cup at Melbourne was faultless and drew high praise from all concerned.

The appointment of James Ashton brought a breath of fresh air to the FIP. Mr. Ashton's New Year address was quite clear: "There is much work to be done now. This should be a period of reflection and study. It is time to redefine the mission of the FIP, to address the concerns of all members small and large, and to clarify our relations with international bodies."[23]

The chairman of the Hurlingham Polo Association, Nicholas Colquhoun-Denvers, succinctly stated: "After all the turmoil of the past six months the FIP is sure to emerge a stronger and more effective global body to represent polo and help its worldwide growth."[24]

Certainly, it was the dawn of a new era of understanding and cooperation among the polo-playing nations. Most regrettably, James W. Ashton, a scion of Australia's first polo family, died as the result of an accident on the polo field in Thailand. His passing caused an irreparable loss to his family and to the world of polo.

Mr. Thomas Biddle, Sr., the most senior among the Big Three chairmen, was appointed temporary president of the FIP. At the annual meeting in Lake Worth, Florida, Eduardo Huergo, a five-goal handicap player and longtime officer in both the Argentine Polo Association and the Federation of International Polo, was elected to finish the presidential term in November 2012.

CHAPTER 23

Literature of British Polo

The literature of polo in Britain is rich in both numbers and quality. The first book to address the modern game is *Polo in India*, by Captain, later Major General, George Younghusband, an officer in the Queen's Own Corps of Guides. The book was published in London in 1890. However, it addresses the game of polo as played in India, and therefore it is outside the scope covered by this work. It is mentioned only to bring attention to its chronological priority.

History

James Moray Brown wrote the section on polo in the book *Riding: Polo*, one of the volumes in the Badminton Library. Moray Brown had played the game at its early stages, when a subaltern in the Cameronian Highlanders; therefore he wrote with knowledge of the game, and after leaving the service he became the doyen of polo writers. This work was published in 1891, and four years later his second book, *Polo*, was published after his untimely passing. Both works cover the historical background to the modern game, the origins of polo in England, the game as played in India, polo ponies, the rules and bylaws, the former closing with an interesting chapter, "How a Polo Game Should Be Played."

The Reverend Thomas Dale produced *The Game of Polo* in 1897. It follows the common pattern of most books published before the onset of the Great War in 1914. They are encyclopedic in their scope, informing the reader about the game's development; training of mount and man; umpiring; management of a polo club; breeding; equipment, including appropriate dress; expenses and danger of the game; notices about the clubs; and that topic so beloved by Victorian authors, recollections and reminiscences.

The Reverend Dale expands his narrative in *Polo — Past and Present* (1905) and culminates with the sumptuous *Polo at Home and Abroad*, which was published in 1915, during the war. The latter is bound in vellum, in a limited edition of one hundred numbered copies. There is also another edition of 150 copies, leather bound, and a third edition, also limited to 150 copies, in cloth. All editions are quite rare.

An unknown editor, "the Sportsman," produced *Polo and Coaching*, a volume in the collection British Sports and Sportsmen, a large folio published during the 1920s. Although undated, the volume on polo can be dated to late 1922 or early 1923. One thousand leather-bound copies were made, as well as the same number in cloth.

Lt. Col. Gerald Hobson wrote the entertaining *Some XII Lancers* (1936) with vignettes about regimental life, including polo, from the early part of the twentieth century until the year of publication.

Herbert Spencer broke new ground with his coffee-table-size *Chakkar: Polo Around the World* (1971). This book set a standard that has not been surpassed forty years after publication. It contains essays by prominent personalities in the game, such as HRH the Duke of Edinburgh, the Earl Mountbatten of Burma, Baron Elie de Rothschild, Hanut Singh, Juan Carlos Harriott, Jr., Ricardo Santamarina, Bob Skene and Cecil Smith. The photography is outstanding, and the passage of time has taken nothing away from this magnificent work. There is a leather-bound edition limited to six hundred copies.

Major J.N.P. Watson's *The World of Polo* (1986) is a good introduction to the history of the game, profusely illustrated. The author was a polo player in the Blues and was polo correspondent to *Country Life*.

John Lloyd wrote *The Pimm's Book of Polo* (1989) with contributions from several personalities, including HH the Rajmata of Jaipur, Hugh Dawnay, Ronald Ferguson, William Loyd, Bryan Morrison, Michael Roberts, and Jack and Marjorie Williams. It is a kaleidoscopic view of the game, focusing mostly in England.

Club Histories

Specific histories of polo clubs in England are very few. Captain Taprell Dorling, RN, wrote *The Hurlingham Club* (1953) and Nigel Miskin's work *History of Hurlingham* (2000) is a meticulously drafted document tracing the venerable club's evolution from a pigeon-shooting establishment to its primordial role in polo's history. The Hurlingham Club published a booklet, mostly photographs, on the occasion of its golden jubilee in 1924 and also *The Hurlingham Club and the Jubilee of Polo 1974–1924*.

Derek Russell-Stoneham and Roger Chatterton-Smith wrote *Polo at Cowdray* (1992), an excellent and concise book tracing the history of the club, with many illustrations and photographs.

Elizabeth Hennessy produced *A History of Roehampton Club* in 1986, which was updated in 2001. The story of the club founded by the Miller brothers is told in a most entertaining style.

Nigel à Brassard, a Cirencester Park member, wrote about Buck's Club in his *A Glorious Victory, A Glorious Defeat* (2001), an excellent book about the 1921 Westchester Cup and the influence upon polo exerted by Buck's, a social club in London.

Herbert Spencer's *A Century of Polo* (1994) describes at length the ups and downs of the Cirencester Park polo club. This is an excellent recounting of the Gloucestershire club by the doyen of polo historians.

Finally, Major John N.P. Watson's last work, *Smith's Lawn: The History of the Guards Polo Club* (2005), is a beautifully produced book telling the development of one of the premier polo clubs in the world.

Instructional: Theory and Practice

Quite obviously, books dedicated to explain and teach the game form the largest category in the literature of polo.

Edward Miller's pioneer work *Modern Polo* was first published in 1896. The book went through six editions, the last one in 1929. This work is one of the few that form the cornerstone of any polo book collection because of its scope, the author's expertise and standing within the polo community, and the sheer quantity and quality of the information provided throughout. Without much doubt, *Modern Polo* was the most influential book on the game.

Close in scope to Miller's opus is *Polo*, by the Scottish player Thomas Drybrough, first published in 1898 and updated and enlarged in 1906. The revised edition is a thick volume that rivals Captain Miller's seminal work.

Maj. Gen. George Younghusband's *Tournament Polo* (1898) is an extension of his proto-endeavor, *Polo in India*, with much emphasis on the competitive aspect of the game.

An extremely rare book is Walter Buckmaster's *Hints for Polo Combination*. Only a handful of copies are known to exist. It is a superb book, concise and to the point, written by one of the top players in the history of the game.

Douglas Godfree, Olympic fencer and a subaltern in the 21st Lancers, wrote *Some Notes on Polo* (1911). This is a thoughtful work, with plenty of practical and sound advice on the game. There are clear diagrams explaining the strokes and the flow of play. Regrettably, and perhaps due to its scarcity, this little volume has not received the recognition it richly deserves.

General John Hardress Lloyd, a ten-goal handicap player and captain on the 1911 Westchester team, penned a short volume titled *Polo: Some Notes on the Game*. Perhaps more a pamphlet than a book, it was originally published by *The Irish Field*. Very few copies are known to exist.

The next decade saw several instructional books offered to the reading public. By far the best is Robert Ricketts' *First Class Polo* (1928). Brigadier Ricketts, one of polo's brightest minds, writes about pace as paramount in success at polo. Pace, extreme pace, according to Ricketts, is not to be confused with wild hitting, which is not conducive to pace, but rather the reverse.

Other books from this period include *Hints on Polo* (1921) by Fearnley Anderson, a six-goal player in the Seaforth Highlanders, and *How to Make a Polo Pony* (1922) by two unknown authors that elected to hide their identities under the pseudonyms "Snaffle-Cavisson" and "Standing-Martingale." Then we have Major Warrington Tylden-Wright, 3rd Hussars, a five-goaler who penned *Notes on Polo* (1927); Colonel Commandant Frank Ramsay's *Polo Pony Training* (1928); and *Practical Polo* by P.O.V. The latter book's author's name came to public light in 1958, when the book was reprinted; it was Brigadier Wilmot Vickers, then living in retirement in Cheltenham. Also from this era is *Ideas on Breaking Polo Ponies* (1931), by Lt. Col. Gerald Hobson. Attached to the main work is *The Polo Crib*, a brief set of basic precepts with much truth in them.

Then appeared two of the most important books on the game. The first was *An Introduction to Polo* by "Marco" (1931). Written by Lord Louis Mountbatten, with some editorial help from his friend Peter Murphy, it is another cornerstone polo book. The original edition was produced for the members of the Royal Navy Saddle Club; several other editions were printed into the 1970s. A gem of a book, it clearly explains everything to do with the game and its mounts.

The Earl of Kimberley, who as Lord Wodehouse was an international ten-goal player, edited *Polo* in 1936. This is volume 21 in the Lonsdale Library of Sports and Pastimes; there are three different bindings: the trade edition with a dust jacket, a quarter-leather edition, and a limited edition in full leather. The latter is a very rare find. The contributors include Brigadier George de la Poer Beresford, Maj. Gen. Geoffry Brooke, Lt. Col. Jack Gannon,

Lord Mountbatten, Brig. Gen. Robert Ricketts and Peter Vischer. Fifteen of the twenty-nine chapters were written by Brigadier Ricketts.

General Beauvoir De Lisle wrote *Hints to Polo Players in India* (1897), originally written for the Durham Light Infantry's officers, and three editions of *Polo in India. Tournament Polo* (1938), by the same author, is an expanded version of his series of lectures done at the request of the Maharaja of Kashmir, which were published in a small book in 1934.

Major John Board wrote *Polo* (1957), profusely illustrated with photographs and the author's own drawings. It is a good instructional book, clearly written and containing good advice. One of the book's highlights is the diagrams explaining the rules of the game, by far the best in polo literature.

George "Bob" Rudkin, a prewar player from Rhinefield and later manager at Hertfordshire Polo Club, wrote a booklet, *Thoughts on Polo*, sometime in the 1950s.

Polo for the Pony Club was published by the British Horse Society at the National Equestrian Centre in 1960. As the title implies, it is a clear explanation of the basic skills in the game.

Peter Grace, who immigrated to England from New Zealand, wrote the comprehensive *Polo* (1991). It is a painstakingly detailed instruction manual of the game, the most complete instructional book since the 1930s. The book went into a second edition.

Two instructional books based upon his teaching courses at Whitfield Court in county Waterford, Republic of Ireland, were produced by Major Hugh Dawnay, 10th Hussars: *Polo Vision*, illustrated by Susanna Holt (1984), and *Playmaker Polo* (2004). Both works carefully explain basic and advanced concepts about the game, according to Major Dawnay's methods of teaching.

Art

George Armour's autobiography, *Bridle and Brush* (1937), contains several sketches of polo scenes. Most interesting are his drawings of the 1913 Westchester Cup at Meadow Brook, when the artist traveled with the English team to America. This proximity with the protagonists also allowed Armour to record pertinent observations about that series of matches.

Major John Watson's *Lionel Edwards: Master of the Sporting Scene* (1986) illustrates "Polo at Tidworth" and a masterful depiction of a polo pony in India.

Two reference works, *The Dictionary of British Sporting Artists* (1985), by Sally Mitchell, and Mary Ann Wingfield's *A Dictionary of Sporting Artists 1650–1990* (1992) contain numerous illustrations of polo bronzes and paintings. Both works are comprehensive in scope and carefully researched.

Sport and the Artist (1988), also by Mary Ann Wingfield, dedicates a full chapter to the game of polo, with many illustrations in both color and black-and-white reproductions.

Also in 1988, John Welcome and Rupert Collins produced *Snaffles*, a well-illustrated book depicting many of Charlie Johnson Payne's celebrated works on polo.

The Sporting Art of Cecil Aldin (1990) is illustrated with many examples of his polo art, including *Dull Polo*, impressions of the final match between British and American Army teams, and two beautiful scenes of polo at Dunster Downs.

The photographer Elizabeth Furth produced *Visions of Polo* (2005). It is a book of high-quality photography, enhanced by captions that include quotes from the participants shown in the illustrations.

Polo Ponies and Equitation

The prolific writer Thomas Francis Dale also wrote about *Riding and Polo Ponies* (1899). He was highly qualified to write on the subject by virtue of his membership in the council of the Polo Pony Society and his expertise on ponies.

Australian Fred Galvayne, sometime manager of the Société du Polo in Paris, included a practical treatise on training ponies and playing polo in his *The XXth Century Book on the Horse* (1905). This work went through three editions.

Major H.P. Young, 4th Bombay Cavalry, wrote *Hints on Sport: Also a Few Practical Suggestions on Polo* (1907), while Colonel Reginald Badger's *A Record of Horses* was privately printed in a fine morocco-bound edition in 1937.

Ponies' Progress by Edward Durand contains good material about the training of polo ponies. This book was published in 1935.

Maj. Gen. Geoffry Brooke's *Horse-sense and Horsemanship of To-day* was one of the most read books on equitation. He also wrote *The Way of a Man with a Horse*, the first volume in the Lonsdale Library of Sports. Both works contain sage information about equitation, the game and the ponies.

Loftus Storey wrote for the County Polo Association *The Training of Mount and Man for Polo* (1948), with a note on "Paddock Polo" by Sir Berkeley Pigott. It is a well-written booklet, offering sound advice and hints to beginners in the game.

Richard Hobson, Colonel Gerald Hobson's son, published *Polo and Ponies* (1976), and followed suit with *Riding: The Game of Polo* (1993).

Competitive Events

Arthur Wells Coaten edited three volumes describing the Westchester Cup series in *International Polo* (1912) and brought the work up to date in 1922.

The same subject was described by the American author Frank Gray Griswold in *The International Polo Cup* (1928). It is an uneven work; while the 1914 series at Meadow Brook, the 1921 matches at the Hurlingham Club and the 1927 competition in America are carefully described, the 1902 contest at Hurlingham is totally ignored. However, it carries the authority of an eyewitness to all the contests, dating back to the inaugural competition in 1886.

The Olympic Games of 1900, 1908, 1920 and 1924 are described in detail in Dr. Bill Mallon's reference works. Ian Buchanan contributed to the 1908 Olympiad and Anthony Bijkerk to the 1920 games.

Seymour Knox describes his team's successful visit to England in *Aurora in England* (1934). "Shorty" Knox's easy style, evident in all his polo books, makes a very interesting reading about polo in the UK in the 1930s from an American perspective.

John Board's *Year with Horses* is a nice recount of the equestrian activity in England in the Coronation year of 1953. The book is fully illustrated with his own drawings.

Nigel à Brassard, Cirencester Park player and a member of Buck's Club, published in 2001 *A Glorious Victory, A Glorious Defeat*. This carefully researched and beautifully written book tells the story of Buck's Club, its involvement in polo since the early days of the nineteenth century to our time, and the story of the 1921 American challenge for the Westchester Cup. Only five hundred copies were printed, the proceeds going to charity.

Biographies and Autobiographies

By and large, polo players are notoriously reluctant to write about themselves, with very few exceptions. Nevertheless, there are quite a number of books describing different aspects of the game, from the social aspect to its context with historical happenings.

Colonel Thomas St. Quintin, who was one of the 10th Hussars that took a whack at a cricket ball at Aldershot in 1869, wrote his life memoirs in *Chances of Sports of Sorts* (1912). Although there is only one full chapter dedicated to polo, the game keeps happily breaking in. Colonel St. Quintin was at the beginnings of polo in England, started the game in Australia and became an iconic figure in the world of polo.

John Buchan wrote *Francis and Riversdale Grenfell*, a biographical study of the famous twins, Francis Octavius and Riversdale Nonus. Francis, an eight-goal handicap player, was awarded the first Victoria Cross of the war. Twice wounded, Grenfell returned to the Western Front and was killed at Ypres in May 1915. Rivy Grenfell, rated at nine goals, was killed after twenty-five days in the field with the 9th Lancers, in September 1914.

Fifty Years of Sport (1925) is a fascinating book of reminiscences by Lt. Col. Edward Miller, 17th Lancers. The game of polo figures prominently in this work, because Colonel Miller was at the epicenter of polo throughout his life.

A large-format, lavish book is *Polo: International Sport*, edited by Alphons Stock about 1930. The book consists of many biographical sketches of famous and not so famous polo players, each one accompanied by a full-page portrait. This book was produced at irregular intervals, because some biographies are missing from apparently identical issues.

Lt. Col. Teignmouth Melvill, sometime in command of that famous polo-playing regiment, the 17th/21st Lancers, wrote his autobiography *Ponies and Women* (1932). It is a first-hand account of his career, which included successes in the Inter-Regimental Tournament and international appearances in the Westchester Cup.

The Spaniard Don Manuel de Escandón, Marqués de Villavieja, wrote *Life has Been Good* (1938). Villavieja describes the game of polo as it was played in the waning years of the nineteenth century in England and on the Continent, proceeding to the 1930s. His acute observations on many personalities, their foibles and virtues, represent a unique perspective of a class that the Great War changed forever, as it also did for polo.

Reminiscences of Sport and War (1939) is a book by Gen. Sir Beauvoir De Lisle. Most of the book is devoted to his military career; however, the chapter on polo provides a vivid description of the tactics and the players on the Durham Light Infantry team that took the Inter-Regimental Tournament and the Indian Open Championship, defeating all the Cavalry regiments and the best Indian teams in the process.

A privately printed book is *Some Memoirs*, the reminiscences of William Riley Smith, the founder of the Toulston Polo Club in Yorkshire. It was published circa 1948.

James Pearce, a five-goal handicap player from the Rugby Club, had an extensive career in England and many parts of the world, including the United States. His recollections are told in *Everybody's Polo* (1949), dotted with sharp observations on the national characters of people from Ireland to Russia, passing through Egypt and Poland.

HRH Prince Philip Sportsman by Helen Cathcart was published in 1961, and Michael Clayton wrote *Prince Charles, Horseman* (1987). The royal involvement in the game is frequently mentioned in those two biographies.

Major Ronald Ferguson wrote his life's story in *The Galloping Major* (1994). The dashing Life Guards officer whose career was placed in jeopardy when the reptile press reported his leaving the Wigmore Club, a repository of women endowed with more charm than virtue, candidly narrates his years of military service, numerous polo tours abroad and his involvement in organizing the International Polo Day at Smith's Lawn.

Brigadier Jack Gannon, longtime secretary of the Hurlingham Polo Association and a seven-goal handicap player in his heyday, recounts many equestrian events in his life in *Before the Colours Fade* (1976). Particularly informative is his narrative regarding the organization of the polo activities for the 1936 Olympic Games in Berlin.

Lt. Col. Alec Harper, another long-serving HPA secretary, tells about his life adventures, including polo, in India, postwar England and Cowdray Park, in *Horse and Foot* (1995). Colonel Harper, an English international, was the organizational guru in Britain after the war, both as a polo player, administrator and constructive critic on many issues affecting the game in his day.

Finally, *Profiles in Polo: The Players Who Changed the Game* (2007) contains short biographies of thirty-four players who exerted a significant impact on the game. The editor, Horace Laffaye, assembled a number of contributors noted for their expertise on polo: Nigel à Brassard, Yolanda Carslaw and Sarah Eakin from England; Americans Dennis Amato and Peter Rizzo; Sebastián Amaya from Argentina; Australian Chris Ashton; Roger Chatterton-Newman from Ireland; and Lady Susan Reeve from South Africa. The featured players from England are Thomas St. Quintin, Edward Hartopp, Francis Herbert, Lord Mountbatten, Lord Cowdray, Claire Lucas Tomlinson, Julian Hipwood and HRH the Prince of Wales, who graciously wrote the foreword to the book.

Umpiring

The only work published in England exclusively devoted to the art of umpiring is "Marco's" *An Introduction to Umpiring*, published by the RNPA in 1934.

Reference

Francis "Tip" Herbert, one of the founders of the Monmouthshire Polo Club in 1872, was the author of the section on "Polo" in *The Encyclopaedia of Sport* (1898), edited by the Earl of Suffolk, Hedley Peek and Frederick Aflalo. The article, bracketed between "Pochard" and "Porcupine," is an excellent description of polo, covering the antiquity of the game, its introduction into England, the ground, polo sticks, the balls, dress, a description of the game itself and a long section on polo ponies. Also included are the Hurlingham Club Polo Rules and Regulations.

The Polo Encyclopedia (2004) by Horace Laffaye contains more than 10,000 entries arranged in alphabetical sequence. This work provides concise information about players, competitions, ponies, polo clubs, artists, authors and their works, and a myriad of other topics. By the same author is *The Evolution of Polo* (2009), a sociological study that traces the development of the game from its origins in Asia to its current manifestation as a professional game.

Annuals and Year Books

The *Polo Players Diary* was published in London from 1910 until 1915. As a supplement to a diary, it contains information about polo clubs, winners of past tournaments, the rules of the game, tournament fixtures and the recent form list.

The *Polo Players Guide* was started by Captain Edward Miller about 1910. This small volume offers much information about provincial polo and the London season.

A larger volume is *The Polo Annual*, edited by L.V.L. Simmonds and Edward D. Miller. This works gives an expanded scope of information compared to the two previous annuals. Regrettably, it became a casualty of the war.

The Polo Year Book was published from 1923 until the start of World War II. In a certain way it can be considered in its scope as the forerunner of the Hurlingham Polo Association Year Book, although it was not an official publication of the Hurlingham Polo Committee.

The *Hurlingham Polo Association Year Book* started publication in 1951. It has grown from a thin volume containing forty pages to the present 2011 hardcover book which offers more than four hundred pages of information. This collection of volumes represents a major reference work for polo historians.

The Horseman's Year, published in London, contains articles related to several equestrian activities at home and abroad. Interesting articles related to polo appeared regularly from 1952 until 1960, a period of time with very limited printed polo coverage in England.

Valerie Halford edited *The Polo World*, which included much information on polo in Britain. Regrettably, only two volumes were published, in 1994 and 1995.

A recent publication, *Polo Collector*, is now in its second year. Edited by polo player Ludovic Pailloncy, this large-format book is a compilation of forty-four important tournaments around the world. It is an invaluable record for researchers and aficionados. Another significant feature of the book is the impressive array of spectacular photographs.

Magazines

Baily's Magazine of Sports and Pastimes is one of the earliest sources about the game of polo in Britain. The reports were written by knowledgeable men about the sport, and the Victorian prose makes for interesting reading.

There was a short-lived *Polo Magazine* edited by Francis Herbert, one of the band of pioneers from Monmouthshire. Subtitled "A Journal of Sport and Fashion," publication started in 1894, with a total of six volumes, the last one issued in 1899.

A very scarce magazine, *Polo at Home and Abroad*, was published from 1901 until 1902. Even rarer is *The Polo and Hunting Journal*, which only comprised three issues in July, August and September of 1925.

The unique *Polo Monthly* was published from 1909 until 1939. Edited by Arthur Coaten, this magazine provides an invaluable record of the game as played at home and overseas throughout that golden period of the game.

Geoffrey Cross edited *Polo Magazine* from 1977 until 1980. With the exception of the HPA yearbooks from that era, it is the only record of polo in Britain along those years, with the exception of newspaper reports.

Polo Quarterly International, initially edited by the capable hands of Roger Chatterton-Newman, the Cowdray Park historian, is a large-format magazine with excellent photography and in-depth articles about historical subjects and contemporary tournaments and institutions. The magazine was launched in 1992, and upon Mr. Chatterton-Newman's retirement, the editorial direction was taken over by Maj. Iain Forbes-Cockell, former polo player with the Life Guards. In 2010, a new editor, Aurora Eastwood, was appointed.

Polo Times started as *The Polo Advertiser* in 1993 by Mrs. Hugh (Margie) Brett in Oxfordshire. Soon the name was changed to *Polo Times*, and it quickly became the most informative monthly polo magazine in Britain. Undoubtedly the most influential contemporary polo magazine, perceptive, informative, irreverent at times, with a fine sense of humor, the game is well served by *Polo Times*. When Margie Brett elected to become publisher, Yolanda Carslaw, who grew up watching polo from her pram at Cowdray, was appointed editor. Her editorial post was recently taken over by James Mullan.

Hurlingham Polo was started by polo player Roderick Vere Nicoll in 2005 and is a semi-official voice for the Hurlingham Polo Association. This well-designed magazine informs the world about polo happenings in the United Kingdom and the rest of the polo world about what is going on at home.

Finally, the *International Journal of History of Sports*, published in London and now in its twenty-eighth year of publication, is the leading publication on this fascinating topic. Its scholarly articles are written by recognized authorities in each field.

CHAPTER 24

Polo in Britain in the Twenty-First Century

The new millennium witnessed tremendous growth of the game of polo worldwide. The increase in the number of players, clubs and ponies defies detailed description.

New Polo Clubs in Britain

The Coworth Park Polo Club, located in Sunninghill between Ascot and Virginia Water, was started in 2001. Situated near Fort Belvedere, sometime home of polo player Edward, Prince of Wales, and later King Edward VIII, the club was the base for polo teams such as Galen Weston's Maple Leafs, Jerudong Park and Ahmiabh Farm. The revived Indian Empire Shield and the Valerie Halford Memorial were some of the trophies.

Nevertheless, the best polo played at Coworth Park was the three events for the all-professional British Polo Championship organized by Nigel à Brassard from 2004 until 2007.

Light Dragoons Polo Club became affiliated with the Hurlingham Polo Association in 2001. The regiment itself was formed in Hohne, Germany, from an amalgamation that encompassed a quartet of original polo-playing cavalry regiments, the 13th/18th Hussars and the 15th/19th Hussars. When the regiment returned to England, the Light Dragoons Club built a new ground at Swanton Morley in Norfolk.

The Rugby Polo Club was established by David and Philip Baker in 2002, using the original polo grounds on Spring Hill laid out by the Miller brothers in the early 1890s.

The Beverly Polo Club was formed in 2002 by Andrew Foreman, with the intention of further promoting polo in Yorkshire. The polo grounds are located at Tickton Hall, in East Yorkshire.

Sussex Polo Club in West Sussex was established in 2002 by Duane and Sallie Anne Lent. The polo grounds are situated at Home Farm in Rowfant. The club caters to beginners and players up to two-goal handicap, in a friendly environment. One of the tournaments is the Rupert Thorneloe Memorial Cup, established in memory of Lt. Col. Thorneloe, Welsh Guards, killed in action in Afghanistan in 2009.

The Druids Lodge Polo Club started as an arena club in 2001 and became an outdoor club two years later. The club is located on the site of a former racing stable within sight of Stonehenge. It is run by Giles Ormerod, whose father, Brigadier Denis Ormerod, had played polo in India with the Gurkhas, Bob Skene's regiment in World War II.[1]

Also in 2003, the St. Albans Polo Club was formed in Hertfordshire by Martin Randall and Steve Collins, a former boxing world champion.

Haggis Farm Polo Club was formed in 2004 in Barton, just a couple of miles outside Cambridge.

Apsley End was a small club started in 2005 by Nichola von Bülow. The field was located between Hitchin and Luton.

Chester Racecourse, with grounds within the Rodee Racecourse in Chester, a short distance from the city center of that beautiful city, was established in 2005. Richard Thomas was the prime mover in the endeavor to create another polo facility in the north, along with Hamilton Ashworth, and with the help of Roddy Wood. The club aims to provide inexpensive polo—if such thing exists—but organizes the highest-handicap tournament in the northern parts, the Twelve-Goal International. A second polo ground was built on the Grosvenor Estate in Churton. The mercurial "Bendor," the late Duke of Westminster, must be smiling somewhere, and perhaps the ghosts of the old Eaton team can be heard smacking a willow polo ball on a moonless night on the Cheshire ground.

The Vale of York Polo Club was started in 2005 on Highwood Farm near Doncaster.

Another club in East Yorkshire appeared in 2006, when the White Rose Polo Club developed grounds at Town End Farm in North Cliffe, in the county's East Riding. The club was founded by Hedley Aylott, who had learned polo at Peter Grace's school in Ascot Park. The Summit Cup and the Yorkshire Open Championship are the club's tournaments.

Suffolk Polo Club was formed in 2006 by Alison Schwabe at the Hare Park Stud in Newmarket. It is a members' club that was formed with the purpose of providing instruction and accessible polo for beginners and advanced players.

Asthall Farm Polo Club was started in 2007 by Nigel and Lynda Walker. The club caters to low-goal players and beginners to the game, the Introduction to Polo Days being a great success.

Other clubs include Lacey Green Polo Club, in the edge of the Chilterns in Buckinghamshire, which was formed in 2007; Stapleford Park in Melton Mowbray, a private polo club also formed in 2007; and Frolic Polo Club in Lode, Cambridge, which was formed in 2008. It must be great fun to play and party in that club. The Leadenham Polo Club in Lincolnshire was formed by James Reeve, Mark Holmes and Raoul Dowding in 2008.

Major Christopher Hanbury, sometime chairman of the Hurlingham Polo Association, established the Longdole Polo Club in Birdlip, between Cirencester and Cheltenham. The club was formed in 1992, when Major Hanbury purchased Longdole Farm, and formally affiliated with the Hurlingham Polo Association in 2008. A polo player for more than forty years, Major Hanbury started playing while a student at the Royal Agricultural College. Following a commission into the Queen's Royal Irish Hussars, he kept

Major Christopher Hanbury, patron of the Lovelocks and Longdole teams, was Hurlingham Polo Association's chairman from 2005 to 2008.

on playing until his retirement from the service and started the Lovelocks Polo team, a showcase for his children and grandchildren. The Lovelocks team has enjoyed more than its share of success in medium- and low-handicap polo.

Dedham Vale in the village of Higham, near the Essex/Suffolk border, was formed by Kyron and Julia Skippen. The Barcome Polo Club was started at Brightling and then moved to Banks Farm in Barcome, near Lewes, East Sussex.

Other clubs include the Burningfold Polo Centre in Dunsfold, Surrey; Fifield Polo Club in Windsor; Ladyswood in Malmesbury, formed by Martyn Meade to develop the younger player; and Little Bentley Polo Park, near Colchester, started by Kelvin and Fred Robinson to encourage low-goal polo.

The Ranksboro Polo Club is located in the North family's Rankborough Farm, in Oakham, Leicestershire. The different spellings appear to be quintessentially English.

RLS Polo club in Royal Leamington Spa continues the tradition of polo in Warwickshire. The club was started in 1999 and affiliated with the HPA in 2003. Set in Stoneythorpe Hall's five hundred acres, RLS is a first-class facility with three polo grounds. David Walton Masters, a former RAF polo player, is the current chairman.

Through the years, other organizations affiliated with the Hurlingham Polo Association.

The Schools and Universities Polo Association was incorporated in 2005 as an outgrowth of the Schools Polo Association which had been started in 1991 and included universities after 1994. The guiding light in this endeavor was American-born Charles Betz, who started playing polo at Ham and later at West Wycombe Park, where he was chairman for seven years.[2]

The Combined Services Polo Association encompasses polo in the Royal Air Force Polo Club, the Royal Naval and Royal Marines Equestrian Association, and the Army Polo Association. The latter includes the Rhine Army PA. Based in Tidworth, the main competitions are the Inter-Regimental Tournament; the Captains and Subalterns Tournament, successor to Ranelagh's Subalterns' Gold Cup; the Rundle Cup between Royal Navy and Army teams; and the Duke of York Cup, between sailors and fliers. The Chapple Cup is a three-game competition between the Combined Services Polo Association and a visiting team. It includes the United Services Cup, usually held at Windsor, and the Indian Army Cavalry Officers' Association Trophy played for at Tidworth.

The British Forces Germany Polo Club, formerly known as the Rhine Army Polo Association, is still responsible for running military polo in Germany. The club has grounds at Bad Lipspringer, Hohne and Fallingbosted, and organizes the Inter-Regimental Tournament in Germany, among other competitions.

Clubs in Ireland

The city of Limerick, perhaps the cradle of polo in Ireland, experienced the revival of a polo club in 2000, an endeavor led by John Fitzgerald, who was the club's first chairman. Limerick Polo Club was based in Crecora at the Greenmount Park racetrack. The polo field was in the middle of the track. Matches were played against close neighbor Clonshire Equestrian and Polo Centre in Adare, and also versus a North Cork polo team.

Polo Wicklow, which had started as an arena polo club in 1993, became affiliated to the HPA in 2005, and the Donaghadee Polo Club in county Down was started in 2009.

Although there was an attempt to restart polo in county Wexford and Enniscorthy in

1960, it was not until 2007 that the game took off at the Bunclody Polo Club. It has two grounds on a wonderful location on the banks of the Slaney River. The long-lost Wexford Challenge Cup, last taken by the 20th Hussars team in 1911, was recently found and was revived one hundred years later.

The Waterford Polo Club has been in existence for some thirty years as the home of the polo school run by Major Hugh Dawnay.

2001: The Year of the Plague

The outbreak of foot-and-mouth disease in England disrupted the polo season in a significant way. Shortly after the epidemic started, the Guards Polo Club communicated to the HPA that all polo activities, including the Queen's Cup and the International Day activities, would be canceled. Several teams elected to pull out at the time. However, the announcement by Beaufort and Cowdray Park that polo would carry on despite the fact that both had dairy herds, gave strength to others to go on and make the season a success. In spite of all the adversities, the season went on, albeit with the usual precautions designed to prevent the spread of the disease.

One team dominated the high-goal season. Ali Albwardy's Dubai took three out of four high-goal tournaments. Adolfo Cambiaso, Lolo Castagnola and the obligatory Englishman, in this case Ryan Pemble, took Cowdray Park's Gold Cup, the Warwickshire Cup at Cirencester's Ivy Lodge ground, and the Indian Empire Shield, brought in as a replacement for the canceled Queen's Cup.

FCT won the Prince of Wales Cup at Berkshire with the team of Roger Carlsson, Martín Vidou, Gabriel Donoso and Ignacio Gonzalez.

In the medium-goal level, Los Locos was the team to beat, because they took their own Arthur Lucas Cup, the Bryan Bethell Cup and the Harrison Cup at Cowdray, thus winning the Victor Ludorum. Caballus, with Tom Morley, Henry Brett, Andrew Hine and Bruce Merivale-Austin, were the winners of the County Cup. The Foxcote eighteen-goal at Inglesham was taken by Laird, who in a rather cheeky manner defeated Oakland Park, a team that had tournament's host Roddy Williams in the lineup.

At Ascot Park, the Women's World Championship was taken by Sue Hodgson from New Zealand, Milly Scott, Emma Tomlinson and Claire Tomlinson. Women players were on several other winning teams. At Beaufort Polo Club, the Prince of Wales Trophy was taken by the host team, which included Emma Tomlinson. In the Cheshire twelve-goal Champion Cup, Lucy Taylor played at number 1 for Emlor, winners over Laird. Nina Vestey won the Gerald Balding Cup at Cirencester, and Kate Seabrook took the Kirtlington Tournament with her family team, Lambourne.

At the international level, Nina Vestey was on the Young England teams that won the Junior Westchester Cup at Myopia Hunt Club in Hamilton, Massachusetts, and the John Cowdray Trophy in Sussex. Lucy Taylor, from Cheshire, took a watered-down Patriotic Cup against Ireland.

Cambridge beat Oxford in the inter-varsity match, and the Light Dragoons defeated the Household Division in the Inter-Regimental Tournament.

Therefore, in spite of the havoc created by the epidemic, the typical determination of polo players to enjoy the game no matter what the circumstances are resulted in an almost full and quite successful season.

2002: Golden Jubilee Celebration

This was a happy time in the United Kingdom because the beloved Queen Elizabeth II reached the milestone of half a century in the throne of England. For those that had witnessed the Coronation at Westminster Abbey in 1953 — most of us obviously through extensive newsreels and motion pictures— it was a time of celebration, and also of reflection. For polo aficionados, 1953 had been a marvelous time to be in England. A new, young Queen, the high expectation of a new Elizabethan Age following the darkness of a worldwide conflict — it all combined to offer a moment of hope and glory.

The dramatic final game for the Coronation Cup at Cowdray Park had signaled the resurgence of polo in Britain, for Harper, Balding, Lakin and Guinness had acquitted themselves nobly against world polo power Argentina.

Some fifty years later, foreign players and patrons of the game dotted England's polo landscape.

In the Prince of Wales Trophy, Ali Albwardy's Dubai, completed by Bartolomé "Lolo" Castagnola, Adolfo Cambiaso and Jamie Peel, beat Swede Roger Carlsson's FCT.

A very good year was enjoyed by Emerging, later victimized at the hands of the Black Bears at Cowdray. Emerging was sponsored by Swiss banker Fabien Pictet, who with Hector Guerrero, Milo Fernández Araujo and Luke Tomlinson took the Queen's Cup by defeating a French-sponsored team, Hubert Perrodo's Labegorce.

English pride was somewhat saved when Foxcote took the venerable Warwickshire Cup, with Tamara Vestey and her band of three players from Down Under, Jack Baillieu, Glen Gilmore and Simon Keyte. They defeated FCT 15–9 after trailing by two goals at halftime. It was a good day — and evening for sure — at Andoversford because Foxcote White, the team formed by Nina Vestey, her brother Benjamin, John Paul Clarkin and Miguel Novillo Astrada, took the subsidiary Bathurst Cup. The Hon. Mark Vestey's sponsored Foxcote capped a good year by winning the Victor Ludorum at both the twelve- and eighteen-goal levels.

Les Lions, those gallant Frenchmen again, took the Indian Empire Shield by defeating Foxcote in the final game. The subsidiary tournament was taken by Los Locos, which were prevented from taking home the trophy of one of the oldest tournaments in the world, the Indian Inter-Regimental Tournament. This event was first taken by the 9th Lancers in 1877.

Urs Schwarzenbach's Black Bears, with the help rendered by three Novillo Astrada brothers, Alejandro, Eduardo and Javier, took Cowdray Park's Gold Cup by defeating Emerging 8–7. Favorites Dubai went out in the semifinal round by a single goal, courtesy of Black Bears; Emerging, riding a high crest, did the same with Labegorce.

The Gold Cup was marred by a show of poor sportsmanship by Argentine Bartolomé Castagnola and Prince Albert Esiri from Nigeria, in a preliminary round. Most regrettably, hard words led to a physical confrontation on the field, which the umpires quickly and rightly ended by sending off both players for the rest of the chukker. The incident was referred to the HPA Disciplinary Committee, which levied a £100 fine upon Lolo Castagnola. This apparent lenient treatment had Cowdray Park's hierarchy by the ears, because the club had suspended Prince Esiri for one match.

Nevertheless, Cowdray Park's polo manager Cheryl Bicket insisted that the Gold Cup had been a smooth affair: "There was bound to be the odd incident — we are dealing with polo players, for goodness sake."[3] It seems that it is perfectly sane to indulge in a boxing bout on the polo grounds.

There were some interesting winners at some of the lower-handicap competitions. The Gerald Balding Cup was taken by Cirencester Park's Flying Pigs, with team sponsor Simon England, Antony Fanshawe, Ben Vestey and Mrs. L. Black, who as Miss Lavinia Roberts was one of the pioneer women players in England. She is the daughter of Squadron Leader Alan Roberts, of Maidensgrove team fame.

The Royal Windsor Cup was taken by Nick Clarke's Careyes, with Roddy Williams, Chilean José Donoso and Roderick Vere Nicoll. Other winners included Bruce Merivale-Austin's blue and gold Caballus, winner of the Harrison Cup and the Eduardo Moore Tournament. In due time, Caballus took the Victor Ludorum sixteen-goal award. Belgian patroness Isabelle Hayen's Groeninghe took the aging County Cup.

The record dryly notes that La Ema — T. Verdon, W. Emerson, M. Emerson, and G.A.D. Emerson — took the Eduardo Rojas Lanusse Cup over Bullfrogs, 6–2½.[4] The Emerson polo lineage dates back to at least 1897, without interruption. Henry Emerson was one of the founders of the polo club at Bell Ville in Córdoba Province, Argentina. George and John Emerson followed, playing at La Ema and at the Hurlingham Club in Buenos Aires. At the onset of World War II, three Emerson brothers, Malcolm, Noel and Roderick, volunteered to serve. They had to draw lots because their father George would allow only two of his sons to volunteer. Malcolm survived, but "Derick" Emerson paid the ultimate price while flying with the Pathfinders Group in 1944. Noel, nicknamed "Tiny" because of his great height, remained in Argentina and became one of the best backs in the country.

One of the season's highlights, also in Argentina, was the international event in which the English team played a two-game series against a representative Argentine team. Luke Tomlinson, William Lucas, Henry Brett and Andrew Hine registered a historic win at Palermo, polo's cathedral, in the first game. Henry Brett was team captain in the first victory of an English international team against Argentina since 1908, when a British Army team won a match at the Hurlingham Club, in the outskirts of Buenos Aires.

For this event the Argentine Polo Association rated Luke Tomlinson at five goals, which gave the English team a half goal on handicap. This minimal advantage was the difference in the match because, trailing by half a goal, England was awarded a thirty-yard penalty that was converted by Andrew Hine to give England a 13½–13 victory.

Andrew Hine was unable to play in the second test because of a previous commitment in Dubai; his place was taken by Satnam Dhillon. The game was lost 11–8½, and therefore the series was also lost on aggregate goals. It is regrettable that professional commitments should rank above international selection honors.

2003: Nina Vestey's Milestone

Carina Patricia Vestey, the youngest daughter of the Hon. Mark and Rosie Vestey, entered the polo history records as the first lady player to win the Cowdray Park Gold Cup, emblematic of the British Open Championship. Nina Vestey, now Mrs. John Paul Clarkin, was on the Hildon Sport team which defeated Labegorce in the final match.

The Royal Military Academy at Sandhurst also made history by taking the Inter-Regimental Tournament. The RMA was represented by three officer-cadets, Lorien McCallum, Benjamin Vestey and Harry Wallace; Captain Caspar West ably led his young players from the number 4 position, just as it was done in John Watson's day more than a century before. Traditions die hard among soldiers.

The high-goal season started with a bang when the unheralded Buzzy Bees— Satnam Dhillon, Roddy Williams, Henry Brett and Jamie Morrison — took the Prince of Wales Trophy at Berkshire. This was the first occasion in three decades in which an all–English team had won a major championship. They defeated FCT in extra time after a thrilling recovery, being down seven goals to one at halftime. Unfortunately, the Buzzy Bees team was disbanded after the tournament. It would have been a stern test for the established teams to play against a well-mounted squad in which all four individuals had respectable handicaps.

In the Queen's Cup at Guards Polo Club, Dubai, absent from the Prince of Wales Trophy because of Ali Albwardy's injured hand, defeated Labegorce, once more finalist, by eleven goals to ten. Lolo Castagnola marked the winning tally with about sixty seconds left in regulation time in the final chukker.

By virtue of their win in the Queen's Cup, Dubai was installed as the favorite to take the Gold Cup as well. However, they fell in the semifinals to Hildon Sport by eleven goals to ten, in a game that a reporter described as "roughhouse tactics" employed by the winners.[5] Adolfo Cambiaso was injured during the course of the game but soldiered on.

There was more of the same in the final game. It was a close-marked, physical game, in which Hildon Sport came out on top, six goals to five. Nina Clarkin, Mark and Luke Tomlinson, and John Paul Clarkin spared neither themselves nor their ponies in wreaking havoc on the Labegorce opponents.

Carlos Gracida, the brilliant Mexican star, said, "It was the roughest British Open final I have ever been involved in. I think they played too rough. They hit you so many times. The umpires were very soft and they should have been more strict about the dangerous riding and riding into players outside play."[6]

Nina Vestey was emphatic that the two nine-goal players on the Labegorce squad, Gracida and Alberto Heguy, "know how to work the umpires. I think we managed to prove that when you have a four-man team and you play in a very male-oriented way, you can beat anyone."[7]

The Goodwood Week at Cowdray Park was a benefit for the teams from Gloucestershire. Los Locos took the Harrison Cup and the Cowdray Park Challenge Cup; Foxcote took the Aotea Cup, subsidiary to the Harrison Cup; and the two teams qualifying from Cirencester, Irongate and Wildmoor, met in the finals of the Holden White Cup, the latter being the victors.

The international polo scene was revived just after Christmas in South Africa, when England met the locals at Kurland in the Cape Province. Jamie Le Hardie, Mark Tomlinson, Luke Tomlinson and Alan Kent defeated Selby Williamson, Douglas Lund, Russell Watson and Gillespie Armstrong by fourteen goals to nine. The English team was mounted on borrowed ponies that were just as good as the ones provided for the local team.

2004: Azzurra's Year of Glory

The first high-goal tournament of the season, the Prince of Wales Trophy at Berkshire, was taken by Azzurra, with Stefano Marsaglia, Marcos Heguy, Juan Martín Nero and Gonzalo Bourdieu. They won over Rick Stowe's Geebungs, a team that lost Miguel Novillo Astrada to injury within three minutes of the ball being thrown into play. Miguel was effectively replaced by older brother Eduardo.

After being finalists for the Queen's Cup in the previous two years, the third time around proved lucky for Labegorce, for they beat Azzurra 7–6 at Smith's Lawn. Hubert Perrodo, Fred Mannix, Jr., Carlos Gracida and Luke Tomlinson played for the red and white French team. The event was marred by Fabien Pictet who, upset at the draw and perceiving injustice in his bracket, did not show up for the initial game with his Emerging team. The Hurlingham Polo Association quite rightly took a jaundiced view of such attitude, and a twenty-eight-day suspension plus a £20,000 fine was imposed upon the guilty party.

The Warwickshire Cup was taken by the Black Bears, with two of the five Novillo Astrada brothers, Eduardo and Javier. Swiss patron Urs Schwarzenbach and Sebastian Dawnay completed the squad. They defeated Foxcote Red in the final match.

The big prize, Cowdray Park's Gold Cup, was won by Stefano Marsaglia's Azzurra, with Marcos Heguy, Alejandro Novillo Astrada and Juan Martín Nero. The other finalist, Dubai, had an off day, losing by the wide margin of seventeen goals to nine, after receiving one goal on handicap.

A most important event was the British Polo Championship played on the immaculate Coworth Park grounds. Two all-professional teams each with an aggregate handicap of twenty-seven goals did battle in a wonderful final match that went into extra time. The Blue Team, sponsored by Williamson Tea, met the Red Audi Team. The White Team, bankrolled by the Gaucho Grill, and the Green Team, sponsored by Solanum, were the losing squads in the semifinals. The Blue Team had Jamie Le Hardy, Glen Gilmore, Henry Brett and Malcolm Borwick. The Red Team aligned with José "Pepe" Araya, Roddy Williams, Jack Baillieu and Nacho Gonzalez. Malcolm Borwick scored in extra time to give the Blues a 7–6 win.

The England versus South Africa international match was again held at Kurland, and again England emerged victorious. Mark Tomlinson, Henry Brett, Luke Tomlinson and Malcolm Borwick, a 27-goal side, defeated "Buster" Mackenzie, Doug Lund, Stuart "Sugar" Erskine and Selby Williamson, 14–13, with a last goal scored by team captain Henry Brett.

2005: A Year for Dubai

A return test match versus South Africa was held at Cowdray Park in September. This time around, James Beim, Malcolm Borwick, Henry Brett and Nacho Gonzalez defended the Rose of England. Selby Williamson, Sugar Erskine, Russell Watson and Gillespie Armstrong represented South Africa. England led throughout the entire game, winning by fourteen goals to six.

In the national high-goal scene, Azzurra, the holders, successfully defended their title in the Prince of Wales Trophy. Jean Gonzalez, Juan Martín Nero, Bautista Heguy and Stefano Marsaglia convincingly defeated Emerging 9–4 in the final game, played on a soggy, badly cut up field. Emerging's Swiss patron Fabien Pictet displayed another bout of unsportsmanlike conduct and eventually was sent off for repeatedly arguing with the referee.[8]

Another team hung on to a trophy, in this case Black Bears hugging the Warwickshire Cup at Cirencester Park. Urs Schwarzenbach, Eduardo and Javier Novillo Astrada, and Nicolás Antinori were on the winning team. They defeated Emlor, a new face in the high-goal circuit, sponsored by Spencer McCarthy and named after his daughters, Emma and Laura. Nacho Gonzalez, Gabriel and José Donoso completed this promising team. After four dull chukkers characterized by close marking and endless tapping, Emlor opened up the game in an effort to close a five-goal gap. Success evaded Emlor; however, they were cheered to an 8–7 final score.

The Queen's Cup was taken by Dubai, led by Adolfo Cambiaso and completed by Ali Albwardy, Alejandro "Piki" Díaz Alberdi and Ryan Pemble, who more than played his four-handicap rating. Just one more example of how young players elevate their level of play when mounted on superior horses. The problem for those players occurs when their handicaps are raised; then they have to leave the team and are left to their own pony resources. In this event, Dubai beat Black Bears, a well-mounted team, with a convincing 12–7 win. An interesting entry was Maidsford, formed by British players Jonny Good, Oliver Hipwood, Malcolm Borwick and Roddy Williams. Partially sponsored by that great supporter of the game Douglas Brown, the squad also received financial help from the HPA, and the entry fee was waived by the Guards Polo Club. Maidsford did well to reach the semifinals, pushing the Black Bears hard to the very end, only to lose 9–7 after a gallant effort.

The British Open Championship for the Cowdray Park Gold Cup was marred by injuries and the curse of tapping the ball. In the semifinal match against Emerging, Adolfo Cambiaso took a fall and broke a bone in his forearm. Adolfito was replaced by eight-goaler Lucas Monteverde; Ryan Pemble (handicap four) was taken off to be substituted by Agustín Nero (handicap six), Juan Martín's older brother. With this new and untried lineup, Dubai had to work hard to defeat Emerging by a single goal.

Dubai met Black Bears in the finals, where Eduardo Novillo Astrada took two nasty hits, one on each leg. The championship game followed the pattern of play displayed earlier in the competition, particularly in the semifinals. Close marking, blocking, tapping the ball, continuously changing the line of the ball, they all combined to make the game boring for the spectators and a nightmare for the umpires. Nevertheless, with the game tied at nine-all in the last chukker, the ability of Agustín Nero and Lucas Monteverde in taking the Novillo Astrada brothers out of Díaz Alberdi's way allowed Dubai to build a two-goal cushion. A late penalty conversion by Black Bears made the final score 11–10 in favor of Dubai.

The all-professional British Polo Championship held its second edition at Coworth Park. Once more, four teams entered. Audi England had Roddy Williams (six-goal handicap), James Beim (six), Ignacio Gonzalez (six) and James Harper (six). The British Lions presented Satnam Dhillon (six), Jamie Le Hardy (six), Will Lucas (six) and Chris Hyde (six). Australasia had Rob Archibald (six), Simon Keyte (seven), Glen Gilmore (seven) and Sam Hopkinson (four). The fourth team, Nigeria, listed Sayyu Dantata (four), Babangida Hassan (four), Jaime García Huidobro alternating with Pepe Araya (eight), and Dawule Daba (four).

Audi England defeated Australasia in the semifinals on Friday evening, with the match going into extra time. In Sunday's final game they faced another all–English squad, the British Lions, on a heavy ground due to rain the previous evening. The turf cut up and a profusion of divots made striking the moving ball quite tricky. Audi England beat the British Lions by eight goals to five. The innovative tournament's organizers, Nigel à Brassard and Derrick Chow, pronounced themselves satisfied with the attendance, some 4,000 spectators, which also benefited from a huge screen showing replays.

The Cowdray Park Challenge Cup was taken by Lambourne, with Kate Seabrook, Francisco "Pancho" Marín Moreno, Tommy Wilson and Robert Thame. They defeated Macereto by ten goals to seven. Also at Cowdray, Farrow and Ball beat Oberhouse 8–7 to win the Holden White Trophy. Martin Ephson, Leroux Hendrix, Ignatius du Plessis and Adrian Wade were on the winning team.

The National Eight-Goal Championship for the Junior County Club at Cheshire Polo

Club was won by Flame Estates. They beat Spinney by the odd goal in eleven. Hamilton Ashworth, Oliver Tuthill, Josh Tuthill and Julian Appleby were the new champions.

On the distaff side, Audi Ladies took the British Ladies Championship, played at Cowdray Park Polo Club. Held as a curtain-raiser for the international test match versus South Africa, the team of Teresa Beresford, Clare Milford Haven, Nina Vestey and Sofia Hamilton defeated Clarita by 7 to 4½ goals. Clare Mathias, Stephanie Haverhals, Marianela Castagnola and Rosa Ross played on the losing finalist.

On a positive note, toward the end of the year the Centaurs, with Jack Baillieu, Mark Tomlinson, Jaime García Huidobro and Mark Tomlinson, a twenty-eight-goal team, qualified for the Hurlingham Club Open and the Argentine Open Championships. At Hurlingham, the Centaurs were beaten by Indios-Chapaleufú II, a Heguy team, and by La Aguada, the Novillo Astradas' squad. Then the Centaurs defeated El Paraíso to record their only win. It was an auspicious start for the lowest-handicapped team in both competitions.

The year ended on a sour note when the international match against South Africa was finished with three players on each side. This traditional test match played between Christmas and the New Year was by all accounts a rough one.

James Beim, Mark Tomlinson, Malcolm Borwick and Nacho Gonzalez played for England, while Gareth Evans, Sugar Erskine, Buster Mackenzie and Doug Lund represented the Springboks. England had a comfortable lead of eight goals to three at halftime. The scoreboard read England eleven, South Africa seven, at the beginning of the last chukker. A violent foul by Doug Lund on James Beim left both players hors de combat. England's coach John Horswell took the option of asking that Buster Mackenzie step down. Matt Pohl, a lower-handicapped player than Lund, entered the field. The game ended with a clear-cut victory for England, by thirteen goals to nine. The loser was the game of polo.

First, it is difficult to understand why one or two substitutes did not travel with the English team, because the option of having a South African player substituting in an international test match was not viable; it just makes a mockery of a contest labeled "international test." Second, it appears that the umpires lost control of the game. The increasing roughness in the course of the contest was quite evident, and the award of a penalty from the spot after a foul that left two players disabled raises concerns about the mind frame of the umpires.

John Horswell was adamant in defending his decision:

> I would not have been doing my job correctly if I had not done what I did. My players are all professionals with careers to think about. I am just their servant. As we had lost James Beim and had no official substitute, I feel that I had no alternative. I regard what I did as being akin to taking out an insurance policy on the result of a game that we deserved to win handsomely — which in the end we did. International polo is a showcase for my players to market their talents in. It was as much a business decision as a sporting one and given a similar set of circumstances in a business scenario, I am sure that none of our major critics would hesitate for a split second to do as we did.[9]

Nevertheless, the feeling lingers on that the situation, both before and during the course of the test match, could have been handled differently. *Polo Times* quoted an unidentified spokesman: "It was unfortunate that the test ended on a sour note. England had been on top for most of the game and one is sure that the decision made may not have been the best one when taking the spirit of the game into consideration."[10]

2006: The Year of the Tap, Tap, Tap

The international scene started in February with a test match at the Kay family's Kihik-ihi Polo Club in Te Awamutu, New Zealand. James Beim, the Tomlinson brothers and Chris Hyde represented England; New Zealand presented Simon Keyte, Tommy Wilson, John Paul Clarkin and Cody Forsyth. The test was played on handicap, New Zealand giving three goals at the start. England dominated play through the first four chukkers, with Luke and Mark Tomlinson showing to advantage their recent experience in the Argentine Open. The score at the beginning of the fifth chukker was eleven goals to five, in England's favor. New Zealand closed the gap to tie the game at thirteen-all in the last chukker, only for Chris Hyde to steal the ball from a New Zealand possession and neatly place it through the goal-posts.

On the following day another English team defeated a foursome named Southern Australia at Werribee Park near Melbourne, Victoria. Matthew Grimes, Kelvin Johnson, Gillon McLachan and Glen Gilmore wore Australia's yellow jerseys, although it was not a representative team. England had Sam Gairdner, Roddy Williams, Andrew Hine and James Harper. Reflecting the increased commercialization of polo, no less than four sponsors' labels appeared on the English team's chests, plus the red rose of England and the national flag. The Australians received two goals by handicap, which were quickly erased in the first chukker, England eventually winning the match 10–8.

A sort of return game was played at Kirtlington Polo Club in July. Peter Webb, Oliver Hipwood, Roddy Williams and Jamie Le Hardy played for England, while Michael Henderson, Jock Mackay, Rob Archibald and Tommy Wilson played for Australasia. Quite fittingly, the game ended with a five-all tie.

South Africa versus England at Cowdray resulted in another victory for England, whose international sides had a banner year. James Beim, Tom Morley, Malcolm Borwick and Nacho Gonzalez defeated the Springboks by eleven goals to nine. Selby Williamson, Ignatius du Plessis, Gareth Evans and Buster Mackenzie fought hard, but their penalty taking was below international standard, and that was the difference.

Up in the northern reaches at the Dundee and Perth Polo Club, the hosts— Peter FitzGerald, Mark Coppez, Alasdair Archibald and Nick Walter — defeated South Africa by six goals to five, with a forty-yard penalty made good by Alasdair Archibald. The South African team was formed by Nicola FitzGerald Coppez, Johan du Plooy, Chris Edwards and Warren Lurie.

The Queen's Cup was retained by the holders, Dubai, in a lackluster game characterized by the never-ending tapping, turning and more tapping. Dubai — Tariq Albwardi, Alejandro Díaz Alberdi, Adolfo Cambiaso and George Meyrick — received a one-goal handicap from the Broncos, which was all important as the final score was 12–11, Dubai on top. George Milford Haven, Facundo Pieres, Gonzalito Pieres and Gareth Evans played for the Broncos.

The tapping epidemic remained alive and well in the Gold Cup, especially in the final game. The Pieres brothers, now sporting Ellerston's black and white shirts, played along with their cousin Jacinto Crotto and patron Jamie Packer. They faced Black Bears, with Guy Schwarzenbach, Eduardo and Javier Novillo Astrada and Lucas James. In front of an impassive crowd, Ellerston was ahead 8–6 in the last chukker, only for the Black Bear to arouse and score three unanswered goals.

If the final game was a bore, there was plenty of action in the quarter and semifinals.

The perennial favorite Dubai, winner of the Prince of Wales Trophy and the Queen's Cup—although with different lineups—beat Warwickshire Cup's winner Oakland Park with ease, only to fall against Ellerston in extra time in the semifinal game. Black Bears defeated Atlantic in the other semifinal, with the winning goal coming alongside the final whistle.

The Royal Windsor Cup was taken by Lovelocks, with Ed Hitchman, Manuel Fernández Llorente, Will Lucas and Charlie Hanbury; they defeated Bateleur by seven goals to five. Lovelocks, with James Beim in Ed Hitchman's place, took the Duke of Beaufort Cup and the Cowdray Park Challenge Cup as well, capping a most successful season by winning the eighteen-goal Victor Ludorum and being runner-up in the fifteen-goal Victor Ludorum.

The old Assam Cup was played at Rutland Polo Club, where the local team Los Gordos, Tom Collie, William Seth Smith, Puff Whiteley and Marcus Collie, defeated Beverley 6–5½. Beverley had two Argentine players on their roster of Ben and Andrew Foreman, Facundo Guevara and Sebastián Funes.

Beaufort Polo Club was the host site for the Women's Polo International, where England—Milly Scott, Tamara Vestey, Nina Vestey and Victoria Grace—beat the Rest of the World by nine goals to four. Marianela Castagnola (Argentina), Lesley-Ann Masterton Fong-Yee (Jamaica), Sunny Hale (United States) and Sherri-Lyn Hensman (Zimbabwe) played for the Rest of the World.

The polo year ended with two international matches. At Campo de Marte in Mexico City, Johnny Good, Henry Brett, Malcolm Borwick and Peter Webb battled to a nine-all draw with Mexico's Billi Steta, Valerio Aguilar, Carlos Gracida and Roberto González Gracida. Down 6–4 at halftime, Peter Webb moved to number 1 and the rest of the players moved back one position. This tactical move worked out quite well, the match ending in a draw.

The usual end-of-year test versus South Africa ended the host's string of defeats at the hands of the Britons. Selby Williamson, Buster Mackenzie, Ignatius du Plessis and Gareth Evans faced Nina Vestey, the first woman to play for England; Roddy Williams; Malcolm Borwick; and Nacho Gonzalez. While Nina was the talk of the town, seventeen-year-old Nachi du Plessis showed all the attributes that may take him to the top of South African polo. The Springboks led throughout the game that ended South Africa's drought in the series with a 10–7 win.

2007: Polo or Pantomime?

Beaufort Polo Club was the venue for the test match between England and New Zealand. England (James Beim, Henry Brett, Luke Tomlinson and Malcolm Borwick), a 26-goal team that received a 1½ goal start from New Zealand (Craig Williams, Simon Keyte, John Paul Clarkin and Tommy Wilson), which proved to be the difference because both teams scored six times. In the third chukker Simon Keyte had to depart due to an injured finger sustained during a bout with the teeth of teammate Craig Williams' horse. The cause of the encounter was not disclosed. Nevertheless, it was a good, open game, with plenty of passing and runs the length of the field, mostly through the center lane following the long-held view of Hanut Singh and his disciple, Australian Sinclair Hill: the shortest way to the goal is through the middle.

The high-goal season suffered a partial casualty when the Prince of Wales Trophy lost its standing as a tournament in its own right. The HPA decided to incorporate the Prince of Wales Trophy into the Queen's Cup, the first eight teams to qualify for the knockout phase of the Queen's Cup and the second eight teams in competition for the Prince of Wales Trophy.

This year the Queen's Cup had twenty-two entries; Ellerston and Loro Piana met in a wonderful final game free of the stop-and-go tactics so prevalent at the time. Loro Piana earned their way to the finals with a win over Apes Hill, an all–British team sponsored by Sir Charles Williams from Barbados, followed by an impressive victory over the holders, Dubai. Ellerston, with the brothers Gonzalito and Facundo Pieres, the promising Richard Le Poer and John Williams, took the game into extra time with a crucial goal with fifteen seconds left on the clock. A foul called against Ellerston on their own doorstep clinched the game 12–11, and the Queen's Cup for Loro Piana.

David Stirling, Alfio Marchini, Juan Martín Nero and Martín Espain played for Loro Piana. Team patron Marchini, an Italian national, was listed at one-goal handicap in England, although he was rated at four goals in Argentina. In essence, Loro Piana was benefited with a three-goal handicap in every game they played. The HPA yearbook dryly reported, "Loro Piana was considered to have half lengthened the handicappers."[11]

On to the Prince of Wales Trophy reserved for the second-best eight teams in the preliminary rounds of the Queen's Cup. Cadenza — Tony Pidgley, Tomás Fernández Llorente, John Paul Clarkin and Nicolás Espain — won the tournament by defeating the Broncos by eleven goals to ten. Santiago Laborde, Pablo MacDonough, Matías MacDonough and Clare Milford Haven played for the Broncos.

"Polo or Pantomime" was the title of *Polo Times'* lead story covering the final match of the English Open Championship for the Cowdray Gold Cup.[12] The chaos began even before the competition started when the Handicap Committee meagerly raised Alfio Marchini's handicap by one goal, thus making Loro Piana's aggregate twenty-three points. The team was allowed to compete; however, Loro Piana had to give Lechuza Caracas one goal on handicap, which proved to be the difference between outright defeat and a possible win in extra time.

The match lasted for almost three hours due to delays caused by injuries, extended discussions regarding who could substitute and who could not, and a frantic search for suitable replacements. It is hard to understand why on such important matches teams are not required to have appropriate substitutes ready and able to enter the game. If the game of polo aspires to be considered a serious sporting endeavor by sponsors and television viewers, it must offer a professional spectacle, well organized and prepared for the unexpected troublesome situation.

The game itself was marred by roughness, which led to constant use of the whistle by the umpires. Gareth Davies wrote, "It might have been more appropriate to have staged this match on an amphitheatre, as the players were more like gladiators on the day than horsemen. It was a match of blood and gore — not least for Pite Merlos, who had to have stitches to his nose. It was full of sound and fury, ultimately signifying nothing."[13]

David Stirling went out with an injured wrist after his pony went down. Stirling was replaced by Pablo Jauretche, who scored the first field goal for Loro Piana. This momentous event occurred in the fourth chukker! Then a nasty crash, well away from the ball in play, between Pite Merlos and Jauretche resulted in a long delay while Merlos was receiving medical treatment in the ambulance. Pite was unable to continue and a search was started for a substitute, with the announcer asking the crowd if there was a nine-goaler among them. Finally, Agustín "Tincho" Merlos was located after a long delay, and the game seemed to be ready to restart. Not so.

Unfortunately, the officials had applied a double standard regarding substitutions. When David Stirling was unable to continue play, Loro Piana's selected a substitute who was not allowed to play because he had been a member of another team in the Gold Cup. A lower-handicapped substitute then took Stirling's place on the team. However, when it was Pite Merlos' turn to leave the stage, two qualified substitutes were available but declined the invitation to play. The Tournament Committee changed its tune and allowed Agustín Merlos, who also had played in a defeated team, to take brother Pite's slot.

Quite rightly, the Loro Piana camp felt aggrieved and refused to continue play. Further delay occurred while the committee tried to persuade the Loro Piana players to return to the field. With the prospect of an unfinished final for the British Open Championship looming large, the Committee's diplomatic efforts prevailed, the Loro Piana players relented, and the game went on.[14]

Juan Martín Nero, who displayed an outstanding performance for Loro Piana, missed two penalty shots in the fifth chukker that could have turned the final result in favor of Lechuza all around. It was not to be.

And so on to the trophy presentation for Víctor Vargas, the three Merlos brothers and Henry Fisher, who was ecstatic with his first Gold Cup trophy.

It is of great interest how perceptions and opinions differ regarding the same event. During a long conversation with "Tincho" Merlos, his recollection of the match was that except for the fact that two falls resulted in injuries that prevented the players from remaining on the field of play, there was nothing unusual about the course of the game. Merlos felt that it was the Gold Cup's final game and everyone tried their best.[15] Who was correct in assessing the game, the witness or the protagonist?

The twice rain-delayed Warwickshire Cup was finally decided in a match for Cowdray Park's Gold Cup—played at Cirencester's Ivy Lodge ground—between Elysian Fields and Cadenza. Australian patron Michael King, with James Beim, José Donoso and Marcos Di Paola took the trophy with a 9–8 win over Cadenza's Tony Pidgley, Tomás Fernández Llorente, John Paul Clarkin and Nicolás Espain. In his first foray in England's high-goal competition, Michael King achieved an outstanding result.

Longdole had a very good season, taking Cirencester Park's eighteen-goal tournament and the Challenge Cup; they were finalists against Los Locos in the undecided Duke of Beaufort's Cup. Longdole took the Victor Ludorum at the eighteen-goal level.

The Longdole Polo Club hosted the annual Dalwhinnie match, in which Halcyon Gallery—Ollie Cudmore, Matt Cudmore, Will Lucas and Dave Miller—defeated Lovelocks, with Charlie Hanbury, George Hanbury, Lolo Castagnola and HRH Prince William. Defeating a royal personage in a charity game was rather cheeky, one should think. It would have never happened in another time.

Prince William also played at Ham Polo Club alongside Adolfo Cambiaso. Thus British Royalty and polo royalty combined forces for worthy charities.

At the Royal Leamington Spa Polo Club in Warwickshire, the Ladies and Gentlemen Challenge finals presented an interesting outcome. Louisa Clothier, Brenda Vandamme, Katie MacDonald and Luis Bermengui convincingly defeated Brenda's husband Mark's team. This is just another example of women being able to compete on even terms in a male-dominated endeavor. Before immigrating to England, John and Audrey Harper, Brenda's parents, were active members of the Fairfield County Hunt Club in America, which had a busy polo season.

The Ladies International at Beaufort pitted the English Ladies— Lucy Taylor, Emma Tomlinson, Nina Clarkin and Tamara Vestey — versus the Ladies of the Rest of the World. South African Sarah van Wyk, Sherri-Lyn Hensman from Zimbabwe and Leslie Ann Fong-Yee from Jamaica were joined by the HPA's own Milly Hodges, who claimed eligibility on account of her having once lived in Zimbabwe. In the event, the English Ladies ran away with a crushing 9–3 victory.

2008: The Resurrection of the Open Game

The first international test match of the year was held in New Zealand at the Kihikihi Polo Club. James Beim, Mark Tomlinson, Malcolm Borwick and Tom Morley played for England, while the All Blacks were Tommy Wilson, Craig Wilson, John Paul Clarkin and Simon Keyte. The match was played on the flat; bring your best and let's play.[16]

England led 6–3 at halftime, which prompted New Zealand's coach Cody Forsyth to enact wholesale changes in the lineup. This worked out quite well for the hosts as they won the test by eleven goals to eight.

The return test match at Beaufort Polo Club was played on a rainy day in June. Luke Tomlinson replaced Tom Morley on the English squad; New Zealand had the brothers Wilson, J.P. Clarkin and Sam Hopkinson. The appointment of Andrew Hine as manager and Javier Novillo Astrada as coach seemed to be of great benefit to the English side. They took off with a quick goal by Beim and were leading 5–3 at the break of a five-chukker game. The final score was England six, New Zealand four.

While the English polo community was licking the wounds inflicted in Mexico at the FIP World Cup, the high-goal season at home was ushered in by the Queen's Cup. The tournament was an unqualified success, not only for Ellerston and its sixth Queen's Cup title, but also for the implementation of the one-tap-only rule, which flattered to deceive. Ellerston's lineup was Max Routledge, Gonzalito Pieres, his cousin Pablo MacDonough temporarily replacing injured Facundo Pieres, and Jamie Packer. Sumaya listed patron Ahmad Aboughazale and three Argentine professionals, Alberto "Pepe" Heguy, Milo Fernández Araujo and Hilario Ulloa.

Sumaya jumped out in front to a 5–2 lead at the end of the second chukker. As time went by, Ellerston's superior horsepower began to incline the balance inexorably toward the black and white shirts. Ellerston ended up the winners by a 10–9 score.

In the Prince of Wales Trophy, George Milford Haven's Broncos defeated Zacara 8–7 in a close encounter. Pablo MacDonough's play was the difference, convincingly justifying his new ten-goal rating in Argentina. Santiago Chavanne and John Fisher completed the team. Zacara — Lyndon Lea, Eduardo and Javier Novillo Astrada, and Juan Harriet — put up a good fight, as the final score showed.

The Warwickshire Cup attracted eight teams, with two entries from the Gottschalk family. Les Lions II, son Max's team, made it to the finals, where they met Lovelocks, led by another "son," in this case Charlie Hanbury. Major Christopher Hanbury also had two entries, Lovelocks and Longdole.

Les Lions II led almost from the start, after a quick goal off Charlie Hanbury's stick following the throw-in. Jaime García Huidobro, Lovelocks' lynchpin, was concussed after two falls, one while warming up and a second one during the game. Jaime was replaced by Marcos Di Paola. Les Lions were leading 8–3 at the conclusion of the fourth chukker; however Lovelocks made an astonishing recovery, holding their opponents scoreless for the last two chukkers while scoring four goals on their own. Unfortunately for Lovelocks it was a case of a little too late, for the scoreboard read 8–7 at the end of a marvelous match.

In the Cowdray Park Gold Cup, Loro Piana, the previous year's finalist, made good this time, defeating Ellerston by a single goal. With Jamie Packer in Australia awaiting the birth of his child, his slot on the team was taken by Tom Barrack. Facundo Pieres was back on the team, joining older brother Gonzalito and Max Routledge.

Loro Piana had David Stirling, Alfio Marchini, Juan Martín Nero and Jamie Peel. Ellerston once more had a slow start, for they were trailing 8–4 at the break. Ellerston then changed its open style of play and followed Loro Piana's tight-marking scheme, crawling to an 11–9 deficit in the last chukker. Loro Piana fouled, and Facundo Pieres converted the forty-yard penalty. With seconds to go and Loro Piana hanging by their nails Facundo took a shot at goal and the ball skewed just wide of the goalpost.

The HPA Handicap Committee remained in a deep slumber regarding Alfio Marchini's two-goal handicap. Still rated at four goals in Argentina, that two-goal differential was the margin of victory for Loro Piana. *Polo Times* succinctly described his performance as "extremely competitive off his handicap."[17]

In the world of medium-goal polo, Zacara took the Royal Windsor Cup by besting Geebung by ten goals to seven. It was the second win for team patron Lyndon Lea in this tournament, for he had taken the trophy with his own Typhoo in 2004.

The Cowdray Park Challenge Cup was taken by the Black Bears, Guy Schwarzenbach, Max Routledge, John Paul Clarkin and Simon Keyte. In the other Goodwood Week tournaments, Emlor won the Harrison Cup with Spencer McCarthy, Joaquín Pittaluga, Nacho Gonzalez and Eden Ormerod. The Holden White Cup went to the well-established team of Lucy Taylor, Emma Tomlinson, Nina Clarkin and Tamara Vestey.

In the County Cup finals at Cirencester, that day belonged, once more, to Los Locos. Claire Tomlinson added another record to her illustrious polo career, because she had taken the County Cup in 1981, while in the family way with Mark, now the number 3 in the winning team. Daughter Emma Tomlinson and Sam Hopkinson completed the Los Locos team. They defeated Ed Magor's Corramore by eleven goals to ten.

The Junior County Cup finals were held at Cheshire Polo Club. Henbury — Simon Taylor, Cristián Chavez, Antony Fanshawe and Matthew Hitchman — defeated Chester Racecourse.

At Rutland, Rathbones— Marcus Collie, Ollie Cudmore, Matías Amaya and Rupert Hegg — defeated Ranksboro in the Assam Cup, which dates back to 1897. The Findlay Trophy, in memory of polo player Sir Roland Findlay, Royal Scots Greys, and the club's first president, was taken by the Felix team, after a close contest with Kingsbridge.

The Wirral Ladies Cup, a trophy dating back more than one hundred years, was played for at Cheshire Polo Club. Newcomers Chester Racecourse — Daniel Loe, Josh Tuthill, Hamilton Ashcroft and Richard Thomas— took the trophy from Simon Taylor's Henbury in the finals.

At Edgeworth Polo Club, the Field Barn Cup was taken by Hotel La Tour, with Victoria Griffiths, Matilda Woodd, Kit Brooks and Robert Freeman-Ker. They defeated Michael Henderson's Minotaurs by 8 goals to 5½ goals.

In the Inter-regimental Tournament, England's oldest polo competition, the holders,

Royal Wessex Yeomanry, retained the title when they defeated the King's Royal Hussars by 6 goals to 4½ goals. Captain Piers Heelis, Lt. Leon Allen, Captain Timothy Verdon and Captain Robert Gourley played for the Yeomanry. Captains Heelis and Verdon were on the winning 2007 team. This was the third win for Timothy Verdon, because he also was a member of the Wessex victorious squad in 1992.

2009: The Westchester Cup Year

The main event of the polo year 2009 was the renewal of the Westchester Cup as the result of a challenge issued to the Hurlingham Polo Association by the U.S. Polo Association. The initial impetus was originated at the 2008 annual meeting of the National Museum and Hall of Fame Board of Directors, chaired by Stephen Orthwein, when one of the directors pointed out that the following year would be the centenary of the historic win by the American "Big Four" team at the Hurlingham Club in Fulham. A small committee of sportsmen was formed, and David Woodd at the HPA was contacted regarding the possibility of a renewal of the international series. The enthusiastic and encouraging support given by the chairman of the Hurlingham Polo Association, Nicholas Colquhoun-Denvers; Colonel Woodd, the chief executive; and John Tinsley, chairman of the HPA's International Committee, allowed the planning to go forward. The event was planned and organized by the Museum of Polo on behalf of the USPA, whose chairman Thomas Biddle, Sr., issued the challenge as stipulated in the deed of gift.

The venue was the International Polo Club at Palm Beach, the site for the U.S. Open Championship and the main location for winter polo in America.

England's selectors nominated James Beim, Mark Tomlinson, Eduardo Novillo Astrada and Luke Tomlinson, with American-based Julian Daniels and Stuart Erskine as reserves. The original American team went through some vicissitudes prior to the match. Julio Arellano had his thumb broken during an international team practice game at Hobe Sound. Just two days before the Westchester Cup, Michael Azzaro had a spill during the Iglehart Cup, and his collarbone was fractured.

With two starters out of the team, America presented Jeffrey Blake, team captain Adam Snow, Nicolás Roldán and Jeffrey Hall, in that order. England received a one-goal handicap, which turned out to be the difference in a very good game, admirably umpired by Car-

John Tinsley, from the Rutland Polo Club, guided the destiny of the Hurlingham Polo Association from 2001 until 2004. Mr. Tinsley continues to serve the game as chairman of the International Committee (Museum of Polo).

los Gracida and Roberto González Gracida, both selected by accord between the two team captains. The game was played by the USPA rules, as specified in the deed of gift that the contest for the Westchester Cup must be played by the rules of the host country. Also by arrangement by the teams' captains, there was to be a stoppage of play around the middle of each chukker to allow players to change mounts. This was done in order to save mounts, most of which had been loaned, while others had been hired by the British team.

Several observers could not fail to notice the different approach to the game by each squad. The American organization appeared to be somewhat lackadaisical, with a bit of an attitude that "Everything will be OK." No one seemed to be in charge. By contrast, the visitors had appointed a manager, Andrew Hine; a chef d'equipe, Andrew Tucker; a coach, Javier Novillo Astrada; and Julian Hipwood overseeing the all-important horse management. The top echelon took the

Mark Tomlinson, the younger of the two brothers, earned his slot on the English international team.

challenge quite seriously, and one of the players remarked to the author the lifting effect caused by the words pronounced before the game by HPA's chairman Nicholas Colquhoun-Denvers, stressing upon the players the honor of representing their country, and the responsibilities carried alongside. This different approach could be felt in the air along the pony lines, just before the start of the contest.

England came out flying, and the score at the break was 6–4 in favor of the visiting team. American coach Owen Rinehart then made some changes: Jeff Hall went to number 1, Snow to number 2 and Jeff Blake moved to back. These changes permitted the American team to tie the score at seven-all in the fourth chukker. The fifth chukker provided an open game with both teams scoring two goals. The sixth chukker was also a fine exhibition of open polo, with both teams trying to score the magic goal. Just three minutes from the bell, England scored the winning tally for a final score of ten goals to nine.

The 2009 Westchester Cup test match was the first one in America since the 1939 contest at Meadow Brook on Long Island, just before the onset of World War II in Europe. It was a momentous occasion. As Stephen Orthwein, chairman of the Museum of Polo stated in the official program, "Regardless of which team wins, this renewal of the Westchester Cup will have delivered to our historic sport a great victory. This is the most significant polo competition to take place in the United States in over a quarter of a century."[18]

At home, two French-sponsored teams battled for the Prince of Wales Trophy, Enigma and Talandracas. Jerome Wirth's Enigma was in dominance, however not by much, along most of the contest, leading 9–7 into the third chukker. Talandracas then elevated its play and took the lead into the last thirty seconds, when James Beim's goal sent the match into extra time. With a little bit of luck, Talandracas edged out Enigma for a 12–11 victory. Edouard Carmignac, Guillermo Terrera, Alejandro Agote and Lucas Monteverde completed the Talandracas squad.

Number 1, that most difficult place to achieve distinction on an international team, has been ably filled by James Beim for England.

As is customary, the Queen's Cup provided good value, with Apes Hill, sponsored by "Cow" Williams from Barbados, facing Sumaya, last year's finalist, in the championship match. Sir Charles Williams abandoned his policy of all-Britain players on the team, and a young six-goal Argentine, Juan Gris Zavaleta, took a place on the Apes Hill squad. Charlie Hanbury and the Tomlinson brothers made up the rest of the team.

Sumaya had Ahmad Aboughazale, Hilario Ulloa, Milo Fernández Araujo and Ignatius du Plessis. Both teams worked hard to get to the finals, because Apes Hill defeated Lechuza Caracas and Sumaya eliminated Dubai, which had Adolfito Cambiaso, albeit an injured one. For a change, the spectators were treated to four-man polo. With Apes Hill up by one goal at the break, Sumaya came out strong and took the lead, and it was very close until near the end, when Charlie Hanbury scored the winner. The Gloucestershire contingent went wild in celebrating a 12–11 win.

The Cowdray Park Gold Cup preliminary rounds left Sumaya to take on La Bamba de Areco, named after patron Jean-François Decaux's estancia in Argentina. Sumaya was on top, 7–4 after three chukkers, 10–8 in the fifth when a crucial play near the Bamba's goal ended up with an injured Milo Fernández Araujo, and his pony with a broken leg. Milo tried to keep on playing but was unable to do so and was replaced by Lucas James. Badly missing their field captain, Sumaya lost the game by one goal. In the other semifinal, Dubai defeated Les Lions II.

The championship game had a sluggish start, with all five goals scored via the penalty route. A field goal by Dubai's Magoo Laprida seemed to galvanize both teams, which suddenly and without warning went into a fast open game. Trailing 5–2 in the third chukker, La Bamba moved on to an 11–10 lead, helped by Cambiaso uncharacteristically missing three penalties from the sixty-yard mark. The final score was La Bamba de Areco thirteen, Dubai ten. Jean-François Decaux, Gonzalito Pieres, Facundo Pieres and Tomás Garbarini Islas, a ringer at one-goal handicap — soon raised to three goals by the Handicap Committee — played for La Bamba de Areco. Rashid Albwardy, Martín Valent, Cristián "Magoo" Laprida, and Adolfo Cambiaso wore the green and white Dubai colors.

The Warwickshire Cup was taken by Emlor/CRL with Spencer McCarthy, Joaquín Pittaluga, Luke Tomlinson and Ignacio Gonzalez, over El Remanso (stillwater), named after the Hanbury's estancia in Argentina. However, El Remanso— George Hanbury, Tom de Bruin, Manuel Fernández Llorente and Jaime García Huidobro— recovered to win the Cowdray Park Challenge Cup over Corovest.

Black Bears, away from high-goal tournaments this season, utilized their considerable resources in the eighteen-goal and fifteen-goal Victor Ludorum, winning both. Along the way they collected the Indian Empire Shield, the Duke of Sutherland Cup, the Coworth Park Challenge and the Eduardo Moore Tournament. Other tournament winners included Ed Magor's Panthers, which team defeated the Black Bears in Cirencester's eighteen-goal tournament and took the Harrison Cup at Cowdray; Lovelocks, winners of the Arthur Lucas Cup at Beaufort; and Hotel La Tour, which gathered the Royal Windsor Cup.

In the Inter-Regimental Tournament, the Household Cavalry — Lt. Col. Crispin Lockhart, Major Rupert Lewis, Captain Jack Mann and HRH Lt. Harry Wales— brought to an end the Royal Wessex Yeomanry's hold on the trophy.

2010: The End of the Decade

The international test match versus South Africa took place in the merry month of May at Cowdray Park. Richard Le Poer, in his first international; Mark Tomlinson; Tom Morley; and Chris Hyde were England's representatives, while South Africa presented Derreck Bradley, Tom de Bruin, Ignatius du Plessis and Gareth Evans. South Africa led 3–1 after one chukker. In a scrappy game, Tom Morley's accurate penalty shooting made the difference; however, the Springboks held tight, and the score at halftime was England seven, South Africa six. England resumed the lead in the fifth chukker, only for South Africa to equalize at the end of regulation time. The extra chukker started on the South African side of the field, and one of the Springboks committed a foul. Morley, who had been near perfection in his penalty taking, had a sixty-yarder stopped and cleared. Chris Hyde took the line, and the whistle went once more. Tom Morley made no mistake from the forty-yard line, and England won 12–11.

England's second international at home was held at Beaufort Polo Club against a team named the Americas, although in fact it was made up of four players from Argentina, Lucas Di Paola, Nicolás Pieres, Marcos Di Paola and Ignacio Toccalino, at twenty-eight goals aggregate. England presented James Beim, Mark Tomlinson, Malcolm Borwick and Luke Tomlinson, a total of 27 goals. Receiving a half goal on handicap, England was beaten 9 to 8½ goals.

In its sometimes mysterious ways, the HPA decided not to select a national eight-goal team to enter the European Eight-Goal Championship. However, four enterprising ladies— Clare Milford Haven, Tamara Vestey, Emma Tomlinson and Nina Clarkin — decided to give it a go. The Hurlingham Polo Association supported the endeavor to the tune of £15,000, and the Marchioness of Milford Haven contributed most of the rest. Along with coach John Paul Clarkin, and reserves Clare Brougham and Harry Tucker, they made the trek to Schloss Eibreichsdorf, a private club owned by Baron Richard Drasche-Wartinberg, located some thirty minutes from Vienna and the tournament's site.

To the surprise of many, but not themselves, the English ladies defeated by comfortable margins Slovakia, Italy and the host country Austria before running into a hiccup against Spain. England then took the bronze medal by defeating Switzerland by 8 goals to 5½. A young French team beat Spain 10–8 to take the European Eight-Goal Championship.

El Remanso took the 2011 Prince of Wales Trophy. Left to right: Jaime Garcia Huidobro, George Hanbury, Mrs. Greta Morrison, Maj. Christopher Hanbury, Charlie Hanbury and David Stirling (photograph by Ana Clara Cozzi, courtesy Sebastian Amaya, PoloLine).

The Prince of Wales Trophy went to Emlor, with Spencer McCarthy, Joaquín Pittaluga, John Paul Clarkin and Nacho Gonzalez. The red-shirted team defeated Talandracas by twelve goals to ten.

In the Queen's Cup stirring finals, Dubai defeated Les Lions II by twelve goals to ten. Rashid Albwardi, Ali's younger son; Francisco Vismara; Pablo MacDonough; and Adolfo Cambiaso played for Dubai. This was the seventh win for Cambiaso in this tournament, an individual record. Les Lions II had seventeen-year-old Chris Mackenzie from South Africa, Buster's son, who mixed in with the superstars with youthful confidence.

Dubai was expected to take the trophy quite comfortably; win they did, but not comfortably. Les Lions fought tooth-and-nail throughout the contest and to most people's surprise, including Cambiaso and company, were leading 10–9 five minutes into the last chukker. Then the magical Adolfito took over and during the remaining time scored two goals from the field and a thirty-yard penalty to bury Les Lions II's hope of achieving a major upset.

Dubai went on to take Cowdray Park's Gold Cup in a final game against Lechuza Caracas that drew mixed reviews. Previous winners Lechuza Caracas had Víctor Vargas, Guillermo Caset, Miguel Novillo Astrada and the obligatory Englishman, Max Routledge.

Dubai took off, scoring four goals to two in the first chukker, and never looked back, for a 14–12 final tally. The story of the game was Adolfito Cambiaso, which was both bad and good. The crowd was treated to another exhibition of stickwork, horsemanship and positional play by one of the game's immortals. On the other hand, his teammates, including a nine-goaler (ten goals in Argentina) in the person of Pablo MacDonough, were reduced to blocking and taking opponents out of Cambiaso's way. Appeals for fouls became a serious epidemic — in fact all of Dubai's goals after the fourth chukker came via penalties — and the game as a whole was rather sticky, with none of the open-play features that had characterized the Queen's Cup final.

The Warwickshire Cup, the oldest high-goal tournament in the realm, was downgraded to twenty goals; it attracted eight entries. Emlor — Spencer McCarthy, Joaquín Pittaluga, Luke Tomlinson and Nacho Gonzalez — held on to the trophy that had gone their way in 2009, a rare instance in which the handicappers left untouched a winning team. In a final game played in the morning at the Ashdon Down field, they defeated Nick Clarke's Salked by nine goals to seven, after trailing 5–4 in the fourth chukker. Capping a most successful season, Emlor also took the Gold Cup at Deauville, and kept on going its merry way with another victory, this time in the Duke of Sutherland Cup. Clinton McCarthy and Miguel del Carril replaced Spencer McCarty and John Paul Clarkin as forwards in this event.

Regrettably, it is sad to record that the Cowdray Park Challenge Cup, which dates back to 1911, was canceled because of lack of interest. The same fate awaited Beaufort's twenty-goal tournament.

In the medium-goal tournaments, the Indian Empire Shield was taken by the Black Bears — Guy Schwarzenbach, Simon Keyte, John Paul Clarkin and Matthew Perry — a well organized team that narrowly bested La Golondrina by eleven goals to ten. The Black Bears once more beat La Golondrina (the Swallow) by a single goal, this time at the Cirencester eighteen-goal tournament. The Duke of Beaufort's Cup saw HB Polo win the trophy from Emlor. Ludovic Pailloncy, Mark Tomlinson, Ignacio Toccalino and Sebastien Pailloncy wore the red and blue jerseys in a 9–8 victory.

At the fifteen-goal level, perennial Los Locos, with Claire Tomlinson, her son Mark, Ignacio Toccalino and George Gemmell, defeated Clarita by one goal; they were the two finalists in the Royal Windsor Cup, out of a field of twenty-two entries.

The Harrison Cup at Cowdray Park was taken by Emlor, with Clinton McCarthy, Eden Ormerod, Joaquín Pittaluga and Nacho González. Home team Laird took the County Cup at Cirencester Park when they defeated Balvanera by a single tally, 8–7. Nick Britten-Long, George Meyrick, Henry Brett and Leroux Hendrik played for Laird.

Beaufort took its own Arthur Lucas Cup, with a team of Simon Tomlinson, Oliver Tuthill, Tom Morley and Jacinto Crotto, Juni's son. Emma Tomlinson replaced Morley in the twelve-goal Queen Mother Trophy, and the blue and white team beat Tayto in the final game by half a goal.

The other two fifteen-goal competitions were won by La Golondrina, Ben Wilson, Diego Cavanagh, Juan Ambroggio and Jack Richardson, in the Eduardo Moore Tournament, and the Black Bears, the winners at the Coworth Park Challenge, beating Altamira.

Ferne Park, with Vere Hamsworth, Eden Ormerod, Will Emerson and James Harper, were the victors in the old Cheltenham Cup. Ferne Park also won the Dollar Cup; Jonathan Rothermere and Joaquín Pittaluga played instead of Harmsworth and Harper for the Prince of Wales Cup at Beaufort. 2010 was a most successful season for the green and grey team.

The low-goal Archie David Cup at Guards was taken by AFB, with Clive Read, James Carr, Sebastian Dawnay and James Harper. Another AFB team took the Julian and Howard Hipwood Trophy at Royal Berkshire. At Cowdray, Nick Dann, Henry Fisher, James Harper and George Milford Haven's Broncos won the Holden White Cup.

The Junior County Cup, which was established in 1905 and is currently the trophy for the National Eight-Goal Championship, was taken by Belgravia Polo, with Hazel Jackson, James Fielding, Grant Collet and Michael Henderson. They defeated Stobart Polo in the final match by the odd goal in seven.

The Victor Ludorum awards went to the Black Bears in the eighteen-goal, Emlor in the fifteen-goal, Ferne Park in the twelve-goal, and AFB in the eight-goal competition.

The UK Women's National Tournament at Ascot Park was won by Pink Power, with Mandie Beitner, Rosie Ross, Sarah Wiseman and Kirstie Otamendi.

In other competitions, Young England defeated Young New Zealand 6–2 in the John Cowdray Trophy. Jack Richardson, Max Charlton, Lanto Sheridan and Eden Ormerod represented Young England.

Oxford University took the varsity match; the Royal Navy the Inter-Regimental Tournament, and Cheshire Polo Club defeated All Ireland in the Patriotic Cup.

Thus a long polo year came to an end. It was a most successful season, and as HPA's chairman Nicholas Colquhoun-Denvers stated in the yearbook, "Despite the many predictions of doom and gloom, I believe that last year was better for polo than most of us had expected and there was certainly an air of optimism after the election."[19]

2011: What's in the Future?

The season started in Sussex with the James Wentworth-Stanley Cup, played at the twenty-two-goal level in early May. The preliminary rounds were held at Cowdray Park and at Trippetts, the Milford Haven's grounds close by. The finalists were Salkeld, with sponsor Nick Clarke, José Donoso, James Beim and Luke Tomlinson, and Sumaya, Oussama Aboughazale's team, completed by Juan Gris Zavaleta, Javier Novillo Astrada and the perennial Carlos Gracida. Due to injury, Luke Tomlinson was replaced in the fifth chukker by Juan Ambroggio. Salkeld limped to a 9–7 win.

In the Queen's Cup tournament, the two semifinals at Guards Polo Club provided good polo, featuring a pair of new teams. Adrian Kirby's Silver Spring 1870, with Australian Ruki Baillieu, John Paul Clarkin and Rob Archibald, led throughout the game against one of the favorites, Enigma. However, in the second half, ten-goaler Juan Martín Nero and Matías MacDonough went into top gear, equalizing the match with just half a minute before the bell. Juan Jauretche scored the winning tally after five minutes of play in extra time, placing Jerome Wirth's team in the finals, with a 10–9 victory.

The second semifinal was equally enthralling. Talandracas, with French patron Edouard Carmignac, Lucas Monteverde, Milo Fernández Araujo and Facundo Sola, battled newcomer Richard Mille to an eight-all standstill through four chukkers. Prince Jefri's team went up two goals, 11–9, in the critical fifth period. In the sixth chukker, goals by Monteverde and Sola made the scoreboard even, and with some sixty seconds left in the game, Facundo Sola scored the winning tally. Max Routledge, Pablo MacDonough and Alejandro Muzzio completed the Richard Mille squad.

The final game was played on a rain-soaked ground. Enigma took off with a vengeance, leading five goals to one after two chukkers. Good work by Lucas Monteverde and Milo Fernández Araujo eventually led to a six-all tie in the fifth chukker. However, Enigma rebounded to take the lead again, 8–6. The rain failed to affect the high level of play, Talandracas drawing level once more on two goals from evergreen Fernández Araujo. On to extra time, when nineteen-year-old Facundo Sola converted a penalty shot to win match and championship for Talandracas.

Eighteen teams allotted into three brackets entered the Cowdray Park Gold Cup. The quarterfinals matched La Bamba de Areco, with Jean-François Decaux, Gonzalo Pieres, Jr., Facundo Pieres and Matt Perry, winners over Sumaya, versus Zacara, which had beaten the holders Dubai, with Adolfo Cambiaso, by a single goal in the elimination round. Zacara had South African Ignatius du Plessis, Lyndon Lea, Hilario Ulloa and Gonzalo Deltour, the latter two former Cambiaso protégés. The other quarterfinals were fought out between unbeaten Piaget and Salkeld, with Nick Clarke, José Donoso, James Beim and Luke Tomlinson, which barely had managed to advance with a 2–2 record. Nevertheless, Salked defeated heavy favorite Piaget by a single goal, and Les Lions, which had Joaquim Gottschalk, Sebastián Merlos, Agustín Merlos and Chris Mackenzie, surprised Loro Piana with a convincing 17–11 win.

In the semifinals, Les Lions continued their good play, beating Salked by two goals, while Zacara surprised La Bamba de Areco with a strong 13–7 victory.

The final match was a close one. Playing well, Les Lions led 10–7 midway through the fourth chukker, the Merlos brothers dominating the midfield. Then Zacara showed its mettle, scoring four unanswered goals to take the lead 11–10. Agustín "Tincho" Merlos equalized the scoreboard with a nice cut shot in the last chukker, some two minutes from time. From the ensuing throw-in, Gonzalo Deltour took off and received a lofted pass from Ulloa to make the winning goal.

This game—as well as many others in the high-goal season—displayed very good polo, a cheerful change brought about by the strict applications of the new rules seen in the polo summer of 2011. Arthur Douglas-Nugent touched the right chord when he wrote, "It does seem that the stricter umpiring directed at those who turn the ball has worsened beyond expectation and the backhand shot is becoming more the norm than the exception. Equally there seems to be less backchat between the players and the umpires as each now can be in no doubt as to where they stand."[20]

It appears that a new dawn is looming in polo's horizon. Perhaps the curse of continuous tapping and the obnoxious custom of disrespect toward the umpires will become a thing of the past. Neither of the two will be mourned.

CHAPTER 25

Some Current Issues in British Polo

Following more than half a century of competition, the Cowdray Park Gold Cup remains the sternest examination of a polo team's ability as well as the quality of its pony string. Not since the Hurlingham Club became the spiritual and legislative home of British polo, and its Champion Cup the most coveted trophy, has a polo club carried such a symbolic burden as Cowdray Park does in contemporary polo.

The Queen's Cup closely follows in terms of prestige. Just four years younger that the Gold Cup, it is the major tournament for the Guards Polo Club. Royalty frequently is on hand to present the handsome silver trophy, which has been played since 1960 with the single interruption brought about by the hoof-and-mouth epidemic of 2001.

Regrettably, both the oldest and one of the newest high-goal tournaments, the Warwickshire Cup and the Prince of Wales Trophy, have been relegated to a secondary role. The latter shares part of the Queen's Cup competition, while the Warwickshire Cup, which dates back to 1894, has been decreased to a twenty-goal tournament. What for many years was the Quadruple Crown of English polo has nowadays been scaled down to only two major tournaments. The wish for playing in many matches has been tempered by the strain in maintaining polo-pony strings at peak condition for an extended period of time, and the alternative offered by straight elimination tournaments is not popular at all among the game's patrons.

Another trend has been the increase in test matches at the international level. Regrettably, they can be too much of a good thing, because some of those labeled "internationals" are just borderline test matches. Sometimes less is better than more. The issue of international handicaps is a very vexing one, with several players sporting three or more different individual handicaps depending upon which country they are in plying their trade.

Following the successful revival of the competition for the Westchester Cup in 2009 at the International Polo Club Palm Beach, its future remains uncertain, even though the understanding between the two Polo Associations at the time was that, regardless of which team won the match, a return challenge would be issued within three years of the event. It appears that there is no will on the part of the U.S. Polo Association to issue, let alone prepare, a challenge for the Westchester Cup. This is not a financial matter, because the USPA's coffers are full, due to the profits accumulated by its marketing branch, Polo Properties.

On the other hand, significant amounts of money have been allotted to the recruiting, coaching and ancillary support for a young team to represent America in the FIP Fourteen-Goal World Championship. The team qualified for the final round to be played in Argentina in September 2011, by defeating Guatemala and Canada in the North American Zone preliminary event in the Dominican Republic.

An England versus America twenty-eight-goal test match at Guards Polo Club should be an unqualified success, both financially and from the sporting point of view. However, it seems that the powers that be in American polo only visualize the difficulties in preparing for such an event, rather than considering the possibilities of success in continuing the longest international rivalry in the world of polo.

The Question of Umpiring

Good umpiring is an art, not a science. There are many officials, both referees and umpires, who might know the rule book by heart and yet fail the stern test of a high-goal level match where so much is at stake. In the pressure cooker of an international test or in the finals of a major tournament, there are tremendous demands inflicted upon the umpires. As the English international player and umpire Paul Withers once said, "The umpires can make or break a polo game."[1]

That almost extinct creature, the perfect umpire, must possess the qualities of equanimity, unflappability and decisiveness, all tempered by a dose of good humor and common sense. Thorough knowledge of the rule book is a given. However, the most important quality is consistency of interpretation of the rules. Early in the game, the players have to understand how the game is going to be called by the umpires.

Most players have a fairly good idea of the rules, not always of the wording. The umpires must be certain that the players are in no doubt whatsoever of the umpires' decisions. Therefore, hesitancy on the part of the umpiring crew, including frequent consultations with the referee, is a sure way of destroying the player's confidence in the umpires.

All this is good and well; however, there is also a burden on the participants. It is essential that the players must ride onto the field with the thought that the umpires are always right, no matter how obviously wrong a call has been. Good sportsmanship,

Paul Withers, an eight-goal handicap player, giving back to the game as an umpire.

that sterling but fading quality in all of sports, is essential in adopting this attitude of respect for the officials.

A long time ago, Dr. James Dwight, a national champion tennis player from Boston in America, pointed out that the "umpire is an unfortunate necessity, and his first object is to make himself as little conspicuous as possible, and to annoy the players as little as he can."[2] Dr. Dwight also suggested that one mistake will outweigh hours of good decisions by the umpires. Players are quick to notice mistakes by the umpires, which in reality are just as important as missing the ball altogether or hitting wide a "sitter" in front of the goalposts.

Nevertheless, there is room for improvement in the quality of umpiring. In 1988, Brigadier Peter Thwaites, at the time chairman of the HPA, wrote in the yearbook:

> The standard of umpiring at almost every level gives cause for concern. Two former Chairmen of the H.P.A. and myself, watching a high-goal final, were dismayed to notice the return of what used to be called "old soldier" tricks, appealing for a foul and worse, the 'manufactured foul' of pulling up to imply a dangerous cross. And of course, the higher the handicap of the player concerned, the more likely is the umpire to be intimidated. These bad habits need a spell of really tough umpiring, if the game is not to suffer."[3]

In the same issue, Lt. Col. Alec Harper added fuel to the fire:

> Our umpires are again increasingly being faced with difficult decisions particularly by the habit of players pulling up, to a halt sometimes, and still claiming the right of way. One feels that if they then take a full shot through the legs of their opponent's pony, they could at least be penalized by dangerous stick work. The whole process is against the spirit of the game and is very boring to watch. Subtle and not so subtle methods of "appealing" are also a constant challenge to the umpire's character.[4]

John Tinsley, at the time the HPA's Chairman, cogently wrote,

> In this increasingly professional and competitive era, many players have become less willing to accept defeat, or indeed a penalty blown against them, in a calm and sportsmanlike way. In addition, the way the game is being played has changed with far more turning of the ball and hence it has become increasingly difficult to umpire. I do not believe that the problem is unique to English polo but it is a problem that we have to sort out. It is not going to be easy and will require strong, fair and, most importantly, consisting umpiring at all levels.[5]

Presciently, Colonel David Woodd, the Hurlingham Polo Association's chief executive, has stated, "The rules of polo should be understandable and user friendly."[6] It is a matter of fact that many current rules, especially the American version, read like a heavy legal treatise.

In reality, the process of lawmaking is one of dialectical exchange between administrators and players. The original rules makers of the game of polo set out with one purpose: to ensure a fair contest. That worthy intention has survived into the present, but with more emphasis on creating and maintaining a flowing spectacle attractive to spectators and also the players. On the other hand, players and coaches rapidly work out how to legally challenge that intention. It is a fact of life that to be any sort of games player is to test the perceived weaknesses of the laws under which one plays. This is part of the culture in modern sports as an endeavor that demands total commitment to their craft by those who carry aspirations of being a champion.

Another peculiar situation is that on the fields of play, games are not strictly governed by their official rules, but by a tenuous understanding between players and umpires as to what is allowed and what is not acceptable. Crafty players will early in the game test the umpires with borderline plays in order to find out how the game will be called.

Sportsmanship

The issue of respect for the rules of the games and the officials charged with their application goes hand in hand with the concept of fair play and sportsmanship. An alarm bell was sounded in 1991 by Peter Thwaites, chairman of the Hurlingham Polo Association. Writing in the HPA's yearbook, Brigadier Thwaites stated,

> Once again during 1990 the behaviour of certain players coupled with the difficulties of umpiring were cause for concern. It is discouraging that with the increasingly high standards of play in this country the sportsmanship and conduct of some of the high goal players should be so noticeably deteriorating. The main problem, of course, is that the umpires are, in most high goal matches, playing in the same tournament and are unwilling to penalize a player who may later be umpiring *them*. In spite of the determined efforts of by Chief Umpire Ronald Ferguson, I believe the job is too much for one man and that a retired high-goal player, perhaps with a sub-committee of umpire supervisors, who have the time to get round more matches, would help to achieve better discipline and uniformity. Again, we are up against professionalism, where a severe decision could affect a player's livelihood. Even so, I believe all members of the H.P.A. share the Stewards' concern at the decline in standards of sportsmanship and fair play.[7]

The concept of sportsmanship goes back a long time; however, it is now under siege by the twin forces of winning at all costs and the lack of graciousness in defeat. Several years ago, Thomas Glynn, a Harvard graduate known as "Mr. Polo" in America, quoted Tommy Hitchcock, a fierce competitor if ever there was one, as saying, "Win as if it is not important, and lose as if you were enjoying it."[8]

Those remarks, expressed in the times of the golden era of polo in the United States, sound totally out of date in today's sporting world. It has been suggested that the idea of sportsmanship was inspired by the myths from the age of chivalry, which also included the inspiration for teams' jerseys.[9]

Nevertheless, the ideal of sportsmanship is ageless. It was an unwritten law, tacitly understood by all and enforced by the dire prospect of ostracism.

Polo in the Olympic Games

At present, the issue of polo in the Olympic Games seems to be moot. If the powers that be failed to include polo in the 2012 Olympiad, there is little hope for the future. The overwhelming superiority of Argentine polo on the world's stage is not the main issue. After all, no one complained about the United States dominance in basketball or the former Soviet Union in gymnastics. The problem is the tremendous cost associated with staging a tournament with very limited mass appeal. What must be preserved is that the Olympic tournament should be played with each country sending their best players, and competed for without handicap. The Olympic Games are only for the very best.

The Issue of Drug Testing

Closely related to the possibility of the renewal of polo as an Olympic sport is the issue of drug testing for man and mount. The International Olympic Committee has delegated the issue to the World Anti-Doping Agency, nowadays based in Montreal, a large bureaucratic organization whose methods are viewed with some reservation by several sporting and legal organizations.

This is a highly charged issue with a clash between those who are doing their best to eradicate drug usage in sports and those who side with the issue of personal rights.

The sad fact is that use of performance-enhancing drugs has tainted many athletes in many sports and games, including Olympic gold medalists, Tour de France bicycle racers, and major league baseball players and football players, just to mention some examples.

The game of polo has the added burden of protecting the ponies from being administered performance-enhancing medications. The darkest day in the history of the game was 19 April 2009, when more than twenty ponies belonging to the Lechuza Caracas organization perished due to an overdose of selenium. The tragedy is that selenium, an essential element in normal metabolism, neither improves performance nor decreases recuperation time to normal after exertion.[10,11]

More than likely, the problem of drug usage by players is not too significant in polo; nevertheless, the Hurlingham Polo Association has taken the lead in instituting a clear policy regarding drug usage: "Doping is the use by an associate member (player or official)—hereafter collectively referred to as 'player'—of any Banned Substance and is strictly forbidden according to the terms of this regulation."[12]

The Rise of Commercialism and the Decline of Civility

Although polo at the high level seems more regimented today than ever before, at this stage in the game's development it appears that the word *fun* has become polo's dirty word; simply stated, the old English tradition of "play the game" is almost forgotten.

Courtesy to opponents, sympathy for the loser, unquestioned obedience to the decision of the umpires are all almost vanished. The wonderful world of the gifted amateur is as much alive as the dodo, and we are all the poorer because of its certain extinction.

The unrelenting rise of commercialism with its increasing pressure to win at all costs is reflected in many facets of the game; however, not all are bad examples. Whether we like it or not, patron polo is a major factor in the survival of the present structure of high-goal polo. The sponsorship of many firms allows the presentation of marvelous spectacles such as the annual match for the Coronation Cup, the largest single-day event in polo. However, the public perception of International Day is slowly changing. Reporting on the event, Antje Derks wrote,

> If polo is ever going to be taken seriously it must be promoted as a competitive sport and not a gigantic party with a match thrown in for good measure. The Federation of International Polo hopes to get our beloved game into the Olympics but, unfortunately, the media are more interested in the personal lives of the players and the celebrities in attendance at our premier events rather than the colossal efforts made by teams, patrons, ponies, players and grooms.[13]

Margaret Brett, at the time Editor of *Polo Times*, struck the right chord when she wrote, "For both polo in general and Cartier in particular, we shouldn't allow our public perception to be one of 'increasingly vulgar events' as suggested by *The Observer*. Our up-and-coming talent will need a better presentation of the sport."[14]

On the other hand, the insatiable thirst for more and more money is evident everywhere. Players' uniforms, including the English international colors and regimental teams, are peppered with large and small advertisements similar to Formula One racers' suits. Several players also sport commercial logos on their white pants, which used to be called breeches in the golden age.

There is nothing wrong with being paid to play polo. The era of the professional polo player began coincidentally with the amateur's days in the sun. Examples from the 1920s abound: the Frenchman Jean de Madré had two Indian ten-goalers on his Tigers team; American Stephen "Laddie" Sanford frequently had on his Hurricanes team another ten-goal handicap player in the person of the talented Irishman Captain Pat Roark; and Seymour Knox loaded his successful Aurora team with English-born Lewis Smith, a nine-goal player in America. The system was well known; however, it was not mentioned in polite circles.

The problem with professionalism occurs when excesses are committed. The most egregious example happened in Beijing in 2011 when three professional players disgraced themselves and their country by threatening to refuse to play for England unless their compensation matched the one offered to other national teams. This was an attitude resembling an industrial action, rather than a problem to be solved through negotiation and mutual professional respect. Eventually, the situation was resolved through the timely intervention of former HPA chairman John Tinsley, now chairman of the International Committee, but the damage had been done.

Perhaps in a moment of obfuscation, the players themselves forgot what an honor it is to be asked to represent your country in an international competition. Twenty pieces of silver or more count for nothing in that situation; furthermore, the fact of being selected to play in an international increases the individual player's exposure in the public and sponsors' eyes, a favorable impression on the marketability of any professional player.

The Question of Scoring

The thought of changing the system of scoring in polo has raised its face. In America, the U.S. Polo Association has legalized in arena polo a two-point score if a goal is made from beyond the center line.[15] The concept of a home run or hitting-for-six thus became part of the indoors game, and raw power overwhelmed exquisite scoring from the field.

Something similar was allowed in a charade game held on the site of the old Hurlingham Club's number-one ground. A goal scored from beyond a sixty-yard semicircle counted as two points. The same system was tried in America at a benefit game featuring eight ten-goal players, past and present. Trailing by a single goal with practically no time left in the match, Adolfo Cambiaso elected to take a sixty-yard penalty from some sixty-five yards. The goal was made and the match won. The innovation met with mixed reviews.

Brigadier Arthur Douglas Nugent, who knows a thing or two about polo, wrote cogently about this issue.[16] Brigadier Douglas-Nugent suggests the possibility of a field goal raised to a value of two points, while a goal from a penalty would remain at one. More radically, a goal scored from more than sixty yards would count three points. In his opinion, this would encourage the early release of the ball and minimize the melees at the goal mouth, painful to watch and rather impossible to umpire.

It is quite possible that the number of fouls committed would rise if the resulting penalty yielded only one goal. As to giving the heavy hitters the advantage of an extra point for a long shot, it takes away the marvel of combination play and the beauty of the goal from the field. Any modification that potentially decreases the number of throw-ins should be carefully drafted and subjected to a period of trial, and perhaps tribulation. However, a way must be found to diminish the number of throw-ins during the course of a game.

Other constructive ideas put forward by Brigadier Douglas-Nugent are to abolish the changing of ends after each goal is scored, with the game being restarted by the side scored upon with a free hit from their sixty-yard line, and a free hit from the nonoffending team when the ball goes out of bounds over the sidelines. All this would significantly reduce the number of throw-ins, a constant source of mischief and a nightmare for the umpires.

All this debate is good because the game of polo occasionally needs a transfusion of ideas and an injection of progress. While considering changes in the rules of the game, the legislative bodies should take into account that polo is more akin to association football or to field hockey than to any other sport or game. It is of interest that hockey's rules do not allow goals scored from beyond the sixteen-yard shooting circle.

The Issue of Handicaps

The question of proper individual handicapping has bedeviled the authorities since the concept was established in America by Henry Lloyd Herbert in 1888. The Hurlingham Polo Committee promulgated the Recent Form List in 1903 at the request of the County Polo Association in an attempt to level the playing field. Every season, the top players were included in a roster, promptly referred to as the "black list." In some tournaments, no more that two players in the Recent Form List were allowed on any given team.

In actual practice, it did not work out satisfactorily because the basic concept was to divide all the registered players into two distinct groups: the very best, and the not so good. The flaw in the system was that there was no real distinction among the players. There was a general sigh of relief when the Hurlingham Polo Committee published the Official Handicap List in 1911. The HPC's example was immediately adopted by the Indian Polo Association and the Polo Association of the River Plate. The arbitrary figure of ten goals as the top handicap has remained as the mark of excellence in polo.

Periodically, there have been calls for increasing the ceiling in handicaps. This reached a crescendo in those times in which an individual player appeared to be way above his contemporaries. In Argentina, Juan Carlos Harriott, the younger, was thought to be a twelve-goal player when compared to his fellow ten-goalers. The same sentiment surfaced when Adolfo Cambiaso reached the summit.

The handicap system has served the game well for the past one hundred years. The powers that be should be very careful if a decision is reached to tamper with the top limit in handicapping. Inflation is not good at all and usually leads to further devaluation of standards that have stood the challenge of time.

However, there are some problems. The main issues are not at the top level; it really makes very little difference when a given player is rated at eight or nine goals. The big problem is at the middle and lower levels. The so-called "ringer" has been part and parcel of the game for a long time, and handicap committees worldwide still struggle with the issue of fair handicapping.

Another issue is that of safety. The question has been asked many times: does a zero-handicap player belong in high-goal polo? George Oliver, the American nine-goal player, gave one answer: "Players now are put on the field before they are ready, and on horses they can't ride."[17]

Nevertheless, the current economics of the game dictate the presence of wealthy patrons in high-goal polo, a situation that will last until the game adopts full professional status.

The Curse of Tapping the Ball

In the 1990s, the practice of tapping the ball ad infinitum by skilled players reached the aspect of an epidemic at all levels of the game. Perhaps it was good and well that superstars like Adolfo Cambiaso showed previously unknown dexterity in handling the ball in the air; however, when less adept practitioners of the art tried in vain to emulate the master, the results reminded seasoned observers of the game of the mess the sorcerer's apprentice got into when left alone in *Fantasia*.

Lt. Col. Alec Harper compared tapping the ball to a virus spreading to all polo ranks, because the tactic was taken up by teams who did not need it.[18]

For the next decade, the game of polo went into a recession with the advent of the two evils, turning on the ball, followed by tapping. Robert Graham, the Hurlingham Polo Association's chief umpire, said, "Some of the games were excruciating [during the 2005 Cowdray Park's Gold Cup]. At our last meeting we discussed how we can stop this style of play by changing the rules. I'm told it happens to a lesser extent in the U.S., where rules on tapping are slightly different, but they blow the whistle more there. It's quite a complicated subject, but we need to work out how to deal with it."[19]

In the same issue of *Polo Times*, former nine-goaler and Captain of England Julian Hipwood, stated, "So much polo is based on possession [compared to several years ago]. Hits are shorter and the line changes often, in contrast to the more classical game. This means that in one way it has become tougher to umpire. But now umpires are given more powers to control the game."[20]

With the change in the rules, the game of polo became more open, at least in high-goal polo in England, America and Argentina. However, many players remain impatient of the backhander, and because turning to the right with possession of the ball is often followed by a whistle, adept players have now perfected a turn to the left, allowing them to keep possession of the ball. Sticky polo is threatening a comeback, if close observation of the twenty-six-goal tournaments in America in 2011 is a predictor of things to come.

International Matches

The major problem in international polo today is the lack of competitive balance among the polo-playing countries. Competitive balance is an important part in professional sports because uncertainty of outcome is a powerful tool for bringing spectators to arenas and stadiums as well as to the ubiquitous television screen.

Currently, Argentina stands alone at the top of the pyramid, with England and America sitting quite comfortably on the second tier. The gap between the second and third tier is as wide as the one enjoyed by Argentina.

However, this discrepancy has proved to be deleterious for polo at its highest level. More than thirty years have passed since the United States and Argentina played for the

Cup of the Americas. England and America have contested the Westchester Cup, the oldest international trophy, only thrice since World War II.

The prospects for a solution in the near future are bleak. Of course, there is always the possibility of Italy becoming a world power in polo if a foursome of Italian passport carriers decides to challenge their country of birth in a world championship with no handicap limits. A team of A. Cambiaso, B. Castagnola, J.M. Nero, and A.N. Other is not to be sneered at, and the precedent has been already set by both Switzerland and Italy, albeit at the fourteen-goal level.

Colophon

In 2011 the game of polo appears to be on the verge of a great change. This most ancient game is played around the world in relatively equal fashion. It was not beset — as football has been — by regional and national modifications of codes, such as Canadian and American football, rugby union and rugby league in England and Australia. There are also creations born out of Australian and Hibernian resistance to a basically English game; thus the great popularity enjoyed by Australian Rules football and Gaelic football in their respective countries. Perhaps it is opportune to quote the delightful Irish saying about football's different codes: "In Rugby you kick the ball, in Association you kick the man if you cannot kick the ball, and in Gaelic you kick the ball if you cannot kick the man."[21]

Major Hugh Dawnay, a former 10th Hussars officer, a winner of the Inter-Regimental Tournament, founder of a polo school and author of two instructional books on the game, was recently interviewed by Chris Ashton, who mentions Major Dawnay grieving the loss of English players to high-goal polo:

> For as long as I've been watching, we've had patrons, but the system of teams blending local and foreign players has almost gone. If you look at the high-goal teams nowadays, very few were English. The patrons count as "home" players, though they are mostly foreigners, while most of the Argentines, with European passports, also qualify as "home" players. The result is that English players no longer figure in high-goal polo.[22]

Just as on American polo grounds, the dearth of local high-goal players in English polo does not bode well for the future of the game at top level.

At present, the game is in a state of flux. There are several difficult issues facing the game's administrators. Among them is the thorny question of European Union passports, the ever-present complaints about the quality of umpiring, the decline of sportsmanship and basic notions of good manners on the field and the need for a comprehensive review and unification of the rules of the game.

Polo has been played in Britain for approximately 150 years. British settlers took the game to North and South America, diplomats to Imperial Russia, Army officers to the African continent from Egypt to the Cape Colony, to the Far East and Australia. It was perfected by remittance men in Canada, estancieros in Argentina, graziers in the Outback, gentry in California, the constabulary in Burma, farmers in South Africa and shepherds in New Zealand.

However, in spite of the distances involved, the game was similar in every continent, submitted to minor local variations, such as subsidiary goals and "behinds," no offside and no hooking. The main reason was that, with the single exception of the United States, every nation followed the Hurlingham Club's rules of the game.

In comparison to other countries, the polo season in England offers a different feeling — the lush turf, the short spells of soft rain, the restrained audience, the unobtrusive umpires, the tradition of old trophies, a touch of royalty, and the unique sense that the intangible values of this most ancient mounted game are preserved and cherished on this island more than in any other place in the world.

APPENDIX 1

Letter to *The Field*, 20 March 1869

Text of the letter to *The Field*, dated 20 March 1869, which prompted Edward Hartopp to try out the game at Aldershot Garrison. Courtesy of Nigel àBrassard, Esq.

Sir,

I am a constant reader of *The Field*, but I have never seen any account in it of this game, which has been played by Europeans in India for some years. Perhaps the following description may be interesting to your readers; and, as there is a good deal of fun, excitement, and skill in the game, might it not be introduced to this country?

The game was originally played by the natives in the district of Munneepoor, from whence it was brought about eight years ago to Calcutta. It was at once taken up by European gentlemen there, who formed a hockey club, and, Government having granted a piece of ground on the Maidan, the club reduced it to good order, and has played there to this day. From Calcutta it found its way to Rangoon, and then to Madras; but it was only in 1868 that it was introduced to Bombay, when a member of the Calcutta Hockey Club brought sticks and balls, and established the game there, where it is now all the rage.

The game is played with sides, as in ordinary hockey or football. There are goals, and the ground is marked out with flags, and all such rules, as "touch," are somewhat similar to our ordinary English game. Each side tries to hit the ball into the adversaries' goal, and thus scores a game. The sticks, made of bamboo (being the lightest and toughest stick we have in India), are about 4½ feet long, with a headpiece. The ball, which must be very light and hard, is made of the root of the bamboo, and is from twice to three times as large as a new cricket ball. The ground must be a piece of flat grass, kept as level as possible by rolling. In Calcutta, we usually play for an hour and a quarter twice a week, this being as much as the ponies can stand in that climate, which will be better understood by my explaining that all, except the goal-keepers, are galloping throughout the game. The Munneepooree (natives) were the best players as late as 1865–66, when they accepted a challenge from the Calcutta Club and, headed by an English captain, came down to Calcutta, and carried off the palm. Whether they are so now is an open question, as some of the members of the C.H.C. are remarkable good players. The Munneepooree ponies used by those natives and by the C.H.C. are very small, not averaging, I should think, more than 11½ hands, which is an advantage; they are also very quick, fast, and, as a rule, have the chief requisite for a hockey pony—good mouths. They are, moreover, very plucky (as I know from experience, having taken a first and second spear in a wild boar off one); and this is also most important, as they often get hard hit in the scrummages. The Munneepooree ponies, after a certain amount of training and play, will follow the ball, stop when it is stopped, and will turn with it, with very little persuasion of rein or spur being required. Whereas the Burmese ponies, which are used in Rangoon and Madras, are both clumsier,

285

and pull too hard after a few months' play. I mentioned all this about the ponies, as I wish to state that the chief difficulty is a good hockey pony. In India we consider the game is the next best fun to pigsticking (or hog hunting, as called by some), and any members of the Calcutta Club would infinitely prefer it to cricket or rackets. Our Calcutta subscription was an entrance fee of one guinea and a half, and six shilling a month, which paid for sticks, balls, pegs, and shandygaff for the members and their friends.

N.S.S.

Polo Player Recipients
of the Victoria Cross

Beresford, Col. Lord William Leslie de la Poer (1844–1900), 9th Lancers, was awarded the Victoria Cross for gallantry in the Zulu War, 1879.

Bingham, Commander (later Rear-Adm.), the Hon. Edward Barry Stewart (1882–1939), RN; HMS *Nestor*, battle of Jutland, 1916.

Bishop, Capt. (later Air Marshal, RCAF) William Avery (1882–1939), 60 Squadron, RFC and Canadian Cavalry; enemy aerodrome near Cambrai, France, 1917.

Brown-Singe-Hutchinson, Maj. Edward Douglas (1861–1940), 14th Hussars; Geluk, South Africa, 1900.

Campbell, Brig. John Charles (1894–1942), Royal Horse Artillery; Sidi Rezegh, North Africa, 1941. A six-goal handicap player, three-time winner of the Inter-regimental Tournament. Killed in February 1942, while a major general in command of the 7th Armoured Division.

Congreve, Capt. Walter Norris (later Gen. Sir Walter) (1862–1927), Rifle Brigade; Colenso, South Africa, 1899. His son Maj. William La Touche Congreve also received the Victoria Cross; they are one of only three father-and-son pairs to win this decoration.

Crutchley, Lt. Victor Alexander Charles (later Adm. Sir Victor) (1893–1986), RN; Ostend and Zeebrugge, Belgium, 1918. Played at Malta on a team with HRH the Duke of York, Lord Mountbatten and Adm. Sir Roger Keyes.

De Montmorency, Lt. (later Capt.) the Hon. Raymond Harvey Lodge Joseph (1867–1900), 21st Lancers; battle of Omdurman, Sudan, 1898. Killed in action in Dordrecht, South Africa.

De Pass, Lt. Frank Alexander (1887–1914), 34th PAVO Poona Horse; near Festubert, France, 1914. Killed in that action.

Dease, Lt. Maurice (1889–1914), Royal Fusiliers; Mons, Belgium. Killed in that action. This was one of the first Victoria Crosses awarded in World War I.

Dugdale, Lt. Frederick Brookes (1877–1901), 5th Lancers; Derby, South Africa, 1901. Was killed while riding with the North Cotswold Hounds.

Dunville, Lt. John Spencer (1897–1917), 1st Royal Dragoons; Epheny, France. Killed in that action.

Fincastle, Viscount Maj. Alexander Edward Murray (later Earl of Dunmor), (1871–1962), 16th Lancers; Tirah Campaign, India, 1893.

FitzClarence, Charles (1865–1914), Royal Fusiliers, later Irish Guards; Mafeking, South Africa, 1899. Killed in action at Polygon Wood, Zonnebeke, Belgium, while in command of the 1st Irish Guards Brigade. Brig. Gen. FitzClarence is the highest-ranking officer inscribed on the Menin Gate Memorial in Ypres, which commemorates those fallen with unknown grave.

Grenfell, Capt. Francis Octavius (1880–1915), 9th Lancers; France, 1914.

Kenna, Capt. (later Brig. Gen.) Paul Aloysius (1862–1915), 21st Lancers; battle of Omdurman, 1898. Killed by a sniper in Gallipoli, Turkey. Colonel Kenna was on the British Olympic equestrian team in 1912.

Keyes, Lt. Col. Geoffrey Charles Tasker (1917–1941), Royal Scots Greys and 11th Scottish Commando; Beda Littoria, North Africa, 1941. Killed while leading the "Rommel Raid."

Maxwell, Lt. (later Brig. Gen.) Francis Aylmer (1871–1917), 18th King's Own Indian Lancers; Korn Spruit, South Africa, 1900. Brigadier Maxwell was in command of the 27th Brigade when he was shot by a German sniper near Ypres, Belgium.

Milbanke, Lt. (later Lt. Col. Sir) John Penniston (1873–1915), 10th Hussars; Colesberg, South Africa, 1900. Killed in Gallipoli, Turkey.

Schofield, Capt. (later Lt. Col.) Harry Norton (1865–1931), Royal Field Artillery; Colenso, South Africa, 1899.

Smyth, Capt. (later Maj. Gen.) Nevill Maskelyne (1868–1941), 2nd Dragoon Guards (Queen's Bays); battle of Omdurman, Sudan 1898.

Warburton-Lee, Commodore Bernard Armitage Warburton (1895–1940), RN; battle of Narvik, Norway. Died of wounds during that engagement. A six-goal player who played mostly in Malta.

Wiart, Lt. Col. Adrian Carton de (later Lt. Gen. Sir Adrian) (1880–1963), 4th Dragoon Guards; La Boiselle, France, 1916. Took the Inter-regimental Tournament and was finalist in the Hurlingham Champion Cup.

Results of Major Championships

The Hurlingham Champion Cup

Open to any polo teams, but teams entered as a club or regiment may only play members of that club or regiment. Presented yearly to each winning team.

1876 **Royal Horse Guards:** Lord Charles Kilmarnock, Frederick Trench-Gascoigne, Hon. Charles Fitzwilliam, John Brocklehurst, Evelyn Atherley

1877 Tie between Monmouthshire and Tyros: 0–0
Monmouthshire: Francis Herbert, Reginald Herbert, Hugh Owen, James Mellor, Edward Curre
Tyros: Cristóbal de Murrieta, Adrián de Murrieta, Sir Bache Cunard, Edward Baldock, Hon. Charles Cavendish

1878 **Monmouthshire:** Francis Herbert, Reginald Herbert, James Mellor, Edward Curre, Sir Charles Wolseley

1879 **Hurlingham:** Edward Baldock, William Ince-Anderton, James Peat, Alfred Peat, Arthur Peat

1880 **Ranelagh:** Francis Herbert, William Ince-Anderton, Edward Baldock, Reginald Herbert, Thomas S. Kennedy

1881 **Sussex County:** Earl of Lewes, Algernon Peyton, James Peat, Alfred Peat, Arthur Peat

1882 **Sussex County:** James Peat, Edward Kenyon-Stow, Algernon Peyton, Arthur Peat, James Babington

1883 **Sussex County:** (w.o.) Capt. Geoffrey Phipps-Hornby, James Peat, Alfred Peat, Arthur Peat

1884 **Freebooters:** Llewellyn Heywood Jones, Thomas Hone, John Watson, Capt. Julian Spicer

1885 **Sussex County:** James Peat, Frank Mildmay, Alfred Peat, Arthur Peat

1886 **Freebooters:** Maj. Bloomfield Gough, Capt. Llewellyn Heywood Jones, Capt. Julian Spicer, John Watson

1887 **Freebooters:** Capt. Malcolm Little, Capt. Llewellyn Heywood Jones, Kenneth MacLaren, John Watson

1888 **Sussex County:** James Peat, Frank Mildmay, Alfred Peat, Arthur Peat

1889 **Sussex County:** James Peat, Frank Mildmay, Alfred Peat, Arthur Peat

1890 **Sussex County:** James Peat, Frank Mildmay, Alfred Peat, Arthur Peat

1891 **Sussex County:** James Peat, Frank Mildmay, Alfred Peat, Arthur Peat

1892 **Sussex County:** James Peat, Frank Mildmay, Earl of Harrington, Alfred Peat

1893 **Sussex County:** (w.o.) James Peat, Frank Mildmay, Alfred Peat, Arthur Peat

1894 **Freebooters:** Gerald Hardy, Lord Charles Southampton, Capt. P.W. Jules Le Gallais, Capt. Denis Daly

1895 **Freebooters:** Gerald Hardy, Lord Charles Southampton, Alfred Rawlinson, Capt. Denis Daly

1896 **Freebooters:** Gerald Hardy, Lord Charles Southampton, Alfred Rawlinson, Walter Buckmaster

1897 **Rugby:** George Miller, Capt. Gordon Renton, Edward Miller, W.J. Drybrough

1898 **Rugby:** George Miller, Capt. Gordon Renton, Edward Miller (Walter Jones), W.J. Drybrough

1899 **Rugby:** Walter Jones, George Miller, Edward Miller, Charles Miller

1900 **Old Cantabs:** Walter A. McCreery, Frederick Freake, Walter Buckmaster, Lawrence McCreary

1901 **Rugby:** Walter Jones, George Miller, Edward Miller, Charles Miller

1902 **Freebooters:** Harold Brassey, Alfred Rawlinson, Walter Buckmaster, Lawrence Waterbury

1903 **Rugby:** Walter Jones, George Miller, Edward Miller, Charles Miller

1904 **Old Cantabs:** Capt. Godfrey Heseltine, Walter A. McCreary, Frederick Freake, Walter Buckmaster

1905 **Roehampton:** Cecil Nickalls, Capt. Herbert Wilson, Patteson Nickalls, Capt. John Hardress Lloyd

1906 **Roehampton:** Cecil Nickalls, Capt. Herbert Wilson, Patteson Nickalls, Capt. John Hardress Lloyd

1907 **Freebooters:** Capt. Leopold Jenner, Riversdale Grenfell, Francis Grenfell, Duke of Roxburghe

1908 **Old Cantabs:** Capt. George Bellville, Frederick Freake, Walter Buckmaster, Lord John Wodehouse

1909 **Roehampton:** Riversdale Grenfell, Capt. Herbert Wilson, A. Noel Edwards, Capt. John Hardress Lloyd

1910 **Old Cantabs:** Capt. George Bellville, Frederick Freake, Walter Buckmaster, Lord John Wodehouse

1911 **Eaton:** Cecil Nickalls, George Miller, Patteson Nickalls, Charles Miller

1912 **Old Cantabs:** Capt. George Bellville, Frederick Freake, Walter Buckmaster, Lord John Wodehouse

1913 **Quidnuncs:** Duque de Peñaranda, Capt. E. William Palmes, Capt. Henry Tomkinson, Capt. Frederick Barrett

1914 **Old Cantabs:** Capt. George Bellville, Frederick Freake, Walter Buckmaster, Lord John Wodehouse

1919 **Freebooters:** Sir John Ramsden, Capt. Ivor Buxton, Walter Buckmaster, Earl Rocksavage

1920 **Freebooters:** Capt. Godfrey Heseltine, Maj. Ivor Buxton, Walter Buckmaster, Lord John Wodehouse

1921 **Freebooters:** Duque de Peñaranda, Thomas Hitchcock Jr., Walter Buckmaster, Lord John Wodehouse

1922 **Argentine Polo Federation:** Juan Miles, Juan Nelson, David Miles, Luis Lacey

1923 **Robots:** Lord Albert Dalmeny, Earle W. Hopping, Lord Cholmondeley, Maj. John Harrison

1924 **Eastcott:** Earle W. Hopping, John A.E. Traill, Maj. Frank Hurndall, Maj. John Harrison

1925 **Jodhpur:** Thakur Prithi Singh, Capt. Austin Williams, Rao Rajah Hanut Singh, Thakur Ram Singh

1926 **Harlequins:** Capt. Richard McCreery, Walter S. McCreery, Wing Cdr. Percival Wise, Lord John Wodehouse

1927 **Hurricanes:** Stephen Sanford, Capt. Charles Roark, Wing Cdr. Percival Wise, Maj. John Harrison

1928 **Hurricanes:** Stephen Sanford, Capt. Charles Roark, Desmond Miller, Maj. John Harrison

1929 **El Gordo:** Duque de Peñaranda, Earle W. Hopping, Marqués de Villabrágima, John A.E. Traill

1930 **Hurricanes:** Stephen Sanford, Gerald Balding, Capt. Charles Roark, Col. Percival Wise

1931 **Merchiston:** John A.E. Traill, John Sanderson, Capt. H. Noel Scott Robson, Humphrey Guinness

1932 **Osmaston:** Sir Ian Walker, Capt. Charles Roark, Capt. G. Errol Prior-Palmer, Maj. John Harrison

1933 **Jaipur:** Prithi Singh, Abhey Singh, Hanut Singh, Maharajah of Jaipur

1934 **Aurora:** Harold Talbot, Elmer Boeseke, Seymour Knox, William Post

1935 **Kashmir:** Maj. Gen. Nawab Khusru Jung, Capt. Charles Roark, Percival Sanger, Maharajah of Kashmir

1936 **Templeton:** Michael Phipps, James Mills, Winston Guest, Robert Strawbridge

1937 **Goulburn:** C. Robertson Skene, Geoffrey Ashton, James Ashton, Robert Ashton

1938 **Texas Rangers:** Charles Wrightsman, Cecil Smith, Aidan Roark, Eric Tyrrell-Martin

1939 **Jaguars:** Capt. Nigel Dugdale, Hon. W. Keith Rous, Hon. John Hamilton-Russell, Capt. Humphrey Guinness

Inter-Regimental Tournament

Instituted in 1878 for a cup given annually by the Hurlingham Club, at first called "the Waterloo Cup." This is the oldest polo tournament in the world.

1878 **5th Lancers:** Julian Spicer, George R. Tufton, Archibald Cosmo Little, Llewellyn Heywood Jones, Capt. Richard St. Leger Moore

1879 **5th Lancers:** Capt. Edward G. Paley, Capt. Joseph S. Benyon, Julian Spicer, A. Cosmo Little, Llewellyn Heywood Jones

1880 **16th Lancers:** Henry R.L. Howard, James M. Babington, Frederick G. Blair, John G.A. Baird, Windham H. Wyndham-Quin

1881 **16th Lancers:** James M. Babington, Frederick G. Blair, John G.A. Baird, Windham H. Wyndham-Quin, Julian Oswald, William B. Browne

1882 **5th Lancers:** A. Cosmo Little, Llewellyn Heywood Jones, Capt. George R. Tufton, Capt. Julian Spicer

1883 **7th Hussars:** Hon. Richard T. Lawley, Thomas Hone, Maj. John L. Hunt, Capt. Robert Roper

1884 **7th Hussars:** Hon. Richard T. Lawley, Thomas Hone, Maj. John L. Hunt, Capt. Robert Roper

1885 **7th Hussars:** Maj. John L. Hunt, Capt. Robert Roper, Thomas Hone, Douglas Haig

1886 **7th Hussars:** Capt. Thomas Hone, George A.L. Carew, Douglas Haig, Capt. Hon. Richard T. Lawley

1887 **5th Lancers:** Llewellyn Heywood Jones, Capt. A. Cosmo Little, Basil St. J. Mundy, Capt. Julian Spicer

1888 **10th Hussars:** Arthur Hughes-Onslow, Edward W.D. Baird, Capt. Charles S. Greenwood, Capt. Hon. Herbert T. Allsop

1889 **9th Lancers:** Capt. Walter K.W. Jenner, Capt. Malcolm O. Little, Capt. Forrester F. Colvin, Capt. Edward L. Lamont

1890 **9th Lancers:** Capt. Forrester F. Colvin, Capt. Walter K.W. Jenner, Capt. Malcolm O. Little, Capt. Edward L. Lamont

1891 **9th Lancers:** Capt. Walter K.W. Jenner, Capt. Hon. Claude H.C. Willoughby, Capt. Forrester F. Colvin, Maj. Edward L. Lamont

1892 **13th Hussars:** Capt. Ernest W.N. Pedder, Duncan F. Robertson-Aikman, Francis H. Wise, Capt. Kenneth MacLaren

1893 **10th Hussars:** Lord George W. Montagu-Douglas-Scott, Capt. Charles T.McM. Kavanagh, Lord William A. Cavendish-Bentinck, Hon. Thomas W. Brand

1894 **13th Hussars:** Capt. Ernest W.N. Pedder, John F. Church, Francis H. Wise, Capt. Kenneth MacLaren

1895 **13th Hussars:** Capt. Ernest W.N. Pedder, John F. Church, Francis H. Wise, Capt. Kenneth MacLaren

1896 **9th Lancers:** David G.M. Campbell, George P. Ellison, Capt. Walter K.W. Jenner, Lord Charles H. Bentinck

1897 **Inniskillings:** Frederick A.B. Fryer, George K. Ansell, Neil W. Haig, Maj. Michael F. Rimington

1898 **Inniskillings:** Holmes C. Higgin, George K. Ansell, Neil W. Haig, Maj. Michael F. Rimington

1899 **7th Hussars:** John Vaughn, Capt. Hon. John G.H.H. Beresford, Maj. George A.L. Carew, Maj. Robert M. Poore

1900 Not played. Boer War.

1901 Not played. Boer War.

1902 Not played. Boer War.

1903 **17th Lancers:** Capt. Ronald J.W. Carden, Maj. William A. Tilney, Alan F. Fletcher, Lt. Col. Bertram P. Portal

1904 **17th Lancers:** Capt. Ronald J.W. Carden, Maj. William A. Tilney, Alan F. Fletcher, Lt. Col. Bertram P. Portal

1905 **Inniskillings:** Capt. George T. Gibson, Maj. George K. Ansell, Capt. Ewing Paterson, Maj. Neil W. Haig

1906 **20th Hussars:** John S. Cawley, Carlyle McG. Dunbar, Capt. Harold C. Hessey, Bernard A.P. Schreiber

1907 **20th Hussars:** John S. Cawley, Bernard A.P. Schreiber, Capt. Harold C. Hessey, Capt. Harry Romer Lee

1908 **11th Hussars:** Francis H. Sutton, Capt. Percy D. Fitzgerald, Michael L. Lakin, Capt. Charles L. Rome

1909 **11th Hussars:** Maj. Thomas T. Pitman, Capt. Percy D. Fitzgerald, Michael L. Lakin, Capt. Francis H. Sutton

1910 **Royal Horse Guards:** Capt. Geoffrey V.S. Bowlby, Capt. Lord Alastair Innes-Ker, Capt. Harold E. Brassey, John F. Harrison

1911 **4th Dragoon Guards:** Capt. Adrian Carton de Wiart, Capt. Charles B. Hornby, Maj. Brownlow H.H. Mathew-Lannowe, Capt. Charles F. Hunter

1912 **Royal Horse Guards:** Capt. Geoffrey V.S. Bowlby, Capt. Lord Alastair Innes-Ker, Capt. Harold E. Brassey, Capt. John F. Harrison

1913 **15th Hussars:** Brian Osborne, Capt. John D.Y. Bingham, Capt. Frederick W. Barrett, Matthew A. Muir

1914 **12th Lancers:** Edward H. Leatham, Capt. Thomas R. Badger, Basil N. Nicholas, Richard S.W.R. Wyndham-Quin

1915 Not played. World War I.

1916 Not played. World War I.

1917 Not played. World War I.

1918 Not played. World War I.

1919 Not played. Replaced by the Military Cup, won by Northamptonshire Yeomanry: Lord

Hugh Stalbridge, Lt. Col. Sir Charles Lowther, Maj. Patteson W. Nickalls and Capt. John G. Lowther.

1920 **17th Lancers:** Lt. Col. Teignmouth P. Melvill, Capt. Herbert B. Turnor, Maj. Vivian N. Lockett, Capt. Dennis C. Boles

1921 **17th Lancers:** Lt. Col. Teignmouth P. Melvill, Capt. Herbert B. Turnor, Maj. Vivian N. Lockett, Capt. Dennis C. Boles

1922 **17th Lancers:** Lt. Col. Teignmouth P. Melvill, Capt. Herbert B. Turnor, Maj. Vivian N. Lockett, Capt. Dennis C. Boles

1923 **17th/21st Lancers:** Lt. Col. Teignmouth P. Melvill, Capt. Clement C. Lister, Maj. Vivian N. Lockett, Capt. Dennis C. Boles

1924 **17th/21st Lancers:** Lt. Col. Teignmouth P. Melvill, Desmond C.J. Miller, Maj. Vivian N. Lockett, Capt. Dennis C. Boles

1925 **17th/21st Lancers:** Ronald B.B.B. Cooke, Hugh C. Walford, Maj. Vivian N. Lockett, Capt. Dennis C. Boles

1926 **17th/21st Lancers:** Ronald B.B.B. Cooke, Hugh C. Walford, Maj. Vivian N. Lockett, Capt. Dennis C. Boles

1927 **Royal Artillery:** Capt. Bryan J. Fowler, Capt. Humphrey G. Morrison, John C. Campbell, Capt. Charles W. Allfrey

1928 **17th/21st Lancers:** Ronald B.B.B. Cooke, Desmond C.J. Miller, Henry W. Forester, Capt. Dennis C. Boles

1929 **17th/21st Lancers:** Ronald B.B.B. Cooke, Hugh C. Walford, Desmond C.J. Miller, Lt. Col. Vivian N. Lockett

1930 **17th/21st Lancers:** Ronald B.B.B. Cooke, Hugh C. Walford, Desmond C.J. Miller, Lt. Col. Vivian N. Lockett

1931 **Queen's Bay:** Capt. George W.C. Draffen, Capt. Alexander H. Barclay, Capt. George H. Fanshawe, Capt. Evelyn D. Fanshawe

1932 **Royal Artillery:** Capt. Bryan J. Fowler, Capt. Horace C. Elton, Capt. Humphrey G. Morrison, Capt. John C. Campbell

1933 **Royal Scots Greys:** Massey H.E. Lopes, Roland L. Findlay, Humphrey P. Guinness, Maj. Cyril H. Gaisford St. Lawrence

1934 **7th Hussars:** Capt. Frederick W. Bass, Capt. Richard B. Sheppard, Capt. Geoffrey Fielden, Lt. Col. Gabriel C.A. Breitmeyer

1935 **3rd Brigade RHA:** Capt. Bryan J. Fowler, Guy P. Gregson, Hugh W.L. Cowan, Maj. John C. Campbell

1936 **12th Lancers:** George J. Kidston, Lt. Col. Richard L. McCreery, Richard W. Hobson, Andrew M. Horsbrugh-Porter

1937 **10th Hussars:** Capt. Michael N.E. Macmullen, Capt. Charles B.C. Harvey, Capt. David Dawnay, Capt. John P. Archer-Shee

1938 **Royal Scots Greys:** Capt. Lord Massey Roborough, Capt. Harry R. Mackenson, Capt. Roland L. Findlay, Capt. Humphrey P. Guinness

1939 **10th Hussars:** Capt. Michael N.E. Macmullen, John W. Malet, Capt David Dawnay, Capt. John P. Archer-Shee

1958 **7th Hussars:** Maj. Hilary Hook, Capt. William H. Richardson, Capt. Michael Q. Fraser, Lt. Col. Charles T. Llewellen Palmer

1959 **Royal Wiltshire Yeomanry:** Theo Douglas Dampney, Lt. Col. Hugh Trefusis Brassey, James Ian Morrison, Lt. Col. Martin St. J.V. Gibbs, Maj. Michael Colvin Watson

1960 **3rd Royal Horse Artillery:** Maj. William D. Mangham, Paul M. Withers, Lt. Col. Philip T. Tower, Capt. Jeremy H. Hemming

1961 **3rd Royal Horse Artillery:** Capt. Jeremy H. Hemming, Capt. Stephen D. Pettifer, Paul M. Withers, Capt. John D.G. Nicholson

1962 **Royal Horse Guards:** Maj. Peter A. Lendrum, Capt. John Hugh Pitman, Capt. Lord Patrick Beresford, Lt. Col. Harry S. Hopkinson

1963 **Life Guards:** Richard Head, Nicholas V.S. Paravicini, Capt. Ronald I. Ferguson, William T.V. Loyd

1964 **Royal Artillery:** John H. Mead, Maj. Aubrey A. Fielder, Maj. Richard B.W. Barber, Maj. Jasper M. Browell

1965 **Queen's Own Hussars:** Capt. Timothy W. Ritson, Michael Q. Fraser, Capt. Malcolm J. Sherwin, Capt. Charles A.R. Lockhart

1966 **Queen's Own Hussars:** David I. McConnel, Capt. Malcolm J. Sherwin, Capt. Charles A.R. Lockhart, Capt. Timothy W. Ritson

1967 **Queen's Own Hussars:** Ian W. Farquhar, David I. McConnel, Capt. Malcolm J. Sherwin, Capt. Charles A.R. Lockhart

1968 **Life Guards:** Capt. Simon T.C. Hanbury, Capt. Victor R.A.S. Law, Maj. Nicholas V.S. Paravicini, Maj. Ronald I. Ferguson

1969 **3rd Carabineers:** Capt. John R. Bower, Richard C.S. Mahoney, Maj. Charles Roland S. Notley, Capt. Peter C.E. Fishbourne

1970 **Royal Hussars:** Maj. Hon. George W.M. Norrie, Capt. David G. Dollar, Maj. Hugh Dawnay, Peter V. Scholfield

1971 **Blues and Royals:** Maj. Brian J. Lockhart, Capt. Andrew H. Parker Bowles, Maj. J. Hugh Pitman, Maj. William S.H. Boucher

1972 **17th/21st Lancers:** Michael J.B. Amoore, Capt. Fiennes M. Strang-Steele, Lt. Col. Arthur R. Douglas-Nugent, Capt. Christopher H. Churton

1973 **Queen's Own Hussars:** Harold M.C. Cunningham, Maj. Charles A.R. Lockhart, Ian W. Farquhar, Capt. Hugh S.R. Boucher

1974 **Blues and Royals:** Nigel Haddon-Paton, Maj. John Hugh Pitman, Maj. Andrew H. Parker Bowles, Lt. Col. William S.H. Boucher

1975 **Blues and Royals:** Lt. Col. J. Hugh Pitman, Maj. Andrew H. Parker Bowles, Nigel Haddon-Paton, T.L. Somerville Livingstone-Learmonth

1976 **Welsh Guards:** Brian J.D. Collins, Lt. Col. Samuel C.C. Gaussen, Capt. C. Redmond Watt, Guardsman E. Jaesopp

1977 **RMA Sandhurst:** Anthony W. Ballard, Capt. Miles T. Ward, Capt. C. Redmond Watt, Maj. Andrew H. Parker Bowles

1978 **Blues and Royals:** Maj. Andrew H. Parker Bowles, Lt. Col. Brian J. Lockhart, Dennis C. Darley, Capt. T.L. Somerville Livingstone-Learmonth

1979 **Life Guards:** Capt. Peter R.L. Hunter, Charles H.N. Graham, Capt. Iain S. Forbes-Cocknell, James L. Hewitt

1980 **Welsh Guards:** Capt. Simon D. Stephenson, Anthony W. Ballard, Maj. C. Redmond Watt, Lt. Col. John F. Rickett

1981 **Welsh Guards:** Capt. Simon D. Stephenson, Anthony W. Ballard, Maj. C. Redmond Watt, Michael K.O. Richardson

1982 **Royal Irish Guards:** Robert A. Noone, Maj. Marcus D. Pilleau, Capt. Jeremy A A Mains, Capt. Adrian C.T. Blackmore

1983 **Welsh Guards:** Capt. Simon D. Stephenson, Anthony W. Ballard, Lt. Col. John F. Rickett, Maj. C. Redmond Watt

1984 **Royal Hussars:** Capt. David P. Wiggin, Maj. John R.D. Kaye, Maj. John J. Rogers, Capt. Peter R.C. Flach

1985 **14th/20th Hussars:** Nigel D.F. Jackson, James B.M. Gordon, Maj. David J.B. Woodd, Maj. Michael J.H. Vickery

1986 **14th/20th Hussars:** James B.M. Gordon, Nigel D.F. Jackson, Maj. David J.B. Woodd, Maj. Michael J.H. Vickery

1987 **14th/20th Hussars:** Michael K. Milne, Rupert Gordon, Maj. David J.B. Woodd, Maj. Michael J.H. Vickery

1988 **Welsh Guards:** Capt. Michael K.O. Richardson, Capt. Anthony W. Ballard, Lt. Col. C. Redmond Watt, Capt. Simon D. Stephenson

1989 **Royal Navy:** Cdr. Robert L. Guy, Capt. Colin L. MacGregor, Lt. Cdr. Richard W. Mason, Lt. Cdr. Philip J. Barber

1990 **Welsh Guards:** Capt. M.K. Oliver Richardson, Maj. Anthony W. Ballard, Lt. Col. C. Redmond Watt, Maj. Simon D. Stephenson

1991 **Welsh Guards:** Capt. M.K. Oliver Richardson, Maj. Anthony W. Ballard, Lt. Col. C. Redmond Watt, Maj. Simon D. Stephenson

1992 **Royal Wessex Yeomanry:** Capt. Paul H. Lucas, James B.M. Gordon, Timothy O. Verdon, Capt. Alexander W. Dabell

1993 **Household Cavalry:** Maj. Hon. James H.A. Broughton, Capt. Anthony J.P. Woodward, Andrew M.K. Barlow, Maj. Hon. Miles R.W. Watson

1994 **Life Guards:** Capt. Christopher N. Mitford-Slade, Capt. William M. Dwerryhouse, Capt. Andrew M.K. Barlow, Maj. Peter R.L. Hunter

1995 **Household Cavalry:** Capt. Jonathan A.L. Wilson, Andrew Fox-Pitt, Capt. Andrew M.K. Barlow, Capt. J. Peter Barclay

1996 **Royal Navy:** Lt. Ian G. Annett, Maj. William D. Peck, Cdr. Richard W. Mason, Capt. Peter Cameron

1997 **The Footguards:** Capt. Andrew F.R. James, Maj. James R. Hayward, Capt. Rupert S.M. Thorneloe, Maj. Michael G.C. O'Dwyer

1998 **RMA Sandhurst:** O/Ct. Nicholas Harrison, Maj. Gen. Anthony G. Denaro, Mark P.F. Dollar, Capt. Alexander D.T. Hawes

1999 **Household Cavalry:** Maj. Peter R.L. Hunter, Rupert Lewis, Mark P.F. Dollar, Capt. Andrew Fox-Pitt

2000 **Household Cavalry:** Lt. Col. Stuart Cowen, Capt. Rupert Lewis, Capt. Andrew Fox-Pitt, Mark P.F. Dollar

2001 **Light Dragoons:** Matthew G. Eyre-Brook, Capt. R. Austen Burden-Cooper, Timothy Smail, Capt. Tom Moon

2002 **Household Cavalry:** Capt. Nicholas Harrison, Capt. Rupert Lewis, Capt. Mark P.F. Dollar, Capt. Andrew Fox-Pitt

2003 **RMA Sandhurst:** O/Ct. Lorien McCallum, O/Ct. Harry Wallace, O/Ct. Benjamin J. Vestey, Capt. Crispin West

2004 **Household Cavalry:** O/Ct. Lorien McCallum, Maj. Peter R.L. Hunter, O/Ct. Benjamin J. Vestey, Maj. Andrew Fox-Pitt

2005 **Household Cavalry:** Capt. James St. John-Price, Capt. Rupert Lewis, Benjamin J. Vestey, Capt. Mark P.F. Dollar

2006 **Household Cavalry:** Lt. Lorien McCallum, Cornet HRH Harry Wales, Maj. Rupert Lewis, Capt. Benjamin J. Vestey

2007 **Royal Wessex Yeomanry:** Capt. Piers Heelis, Capt. James B.M. Gordon, Capt. Timothy O. Verdon, O/Ct. James Horton

2008 **Royal Wessex Yeomanry:** Capt. Piers Heelis, Lt. Leon Allen, Capt. Timothy O. Verdon, Capt. Robert Gourley

2009 **Household Cavalry:** Lt. Col. Crispin Lockhart, Maj. Rupert Lewis, Capt. Jack Mann, HRH Lt. Harry Wales

2010 **Royal Navy:** Lt. Cdr. Allan Wilson, Sub Lt. Hiro Suzuki, Cdr. Richard Mason, Capt. Adrian Aplin

All Ireland Open Cup

Open to all bona fide club, county, Irish County Polo Club Union, Regimental and Vicere-gal teams. A bona fide club, according to the Hurlingham Committee's definition, is one which has a ground of its own and regular playing members.

1878 **7th Royal Fusiliers:** Henry Mansel-Pleydell, Lord Percy St. Maur, Robert Saunders, George Hayhurst, Francis Sartoris

1879 **7th Hussars:** Capt. Robert Roper, Capt. Phillips, Hon. Richard Lawley, Lord Alfred Lumley, John Hunt

1880 **Royal Scots Greys:** William Middleton, William Hippisley, John Torrens, Richard Wolfe

1881 **5th Lancers:** Christian Combe, George Tufton, Julian Spicer, Llewellyn Jones

1882 **All Ireland PC:** Capt. William Montague, Herbert Dugdale, Geoffrey Hone, John Watson

1883 **Carlow:** William Edge, Richard Wolfe, Thomas Hone, John Watson

1884 **5th Lancers:** Basil Mundy, John Sinclair, Capt. Llewellyn Jones, Capt Julian Spicer

1885 **Freebooters:** William Edge, W. Anderson, James Jameson, John Watson

1886 **Freebooters:** Douglas Haig, William Edge, Capt. Hon. Richard Lawley, John Watson

1887 **All Ireland PC:** J.D. Calley, Capt. James Babington, James Locke, John Watson

1888 **All Ireland PC:** James Reilly, Capt. George Middleton, James Jameson, John Watson

1889 **Freebooters:** Capt. Francis Fetherstonhaugh, James Jameson, H. Thomas Fenwick, John Watson

1890 **All Ireland PC:** James Reilly, Capt. Thomas Hone, James Jameson, John Watson

1891 **13th Hussars:** Capt. Ernest Pedder, Francis Wise, Duncan Robertson Aikman, Capt. Kenneth MacLaren

1892 **9th Lancers:** Capt. Walter Jenner, Capt. Malcolm Little, Capt. Forrester Colvin, Maj. Edward Lamont

1893 **13th Hussars:** Capt. Ernest Pedder, Francis Wise, Duncan Robertson Aikman, Capt. Kenneth MacLaren

1894 **15th Hussars:** Capt. Frederick Dalgety, Capt. Henry Dundas, Capt. Basil Mundy, Capt. Tyrrell de Crespigny

1895 **Freebooters:** Lord Shrewsbury, Alfred Rawlinson, Walter Buckmaster, Capt. Bernard Daly

1896 **13th Hussars:** Capt. Ernest Pedder, John Church, Francis Wise, Capt. Kenneth MacLaren

1897 **Rugby:** Charles Miller, George Miller, Edward Miller, W.J. Drybrough

1898 **Rugby:** Frank Hargreaves, George Miller, Edward Miller, W.J. Drybrough

1899 **Inniskilling Dragoons:** Capt. Camborne Paynter, George Ansell, Holmes C. Higgin, Neil Haig

1900 **Freebooters:** Frank Hargreaves, Capt. Hon. John Beresford (Oliver Haig), Frederick Freake, John Watson

1901 **Nomads:** Patteson Nickalls, Capt. Hollwey Steeds, George Miller, Charles Miller

1902 **Wanderers:** John Hargreaves, Maj. George Ansell, Frederick Freake, Capt. Neil Haig

1903 **Wanderers:** Alfred Rawlinson, Frederick Freake, Capt. Neil Haig, Gen. Michael Rimington

1904 **Woodpeckers:** William Bass, Hon. Aubrey Hastings, Capt. Herbert Wilson, Capt. John H. Lloyd (Edward Miller)

1905 **Irish County PCU:** Auston Rotherham, Samuel Watt, Maj. Charles O'Hara, Percy O'Reilly

1906 **Woodpeckers:** William Bass, Hon. Aubrey Hastings, Capt. Herbert Wilson, Capt. John H. Lloyd

1907 **Rugby:** Duke of Westminster, Riversdale Grenfell, George Miller, Charles Miller
1908 **Old Cantabs:** Isaac Bell, Frederick Freake, Walter Buckmaster, Lord John Wodehouse
1909 **Woodpeckers:** Sir William Bass, Hon. Aubrey Hastings, Capt. Herbert Wilson, Capt. John H. Lloyd
1910 **Woodpeckers:** Sir William Bass, Hon. Aubrey Hastings, Capt. Herbert Wilson, Capt. John H. Lloyd
1911 **Eaton:** Cecil Nickalls, Duke of Westminster, Patteson Nickalls, Earl of Rocksavage
1912 Abandoned due to wet weather
1913 **Hillmorton:** Harry Rich, William Balding, John Drage, Stanley Barton
1919 **Hillmorton:** Capt. William Goulding, John McCann, William Balding, Asa Balding
1920 **All Ireland Club:** John Trench, Capt. Charles Roark, Capt. Richard Wyndham-Quin, Edmund Roark
1921 **Hillbrook:** John Trench, Capt. William Goulding, William Balding, Asa Balding

County Cup

Instituted by the Hurlingham Club. Control of tournament undertaken and Challenge Cup presented in 1898 by the County Polo Association.

1885 **Gloucestershire:** Edward Kenyon Stow, Lord Harrington, Frank G. Matthews, T.S. Baxter
1886 **Gloucestershire:** Edward Kenyon Stow, Lord Harrington, Frank G. Matthews, Malcolm Little
1887 **Derbyshire:** Edward Kenyon Stow, Lord Harrington, Gerald Hardy, Capt. Francis Herbert
1888 **Kent:** Robert Stewart-Savile, Capt. Edwin A.H. Alderson, Maj. Cecil W. Peters, George Russell
1889 **Barton:** Gerald Hardy, John Reid Walker, William Hall Walker, Lord Harrington
1890 **Berkshire:** Capt. Victor J.F. Ferguson, Henry T. Fenwick, Hon. William H. Lambton, Capt. Julian Spicer
1891 **Liverpool:** G. Herbert Pilkington, C.E. Mason, Alfred Tyrer, William H. Walker
1892 **Meath:** William Gore Lambarde, Frederick H.W. Fetherstonhaugh, James O. Jameson, Thomas Hone, John Watson
1893 **Edinburgh:** William Younger, Cortlandt Gordon Mackenzie, W.J. Drybrough, Thomas Drybrough
1894 **Edinburgh:** William Younger, Francis Egerton Green, W.J. Drybrough, Thomas Drybrough
1895 **Rugby:** Lord Shrewsbury, George Miller, Edward Miller, Capt. Denis St. G. Daly
1896 **Stansted:** Guy Gilbey, Gerald Gold, Arthur Gold, Walter Buckmaster
1897 **Rugby:** Walter Neilson, Frank Mackey, Lord Shrewsbury, Capt. Gordon Renton
1898 **Chislehurst:** Cecil Nickalls, Henry Savill, Morres Nickalls, Patteson Nickalls
1899 **Stansted:** Philip Gold, Capt. George B. Gosling, Tresham Gilbey, Gerald Gold
1900 **Rugby:** John Drage, Comte Jean de Madré, Keith Marsham, Sir Humphrey de Trafford (Edgar S. Prince)
1901 **Eden Park:** Harry Rich, Percy Bullivant, Hubert Marsham, Hugh Cardwell
1902 **Eden Park:** Leonard Bucknell, John Clement de Las Casas, Alfredo de Las Casas, Hugh Cardwell
1903 **Blackmore Vale:** Arthur Tyrwhitt-Drake, John Hargreaves, Frank Hargreaves, Capt. Geoffrey S. Phipps-Hornby (Manuel de Las Casas)
1904 **Cirencester:** James Mason, Hon. Aubrey Hastings, Reginald Barker, John Adamthwaite

1905 **Rugby:** James Pearce, John Drage, Walter Balding, Hon. Osmond Hastings

1906 **Rugby:** James Pearce, William Bellville, John Drage, Hon. Osmond Hastings

1907 **Hutton:** Malcolm Pilkington, C.K. Carr, Laurence Carr, Raymond Courage

1908 **Wirral:** Thomas Royden, George Lockett, Stanley Watson, Frederick Wignall

1909 **Kingsbury:** Julian Winans, Harry Rich, Gordon Withers, Paul Winans

1910 **Salibury Plain:** Capt. Walter Long, Malcolm Borwick, John Readman, Maj. Charles Bulkeley-Johnson

1911 **Cirencester:** Walter Burdon, Hon. Aubrey Hastings, Hugh Baker, James Mason

1912 **Vale of White Horse** (Swindon): Maurice Kingscote, Hon. Aubrey Hastings, A. Noel Edwards, Jesse Gouldsmith

1913 **Norwich:** Lt. Edward H. Leatham, Capt. T. Reginald Badger, Lt. Basil Nicholas, Frederick Wormald

1914 **Wellington:** Kenneth Palmer, Guy Hargreaves, Capt. Frank Hurndall, Lt. Col. Thomas Pitman

1919 **Wellington:** Lt. Col. Henry Playdell-Railston, Maj. Hugh Ashton, Brig. Gen. Otway C. Herbert, Maj. Francis Penn-Curzon

1920 **Aldershot:** Capt. Hubert Chinnock, Lt. Col. Edward Peel, Lt. Col. William Winwood, Brig. Gen. Antony E.W. Harman

1921 **Wellington:** Lt. Leslie Ormrod, Guy Hargreaves, Col. Comdt. Antony E.W. Harman, Lt. Col. George Philippi

1922 **Rugby:** Colin Patrick, John Drage, Eric Forwood, Maj. John Lowther

1923 **Cheltenham:** Capt. William McMullen, Capt. Walter Steel, Capt. Charles Roark, W.F. Holman

1924 **Rugby:** Maj. William Styles, Capt. Arnold Wills, Eric Forwood, Lt. Robert Greenshields

1925 **Fleet:** Lt. John Hirsch, Lt. Leslie Ormrod, Capt. George Fanshawe, Capt. Francis Spooner

1926 **Fleet:** Capt. Hubert Chinnock, Lt. Desmond Miller, Lt. Col. Teignmouth Melvill, Capt. Francis Bucher

1927 **King's Dragoon Guards:** Maj. Edward Sprot, Maj. Thomas Gladstone, Maj. Herbert Hatfeild, Capt. Robert Greenshields

1928 **Rugby:** Charles Aldridge, Walter Duckworth, Herbert Sutton, Capt. Clement Barton

1929 **Aldershot** (KDG): John Wilder, Maj. Edward Sprot, Maj. Herbert Hatfeild, Capt. Robert Greenshields

1930 **Rugby:** Charles Aldridge, Capt. R.C. Over, Capt. Geoffrey Shaw, Eric Forwood

1931 **Beaufort:** Capt. Maurice Kingscote, Alexander Bullock, Capt. Frank Spicer, Maj. Trevor Horn

1932 **Aldershot:** Charles Davies-Gilbert, Capt. Frederick Byass, Capt. Geoffrey Fielden, Maj. Gabriel Breitmeyer

1933 **Toulston:** J.F. Holdsworth, Raymond Hill-Forster, Capt. Walter Griffiths, William Riley-Smith

1934 **Bordon** (19th Field Brigade, RA): John Evatt, Capt. Charles Rugge-Price, William Holman, Maj. Charles Allfrey

1935 **Aldershot:** Capt. Bryan Fowler, Capt. Horace Elton, Hugh Cowan, Maj. William Morgan

1936 **Toulston:** Lt. Col. Cecil Emsley, Thomas Paisley, Raymond Hill-Forster, Capt. Walter Griffiths

1937 **Rugby:** William Horbury, Harold Freeborn, Eric Forwood, C. Drage

1938 **Tidworth:** Lt. Leslie Richmond, Lt. John Malet, Capt. Michael Macmullen, Lt. Robert Kaye

1939 **Aldershot Command** (4th Dragoon Guards): Lt. Thomas Bell, Lt. Guy Cunard, Lt. Claud Stretton Dixon, Capt. Thomas Cooper
1951 **Beechwood:** William Wallace, Harold Freeborn, Brig. Henry Young, Juan J. Reynal
1952 **Polo Cottage:** Lord David Brecknock, Fred Withers, Hanut Singh, Col. James Pell-Archer
1953 **Cotswold Park:** Lt. Col. Martin St. J. V. Gibbs, Col. Alastair Gibb, Gerald Balding, Maj. Michael Watson
1954 **Henley:** Capt. Michael Cain, Sinclair Hill, Clement Barton, Ernesto Lalor
1955 **Polo Cottage:** Fred Withers, William Riley-Smith, Maj. Claud Stretton Dixon, Maj. Gen. David Dawnay
1956 **Ancient Mariners:** Cdr. Robert de Pass, Capt. Peter Wilson, Lt. Col. Alec Harper, Lt. J.W. Mathwin Maunder
1957 **Media Luna:** Juan P. Nelson, Luis Nelson, Arturo Reynal, Lt. Col. Peter Dollar
1958 **Silver Leys:** Arthur Boyd Gibbins, John Lucas, Capt. Kishen Singh, Rasik Jaitha
1959 **Jersey Lilies:** Maharajah of Cooch Behar, John Lucas, Charles Smith-Ryland, Eric Moller
1960 **Silver Leys:** Arthur Boyd Gibbins, Richard Harding, Brian Bethell, Maj. Kishen Singh (Risaldar Gaje Singh)
1961 **Jersey Lilies:** Kumwar Bijai Singh, Eric Moller, Hanut Singh, Jeremy Barber
1962 **Ambersham:** Lt. H.S. (Billy) Sodhi, João Adao, Lt. Col. Alec Harper, Ronald Driver
1963 **Cirencester Park:** Maj. John Mayne, Eduardo Rojas Lanusse, Jack R. Williams, Eduardo Moore
1964 **Jersey Lilies:** Ricardo Díaz Dale, Patrick Kemple, Hanut Singh, Eric Moller
1965 **Cholmondeley:** Lord Rocksavage, Peter Hunter, Ricardo Díaz Dale, Eduardo Moore
1966 **Todham:** Ronald Driver, Rodolfo Lagos Mármol, Ricardo Díaz Dale, Carlos Debaisieux
1967 **Buccaneers:** Lord Samuel Vestey, Capt. John Macdonald-Buchanan, Eduardo Moore, Peter Gifford
1968 **Buccaneers:** J. Robert Hodgkinson, Lord Samuel Vestey, Clement Barton, Eduardo Moore
1969 **Jersey Lilies:** Eric Moller, Juan R. Moore, Julian Hipwood, Maj. Pradeep Mehra
1970 **Lushill:** Capt. Frederick Barker, Peter Gifford, Ricardo Arechavaleta, Jack Williams
1971 **San Flamingo:** John E.A. Kidd, Timothy Harding, Julian Hipwood, Ronald Driver
1972 **Los Locos:** Mrs. Claire Tomlinson, Capt. Simon Tomlinson, John Lucas, Hon. George Bathurst
1973 **San Flamingo:** John E.A. Kidd, Timothy Harding, Julian Hipwood, Ronald Driver
1974 **Foxcote:** Lord Samuel Vestey, Hon. Mark Vestey, Aníbal García, John Horswell
1975 **Foxcote:** Robert Bayston, Hon. Mark Vestey, Juan R. Moore, Lord Samuel Vestey
1976 **Langley Priors:** John Hine, José Luis Merlos, George Barlow, Daniel Devrient
1977 **Los Locos:** Joey Newton, Mrs. Claire Tomlinson, Capt. Simon Tomlinson, Héctor Barrantes
1978 **Pahang:** Prince Abdul Rahman, Lord Patrick Beresford, Eduardo Moore, Dougal Lang
1979 **Falcons:** Alexandre Ebeid, Guillermo Olivero, Juan B. Castilla, Juan J. Díaz Alberdi
1980 **Chopendoz:** Philip Elliott, Eduardo Moore, Bryan Morrison, Hal Henderson
1981 **Los Locos:** Mrs. Claire Tomlinson, Capt. Simon Tomlinson, Cody Forsyth, Martin Brown
1982 **Ewen House:** Andrew Hine, John Hine, Graham Thomas, Patrick Churchward
1983 **Ingwenya:** Nicki Hahn, John Horswell, Howard Hipwood, Ian Hunt
1984 **BBs:** Christian-Leopold Heppe, Capt. Michael Amoore, Maximiniano Errázuriz, Charles Seavill
1985 **Saracens:** Jock Green-Armitage, Andrew Hine, Cody Forsyth, John Kidd

1986　**Los Locos:** Antony Fanshawe, Eugene Fortugno, Mrs. Claire Tomlinson, Capt. Simon Tomlinson

1987　**Sladmore:** Alexander Brodie, Patrick McIlldowie, John Horswell, Edward Horswell

1988　**Sladmore:** Alexander Brodie, Patrick McIlldowie, John Horswell, Edward Horswell

1989　**Levitt:** Libor Krejci, Andrea Vianini, Alan Kent, Michael St. Aubyn

1990　**Rough Park:** Gordon Roddick, William Lucas, Stuart Mackenzie, Terry Hanlon

1991　**Panache:** Mike Rutherford, Francisco Marín Moreno, Alan Kent, George Milford Haven

1992　**Los Locos:** Mrs. Claire Tomlinson, Capt. Simon Tomlinson, Milo Fernández Araujo, Jack Kidd

1993　**Palmera:** Alexander Brodie, Roderick Wood, Howard Hipwood, Sheik Mohammed Alhamrani

1994　**Lambourne:** Jonathan Wade, William Hine, Francisco Marín Moreno, John Seabrook

1995　**Dubai:** Ali Saeed Albwardi, Robert Thame, William Lucas, Glen Gilmore

1996　**Palmera:** John Fisher, Roderick Wood, Julian Daniels, Ignacio Gonzalez

1997　**Laird:** Fergus Prentice, Jonathan Wade, William Lucas, Richard Britten-Long

1998　**Timbavati:** Jamie Dickson, Francisco Marín Moreno, Andrew Hine, Simon Grinstead

1999　**Los Locos:** Mark Tomlinson, Luke Tomlinson, Guillermo Willington, Mrs. Claire Tomlinson

2000　**Oaklands Park:** Martyn Ratcliffe, Oliver Hipwood, Roderick Williams, Roderick Matthews

2001　**Caballus:** Thomas Morley, Henry Brett, Andrew Hine, Bruce Merivale-Austin

2002　**Groeninghe:** Isabelle Hayen, Jonathan Good, Glen Gilmore, Thomas Morley

2003　**C.S. Brooks:** Senter Johnson, James Beim, Mark Tomlinson, Thomas Morley

2004　**Corramore:** Edward Magor, Ryan Pemble, John P. Clarkin, David Allen

2005　**Groeninghe:** Isabelle Hayen, Simon Keyte, Glen Gilmore, John Martin

2006　**Wildmoor:** Lord Richard Le Poer, Robert Archibald, James Beim, Mark Booth

2007　**Al Burak:** Sehr Ahmad, Max Charlton, John P. Clarkin, Gareth Evans

2008　**Los Locos:** Miss Emma Tomlinson, Sam Hopkinson, Mark Tomlinson, Mrs. Claire Tomlinson

2009　**Laird-Corovest:** Richard Britten-Long, George Meyrick, Glen Gilmore, Alan Kent

2010　**Laird:** Nicholas Britten-Long, George Meyrick, Henry Brett, Leroux Hendriks

Westchester Cup

Presented by the playing members of the Westchester Polo Club to be competed by teams representing the Hurlingham Club and the Westchester Polo Club. In 1911, a deed of gift transferred the trophy to the Polo Association of America.

1886　at Westchester Polo Club. **Hurlingham:** Thomas Hone, Hon. Richard Lawley, Malcolm Little, John Watson

1900　at Hurlingham Club. **Hurlingham:** Hon. John Beresford, Frederick Freake, Walter Buckmaster, John Watson

1902　at Hurlingham Club. **Hurlingham:** Cecil Nickalls, George Miller, Patteson Nickalls, Walter Buckmaster

1909　at Hurlingham Club. **America:** Lawrence Waterbury, James M. Waterbury, Harry P. Whitney, Devereux Milburn

1911　at Meadow Brook Club. **America:** Lawrence Waterbury, James M. Waterbury, Harry P. Whitney, Devereux Milburn

1913　at Meadow Brook Club. **America:** Louis Stoddard, Lawrence Waterbury, Harry P. Whitney, Devereux Milburn

1914 at Meadow Brook Club. **Great Britain:** Henry Tomkinson, Leslie Cheape, Frederick Barrett, Vivian Lockett

1921 at Hurlingham Club. **America:** Louis Stoddard, Thomas Hitchcock Jr., J. Watson Webb, Devereux Milburn

1924 at Meadow Brook Club. **America:** J. Watson Webb, Thomas Hitchcock Jr., Robert Strawbridge Jr., Devereux Milburn

1927 at Meadow Brook Club. **America:** J. Watson Webb, Thomas Hitchcock Jr., Malcolm Stevenson, Devereux Milburn

1930 at Meadow Brook Club. **America:** Eric Pedley, Earle A.S. Hopping, Thomas Hitchcock Jr., Winston Guest

1936 at Hurlingham Club. **America:** Eric Pedley, Michael Phipps, Stewart Iglehart, Winston Guest

1939 at Meadow Brook. **America:** Michael Phipps, Thomas Hitchcock Jr., Stewart Iglehart, Winston Guest

1992 at Guards Polo Club. **America:** John Gobin, Adam Snow, Owen Rinehart, Robert E. Walton

1997 at Guards Polo Club. **Great Britain:** William Lucas, Cody Forsyth, Howard Hipwood, Andrew Hine

2009 at International Palm Beach Polo Club. **Great Britain:** James Beim, Mark Tomlinson, Eduardo Novillo Astrada, Luke Tomlinson

Warwickshire Cup

Instituted in 1894 for a Challenge Cup presented to the Warwickshire Polo Club by the townspeople of Leamington. The tournament was dormant from 1914 until 1932 when Mr. Frank Hargreaves, the winning team's captain in 1913, presented the cup to the Roehampton Club to be played in a match between Roehampton and Hurlingham, or a visiting team from overseas. Competition for the Warwickshire Cup was resumed in 1959.

1984 **Mr. E.D. Miller's Team:** A.L. Bellville, Percy Leaf, H. Jasper Selwyn, Edward D. Miller

1895 **Mr. E.D. Miller's Team:** Walter J.H. Jones, Luis de Errazu, Hugh Scott Robson, Edward D. Miller

1896 **Rugby:** Walter J.H. Jones, Earl of Shrewsbury, George A. Miller, Edward D. Miller

1897 **Winwick:** Earl of Shrewsbury, Frederick M. Freake, Charles D. Miller, Alfred Rawlinson

1898 **Winwick:** George K. Ansell, Alfred Rawlinson, Neil W. Haig, Capt. Kenneth MacLaren

1899 **Old Cantabs:** Walter A. McCreery, Fredrick M. Freake, Walter S. Buckmaster, Godfrey Heseltine

1900 **Mr. W. Buckmaster's Team:** Frank J. Mackey, Frederick M. Freake, Walter S. Buckmaster, Maurice Raoul-Duval

1901 **Old Cantabs:** Godfrey Heseltine, Frederick M. Freake, Walter S. Buckmaster (Charles D. Miller), Frank Hargreaves

1902 **Mr. W. Buckmaster's Team:** John Drage, Frederick M. Freake, Walter S. Buckmaster, Frank Ellison

1903 **Stockton House:** Walter A. McCreary, W.D. Holden, Walter S. Buckmaster, Frank Bellville

1904 **Friz Hill:** Walter A. McCreary, John Hargreaves, Frank Hargreaves, Frederick M. Freake

1905 **Oakham House:** William V. Beatty, William Harrison, Frank Bellville, Maj. Arthur Pirie (Lord John Wodehouse)

1906 **Oakham House:** William V. Beatty, Capt. Leopold Jenner, Capt. Guy Mort, Maj. Arthur Pirie

1907 **Tigers:** Comte Jean de Madré, Leslie St. C. Cheape, Capt. Frederick W. Barrett, Capt. Brownlow Mathew-Lannowe

1908 **Old Cantabs:** Norman Loder, Isaac Bell, Frederick M. Freake, Lord John Wodehouse

1909 **Tigers:** Comte Jean de Madré, Capt. Hon. Denis Y. Bingham, Capt. Brownlow Mathew-Lannowe, Col. Chunda Singh

1910 **Tigers:** Comte Jean de Madré, Capt. Henry A. Tomkinson, William Llewellen Palmer, Capt. Charles Hunter

1911 **Thornby:** Capt. John P. Fitzgerald, James Sydney Mason, Sir Charles Lowther, Patteson Nickalls

1912 **Friz Hill:** Philip Magor, Sir Francis Waller, Capt. Leslie St. C. Cheape, Frank Hargreaves

1913 **Friz Hill:** Lord William Ednam, Capt. Edward Wienholt, Capt. Leslie St. C. Cheape, Frank Hargreaves

1932 **Roehampton:** Capt. Ronald Cooke, Col. Sir Harold Wernher, Humphrey P. Guinness, Capt. Hugh Walford

1933 **Roehampton:** Hugo S. Backhouse, Rao Rajah Abhey Singh, Rao Rajah Hanut Singh, Capt. Hugh Walford

1934 **Kashmir:** Rao Rajah Abhey Singh, Capt. Charles I.T. Roark, Capt. Percival Sanger, Maharaja of Kashmir

1937 **Goulburn:** Philip Ashton, Geoffrey Ashton, James Ashton, Robert Ashton

1939 **Roehampton:** Capt. John P. Robinson, Hon. Marcus Samuel, Capt. Humphrey Morrison, Capt. Humphrey Guinness

1959 **Kirtlington:** Lt. Col. Anthony Taylor, Miss Judy Forwood, Alan Budgett, Brig. George Fanshawe

1960 **Argentina:** Dr. Jorge Marín Moreno, Luis H. Garrahan, Alejandro Mihanovich, Juan R. Ross

1961 **Sud America:** Wallace Simonsen, João Adao, Col. Mario H. Laprida, Alejandro Mihanovich

1962 **Ratanada:** Maj. Kishen Singh, John L. Lucas, Rao Rajah Hanut Singh, Lt. Gaje Singh

1963 **Buccaneers:** Jonathan Ramsden, Capt. John MacDonald-Buchanan, Juan L. Cavanagh, Wyndham Lacey

1965 **Jersey Lilies:** Ricardo Díaz Dale, Patrick Kemple, Rao Rajah Hanut Singh, Eduardo R. Moore

1966 **Windsor Park:** Lord Waterford, Lord Patrick Beresford, Gonzalo J. Tanoira, HRH Prince Philip

1967 **Checkers Manor:** Peter Palumbo, Roberto James, Juan J. Díaz Alberdi, Edward Bowlby

1968 **Cirencester Park:** Lord Samuel Vestey, Eduardo R. Moore, Peter Perkins, Capt. Frederick Barker

1969 **Buccaneers:** Lord Samuel Vestey, Robin Willans, Eduardo R. Moore, Hon. Mark Vestey

1970 **Todham:** C. Ronald Driver, Howard Hipwood, Julian Hipwood, Jorge Tassara

1971 **San Flamingo:** Anthony Devcich, Howard Hipwood, Julian Hipwood, C. Ronald Driver

1972 **Stowell Park:** Hon. Mark Vestey, Lord Samuel Vestey, Eduardo Moore, Héctor Barrantes

1973 **Stowell Park:** Hon. Mark Vestey, Lord Samuel Vestey, Eduardo Moore, Héctor Barrantes

1974 **Cowdray Park:** Alexander Harper, Hon. Michael Hare, Paul Withers, Celestino Garrós

1975 **Cowdray Park:** Hon. Michael Hare, Richard Walker, Paul Withers, W. Patrick Churchward

1976 **Golden Eagles:** Edward Horswell, Luis Sosa Basualdo, Sinclair Hill, David Gemmell

1977 **Cowdray Park:** Hon. Michael Hare, Gonzalo Pieres, Paul Withers, W. Patrick Churchward

1978 **Stowell Park:** J. Nicholas Williams, Lord Charles Beresford, Eduardo Moore, Héctor Barrantes

1979 **Roundwood Park:** W. Galen Weston Sr., Anthony Devcich, Howard Hipwood, Stuart Mackenzie

1980 **Cowdray Park:** Hon. Charles Pearson, Paul Withers, Antonio Herrera, Patrick Churchward

1981 **Maple Leafs:** W. Galen Weston Sr., Stuart Mackenzie, Howard Hipwood, Maj. C. Redmond Watt

1982 **Southfields:** David Yeoman, Carlos Gracida, John Walker, Lord Charles Beresford

1983 **Boehm Team:** Lord Patrick Beresford, Graham Thomas, Howard Hipwood, Philip Elliott (Hon. Mark Vestey)

1984 **Southfields:** David Yeoman, Alan Kent, Owen Rinehart, David Jamison

1985 **Centaurs:** David Yeoman, Alan Kent, Owen Rinehart, David Jamison

1986 **Falcons:** Martin Brown, Jesús Baez, Carlos Gracida, Alexandre Ebeid

1987 **Southfield:** Adrian Wade, Alan Kent, Owen Rinehart, Martin Brown

1988 **Black Bears:** Jonathan Wade, Michael Azzaro, Dale Smicklas, Martin Brown

1989 **Southfield:** John Yeoman, Alan Kent, Owen Rinehart, Christopher Bethell

1990 **Ellerston White:** Adrian Wade, Gonzalo Tanoira, Gonzalo Pieres, Kerry Packer

1991 **Black Bears:** Urs Schwarzenbach, Michael Azzaro, Dale Smicklas, Oliver Ellis

1992 **Los Locos:** Mrs. Claire Tomlinson, Milo Fernández Araujo, Héctor Crotto, Capt. Simon Tomlinson

1993 **Ellerston White:** Tarquin Southwell, Adolfo Cambiaso, Gonzalo Pieres, Kerry Packer

1994 **Black Bears:** Urs Schwarzenbach, Sebastián Merlos, Juan I. Merlos, Tarquin Southwell

1995 **Royal Pahang:** James McLeavy, Tomás Fernández Llorente, Howard Hipwood, Simon Lucas

1996 **Ellerston White:** Julian Daniels, José Donoso, Gonzalo Pieres, Darren Smith

1997 **Black Bears:** Urs Schwarzenbach, Tomás Fernández Llorente, Michael Azzaro, John Fisher

1998 **Lovelocks:** Robert Cudmore, Adrian Wade, Alan Kent, James Dixon

1999 **Pommery:** John Manconi, Henry Brett, Alejandro Díaz Alberdi, Juan Bollini

2000 **Woodchester:** Craig McKinney, Silvestre Garrós, Milo Fernández Araujo, Henry Brett

2001 **Dubai:** Ali Albwardi, Bartolomé Castagnola, Adolfo Cambiaso, Ryan Pemble

2002 **Foxcote:** Miss Tamara Vestey, John Baillieu, Simon Keyte, Glen Gilmore

2003 **FCT:** Roger Carlsson, John Baillieu, Henry Brett, Jaime García Huidobro

2004 **Black Bears:** Urs Schwarzenbach, Eduardo Novillo Astrada, Javier Novillo Astrada, Sebastian Dawnay

2005 **Black Bears:** Urs Schwarzenbach, Eduardo Novillo Astrada, Javier Novillo Astrada, Nicolás Antinori

2006 **Oaklands:** Martyn Ratcliffe, Gastón Laulhé, Alberto Heguy, George Meyrick

2007 **Elysian Fields:** James Beim, Michael King, José Donoso, Marcos Di Paola

2008 **Les Lions II:** Max Gottschalk, Ignatius Du Plessis, Mariano González, Ignacio Novillo Astrada

2009 **Emlor-CLR:** Spencer McCarthy, Joaquín Pittaluga, Luke Tomlinson, Ignacio Gonzalez

2010 **Emlor-CLR:** Spencer McCarthy, Joaquín Pittaluga, Ignacio Gonzalez, Luke Tomlinson

Ranelagh Open Cup

Challenge Cup presented by the golfing members of the Ranelagh Club. Until 1908 the holders defended the cup in the final game.

1897 (June) **Rugby:** Walter Jones, Charles Miller, George Miller, Edward Miller. Challenged in July by **Ranelagh:** Alfred Rawlinson, Dohkal Singh, Walter Buckmaster, W.J. Drybrough

1898 **Freebooters:** Alfred Rawlinson, Frederick Freake, Walter Buckmaster, John Watson

1899 **Freebooters:** John Vaughn, George Ansell, Alfred Rawlinson, Hon. John Beresford

1900 **Old Cantabs:** Walter A. McCreery, Frederick Freake, Walter Buckmaster, Lawrence McCreery

1901 **Rugby:** Walter Jones, George Miller, Earl of Shrewsbury (Edward Miller), Charles Miller

1902 **Rugby:** Walter Jones, Earl of Shrewsbury, Capt. Edward Miller, Charles Miller

1903 **Old Cantabs:** Walter A. McCreery, Frederick Freake, Walter Buckmaster, Capt. Godfrey Heseltine

1904 **Roehampton:** Capt. Herbert Wilson, Morres Nickalls, Patteson Nickalls, Capt. John Hardress Lloyd

1905 **Roehampton:** Capt. Herbert Wilson, Morres Nickalls, Patteson Nickalls, Capt. John Hardress Lloyd

1906 **Roehampton:** Capt. Herbert Wilson, Morres Nickalls, Patteson Nickalls, Capt. John Hardress Lloyd

1907 **Roehampton:** Capt. Herbert Wilson, Morres Nickalls, Patteson Nickalls, Capt. John Hardress Lloyd

1908 **Ranelagh:** Capt. Leopold Jenner, Frederick Freake, Frederick Gill, Duke of Roxburghe

1909 **Meadow Brook:** Lawrence Waterbury, James Waterbury, Harry P. Whitney, Devereux Milburn

1910 **Old Cantabs:** Capt. George Belville, Frederick Freake, Walter Buckmaster, Lord John Wodehouse

1911 **Royal Horse Guards:** Capt. Geoffrey Bowlby, Capt. Harold Brassey, Capt. Lord Alastair Innes-Ker, John Harrison

1912 **Old Cantabs:** Capt. George Melville, Frederick Freake, Walter Buckmaster, Lord John Wodehouse

1913 **Tigers:** Comte Jean de Madré, Henry Moreton Railston, Capt. R. Gerald Ritson, Capt. Leslie Cheape

1914 **Cavalry Club:** Brian Osborne, Geoffrey H. Phipps-Hornby, Capt. Frank Hurndall, Capt. A. Noel Edwards

1919 **Thornby:** Capt. Arnold Wills, Maj. Frank Hurndall, Maj. Frederick Barrett, Maj. Vivian Lockett

1920 **Freebooters:** John A.E. Traill, Lt. Col. Hugh Ashton, Lord George Rocksavage, Maj. John Harrison

1921 **Foxhunters "A":** James Montagu, Earle W. Hopping, Charles Rumsey, Capt. Frederick Gill

1922 **Cowdray:** Maj. Hon. Harold Pearson, Lord Albert Dalmeny, Walter Buckmaster, Lord George Cholmondeley

1923 **Freebooters:** Duque de Peñaranda, Sir Charles Lowther, Walter Buckmaster, Lord George Cholmondeley

1924 **Eastcott:** Stephen Sanford, Earle W. Hopping, Maj. John Harrison, John A.E. Traill

1925 **Eaton:** William Filmer-Sankey, Marqués de Villabrágima, Lt. Col. Charles Hunter, John A.E. Traill

1926 **El Gordo:** Duque de Peñaranda, Marqués de Villabrágima, Lewis Lacey, John A.E. Traill

1927 **Hurricanes:** Stephen Sanford, Capt. Charles Roark, Wing Cdr. Percival Wise, Maj. John Harrison

1928 **El Gordo:** Duque de Peñaranda, Marqués de Villabrágima, Lewis Lacey, John A.E. Traill

1929 **Hurricanes:** Stephen Sanford, Capt. Charles Roark, Wing Cdr. Percival Wise, Maj. John Harrison

1930 **Hurricanes:** Stephen Sanford, Gerald Balding, Capt. Charles Roark, Wing Cdr. Percival Wise

1931 **Merchiston:** Maj. Geoffrey H. Phipps-Hornby, John Sanderson, Capt. Hugh N. Scott Robson, Humphrey Guinness

1932 **Cavaliers:** Arthur Milborne-Swinnerton-Pilkington, Lt. Col. Vivian Lockett, Henry Scott, John A.E. Traill

1933 **Jaipur:** Prithi Singh, Abhey Singh, Hanut Singh, Maharajah of Jaipur

1934 **Knaves:** Capt. Arthur Milborne-Swinnerton-Pilkington, Capt. Charles Roark, Capt. G. Errol Prior-Palmer, Maj. John Ferguson

1935 **Optimists:** Maj. Geoffrey H. Phipps-Hornby, Michael Phipps, Hesketh Hughes, Tom Guy

1936 Not finished

1937 **Bhopal:** Prithi Singh, Maj. Claude Pert, Hanut Singh, Capt. Hugh Walford

1938 **Texas Rangers:** Charles Wrightsman, Cecil Smith, Aidan Roark, Eric Tyrrell-Martin

1939 **Giant Pandas:** Capt. Nigel Dugdale, Hon. W. Keith Rous, Hon. John Hamilton-Russell, Capt. Humphrey Guinness

Roehampton Cup

Trophy presented by Mrs. John (Alison) Cuninghame of Craigends, Ayrshire.

1902 **Buccaneers:** Harold Brassey, Hon. Reginald Ward, Frederick Menzies, Capt. Hon. George Marjoribanks

1903 **Magpies:** Capt. Leopold Jenner, Capt. Godfrey Heseltine, Capt. John Hardress Lloyd, Ulric Thynne

1904 **Students:** Cecil Grenfell, Riversdale Grenfell, Morres Nickalls, Patteson Nickalls

1905 **Roehampton:** Cecil Grenfell, Riversdale Grenfell, Morres Nickalls, Patteson Nickalls

1906 **Woodpeckers:** Capt. Herbert Wilson, Frederick Menzies, Capt. Brownlow Mathew-Lannowe, Capt. John H. Lloyd

1907 **Leopards:** Capt. Leopold Jenner, Malcolm Pilkington, Morres Nickalls, Capt. Claude Champion de Crespigny

1908 **Leopards:** Capt. Leopold Jenner, Capt. Herbert Wilson, Capt. Claude Champion de Crespigny, Hon. Ivor Guest

1909 **Beauchamp Hall:** Capt. Leopold Jenner, Capt. Percy Fitzgerald, Frederick Gill, Capt. Charles Hunter

1910 **Ranelagh:** Capt. Leopold Jenner, Frank Hurndall, Capt. Percy Fitzgerald, Maj. H. Romer Lee

1911 **Tigers:** Comte Jean de Madré, Capt. Carlyle MacG. Dunbar, Capt. R. Gerald Ritson, Capt. Leslie Cheape

1912 **Wanderers:** Capt. George Bellville, Maj. Percy Fitzgerald, Maj. Edgar Brassey, Frederick Gill

1913 **Pilgrims:** Capt. Teignmouth Melvill, Alfred Grisar, Capt. Edward Wienholt, Frank Rich

1914	**Old Etonians:** Geoffrey Phipps-Hornby, Capt. John Astor, Lord Rocksavage, Capt. John Harrison

1919	**Scouts:** Maj. W. T. Miles, Brig. Gen. Percy Fitzgerald, Capt. Hon. Frederick Guest, Maj. Frederick Barrett

1920	**Roehampton:** Capt. Arnold Wills, Lt. Col. Hugh Ashton, Maj. Francis Penn-Curzon, Lt. Col. Charles Miller

1921	**Eastcott:** Stephen Sanford, Earle W. Hopping, Maj. Philip Magor, John A.E. Traill

1922	**Cirencester:** Capt. Maurice Kingscote, Hon. Aubrey Hastings, Capt. Rex Smart, Capt. Lindsay Shedden

1923	**Cirencester:** Capt. Maurice Kingscote, Hon. Aubrey Hastings, Capt. Rex Smart, Capt. Lindsay Shedden

1924	**Optimists:** Hon. Kenneth Mackay, Maj. Horace Colmore, Capt. Charles Tremayne, Maj. Alfred Tate

1925	**La Pampa:** Juan D. Nelson, Marqués de Villavieja, Alfredo Peña, Juan A.E. Traill

1926	**Templeton:** Philip Forsyth-Forrest, Maj. Geoffrey Phipps-Hornby, Maj. Frederick Barrett, Capt. Hon. Frederick Guest

1928	**Hurricanes:** Stephen Sanford, Capt. Charles Roark, Lt. Desmond Miller, Maj. John Harrison

1929	**Pilgrims:** Capt. Maurice Kingscote, Maj. Geoffrey Phipps-Hornby, G. Errol Prior-Palmer, Alfred Grisar

1930	**17th/21st Lancers:** Lt. Ronald Cooke, Lt. Desmond Miller, Lt. Hugh Walford, Lt. Col. Vivian Lockett

1931	**Hurricanes:** Stephen Sanford, William Whitbread, Capt. C.T.I. Roark, Col. Percival Wise

1932	**Merchiston:** Dudley Frost, Hesketh Hughes, F. H. George, Maj. Evelyn Fanshawe

1933	**Friar Park:** Archie David, Capt. Patrick J. Butler, Capt. Humphrey Morrison, John Robinson

1934	**Panthers:** Earl of Erne, Maj. Geoffrey Phipps-Hornby, Eric Tyrrell-Martin. Maj. Philip Magor

1935	**Panthers:** Maj. Noel Leaf, Stephen Sanford, Eric Tyrrell-Martin, Capt. Dudley Norton

1937	**Someries House:** Col. Sir Harold Wernher, Maj. Claud Pert, Capt. David Dawnay, Andrew Horsbrugh-Porter

1938	**Someries House:** Col. Sir Harold Wernher, Capt. Hon. Richard Hamilton-Russell, Capt. David Dawnay, Capt. Andrew Horsbrugh-Porter

1939	**Pandas:** Archie David, Lt. Kenrick J. Price, Capt. John Montagu Douglas-Scott, Maj. John Harrison

1947	**Ham:** Mrs. Peter (Celia) Fleming, William Walsh

1950	**Sussex:** Alastair Gibb, Lt. Col. Geoffrey Phipps-Hornby, Lt. Col. Peter Dollar, John Lakin

1951	**La Espadaña:** Juan J. Reynal, Luis H. Garrahan, Juan R. Ross, Carlos R.B. Buchanan

1952	**Friar Park:** Maj. Archie David, Lt. Col. Andrew Horsbrugh-Porter, Lt. Col. Humphrey Guinness, William Walsh

1953	**Park House:** Fred L. Withers, Ernesto J. Lalor, Juan R. Ross, José I. Domecq

1954	**Cowdray Park:** Peter Cruden, Lt. Col. Peter Dollar, Rao Rajah Hanut Singh, John Lakin

1955	**Greyhounds:** J. Sinclair Hill, Col. Gerald Critchley, Lt. Col. Alec Harper, Charles Smith-Ryland

1956	**Cowdray Park:** Brig. Masud "Hesky" Baig, Charles Smith-Ryland, Rao Rajah Hanut Singh, John Lakin

1957–1966: Trophy played as prize for a golf tournament at Roehampton Club

1967 **Silver Leys:** Arthur Boyd Gibbins, Capt. Gaje Singh, Luis Sosa Basualdo, C. Reddy Watt

1972 **Squires Farm:** Geoffrey Lawson, Norman E. Wates, Brian Bethell, Colin A. "Tim" Brodie

1974 **Toulston:** Peter Gaunt, R. Rossiter, Lt. Col. Kishen Singh, John N. Hinchliffe

1975 **Wilmer Cottage:** Christopher Tauchert, Maj. Brijendra Singh, Capt. Charles Lowther, Sam Houston

1976 **The Bees:** Richard Maple-Brown, Bryan Morrison, Bertram Arbeid, Marcus Emerson

1977 **Invicta:** Denzil Fernandez, Christopher Tauchert, Derek Copeland, Sam Houston

1978 **Wanderers:** Geoffrey Godbold/Michael Stewart, David Pearl, Geoffrey Lawson, Roger White

1979 **Travelwise Tortugas:** William Healy, Christopher Tauchert, Juan J. Díaz Alberdi, Denzil Fernandez

1981 **Equus:** Quentin Davis, Michael Willoughby, William Roberts, David Anderson

1983 **The Watergate:** Norman Lobel, Geoffrey Lawson, Martin Glue, David Anderson

1986 **Maidford:** J. Nicholas Williams, E.B. "Ted" Marriage, Derek Copeland, Douglas Brown

1994 **Freebooters:** Ray Barnes, Mrs. Pamela Bannister, Peter McCormack, Christopher Graham

1995 **Redcliffe Square:** Don Christian, Steve Allen, Michael Ventura, Tim Healy

1996 **Dubai Exiles:** Peter McCormack, Neil McLean, Martin Glue, Steve Lamprell

1997 **Twelve Oaks:** Ian Wooldridge, Graham Wooldridge, John Horswell, Nick Brister

1998 Not played: rain.

1999 **Black Cats:** Mark Wadhwa, Tristan Phillimore, Marcus Hancock, Laird Ward

2000 **Ravenscourt:** Miss Virginia Featherstone-Witty, Andrew Blake-Thomas, Oscar Mancini, Simon McLaren-Tosh

2001 **Regal:** Raphael Singh, Sergio Baselli, Tarquin Southwell, Martin Stegeman

2002 **Los Pinguinos:** Mark Persaud, Alan Ruzzaman, Martin ffrench-Blake, Sam Gairdner

2003 **Clarita:** Clare Mathias, Sam Gairdner, James Lucas, Chris Mathias

2004 **Clarita:** Clare Mathias, Chris Mathias, Sam Gairdner, James Lucas

2005 **Clarita:** Clare Mathias, Chris Mathias, Sam Gairdner, Corin Gibbs

2006 **Montana Polo:** Tony Gerrard, Martin Roman, Ariel Tapia, Adam Leech

2007 **Los Dientes:** Matthew Tooth, Lucas Fernandez, Sebastian Dawnay, Oscar Mancini

2008 **Avalon Polo:** Christopher Caesar, Jeffrey Schlesinger, Nicolas Talamoni, Greg Keyte

2009 **Tchogan:** Jason Norton, Heiko Voelker, Nicolas Talamoni (Adolfo Casabal), Greg Keyte

2010 **Rios Profundos:** Hugo Davis, Benjie Davis, Matias Machando, Martin Valent

Junior County Cup

Instituted for a challenge cup presented by the Blackmore Vale Polo Club. Open to teams representing any county polo club, provided that the aggregate handicap did not exceed twelve points, no player handicapped above five points being eligible. In 1907 control was passed on to the County Polo Association.

1905 **Aldershot:** James Blakiston Houston, Capt. Sir Charles Lowther, Capt. Guy Mort, Capt. John van der Byl

1906 **Aldershot:** William Armitage, Capt. Sir Charles Lowther, Capt. Guy Mort, Capt. John van der Byl

1907 **Blackmore Vale:** Charles Lambe, H.S. Harrison, John Holford, Robert Eden

1908 **Cambridge University:** Frederick Wingfield Digby, Norman Loder, Herbert Rich, Hon. Clive Pearson

1909   **Stoke D'Abernon:** Roland Burn, Noel Price, Aubrey Price, Clifford Trollope

1910   **Stoke D'Abernon:** Edmund Bennett, Noel Price, Aubrey Price, Clifford Trollope

1911   **Cirencester:** Hugh Baker, Stanley Barton, Jesse Gouldsmith, James Mason

1912   **York:** Hon. Alexander Leslie-Melville, Hugh Noel Scott Robson, Capt. Douglas Duguid-McCombie, Ralph Whitehead

1913   **Norwich:** Maj. Cecil Fane, Capt. T. Reginald Badger, Edward Leatham, John Eden

1914   **Stoke D'Abernon:** Hon. Robert Douglas-Scott-Montagu, Hon. Charles Douglas-Pennant, Arthur B. Hankey, Clifford Trollope

1920   **Wellington:** Lt. Col. Balfour Hutchinson, Lt. Col. Rex Osborne, Capt. Dereck Richardson, Maj. Donald McLeod

1921   **Rugby:** Ronald Deterding, Capt. Harry Rich, Hon. Kenneth Mackay, Capt. Clement Barton

1922   **Tidworth:** Geoffrey Clifton-Brown, Walter S. McCreery, Richard McCreery, James Bailey

1923   **Tidworth:** Geoffrey Clifton-Brown, Walter S. McCreery, Richard McCreery, Alexander Cadogan Brown

1924   **Fleet** (Los Gringos): Gerald Royce Tomkin, Lionel Peel Yates, Capt. Harold Watkis, Robert Lambert

1925   **Weedon:** William Carr, Capt. Arthur Moubray, Thomas Meyrick, William Brough Scott

1926   **Cheltenham:** Wilfred Bailey, Capt. David Mitchell, W.F. Holman, Arthur Cresswell

1927   **Rugby:** Cdr. Francis J. Alexander, Capt. Lord Robert Cromwell, John Drage, Herbert Sutton

1928   **Toulston:** J.F. Holdsworth, Cecil Drabble, William Riley-Smith, Maj. Harold Nichols

1929   **Toulston:** J.F. Holdsworth, Col. Cecil Emsley, Raymond Hill-Forster, William Riley-Smith

1930   **Aldershot:** Peter Wiggin, John Dugdale, Rodney Verelst, Rodney Schreiber

1931   **Stoke D'Abernon:** W. Payne, William Withycombe, James Withycombe, Noel Docker

1932   **Aldershot:** Nevill Dunne, James Vernon-Miller, Capt. Rupert Kilkelly, Charles Duff

1933   **Toulston:** J.F. Holdsworth, Raymond Hill-Forster, Capt. Walter Griffiths, Wiliam Riley-Smith

1934   **Toulston:** Col. Cecil Emsley, Thomas Paisley, William Riley-Smith, Capt. Walter Griffiths

1935   **Tidworth:** Col. Richard Grubb, William Ritson, Maj. Charles Clark, Richard Bertram

1936   **Toulston:** Col. Cecil Emsley, Thomas Paisley, William Riley-Smith, Capt. Walter Griffiths

1937   **Aldershot:** Capt. Humphrey Lambert, Capt. John Collingwood, Capt. Peter Dollar, Maj. Cuthbert Todd

1938   **Toulston:** Raymond Hill-Forster, J.F. Holdsworth, Thomas Paisley, Capt. Walter Griffith

1939   **Aldershot:** Thomas Bell, Guy Cunard, Claud Stretton Dixon, Capt. Thomas Cooper

1948   **Birkdale:** Mrs. Dorothy Kitson, L. Arthur Lucas, Capt. Patrick Butler, Maj. Thomas Hilder

1949   **Birkdale:** John Lucas, L. Arthur Lucas, James Withycombe, H. Edward Taucher

1950   **Henley:** Mrs. Celia Fleming, Sqn. Ldr. Alan Roberts, Thomas Hilder, William Walsh

1951   **Maidengrove:** Capt. John Lovegrove, Sqn. Ldr. Alan Roberts, Maj. Hugh Brassey, Lt. Col. Alan Scott

1952   **Hertfordshire:** Edmund Roark, John Lucas, James Withycombe, L. Arthur Lucas

1953   **Cowdray Park:** Lord John Cowdray, Lt. Col. Alec Harper, Lt. Col. Peter Dollar, HRH Prince Philip

1954 **Ancient Mariners:** Lt. Cdr. Robert de Pass, HRH Prince Philip, Lt. Col. Alec Harper, Lt. J.W. Mathwin Maunder

1955 **Friar Park:** Maj. Archie David, Lord Patrick Beresford, Ernesto Lalor, Sir Andrew Horsburgh-Porter

1956 **Windsor Park:** Col. William H. Gerard Leigh, Clement Barton, Ernesto Lalor, Ronald Ferguson

1957 **Cirencester Park:** Col. Raymond Barrow, Brian Bethell, Lt. Col. Anthony McConnel, Hon. George Bathurst

1958 **Kirtlington:** Lt. Col. Anthony D. Taylor, Miss Judy Forwood, Clement Barton, R. Alan Budgett

1959 **Jersey Lilies:** Maj. Dennis Grehan, Capt. Robert Baxter, Lt. Col. Alec Harper, Eric Moller

1960 **Tidworth:** Capt. James Ormrod, Hon. George Bathurst, Paul Withers, Jimmy Edwards

1961 **Cirencester:** Dirk Sellschopp, Hon. George Bathurst, Lt. Col. Anthony McConnel, Andrew Summers

1962 **Cowdray Park:** Edward Graham-Wood, Eduardo Rojas Lanusse, Hanut Singh, Ross Bramma

1963 **Cowdray Park:** Alexander J. Harper, Lord Samuel Vestey, Lt. Col. Alec Harper, John Chart

1964 **Windsor Park:** Capt. Nigel Corbally-Stourton, Maj. Peter Thwaites, HRH Prince Philip, Capt. Robert Combe

1965 **Cheshire:** George Barlow, Manuel Lainez, Michael G. Moseley, Peter Hunter

1966 **Cowdray Park:** Alexander Harper, Fred Withers, Lt. Col. Alec Harper, Sir Vyvyan Naylor-Leyland

1967 **Windsor Park:** HRH Prince Charles, Lt. Col. Peter Thwaites, HRH Prince Philip, George Routledge

1968 **Tidworth:** Capt. D. Ian McConnel, Peter Gifford, Timothy Harding, Maj. Charles Lockhart

1969 **Cowdray Park:** Henry Jurgens, Hon. Michael Hare, Lt. Col. Alec Harper, John Tylor

1970 **Cheshire:** George Barlow, John Barlow, Michael G. Moseley, Dougal Long

1971 **La Ema:** G. Anthony Emerson, Richard Clifford, Capt. D. Ian McConnel, Robert Graham

1972 **Kerfield:** Sebastian B. de Ferranti, Philip Crompton, Capt. Timothy Ritson, Maj. James Ormrod

1973 **Rhinefield:** James Daniels, Maj. Peter Bruxnell-Randall, Col. David Sylvester-Bradley, Nigel Kennard

1974 **Langley Priors:** Raymond Ashworth, John Hine, George Barlow, Daniel Devrient

1975 **Los Locos:** John Bayston, Robert Bayston, Mrs. Claire Tomlinson, Capt. Simon Tomlinson

1976 **Los Locos:** Maj. F. Michael Strand-Steel, Joey Newton, Mrs. Claire Tomlinson, Capt. Simon Tomlinson

1977 **Los Locos:** Joey Newton, Marcos Bignoli, Mrs. Claire Tomlinson, Capt. Simon Tomlinson

1978 **Silver Bears:** David Yeoman, Robert Bayston, Graham Thomas, Robert Hall

1979 **Silver Bears:** J. Taylor, Richard Clifford, Paul Clarkin, Robert Hall

1980 **Langley Priors:** Andrew Hine, John Hine, Richard Kimber, James Lucas

1981 **Satnam Dorcas:** Kuhldip S. Dhillon, Mark Barlow, Cody Forsyth, James Cunningham

1982 **Peoverwood:** Mrs. Ninanne Hancock, Marcus Hancock, Graham Thomas, Randle Brooks

1983 **Woodhill:** Mrs. Ninnane Hancock, Marcus Hancock, Graham Thomas, Grenville Waddington

1984 **Kirtlington:** Christopher Courage, Roderick Matthews, John Tylor, Crispin Matthews
1985 **Phoenix Park:** Stephen Hutchinson, John Kavanagh, Michael Meenaghan, Peter Newell
1986 **Satnan Outlandos:** Bruce Green, Kuhldip S. Dhillon, Timothy Keyte, Julian Llewellen Palmer
1987 **Satnam:** Nicholaus Hahn Jr., Kuhldip S. Dhillon, Ian Hunt, Mark Barlow
1988 **Stoneyhill:** Robert Bayston, J. Nicholas Williams, Robert Cudmore, Jason Dixon
1989 **Tayto:** Stephen Hutchinson, Howard Taylor, Eduardo Lalor, Jeff Pearce
1990 **Whitehall:** Oliver Taylor, Stephen Hutchinson, Eduardo Gómez Romero, Howard Taylor
1991 **Kirtlington:** Andrew Barlow, Christopher Whiteley, John Tylor, Crispin Matthews
1992 **Woodchester:** Craig McKinney, Germán Llorens, Chris Atkinson, Lawrence O'Mahony
1993 **Tayto:** Andrew Fox-Pitt, Stephen Hutchinson, Andrea Vianini, Jonathan Kavanagh Jr.
1994 **Whitehall:** Howard Taylor, Oliver Taylor, Pablo Crespin, Henry Stevens
1995 **Whitehall:** Derrick Lyons, Pablo Crespin, Charles Seavill, Howard Taylor
1996 **Woodchester:** Craig McKinney, Sebastián Funes, Sebastian Dawnay, Oliver Hipwood
1997 **Woodchester:** Craig McKinney, Sebastián Funes, Sebastian Dawnay, Jonathan Good
1998 **Talacrest Boxers:** John Collins, Peter Webb, Chris Hyde, Shane Borland
1999 **Tayto:** Raymond Hutchinson, Stephen Hutchinson, Martín Rodríguez, Jonathan Kavanagh Jr.
2000 **Los Cazadores:** Ronnie Walker, Alexander Brodie, Carlos Mayón, Mark Keegan
2001 **Los Cazadores:** Ronnie Walker, Ben Turner, Carlos Mayón, Tristan Pemble
2002 **Eurocall:** Nigel Warr, Nicolás San Román, James Glasson, Corin Gibbs
2003 **Henbury:** Simon Taylor, Antony Fanshawe, James Harper, Cristián Chaves
2004 **Pavilion:** Nigel Warr, Henry Fisher, Kelvin Johnson, John Fisher
2005 **Flame Estates:** Hamilton Ashworth, Oliver Tuthill, Josh Tuthill, Julian Appleby
2006 **Autodex:** Richard Fagan, Dominic Barnes, Peter Webb, Tim Brown
2007 **Chester Racecourse:** Elliot Sands, Marcus Hancock, Nico Fontanarrosa, Richard Thomas
2008 **Henbury:** Simon Taylor, Cristián Chaves, Antony Fanshawe, Matthew Hitchman
2009 **Henbury** (Eversheds): Simon Taylor, Cristián Chaves, Antony Fanshawe, Mark Baldwin
2010 **Belgravia Polo:** Hazel Jackson, James Fielding, Grant Collett, Michael Henderson

Coronation Cup

Instituted in 1911 for a £250 Challenge Cup given by the Ranelagh Club Committee in celebration of the coronation of King George V. Open to the winners of the Hurlingham Champion Cup, Ranelagh Open Cup and Inter-regimental Tournament. Visiting foreign teams might be invited. In 1913 the winner of the Roehampton Open Cup was added to the roster. In 1953, Argentina, Chile, Spain and the United States were invited to participate in a tournament that also included England, Cowdray Park and Woolmers Park. From 1971 on, it is a single match between England and an invited nation or team.

1911 **Indian Polo Association:** Capt. Leslie Cheape, Maj. Shah Mirza Beg, Capt. R. Gerald Ritson, Capt. Vivian Lockett
1912 **Old Cantabs:** Capt. George Bellville, Frederick Freake, Walter Buckmaster, Lord John Wodehouse
1913 **Quidnuncs:** Duque de Peñaranda, Capt. E. William Palmes, Lord Ivor Ashby St. Ledgers, Capt. Frederick Barrett
1914 **12th Lancers:** Edward Leatham, Capt. T. Reginald Badger, Basil Nicholas, Richard Wyndham-Quin

1919 **Freebooters:** Sir John Ramsden, Capt. Ivor Buxton, Lord George Rocksavage, Maj. John Harrison

1920 **Freebooters:** John A.E. Traill, Lt. Col. Henry Ashton, Lord George Rocksavage, Maj. John Harrison

1921 **Foxhunters:** James Montagu, Rodman Wanamaker, Earle W. Hopping, Capt. Frederick Gill

1922 **17th Lancers:** Lt. Col. Teignmouth Melvill, Capt. Herbert Turnor, Maj. Vivian Lockett, Capt. Dennis Boles

1923 **Tigers:** Comte Jean de Madré, Maj. Jaswant Singh, Maj. Eric Atkinson, Col. Jagindar Singh

1924 **Eastcott:** Alfred Grisar, John A.E. Traill, Maj. Frank Hurndall, Maj. John Harrison

1925 **Eaton:** William Filmer-Sankey, Marqués de Villabrágima, Earle W. Hopping, John A.E. Traill

1926 **El Gordo:** Duque de Peñaranda, Marqués de Villabrágima, Lewis Lacey (Capt. George Scott-Douglas), John A.E. Traill

1927 **El Gordo:** Duque de Peñaranda, Marqués de Villabrágima, Lewis Lacey, John A.E. Traill

1928 **El Gordo:** Duque de Peñaranda, Marqués de Villabrágima, John A.E. Traill, Lewis Lacey

1929 **Hurricanes:** Stephen Sanford, Capt. Charles T.I. Roark, Wing Cdr. Percival Wise, Maj. John Harrison

1930 Not played. Westchester Cup.

1931 **Panthers:** Eric Tyrrell-Martin, Capt. Charles Roark, Maj. Philip Magor, John A.E. Traill

1932 **Osmaston:** Sir Ian Walker, Capt. Charles Roark, Capt. G. Errol Prior-Palmer, Maj. John Harrison

1933 **Jaipur:** Rao Kumar Prithi Singh, Rao Rajah Abhey Singh, Rao Rajah Hanut Singh, Maharajah of Jaipur

1934 **Knaves:** Capt. Arthur Milborne-Swinnerton-Pilkington, Capt. Charles Roark, Capt. G. Errol Prior-Palmer, Maj. John Ferguson

1935 **Panthers:** Stephen Sanford, Capt. G. Erroll Prior-Palmer, Eric Tyrrell-Martin, Maj. Philip Magor

1936 **Templeton:** Michael Phipps, James Mills, Winston Guest, Robert Strawbridge Jr.

1937 **Jaguars:** Hon. W. Keith Rous, Capt. Charles Roark, Gerald Balding, Stephen Sanford

1938 **Texas Rangers:** Charles Wrightsman, Cecil Smith, Aidan Roark, Eric Tyrrell-Martin

1939 **Someries House:** Maj. John Robinson (Sir Harold Wernher), Capt. Andrew Horsburgh-Porter, Capt. Erroll Prior-Palmer, John Lakin

1951 Played for the Festival Cup. **Hurlingham:** Lt. Col. Alec Harper, Gerald Balding, Lt. Col. Humphrey Guinness, John Lakin

1953 **Argentina:** Eduardo Braun Cantilo, Ernesto Lalor, Alejandro Mihanovich, Juan C. Alberdi

1971 **America:** Ronald Tongg, William R. Linfoot, Harold L. Barry, Harold A. Barry

1972 **America:** William C. Linfoot, William R. Linfoot, Roy Barry Jr., Harold L. Barry

1973 **America:** William Ylvisaker, Thomas Wayman, William R. Linfoot, Harold L. Barry

1974 **America:** William Ylvisaker, Thomas Wayman, Roy Barry Jr., Lester Armour

1975 **South America:** Gonzalo Pieres, Eduardo Moore, Juan J. Díaz Alberdi, Héctor Barrantes

1976 **South America:** Gonzalo Pieres, Antonio Herrera, Eduardo Moore, Aníbal García

1977 **South America:** Luis Sosa Basualdo, Gonzalo Pieres, Eduardo Moore, Héctor Crotto

1978 **South America:** Abel Aguero, Gonzalo Pieres, Alejandro Garrahan, Héctor Crotto

1979 **England:** H. John Horswell, Paul Withers, Julian Hipwood, Howard Hipwood
1980 **Rest of the World:** S. Jake Sieber, Antonio Herrera, Héctor Crotto, Jaime MacKay
1981 **South America:** Alvaro Pieres, Martín Zubía, Gonzalo Pieres, Héctor Crotto
1982 **England:** Lord Charles Beresford, Alan Kent, Julian Hipwood, Howard Hipwood
1983 **England:** Lord Charles Beresford, Alan Kent, Julian Hipwood, Howard Hipwood
1984 **Rest of the World:** Cody Forsyth, Carlos Gracida, Silvio Junqueira Novaes, Owen Rinehart
1985 **Mexico:** Rubén Gracida, Carlos Gracida, Guillermo Gracida, Jesús Baez
1986 **Mexico:** Rubén Gracida, Carlos Gracida, Guillermo Gracida, Antonio Herrera
1987 **North America:** Michael Azzaro, Robert Walton, Owen Rinehart, Dale Smicklas
1988 **England:** Andrew Seavill, Julian Hipwood, John Horswell, Lord Charles Beresford
1989 **England:** Andrew Hine, Julian Hipwood, Alan Kent, Lord Charles Beresford
1990 **England:** William Lucas, Julian Hipwood, Howard Hipwood, Roderick Matthews
1991 **New Zealand:** Andrew Parrott, Stuart Mackenzie, Cody Forsyth, Greg Keyte
1992 Not played. Westchester Cup.
1993 **England:** William Lucas, Julian Hipwood, Howard Hipwood, Lord Charles Beresford
1994 **England:** Julian Daniels, Adrian Wade, Lord Charles Beresford, James Lucas
1995 **Argentina:** Gastón Laulhé, Tomás Fernández Llorente, Benjamín Araya, Julio Zavaleta
1996 **England:** Julian Daniels, Adrian Wade, Howard Hipwood, Henry Brett
1997 Not played. Westchester Cup.
1998 **Chile:** José Donoso, Jaime García Huidobro, Gabriel Donoso, José Iturrate
1999 **England:** Julian Daniels, Henry Brett, William Lucas, Andrew Hine
2000 **Argentina:** Jorge Healy, Milo Fernández Araujo, Eduardo Heguy, Matías MacDonough
2001 **England:** Julian Daniels (Roderick Williams), William Lucas, Henry Brett, Andrew Hine
2002 **Rest of the Commonwealth:** Frederick Mannix Jr., John Bailllieu, Glen Gilmore, Simon Keyte
2003 **England:** William Lucas, Luke Tomlinson, Henry Brett, Andrew Hine
2004 **Chile:** Alejandro Vial, José Donoso, Gabriel Donoso, Jaime García Huidobro
2005 **Australia:** Damien Johnston, John Baillieu, Glen Gilmore, Michael Todd
2006 **England:** James Beim, Mark Tomlinson, Henry Brett, Luke Tomlinson
2007 **Chile:** José Zegers, Martín Zegers, José Donoso, Jaime García Huidobro
2008 **England:** James Beim, Mark Tomlinson, Malcolm Borwick, Luke Tomlinson
2009 **Argentina:** Gustavo Usandizaga, Martín Valent, Adolfo Cambiaso, Facundo Pieres
2010 **England:** James Beim, Mark Tomlinson, Malcolm Borwick, Luke Tomlinson
2011 **England:** James Beim, Mark Tomlinson, Luke Tomlinson, Ignacio Gonzalez

Cowdray Park Challenge Cup

An invitation tournament. No team to exceed twenty-four points or to claim less than twelve points.

1911 **Cowdray:** Norman W. Loder, Hon. Bernard Clive Pearson, Capt. Hugh C.S. Ashton, Capt. Eustace W. Morrison-Bell
1912 **Mentmore:** Pelham C. Puckle, Evelyn A. de Rothschild, Walter S. Buckmaster, Lord Albert Dalmeny
1913 **Mentmore:** Evelyn A. de Rothschild, Lord Albert Dalmeny, Walter S. Buckmaster, Ernest B. Horlick
1914 **Cowley Manor:** Sir Humphrey de Trafford, Maurice J. Kingscote, Charles D. Miller, Ernest B. Horlick

1919 **Cavalry:** Capt. Harold A. Wernher, Lord Hugh Stalbridge, Maj. Hugh C.S. Ashton, Capt. John F. Harrison

1920 **Anglesey House:** Brig. Gen. Edward J.R. Peel, Lt. Col. James J. Richardson, Capt. Dennis C. Boles, Brig. Gen. Arthur C. Daly

1921 **Cowdray:** Hon. Harold Pearson, Hon. B. Clive Pearson, Lord Albert Dalmeny, Capt. John G. Lowther

1922 **Cowley Manor:** William P. Filmer-Sankey, Marquess John Blandford, Sir Ernest Horlick, Maj. John F. Harrison

1923 **Cowley Manor:** William P. Filmer-Sankey, Maj. Harold A. Wernher, Sir Ernest Horlick, Maj. John F. Harrison

1924 **Cavalry Club:** Capt. Richard L. McCreery, Walter S. McCreery, Capt. Charles H. Tremayne, Maj. Harold V.S. Charrington

1925 **17th/21st Lancers:** Lt. Col. Teignmouth P. Melvill, Hugh C. Walford, Maj. Vivian N. Lockett, Henry W. Forester

1926 **Someries House:** Lord Edward Digby, Maj. Harold A. Wernher, Lt. Col. Hugh C.S. Ashton, Capt. James N. Bailey

1927 Not played.

1928 **Scopwick:** Col. Hon. Frederick V. Willey, Edmund C. Roark, Capt. Hugh N. Scott Robson, Maj. Dennis C. Boles

1929 **Optimists:** Hon. William W. Astor, Capt. Andrew H. Ferguson, Capt. Charles H. Tremayne, Capt. Dudley J.E. Norton

1930 **Cowdray:** Hon. W. John C. Pearson, Hon. B. Clive Pearson, Peter W. Dollar, Maj. John F. Harrison

1931 **Remnants:** Terence A.A. Watt, John Lakin, Capt. Dudley J.E. Norton, John G. Morrison

1932 **Lakers Lodge:** Hugh Nelson, Capt. Frederick W. Bass, Capt. Humphrey G. Morrison, Capt. John P.B. Robinson

1933 **Someries House:** Capt. Frederick E.B. Wignall, Col. Sir Harold Wernher, Capt. Ronald B.B.B. Cooke, Cdr. Lord Louis Mountbatten

1934 Not played.

1935 **Cowdray:** Lord John Cowdray, John Lakin, Capt. Peter W. Dollar, Maj. John F. Harrison

1936 **Cowdray:** Lord John Cowdray, John Lakin, F. Winston C. Guest, Maj. John F. Harrison

1937 **Adsdean:** John P.B. Robinson, Hon. Marcus R. Samuel, Capt. Humphrey G. Morrison, Capt. Lord Louis Mountbatten (Maj. John F. Harrison)

1938 **Jaguars:** E.C.F. Nutting, Hon. W. Keith Rous, Capt. Peter W. Dollar, Capt. Humphrey P. Guinness

1939 **The Knaves:** George H. Lowther, Maj. Peter W. Dollar, John Lakin, Maj. John F. Harrison

1948 **Cowdray:** Maj. Colin Davenport, Hon. Mrs. John (Daphne) Lakin, Lord John Cowdray, John Lakin

1949 **Henley:** Mrs. Philip (Celia) Fleming, William Walsh, Sqn. Ldr. A.J. Alan Roberts, Capt. Patrick J. Butler

1950 **Sussex:** Lord John Cowdray, Maj. Gen. Robert A.R. Neville, Lt. Col. Peter W. Dollar, John Lakin

1951 **Cowdray Park:** Lord John Cowdray, Lt. Col. Alec F. Harper, Lt. Col. Peter W. Dollar, John Lakin

1952 **Beechwood:** William E. Wallace, Charles Smith-Ryland, Rao Rajah Hanut Singh, Col. Gerald H. Critchley

1953 **Hertfordshire:** Francisco Astaburuaga, Carlos O. de la Serna, Col. Prem Singh, John L. Lucas

1954 **Cowdray Park:** Lt. Col. Peter W. Dollar, Kanwar Bijai Singh, Rao Rajah Hanut Singh, Maj. Gen. David Dawnay

1955 **Friar Park:** Maj. Archie David, Lt. Col. Anthony H. McConnel, Col. Humphrey P. Guinness, Ernesto J. Lalor

1956 Not played.

1957 **Cowdray Park:** Lt. Col. Peter W. Dollar, John Lakin, Lt. Col. Alec F. Harper, Col. Gerald H. Critchley

1958 **Friar Park:** Maj. Archie David, Capt. Ronald I. Ferguson, Ernesto J. Lalor, Alejandro Mihanovich

1959 **Centaurs:** Lt. Col. Peter W. Dollar, Guillermo Gracida, Gabriel Gracida, Sir Evelyn de Rothschild

1960 **Cowdray Park:** Paul M. Withers, Lt. Col. Alec F. Harper, Rao Rajah Hanut Singh, Alejandro Mihanovich

1961 **Centaurs:** Dr. Jorge N. Marín Moreno, John L. Lucas, Gabriel Gracida, Sir Evelyn de Rothschild

1962 **Windsor Park:** Capt. Lord Patrick Beresford, HRH the Duke of Edinburgh, Juan L. Cavanagh, Maj. Ronald I. Ferguson

1963 **Sao Silvestre:** Ricardo Díaz Dale, Juan J. Díaz Alberdi, Horacio A. Heguy, Alejandro Mihanovich

1964 **Jersey Lilies:** Ricardo Díaz Dale, Patrick Kemple, Rao Rajah Hanut Singh, Eduardo R. Moore

1965 **Jersey Lilies:** Ricardo Díaz Dale, Patrick Kemple, Rao Rajah Hanut Singh, Eduardo R. Moore

1966 **Templeton:** Alejandro Mihanovich, Jorge A. Tanoira, Edward F.S. Bowlby, Alfredo Goti

1967 **Woolmers Park:** Dr. Jorge N. Marín Moreno, Enrique A. Zorrilla, John L. Lucas, Celestino Garrós

1968 **Kerfield House:** Sebastian B.J.Z. de Ferranti, Rodolfo Lagos Mármol, Alejandro Mihanovich, George D. Rollinson

1969 **Pimms:** Lord David Brecknock, Héctor Merlos, Daniel González, Brian B. Bethell

1970 **Stowell Park:** Lord Samuel Vestey, Hon. Mark W. Vestey, Eduardo R. Moore, Héctor E. Barrantes

1971 **Pimms:** Lord David Brecknock, Enrique A. Zorrilla, Daniel González, Maj. Ronald I. Ferguson

1972 **Stowell Park:** Lord Samuel Vestey, Hon. Mark W. Vestey, Eduardo R. Moore, Héctor E. Barrantes

1973 **San Flamingo:** Juan R. Moore, Douglas MacDonald, Julian B. Hipwood, C. Ronald Driver

1974 **San Flamingo:** Alan J. Kent, Howard J. Hipwood, Julian B. Hipwood, C. Ronald Driver

1975 **Jersey Lilies:** Alan J. Kent, Ezequiel Fernández Guerrico, Daniel Devrient, John E.A. Kidd

1976 **Jersey Lilies:** Alan J. Kent, Gonzalo Pieres, Ezequiel Fernández Guerrico, John E.A. Kidd

1977 **Stowell Park:** Julian B. Hipwood, Abel A. Aguero, Lord Samuel Vestey, Guy Wildenstein

1978 **Sladmore:** Edward Horswell, H. John Horswell, Abel A. Aguero, Alejandro Garrahan

1979 **Songhai:** Alan J. Kent, Alvaro Pieres, Gonzalo Pieres, Oliver J. Ellis

1980 **Stowell Park:** Hon. Mark W. Vestey, Gonzalo Pieres, Héctor E. Barrantes, Philip N.W. Elliott

1981   **Sladmore:** Edward Horswell, Alvaro Pieres, H. John Horswell, Maj. Ronald I. Ferguson
1982   **Boehm Team:** Lord Patrick Beresford, Philip N.W. Elliott, Stuart Mackenzie, Hon. Mark W. Vestey
1983   **Maple Leafs:** W. Galen Weston Sr., Alan J. Kent, Anthony Devcich, Cody Forsyth
1984   **Maple Leafs:** W. Galen Weston Sr., Carlos Gracida, Anthony Devcich, Martin Glue
1985   **Tramontana:** Anthony N.C. Embiricos, Rodrigo Vial, Carlos Gracida, Lord Charles Beresford
1986   **Los Locos:** Capt. G. Simon Tomlinson, Eugene Fortugno, Mrs. Claire J. Tomlinson, Stephane Macaire
1987   **Windsor Park:** Geoffrey J.W. Kent, Cody Forsyth, Stuart Mackenzie, HRH the Prince of Wales
1988   **Maple Leafs:** Andrew C. Hine, Julian B. Hipwood, Robert E. Walton, W. Galen Weston Sr.
1989   **Chateau Giscours:** Louis Tari, Santiago Gaztambide, Lionel Macaire, Adrian M. Wade
1990   **Rosamundo:** David Pearl, Antonio Herrera, Alejandro Díaz Alberdi, Roderick D. Matthews
1991   **Los Locos:** Mrs. Claire J. Tomlinson, Martín Vidou, Milo Fernández Araujo, Capt. G. Simon Tomlinson
1992   **Alcatel:** John W. Manconi, Horacio Fernández Llorente, Alejandro Díaz Alberdi, Antony Fanshawe
1993   **Maple Leafs:** W. Galen Weston Jr., Michael V. Azzaro, Guillermo Gracida, Harry Pearl
1994   **Black Bears:** Urs E. Schwarzenbach, Sebastián Merlos, Juan I. Merlos, Jason Dixon
1995   **Cowdray Park:** Hon. Charles Pearson, Alan J. Kent, Gustavo Courreges, Lord Charles Beresford
1996   **C.S. Brooks:** Mike Rutherford, Martín Vidou, Lord Charles Beresford, Adam Buchanan
1997   **C.S. Brooks:** Senter Johnson, Lord Charles Beresford, Miguel Novillo Astrada, Charles S. "Brook" Johnson
1998   **C.S. Brooks:** Senter Johnson, Andrew J.S. Seavill, Henry A.D. Brett, Jaime A. García Huidobro
1999   **Azzurra:** Stefano Marsaglia, Adrian M. Wade, Alan J. Kent, Mauricio Devrient-Kidd
2000   **Groeninghe:** Isabelle Hayen, James Dixon, Glen A. Gilmore, Malcolm P. Borwick
2001   **Vampire Bats:** Jack Kidd, Andrea Vianini, Henry A.D. Brett, Rory Sweet
2002   **Vampire Bats:** Rory Sweet, Henry A.D. Brett, Andrea Vianini, Thomas Morley
2003   **Los Locos:** Satnam S. Dhillon, Mark L. Tomlinson, William Lucas, Mrs. Claire J. Tomlinson
2004   **Los Locos:** Miss Emma Tomlinson, Satnam S. Dhillon, Matías MacDonough, Mrs. Claire J. Tomlinson
2005   **Lambourne:** Miss Katie Seabrook, Francisco Martín Moreno, Thomas Wilson, Robert Thame
2006   **Lovelocks:** Manuel Fernández Llorente, James R. Beim, William Lucas, Maj. Charles O. Hanbury
2007   **Longdole:** Maj. Charles O. Hanbury, Robert Archibald, Malcolm P. Borwick, Thomas Morley
2008   **Black Bears:** Guy Schwarzenbach, Max Routledge, John P. Clarkin, Simon Keyte
2009   **El Remanso:** George Hanbury, Tom de Bruin, Manuel Fernández Llorente, Jaime García Huidobro
2010   Not played.

Roehampton Open Challenge Cup

Open to any team without restrictions. For a Challenge Cup presented by the golf players in 1913.

1913 **Pilgrims:** Capt. Teignmouth Melvill, Alfred Grisar, Capt. Edward Wienholt, Frank Rich

1914 **Old Etonians:** Geoffrey H. Phipps-Hornby, Capt. Francis Grenfell, Earl Rocksavage, Capt. John Harrison

1920 **Old Cantabs:** Sir John Ramsden, Maj. Ivor Buxton, Walter Buckmaster, Lord John Wodehouse

1921 Abandoned due to American and English practice games.

1922 **Argentine Polo Federation:** Juan Miles, Juan Nelson, David Miles, Luis Lacey

1923 **Freebooters:** Duque de Peñaranda, Sir Charles Bingham, Walter Buckmaster, Lord John Wodehouse (Capt. Hugh N. Scott Robson)

1924 **Freebooters:** Alfred Grisar, Capt. Eric Atkinson, John A.E. Traill, Lewis Lacey

1925 **Jodhpur:** Thakur Prithi Singh, Capt. Austin Williams, Rao Rajah Hanut Singh, Thakur Ram Singh

1926 **El Gordo:** Duque de Peñaranda, Marqués de Villabrágima, Lewis Lacey, John A.E. Traill

1927 **Hurricanes:** Stephen Sanford, Capt. Charles Roark, Wing Cdr. Percival Wise, Maj. John Harrison

1928 **Hurricanes:** Stephen Sanford, Capt. Charles Roark, Wing Cdr. Percival Wise, Maj. John Harrison

1929 **El Gordo:** Duque de Peñaranda, Earle W. Hopping, Marqués de Villabrágima, John A.E. Traill

1930 **Hurricanes:** Hanut Singh, Gerald Balding, Capt. Charles Roark, Col. Percival Wise

1931 **Panthers:** Geoffrey H. Phipps-Hornby, Eric Tyrrell-Martin, Maj. Philip Magor, John A.E. Traill

1932 **Panthers:** Marqués Antonio de Portago, Eric Tyrrell-Martin, Maj. Philip Magor, John A.E. Traill

1933 **Jaipur:** Prithi Singh, Abhey Singh Hanut Singh, Maharajah of Jaipur

1934 **Aurora:** Harold Talbott, Elmer Boeseke, Seymour Knox, William Post

1935 **Panthers:** Stephen Sanford, Michael G. Phipps, Eric Tyrrell-Martin, Maj. Philip Magor

1936 **Templeton:** Michael Phipps, James Mills, Winston Guest, Robert Strawbridge

1937 **Jaguars:** Hon. W. Keith Rous, Stephen Sanford, Gerald Balding, Winston Guest

1938 **Texas Rangers:** Darryl Zanuck, Cecil Smith, Aidan Roark, Eric Tyrrell-Martin

1939 **Someries House:** Sir Harold Wernher, Capt. Andrew Horsburgh-Porter, Capt. G. Errol Prior-Palmer, Capt. David Dawnay

Cowdray Park Gold Cup

Established by Lord Cowdray in 1956. Eventually became emblematic of the English Open Polo Championship

1956 **Los Indios:** Jorge Marín Moreno, Pablo Nagore, Antonio Heguy, Juan Echeverz

1957 **Windsor Park:** Juan P. Nelson, Ernesto Lalor, Lt. Col. Humphrey Guinness, HRH Prince Philip

1958 **Cowdray Park:** Lt. Col. Peter Dollar, Lt. Col. Alec Harper, Hanut Singh, John Lakin

1959 **Casarejo:** Baron Elie de Rothschild, Rubén Gracida Hoffman, Alejandro Gracida Hoffman, Pedro Domecq de la Riva

1960 **Laversine-Casarejo:** Baron Elie de Rothschild, Rubén Gracida Hoffman, Alejandro Gracida Hoffman, Pedro Domecq de la Riva

1961 **Cowdray Park:** Brig. Gen. Masud A.A. Baig, Paul Withers, Lt. Col. Alec Harper (John Lakin), Charles Smith-Ryland

1962 **Cowdray Park:** Brig. Gen. Masud A.A. Baig, Brian Bethell, Paul Withers, Charles Smith-Ryland

1963 **La Vulci:** Marchese Giacinto Guglielmi de Vulci, José M. Torres Zavaleta, Carlos de la Serna, Daniel González

1964 **Jersey Lilies:** Ricardo Díaz Dale, Patrick Kemple, Hanut Singh, Eduardo Moore
1965 **Jersey Lilies:** Ricardo Díaz Dale, Patrick Kemple, Hanut Singh, Eduardo Moore
1966 **Windsor Park:** Lord Patrick Beresford, Lord Waterford, Gonzalo Tanoira, HRH Prince Philip
1967 **Woolmers Park:** John Lucas, Dr. Jorge Marín Moreno, Enrique Zorrilla, Celestino Garrós
1968 **Pimms:** Lord David Brecknock, Julian Hipwood, Daniel González, Alfredo Goti
1969 **Windsor Park:** Lord Patrick Beresford, Lord Waterford, HRH Prince Philip, Paul Withers
1970 **Boca Raton:** Joseph Casey, John C. Oxley, Roy Barry Jr., John T. Oxley
1971 **Pimms:** Lord David Brecknock, Enrique Zorrilla, Daniel González, Maj. Ronald Ferguson
1972 **Pimms:** Lord David Brecknock, Ronald Tongg, Daniel González, Maj. Ronald Ferguson
1973 **Stowell Park:** Hon. Mark Vestey, Lord Samuel Vestey, Eduardo Moore, Héctor Barrantes
1974 **Stowell Park:** David Gemmell, Lord Samuel Vestey, Eduardo Moore, Héctor Barrantes
1975 **Greenhill Farm:** James Sharp, Thomas Wayman, Lester Armour, Maj. Ronald Ferguson
1976 **Stowell Park:** J. Nicholas Williams, Hon. Mark Vestey, Eduardo Moore, Héctor Barrantes
1977 **Foxcote:** Peter Palumbo, Hon. Mark Vestey, Eduardo Moore, Daniel Devrient
1978 **Stowell Park:** J. Nicholas Williams, Lord Samuel Vestey, Eduardo Moore, Héctor Barrantes
1979 **Songhai:** Alan Kent, Alvaro Pieres, Gonzalo Pieres, Oliver Ellis
1980 **Stowell Park:** Philip Elliott, Hon. Mark Vestey, Eduardo Moore, Héctor Barrantes
1981 **Falcons:** Alexandre Ebeid, Gonzalo Pieres, Héctor Merlos, Luis Amaya
1982 **Southfield:** David Yeoman, Carlos Gracida, Lord Charles Beresford, John Walker
1983 **Falcons:** Andrew Hine, Carlos Gracida, Guillermo Gracida, Alexandre Ebeid
1984 **Southfield:** David Yeoman, Alan Kent, Owen Rinehart, David Jamison
1985 **Maple Leafs:** W. Galen Weston Sr., Julian Hipwood, Martin Glue (Luis Amaya), Anthony Devcich
1986 **Tramontana:** Anthony Embiricos, Jesús Baez, Carlos Gracida, Martin Brown
1987 **Tramontana:** Anthony Embiricos, Roberto González Gracida (Michael Azzaro), Carlos Gracida, David Jamison
1988 **Tramontana:** Anthony Embiricos, Valerio Aguilar, Carlos Gracida, David Jamison
1989 **Tramontana:** Anthony Embiricos, Roberto González Gracida, Carlos Gracida, David Jamison
1990 **Hildon House:** Capt. Michael Amoore, Norman Lobel, Tomás Fernández Llorente, Howard Hipwood
1991 **Tramontana:** Adam Buchanan, Adolfo Cambiaso, Carlos Gracida, Anthony Embiricos
1992 **Black Bears:** Urs Schwarzenbach, Sebastián Merlos, Juan I. Merlos, Martin Brown
1993 **Alcatel:** Peter Webb, Gabriel Donoso, Alejandro Díaz Alberdi, Ignacio González
1994 **Ellerston Black:** Oliver Taylor, Roberto González Gracida, Carlos Gracida, James Packer
1995 **Ellerston White:** Oliver Hipwood, Carlos Gracida, Gonzalo Pieres, Kerry Packer
1996 **C.S. Brooks:** John C. Fisher, Ignacio Heguy, Eduardo Heguy, Charles S. "Brook" Johnson (Sebastian Dawnay)
1997 **Labegorce:** Hubert Perrodo, Javier Novillo Astrada, Carlos Gracida, Jamie Le Hardy

1998 **Ellerston:** James Beim, Adolfo Cambiaso, Gonzalo Pieres, John C. Fisher
1999 **Pommery:** John Manconi, Henry Brett, Alejandro Díaz Alberdi, Juan Bollini
2000 **Geebung:** Rick Stowe, Bautista Heguy, Adolfo Cambiaso, David Allen
2001 **Dubai:** Ali Albwardi, Adolfo Cambiaso, Bartolomé Castagnola, Ryan Pemble
2002 **Black Bears:** Urs Schwarzenbach, Javier Novillo Astrada, Eduardo Novillo Astrada, Alejandro Novillo Astrada
2003 **Hildon Sport:** Miss Carina Vestey, Mark Tomlinson, Luke Tomlinson, John P. Clarkin
2004 **Azzurra:** Alejandro Novillo Astrada, Juan M. Nero, Marcos Heguy, Stefano Marsaglia
2005 **Dubai:** Tariq Albwardi, Lucas Monteverde, Alejandro Díaz Alberdi, Agustín Nero
2006 **Black Bears:** Guy Schwarzenbach, Eduardo Novillo Astrada, Javier Novillo Astrada, Lucas James
2007 **Lechuza Caracas:** Víctor Vargas, Sebastián Merlos, Juan I. Merlos (Agustín Merlos), Henry Fisher
2008 **Loro Piana:** David Stirling, Alfio Marchini, Juan M. Nero, James Peel
2009 **La Bamba De Areco:** Jean-François Decaux, Gonzalo Pieres Jr., Facundo Pieres, Tomás Garbarini Islas
2010 **Dubai:** Rashid Albwardi, Francisco Vismara, Pablo MacDonough, Adolfo Cambiaso

Queen's Cup

Trophy donated by HM Queen Elizabeth II in 1960

1960 **The Centaurs:** Dr. Jorge Marín Moreno, John L. Lucas, Gabriel Gracida, Sir Evelyn de Rothschild
1961 **Silver Leys:** Arthur G. Boyd Gibbins, Capt. J. Hugh Pitman, Maharaj Prem Singh, Risaldar Gaje Singh
1962 **Sao Silvestre:** Wallace Simonsen, João Adao, Juan J. Díaz Alberdi, Alejandro Mihanovich
1963 **Cowdray Park:** Lt. Col. Alec F. Harper, Paul M. Withers, J. Sinclair Hill, Brian B. Bethell
1964 **The Centaurs:** Dereck Goodman, Dr. Jorge N. Marín Moreno, John L. Lucas, Sir Evelyn de Rotschild
1965 **Pimms:** Lord George Brecknock, Dr. Jorge Marín Moreno, John L. Lucas, Daniel González
1966 **Pimms:** Lord George Brecknock, Dr. Jorge Marín Moreno, John L. Lucas, Celestino Garrós
1967 **Woolmers Park:** Dr. Jorge Marín Moreno, Enrique A. Zorrilla, John L. Lucas, Celestino Garrós
1968 **Woolmers Park:** Dr. Jorge Marín Moreno, Hernán H. Valenzuela, John L. Lucas, Sir Evelyn de Rothschild
1969 **Pimms:** Lord George Brecknock, Alejandro Soldati, Daniel González, Brian B. Bethell
1970 **Cowdray Park:** Lt. Col. Alec F. Harper, Howard J. Hipwood, Julian B. Hipwood, Hon. Michael Hare
1971 **Stowell Park:** Lord Samuel Vestey, Hon. Mark W. Vestey, Eduardo R. Moore, Héctor E. Barrantes
1972 **Cowdray Park:** William C. Linfoot, Howard J. Hipwood, William R. Linfoot, Hon. Michael Hare
1973 **Stowell Park:** Lord Samuel Vestey, Hon. Mark Vestey (Chris Bethell), Eduardo R. Moore, Héctor E. Barrantes
1974 **San Flamingo:** C. Ronald Driver, Howard J. Hipwood, Julian B. Hipwood, William T. Ylvisaker

1975 **Foxcote:** Lt. Col. Alec Harper, Hon. Mark W. Vestey, Eduardo R. Moore, Stuart T. Mackenzie

1976 **San Flamingo:** C. Ronald Driver, Howard J. Hipwood, Antonio Herrera, H. John Horswell

1977 **Foxcote:** Peter Palumbo, Hon. Mark W. Vestey, Eduardo R. Moore, Daniel Devrient

1978 **Stowell Park:** John N. Williams, Lord Samuel Vestey, Eduardo R. Moore, Héctor Barrantes

1979 **Los Locos:** Mrs. Claire J. Tomlinson, Capt. G. Simon Tomlinson, Héctor J. Crotto, David S. Gemmell

1980 **Stowell Park:** Hon. Mark W. Vestey, Eduardo R. Moore, Héctor E. Barrantes, Philip M.W. Elliott

1981 **Cowdray Park:** Hon. Charles A. Pearson, Carlos E. Jauregui, Paul M. Withers, Alexander J.C. Harper

1982 **Boehm Team:** Lord Patrick Beresford, Howard J. Hipwood, Stuart T. Mackenzie, Hon. Mark Vestey

1983 **Cowdray Park:** Hon. Charles A. Pearson, Cody Forsyth, Paul M. Withers, W. Patrick Churchward

1984 **Foxcote:** Lord Samuel Vestey, Lord Charles Beresford, Silvio Novaes, Philip M.W. Elliott

1985 **Centaurs:** David Yeoman, Alan J. Kent, Owen R. Rinehart, David L. Jamison

1986 **Les Diables Bleus:** Guy Wildenstein, Rodrigo Vial, Guillermo Gracida, HRH the Prince of Wales

1987 **Southfield:** John F. Yeoman, Alan J. Kent, Owen R. Rinehart, Martin R.R. Brown

1988 **NPC Broncos:** Marquess George Milford Haven, Cody Forsyth, Gabriel Donoso, Martin Glue

1989 **Hilditch and Key:** Andrew C. Hine, Julian B. Hipwood, Robert D. Walton, W. Galen Weston Sr.

1990 **Santa Fe:** Andrew C. Hine, Cody Forsyth, Héctor J. Crotto, William Bond-Elliott

1991 **Ellerston White:** Alasdair Archibald, Alfonso Pieres, Gonzalo Pieres, Kerry F.B. Packer

1992 **Ellerston White:** Henry Brett, Bautista Heguy, Alberto Heguy, Alasdair Archibald

1993 **Black Bears:** Oliver Hipwood, Sebastián Merlos, Juan I. Merlos, James Dixon

1994 **Black Bears:** Urs E. Schwartzenbach, Sebastián Merlos, Juan I. Merlos, Tarquin Southwell

1995 **Labegorce:** Hubert Perrodo, Martin Brown, Alberto Heguy, Milo Fernández Araujo

1996 **Ellerston White:** Julian Daniels, Javier Novillo Astrada, Gonzalo Pieres, Kerry F.B. Packer

1997 **Isla Carroll:** Matthew Pennell, Juan I. Merlos, Guillermo Gracida, John B. Goodman

1998 **Ellerston:** James Beim, Adolfo Cambiaso, Gonzalo Pieres, John C. Fisher

1999 **Ellerston:** James Beim, Adolfo Cambiaso, Gonzalo Pieres, Tristan Wade

2000 **Geebung:** David Allen, Adolfo Cambiaso, Bautista Heguy, Rick Stowe

2001 Not played. Hoof-and-mouth disease.

2002 **Emerging:** Fabien Pictet, Héctor Guerrero, Milo Fernández Araujo, Luke Tomlinson

2003 **Dubai:** Ali Albwardi, Bartolomé Castagnola, Adolfo Cambiaso, Matthew Lodder

2004 **Labegorce:** Hubert Perrodo, Frederick Mannix Jr., Carlos Gracida, Luke Tomlinson

2005 **Dubai:** Ali Albwardi, Alejandro Díaz Alberdi, Adolfo Cambiaso, Ryan Pemble

2006 **Dubai:** Tariq Albwardi, Alejandro Díaz Alberdi, Adolfo Cambiaso, George Meyrick

2007 **Loro Piana:** David Stirling, Alfio Marchini, Juan M. Nero, Martín Espain

2008 **Ellerston:** Max Routledge, Gonzalo Pieres Jr., Pablo MacDonough, Jamie Packer

2009 **Apes Hill:** Charles Hanbury, Mark Tomlinson, Juan Gris Zavaleta, Luke Tomlinson

2010 **Dubai:** Rashid Albwardi, Francisco Vismara, Pablo MacDonough, Adolfo Cambiaso

2011 **Talandracas:** Edouard Carmignac, Lucas Monteverde, Milo Fernández Araujo, Facundo Sola

Silver Jubilee Cup

Presented in 1977 by Mr. John Wilson, chairman of W.D. & H.O. Wills, to the Hurlingham Polo Association as a perpetual challenge trophy to commemorate the twenty-fifth anniversary of the accession of HM Queen Elizabeth II to the throne.

1977   **France:** Stéphane Macaire, Guy Wildenstein, Lionel Macaire (Abel Aguero), Jacques Macaire

1978   **The Commonwealth:** HRH the Prince of Wales, Anthony Devcich, Sinclair Hill, Ahmadu Yakubu

1979   **England II:** Alan Kent, Patrick Churchward, Maj. Ronald Ferguson, HRH the Prince of Wales

1980   **England II:** Lord Charles Beresford, Alan Kent, Robert Graham, HRH the Prince of Wales

1981   **England II:** Martin Brown, John Horswell, Robert Graham, HRH the Prince of Wales

1982   **Young America:** William Ylvisaker Jr., Stewart Armstrong, Charles Bostwick, Richard Bostwick

1983   **France:** Guy Wildenstein, Alain Bernard, Lester Armour III, Stéphane Macaire

1984   **Spain:** Vicente Prado, Pedro Domecq, Ignacio Domecq, Rafael Echevarrieta

1985   **England II:** HRH the Prince of Wales, John Horswell, Robert Graham, Lord Charles Beresford

1986   **Chile:** Alejandro Fantini, Rodrigo Vial, Samuel Moreno, Fernando Fantini

1987   **Prince of Wales' Team:** Geoffrey Kent, HRH the Prince of Wales, Stuart Mackenzie, Martin Brown

1988   **France:** Alain Bernard, Louis Tari, Lionel Macaire, Stéphane Macaire

1989   **North America:** Roberto González Gracida, Michael Azzaro, Owen Rinehart, Dale Smicklas

1990   **Ellerston White:** Adrian Wade, Alfonso Pieres, Gonzalo Tanoira, Stuart Mackenzie

1991   **Prince of Wales' Team:** Javier Celis, Carlos Gracida, Guillermo Gracida, HRH the Prince of Wales

1992   **Hurlingham:** Philip Elliott, Lord Charles Beresford, Julian Hipwood, HRH the Prince of Wales

1993   **Canada:** Galen Weston Jr., Todd Offen, David Offen, Steve Dalton

1994   **The Brothers Blue:** José Donoso, Clemente Zavaleta, Gabriel Donoso, Julio Zavaleta

1995   **Labegorce:** Hubert Perrodo, Milo Fernández Araujo, Alberto Heguy, Martin Brown

2002   (UBS, at Cowdray Park) **Los Tamaraos:** Bobby Aguirre, Gabriel Donoso, Milo Fernández Araujo, Ignacio Gonzalez

2003   **Lamrei:** Santiago Gaztambide, Charlie McCowen, Marcos Di Paola, Luke Tomlinson

2004   **Bateleur:** Alan Kent, Martín Vidou, Andrea Vianini, Lord Charles Beresford

2005   **Lamrei:** Gastón Moore, Santiago Gaztambide, Marcos di Paola, Charlie McCowen

2006   **Lamrei:** Gastón Moore, Santiago Gaztambide, Marcos di Paola, Charlie McCowen

2007   **Lamrei:** Gastón Moore, Santiago Gaztambide, Marcos di Paola, Charlie McCowen

Prince of Wales Trophy

Established in 1986 by the Royal County of Berkshire Polo Club.

1986   **Kennelot:** Henryk de Kwiatowski, Warren Scherer, Howard Hipwood, Oliver Ellis

1987   **Southfield:** David Jamison, Alan Kent, Owen Rinehart, Martin Brown

1988   **Hildon House:** Wicky El Effendi, Norman Lobel, Howard Hipwood, Lord Charles Beresford

1989   **Tramontana:** Anthony Embiricos, Roberto González Gracida, Carlos Gracida, David Jamison

1990 **Tramontana:** Anthony Embiricos, Roberto González Gracida, Carlos Gracida, Patrick
       Cowley
1991 **Munipore:** Peter Scott, Bautista Heguy, Eduardo Heguy, Bryan Morrison
1992 **Ellerston White:** Henry Brett, Bautista Heguy, Eduardo Heguy, Alasdair Archibald
1993 **Maple Leafs:** Justin Gaunt, Michael Azzaro, Guillermo Gracida, Galen Weston Sr.
1994 **Cowdray Park:** Hon. Charles Pearson, Alan Kent, Gustavo Courreges, Lord Charles
       Beresford
1995 **Alcatel:** John Manconi, Gabriel Donoso, Alejandro Díaz Alberdi, Antony Fanshawe
1996 **Alcatel:** John Manconi, Gabriel Donoso, Alejandro Díaz Alberdi, Tarquin Southwell
1997 **Geebung:** Andrew Hine, Santiago Araya, Bartolomé Castagnola, Rick Stowe
1998 **Jerudong Park:** Bahar Jefri Bolkiah, Bautista Heguy, Eduardo Heguy, Neil Dickson
1999 **Ellerston:** James Beim, Adolfo Cambiaso, Gonzalo Pieres, Tristan Wade
2000 **Royal Pahang:** Prince Rahman, Martín Vidou, Alberto Heguy, Malcolm Borwick
2001 **FCT:** Roger Carlsson, Martín Vidou, Gabriel Donoso, Ignacio Gonzalez
2002 **Dubai:** Ali Albwardi, Bartolomé Castagnola, Adolfo Cambiaso, James Peel
2003 **Buzee Bees:** Satnam Dhillon, Roderick Williams, Luke Tomlinson, Jamie Morrison
2004 **Azzurra:** Stefano Marsaglia, Marcos Heguy, Juan Martín Nero, Gonzalo Bourdieu
2005 **Azzurra:** Jean Gonzalez, Juan M. Nero, Bautista Heguy, Stefano Marsaglia
2006 **Dubai:** Tariq Albwardi, Jonny Good, Ignacio Toccalino, Adolfo Cambiaso
2007 **Cadenza:** Tony Pidgley, Tomás Fernández Llorente, John P. Clarkin, Nicolás Espain
2008 **Broncos:** George Milford Haven, Santiago Chavanne, Pablo MacDonough, John Fisher
2009 **Talandracas:** Edouard Carmignac, Guillermo Terrera, Alejandro Agote, Lucas Mon-
       teverde
2010 **Emlor:** Spencer McCarthy, Ignacio Gonzalez, John P. Clarkin, Joaquín Pittaluga

Prince Philip Trophy

1992 **Tramontana:** Anthony Embiricos, Carlos Gracida, Guillermo Gracida, Martin Brown
1996 **Ellerston White:** Julian Daniels, Javier Novillo Astrada, Cerlos Gracida, Darren Smith
1997 **Labegorce:** Hubert Perrodo, Javier Novillo Astrada, Carlos Gracida, Jamie Le Hardy
1998 **Ellerston White:** James Beim, Adolfo Cambiaso, Gonzalo Pieres, John Fisher
1999 **Pommery:** John Manconi, Henry Brett, Alejandro Díaz Alberdi, Juan Bollini
2000 **Black Bears:** Urs Schwarzenbach, Javier Novillo Astrada, Miguel Novillo Astrada,
       Sebastian Dawnay
2001 **England I:** Satnam Dhillon, Ignacio Gonzalez, Luke Tomlinson, Roderick Williams
2002 (European Open) **Beaufort:** Satnam Dhillon, Gastón Laulhé, José Araya, Luke Tom-
       linson

Golden Jubilee Cup

2002 **Prince of Wales' Team:** James Beim, Oliver Hipwood, Roderick Williams, Chris Hyde
2003 **Prince of Wales' Team:** HRH Prince Harry of Wales, Mark Tomlinson, Roderick
       Williams, Chris Hyde
2004 **Hurlingham:** Richard Le Poer, Satnam Dhillon, Malcolm Borwick, Chris Hyde
2005 **Prince of Wales' Team:** HRH Prince Harry of Wales, James Harper, Andrew Hine,
       Ignacio Gonzalez
2006 **Prince of Wales' Team:** HRH Prince Harry of Wales, Satnam Dhillon, Malcolm Bor-
       wick, Ignacio Gonzalez
2007 **Hurlingham:** Satnam Dhillon, James Harper, Tom Morley, Roderick Williams
2008 Jamie Le Hardie, Henry Brett, Chris Hyde, Jonny Good
2009 **Hurlingham:** Max Routledge, Satnam Dhillon, Tom Morley, Chris Hyde
2010 **Hurlingham:** Oliver Cudmore, Richard Le Poer, Satnam Dhillon, Ryan Pemble

Chapter Notes

Chapter 1

1. Valentine Irwin (1838–1873) was born in Rathmoylan, county Roscommon.
2. Norman J. Cinnamond, *El Polo* (Barcelona: Librería Catalonia, no date [1929]), 27.
3. *Stonyhurst Magazine* 14, no. 272 (December 1927), 388.
4. Cinnamond, op. cit., 29.
5. *Polo Monthly*, June 1929.
6. Henry Manners Chichester and George Burges-Short, *The Records and Badges of Every Regiment and Corps in the British Army* (London: Gale & Polden, 1900), 85.
7. Lionel Dawson, *Sport in War* (London: Collins, 1936), 93.
8. T. Levins Moore, *Polo in Ireland*, in *Polo-Coaching*, ed. "The Sportsman" (London: Sports and Sportsmen, no date), 73.
9. Robert Weir and J. Moray Brown, *Riding: Polo* (London: Longmans, 1891), 345.
10. *London Gazette*, 5 March 1869, 1515.
11. *The Field*, 20 March 1869.
12. T.A. St. Quintin, *Chances of Sports of Sorts* (Edinburgh: Blackwood, 1912), 329.
13. R.S. Liddell, *The Memories of the Tenth Royal Hussars* (London: Longmans, 1891), 552. Col. Robert Spencer Liddell (1841–1903), the son of Sir John Liddell, KCB, MD, director-general of the Medical Department of the Navy, was educated at Harrow School and joined the 10th Hussars as an ensign in 1858. He was Junior Lt. Col. from 1881 to 1886 in Sudan and retired from command under the six-years rule.
14. For a discussion on the correct date for this match, see Horace Laffaye, *The Evolution of Polo* (Jefferson, NC: McFarland, 2009), 21.
15. Frank H. Reynard, *The Ninth (Queen's Royal) Lancers, 1715–1903* (Edinburgh: Blackwood, 1904), 82.
16. For additional information on Captain St. Quintin, see Chris Ashton, "Thomas St. Quintin: A Great Polo Pioneer," in *Profiles in Polo* (Jefferson, NC: McFarland, 2007), 17. For biographical information on Captain Hartopp, see Roger Chatterton-Newman, "Edward Hartopp: This Must Be a Good Game," in *Profiles in Polo*, 13.
17. Weir and Moray Brown, op. cit., 255.
18. "Our Van," *Baily's*, August 1872, 180.
19. *Illustrated London News*, 20 June 1874, 579.
20. See Roger Chatertton-Newman, *Profiles in Polo*, "Francis Herbert: Killed a Salmon, Shot Some Grouse and Played Polo," 28.
21. E.D. Miller, *Polo Players Guide & Almanack* (Rugby: Pepperday, 1910), 146.
22. J. Moray Brown, "About Some Polo Clubs" *Baily's*, June 1894, 380.
23. The cup is a Cashmere raised design with three snake handles and cover to match, mounted with an elephant.
24. G.W. Hobson, *Some XII Lancers* (Long Compton: King's Stone, 1936), 151.
25. "The Sportsman," ed., "The Story of the Clubs," in *Polo-Coaching* (London: Sports & Sportsmen, no date), 65.

Chapter 2

1. "Our Van," *Baily's*, "Polo at Bedford, St. Neots and in York," October 1900, 294.
2. J. Moray Brown, *Polo* (London: Vinton, 1895), 113.
3. J. Moray Brown, "About Some Polo Clubs," *Baily's*, June 1894, 373.
4. "County Polo Clubs: The North Devon," *Polo Monthly*, March 1909, 61.

5. Arthur W. Coaten, *The Polo Player's Diary for 1912* (London: Vaughn, 1912), 174.

6. Brown, *Polo*, 115.

7. L.V.L. Simmonds and E.D. Miller, *The Polo Annual* (London: Cox, 1913), 200.

8. Coaten, op. cit., 166.

9. J. Moray Brown, "About Some Polo Clubs," *Baily's*, June 1894, 368.

10. Coaten, op. cit., 166.

11. *British Hunts*, op. cit., vol. 1, 1908, 165.

12. John James Scott-Chisholme, 9th Lancers, was a joint winner of the Indian P.A. Open Championship in 1899. Col. Scott-Chisholme (1851–1899) was military secretary to the governor of Madras. During the Anglo-Boer War he was killed at Elandslaagte while in command of the Imperial Light Horse.

13. E.D. Miller, *Modern Polo* (London: Hurst & Blackett, 1911), 4.

14. Anthony Blight, *Georges Roesch and the Invincible Talbot* (London: Grenville, 1970), 5.

15. J. Moray Brown, "About Some Polo Clubs," *Baily's*, July 1894, 80.

16. Joseph Foster, *Alumni Oxonienses* (Oxford: Parker, 1888–1892).

17. J.A. Venn, *Alumni Cantabrigienses* (London: Cambridge U. Press, 1922–1954).

18. Walter, 1st Viscount Long (1854–1924), held the offices of president of the Board of Agriculture, chief secretary for Ireland, secretary of state for the colonies, and first lord of the Admiralty. He was also appointed to the Privy Council.

Chapter 3

1. Jean-Luc Chartier, *Cent Ans de Polo en France* (Paris: Polo Club Editions, 1992), 29.

2. This cartoon was reproduced in *Polo*, December 1930, 14.

3. Robert Weir and J. Moray Brown, *Hunting: Polo* (London: Longmans, 1891), 259.

4. John Elliott Cowdin, "Polo in America," in *The Book of Sport*, ed. William Patten (New York: J.F. Taylor, 1901), 140.

5. F. Gray Griswold, *The International Polo Cup* (New York: Dutton's, 1928), 11.

6. Alden Hatch and Foxhall Keene, *Full Tilt* (New York: Derrydale, 1938), 129.

7. John Hanlon, "A Posh Game in a Posh Town," *Sports Illustrated*, 22 September 1969, 125.

8. *New York Times*, 26 August 1886, 2.

9. "The First Matches in America," in *International Polo*, ed. Arthur W. Coaten (London: Vaughn, 1912), 10.

10. E.D. Miller, *Fifty Years of Sport* (New York: Dutton, no date [1925]), 67.

11. J.C. Cooley, "A Champion of America," *Polo*, June 1930, 23.

12. *Outing*, "International Polo," June 1911, 380. These gentlemen were Frederick Beach, Raymond Belmont, Oliver Bird, Griswold Lorillard, Edwin Morgan, Elliott Roosevelt, John Sanford, William Thorn Jr., Cornelius Vanderbilt and Egerton Winthrop.

13. Griswold, op. cit., 12.

14. Nigel à Brassard, *A Glorious Victory, A Glorious Defeat* (Chippenham: Antony Rowe, 2001), 19.

15. Ibid., 20.

16. *The Westchester Cup Commemorative Program* (Lake Worth: Museum of Polo and Hall of Fame, 2009), 48.

17. Nigel à Brassard, "The Westchester Trophy: A Tiffany Design," in *The Westchester Cup Commemorative Program* (Lake Worth: Museum of Polo, 2009), 46.

18. J.C. Cooley, "Post and Paddock," *Polo*, September 1935, 18.

19. St. Quintin, op. cit., 237.

20. *Polo Monthly*, "Polo in Argentina," March 1909, 65.

Chapter 4

1. *Polo Monthly*, "Players Past and Present: The Famous Sussex Team," March 1909, 15.

2. Weir and Brown, op. cit., 349.

3. *Polo Monthly*, September 1932, 377.

4. Edward D. Miller, *Fifty Years of Sport* (New York: Dutton, no date), 64.

5. Miller, op. cit., 182.

6. Frederick William L.S.H. Cavendish was on the regimental team that took the Beresford Cup and the Inter-regimental Tournament in 1909 in South Africa. His nickname, "Caviar," pays eloquent testimony to his tastes and profligacy. He lost a substantial fortune, whereupon he became a serious officer, passing Staff College. Brig. Gen. Cavendish (1878–1931) was a staff officer in France during World War I.

7. Frank H. Reynard, *The Ninth (Queen's Royal) Lancers 1715–1903* (Edinburgh: Blackwood, 1904), 125.

8. G.W. Hobson, *Some XII Lancers* (Long Compton: King's Stone, 1936), 230.

9. Alphabetical list of polo players who were killed in the Anglo–South African War, 1899–1902:

The Earl of Airlie's fate has been mentioned above.

Lt. Lord Archibald Ava, formerly 17th Lancers, who was in South Africa as a war correspondent; was mortally wounded carrying messages from Ladysmith, 1900.

Lt. Robert Bellew, 16th Lancers, killed at Fourteen Streams, Piquetberg Road, 1901.

Lt. Percy Frederick Brassey, 9th Lancers, killed during the relief of Kimberley, 1900.

Lt. Hon. Charles William Hugh Cavendish, 17th Lancers. Killed in action at Diamond Hill, near Pretoria, 1900.

Lt. Thomas Connolly, Royal Scots Greys. Killed in action at Kaalboschfontein in 1900.

Capt. George Percy Brasier Creagh, 9th Hodson's Horse. While in command of Robert's Horse was wounded at Kareefontein; died four days later at Eirslaagte, in 1900.

Maj. Henry Shelly Dalbiac, Imperial Yeomanry, was killed in action in 1900 at Senekal. A famous athlete, jockey, and writer for sports papers, he had served in the Royal Artillery.

Capt. George Paget Ellison, 9th Lancers. Died of enteric fever (typhoid) at Kroonstad, in 1900.

Commander Alfred Peel Ethelston, HMS Powerful, an officer in the Naval Brigade. Killed in action at Graspan, 1899. Commander Ethelston had played on the initial polo games on Victoria Island, Canada.

Maj. Joseph "Jack" Hanwell, Royal Field Artillery. Killed in action near Ventersburg, 1900.

Lt. William Henry Tucker Hill, 5th Lancers, who was on the winning team of the Beresford Cup in South Africa, died in action at Waggon Hill, Ladysmith, in 1900.

Capt. Lord William Kensington, 2nd Life Guards, was wounded at Houtne on 30 April 1900 and died in Bloemfontein on 24 June.

Maj. Philip Walter Jules Le Gallais, 8th Hussars, already mentioned.

Lt. Col. Norton Legge, 20th Hussars, was killed in action at Nooitgedacht, 1900.

Capt. Thomas Eyre Lloyd, Coldstream Guards, died of wounds at Brakenlaagte, in 1901.

Capt. Cortlandt Gordon McKenzie, Royal Artillery, one of the top players for the Edinburgh Polo Club and a two-time winner of the County Cup, died of the dreaded enteric fever at De Aae, in 1900.

Capt. the Hon. Raymond de Montmorency, VC, 21st Lancers, was killed in action near Stormbers, in 1900.

Lt. Robert Alexander Morritt, 17th Lancers, killed in action near Moddefontein, in 1901. His fellow officers Lt. Russell and Lt. Sheridan were killed in the same action.

Maj. James Alexander Orr-Ewing, Warwickshire Yeomanry, killed at Kleis, was an old 16th Lancers officer.

Lt. Thomas Douglas Pilkington, 1st Royal Dragoons, killed in action at Kaalboshfontein, 1900.

Capt. Robert Egerton Rasbotham, Durham Light Infantry, was killed in action at Eden Kop, in 1901.

Lt. Bertram Temple Rose, Royal Horse Guards, died of enteric fever at Base Hospital in Pietermaritzburg, in 1900.

Capt. Charles Ernest Rose, Royal Horse Guards, brother of the above mentioned officer, was killed in action near Wellow, just thirty-four days after his brother's death.

Lt. Philip Leslie Russell, 17th Lancers.

Lt. Albert Savory, 4th Hussars, one of Winston Churchill's teammates in the Indian Inter-regimental Champion team, was killed in Natal, while attached to the South African Light Horse.

John James Scott-Chisholme, 9th Lancers, killed in 1899 at Elandslaagte, while in command of the Imperial Light Horse, a unit that he had raised himself.

Lt. Richard Brinsley Sheridan, 17th Lancers.

Lt. Col. John Sherston, Rifle Brigade, killed in action near Talanal Hill, 1899.

Lt. Col. Cecil Foster Seymour Vandeleur, Coldstream Guards, was killed in a train ambush near Isaterval, in 1901.

Chapter 5

1. Nigel Miskin, *History of Hurlingham* (No place: private printing, 2000), 23.
2. Pedro F. Christophersen, *Teoría y Práctica del Juego de Polo* (Buenos Aires: A.A. de Polo, 1948), 241.
3. T.B. Drybrough, *Polo* (London: Vinton, 1898), 46.
4. Miskin, op. cit., 78.
5. Taprell Dorling, *The Hurlingham Club* (London: private printing, no date [1953]), 31.
6. Ibid., 121. Mr. Nigel Miskin, the Hurlingham Club's historian and honorary member, was a most charming host during the author's and his wife's visit to the club.
7. In his inimitable style, Samuel Pepys recorded in his diary, "17th Jan … all the discourse of the Duel yesterday between the Duke of Buckingham, Holmes, and one Jenkins on one side, and my Lord of Shrewsbury,

Sir Jo. Talbot, and one Bernard Howard, on the other side; and all about my Lady Shrewsbury, who is a whore and is at this time, and hath for a great while been, a whore to the Duke of Buckingham; and so her husband challenged him, and they met yesterday in a close near Barne Elmes and there fought; and my Lord Shrewsbury is run through the body from the right breast through the shoulder, and Sir Jo. Talbot all along up one of his arms, and Jenkins killed upon the place, and the rest all in a little measure wounded." This formidable duel involving three against three swordsmen was one of the most notorious in England. Lord Shrewsbury died of his wound months later.

8. Edward D. Miller, *Fifty Years of Sport* (New York: Dutton, no date), 152.

9. Ibid., 155.

10. *Polo Monthly*, "The Cirencester Club," June 1909.

11. *Polo Monthly*, "The Passing of Cirencester Club," August 1932, 26.

12. The story of polo at Cirencester is told in Herbert Spencer's *A Century of Polo*, published in 1994.

13. Elizabeth Hennessy's *A History of Roehampton Club, 1902–2001*, privately printed by the club, contains much information about the various activities developed since its foundation.

14. Dereck Russell-Stoneham and Roger Chatterton-Newman wrote *Polo at Cowdray*, a comprehensive history of the club.

15. T.F. Dale, *Polo: Past and Present* (London: Country Life, 1904), 75.

16. T.B. Drybrough, *Polo* (London: Longmans, 1906), 205.

17. "The 1909 Recent Form List," *Polo Monthly*, March 1909, 34.

18. T.F. Dale, *Polo: Past and Present* (London: Country Life, 1905), 273.

19. "Polo's Progress in England," *Polo Monthly*, November 1923, 93.

20. T.F. Dale ("Stoneclink"), *Polo at Home and Abroad* (London: London & Counties, 1915), 135.

21. Ibid., 143.

Chapter 6

1. Horace William Noel Rochfort, BA, JP, DL, High Sheriff for county Carlow (1809–1891), was also the founder of Carlow Cricket Club and founder and first president of the County Carlow Rugby Football Club in 1873, the oldest extant provincial rugby club in Ireland. Rochfort was succeeded as president by another polo player, Steuart Duckett.

2. E.D. Miller, *Modern Polo* (London: Hurst & Blackett, 1911), 496.

3. For a biographical sketch of John Watson, see Roger Chatterton-Newman, "John Watson: The Founding Father," in *Profiles in Polo* (Jefferson, NC: McFarland, 2007), 23.

4. T. Moore Levins, "Polo in Ireland," in *Polo and Coaching*, ed. "the Sportsman," (London: Sports & Sportsmen, no date), 79.

5. *British Hunts and Huntsmen* (London: Biographical, 1911), 346.

6. Information about the polo clubs in Ireland was obtained from many sources: several editions of *The Polo Player's Guide*, *The Polo Annual*, *The Polo Player's Almanack* and the above-cited article by Thomas Moore Levins.

7. *British Hunts*, op. cit., 336.

8. T.F. Dale, ed., *Polo at Home and Abroad* (London: London & Counties, 1915), 303.

Chapter 7

1. Letter to the editor, *The Field*, 19 March 1870, 260.

2. The players were the British Consul in Rosario, Lewis Joel; Mr. Lane; Mr. Dana; Peter Schnack, owner of a model rural establishment in Cañada de Gómez; and Mr. Hope, a member of a family whose descendants are recorded in the polo handicap lists until the 1980s. Two brothers Hope leased land in that area and eventually would become large landowners. Their opponents were Mr. Weldom; Mr. Krell; E. Soppe, mentioned in the records of St. Bartholomew's Anglican Church in Rosario; Mr. James; and Mr. Markham. The umpire was Joseph Greenwood, owner of Estancia Irwell, named for a river in his native Lancashire.

3. Horacio A. Laffaye, *El Polo en la Argentina en el Siglo XIX* (Lake Worth, FL: Museum of Polo, 2009), 3.

4. *River Plate Sport and Pastime*, 28 September 1892, 9. Resolution of the Polo Association of the River Plate: "Two annual championships to be held…."

5. *The Indian Polo Association Calendar* (Meerut: Station Press, 1927), 20.

6. *River Plate Sport and Pastime*, 13 July 1892, 10.

7. Frank J. Balfour, "Polo in South America," in *Polo at Home and Abroad*, ed. T.F. Dale (London: London & Counties, 1915), 183.

8. *Baily's*, "Our Van," August 1896, 168.

9. *Polo Monthly*, "Brilliant Argentine Players," June 1912, 248.

10. Eduardo P. Archetti, *Masculinities: Football, Polo and the Tango in Argentina* (Oxford: Berg, 1999), 93.

11. Chris Ashton, *Geebung: The Story of Australian Polo* (Sydney: Hamilton, 1993), 29.

12. Ibid., 30.

13. Ibid., 31.

14. H.T. Denny, *Polo of Course: A History of Polo in W.A.* (Perth: Private printing, 1997), 11.

15. Quoted in K.M. Little, *Polo in New Zealand* (Wellington: Whitcombe and Tombs, 1956), 16.

16. Donald C. McKenzie and John R. McKenzie, *Polo in South Africa* (Pietermaritzburg: Teeanem, 1999), 1.

17. Ibid., 1.

18. Ibid., 356.

19. "Shinney on Horseback," *San Francisco Call*, 4 April 1895, 5.

20. Capt. William Michael Glynn Turquand was commissioned as an ensign in the Coldstream Guards on 22 May 1866 and was eventually promoted to lieutenant — in 1868 — and then captain, before resigning his commission on 6 January 1875. Captain Turquand married Eleanor Duff, from Fetteresso Castle, Scotland; they had a daughter, Ann, who died in infancy, and a son, William, who eventually was manager of the Coronado Hotel near San Diego, when it was a mecca of polo in California. Captain Glynn Turquand died, age forty-one, on 14 September 1887, in Green Spring, Ohio, and is buried in Bexar County Cemetery, San Antonio, next to his children.

21. Information provided by Debra Gracy: "In Southwest Texas (Boerne) is the famous Balcones Ranch (owned by Capt. Turquand). It is a monument to a class who helped to give Texas her peculiar reputation. Balcones Ranch was improved by a wealthy Englishman who came out from the old country with a pocketful of money and his head full of ideas of a good time. He put on the raw land the usual improvements and then he added a race track, a polo ground and various diverting institutions. While the money lasted. The fun was fast and furious for everybody who chose to come. But the end of a check book and of a fast life was reached together." Ms. Gracy is restoring the Phillip Manor, one of the oldest buildings in Texas, where several of the polo players lodged and met as a clubhouse. Phillip Manor's bar is named Captain Turquand's Saloon in honor of the 1883 Boerne Polo Club." Personal communications, 8 November 2007 and 11 September 2009.

22. *London Gazette*, 21 July 1871, p. 3264. Egremont Eadon Shearburn was born in Manstead House, Goldaming, county of Surrey, in 1853, the son of Captain Thomas and Sarah Shearburn, and was educated at Marlborough College. He was commissioned into the 3rd Regiment (Light Infantry) West York Militia, in 1871. Later, on 1 January 1880, he transferred to the 9th Lancers and on 10 November of the same year resigned from the service. Captain Shearburn served in the Afghan War with the 9th Lancers before his retirement.

23. Lawrence M. Woods, *British Gentlemen in the Wild West* (New York: Free Press, 1989), 127.

24. Curtis Harnack, *Gentlemen on the Prairie* (Ames: Iowa State University, 1985), 208.

25. Woods, op. cit., 6.

26. J.B. Macmahan, "Polo in the West," *Outing*, September 1895, 472.

27. Personal visit, August 2010.

28. Bucky King, *Big Horn Polo* (Sheridan: Still Sailing, 1987), 2.

29. Ibid., 6.

30. Quoted in Marshall Sprague, *The Grizzlies* (No place: Cheyenne Mountain Country Club, 1983), 59.

31. Dennis Amato, "Early California Polo," *Polo*, April 1996, 35.

32. James Campbell Besley was born in 1874 and received his education at Eton and Oxford, where he started playing polo. He immigrated to Australia, where he gained a degree at the Broken Hill School of Mines in New South Wales. Then Besley made a fortune in the gold fields of Kalgoorlie and Coolgardie in Western Australia. The gold fever took him to the Klondike gold rush, where he added to his considerable patrimony. At the end of the Boer War in South Africa, Besley worked for Cecil Rhodes, drawing up geological reports. Always on the move, he returned to the Klondike to sell his interests and went to Mexico to mine silver and copper, while managing a 50,000-acre ranch. Then Besley went on to Lima, Peru, to look for the source of the Amazon River and rafted down 4,000 miles to the Atlantic Ocean.

33. Tony Rees, *Polo: The Galloping Game* (Cochrane: Western Heritage, 2000), 13.

34. Ibid., 237.

35. Ibid., 15.

36. Geoffrey W. Rice, *Heaton Rhodes of Otahuna* (Christchurch: Canterbury University Press, 2001), 62. This book is a biography of Sir Heaton Rhodes, Arthur's cousin and teammate.

37. *Press*, Christchurch, 9 March 1886, 2d.

38. Three of these officers reached Flag rank. Admiral Sir Reginald Tyrwhitt was the hero of the battle of Dogger Bank in the North Sea in 1914. Admiral William Oswald Story retired in 1912 and went to live in Canada; when the war started, he volunteered and was transferred to the Royal Canadian Navy. The third flag officer was Vice-Admiral Seymour Elphinstone Erskine, who commanded the Royal Navy Barracks in Chatham.

39. Gabriel Ellison and Kim Fraser, *Harmony of Hooves: A Celebration of Racing and Polo in Northern Rhodesia and Zambia* (No place: Natal Witness, 1999), 110.

40. Personal communication from Nicholas Colquhoun-Denvers, 26 May 2011.

41. E.F. Bolton, *Horse Management in West Africa* (Norwich: Jarrold, 1931), 47.

42. Wendy Hutton, *The Singapore Polo Club: An Informal History* (Singapore: Girdwood, 1983), 10.

43. Ibid.

44. "From All Quarters," *Polo Monthly*, May 1912, 218.

45. "Early Polo in Valparaiso," *Polo Monthly*, May 1934, 77.

46. Ignácio de Loyola Brandão, *Polo Brasil* (São Paulo: Markmidia, 1992), 137.

47. Ibid., 142.

48. Robert Weir and J. Moray Brown, *Riding: Polo* (London: Longmans, 1899), 292.

49. Prior to entering the diplomatic service, Sir Thomas Berry Cusack-Smith, KCMG (1859–1929), was a lieutenant in the 1st Volunteer Battalion, Essex Regiment. During the war he served as a major in the Royal Field Artillery.

Chapter 8

1. Halden and Keene, 131.

2. Ibid., 134.

3. Minutes of the Polo Association, 1890–1900. Typewritten documents at the Museum of Polo, Wellington, Florida.

4. Perry R. Duis, *Challenging Chicago: Coping with Everyday Life, 1937–1920* (Chicago: University of Illinois, 1998), 308.

5. Our Van, "The America Cup," *Baily's*, August 1900, 135.

6. Ibid.

7. "The Sportsman," *Polo & Coaching* (London: Sports and Sportsmen, no date), 224.

8. E.D. Miller, *Fifty Years of Sport* (New York: Dutton's, no date), 306.

9. Hurlingham Polo Association, 2009 Yearbook (Faringdon: HPA, 2009), 338.

10. *The Field*, 7 June 1902, 861.

11. Ibid.

12. The oldest rules of polo, those of the Silchar Club in Assam, specified that when a defending team hit the ball behind their own backline, a free shot from the intersection of the back- and sidelines was awarded to the attacking team, just like in hockey and soccer. This is the origin of the term "corner" in Argentina referring to what in the United States is called a "safety."

13. *Country Life*, 28 June 1902, 851.

14. *Baily's*, "Our Van," March 1902, 239.

15. For a biographical study of Harry P. Whitney, see Nigel à Brassard, "Harry Payne Whitney: 'Total Polo,'" in *Profiles in Polo* (Jefferson, NC: McFarland, 2007), 42.

16. Halden and Keene, op. cit., 136.

17. Ibid., 144.

18. Ibid., 143.

19. A.W. Coaten , ed., *International Polo Matches* (London: Vaughn, 1912), 54.

20. Henry Holmes, "The English Team in America, 1911," in Coaten, op. cit., 60.

21. J.C. Cooley, "1927, An International Year in Polo," *The Sportsman*, February 1927, 70.

22. Polo Association, 1919 Yearbook, "Chairman's Report," 121.

Interlude 1

1. Lionel Dawson, *Sport in War* (London: Collins, 1936), 68.

2. Lionel James, *The History of King Edward's Horse* (London: Sifton, 1921), 344.

3. E.D. Miller, *Fifty Years of Sport* (New York: Dutton, no date), 189.

4. C.H. Dudley Ward, *History of the Welsh Guards* (London: Murray, 1920), 224.

Chapter 9

1. Arthur W. Coaten, ed., *The Polo Players' Diary* (London: Vaughn, 1912), 74.

2. *Polo Monthly*, June 1921, 183.

3. Marqués de Villavieja, *Life Has Been Good* (London: Chatto & Windus, 1938), 253.

4. Ibid., 253.

5. The Argentine Polo Federation was a short-lived organization. It was founded by Argentine and British players as a reaction to the Polo Association of the River Plate negative attitude in respect to foreign tours and its refusal to have Hurlingham's Laws of the Game of Polo printed in Spanish. In September 1922, the two entities merged to establish the Argentine Polo Association.

6. U.S. Polo Association, 1923 Yearbook, "The 1922 Special Invitation Matches," 32.

7. "Polo Returns to Ireland," *Polo*, January 1929, 28.

8. "At Phoenix Park," *Polo Monthly*, September 1932, 404.

9. Newell Bent, *American Polo* (New York: Macmillan, 1929), 130.

Chapter 10

1. Bill Mallon and Ian Buchanan, *The 1908 Olympic Games* (Jefferson, NC: McFarland, 2000), 1.

2. Dr. William Penny Brookes (1809–1895) studied medicine at Guy's Hospital and St. Thomas Hospital in London but finished his studies at the medical schools in Paris and Padova. Then he returned to his hometown to continue the practice that his father had started. Dr. Brookes founded in 1865 the National Olympian Association, which eventually became the British Olympic Association. In 1881, Dr. Brookes proposed that an International Olympic Festival be held in Athens. He was invited as a guest of honor at the Sorbonne Congress in 1894 but was unable to attend due to illness.

3. Mallon and Buchanan, op. cit., 2.

4. John J. MacAloon, *This Great Symbol: Pierre de Coubertin and the Origins of the Modern Olympic Games* (Chicago: University of Chicago, 1981), 272.

5. Bill Mallon, *The 1900 Olympic Games* (Jefferson, NC: McFarland, 1998), 5.

6. David Wallechinsky, *The Complete Book of the Olympics* (London: Penguin, 1988), xxi.

7. Mallon, op. cit., 142.

8. Reet Ann Howell and Max Howell, *Aussie Gold: The Story of Australia in the Olympics* (South Melbourne: Brooks, 1988), 17.

9. *British Hunts and Huntsmen*, op. cit., 3: 451.

10. Pierre de Coubertin, *Olympic Memoirs*, trans. Geoffrey de Navacelle (Lausanne: IOC, 1997), 178.

11. *Time*, 9 August 1943.

12. The correct spelling is "Vyvyan," as described in the *London Gazette*; however, he is invariably mentioned in the polo literature as "Vivian." For the sake of simplification, the latter spelling is used throughout this book.

13. Norman J. Cinnamond, *El Polo* (Barcelona: Librería Catalonia, no date), 187.

14. Ibid., 198.

15. Jack Gannon, *Before the Colours Fade* (London: J.A. Allen, 1986), 44.

16. Ibid., 51.

17. Eduardo A. Coghlan, *Los Irlandeses en la Argentina* (Buenos Aires: Abraxa, 1987), 289.

18. Raúl Ortigüela, *Raíces Celtas* (Córdoba: Graziani, 1998), 19.

Chapter 11

1. For a comprehensive narrative of the 1921 Westchester Cup competition and surrounding festivities, see Nigel àBrassard, *A Glorious Victory, A Glorious Defeat*, published in 2001.

2. American poet (1837–1913), the "Poet of the Sierras" and the "Byron of the Rockies." Miller achieved more recognition in England than in America.

3. *Polo Monthly*, October 1924, 47.

4. Ibid.

5. *Polo Monthly*, October 1924, 49.

6. "Various Points of View," *Polo Monthly*, November 1923, 104.

7. "Polo's Progress in England," *Polo Monthly*, November 1923, 92.

8. Ibid., 93.

9. *Morning Post*, October 11, 12, and 13, 1924.

10. Sir Harold Edward Snagge, KBE (1872–1949), was chairman of Napiers and a director of Barclays Bank.

11. *Polo Monthly*, December 1924, 189.

12. Peter Vischer, "Britain's Challenge to American Polo," *Polo*, June 1927, 5.

13. Frank S. Butterworth, "Polo Notes and Comment," *The Sportsman*, November 1927, 69.

14. Peter Vischer, "America Keeps the International Challenge Cup," *Polo*, October 1927, 24.

15. "The International Matches: Lord Cowdray on England's Prospects," *Polo Monthly*, April 1930, 27.

16. "International Trial Matches," *Polo Monthly*, May 1930, 119.

17. U.S. Polo Association, 1931 Yearbook, "International Polo," 24.

18. "America Keeps the Cup," *Polo*, October 1930, 35.

19. R.L. Ricketts, "Tactics: Combination," in *Polo*, ed. Earl of Kimberley (London: Seeley, 1936), 73.

20. Brig. Gen. R.L. Ricketts, "Britain's International Failures," *Polo*, July 1931, 17.

21. Ibid., 17.

22. Ibid., 18.

Chapter 12

1. "The Coming Season at Ranelagh," *Polo Times*, April 1932, 21.
2. *Polo Monthly*, "Current Topics," August 1931, 354.
3. Hurlingham Polo Association, 1990 Yearbook, 36.
4. *Polo Monthly*, April 1932, 22.
5. Chris Ashton, *Geebung* (Sydney: Hamilton, 1993), 91.
6. *Polo Monthly*, "Ranelagh Open Cup," July 1931, 278.
7. *County Polo Association Red Book*, 1937, 131–145.
8. Elizabeth Keyes, *Geoffrey Keyes, V.C.* (London: Newnes, 1956), 64.
9. Keyes, op. cit., 101.
10. Seymour Knox, *Aurora in England* (Buffalo: private printing, 1934).
11. Thakur, a noble; Rao Rajah, of royal blood, but not in line of succession.
12. John H. Tunis, "England's Polo Season," *Polo*, August 1933, 16.
13. For a full account of this tour, consult Seymour H. Knox, *Aurora in England* (Buffalo: private printing, 1934).
14. Ibid., 30.
15. Ibid., 65.
16. *Polo Monthly*, Current Topics, June 1934, 130.
17. *Polo Monthly*, Current Topics, "Blow to Lovers of the Game," May 1932, 84.
18. *Polo y Campo*, May 1936, 31.
19. *County Polo Association Red Book*, 1939, 88.
20. Donald C. McKenzie and John R. McKenzie, op. cit., 345. Ginger Bain (seven), Gordon Campbell (seven), L.S. Langridge (seven) and G. Truter (three) played for Harrismith. The Kokstad team was Douglas Stubbs (four), Robin Scott (four), Kaiser Scott (six) and Eric Scott (five).
21. *Polo Monthly*, "Match at Belfast," August 1938, 14.
22. *Polo Monthly*, "Irish Fortnightly Cup," August 1938, 15.
23. Peter Vischer, "The International Polo Matches," *Horse & Horseman*, July 1936, 18.
24. Peter Vischer, "American Triumph," *Country Life*, July 1939, 17.
25. U.S. Polo Association, 1940 Yearbook, 24.
26. Personal communication from Bob Skene, Santa Barbara, November 1978.
27. U.S. Polo Association, 1940 Yearbook, 25.

Chapter 13

1. T.F. Dale's *Polo at Home and Abroad* (London: London & Counties, 1915), plate 21.
2. Roy Heron, *The Sporting Art of Cecil Aldin* (London: Sportsman's, 1990), 86.
3. Heron, op. cit., 12.
4. Heron, op. cit., 85 and plate 15.
5. G.D. Armour, *Bridle and Brush* (New York: Scribner's, 1937), 205, 215, 217, 221, 223, 227, 230–231, 237.
6. Badger, T.R., *A Record of Horses* (Leicester: Rathby, 1937), 74.
7. Sally Mitchell, *The Dictionary of British Equestrian Artists* (Woodbridge: Antique Collectors, 1985), 104.
8. Earl of Suffolk and Hedley Peek, *The Encyclopaedia of Sport* (London: Lawrence and Bullen, 1898), 2: 125.
9. *Polo*, March 1986, 33.
10. W.E. Lyon, ed., *The Pegasus Book* (New York: Smith, 1931), 130.
11. J.N.P. Watson, *The World of Polo* (Topsfield, MA: Salem, 1986), full page between 76 and 77.
12. Mitchell, op. cit., 138.
13. *Fores' Sporting Notes and Sketches* 26 (1911).
14. Watson, op. cit,, 101.
15. Mary Ann Wingfield, *Sport and the Artist* (Woodbrige: Antique Collectors, 1985), 272.
16. Watson, op. cit., 148.
17. *Polo*, November 1993, 19.
18. Mary Ann Wingfield, *A Dictionary of Sporting Artists, 1650–1990* (Woodbridge, Suffolk: Antique Collector's Club, 1992), 74.
19. Marc Jeffery, "Terence Cuneo," *PQ International*, Winter 1992, 32.
20. Illustrated in *Polo*, November 1989, 52; *Polo*, November 1990, 23; *Polo*, November 1990, 32, and *PQ International* 28: 64–65.
21. Wingfield, *Sport and the Artist*, op. cit., 279.
22. Ibid., 265.
23. T.B. Drybrough, *Polo* (London: Longmans, 1906), fig. 159.

24. Illustrated in Sally Mitchell's *Dictionary of Sporting Artists*, 234, and in *Polo*, July 1978, 24.

25. *Polo Monthly*, June 1928, 257.

26. Mitchell, op. cit., 240.

27. Wingfield, *Sport and the Artist*, op. cit., 291.

28. Mitchell, op. cit., 270.

29. Wingfield, *Sport and the Artist*, op. cit., 290.

30. Reference to this match is made in *Polo Monthly*, August 1921.

31. Edward Horswell, Esq., personal communication. In 1984 a limited edition of nine was sold on behalf of the Royal Veterinary College Duncan's Horse Appeal.

32. There is a reference to this painting in *Baily's*, vol. 74, July 1900, 55.

33. Wingfield, *Sport and the Artist*, op. cit., 278.

34. *PQ International*, 1992, 46.

35. "The Sportsman," ed., *Polo-Coaching* (London: Sports & Sportsmen, 1922), 232.

36. T.F. Dale, *Riding and Polo Ponies* (London: Unwin, 1899), plate facing p. 60.

37. H.B. De Lisle, *Reminiscences of Sport and War* (London: Eyre & Spotiswoode, 1938), 184.

38. *Polo*, October 1986, 23.

39. *Hurlingham Polo*, Spring 1991, 12.

40. Wingfield, *Sport and the Artist*, op. cit., 272.

41. Mitchell, op. cit., 433.

42. *Polo*, October 1988, 49.

Interlude 2

1. John Frayn Turner, *V.C.'s of the Royal Navy* (London: Harrap, 1956), 41.

2. Elizabeth Keyes, *Geoffrey Keyes of the Rommel Raid* (London: Newnes, 1956), 260. Elizabeth Keyes was Geoffrey's younger sister.

3. Alan Moorehead, *A Year of Battle* (London: Hamilton, 1943), 61.

Chapter 14

1. Major John Board, "Polo Club Gossip," undated newspaper clipping.

2. Personal communication from N.J.A. Colquhoun-Denvers, 26 May 2011.

3. L.R., "Two Guinea Membership," *PQ International* 30 (Winter 1999): 67.

4. Quoted in Derek Russell-Stoneham and Roger Chatterton-Smith, *Polo at Cowdray* (London: PBI, 1992), 36.

5. Ibid., 38.

6. Graham Dennis, "Suffolk Splendour," *PQ International* 39 (Spring 2002): 87.

7. Hurlingham Polo Association, 1951 Yearbook, 38.

8. The author is indebted to Brigadier Douglas-Nugent for providing this information. Personal communication, 14 June 2011.

9. Sir Leslie Rundle (1856–1934), Royal Artillery, fought in several campaigns, including the Boer War, and was governor and commander in chief in Malta from 1909 to 1915.

10. J.R.C. Gannon, "Polo in 1951," *Horseman's Year* (London: Collins, 1952), 100.

11. *Times*, 26 July 1951. There is a photograph with the caption "Princess Elizabeth presenting the Festival Cup to G. Balding of the Hurlingham team, after they had beaten la Espadana at Roehampton." The author is grateful to Nigel à Brassard for unearthing this information.

12. Hurlingham Polo Association, 1957 Yearbook, 12.

13. For a full story of the club, consult J.N.P. Watson, *Smith's Lawn: The History of Guards Polo Club, 1955–1005*.

14. Elizabeth Hennessy, *A History of Roehampton Club* (No place: Roehampton Club, 2001), 43.

15. Quoted in Hennessy, op. cit., 43.

16. K.M. Little, *Polo in New Zealand* (Wellington: Whitcombe, 1956), 45.

17. Geoffrey Ashton was the son of Geoff Ashton, one of the famous brothers that made up the Goulburn team that toured England in 1930 and won Hurlingham's Champion Cup in 1937. Tom Barlow was the son of Charles "Punch" Barlow, Caius and Gonville College, who played rugby for Cambridge, being team captain in 1926, leading the Light Blues to a thirty-point victory over Oxford. Punch Barlow was captain of the Natal side and was in the Springboks Trials in 1928. He was a fine cricketer, being captain of his high school and college teams, and played county cricket for Somerset during the university vacation. A seven-goal player, Barlow was the captain of the South African polo team that toured Argentina in 1952 and was president of the South African Polo Association from 1939 to 1958. Jonathan Riley-Smith was the son of Douglas and grandson of William Riley-Smith, of Toulston Polo Club fame.

18. Dr. Edward de Bono was a Rhodes Scholar at Oxford, an MD, PhD and PhilD. A philosopher, he is the creator of the term "lateral thinking." Dr. Anthony de Bono became a renowned cardiovascular surgeon.

19. Harold Sebag Montefiore, "Polo Retrospect," *Horseman's Year* (London: Collins, 1960), 109.

20. Trudi Morgan, *Polo Magazine*, April 1978, 26.

21. W. Holden White, "Polo Retrospect," *Horseman's Year* (London: Collins, 1959), 101.

22. Ibid., 104.

Chapter 15

1. Nicholas Courtney, *Sporting Royals, Past and Present* (London: Hutchinson, 1983), 79.

2. Sir Bryan Godfrey-Faussett, GCVO, CMG (1863–1945), gained the rank of captain in the service of the Royal Navy. The then Lieutenant B. Godfrey-Faussett, RN, also played polo with HRH Prince George at Malta.

3. "The Game in the Navy," *Polo Monthly*, July 1932, 233.

Chapter 16

1. Hurlingham Polo Association Yearbooks, 1957–2011.

2. Hurlingham Polo Association, 1965 Yearbook, 1.

3. W. Russell G. Corey, *Alan Corey: 9 Goals* (No place: private printing, 2010), 223.

4. Personal communication from Mr. Thomas Burke Glynn.

5. Elizabeth Y. Layton, *The Golden Mallet* (Kauai: Grey Lady, 2003), 37.

6. J.C.R. Gannon, "Introduction," HPA 1970 Yearbook, 1.

7. Gen. Sir Alexander Godley, MFH, was a keen sportsman and played on the British military team that defeated their Argentine counterparts in the first international game in 1908, held at the Hurlingham Club in the outskirts of Buenos Aires. Gen. Godley was instrumental in the training of the New Zealand Army prior to the First World War.

Chapter 17

1. U.S. Polo Association, 1973 Yearbook, "The Coronation Cup," 91.

2. Charles Froggart, "The Hand of Gabriel," *Polo Times*, September 2007, 40.

Chapter 18

1. Marc Jeffery, "Terence Cuneo," *PQ International*, Winter 1992, 32.

2. J.N.P. Watson, *Smith's Lawn: The History of Guards Polo Club, 1955–2005*. Wykey, Shrewsbury: Quiller, 2005.

3. For a short biography of Claire Lucas, see Yolanda Carslaw, "Claire Tomlinson: The Most Influential Lady Player," in *Profiles in Polo* (Jefferson, NC: McFarland, 2007), 206.

4. Hurlingham Polo Association Yearbooks, 1971–1980.

5. Margie Brett, "From the Editor," *Polo Times*, September 2007, 4.

6. Hurlingham Polo Association Yearbooks, 1971 and 1980, pp. 8 and 17.

7. *Polo Magazine*, September 1977, 42.

Chapter 19

1. Lord Cowdray, "Introduction," 1961 HPA Yearbook, 2.

2. Ibid.

3. Chris Ashton, "Sinclair Hill: I'll Give you Fancy Pants!" in *Profiles in Polo* (Jefferson, NC: McFarland, 2007), 151.

4. Kathleen Beer, "Diary of a Visiting Team," *Polo Newsletter*, January 1973, 5.

5. Ibid., 6.

6. Lord Cowdray, "Introduction," 1967 HPA Yearbook, 1.

7. Donald C. McKenzie and John R. McKenzie, *Polo in South Africa* (Dargle: private printing, 1999), 73.

8. Ibid., 159.

9. Quoted in T.P. McLean, *The Savile Cup* (Cambridge: New Zealand Polo Association, 1989), 104.

10. Ibid., 109.

11. Ibid.

12. "White Horse in Mexico," *Polo Magazine*, April 1979, 18.

Part IV

1. "Burma Polo: Past and Present," *Polo Magazine*, June 1930, 249.

2. "Keeping Cool," *PQ International*, Spring 2003, 77.

Chapter 20

1. Hurlingham Polo Association, 2001 Yearbook.
2. *Polo Quarterly International* (1997): 56.
3. David Edelsten, "Orchard Polo Club," *Polo Times*, May 2004, 45.
4. Lt. Col. A.F. Harper, "Review of the Season." 1982 HPA Yearbook, 5.
5. Ibid.
6. Crocker Snow Jr., "Worth the Wait," *Polo*, October 1992, 44.
7. Crocker Snow Jr., "On the Sidelines: Gracida vs. Gracida," *Polo*, October 1992, 43.
8. Ibid.

Chapter 21

1. *The Bystander*, "Lady Polo Players at Ranelagh," 26 July 1905, 172.
2. Ladies' Polo Association, "Reports and Fixtures," *Polo Monthly*, June 1939, 62.
3. *Polo Monthly*, July 1920, 321.
4. *Polo Monthly*, September 1920.
5. *Polo Monthly*, July 1920, 321.
6. *Polo Monthly*, September 1921, 442.
7. *Polo Monthly*, August 1930, 419.
8. *Polo Monthly*, September 1931, 434.
9. *Polo Monthly*, September 1933, 333.
10. *Polo Monthly*, August 1938, 52.
11. Graham Dennis, "Suffolk Splendour," *PQ International*, Spring 2002, 86.
12. *Polo Monthly*, August 1938, 17.
13. *Polo Monthly*, August 1938, 18.
14. "Finding the Dream," *Polo Times*, May 2006, 31.
15. County Polo Association 1937 Red Book, 42.
16. For a biographical study of Claire Lucas Tomlinson, see Yolanda Carslaw, "Claire Tomlinson: The Most Influential Lady Player," in *Profiles in Polo* (Jefferson, NC: McFarland, 2007), 206.
17. Editorial, *Polo Magazine*, September 1977, 4.
18. Hurlingham Polo Association, 1976 Yearbook, 91.
19. Hurlingham Polo Association, 1978 Yearbook, 1.

Chapter 22

1. "Letters," *Polo Times*, June 2001, 10. Text of the letter sent by Mr. Chris Jones to the heads of FIP, AAP, HPA and USPA:

Sirs,

As you are aware I was the Tournament Director at the recently concluded FIP World Cup in Melbourne, Australia. That tournament was a great success in all regards but an umpiring incident and a number of discussions I had during the tournament has prompted me to write this letter.

FIP tournaments are run under FIP rules for International Polo. These rules are the result of a series of meetings and agreements between the three major international polo countries— Argentina, United States and England. Prior to those meetings, there were three major sets of rules with all other polo playing countries affiliating themselves to one of those rule making bodies, although the game was basically the same. There were interpretations and some minor differences which were inconsistent. The international rules have been well received, most of the differences have been eliminated and it seems natural that all Associations should adopt and play under these international rules.

FIP is doing an excellent job of bringing the world of polo together, but with the details of the rules it is really in the hands of the three Associations, or their rules committees, to co-ordinate the production of a final set of rules.

The incident in the tournament to which I referred involved the taking of a Penalty 2, when one umpire, in a moment of indecision, lapsed back into the rules he was familiar with rather than the presiding FIP rule for the carrying out of a Penalty 2. The incident was minor and fortunately not critical to the outcome of the game, but it highlighted the need for not only an international agreed set of rules, but one set of rules under which all three Associations and their affiliates play. This would be an important step toward the aim of Olympic and more international high goal competition.

There are two challenges to be met in order to achieve one set of rules. Firstly it requires the political will of the three major Associations to achieve that aim and to consider a wider perspective than rules introduced for local conditions or requests. Each country or Association may have additional bye-laws for local conditions, but these should not alter the underlying rules. It will be essential for the Associations to go to the negotiating table with an acceptance that change may be necessary and, if made, will be accepted and "championed" at home. It is going to take strong presidents and chairmen to alter local majorities' views in the interests of world polo progress.

The second challenge is the mechanics. The remaining difficulties in common rules will need more than political will to succeed. Discussion and perhaps wider opinions from other FIP members may need to be sought to consider advantages and disadvantages. The remaining difficulties are:

    a. Penalty 2.
       Undefended or not?
       One hit or unlimited hits?
       Penalty 3.
       Undefended or not?
    b. Length of a chukka.
       7 or 7 ½minutes?
    c. Rule 1. Interpretation.

I have different opinions on all of these but have purposely not expressed them in this letter as it needs the philosophy and mechanics of communication, opinion, discussion, decision and communication/promotion of that decision to be set first.

If the three Associations could agree a compromise in these three areas and adopt those compromises in their own country rules, it would help FIP and international polo move forward significantly.

There a number of other aspects which will need to be addressed in time. Drugs in polo are probably at present not of great significance, but it is an emotive issue and a difficult one in many Olympic sports and countries. FIP carried out drug testing at the World Cup but under a protocol which I suspect was not clear enough to avoid being challenged. As the Olympic representative, FIP is the best body to introduce that protocol, but again, only if it is accepted by all Affiliates.

Although FIP World Cup tournaments may use pooled horses, future international games may not and a drug protocol for horses also needs to be adopted.

There may be some rule changes which would make it easier for spectators to understand the game, and to make it easier to televise. An example is not changing ends after a goal. But these aspects are not fundamental to the present rules and it is better to target the existing significant issues without having the fundamental process disrupted by diversions.

Like I am sure many players in the world, I implore you and your successors to grasp this issue and politically nurse it through to its conclusion and acceptance.

                              Respectfully yours,
                              Chris Jones
                              Auckland, New Zealand

  2. Text of the HPA communication to the author:

Hard to be very succinct but will have a go. Basically first thought reasons are:

Welfare — different emphasis in different countries.

Different nationalities have different view as to the detail required — the lawyer induced mentality that every eventuality must be covered. The infantry have to be told where to dig and die, the cavalry only need to be given the intent and how it is achieved is left largely up to them. The U.S. need chapter and verse, the Argentines do not worry too much what is written in the rules.

It is a different game at different levels and with a predominance of patron polo there is no great incentive to play 4 man polo for which the original rules were written.

Each prefers their own and is reluctant to give up the independence of being able to change them when they want.

There is insufficient international polo played or watched to drive associations to one set of rules. Of the 20,000 players, very few are fussed that there are different rules and most of the spectators do not understand them anyway.

  3. Text of the USPA communication to the author: "To add a little levity to your concern. We can't even get 12 high goal sponsors to play by our rules. It ain't easy my friend."

  4. Text of the FIP reply.

It is a good question.

One answer would be that AAP, HPA and USPA are satisfied with their rules and — at the local level — they are not interested in any changes.

However, on the other hand, the rules' unification has been discussed at least since 1995 by the three Associations, and also through the FIP. Meanwhile, appropriate rules for international matches have been approved, different from each one but incorporating parts from each one. These are the FIP's Rules of the Game, which are periodically brought up to date and are in force in the World Championships with Handicap.

Ever since, each Association's Rules Committee have formalized changes; some — like the USPA — quite frequently, others rarely, such as the AAP.

Lately, there is a trend toward convergence in certain matters, and somehow the Argentine rules are taken as example; for instance, the duration of each chukker: both the HPA and the AAP are similar, with the exception of how the last chukker ends in case of a tie. The USPA has something similar; however, in my opinion, on the wrong track.

Regarding the penalties, things get a bit complicated. Some time ago, the USPA decided that the 30 and 40 (yards) can not be defended; later in high handicap matches only the 30-yard penalty is not allowed to be defended. The HPA as well does not allow the 30-yard (penalty) to be defended. The AAP allows both 30 and 40-yards penalties to be defended. Personally, I believe that here in Argentina this could be unified, allowing the 30-yarder to be defended only in the Abiertos and high-goal handicap tournaments; however, that is another story.

As to the other penalties, the differences are minor. The AAP has pioneered outlawing turning on the ball, without changing the rules but instructing the umpires to call a foul in the play. The HPA and the USPA are doing the same, with the HPA making it part of the rules.

As you can see, your question receives explanations, but the issue remains without formal resolution.

5. Interview with Marcos Uranga, 20 March 2006.
6. Venues and results of the FIP Fourteen-Goal World Championships are as follow:

Year	Place	Gold	Silver	Bronze
1987	Buenos Aires	Argentina	Mexico	Brazil
1989	Berlin	America	England	Argentina
1992	Santiago	Argentina	Chile	England
1995	St. Moritz	Brazil	Argentina	Mexico
1998	Santa Barbara	Argentina	Brazil	England
2001	Melbourne	Brazil	Australia	England
2004	Chantilly	Brazil	England	Chile
2008	Mexico City	Chile	Brazil	Mexico

7. Marty LeGrand, "Of Olympic Proportions," *Polo*, June/July 1989, 29.
8. Ibid., "The Road to Berlin."
9. William Loyd, "The New World Champions," *Polo*, November 1989, 27.
10. "Numero Uno," *Polo*, August 1992, 23.
11. Luke Borwick, "14-Goal World Polo Championship," *Polo Times*, November 1998, 8.
12. Gwen Rizzo, "Polo Maximus," *Polo Players' Edition*, November 1998, 20.
13. J.W.M. Crisp, "Review of the Season," 1999 HPA Yearbook, 9.
14. Charles Froggart, "The World Championship: Brazil by a Whistle," *Polo Times*, October 2004, 28.
15. "Viva Brazil," *Polo Players' Edition*, November 2004, 27.
16. Charles Froggart, "Los Conquistadores: Chile," *Polo Times*, July 2008, 43.
17. Personal communication from Marcos Uranga, April 2011.
18. Charles Froggart, "The World Championship: Brazil by a Whistle," *Polo Times*, October 2004, 31.
19. Quoted in "From the Editor," *Polo Times*, July 2008, 4.
20. Ibid.
21. Pascal Renauldon, "PGH Defends His Presidency," *Polo Times*, November/December 2009, 10.
22. Personal communication from N.J.A. Colquhoun-Denvers Esq., May 2011.
23. "FIP Regroups after Crisis," *Polo Times*, January/February 2010, 9.
24. Ibid.

Chapter 24

1. Personal communication from Brigadier Denis Ormerod, CBE, 26 April 2000.
2. Herbert Spencer, "Charles Betz: The Regeneration Game," *Polo Times*, June 2009, 14.
3. Gareth A. Davies, "Battling Bears Take Gold," *Polo Times*, August 2002, 23.
4. Hurlingham Polo Association, 2003 Yearbook, 252.
5. Gareth A. Davis, "Hildon Sport Claim Historic Victory," *Polo Times*, August 2003, 22.
6. Ibid.
7. Ibid.
8. Adrian Gahan, "Azzurra Endure," *Polo Times*, July 2005, 43.
9. *Polo Times*, January/February 2006, 43.
10. Ranelagh, "South African International Ends in Controversy," *Polo Times*, January/February 2006, 4.
11. Hurlingham Polo Association, 2008 Yearbook, "Review of the Season," 4.
12. Gareth Davies, "Polo or Pantomime," *Polo Times*, August 2007, 37.

13. *Polo Times*, August 2007, 38.

14. Arthur Douglas-Nugent, "Umpire's Corner," *Polo Times*, September 2007, 19.

15. Personal communication from Agustín Merlos, 10 April 2011.

16. Brett O'Callahan, "A Game of Two Halves," *Polo Times*, April 2008, 40.

17. Gareth A. Davies, "The Gold Cup Cowdray Park Polo Club," *Polo Times*, 41.

18. Stephen Orthwein, "Welcome from the Chairman," *The Westchester Cup Commemorative Program* (Lake Worth, FL: Museum of Polo and Hall of Fame, 2009), 8.

19. Nicholas Colquhoun-Denvers, "Chairman's Foreword," 2011 HPA Yearbook, 2.

20. Arthur Douglas-Nugent, "Glowing Mid-term Report for English Season as Players Embrace New Rules," *Polo Times*, July 2011, 24.

Chapter 25

1. Personal communication.

2. James Dwight, *Lawn-Tennis* (Boston: Wright & Ditson, 1886), 69.

3. Brigadier P.T. Thwaites, "Foreword," 1988 HPA Yearbook, 5.

4. Lt. Col. A.F. Harper, ibid., 8.

5. John Tinsley, "Chairman's Statement," 2003 HPA Yearbook, 2.

6. David Woodd, "Letters," *Polo Times*, March 2002, 10.

7. Brigadier P.T. Thwaites, "Foreword," 1991 HPA Yearbook, 5.

8. Personal communication from Mr. Thomas B. Glynn.

9. Mark Girouard, *The Return of Camelot* (New Haven, CT: Yale University, 1981), 240.

10. *Ellenhorn's Medical Toxicology* (Baltimore, MD: William & Wilkins, 1997), 1607.

11. *Haddad & Winchester's Clinical Management of Poisoning and Drug Overdose* (Philadelphia: Saunders Elsevier, 2007), 1164.

12. Hurlingham Polo Association, 2009 Yearbook, 64.

13. Antje Derks, "England Victorious on Cartier Day," *Polo Times*, September 2008, 40.

14. From the Editor, "Polo's Image," *Polo Times*, September 2008, 4.

15. U.S. Polo Association, 2009 Yearbook, 141.

16. Arthur Douglas-Nugent, "Stage Set for a Scoring Structure Switch," *Polo Times*, March 2008, 23.

17. Daniel Wallace, "Umpire Abuse: Getting Tough Isn't Enough," *Polo*, September 1991, 14.

18. Col. Alec Harper, "Polo Virus," *PQ International*, Winter 1995, 52.

19. Yolanda Carslaw, "The Veuve Cliquot Gold Cup 2005," *Polo Times*, August 2005, 37.

20. Ibid.

21. W. John Morgan and Geoffrey Nicholson, *Report on Rugby* (London: Heinemann, 1959), 94.

22. Chris Ashton, "Major Accomplishments," *Polo Times*, September 2010, 14.

Bibliography

à Brassard, Nigel. *A Glorious Victory, A Glorious Defeat*. Chippenham: Rowe, 2001.
_____. *Tommy Hitchcock: A Tribute*. Cirencester: Letter Press, 2003.
Aldrich, Nelson W., Jr. *Tommy Hitchcock: An American Hero*. No place: Fleet Street, 1984.
Anderson, F. *Hints on Polo*. Allahabad: Pioneer, 1921.
Armour, G.D. *Bridle and Brush*. New York: Scribner's, 1937.
Ashton, Chris. *Geebung: The Story of Australian Polo*. Sydney: Hamilton, 1993.
Badger, T.R. *A Record of Horses*. Leicester: Rathby, 1937.
Baltzell, E. Digby. *Sporting Gentlemen*. New York: Free Press, 1995.
Barnes, Simon. *The Meaning of Sport*. London: Short Books, 2006.
Bent, Newell. *American Polo*. New York: Macmillan, 1929.
Board, John. *Year with Horses*. London: Hodder & Stoughton, 1954.
British Hunts and Huntsmen. 4 vols. London: Biographical, 1908–1911.
Brooke, Geoffrey. *Horse-Sense and Horsemanship of To-day*. London: Constable, 1934.
_____. *Horsemanship*. London: Seeley, 1948.
Brown, J. Moray. *Polo*. London: Vinton, 1895.
Buchan, John. *Francis and Riversdale Grenfell*. London: Nelson, 1920.
Buckmaster, Walter. *Hints for Polo Combination*. London: Vinton, no date [1909].
Burke, Bernard. *A Genealogical and Heraldic History of the Landed Gentry in Ireland*. London: Harrison, 1899.
Chartier, Jean-Luc A. *Cent Ans de Polo en France*. Paris: Média France, 1988.
_____. *Polo de France*. Paris: Polo Club Editions, 1993.
Chichester, Henry Manners, and George Burges-Short. *The Records and Badges of Every Regiment and Corps in the British Army*. London: Gale & Polden, 1900.
Christensen, Karen, Allen Guttmann and Gertrude Pfister. *International Encyclopedia of Women Sports*. New York: Macmillan, 2001.
Cinnamond, Norman J. *El Polo*. Barcelona: Librería Catalonia, no date [1929].
Coaten, A.W., ed. *International Polo*. London: Vaughn, 1912.
Corey, W. Russell G. *Alan Corey: 9-Goals*. No place: private printing, 2009.
County Polo Association. *The Training of Mount and Man for Polo*. London: CPA, 1948.
Courage Exhibition of National Trophies. *Sporting Glory*. London: Sporting Trophies Exhibition, 1992.
Courtney, Nicholas. *Sporting Royals: Past and Present*. London: Hutchinson, 1983.
Dale, T.F. *The Game of Polo*. Westminster: Constable, 1897.
_____. *Riding and Polo Ponies*. London: Unwin, 1899.
_____. *Polo: Past and Present*. London: Country Life, 1905.
_____. *Polo at Home and Abroad*. London: London & Counties, 1915.
Dawnay, Hugh. *Playmaker Polo*. London: Allen, 1984.
_____. *Polo Vision*. London: Allen, 2004.
Dawson, Lionel. *Sport in War*. London: Collins, 1936.
De Lisle, H. deB. *Tournament Polo*. London: Eyre & Spottiswoode, 1938.
_____. *Reminiscences of Sport and War*. London: Eyre & Spottiswoode, 1939.
Dorling, Taprell. *The Hurlingham Club*. London: private printing, 1953.
Drybrough, T.B. *Polo*. London: Vinton, 1898.
Dwight, James. *Lawn-Tennis*. Boston: Wright & Ditson, 1886.
Edinburgh, H.R.H. The Duke of. *Men, Machines, and Sacred Cows*. London: Hamilton, 1988.

Ellenhorn's Medical Toxicology. Baltimore, MD: William & Wilkins, 1997.

Ellison, Gabriel, and Kim Fraser. *Harmony of Hooves: A Celebration of Racing and Polo in Northern Rhodesia and Zambia.* No Place: Natal Witness, 1999.

Ferguson, Ronald. *The Galloping Major.* London: Macmillan, 1994.

Foster, Joseph. *Alumni Oxonienses.* Oxford: Parker, 1888–1892.

Furth, Elizabeth. *Visions of Polo.* Addington: Kenilworth, 2005.

Gannon, Jack. *Before the Colours Fade.* London: Allen, 1976.

Girouard, Mark. *The Return of Camelot.* New Haven, CT: Yale University, 1981.

Godfree, D.W. *Some Notes on Polo.* Newport: Blake, 1911.

Grace, Peter. *Polo.* New York: Howell, 1991.

Griswold, Frank Gray. *The International Polo Cup.* New York: Dutton's, 1928.

Haddad & Winchester's Clinical Management of Poisoning and Drug Overdose. Philadelphia: Saunders Elsevier, 2007.

Harnack, Curtis. *Gentlemen on the Prairie.* Ames: Iowa State University, 1985.

Harper, Alec. *Horse and Foot.* Petergat: Quacks Books, 1995.

Hatch, Alden, and Foxhall Keene. *Full Tilt.* New York: Derrydale, 1938.

Hennessy, Elizabeth. *A History of Roehampton Club.* No place: Roehampton Club, 2001.

Herbert, F.A. "Polo." In Suffolk, Earl of, and F.G. Aflalo, *The Encyclopaedia of Sport.* London: Lawrence & Bullen, 1898.

Heron, Roy. *The Sporting Art of Cecil Aldin.* London: Sportsman's Press, 1990.

Hobson, G.W. *Ideas on Breaking Polo Ponies.* No place: private printing, 1927.

Hobson, Richard. *Polo and Ponies.* London: Allen, 1976.

_____. *Riding: The Game of Polo.* London: Allen, 1993.

_____. *Some XII Lancers.* Shipton-on-Stour: King's Stone, 1936.

Kimberley, Earl of, ed. *Polo.* London: Seeley, 1936.

King, Bucky. *Big Horn Polo.* Sheridan: Still Sailing, 1987.

Knox, Seymour H. *Aurora in England.* Buffalo: private printing, 1934.

Laffaye, Horace A. *The Evolution of Polo.* Jefferson, NC: McFarland, 2009.

_____. *The Polo Encyclopedia.* Jefferson, NC: McFarland, 2004.

_____, ed. *Profiles in Polo: The Players Who Changed the Game.* Jefferson, NC: McFarland, 2007.

Lidell, R.S. *The Memoirs of the Tenth Royal Hussars.* London: Longmans, 1891.

Little, K.M. *Polo in New Zealand.* Wellington: Whitcombe & Tombs, 1956.

Lloyd, John. *The Pimm's Book of Polo.* North Pomfret: Trafalgar, 1989.

Loyola Brandão, Ignácio de. *Polo Brasil.* São Paulo: Markmidia, 1992.

Mackay, James. *The Animaliers.* New York: Dutton, 1973.

Mallon, Bill. *The 1900 Olympic Games.* Jefferson, NC: McFarland, 1997.

_____, and Ian Buchanan. *The 1908 Olympic Games.* Jefferson, NC: McFarland, 1999.

_____, and Anthony Th. Bijkerk. *The 1920 Olympic Games.* Jefferson, NC: McFarland, 2009.

"Marco." *An Introduction to Polo.* London: Country Life, 1931.

McKenzie, Donald C., and John R. McKenzie. *A History of Polo in South Africa.* Dargle: private printing, 1999.

McLean, T.P. *The Savile Cup.* Cambridge: New Zealand P.A., 1990.

Melvill, T.P. *Ponies and Women.* London: Jarrolds, 1932.

Miller, E.D. *Fifty Years of Sport.* New York: Dutton, no date [1925].

_____. *Modern Polo.* London: Thacker, 1896.

Miskin, Nigel. *History of Hurlingham.* No place: private printing, 2000.

Mitchell, Sally. *The Dictionary of British Sporting Artists.* Woodbridge: Antiques Collector's Club, 1985.

Moorehead, Alan. *A Year of Battle.* London: Hamilton, 1943.

Morgan, W. John, and Geoffrey Nicholson, *Report on Rugby.* London: Heinemann, 1959.

Patten, William. *The Book of Sport.* New York: Taylor, 1901.

Pearce, J.J. *Everybody's Polo.* London: Hale, 1949.

Ramsay, F.W. *Polo Pony Training.* Aldershot: Gale & Polden, 1928.

Rees, Tony. *The Galloping Game.* Cochrane: Western Heritage, 2000.

Reynard, Frank H. *The Ninth (Queen's Royal) Lancers, 1715–1903.* Edinburgh: Blackwood, 1904.

Ricketts, R.L. *First Class Polo.* Aldershot: Gale & Polden, 1928.

Roberts, Mike. *40 Years Behind the Lens.* No place: private printing, 2010.

Ross-of-Bladensburg, Sir Foster George. *A History of the Coldstream Guards.* London: Innes, 1896.

Russell-Stoneham, Derek, and Roger Chatterton-Smith. *Polo at Cowdray.* London: PBI, 1992.

St. Quintin, T.A. *Chances of Sports of Sorts.* Edinburgh: Blackwood, 1912.

Spencer, Herbert. *A Century of Polo*. No place: World Polo, 1994.
_____. *Chakkar: Polo around the World*. New York: Drake, 1971.
"Sportsman, the." *Polo and Coaching*. London: Sports & Sportsmen, no date [1923].
Stock, Alphons. *Polo: International Sport*. London: Universal Bridge of Trade, no date [1930].
Tanoira, Javier. Unpublished manuscript.
Tucoo-Chala, Pierre. *Histoire de Pau*. Toulouse: Privat, 1989.
Tylden-Wright, W.R. *Notes on Polo*. London: Butterworth, 1927.
Van Der Zee, Jacob. *The British in Iowa*. Iowa City: Historical Society of Iowa, 1922.
Venn, J.A., compiler. *Alumni Cantabrigienses*. London: Cambridge University Press, 1922–1954.
Villavieja, Marqués de. *Life Has Been Good*. London: Chatto & Windus, 1938.
Walford, Edward. *The County Families of the United Kingdom*. London: Spottiswoode: 1919.
Wallechinsky, David. *The Complete Book of the Olympics*. New York: Penguin, 1988.
Watson, J.N.P. *Lionel Edwards: Master of the Sporting Scene*. London: Sportsman's, 1986.
_____. *Smith's Lawn: The History of Guards Polo Club, 1955–2005*. Wykey, Shrewsbury: Quiller, 2005.
_____. *The World of Polo*. Topsfield: Salem, 1986.
Weir, Robert, and J. Moray Brown. *Riding: Polo*. London: Longmans, 1891.
Wilson, Hamish. *Polo in New Zealand, 1956–1976*. Auckland: Viking, 1976.
Wingfield, Mary Ann. *A Dictionary of Sporting Artists, 1650–1990*. Woodbridge, Suffolk: Antique Collector's Club, 1992.
_____. *Sport and the Artist*. Woodbridge, Suffolk: Antique Collector's Club, 1988.
Woods, Lawrence M. *British Gentlemen in the Wild West*. New York: Free Press, 1989.
Young, H.P. *Hints on Sport: Also a Few Practical Suggestions on Polo*. Leamington: private printing, 1907.
Younghusband, G.J. *Polo in India*. London: W.H. Allen, 1890.

Annuals and Year Books

Asociación Argentina de Polo. *Centauros*. Buenos Aires, 2002–2006.
_____. *Libro Anual*. Buenos Aires, 1930–1980.
Hurlingham Polo Association Yearbook. London, Billingshurst, Kirtlington and Little Coxwell, 1951–2011.
Lyon, W.E. *The Horseman's Year*. London, 1951–1960.
Newman, Josiah. *International Polo Club Guide for the Coronation Year*. Bristol: W. Crofton Hemmons, 1902–1903.
The Polo Association Yearbook. New York: The Polo Association, 1890–1922.
The Polo Year Book. London: 1928–1937.
Simmonds, L.V.L., and E.D. Miller. *The Polo Annual*. London, 1913.
Spalding's Polo Guide. New York, 1921–1923.
U.S. Polo Association Year Book. New York, Oak Brook, and Lexington, 1923–2008.

Magazines and Newspapers

Automobile Quarterly. Kutztown, 1962–2009.
Baily's Magazine of Sports and Pastimes. London, 1875–1915.
El Caballo. Buenos Aires, 1949–1989.
Centauros. Buenos Aires, 1955–1983.
Country Life.
Galveston Daily News, 1876–1883.
El Gráfico. Buenos Aires, 1924–2007.
Horse and Horseman. New York, 1936–1938
International Journal of Sport. London, 2001–2003.
The Le Mars Sentinel. Le Mars, 1878–1887.
The London Gazette. London, 1845–2007.
Outing Magazine, 1891–1923.
Polo. New York, 1927–1936.
Polo. Gaithersburg and Wellington, 1972–1996.
Polo & Campo. Buenos Aires, 1933–1939.
Polo & Equitación. Buenos Aires, 1924–1932.
The Polo Magazine, 1977–1979.
Polo Monthly. London, 1909–1939.

Polo Players Diary. London, 1910.
Polo Players' Edition. Wellington, 1997–2011.
Polo Players Guide. London, 1910–1912.
Polo Quarterly International, 1992–2011.
Polo Times. North Leigh, 1993–2011.
San Antonio Light. San Antonio, 1883.

Index

Numbers with *bold italics* indicate pages with illustrations.

Abadie, Maj. Eustace 16
Abergavenny, Marquess of 100
Abergavenny Tournament 56
Aboughazale, Ahmad 264, 268
Aboughazalem, Oussama 272
à Brassard, Nigel C. 35, *C6*, 242, 245, 247, 250, 258
Accra Polo Club 76
Adam, Maj. 99
Adamthawite, John 52, 53
Adao, João 186
Addington, William 15
Aden Polo Club 77
AFB (team) 272
Afghanistan 66, 250
Aflalo, Frederick G. 247
Agassiz, Rodolphe L. "Dolph" 83, 85
Agnew, Maj. John 24
Agote, Alejandro 268
Aguero, Abel A. "Negro" 190
Aguilar, Valerio "Vale" 225, 261
Ahmiabh Farm (team) 250
Airlie, Tenth Earl of 71
Airlie, David Olgivy, 10th Earl of 44, 71, 325
Alberdi, Enrique J. "Quito" 172
Alberdi, Juan C. "Bebé" 172, 217
Alberta Province 74
Albwardy, Ali 253, 254, 256, 258
Albwardy, Rashid 268, 270
Albwardy, Tariq 260
Alcatel (team) 220, 222
Aldershot (team) 17, 27
Aldershot Cup 50
Aldershot Garrison 8, 37, 50, 167, 201, 246
Aldershot Infantry Cup 50, 64
Aldin, Cecil C.W. 145
Alexander, Henry Bruen 74
Alexander, Capt. K. 139
Alexander, Dr. William 18
Alexander of Tunis, F.M. Lord Harold 163
HMS Alexandra 181
Alexandra, H.M. Queen 9, 47, 109, 117, 180, 225
Alexandria 28
Alfonso X 30, 117, *128*
All-Ireland Military Challenge Cup 63

All-Ireland Novices' Tournament 63
All Ireland Open Cup 59, 63, 296
All Ireland Polo Club 59–63, 104, 109, 138, 139, 178, 272
All-Ireland Social Club's Cup 63
All-Ireland Subalterns' Tournament 63
Allen, David 222
Allen, Lt. Leon 266
Allen, Brig. Gen. Terry de la M. 110, 111
Allenby, Lt., R.N. 181
Allfrey, Maj. Charles W. 99
Allfrey, Capt. Nugent 53
Allsopp, Maj. Ranulf 77
Allwoodley Polo Club 26
Altamira (team) 271
Alva Cottage (team) 23
Amato, Dennis J. 73, 247
Amaya, Luis 216
Amaya, Matías 265
Amaya, Sebastián 247
Amberjack (pony) 154
Ambroggio, Juan 271, 272
America 47, 57, 68–71, 83, 90, 97, 187, 188, 196, 206, 239, 240, 241, 266, 267, 279–281
America (team) 66, 91, 113, 117, 120, 122, 141, 172, 190, 191, 223, 224, 232, 235, 236, 274, 335
Americas, Cup of the 115, 119, 137, 140, 206, 282
Amoore, Capt. Michael J.B. 201, 219
Amsink, Heinrich 114
Analandia 80
Ancrum, William 78
Anderson, David 213
Anderson, Maj. Fearnley 243
Anderson, Richard "Harry" 79
Andrada, Manuel A. 114, 115
Anglesey Polo Club 213
Anker, Ronnie 195
Anne, HRH Princess 183
Anningsdale Polo Club 215
Annual Summer Tournament (Kirtlington) 226
Ansell, Col. George K. 54, 60
Ansell, Capt. Michael 139
Ansty Polo Club 215

Antinori, Nicolás 257
Antrim Polo Club 61
Antwerp 110
Antwerp Polo Club 111
Aotea (team) 76, 174, 175, 208
Aotea Cup 256
Apes Hill (team) 262, 268
appeals for fouls 83, 276
Appleby, Julian 259
Apsley End Polo Club 251
Araya, José I. "Pepe" 257, 258
Arbuthnot, Rear-Adm. Sir Robert 73, 74
Archdale, Edward 62
Archer-Shee, Brig. John P. 134, 194
Archetti, Prof. Eduardo P. 66
Archibald, Alasdair 220, 221, 235, 236, 260
Archibald, Rob 258, 260
Archie David Cup 160, 272
Arellano, Julio F. 224, 266
Argentina 64–67, 165, 206, 232, 239, 274, 281
Argentina (team) 37, 38, 78, 112–114, 172, 192, 206, 233–237, 255
Argentine Ambassador's Cup 171
Argentine Club 37, 66
Argentine Open Championship 18, 65, 137, 165, 206, 239
Argentine Polo Association 47, 65, 164, 168, 206, 232, 233, 255, 328
Argentine Polo Federation 103, 328
Arkwright, Miss Lillian 225
Armit, Lt. John Lees 72
Armitage, Lt. William 17
Armour, George D. 145, 146, 148, *C2*, 244
Armour, Lester, III "Red" 151, 184, 190, 200
Armstrong, Charles M. 188
Armstrong, Gillespie "Gippie" 256, 257
Armstrong, John 188
Armstrong, Simon "Solly" 208
Army Championship Cup 168
Army Cup 50
Army-in-India 37, 120, 121, 208
Army Polo Association 252
Army Polo Committee 51, 189
Army Saddle Club 204

Arnold, Maj. W.J. 139
Arnott, Maxwell 60
Arthingworth Hall Cup 99
Arthingworth Polo Club 99
Arthur Lucas Cup 253, 269, 271
Ascot Park Polo Club *C4*, *C7*, 213, 214, 230, 231, 251, 253, 272
Asdean (team) *162*
Ashfields Polo Club 214
Ashtead Polo Club 56
Ashton, Alfred 16
Ashton, Chris 205, 247, 282
Ashton, Geoffrey G. 122, *128*, 129, 130
Ashton, Geoffrey, Jr. 177
Ashton, Mrs. Helen *128*
Ashton, Lt.-Col. Hugh C.S. 54, 55, 116
Ashton, James H. "Jim" *128*, 129, *130*
Ashton, James, Sr. *128*
Ashton, James W. 235, 238, 240
Ashton, Philip S.K. *128*
Ashton, Robert R. "Bob" *128*, 129, 130, 141
Ashworth, Hamilton 251, 259
Astaburuaga, Francisco 164, 165, 172
Asthall Farm Polo Club 251
Atherley, Capt. Evelyn G.H. 29, 39
Atkinson, Maj. Eric G. "Joey" 103–106, 118, 120–122, 128
Atlantic (team) 261
Assam Cup *C5*, 195, 261, 265
Astor, John Jacob 109, 110
Astor, William Waldorf 35
Auckland 75
Auckland Polo Club 75
Auriol-Baker, A. 56
Auriol-Baker, D. 56
Aurora (team) 129, 132–135, 137, 253, 279
Austin, Ken 209
Australasia (team) 83, 191, 192, 258, 260
Australia 29, 35, *36*, 67, 68, 175, 192, 232, 234, 236, 238
Austria 110, 277
Autumn Cup 52
Ava, Lord Archibald 325
Avery, Maj. Leonard 226
Aylott, Hedley 251
Ayrshire Polo Club 14
Azzaro, Michael V. 224, 266
Azzurra (team) 222, 256, 257

Babington, Lt.-Gen. Sir James M. 40, 44, 60
backhander 34, 44, 59, 119, *153*, 223, 281
Backhouse, Hugo S. 132
Bad Lippspringe 166, 252
Bader, Douglas 161
Badger, Lt.-Col. T. Reginald 22, 146, 150, 245
Baez, Jesús 217
Bagatelle Polo Club 32, 108, 109, 112, 113, 137
Bagnell, David 203

Bagorita (pony) 154
Baibiene, Horacio 187
Baig, Brig. Masud A.A. "Hesky" 185
Baillieu, Colin 203
Baillieu, John "Ruki" 192, 254, 257, 259, 272
Bain, Ginger 330
Baird, Lt. John G.A. 44
Baker, David 250
Baker, Hugh 53
Baker, Philip 250
Baker, Reginald L. "Snowy" 110
Baker, William 15
Bakewell, John S. 20
Bakewell, Maj. William 99
Balada (pony) 87
Balcones Ranch 69, 327
Balding, Arthur 25
Balding, Asa 22, 62
Balding, Miss B. 226, 227
Balding, "Baby" 227, 235
Balding, Judy 227
Balding, Gerald M. 102, 122, *123*, 128, *130*, 133, 135, 139–142, 144, 150, 168, *169*, 170, 172, 194, 226, 254, 331
Balding, William 15, 22, 57
Baldock, Col. Edward H. 24, 32, 39, 40, 50
Baldock, John 8
Baldwin, Charles 72
Baldwin, G. 15
Baldwin, Air Vice-Marshal Sir John 138
Balfour, Frank J. 20, 23, 65, 66
Ball, Robert 18, 82
Ball, William 16
Ballard, Maj. Anthony W. *201*
Ballin a Hone (pony) 87
Balvanera (team) 271
Bamberger, Arnaud *C5*
Bampfield, Mrs. 225
Banket Polo Club 76
Bar XY Ranch 74
Barakat, Ashrak 213
Barbados 78, 262, 268
Barbour, Lt.-Col. David 166, 201
Barbour, Frank 60, 61
Barcelona, Real Polo Club de 7
Barclay, Capt. Alexander H. 133
Barclay, Hugh Petre 189
Barcome Polo Club 252
Baring, Lt.-Col. Thomas M. 189
Barker, Capt. Frederick G. 53, 171, 189
Barker, Reginald R. 53
Barker, Wright 146
Barlow, Capt. Andrew M.K. 173
Barlow, Charles S. "Punch" 331
Barlow, Mark H.D. 173
Barlow, Tom 177, 331
Barn Elms 50, 51, 326
Barnard, Capt. H.W. 13
Barnard, Thomas 15
Barne, Seymour 61
Barnett, W. 15
Barrack, Thomas J., Jr. 65
Barraclough, Ernest 99

Barrantes, Héctor E. 194, *195*, *197*, 199, *200*, 208
Barrett, Mr. (Staffordshire player) 29
Barrett, Frederick W. "Rattle" 43, 63, 89, 91, 110–113, 116, 117
Barrow, Miss N. 225
Barrow, Col. Raymond C. 53, 171
Barrow, Col. Richard 179
Barry, Harold A. "Joe" 190, 224
Barry, Harold L. "Chico" 190, 205, 206
Barry, Roy M. 186
Bartalis, Kálmán von 114
Barthorp, Capt. Arthur 9
Barton, Clement M. "Clem" 173, 176, 204
Barton, H.A. 73
Barton, Stanley J. 53
Barton Abbey (team) 160, 176, 226
Barton Polo Club 46, 148
Bartram, Walter 114
Bass, Capt. Frederick W. 134
Bateleur (team) 261
Bateman, Lt. Anthony 166
Bath Bun (pony) 153
Bath Club 49, 67
Bathurst, 7th Earl 52
Bathurst, 8th Earl 170
Bathurst, Hon. George B. 53, 170, 171, 179, 204
Bathurst Cup 254
Battenberg, Prince Louis 180
Bauer, Carl Ferdinand 146
Baxter, Capt. Robert D. 177
Baxter, T.S. 45
Bayford, Maj. Edmund 37
Bayley, Edward 61
Bayley, R.A. 31
Bayly, John 17, 79
Baynes, Capt. Geoffrey 61
Bazley, Capt. Gardner 52
Beach, Frederick 34, 324
Beard, Maj. Louis A. 105, 106
Beatty, Sir Kenneth 99
Beatty, Philip Vandeleur 22, 61
Beatty, William 25
Beauchamp Hall (team) 25, 82, 87
Beaufort Polo Club (1872) 19
Beaufort Polo Club (1929) 19, 53, 101, 122, 124, 127, 137, 226
Beaufort Polo Club (1989) 19, 178, 214, 253, 261, 264, 269, 271
Beauty Spot (pony) 133
Beckton Polo Club 71
Beddington, Lt. Edward 16, 20
Bedford, Henry 66
Bedford County Polo Club 15
Beechanger (team) 176, 177
Beechwood (team) 168
Beeckman, Robert L. 87
Beer, Robert 205
behinds 282
Beim, James R. 192, 193, 220, 222, 235, 257–261, 263, 264, 266, *268*, 269, 272, 273
Beitner, Mandie 272
Belcher, Col. Paul *C8*
Belgium 110, 112, 138

Belgrano Polo Club 65
Belgravia Polo 272
Belize Colony and Athletic Club 78
Bell, Charles 25
Bell, Capt. Henry 19
Bell, H.S. 23
Bell, Isaac "Icky" 25, 60
Bell, John 14
Bell, Dr. William 72
Bell Ville Polo Club 255
Bellaco Polo Club 65
Bellemy, Ernest 61
Bellew, Lt. Robert 325
Bellville, A.L. 22
Bellville, Capt. George E. 20, 42
Belmont, Raymond R. 34, 324
Beloe, Mrs. A. 173
Bendigo (pony) 82
Bengal-Nagpur Railway Polo Club
    65
Bengough, Col. Sir Piers 194
Benítez, Francisco 65
Bennett, Edmund R. 56
Bennett, James Gordon 32, 68, 69
Bennett, Thomas 26
Bennetts, A.W. 75
Bentley, Henry Cumberland 31
Benyon, Sir John 12
Benyon, Capt. Joseph S. 43
Beresford, Lord Charles *C5*, 190,
    192, 208, 216, 222, *223*
Beresford, Lt.-Col. George de la
    Poer 120, 243
Beresford, Maj. Hon. John G.H.H.
    37, 68, 82, 108, 207
Beresford, Lord Patrick T. 154,
    173, 176, 177, 185, 186, 190, *196*,
    204, 207, 209, 216, *223*
Beresford, Lady MaríaTeresa 259
Beresford, Gen. Sir William 211
Beresford, Lord William L. 9, 10
Beresford Cup 68, 207
Berkshire Polo Club 15, 46, 56
Berlin 335
Bermengui, Luis 263
Berryman, Capt. Montagu 167
Besley, James Campbell 73, 327
Bethell, Brian B. 53, 148, 163, 185–
    188
Bethell, Christopher J. "Chris"
    195, 218
Bethlen, Graf István 114
Bettner, Robert Lee 73
Betz, Charles 252
Beveridge, Robert D. 206
Beverly Hills 165
Beverly Polo Club 250
Bhamo Polo Club 78
Bhopal (team) 131, 135
Bhopal, Col. Sir Muhammad,
    Nawab of 130
Bicket, Cheryl 254
Biddle, Thomas J., Sr. 239, 248,
    266
"Big Four" (team) 58, 82, 86–88,
    90, 91, 118, 136, 266
Big Horn Polo Club 71, 72
Bijkerk, Anthony T. 245
Billericay Polo Club 166

Billy (pony) 152
Billy Walsh Cup 214
Bindura Polo Club 76
Binfield Heath Polo Club 214
Bingham, Capt. Hon. J. Denis Y.
    63, 112, 113
Bingley, Capt. Robert 137
Binnie, T. 13
Bird, John A.H. 146
Bird, Oliver 324
Birkdale (team) 168
Birkhill (team) 186
Birley, G. 99
Birmingham Polo Challenge Cup
    25
Bishop's Stortford (team) 18
Bissacia, Duc Armand de 108
Black, Mrs. Lavinia 255
Black Bears (team) *C6*, 218, 221,
    222, 254, 257, 258, 260, 261,
    265, 269, 271, 272
Black Robin Farm 99
Blackbirds (team) 139
Blackbourn, Miss J.163
Blackburne, Capt. Charles 21
Blackett, William 27
Blackmore Vale Polo Club 17, 18
Blackwood, Lt. Lord Frederick 44
Blain, F.W. 16
Blair, Lt.-Col. Frederick G. 43, 44
Blair Polo Club 70
Blake, Jeffrey 266, 267
Blake-Thomas, Andrew 236
Blakiston-Houston, Edward 61
Blakiston-Houston, John 61, 134
Blakiston-Houston, Richard 61
Blakiston-Houston Cup 134
Blandford Meg (pony) 147, *C3*, 161
Blasson, Harry 69
Bloemfontein Polo Club 207
Blofeld, Frank D'Arcy 23
Blue Sleeve (pony) 152
Bluejackets (team) 28
Bluejackets Cup 162
The Blues *see* Royal Horse Guards
Blues and Royals 200
Blumson, W. 52
Blundell Brown, T. 19
Blyth, Ormond 19
Blyth, Rupert 19
Board, Maj. John A. 146, 159, 244,
    245
Bobbet, John 61
Boca Raton (team) 186
Boden, Henry 18, 29
Boehm's Team 216
Boerne 69, 327
Boeseke, Elmer J., Jr. 112, 132, 137
Boileau, Harry 15
Boles, Maj. Dennis C. 102, 103, 106
Bolkiah, Bahar Jefri 221
Bollini, Juan M. 222
Bond-Cabbell, Benjamin 25
Bond-Elliott, William 219
Bordon Challenge Cup 55
Bordon Officers' Polo Club 99
Bordon Silver Cup 99
Border Regiment 166
Bordeu, Teófilo V. "Toti" 162

Borwick, Luke 202, 235
Borwick, Lt.-Col. Malcolm 46
Borwick, Malcolm P. 46, 192, 193,
    235, 236, 257–261, 264, 269
Boscawen, Hon. Hugh 10
Boston Spa (team) 228
Bostwick, George H., Jr. "Pete" 142
Bott, Mrs. Judith 226, 227
Boucher, Capt. Hugh 201
Boucher, Maj. William S.H. 200
Bourdieu, Gonzalo 256
Boussoud, Jean 108
Bovill, Capt. Bristow 205
Bowden, Sir George 67
Bowden-Smith, Philip 113
Bowdon Polo Club 16, 170
Bowlby, Edward F.S. 186
Bowles, W.A. 24
Boyd-Gibbins, Arthur G. "Alfie"
    19, 163, 176, 186
Bradford, James 20
Bradley, Cuthbert 146
Bradley, Derreck 269
Bradshaw, Frederick 18
Braine, Col. Herbert 99
Brammall, Mr. (London P.C.) 55
Bramwell, Hugh 12
Brand, Hon. Thomas W. *36*, 37
Brandon Polo Club 74
Brandywine Polo Club 205
Brannockstown Polo Club 215
Brassey, Edwin 24
Brassey, Lt. Percy F. 325
Braun Cantilo, Eduardo 172
Braun Cantilo, Rafael "Rafi" 175
Braund, David 202
Brazil 79, 80, 192, 233, 235–238,
    335
Brecknock, David, Earl of 155,
    177, 186, 199
Breeks, Capt. Richard 19
Breitmeyer, Lt.-Col. Gabriel C.A.
    134
Brent Walker (team) 218
Brett, Henry D. *C7*, *191*, 192, 199,
    220–222, 234, 253, 255–257,
    261, 271
Brett, Mrs. Hugh (Margie) 249, 278
Brewhurst (team) 176, 177
Brian Bethell Cup 253
Bridges, Capt. Thomas McG. 22
Brigade of Guards Polo Club 28
Brigg, Capt. Tom 159, 160
Bright, Herbert 150
Brighton and County Polo Club 24
Brinquant, Raoul de 32
Bristow, F.S. 20
British Army – American Army
    Series 104–106
British Army of the Rhine 166
British Army of the Rhine's Inter-
    Regimental 166–168
British Army Team 28, 37, 167,
    204, 205, 252, 255
British East Africa 76
British Forces Germany Polo Club
    252
British Honduras 78
British Lions (team) 58

British Polo Championship 250, 257, 258
Britten-Long, Nicholas 271
Brixworth (team) 24
Broadbent, Lt. Edgar 17
Broadhead, W. Smithson 146
Brocas-Clay, Alfred 51
Brock, Col. B.J. 13
Brockenhurst Polo Club 20
Brocklebank, Capt. Richard 53
Brocklehurst, Capt. John F. 35, 39
Brodie, Alex C. *218*, 234
Broncos 217, 260, 262, 264, 272
Bronze Horse Trophy 196
Brooke, Maj.-Gen. Geoffry H. 37, 113, 152, 243, 245
Brookes, Dr. William P. 107
Brooks, Henry Jamyn 146
Brooks, John 59
Brooks, Kit 265
Brougham, Claire 269
Brown, Maj. Cecil 146
Brown, Sir David 186
Brown, Douglas *C6*, 258
Brown, James Moray 8, 13, 32, 41, 241
Brown, Lt. Col. Lewis 105
Brown, Sir Martin 214
Brown, Martin R.R. 217, 222
Brown, Paul D. 146, 147
Brown, Tom 67
Brown-Clayton, Maj. Robert 68, 154
Browne, W. Byron 44
Brune, Capt. Prideaux 17
Brunker, Capel 113
Brunskill, Elliot R.F. 23
Bryan, Hon. Maj. George *36*
Bryant, Harold 72
Bryant, Capt. Loftus 17
Bryn Mawr Polo Club 104
Buccaneers (team) 187
Buchan, John 246
Buchanan, Adam 221, 222
Buchanan, Carlos R.B. "Laddie" 169
Buchanan, Donald 207
Buchanan, Ian 245
Buchanan, Peter R.G. "The Tout" 147
Buckenham, F.H. 99
Buckenham, Peter 171
Buckmaster, Capt. Herbert 203
Buckmaster, Walter S. 18, 19, 31, 42, 55, 57, 60, 82, 83, 85, 87, 90, 101, 103, 108, 109, 111, 116, 117, 119, 151, 203, 251
Bucknell, Leonard C. 16, 25, 56
Bucknell, Capt. William 227
Bucknill, Sir Thomas 56
Buck's Club 116, 147, 179, 203, 250
Budgett, Mrs. Alan 173
Budgett, Arthur 138
Budgett, Charles 100
Budgett, Heather (Mrs. John Tylor) 147
Budgett, Hugh 100, 172
Budgett, R. Alan 138, 170, *172*, 173, 202

Buenos Aires 29, 79, 206, 238, 335
Buenos Aires (team) 66
Buenos Aires & Rosario Railway Polo Club 65
Buenos Aires Polo Club 65
Buffalo Polo Club 71
Bulkeley, Capt. Arthur "Donjy" 9, 10
Bulkeley-Johnston, Brig.-Gen. Charles B. 46
Bullard, Gen. Robert *105*
Bullfrogs (team) 255
Bullivant, Percy 25, 55, 56
Bullough, Ian 62
Bunclody Polo Club 253
Burdett-Fisher, Gen. Sir Bertie Drew 167
Burdon, Walter B.C. 53
Burdon, William Wharton 23
Burgess, Dr. Richard 18
Burghley Park Polo Club 22
Burke, Carleton F. 122
Burma 77, 78
Burma Polo Association 77
Burma Polo Association Cup 77
Burn, Sir Roland C.W. 54, 56
Burnaby, Algernon 29
Burnard, Lt. Charles 17
Burningfold Polo Centre 252
Burrell, Anthony 214
Burrell, Charlie 214
Burton, Sir William 24
Bury, Oliver 99
Busby, C.J. 164
Buscarlet, Mrs. Bowen 56
Butler, Maj. Francis 52
Butler, James 8
Butler, Michael W. 196
Butler, Capt. Patrick J. 163, 168
Butler, Paul 204
Butler, Sir Spencer Harcourt 78
Butler National Handicap 204
Butson, Henry 61
Butson, Maj. Sinclair 61
Butter, Jim 163
Butterworth, Frank, Sr. 121
Buxton, Capt. Ivor 22, 97, 98
Buxton, John 22
Buxton, Richard 22
Buzzy Bees (team) 256
Byner, C.J. 25

Caballus (team) 253, 255
Cachar 62
Cadenza (team) 262, 263
Calcutta 7, 35, 62
Calcutta Cup 13
Calcutta Polo Club 19
Calcutta Rugby Football Club 13
Calgary Polo Club 74
California 73, 142, 212, 335
Calley, J.D. 60
Calley, Maj. Thomas C.P. 25
Camarena, Francisco "Paco" 209
Cambiaso, Adolfo 221, 222, 253, 254, 258, 260, 264, 268, 270, 271, 273, 279–282
Cambridge, Duke of 9

Cambridge & Newmarket Polo Club 214
Cambridge University Polo Club 18, 30, *31*, *C4*, 164, 170, 185, 214, 229, 253
Cambridge University Open Cup 16
Cambridgeshire Hunt (team) 15
Camden, Lady 10
Camden, Marquis 10
Camp Polo Club of Uruguay 65
Campbell, Capt. Charles 20
Campbell, Col. Colin 26
Campbell, D.E. 23
Campbell, Gordon 139, 330
Campbell, John A. 66, 67
Campbell, Maj.-Gen. John C. "Jock" 129, 134, 156
Campbell, Miss Nell 227
Campbell, Maj. Noel 17
Campbell, W. 61
Campbell-Preston, Hon. Angela 165
Campbell-Preston, Col. Robert 165
Camperdown Polo Club 36
Campo de Marte 209, 261
Canada 29, 73–75, 178, 236, 274, 282
Cañada de Gómez Polo Club 64–66, 326
Candy, Capt. Cairnes-Derrick 67
Candy, Capt. Henry "Sugar" 69
Canford Magna Polo Club 166, 228
Canterbury Polo Club 27, 28, 189
Cárcano, Miguel 187
Cardiff and County Polo Club 12, 13
Cardwell, Hugh B. 56
Cardwell, R.M. 99
Careyes (team) 255
Carlow 8, 60
Carlsson, Roger E. 253, 254
Carlton, Viscount 99
Carmichael, Lt. H. 78
Carmignac, Edouard 268, 272
Carnival Cup 76
Carr, C.K. 19
Carr, James 272
Carr, L.R. 19
Carr, Brig. William G. 28
Carrara, A. 164
Carslaw, Yolanda 247, 249
Carton de Wiart, Adrian 98
Casarejo 175, 177
Casares, Col. Samuel A. 37, 38
Case, Henry A. 40
Caset, Guillermo 270
Casey, Joey 186
Casson, Joseph 61
Castagnola, Bartolomé "Lolo" 253, 254, 256, 264, 282
Castagnola, Marianela 259, 261
Castlereagh, Lord Charles 11, 29
Castro Maya, Raymundo 79
The Cat (pony) 82
Cathcart, Helen 246
Catterick Garrison 157
Catteridge Bridge Polo Club 26, 27

Cattle, C.F. 24
Cattley, George A. 147
Catto, G.K. 16
Cavaliers (team) 131, 135
Cavalry Club 49, 66, 120, 171, 203
Cavalry Cup 76
Cavalry School Polo Club 27, 55
Cavan, Earl of 104
Cavanagh, Diego, Jr. 271
Cavanagh, Juan L. 187
Cavanagh, Roberto L. 114, 115, 138
Cavendish, Capt. Hon. Charles W.H. 39, 43, 325
Cavendish, Brig-Gen. Frederick W.L.S.H. "Caviar" 44, 324
Cawley, Capt. John S. 20
Cawthorne, Neil 147
Cayzer, Henry 14
Cazalet, Edward 177
Cazón, Nicolás E. 165
Centaurs (team, 1950s) 175, 178, 186–188
Centaurs (team, 1980s) 217
Centaurs (team, 2000s) 259
Central America 78
Ceylon 29
Chadwick, Alfonso "Pollo" 165
Chagrin Valley Hunt Club 161
Chaine, Capt. William 8–10
Chakari 76
Chambers, Maj. Arthur 16
Chamois (team) 146
Champion de Crespigny, Lt. Vivian 75
changing ends 280, 334
Channing, W.E. 203
Chantilly 236, 238, 335
Chaplin, Gavin C. 208
Chaplin, Julian W.R. "Buddy" 207
Chaplin, Ronald 152
Chapman, T. 18
Chapple Cup 252
Charley, Arthur 61
Charlton, Max 272
Charmer (pony) 152
Charrington, Hugh 25
Chateau Giscours (team) 218
Chatterton-Newman, Roger 147, 242, 247–249, 326
Chavanne, Santiago 264
Chavez, Cristián 265
Chaytor, Capt. Joshua 104, 139
Cheape, Lt. George 8
Cheape, Capt. Leslie St. C. 89–92, **94**, 98, **C2**
Checkendon Polo Club 215
Cheetahs (team) 227
Cheltenham Cup 171, 271
Cheltenham Polo Club 19, 24, 53, 65
Chequers Manor (team) 186, 187
Cherry Tree (ground) 213
Chesham, Lord Charles 44
Chesham, Lady Margot 226
Cheshire Champion Cup 21
Chester County Club 16
Chester Racecourse Polo Club 251, 265
Cheyenne Club 69

Cheyenne Mountain Country Club 72
Child, Sir Smith Hill 24, 54
Childwall (ground) 21
Chile 78, 79, 165, 172, 191, 192, 217, 233, 234, 237, 335
Chillesford Polo Ground 126, 163, 164, 227
Chinchillas (team) 126
Chisenhale-Marsh, Atherton H. 18
Cholmondeley, Lord George 30, 55, 67, 74, 97, 98, 116, **102**
Chopendoz (team) 213
Chow, Derrick 258
Christchurch Polo Club 75
Churchill, Sir Winston 51, 98, 156
Churchward, W. Patrick **198**, 199, 208, 216
Churton, Capt. Christopher H. 201
Cicely (pony) 151
Cicero Cup 56, 57, 126
Cinderella (pony) 87
Cinders (pony) 87
Cinnamond, Norman J. 7
Cirencester Challenge Cup 52
Cirencester 18-goal Tournament 263, 269, 271
Cirencester Park Polo Club 45, 53, 148, 151, 156, **C3**, 170, 171, 179, 218, 242
Cirencester Polo Club 19, 52, 53, 126
Cirencester Spring Tournament 53
Civilians (team) 165
Clagett, Jean 147
Clanbrassil Cup 227, 228
Clarence, Prince Albert Victor, Duke of 180
Clarita (team) 259, 271
Clark, Forrester "Tim" 19
Clark, Lyons 17
Clarke, Arundell 17
Clarke, J. Percival "Percy" 79
Clarke, Nick 255, 271, 273
Clarke, S.T. 177
Clarkin, John P. 254, 256, 260–265, 270, 271
Clarkin, Mrs. John P. *see* Vestey, Nina
Clayton, Michael 246
Clayton-Clayton, Capt. William "Dick" 9, 10
Clegg, Assheton 21
Clegg, Capt. Humphrey 17
Clément, Albert 30
Clément, Gustave-Adolphe 29
Clerke, Maj. Albert 61
Cleveland Polo Club 27
Clibborn, Cuthbert J. "Bertie" 62
Clifford, Richard W.C. 173
Clitheroe Polo Club 22
Clonshire Equestrian and Polo Centre 252
Close, Frederick B. 70
Close, James B. 70
Close, John B. 70
Close, William B. 70
Clothier, Louisa 263
Clowes, Winchester 30

Clunie, Frank W. 79
Coaker, Lt.-Col. Ronald 166, 167, 201
Coaten, Arthur W. 245, 248
Cobbold, R.N. 227
Cobnut (pony) 87, 150
Cochrane Cup 104
Coghill, Lt. Nevill 111
Cola (pony) 148
Colchester Garrison Polo Club 213
Colchester Polo Club 27
Cole, Lt. Arthur 76
Colgan, Dr. Francis 60
Collet, Grant 272
Collie, Marcus 265
Collie, Tom 261
Collier, Imogen 147
Collins, Declan 178
Collins, Rupert 244
Collins, Steve 251
Collis, Capt. Robert 20
Collyer-Bristow, J. 56
Colmore, Lt.-Col. Horace 147
Colmore, Mrs. Horace "Nina" 147, **C3**, **161**
Colombia 204, 233
Colonia Polo Club 79
Colorado Springs 72
Colquhoun-Denvers, Nicholas J.A. **C5**, 159, 178, 239, 240, 266, 267, 272
Colt, Henry 116
Coltbridge Park 13
Colts Cup 127
Columbia (team) 190, 199
Colville, Lt. Hon. Stanley 181
Combe, Samuel Barbour 61
Combermere Barracks 28, 173
Combermere Cup 176
Combined Northern Provinces (team) 207
Combined Services Polo Association 252
Comins, D. 68
Commandant's Cup 76
Commission Cup 77
Commonwealth Games 178, 179
Compiègne (team) 108
Conceit (pony) 152
Connaught, Prince Arthur of 13, 76
Connaught Cup 76
Connell, J. Arthur 72
Connolly, P.W. 61
Conte McDonnell, Jorge 187
Conway, F. 99
Conyngham, Marquis Victor 61
Cooch Behar, Maharajah of 177
Cook, Frank 79
Cooke, John 22
Cooke, John F. 62
Cooke, Lt. Ronald B.B.B. 102, 122
Cookson, Maj.-Gen. Gerald 73
Cookson, Thomas 21
Cooley, James C. 35, 91
Coombe Farm (team) 230
Copa República Argentina 45
Coppez, Mark 260
Coppez, Nicola FitzGerald 260

Corbett, Roland 226
Corell, Marie 25
Corey, Alan L., Jr. 187, 188
Corey, Alan L., III 187, 188
Corinthian Trophy 196
Cork 8, 62
Cornell University 196
Coronation Cup 54, 97, 98, 101–103, 134, *135*, 136, 137, *C5*, 164, *169*, 172, 175, 190, *191*, 192, 193, 254, 278
Coronel Suárez Polo Club 90, 175, 195, 206
Corovest (team) 269
Corramore (team) 265
Cory, Sir Clifford 12
Cotswold (team) 160
Cottontail (pony) 87, 150
Coubertin, Baron Pierre de Fredí 107–110
County Cup 13, 45, 46, 48, 146, 174, 176, 218, 265
County Meath (team) 8, 46, 61–63
County Polo Association 45, 51, 57, 100, 127, 159, 228, 280
Couper, Lt. George 147
Courage, Christopher 173
Courage, Ernest 56
Courage, Hugh 20
Courage, Raymond 19
Courtenay (team) *C6*
Couturié, Henri 138
Cowan, Lt. Hugh W.L. 134
Coward, John 79
Cowdin, John E. 32, 83, *84*
Cowdray, 1st Viscount 54, 55
Cowdray, Harold Pearson, 2nd Viscount 54, 55, 122
Cowdray, John, 3rd Viscount 55, 142, *143*, 148, 159–161, 165, 170, 174, 175, 177, 188, *198*, 202, 229
Cowdray Park Challenge Cup 54, 160, 188, 216, 219, 220, 258, 265, 271
Cowdray Park Gold Cup 174, 175, 177, 185, 188, 216, 221, 258, 262, 265, 268, 271, 273, 274
Cowdray Park Polo Club 54, 55, 99, 103, 160, 161, 165, 166, 170, 172, 174, 177–179, 185–187, 189, *198*, 199, 200, 204, 205, 228, 253
Cowlard, Lt. John 61
Cowley, David 202
Cowley, Patrick 218
Cowley, William Payne 22
Coworth Park Challenge 269, 271
Coworth Park Polo Club 250
Cox, Douglas 61
Cox, Herbert C. "Bert" 19, 127
Cox, Maj. M. 133
Craddock, Adm. Christopher 27, 61
Craig, John 13
Craig, Capt. (R.A.) 77
Craig, Terence R. 207
Crawford, Susan L. 147
Crawhall, Joseph E. 147, 148
Crawley, Midshipman John 76
Cresswell, Arthur J.G. 19

Crewdson, A.F., Jr. 17
Crewdson, F. 17
Crewdson, H. Douglas 17
Crewdson, J. 21
Crichton, Maj. Hubert 54
Crisp, J.W.M. "Buff" *202*
Croshaw, Capt. Oswald 14
Cross, Geoffrey 203, 229, 248
Crossley, Eric 25
Crossley, Francis 22
Crossley, Sir Kenneth 21
Crotto, Héctor J. "Juni" 190, 219, 230
Crotto, Jacinto 260, 271
C.S. Brooks (team) 222
Cubitt, Hon. Charles Guy 201
Cudmore, Matt 263
Cudmore, Oliver "Ollie" 263, 265
Cullinan, P. Dunne 61
Culverwell, Davis 207
Cumings, Lt. George 75
Cunard, Sir Bache E. 11, 39, 47, 69
Cunard, Lt. Edward 11
Cuneo, Terence T. 148, 194
Cuningham of Craigends, Mrs. John (Alison) 53
Cunningham, Glen 14
Cunningham, Lt. Harold M.C. 201
Cunninghame, H. 23
Cuppage, Louis 74
Curr, John 72
Curraghmore Polo Club 215
Curre, Sir Edward 12, 39
Currie, A. 77
Cursham, Juliet 148
Cusack-Smith, Sir Thomas Berry 80, 328
Cushing, Charles Phelps 72
Cushing, Harry B. IV 151
Cyclops (pony) 59
Czar (pony) 151

Daba, Dawule 258
D'Acosta, F. 64
Dacres-Dixon, Capt. Anthony 166
Dadd, Frank *31*
Dainty (pony) 150, 152, *C1*
Dalbiac, Maj. Henry S. 325
Dale, Rev. Thomas F. 57, 58, 241, 245
Dalgety, Alexander 27
Dalmahoy Polo Club 178
Dalmeny, Lord Albert 54, 55, 67, *102*, 116, 118
Dalton, Rev. John N. 180
Dalwhinnie (match) 263
Daly, Maj.-Gen. Arthur C. 99
Daly, Capt. Bernard 60
Daly, Capt. Denis St. G. 40, 83, 108
Daly Cup 99
Dalziel, Peter 99
Daniels, Julian J. 192, 221, 234, 266
Dann, Nick 272
Dansey, Capt. Edward 10
Danson Park 28
Dantata, Sayyu 258
Darby, John 51
D'Arcy, Matt 59

Darley, Lt. Dennis C. 200
Darling (pony) 89
Darlington Polo Club 27
Darwin, Bernard 146
Davenport, Maj. Claude 201
Davenport, Maj. Colin 161
David, Maj. Archie 148, 162, 163, 173
Davidson, James 62
Davidson, T.N. 99
Davis, H.R. 62
Davis, Peter 189
Davison, Capt. Thomas 43
Dawkins, Sir Clinton 56
Dawnay, Maj.-Gen. Sir David 114, 133, 134, 188
Dawnay, Maj. Hugh 194, 242, 244, 253, 282
Dawnay, Sebastian H. 222, 257, 272
Dawson, George 18
Dawson, Hugh 24
Dawson, Lionel 7
Deacon, Mr. (Swindon player) 25
de Alba, Santiago "Jimmy," Duque 43, 110, 111
Dease, William 61
Deauville 164, 173, 187, 239
Deauville Gold Cup 164, 188, 271
De Bono, Dr. Anthony 177, 332
De Bono, Dr. Edward 177, 332
de Bruin, Tom 269
Decaux, Jean-François 221, 268, 273
Deccan Horse 168
Deceive (horse) 111
Decies, Lord *see* Beresford, John
de Clermont, Edward 20, 56
de Condamy, Charles-Fernand 32
Decoy Club 195
Dedham Vale Polo Club 252
de Ferrante, Sebastian Z. 155, 187
Defries, Miss D'Arcy 226
de Ganay, Paul 233
de Guiche, Duc Armande 32
de Janze, Vicomte Frédéric L. 32
de Jaucourt, Marquis Pierre 22
de Jumilhac, Comte Pierre 112
de La Maza, Conde Leopoldo 110, 111, 113
Delamer, Lord Hugh 16
de La Rochefoucauld, Vicomte Charles 108
de Las Casas, Alfredo 17, 23, 56
de Las Casas, Juan Clemente 17, 56, 57
de Las Casas, Luis 17
de Las Casas, Manuel 17
de la Serna, Carlos O. 164, 172, 185
del Carril, Miguel 271
De Lisle, Edwin 195
De Lisle, Gen. Sir Henry deB. 43, 153, 244, 246
De Little, Ernest 36
Del Monte 142, *143*
Deltour, Gonzalo 273
de Madré, Comte Jean 87, 103, 108, 151, 152, 279
Demetriade Cup 170

de Monbrison, Hubert C. 113, 138
de Montaigu, Count René 25, 52
de Murrieta, Adriano L. 11, 24, 39, 47
de Murrieta, Cristóbal 11, 39, 47
Denby, E. 52
Dening, Capt. John P. (Jack) 106, 120, 121
Dennis, Capt. Morley 62
de Peñaranda, Duque Hernando 110, 112
de Polignac, Comte Charles 112
de Portago, Marqués Antonio 129, 130, 132
Derbyshire Open Tournament 29
Derbyshire Polo Club 21, 40
Derks, Antje 278
de Robeck, Baron Henry 60
Derry, County 62
Derryhouse, Peter 194
de Salis, Lt.-Col. Rodolph 164
de Savory, Marcia 154
Desborough, Lord William 109
de Trafford, Capt. Humphrey 99
de Trafford, Sir Humphrey F. 21, 22, 147, 152, *C1*
Devcich, Anthony "Tony" 199, 216, 217
Devenish, Charles 53
Devenish, Jesse 53
Devereux, Horace 72
Devereux, Walter B., Jr. 72
Devereux, Walter B., Sr. 72
Devereux, William 72
de Villabrágima, Alvaro Figueroa, Marqués de 110, 113
Devon Polo Club 17
Devrient, Daniel 200
Dewar Cup 45
de Winton, Sir Francis 74
de Winton, Richard Stretton 19
Deykin, Henry Cotterill 148
Dhillon, Satnam S. 255, 256, 258
Les Diables Bleus 184, 199, 217
Díaz Alberdi, Alejandro (Piki) 219, 220, 222, 258, 260
Díaz Alberdi, Juan J. 170, 186
Dickel's Riding Academy 69
Dickinson, B. 18
Dickinson, H.B. 148
Dickson, A. Gordon 19
Dienes-ohem, Lt. Tivadar 114
Dieppe 32
Digle, Maj. (Occasional P.C. player) 99
Di Paola, Lucas 269
Di Paola, Marcos (Negro) 263, 265, 269
Dixon, James 221
Dixon, Jason 234, 235
Dixon, Mr. (Market Harborough player) 22
Dobrée, Nicholas 26
Docker, Noel H. 56
Dollar, Lt.-Col. Peter W. 148, 161, 165, 170, 172, 174, 175, 177, 178
Dollar Cup 161, 271
Domecq de la Riva, Pedro 172, 175

Domecq González, José Ignacio 172
Donaghadee Polo Club 252
Donoso, Gabriel 192, 217, 220, 222, 253, 257
Donoso, José 192, 255, 257, 263, 272, 273
Dorignac, Gastón R. 183, 187, 206
Dorling, Capt. H. Taprell "Taffrail" 242
Dorman, Charles 27
Dorman, George 27
Dorrington, Hubert 27
Douglas, John *see* Morton, Earl of
Douglas, John 110
Douglas, Walter 72
Douglas-Nugent, Brig. Arthur R. 166, 167, 201, 273, 279, 280
Douglas-Pennant, Hon. Charles 56
Douglas-Scott-Montagu, Hon. Robert 56
Douro, Maj. The Marquess 173
Dowding, Raoul 251
Dower, Gandar 226
Down Farm 19, 127, 214
Draffen, Capt. George W.C. 133
Drage, John 15, 57
Drasche-Wartinberg, Baron Richard 269
Driver, C. Ronald 187, 199
Druids Lodge Polo Club 250
The Drum Polo Club 178
Drummond, Capt. Alexander 100
Drummond, Mortimer 73
Drummond-Hay, Lady Margaret 227
Drummond-Moray, David 178
Drummond Moray, William 178
Drury, Hugh 73
Drybrough, Andrew 13
Drybrough, Thomas B. 13, 243
Drybrough, W.J. "Jack" 13, 42, 52, 60
Drysdale, Bill 68
Dubai 253, 254, 256–258, 260–262, 268, 270, 271, 273
Dubai Trophy 214
Dublin 59, 61, 62, 139
Duckett, Lt. John 44
Duckett, Steuart 8, 60, 326
Duddingstone Cottage Park 13
Dudley, Lord 50
Dugdale, Capt. Nigel 130, 131, 136
Duggan, Heriberto 172
Duggan, Luis J. 114, *115*
Duguid-McCombie, Capt. Douglas M. 28
Duke of Beaufort Cup 261, 263, 271
Duke of Cornwall Light Infantry 68
Duke of Sutherland Cup 188, 269, 271
Duke of York Cup 28, 127, 252
Dulverton Polo Club 30, 126
Dunbar, Col. Carlyle M. 117
Dundas, Robert "Bobby" 237
Dundee, Earl of 178
Dundee and Perth Polo Club 178, 260

Dundee Polo Club 178
Dunkerley, William 21
Dunville, John 61
Dunville, Robert G. 61
du Plessis, Ignatius *C7*, 258, 260, 261, 268, 269, 273
du Plooy, Johan 260
Durand, Sir Edward P.M. 245
Durham North Polo Club 27
Düsseldorf 166, 234
Dwight, Dr. James 276
Dynamite (pony) 151

Eakin, Sarah 247
Earl, George 35, 148
Early Dawn (pony) 82
East Griqualand 207
East Kent Regiment (Buffs) 77
East Lancashire Polo Club 22
Eastbourne Polo Club 99
Eastcott (team) 103
Eastwood, Aurora 249
Eaton (team) 30, 60, 67, 97, 251
Eaton Tournament 30
Ebeid, Alexandre 216, 217
Eccles, Maj. G.M. 61
Echeverz, Juan 175
Eden, J.C. 99
Eden, Lt. John 22
Eden, Robert H.H. 17, 18, 23
Eden Park Polo Club 45, 56
Edgbaston Polo Club 25
Edgecumbe, Lord 17
Edgeworth Polo Club 214, 265
Edinburgh, Duke of (1874) 47
Edinburgh Polo Club 13, 21, 26, 31, 46, 178
Edinburgh, Prince Philip Mountbatten, Duke of 148, 152, 173, 174, 176, 179, *182*, 183, 185, 186, 188, 194, 206, 242
Edmonson, Edward W. 78, 79
Eduardo Moore Tournament 255, 269, 271
Eduardo Rojas Lanusse Cup 170, 255
Edward VII, H.M. King 180
Edward VIII, H.M. King 181, 183, 250
Edwards, Chris 260
Edwards, F.A. 20
Edwards, Lionel D.R. 145, 148, *149*, 150–152
Edwards, Capt. A. Noel 18, 26, 43, 53, 60, *89*, 90, 91, 94
Egan, Frederick W. 55
Egerton-Green, Maj. Francis 13, 87
18th Hussars 37, 52, 68
8th Hussars 8, 10, 17, 44, 98
Eisinger, Rennie 205
El Bagual *see* Wild Horse Team
11th Hussars 45, 71, 137, 166
Eley, Lt. William 152
El Gordo (team) 102, 111
Elizabeth II, HM Queen *C5*, *C8*, 171, 172, 174, 183, 186, 254
Ellerston 218, 220–222, 260–262, 264, 265

Ellerston Black 221, 222
Ellerston White 219, 221, 222
Ellerston's 18-goal Tournament 236
Elliott, Philip N.W. 194, 199, 216, 217
Ellis, Oliver J. 200
Ellis, William Chute 31
Ellison, Charles C. 26, 153, *C2*
Ellison, Frank O. 13, 25, 29
Ellsworth, Wilson 148
El Paraíso (team) 259
El Remanso (team) 269, *270*
El Rincón Polo Club 170
Elton, Brig. Horace C. 129, 134
Elysian Fields (team) 263
Embiricos, Anthony N.C. 217, 218, 221
Emerging (team) 254, 257, 258
Emerson, G.A.D. "Tony" *C5*, 255
Emerson, George 255
Emerson, Henry W. 255
Emerson, J. Malcolm 255
Emerson, John 255
Emerson, Mark *C5*, 255
Emerson, Noel A. "Tiny" 255
Emerson, Roderick "Derick" 255
Emerson, William R. "Will" *C5*, 255
Emlor *C8*, 253, 257, 265, 270–272
Emlor/CRL 258
Emmet, Robert 25
England (team) *36*, 37, 63, 66, 82, 83–92, 110–114, 116–118, 122, 123, 137, 139–141, 144, 164, 165, 169, 170, 172, 190–193, 206, 224, 234–238, 259, 260, 266, 267
England, Simon 255
English Ladies (team) 264
English Women's Open Championship 227
Enniscorthy Polo Club 252
Ephson, Martin 258
Epsom Polo Club 213
Equitation School (Weedon) 27
Eridge Polo Club 100
Erskine, Francis 189
Erskine, Vice-Adm. Seymour E. 75, 327
Erskine, Stephen 208
Erskine, Stuart "Sugar" 257, 259, 266
Escandón, Eustaquio de 108
Escandón, Pablo de 108
Esiri, Prince Albert 254
Espain, Martín 262
Espain, Nicolás 262, 263
Ethelston, Comm. Alfred Peel 73, 74, 325
European 8-goal Championship 269
Eustace, Maj. John 60
Eustis, William C. 83
Evans, David 13
Evans, Gareth 259–261, 269
Evans, George 15, 16
Evans, Robert 20
Evatt, Lt.-Col. John H.B. 99
Eve, Col. Stephen 196

Eveleigh, Michael 148
Exeter Polo Club 17

Fabiola (pony) 194
Fagan, Sir Edward A. 109
Fairfax-Lucy, Sir Henry 24, 25
Fairfield County Hunt Club 264
Fairy Story (pony) 102
Falcons 216, 217
Fallingbosted 252
Fane, Maj. Cecil 22
Fane, Sir Vere Bonamy Fane 78
Fane Junior Cup 78
Fane Senior Cup 78
Fannin, Lt. V.G. 93
Fanshawe, Antony G. 220, 235, 255, 265
Fanshawe, Maj.-Gen. Sir Evelyn D. 104, 114, 133, 138
Fanshawe, Lt.-Col. George H. 133
Farewell Cup 162
Farmer, Heywood 53
Farmer, James 52
Farmer, Leslie G.H. 29
Farquhar, Capt. Ian W. 201
Farran, Capt. George 19
Farrington, Col. Sir Henry 166
Farrow and Ball (team) 258
Faulkner-Horne, Shirley 227
Fauquet-Lemaître, Auguste 108
Faussett, Lt. Godfrey 17
Federation of International Polo 233, 238–240
Felix (team) 265
Felton, W.F. 52
Fenwick, Col. Henry T. 15, 46, 147
Fenwick, Lt. Maurice 75
Ferguson, Maj. Ronald I. 46, 188, 199, 200, 204, 206, 207, 216, 242, 246, 277
Ferguson, Capt. Victor J.F. 15, 46
Fermanagh, County 62
Fernández Araujo, Milo 254, 264, 268, 272, 273
Fernández Llorente, Manuel 261, 269
Fernández Llorente, Tomás 219, 262, 263
Fernández Sarraua, Maj. Rubén A. 165
Ferne Park (team) 271, 272
Fernham (team) 148
Fernhurst (team) 161
Festival Cup 168–170
Fetcham Park Polo Club 56
Fetherstonhaugh, Capt. Frederick H.W. 60, 61
ffrench Davis, F. 19
FHM Polo Club 215
Field Barn Cup 265
Fielden, Col. Geoffrey 134
Fielding, James 272
Fiennes, Capt. Henry 44
Fife, Lt. William 9
Fifield Polo Club 252
15th Hussars 45, 60
5th Fusiliers 77, 99
Findlater, Dr. Alexander 55
Findlay, Lady 196

Findlay, Col. Sir Roland L. 134, 195, 196, 265
Findlay Cup 196, 265
First (pony) 148
First Sibsagar Cup 195
Fish Creek Polo Club 74
Fisher (ground) 167
Fisher, Henry 237, 238, 263, 272
Fisher, John 221, 222, 237, 264
Fisher-Rowe, Capt. Conway 99
Fitz (pony) 147
FitzGerald, J. 61
FitzGerald, John 252
FitzGerald, Peter 260
Fitzgerald, Wilfred 60
FitzWilliam, Hon. Charles 39, 47
FitzWilliam, Hon. John 30
FitzWilliam, Hon. Thomas 8–10
Fitzwilliam, William, 6thth Earl 26, 51
FitzWilliam, William, 7th Earl 99
Fitzwilliam, Lord William C.W. 11, 12
Flame Estates (team) 259
Flamingo (team) 144
Fleet Polo Club 27
Fleming, Nicholas 176
Fleming, Maj. R. Peter 226
Fleming, Mrs. Peter (Dame Celia Johnson) 163, 173, 176, 226–228
Flower, A.D. 24
Flower, Spencer 24
Flying H Polo Club 72
Fong-Yee, Lesley Ann M. 261, 264
Fontwell Magna (team) 227
Forbes-Cockell, Maj. Iain S. 249
Fordham, Wolverley 15, 16
Foreman, Andrew 250, 261
Foreman, Ben 261
Forester, Lt. Henry W. 102
Forestier-Walker, Lt.-Col. Roland 50
Forster, Capt. (Norwich player) 22
Forsyth, Cody 216, 217, 219, 223, 224, 260, 264
Fort Belvedere 250
Fort Grange Aerodrome 20
Fort Macleod Polo Club 74
Fort Needham 73
Fortescue, Lt. Hon. Seymour 181
Fortnightly Challenge Cup 99
Fortugno, Alfred E. "Fred" 205
Forwood, Eric B. 99, 229
Forwood, Miss Judy 173, 226, 227, 229
Foster, Sir Vere 23, 62
Fothergill, George A. 149
Four Winds (team) 133
Fournier-Sarlovèze, Capt. Henri-Robert 108
14th/20th Hussars 104, *216*
4th Dragoon Guards 45, 97, 98
4th/7th Dragoon Guards 166
Fowler, Capt. Bryan J. "Friz" 114, 129, 133, 134, 139, 141
Fowler, C. Leslie 18
Fox, Edward Lane 26
Fox-Pitt, Capt. Mervyn 178
Foxbury (team) 226

Foxcote (team) 171, 194, 200, 216, 220, **230**, 254, 256, 257
Foxcote 18-goal Tournament 253
Foxhunters (Olympic team) 81, 82, 108
Foxhunters (team) 99
France 32, 112–113, 137, 138, 236, 269
Franco, J.J. 78
Fraser, Maj. Michael Q. *167*, 168, 177
Fraser-Tytler, William 56
Freake, Sir Frederick 29, 42, 52, 57, 60, 82, 84, 87, 91, 108, 109, *C2*
Freebooters (teams) 40, 59, 60, 82, 97, 98, 101, 103, 136, 139
Freeborn, Harold E. 168
Freeman-Ker, Robert 265
French, M.M. King 61
Frewell, Moreton 69, 70
Frewell, Richard 69
Frewell, Stephen 69
Friar Park 160, 163, 174, 187, 189
Friar Park Cup 173, 177
Frolic Polo Club 251
Frontier Cup 78
Frost, Dudley 132
Frost, Mrs. (Rugby P.C. player) 226
Fuller, William 55
Funes, Sebastián 261
Furber, Frank 66
Furber, Stanley 66
Furness, H.R. 78
Furth, Elizabeth 244
Fusilier (pony) 82

Gaddum, Harry 16
Gaddum, Mr. (Bowdon player) 16
Gairdner, Maj. Charles 104
Gairdner, Lt.-Comdr. C.R.W. 18
Gairdner, Hubert 61
Gairdner, Sam 260
Gaisford St. Lawrence, Lt.-Col. Cyril H. 134
Galindo, Héctor 208
Galvayne, Fred 245
Game, George 19, 25
Gannon, Brig. Jack R.C. 114, 179, 188, 201–203, 247
Gannon Trophy 202
Garbarini Islas, Tomás 268
García Huidobro, Jaime A. 192, 258, 259, 264, 269, *270*
Garforth, Francis 75
Garland, Mrs. Charles 25
Garland, Charles T. 25, 26, 30
Garland, Lt. Edward 75
Garrahan, Alejandro T. "Alex" 190
Garrahan, Luis H. 169
Garrós, Celestino 186, 187, 199
Garza (pony) 148
Gauchos (team) 136, 138
Gautier, Robert 138
Gaztambide, Santiago 191, 218
Gazzotti, Andrés 114, 115
Gebhard, Frederick 35

Geebungs (team) 220–222, 256, 265
Gemmell, David S. 194, 199, 209, 230
Gemmell, George 271
The General (pony) 152
George V, H.M. King 28, 97, 106, 116, 117, 180, 181
George VI, H.M. King 28, *181*
George, Capt. Richard 120, 122
Georgian Cup 76
Georgios, King of Greece 107
Gerald Balding Cup 176, 230, 253, 255
Gerhardt, Maj. Gen. Charles H. 106
Germany 110, 114, 166, 233, 234, 236, 252
Gerry, Elbridge T. 140–142
Ghana 76
Giant Pandas (team) 131, 136
Gibb, Col. Alastair M. 161, 165
Gibb, Mrs. Alistair (Yoskyl Pearson) 162
Gibb, Duncan Hoyle 14
Gibson, J.S. "Johnny" 68
Giffard, Miss R. 227
Gifford, Peter 27, 189
Gigolos (team) 227
Gilbert, Terence J. 149
Gilbey, Guy 19
Gilbey, Tresham 19, 45, 163
Gilbey, Sir Walter 147, 153
Giles, C.R. 78
Giles, Godfrey D. 149
Gilks, Col. A. Pearson "Tony" 195
Gill, Frederick A. 50, 57, 74, 104, 108, 109
Gill, R. 139
Gillard, Philippa "Pippa," née Grace 230
Gilmore, Glen A. 192, 254, 257, 258, 260
Girardot, Ernest-Gustave 149
Gisborough, Lord Richard 27
Gladstone, Maj. T. Hugh 21
Gladstone, William 149
Gladstone, W.L. 21
Glasson, James 235
Glazebrook, Derrick 174
Glenwood Springs 72
Gloucester, Prince Henry, Duke of 183
Gloucester, Prince William of *196*
Gloucester Militia 52
Gloucestershire (team) 29, 45
Glue, Martin V. 217
Glynn, Thomas B. 277
goalkeeper 9, 11, 32, 64
Gobin, John S. 223, 224
Godfree, Douglas W. 243
Godfrey-Fawcett, Sir George 180, 332
Godley, Gen. Sir Alexander 37, 332
Godley Memorial Tournament 189
Gold (pony) 152, *C1*
Gold, Arthur 19
Gold, Gerald 19
Gold, Harcourt 19
Gold, Philip 19

Gold Coast 76
Golden Eagles 199
Golden Jubilee Cup 192
Goldschmidt, Maj. Sidney 21, 152
Gómez Thwaites, Julio 169
Goñi Durañona, Guillermo "Willy" 176
González, Daniel 183, 185–188, 199, 206
Gonzalez, Ignacio "Nacho" *C8*, 222, 253, 257–261, 265, 267, 269–271
Gonzalez, Jean 257
González, Mariano *C7*
González Gracida, Roberto 192, 217, 218, 222, 261
Good, Jonathan M.W. "Jonny" 236, 258, 261
Goodlake, Capt. Henry 52
Goodman, Dereck 186
Goodman, John B. 221, 224
Gordon, J. Alastair 207
Gordon Highlanders 68, 181
Gore, Sir Ralph 19
Gormanstown Strand 8
Gosling, Capt. George 19, 39
Goti, Alfredo L. "Negro" 186
Gottschalk, Joaquim 264, 273
Gottschalk, Max *C7*, 264
Gough, Col. Hubert 20
Gough, Capt. Hugh 9
Goulburn 122, *128*, 129, 130, 135
Gould, Charles 8
Gould, George 110
Gould, Jay, Jr. 110
Goulding, Lady Lingard 139
Goulding, Sir William L.A. 104
Gouldsmith, Jesse D. 26, 52, 53
Gourley, Capt. Robert 266
Gower, Viscount 73
Grace, Jane E.R. "Janey" *C4*, 230
Grace, Katie L.R. *C4*, 230
Grace, Peter R. *C4*, 213, 244, 251
Grace, Philippa M.R. "Pippa" *C4*, 214, 230, 231
Grace, Victoria A.R. "Tor" *C4*, 230, 261
Gracia Zazueta, Maj. Juan 114
Gracida, Alejandro "Cano" 175, 177
Gracida, Carlos 191, 192, 209, 216, 217, 221–223, 256, 257, 261, 267, 272
Gracida, Gabriel "Chino" 175, 186, 188
Gracida, Guillermo 175
Gracida, Guillermo, Jr. "Memo" 191, 192, 209, 216, 217, 222–224
Gracida, Rubén "Pato" 175, 177
Gracida, Rubén, Jr. 192
Gracy, Debra 327
Graham, Chris 178
Graham, Robert 208, 281
Grahn, Bertil A. 187
Grant, Jasper 61
Grant Cup 78
Grant-Lawson, Sir Peter 99
Graves, R.E. "Tannar" 21
Gray, Capt. Frederick 18

Gray, H.G. Wyndham 18
Gray, Lt. S.H. 78
Green, Edward 8
Green, Maj. (Warwick player) 24
Green, Capt. Philip 9, 10
Green-Price, Herbert 31
Greenall, Hon. Mrs. Edward
  (Josephine) 226
Greenall, Hon. Mrs. Gilbert
  (Betty) 226, 227
Greenbury, Toby 214
Greenhil Farm (team) 190, 196,
  198–200
Greenwell, Walpole 21
Greenwood, Joseph 326
Gregg, Charles 8
Gregson, Lt. Guy P. 134
Grehan, Maj. Dennis S. 177
Grenfell, Arthur 75
Grenfell, Francis O. 74, 94, 246
Grenfell, Riversdale N. "Rivy" 43,
  60, 75, 87, 94, 246
Grenfell Cup 75
Gresson, R.H.A. 19
Greswolde-Williams, Francis 20
Greville, Capt. Hon. Robert 29
Grey Legs (pony) 152
Greyling (pony) 87
Griffiths, Victoria 265
Griffiths, Capt. Walter S. 228
Grigg, Wing-Commdr. Louis 183
Grimes, Matthew 260
Grimsthorpe (team) 227
Grindley, H. Hugh 138
Grinstead, Dianne 68
Grisar, Alfred F. 103, 110, 112
Grissell, Capt. Frank D. 9, 24, 71
Griswold, Frank Gray 33, 35, 245
Groeninghe (team) 222, 230, 255
Grogan, William 60
Groome, S.T. 62
Grosse, Col. Julio W. 165
Grosvenor, Lord Arthur 16
Grosvenor, Lord Hugh W. 74
Guards Polo Club 151, *C6*, *C8*,
  173, *191*, 239, 253, 258, 272, 274
Guatemala 234, 235, 274
Guelph Agricultural College 74
Guerrand-Hermès, Patrick 238–
  240
Guerrero, Héctor 254
Guest, Mrs. Ann Phipps 113
Guest, Capt. Hon. Frederick E. 51,
  87, 112, 113, 154
Guest, Ivor see Wimborne
Guest, Raymond R. 143, 154
Guest, Winston 113, 119, 122, 130,
  133, 135, 140–144, 150, 154
Guevara, Juan Facundo 261
Guggisberg, Brig.-Gen. Sir Freder-
  ick G. 76
Guinness, Lt.-Col. Humphrey P.
  114, *115*, 120, 122, *123*, 129, 131,
  133, 134, 136, 139, 140, 141, 150,
  164, 165, 168, *169*, 172, 173, 175,
  176, 188, 203, 254
Gunnersbury Polo Club 30
Gurdon, Hon. Mrs. Yoskyl, née
  Pearson 227

Gurney, Quintin 22
Guthrie, Lt. John 54
Guy, Tom 131
Gwyer, Keats 25

Hackett-Jones, Anthony 213
Haddelsey, Vincent 149
Haddon-Paton, Lt. Nigel 200
Haggis Farm Polo Club 251
Hahn, Nicholaus A. "Nicki" 216
Haig, Maj-Gen. Neil W. 25, 35,
  36, 37, 57, 149
Haig, Oliver 25
Haig, Roland 16, 21
Haigh, Alfred G. 150
Halcyon Gallery (team) 263
Hale, Sunset "Sunny" 261
Haley, Mrs. (Invaders player) 226
Halford, Valerie 248
Halifax, Nova Scotia 73
Hall, Harry 68
Hall, Jeffrey S. 266, 267
Hall, Rob 68
Ham Common Polo Club 100, 159
Ham House Tournament 214
Ham Polo Club 159, 160, 166, 174,
  177, 178, 214, 263
Hamburg Polo Club 114
Hamilton, Comdr. Bryan 79
Hamilton, Sofia 259
Hamilton-Russell, Hon. John 130,
  131, 136
Hampden, Viscount 36
Hampshire Carabineers Yeomanry
  20
Hampshire County Polo Club 20
Hampshire Hunt (Pony Club
  branch) 202
Hampstead Polo Club 215
Hanbury, Charlie 261, 263, 264,
  268, *270*
Hanbury, Maj. Christopher O.P.
  C6, 221, *251*, 264, *270*
Hanbury, George 263, 269, *270*
Hanbury-Williams, Capt. Ferdi-
  nand C. 11, 12
Handicap Challenge Cup 17
Handley Cross (team) 16, 25, 29
Handley Cross Cup 202
Hankey, Arthur B. 56
Hankey, J. Barnard 56
Hankow 28
Hanlon, A.E. 99
Hanly, John 61
Hann, Priscilla *150*
Hardcastle, William 27
Harding, Richard C. 163, 166
Harding, Maj. Robin 166
Harding, Timothy R. 27, 166
Hardy, Gerald H. 29, 40
Hardy, N. 228
Hare, Hon. Michael 186, *198*, 199,
  203
Hare Park Stud 251
Harford, Lt.-Comdr. Arthur 75
Hargreaves, Frank 52
Hargreaves, John 18
Harlequins (team) 102
Harman, Lt.-Col. Jackes W. 204

Harman, Lt. Thomas 61
Harmsworth, Vere 271
Harper, Lt.-Col. Alexander F.
  "Alec" 168, *169*, 170, 172, 173,
  175, 177, 179, 185, 186, 188, 202,
  203, 219, 233, 247, 254, 276, 281
Harper, Alexander J.C. "Sandy"
  199, 215
Harper, James 236, 237, 258, 260,
  271, 272
Harper, John 263
Harper, Mrs. John (Audrey) 263
Harriet, Juan 264
Harrild, Walter C. 27, 31
Harrington, Charles, Earl 16, 29,
  40, 45, 46, 50, 51, 59, 82
Harrington, W. Ray 188, 205
Harriott, Alfredo 183, 206
Harriott, Juan C., Jr. "Juancarlitos"
  165, 183, 186, 187, 206, 242, 280
Harriott, Juan C., Sr. 165
Harris, Maj. Arthur R. 110, 111
Harris, H.M. 24
Harrismith Polo Club 139
Harrison, David 12
Harrison, Miss Hilda 138
Harrison, H.S. 23
Harrison, Lt. John 52
Harrison, Maj. John F. "Jack" 97,
  98, *102*, 103, 116, 118, 128, 130,
  135, 136, 137, 150, 160
Harrison Cup 160, 161, 170, 188,
  218, 253, 255, 256, 265, 269, 271
Harrogate Polo Club 126
Hartopp, Capt. Edward 9, 10, 11,
  62, 64, 232, 247, 323
Hartopp Cup 167
Harvey, Brig. Charles B.C. 134
Harvey, Capt. Crosbie 61
Harvey, D. 139
Harvey, Lt. John 54
Harvey, Peter 195
Harvey, Brig. Roscoe 194
Harwood, Adm. Henry 79
Haseltine, Herbert 87, 150, 160
Hassall, Alfred 16, 17
Hassan, Babangida 258
Hastings, Hon. Aubrey A.C.T. 26,
  53
Hastings, Sir George 50
Hastings, Hon. Osmond W.T.W. 26
Hatch, Alden 81
Hatfield Polo Club 20
Havelock-Allan, Sir Henry 27
Haverhals, Stephanie 259
Hawaii 188
Hawden, Miss Binks 227
Hawke, Lord 66
Hawke's Bay Polo Club 174
Hayen, Isabelle 222, 230, 255
Hayes, G. Constable 26
Hayhurst, George 59
Hazard, William A. 54
Hazaribagh 64
HB Polo (team) 271
Head, Maj. Charles 61
Healy, Mrs. Peggy 214
Healy, Tim 178, 214
Healy, William 214

Heatherington, John 251
Heatley, A.E. 99
Heaton-Ellis, David 215
Heaton-Ellis, Kristin 215
Heaton-Nicholls, Murray 208
Heave Ho (pony) 147
Heavy Cavalry (team)10
Hedley, Capt. Gordon 166
Heelis, Capt. Piers 266
Hegg, Rupert 265
Heguy, Dr. Alberto P. 183, 206
Heguy, Alberto "Pepe" 221, 256, 264
Heguy, Antonio 175
Heguy, Bautista 220–222, 257
Heguy, Eduardo "Ruso" 220, 222
Heguy, Gonzalo A. 175
Heguy, Horacio A. 183, 187, 205
Heguy, Horacio S. 175
Heguy, Ignacio "Nachi" 222
Heguy, Luis M. 165
Heguy, Marcos 256, 257
Helen (pony) 153
Helme, Capt. Burchall 11, 12
Hemming, Capt. Jeremy H. 168
Henbury (team) 265
Henderson, Michael 260
Hendrix, Leroux 258
Henley Polo Club 148, 160, 162, 163, 166, 170, 173, 228
Hennessy, Elizabeth 242
Henry, Capt. Frank 19
Henry, Richard A.B. 62
Hensman, Sherri-Lyn 261
Herbert, Francis J.A. "Tip" 9–12, 15, 24, 29, 32, 35, 39, 40, 50, 55, 146, 213, 232, 247, 248
Herbert, Henry L. 57, 92, 280
Herbert, W.Reginald J.F. "Reggie" 11, 12, 15, 24, 32, 39, 40, 50, 73, 213, 232
Herbert Memorial Trophy 104
Hermon-Hodge, Henry 226
Heron, Roy 145
Herr, Maj. John K. 105
Herrera, Antonio 173, 199, 219
Hertfordshire Polo Club 164, 166, 228, 244
Hervey, Keith 113
Heseltine, Godfrey 31, 42, 57, 101
Heseltine, Michael 150
Hetherington, Charles 178
Heygate, Capt. Edward 20
Heygate, Capt. Richard 20
Heywood, Capt. G. Percival 16
Heywood Jones, Llewellyn "Wengy" 21, 43
Heywood Jones, Oliver "The Boss" 21
Heywood Jones, Richard "Bengey" 21
Heywood-Lonsdale, Lt. Edward 28
Heyworth-Savage, Col. Cecil 20
High River Polo Club 74
Highwood Farm 251
Hilder, Col. Frank 99
Hilder, Maj. Thomas M. 104, 168
Hilder, Winnie 226

Hilditch & Key (team) 218
Hildon House (team) 219
Hildon Sport (team) 230, 255, 256
Hill, Alexander Staveley 74
Hill, Bertie *36*
Hill, J. Sinclair 184, 186, 203–206, 209, 261
Hillier, Joseph 12
Hillmorton (team) 60, *181*
Hinchcliff, Chamberlain "Jumbo" 18
Hinde, Sir W. Robert N. 114
Hine, Andrew C. 192, 216, 218, 219, 224, 234, 253, 255, 260, 264, 267
Hine, John S. 203
Hine, William (Will) 235
Hipwood, Howard J. 149, 186, 189, 190, *191*, 192, 199, 202, 207, 215, 216, 219, 223, 224
Hipwood, Julian B. 147, 186, 190, *191*, 199, 202, 207, 217, 218, 247, 267, 281
Hipwood, Oliver "Ollie" 221, 222, 258, 260
"hired assassins" 211
Hitchcock, Thomas 34
Hitchcock, Thomas, Jr. "Tommy" 101, 112, 116, 117, 119–123, 140, 142–144, 277
Hitchman, Edward 236–238, 261
Hitchman, Matthew 265
Hoare, Oliver 18
Hobart Polo Club 68
Hobson, Lt.-Col. Gerald W. 13, 30, 99, 241, 143
Hobson, Richard W. 134, 245
Hodges, Milly, née Scott *C7*, 253, 264
Hodgkinson, J. Robert 198
Hodgson, Edward 26
Hodgson, Philip 26
Hodgson, Sue *C7*, 253
Hofius, E. 78
Hohne 166, 250, 340
Hoison-Craufurd, Maj. John 14
Holden, Hon. Glen A., Sr. 238, 240
Holden White Challenge Cup 161, 177, 228, 256, 258, 265, 272
Holderness Polo Club 26
Holford, John C. "Jack" 17, 18
Holford Cup 130
Holiday, C. Gilbert J. 145, 150, 151, *C1*
Holland 236
Holland, Lt.-Gen. Sir Arthur 93
Holland, William F.C. 19
Hollingsworth, S. 25
Holman, William 99
Holmes, Capt. A.V.C. 62
Holmes, Mark 251
Holt, Miss Denis 226
Holt, Susanna 244
Holtby, Thomas 26
Hone, Capt. Thomas *33*, 60–62
Hook, Maj. Hilary *167*, 168
Hooper, Maj. Richard Grenside 99
Hopkinson, Samuel 258, 264, 265

Hopping, Earle A.S. 119, 122
Hopping, Earle W. *102*, 103, 117
Horbury, William L. 132
Hornby, Capt. Charles B. 98
Horne, G.B. 24
Horne, Capt. Geoffrey 24
Hornets (team) 126, 127
Hornsby, J. 22
Horsburgh-Porter, Lt.-Col. Sir Andrew M. 133, 134, 170
Horse and Hound Cup 177, 188
Horswell, Edward *218*
Horswell, H. John 190, 191, 203, 207, 209, *218*, 259
Horswell, Harry 203
Hotel La Tour (team) 265, 269
Houlder, Frank 56
Houlder, Fred 56
Houldsworth, William 14
Houldsworth Cup 17
Houlton, George 26
Hounslow Heath 8, 10, 71
House, M.H.N. 20
House, Philip 20
House of Commons (team) 51, 55
House of Lords (team) 51
Household Brigade Polo Club 162, 173, 183
Household Cavalry Polo Club 28, 173, 183
Household Division (team) 253
Howard, Henry Lloyd 40, 43, 44
Howard, W. 23
Howell, Howard 137
Howes, Comdr. P. 148
Howes, S.H. 25
Hudson, William 188
Huergo, Eduardo J. 115, 187, 240
Hughes, H. Hesketh 131, 132, 133, 138–142, 150
Hughes, J. Watson 21
Hulse, Lt. Harold H. 68
Hume-Campbell, Sir John 19
Humfrey, Charles 195
Hungary 110, 114
Hunt, Maj. John L. 29
Hunt Cup 51, 151
Hunter, Capt. Charles F. 13, 98, 116
Hunter, Ian 148
Hunter, W.T. 104
Hunter-Weston, Col. Aylmer 14
Huntingdon, Earl of 55, 61
Hurley, Sir George 20
Hurlingham (team) 12, *33*, 34, 40, 50, 109, 137, 138, *169*, 170, 173, 174, 204
Hurlingham Champion Cup 39–40, 42, 43, 51, 101, 103, *128*, 129, 130, 274
Hurlingham Club (Argentina) 37, 65, 110, 176, 183, 206
Hurlingham Club (Fulham) 11, *31*, 32, *33*, 35, 45, 47, *48*, 49, 50, 101, 109, 138, 159, 174, 227, 242, 274
Hurlingham Club Committee 10, 55, 57, 58, 113, 116, 126, 159, 228, 280
Hurlingham Polo Association 19,

159, 164, 166, 168, 172, 189, 202, 232, 233, 238, 266, 269
Hurlingham Rovers (team) 178, 206, 207
Hurndall, Maj. Frank B. *105*, 116, 118, 137
Hurricanes 102, 128, 130, 279
Hurtley, Edward 26
Hurtley, Fred 26
Hurtley, Joseph 26
Hurtwood Park Polo Club 214
Hurworth Polo Club 27
Hutcheson, Capt. (California player) 73
Hutton, Richard 72
Hutton Polo Club 19, 99
Hyde, Christopher "Chris" 258, 260, 269

Ibadan Polo Club 76
Iglehart, D. Stewart B. 140–144, 150
Iglehart, David S. 122
Iglehart Cup 266
Ilorin Polo Club 76
Inanda Country Club 206, 206
Ince-Anderton, Capt. William A.A.J. 32, 39, 40, 50
Inchbald, Maj. Pierre 99
Indart, Miguel 170
Indart Cup 170
Indian Army Cavalry Officers' Association Trophy 252
Indian Polo Association 97, 98, 232, 280
Indian Princes' Empire Shield 136, 250, 253, 254, 269, 271
Indios-Chapaleufú II (team) 259
Ingestre, Lord Charles 30, 59
Inglesham Polo Centre 215, 253
Ingwenya (team) 216
Innes, Malcolm 213
Innes-Ker, Lord Alastair R. 73
Inniskilling Dragoons 44, 45, 60, 149
Inter-Colonial Challenge Cup 78
International Equestrian Federation 239
International Gun and Polo Club 24
International Olympic Committee 107, 109, 277
International Polo Club Palm Beach 35, 239, 274
International Tournament (Paris) 29
International Tournament (Ranelagh) 66
International 24-goal Tournament (Palermo) 165
International Women's Polo Association 214, 230, 231
Inter-Regimental Tournament 43–45, 48, 97, 102, 103, 131, 133, 134, *167*, 168, 177, 200, *201*, *216*, 252, 253, 265, 266, 269, 272
Inter-Regimental Tournament (B.A.O.R.) 166, 252
Inter-Regimental Tournament (India) 246, 254

Invaders (team) 226
Invicta Polo Club 189
Irish County Cup 62, 63
Irish County Polo Union 60, 62, 63
Irish Fortnightly Cup 139
Irongate (team) 256
Irvine, Charles D'Arcy 62
Irvine, D. 21
Irvine, J. 21
Irwin, Fr. Francis Joseph 7
Irwin, H.J. 139
Irwin, Valentine 7
Isaac, Capt. John 73
Isla Carroll (team) 221, 222, 224
Italy 150, 233, 235–237, 269, 282
Ivester-Lloyd, Thomas 151
Ivy Lodge Ground 148, 156, 170, 171, 199, 253, 163
Izzard's Field 34

Jacinto, Nicky 208
Jackman, Miss E. 226
Jackman, Miss K. 226
Jackman, Miss M. 226
Jackson, Bramwell 24
Jackson, C.B.A. 24
Jackson, Hazel 272
Jacobs, Edgar 66
Jaipur (team) 129, 135, 136, 162
Jaipur, Maharajah of "Bubbles" 238
Jaipur, Maharajah of "Jai" 128, 186, 188
Jaipur, HH Rajmata of 242
James, Capt. A.G. 53
James, Col. A.P. 12
James, Lucas 260, 268
James, Roberto A. 186
James-Moore, J.H. 23
James Wentworth-Stanley Cup 272
Jameson, Henry R. 31
Jameson, James O. 60–62
Jamison, David L. 208, 217, 223
Jamison, H.R. 74
Jaucourt Cup 22
Jauregui, Capt. Carlos E. "Negro" 215
Jauretche, Juan 272
Jauretche, Pablo 262
Jeaves, Capt. (Wellington player) 16
Jefferies, Harry H. 79
Jenner, Lt.-Col. Leopold C.D. 50, 54, 57, 153
Jericho Priory Polo Club 166
Jersey Lilies (team) 162, 171, 177, 185, 186, 198, 199
Jerudong Park 221, 250
Jewell, Charles 65
Jewell, Ernest 65
Joanina (pony) 148
Jodhpur (team) 103, 104
Joel, Lewis 326
John Cowdray Trophy 253, 272
Johnson, Charles Senter "Brook" 222
Johnson, Hon. Diana 214
Johnson, Sir G. Lloyd 20
Johnson, J. 138

Johnson, Kelvin 260
Johnson, Senter 222
Johnston, A. Lawson 53
Johnston, Col. N.H. 13
Johnston, S.K., Jr. 72
Johore, H.H. Sultan of 77
Jones, Adrian 151
Jones, Albert 24, 29
Jones, Chris 232
Jones, Kenny 214
Jones, Walter J.H. 42, 52, 54, 57, 109, 149, 152
Jordan, Alfred 16, 24
Joyce, Arthur 60
Julian and Howard Hipwood Trophy 272
Jung, Maj.-Gen. Nawab Khusru 129
Junior Championship (Roehampton) 54, 55, 103, 111
Junior Colts Cup 127, 134
Junior County Cup 19, 22, 27, 28, 30, 51–53, 56, 168, 171, 173, 177, 183, 228, 258, 265, 272
Junior Springboks (team) 207
Junior Westchester Cup 253
Jupiter (pony) 102, 146

Kaduna Polo Club 76
Kano Polo Club 76
Karkloof Polo Club 78
Kashmir (team) 129
Kashmir, Maharajah of 129, 244
Katsina Polo Club 76
Kavanagh, Walter McM. 31
Kay, Tony 174
Kearsley, Edward 17
Keating, Capt. M. Dew 52
Keene, Foxhall P. "Foxie" 33, 34, 81, 83, 85, 86, 89, 91, 108
Kelburn, Comm. Viscount 14, 68, 76, 174
Kelley, Dunbar 56
Kelly, Elizabeth 227
Kelly, Miss P. 227
Kemp, Alfred 18
Kemp, Sydney 18
Kemple, Patrick 185, 206, 207
Kempson, Thomas P. 29, 40
Kennard, Vivian G. 18
Kennedy, Lt.-Col. Sydney 133, 179
Kennedy, T. Stuart 29, 40
Kenny, Arturo J. 112
Kensington, Capt. Lord William 325
Kent (team) 46
Kent, Alan J. 190, 192, 216–218, 223, 224, 256
Kent, Geoffrey J.W. 217
Kenya 189, 195, 200, 204
Kenyon-Fuller, A.C.C. 15
Kenyon Stow, Edward 27, 40, 45, 50
Keppel, Lt. Colin 180
Kerfield (team) 187
Kestrels (team) 139
Kevill-Davies, Hugh 20
Keyes, Lt.-Col. Geoffrey C.T. 156
Keyes, Adm. Sir Roger 18, 156

Keyte, Simon 192, 254, 258, 260, 261, 264, 265, 271
Kidd, Malcolm 215
Kidston, Mrs. Dorothy 228
Kidston, George J. 134
Kidston, Richard 14
Kihikihi Polo Club 174, 260, 264
Kilburne, George G., Jr. 151
Kildare, County 61
Kildare Polo Club 215
Kilkenny, County 62
Kilmarnock, Lord Charles 11, 39, 47
Kilworth Sticks (team) 22
Kimber, Richard 208
Kimberley, Earl of *see* Wodehouse
Kinchant, Frank E. 56, 65
King, John Gregory 151
King, Michael 263
King Edward's Horse 93
King William's Town 68
King's African Rifles 76
King's County 61
King's Royal Hussars 266
Kingsbridge (team) 265
Kingsbury Polo Club 55
Kingscote, Capt. Maurice J. 26, 53, 122, 171, 226
Kingscote, Mrs. Maurice (Violet) 225
Kingscote Cup 171
Kinta (pony) *C3*
Kipling, Rudyard 153
Kirby, Adrian P. 272
Kirtlington Cup 100, 138, 173, 253
Kirtlington Park Polo Club 99, 138, 147, 172, 173, 177, 219, 226, 229, 280
Kirkwood, Maj. Thomas W. "Billy" 103, 104, 118, 138, 139
Kitson, Mrs. Roland (Dorothy) 168
Knaves (team) 128, 130, 131, *135*, 137
Knepp Castle Polo Club 214
Knight, J.G. 24
Knowles, George 163
Knox, Seymour H., Jr. 132, 134, 137, 143, 279
Kokstad Polo Club 139
Kokstad Tournament 139
Köser, Arthur 114
Kouros (team) 217
Kurland 256, 257

La Aguada 259
La Bamba de Areco (team) 268, 273
Labegorce (team) *C6*, 221, 222, 224, 254–257
Laborde, Santiago 262
La Buena Suerte (estancia) 65
Lacey, Lewis L. 65, 93, 102, 103, 118, 122, *123*, 132, 137, 146, 148, 154, 161
Lacey, William 37
Lacey, Wyndham H.D. 161, 179, 187, 206, 207
Lacey Green Polo Club 251

Ladies and Gentlemen Challenge 263
Ladies Invitation Cup (Ranelagh) 227
Ladies' Nomination Cup 54
Ladies of the Rest of the World (team) 264
Ladies' Polo Association 228
Lady Jane (pony) 151
Ladyswood Polo Club 252
La Ema (team) *C5*, 255
La Espadaña Polo Club 168, 169, 170, 188
Laffaye, Horace 247
Lafford Polo Club 22
La Fontaine, Thomas S. 151, *C3*
Lagos Mármol, Rodolfo 187
Lagos Polo Club 76, 155, 178
La Golondrina (team) 271
Laird (team) 253, 271
Lakewood Polo Club 89, 110
Lakin, Henry 25
Lakin, John 144, 161, 164, 165, 168, *169*, 170, 172, 174, 175, 177, 178, 185, 188, 254
Lakin, Mrs. John (Hon. Helena Daphne) 161, 162, 174, 228
Lakin, Michael L. 25
Lakin, Richard 25
Lalor, Alfredo 165
Lalor, Ernesto J. "Tito" 165, 172, 175, 176
Lalor, Luis A. 165
Lalor, Luis E. 165, 230, 240
Lamb, Montague 15
Lambarde, William Gore 60, 61
Lambart, Lt. Lionel 17
Lambe, Lt.-Comdr. Charles 28
Lambe, Maj. H.E. 17, 18, 23
Lambert, Septimus 21
Lambourne (team) 230, 253, 258
Lambton, Brig.-Gen. Hon. Charles 33, 34
Lambton, Sir Hedworth 73
Lambton, Sir William H. 15, 46
La Montagne, René 89, 91
Lancaster, Mrs. Marjorie 138
Lancaster, Oliver 138
Landry, Juan C. 165
Lane, C. 16
Langford, Col. Patrick 202
Langridge, L.S. 330
Langtry, Mrs. Edward 70
Lanyon, Miss (Fontwell Magna player) 227
La Pampa (team) 38
Laprida, Cristián J. "Magoo" 268
Laprida, Brig.-Gen. Manuel A. 165
Laprida, Brig.-Gen. Mario H. 165
Larrain, Gustavo 172
Las Petacas (team) 65
Las Tres Lagunas (estancia) 66
Lass (pony) 194
Laulhé, Gastón *197*
Lavender Hill (team) 198, 199
Laversine (team) 185, 187
La Vulci (team) 185
Law, Capt. Victor R.A.S. 203

Lawley, Hon. Richard T. *33*, 34, 44, 82
Lawns (ground) 54, 172, 177
Lea, Lyndon 264, 265, 273
Leadenham Polo Club 251
Leaf, Lt. James *105*
Leaf, Maj. Nöel W. 138, 142
Leamington 52
Leatham, Lt. Edward H. 22, 94
Lechdale Polo Club 23
Lechmere, Anthony Hungerford 26
Lechuza Caracas 262, 263, 268, 270, 278
Lee, Thomas 74
Leeds Polo Club 26
Leesthorp, Lord 35
Leetham, Ian 195
Le Gallais, Lt.-Col. P.W. Jules 40, 44
Le Ggatt, Laurance 214
Le Hardy, Jamie 222, 236, 256–258, 260
Leigh, Hon. Dudley 25
Leigh, John Blundell 31
Le Mars Polo Club 70
Lent, Duane 250
Lent, Sallie Anne 250
Leominster Polo Club 20
Leonard, John 60, 61, 63
Leonard, John A., Jr. 139
Le Poer, Richard *223*, 262, 269
Leslie-Melville, Hon. Alexander 28
L'Estrange, Henry G. 61
Lewes, William Nevill, Earl of 40, 50
Lewis, Evan 12
Lewis, Maj. Rupert 269
Lewis Lacey Field 37
Liddell, Sir John 323
Liddell, Capt. Lionel 99
Liddell, Col. Robert S. 8–10, 323
Life Guards 10, 25, 28, 47, 67, 173, 201
Light Cavalry (team) 10
Light Dragoons Polo Club 250
Lillie Bridge (Royal Polo Club) 11, 12, 21, 47
Lim Ching Tsong (tournament) 78
Lima Polo and Hunt Club 21, 79
Limerick 7, 8
Limerick Polo Club 7
Linborne (team) 227
Lindsay, Capt. Lionel 12
Lindsay, Capt. Walter 62
Lindsay, William 71
Linfoot, William C. "Corky" 199
Linfoot, Dr. William R. 188, 190, 199
Les Lions 254, 273
Les Lions II 264, 265, 268, 270
Lion's River Polo Club 207
Lister, Maj. C. Charles 54, 102
Little, Sir Archibald C. 45
Little, Cosmo 43
Little, "Josey" 46
Little, Lt.-Col. Malcolm A.A. 46
Little, Capt. Malcolm O. *33*, 34, 45

Little Bentley Polo Park 252
Little Mary (pony) 87, 150
Liverpool Polo Club 13, 17, 21, 26
Livingstone-Learmonth, Lestock 18
Livingstone-Learmonth, Capt. Nigel 18
Livingstone-Learmonth, Capt. Somerville 200
Llandaff Field 178
Llanfairfechan (team) 16
Llantartam Abbey 12
Llantartam Park 12
Llewellyn, Sir Leonard 12
Llewellen Palmer, Lt.-Col. Charles T. "Tim" *167*, 168
Llorente, Pedro G. 175
Lloyd, John 242
Lloyd, Brig.-Gen. John Hardress 43, 57, 60, 61, 63, **88**, 89, 90, 92, 109, 119, 243
Lobb, Arthur 19
Lobel, Norman A. 213, 219
Locke, James H. 60
Lockett, George A. 16, 21, 79
Lockett, George G. 17
Lockett, Robert 17
Lockett, Col. Vyvyan N. 17, 90, 91, 98, 102, 103, *105*, 106, 110–112, 116, 117, 122, 131, 137, 147, 201
Lockett William 17
Lockhart, Maj. Brian J. 200
Lockhart, Maj. Charles A.R. 27, 201
Lockhart, Lt.-Col. Crispin 269
Lodge, K.R. 214
Loder, Matthew 236
Loder, Norman 54
Loder, Simon 173
Loe, Daniel 265
Loewenstein, Robert 138
Loftus, Capt. St. John D. 22
London Country Club 99
London Polo Club 95
Londonderry, Marquess Charles of 11
Long, Brig.-Gen. Viscount Walter Hume "Toby" 31, 46, 324
Long, Capt. W.B. 22
Longdole Polo Club 251, 263, 264
Longmoor Camp 27, 99
Longueville, Maj. Edward 151
Longworth, Maj. Thomas 19, 127
Lopes, Capt. Massey H.E. *see* Roborough
López de Carrizosa, Francisco "Paco" 172
Lorillard, Nathaniel G. 33, 324
Lorne, Marquis of 74
Loro Piana 262, 263, 265, 273
Los Angeles 73
Los Gordos (team) 261
Los Indios Polo Club 165, 174, 175
Los Locos 171, *197*, 198, 217, 221, 222, 229, 230, 253, 256, 263, 265, 271
Louth, County 62
Lovat, Simon 44
Lovelocks (team) 221, 251, 252, 261, 263–265, 269

Low, W.M. 25
Lowry, T.C. 194
Lowther, Lt.-Col. Sir Charles 66, 98
Lowther, Capt. John G. 98, 99
Loyd, Maj. William T.V. 203, 242
Lucas, Mrs. Ethel B. 164, 229
Lucas, James 234
Lucas, John L. 164, 175, 177, 186–189, 229
Lucas, L. Arthur 159, 164, 168, 170, 172, 175, 229
Lucas, Patricia 164, 229
Lucas, William (Will) 192, 218, 223, 224, 234, 255, 258, 261, 263
Lucas-Lucas, Henry F. 151, 152
Lucero, Eduardo 66
Lucilla (pony) 152
Luckton, Lt. H.V. 13
Ludlow Polo Club 23
Luffenham Airfield 195
Lukshumeyesh, V. 177
Luna (pony) 152
Lund, Douglas 256, 257, 259
Lurie, Warren 260
Lushill (team) 189
Lyell, Malcolm 203
Lyle, F. Hervey A. 72
Lynch-Staunton, Leonard A. 66, 67
Lyne, C.E. Michael 152
Lynt Farm 215
Lyon, Horace 79
Lyon, Jorge 165
Lysen, Maurice 110, 111
Lyster, L.C. 99

Macaire, Jules F. 112, 138
Macaire, Lionel 218
Macan, Col. Thomas T. 225
MacDonald, Katie 263
Macdonald, Midshipman W.B. 78
Macdonald-Buchanan, Capt. John 155
MacDonough, Matías 262, 272
MacDonough, Pablo 262, 264, 270–272
MacDougall, Maj. Hartland B. 75
Macereto (team) 258
MacIntire, Kenneth S. 152
MacIver, Ian 79
Mackay, Jaime 208
Mackay, Jock 260
Mackenson, Harry 134
Mackenzie, A. 67
Mackenzie, A.F. "Sandy" 174
MacKenzie, Bruce "Buster" 257, 259–261
Mackenzie, Chris 270, 273
MacKenzie, Capt. Cortland G. "Corty" 13
Mackenzie, Stuart T. 215–217
Mackey, F. Jay 16, 25, 66, 81, 82, 108
Mackintosh of Mackintosh 12
Maclaren, Maj. Kenneth "Boy" 109
Macmullen, Capt. Michael N.E. 134
Madlener, Geoffrey 129, 130

Madrid (team) 54
Madrid Cup 54
Magee, W. 138
Magic Spell (pony) 149
Magor, Edward 265, 269
Magor, Maj. Philip 18, 99, 103, 119, 130, 131, *132*, 133, 135
Maidensgrove (team) 230, 255
Maidsford (team) 258
Maidugari 76
Maifeld (field) 113, *115*, 234
Mains, Jeremy 215
Mainspring (pony) 82
Malcolmson, G.V. 139
Malet, Capt. John W. 134
Malet de Carteret, Guy 194
Malhado, H. 78
Mallon, Dr. Bill 108, 245
Malta 28, 29, 167
Manchester Polo Club 16, 21, 26, 170
Manclark, James 178
Manconi, John W. 220–222
Mandalay 78
Mandel-Pleydell, Henry 59
Mandeville, Lord George 69
Mangham, Maj. William D. 168
Manipur 7, 35, 62
Mann, Capt. Jack 269
Mannequins (team) 227
Manning, C. Heath 199
Mannix, Fred 192, 257
Mansfield, Earl of 178
Maple Leafs 215, 216, *217*, 218, 220, 222, 250
Marandellas 76
Marchini, Alfio 262, 265
Marden, Capt. Sir Thomas 99
Mardon Cup 17
Margaret, HRH Princess 168
Margetts, Col. Nelson E. "Nels" 110, 111
Marie Sol (pony) 143
Marín Moreno, Francisco "Pancho" 258
Marín Moreno, Dr. Jorge N. 175, 186–188
Marjoribanks, Hon. Dudley 54
Market Harborough Polo Club 22, 99
Marriage, E.B. "Ted" 166
Marsa (grounds) 28
Marsaglia, Stefano 256, 257
Marsh Mallow (pony) 153
Marshall, George 24
Marsham, Hubert W. 56
Marsham, Keith H. 152
Martin, Hugo 23
Martin, J. 138, 139
Martin, John 237
Martínez, José 65
Martínez, Sixto 65
Martyr, Lt.-Col. Cyril 53
Mary Morrison (pony) 153
Maseru 207
Mashonaland 76
Mason, C.E. 21
Mason, James S. 52, 53
Master, Col. Chester 52

Master, Digby 52
Masters, Capt. Godfrey 12
Masters, Jack W. 174
Masterton Fong-Yee, Lesley-Ann 261
Matabele 76
Mathew-Lannowe, Lt.-Col. Brownlow H.H. 15, 87, 98
Mathias, Chris 178
Mathias, Claire 259
Matthews, Crispin 173
Matthews, Francis 215
Matthews, Frank G. 45
Matthews, Roderick 173, 219
Maude, Capt. Anthony 61, 62
Maudsley, Eustace 43
Maunder, Lt. Mathwin "Matt" 155
Maxwell, Capt. Charles 52
Maxwell, W. 67
Mayne, Maj. John 53, 171
Mayne, Maj. Robert 61
Mayo, Earl of 11
McCallum, Lt. Lorien 255
McCalmont, Dermot 24
McCann, Arthur 60, 63
McCann, John Paul 60, 63, 104, 109
McCann, P. 139
McCarthy, Clinton 271
McCarthy, Spencer *C8*, 257, 265, 268, 270, 271
McConnel, Lt.-Col. Anthony H. 53, 171, 179
McConnel, Capt. David Ian 27
McConnel, Capt. Frederick 14
McCreery, Andrew B. 42
McCreery, Lawrence 31, 42, 81
McCreery, Sir Richard L. 102, 106, 134, 163
McCreery, Lt. Thomas 106
McCreery, Walter A. 42, 66, 81, 108, 134
McCreery, Walter S. 102, *105*, 106, 128
Mcculloch, Capt. D.B. 61
McCulloch, Lt. William 93
McDonald, Douglas "Dougie" 207
McGillycuddy, D. 139
McIldowie, Patrick *218*
McIvor, Graham 151
McKean, Lorne 152
McKenzie, Donald C. 58
McKenzie, John 58
McKergow, Lt.-Col. Robert 24, 54
McKinney, Craig 221
McLachan, Gillon 260
McLean, Dr. John C. 25
McMicking, Maj. Harry 17
McMicking, T. 23
McPherson, Insp. Duncan 74
McVicker, Lt.-Col. Samuel 139
Meacham, Phyllida 152
Mead, George H. 122
Meade, Martyn 252
Meadow Brook (team) 87, 136, 144, 150, 172, 187, 188
Meadow Brook Club 60, 89–92, 104, 105, 115, 117, 118, 120, 121, *123*, 137, 244
measurement of ponies 57, 58

Meath *see* County Meath
Media Luna Polo Club 18, 176, 187
Melbourne 235, 240
Mellor, Sir James R. 11, 12, 24, 39
Mellor, J.G. 22
Melly, Col. Hugh 16, 21
Melton Ladies (team) 226
Melton Mowbray Polo Club 22, 126
Melton Mowbray Tournament 22
Melvill, Lt. Teignmouth 111
Melvill, Lt.-Col. Teignmouth P. 102, *105*, 110, 111, 116, 118, 201, 246
Mendiguy, Carlos A. "Charlie" 187
Menzies, Keith 94
Merchiston (team) 129–131
Merck, Harold 188
Merckel, Mrs. Henry 226
Merivale-Austin, Bruce 253, 255
Merlos, Agustín "Tincho" 263, 273
Merlos, Héctor O. "Cacho" 216
Merlos, Juan I. "Pite" 221, 222, 224, 262, 263
Merlos, Sebastián 221, 222, 273
Metcalfe, Capt. Edward 183
Metcalfe, Capt. Geoffrey 53
Metcalfe, John C. 53
Mews, Lt. Roy 129
Mexico 108, 114, 164, 190–192, 233, 235, 236, 238, 335
Mexico City 209, 237, 261
Meyrick, George (1908) 24
Meyrick, George 237, 260, 271
Meyrick, Sir Thomas F. 28
Micklem, Col. Henry 162
Mid-Cheshire Polo Club 170
Mid-Essex Polo Club 19, 99
Middlesex Polo Club 55
Middleton, Capt. George 60
Middlewood Polo Club 26, *C2*
Midhurst Town Cup 177, 188, 199, 216
Midtoi (pony) 133
Midwood, Arthur 22
Miguens, Carlos 187
Mihanovich, Alejandro "Alex" 170, 172, 186
Mihurst Town Cup 177, 188, 199, 216
Milburn, Devereux 19, 54, 58, 85, 86, 91, 92, 116, 117–121, 144, 150, 152
Milburn, John G. 72
Mildmay, Lord Francis 29, 40, *41*
Miles, Audley C. 31
Miles, David B. 103
Miles, Juan B. 103, 112
Miles City 71
Milford Haven, Clare, Marchioness of 259, 262, 269
Milford Haven, George I., Marques of *C3*, 217, 218, 260, 264, 272
Military Cup 98
Military Handicap Tournament 28, 131
Mill Reef (horse) 153

Millarville Polo Club 74
Miller, Charles D. 30, 42, 43, 52–54, 57, 60, 67, 82–84, 87, 109, 133, 152, 174
Miller, Dave 263
Miller, Lt. Desmond C.J. 102, 122, 129
Miller, Lt.-Col. Edward D. "Ted" 29, 35, 42–44, 51, 52, 54, 57, 58, 60, 83, 90, 93, 117, 118, 119, 152, 242, 246, 248
Miller, George A. 29, 30, 42, 43, 51, 52, 54, 57, 60, 84, 109, 152
Miller, Joachim 118
Miller, Michael F. "Mike" 207
Mills, James P. "Jimmy" 130, 133, 135, 142
Milne, Alexander 79
Milne, G. Lees 29, 52
Milwaukee Polo Club 204, 205
Minotaurs (team) 265
Miskin, Nigel 49, 242
Miss Edge (pony) 152, *C1*
Mitchell, Maj. Alexander 99
Mitchell, J.E. 26
Mitchell, Sally 146, 154, 244
Mitchell, S.C. 31
Mitchell, T.H.W. 26
Mitchell, William 61
Molineux, Hon. Osbert 16
Molineux, Hon. Richard 16
Moller, Eric B. 162, 171, 176, 177, 185, 186
Moller, Ralph 171
Molloy, J.W. 139
Mona Airfield 213
Monaveen (horse) 41
Moncrieffe, Lady Louisa 71
Moncreiffe, Malcolm 71
Moncreiffe, Sir Thomas 71
Moncrieffe, William 71
Monmouthshire Polo Club 10–12, 15, 21, 24, 35, 39, 40, 213, 232, 247
Monmouthshire Polo Club (2000) 213
Monsell, Lt. Bolton Eyres 20
Montaigu Cup 52
Monteverde, Lucas 258, 268, 272, 273
Montevideo Polo Club 65, 79
Montgomerie, Lord 14
Montgomery, Henry 61
Montgomery, H.W. 15, 16
Montgomery, Col. John C. 110, 111
Montmorency, Capt. the Hon. Raymond de 325
Monty Waterbury Cup 104, 139
Mooi River Polo Club 68
Moon, Arthur 53
Mooney, F. Morgan 61
Moore, A. Levins 139
Moore, Eduardo R. "Gordo" 53, 171, 185, 187, 194, *195*, *197*, 200, 208
Moore, Chaplain Hugh 76
Moore, Capt. Richard St. Leger 43
Moore, Robert St. Leger 9, 10
Moore, Thomas Levins 61

Moore Park (Sidney) 67
Moorehead, Alan 156
Moray, David Drummond 178
Moray, William Drummond 178
More-Nesbitt, Alan 78, 178
Moreno, Pablo 165, 172
Moreton Morrell Polo Club 25
Moreton Morrell Tournament 25, 37
Morgan, Edwin D. 34, 324
Morgan, George 208
Morisset, Capt. 67
Morley, David 235
Morley, Thomas O. 236–238, 253, 260, 264, 269, 271
Morot, Aimé 150
Morris, A.E. 52
Morrison, Bryan A. 213, 220, 242
Morrison, Mrs. Greta *270*
Morrison, Capt. Humphrey G. 55
Morrison, Jamie T. 256
Morrison, John G. 138
Morrison-Bell, Lt.-Col. Eustace W. 54, 55
Morrogh-Ryan, J. 63
Morrogh-Ryan, Leonard 61, 63
Mort, Col. Guy M. 99
Morton, John Douglas, Earl of 178
Moseley, Michael G. "Micky" 155, 170, 228
Moseley, Oswald G. 22, 170
Mosselmans, Adriaan "Mossy" 100
Motspur Park 56
Moubray, Capt. Arthur R. St. J. 28
Mount Edgecumbe Cup 17
Mountbatten, Lady Edwina *162*
Mountbatten, Lord Louis 28, 47, 98, *162*, 180, 183, 194, 232, 242–244, 247
Mounted Infantry Polo Club 27
Mowry, Capt. Nell 73
Much Wenlock (games) 107
Mullan, James 249
Muller Luján, Julio 114
Munby, Edward 20
Munipore (team) 220
Munnings, Sir Alfred 37, 145, 152
Munster 166
Murphy, Chris 178
Murphy, John "Jackie" 206
Murphy, Peter 243
Murphy, Capt. Reginald 60
Murphy, Vere Brudenell 60
Murray, Hon. Mrs. Angela 227
Murray, Lt. E.M. 93
Murray, Marshall 60
Murrayfield 13
Museum of Polo & Hall of Fame 154, 266, 267
Musker, Capt. Herbert 24
Muzzio, Alejandro 272
My Girl (pony) 102, 152
Mynors, Stella 152
Myopia Hunt Club 253
Mytikyina 78

Nagore, Pablo P. 175
Napper, Capt. Alexander 61
Natal 207, 331

Nathan, Sir Matthew 76
National 8-goal Championship *see* Junior County Cup
National Olympic Association 107
National Polo Pony Society 10
National School of Equitation 226
National 16-goal Championship *see* County Cup
Nava Castillo, Capt. Antonio 114
Naylor, Richard 47
Neave, Capt. Richard 19
Neave, Sheffield 18, 99
Negrete (estancia) 65, 180
Neil Haig Cup 174
Neilson, A.T. 21
Neilson, H.C. 21
Neilson, Capt. Walter G. 27, 53
Nelson, Juan D. "Jack" 103, 112, 141, 161, 172, 176
Nelson, Juan P. "John" 175, 176
Nelson, Luis T. 103, 176
Nelson, Luis T., Jr. 176
Nelson, Tomás B. "Tommy" 137
Nelson, W. Hope 17
Nero, Agustín 236, 258
Nero, Juan M. 236, 256, 257, 262, 263, 265, 272, 282
Neville, Maj.-Gen Sir Robert 28
New Forest Polo Club 228
New Park Farm 160
New South Wales 67, 209
New Zealand 14, 29, 46, 75, 76, 174, 208, 209
New Zealand (team) 175, 191, 192, 193, 260, 261, 264
New Zealand Polo Association 75, 208
Newman, J. Colin 55
Newton, H.F. 73
Nicholas, Lt. Basil G. 22
Nicholas, Hubert 25
Nicholson, Maj. J. David G. 205
Nickalls, Cecil P. 30, 43, 46, 60, 67, 83, 84
Nickalls, Miss Cicely 226
Nickalls, Miss J. 227
Nickalls, Morres "Bobby" 43, 46, 57, 152
Nickalls, Brig.-Gen. Norman T. 29
Nickalls, Patteson W. "Pat" 30, 43, 46, 57, 60, 83, 84, 87, 98, 109, 152
Nickalls, Miss "Tinker" 226
Nigeria 76, 233, 258
Nigerian Cup 76
Nigerian Polo Association 76
Nightingale, Basil 152, *C2*
Nimble (pony) 151
Nimmo, Johnnie 189
Nimrod Club 49
Nimrod Vase 99
Nine Acres (ground) 59, 60, 139
9th Lancers 8–10, 44, 60, 62, 71, 194, 254
Nkana Polo Club 76, 217
Noakes, J. Norman 56
Nolans, J.W. 61
Nomads (team) 60

Norrie, Lord George Willoughby 139, 194
North, Capt. Albert 26
North Cork (team) 252
North Devon Polo Club 17
North Stafford Tournament 24
North Staffordshire Polo Club 24
North Westmeath Polo Club 60
North Wiltshire Polo Club 26
Northampton County Polo Club 23
Northamptonshire Yeomanry 98
Northern Ireland 139, 213
Northern Ireland Polo Club 215
Northern Nigeria 76
Northern Rhodesia 76
Northumberland Polo Club 23
Northwestern Polo League 70
Norton, Capt. Dudley J. 129
Norwich Polo Club 22
Notley, Maj. C. Roland S. 205
Novaes, Silvio 217
Novices' Cup 51, 55, 98, 111
Novillo Astrada, Alejandro "Negro" 254, 257
Novillo Astrada, Eduardo 254, 257, 258, 260, 266
Novillo Astrada, Ignacio "Nacho" *C7*
Novillo Astrada, Javier 221, 222, 254, 257, 260, 264, 267, 272
Novillo Astrada, Miguel 254, 256, 270
NPC Broncos 217
Nuttall, M.F. 153

Oak Brook Polo Club 196, 198, 204, 205
Oakland Park 253, 261
Oakley Hunt (team) 15
Oberhouse (team) 258
Occasional Polo Club 99
O'Connell, James 178
Oddments (team) 227
Odell, Thomas Smyth 61
O'Driscoll, John 178
O'Dwyer, Lt.-Col. Sean *196*
Oelrichs, Hermann 68, 69
O'Farrell, Jaime 138
O'Farrell, Jorge E. 138
Offchurch Bury Polo Club 214
Off-side rule 57, 58
Ogilvy, David *see* Airlie
Ogilby, Capt. Robert 26
Ogilvie, Frank 13
O'Hara, Maj. Charles K. 60, 61
Olazábal, Francisco 209
Old Cantabs 42, 60, 67, 81, 101, 111
Old Childwallians 21
Old Etonians 98, 128
Old Harrovians 54
Old Malburians 54
Oldfield, John 153
Ollerhead, Dr. Thomas 23
Olympic Games: 1900, Paris 108–109; 1908, London 109–110; 1920, Antwerp 110–112; 1924, Paris 112–113; 1936, Berlin 113–115, *115*

Omaha Polo Club 70
O'Mahony, Fr. James 7
O'Neill, Hon. Arthur 61
Onslow, William Hillier, Earl of 46, 75
Optimists (team) 131, 132
Orange Free State 206, 207
Orchard Polo Club 215
O'Reilly, Ken 178
O'Reilly, Percy P. 60, 109
Orford Polo Club 164, 166
Orleans Club 49
Ormerod, Brig. Denis 250
Ormerod, Eden 265, 271, 272
Ormerod, Giles 250
Ormrod, Lt. Leslie A. 22
O'Rorke, Edward D. "Teddy" 65
Orthwein, Peter B. 188
Orthwein, Stephen A., Sr. 188, 240, 266, 267
Osborne, Lt. Brian 94
Osborne, Francis C. 62
Osbourne, Charles E. 180
Osmaston (team) 129, 131, 135, 136
Ostende 110
Oswald, Patrick 178
Otamendi, Kirstie 272
Otter Vale Challenge Cup 17
Otter Vale Polo Club 17
Owen, Hugh 12, 24, 39
Oxenbould, Amy *153*
Oxford-Cambridge match 30, *31*, 43, 48, 82, *C4*, 168, 170, 177, 253, 272
Oxford University 31, 54, 170, 177
Oxley, John C. "Jack" 186
Oxley, John T. 186, 205
Oxley Ranche 74

Pacey, Mrs. Betty 173
Pacey, Miss P. 227
Pacific Coast Polo & Racing Assoc. 73
Packer, Jamie 222, 260, 264, 265
Packer, Kerry F.B. 211, 218, 219, 221, 222
Padilla, Col. Enrique 112
Paget, Maj. Arthur 52
Paget, Lady Louisa 213
Paget Boots (trophy) 213
Paice, George 153
Pailaret, Capt. Charles 9
Pailloncy, Ludovic 248, 271
Pailloncy, Sebastien 271
Paine, Lewis 56
Pakenham, Lady Violet 226
Pakistan 166, 236
Palacios, Carlos 233
Palermo (grounds) 45, 137, 160, 165, 206, 233, 238, 255
Palethorpe, C.H. 25
Paley, Capt. Edward G. 8, 43
Palfrey, Henry P. 153
Palmer, James L. 153
Palmer, Joseph G.F. 75
Palmer, Oliver 67
Palmes, Capt. Edward W.E. "Bill" 43, 89
Palmes, Guy St. Maur 28

Palumbo, Baron Peter G. 177, 186, 194, 198, 200, 203
Pampero (pony) 161
Pannell, Matthew 224
Parker, Gillian 153
Parker, Jonty 178
Parker, R.E. 22
Parker Bowles, Brig. Andrew H. 200
Parry-Okeden, Capt. Uvedale 9, 10
Paterson, A.B. "Banjo" 222
Paterson, Capt. Ewing 17
Patricia (pony) 82
Patriotic Challenge Cup 48, 61, 63, 104, 178, 253, 272
Paul, Grahame "Toby" 103
Paul, Joseph 22
Paullin, Daniel 70
Payne, Charlie J. "Snaffles" 153, 244
Payne, W. 56
Peake, Walter 56
Pearce, James 17, 57, 246
Pearl, David 219
Pearse, Lt. C. St. A. 73, 74
Peerson, Hon. B. Clive 54, 99, 103
Pearson, Hon. Charles A. 199, 215
Pearson, Staff-Surgeon Christopher 73
Pearson, Hon. H. Dahpne *see* Mrs. John Lakin
Pearson, Hon. Harold 54, 55, 99, 103
Pearson, Hon. Weetman 55, 57
Pearson, Hon. Yoskil 226
Pease, Claud 27
Pease, Joseph 27
Pease, William E. 27
Peat, Alfred E. "Boy" 39, 40, *41*, 50
Peat, Arthur R. 40, *41*, 50
Peat, James E. "Johnnie" 39, 40, *41*, 50
Pedley, Eric L. 119, 122, 123, 140–142, 150
Peek, Hedley 247
Peel, Jamie 254, 265
Peers de Niewburg, Baron Gastón 110, 111
Pegasus (team) 222
Pegasus Polo Centre 214
Pekisko Polo Club 74
Pemble, Ryan 253, 258
Pemble, Tristan 236
Pembroke, Earl of 73
Pembrokeshire 12
Pembrokeshire Polo Club 13
Peña Unzué, Alfredo M. 103
Pender, Miss Denison 227
Penn-Curzon, Lt.-Col. Francis R.H. 17
Pennell, Vane 109
Pepys, Samuel 325
Pepys, Capt. Walter 25
Perfection (pony) 150, *160*
Perkins, Arthur P. 188, 189
Perkins, Norman 99
Perkins, Peter 53, 171, 188, 199
Perrodo, Hubert *C6*, 221, 222, 224, 254, 257
Perry, Matthew 271, 273

Pershing, Gen. John "Black Jack" 104
Pert, Maj.-Gen. Claude E. 120, 121, 131
Perth Cup 178
Peru 21, 29, 79, 233
Pessoa, Maj. José 80
Peter (pony) 152
Peyton, Sir Algernon 40
Philadelphia Country Club 104
Philippi, Mrs. George 226
Phillimore, Lord 214
Phillips, Hon. Colwyn 12
Phillips, Miss F. 226, 227
Phillips, Frederick 56
Phillips, Capt. Noel 56
Phipps, Harold C. 91
Phipps, Michael G. 130, 131, 133, 135, 140, 142, 144, 150
Phipps-Hornby, Geoffrey H. 18, 103, 118, 122, 131, *132*, 137, 161
Phipps-Hornby, Geoffrey S. 18, 40
Phoenix Park 59, 60, 62, 63, 104, 138, 139, 178, 189
Piaget, (team) 273
Picard, Alfred 107
Pickersgill, Joseph 26
Pictet, Fabien 254, 257
Pidgley, Tony K. 262, 263
Pieres, Alfonso T. 216
Pieres, Dr. Alvaro C. 200
Pieres, Facundo *C8*, 193, 260, 262, 264, 265, 268, 273
Pieres, Gonzalo 190, *198*, 199, 200, 216, 219, 220, *221*, 222
Pieres, Gonzalo, Jr., "Gonzalito" *221*, 260, 262, 264, 265, 268, 273
Pieres, Nicolás "Nico" 269
Piershill Barracks 13
Pigott, Sir Berkeley 245
Pilkington, Capt. Arthur W.M.S. 128, 131, *135*, 137
Pilkington, Charles 19
Pilkington, G. Herbert 21
Pilkington, Malcolm C. 19
Pilkington, William L. 21
Pimms (team) 186, 187, 189, 198, 199
Pincher Creek Polo Club 74
Pinhorn, Stanley 74
Pink Power (team) 272
Pinney, Maj. George 99
Piper (pony) 152, *C1*
Piping Rock Club 90, 122
Pirates (team) 63, 129, 130
Pitman, Lt.-Col. John Hugh 163, 186, 200, 205
Pitman, Maj.-Gen. Thomas T. 25
Pittaluga, Joaquín *C8*, 265, 268, 270, 270
Plainsmen (team) 188, 189
Platt, James 21
Platt, Sydney 16
Playdell-Railston, Lt.-Col. Henry G. 93, 146
Pohl, Matt 259
Polehampton, Frederick 25
Pollock, Capt. Allan 24

Polo Association (1890) 35, 47, 54, 73, 81, 83, 85, 116, 232
Polo Association of the River Plate 18, 20, 65, 79
Polo Association of Uruguay 138
Polo Cottage (team) 147, 161, 179
Polo Monthly Cup 104
Polo Ranch 71
Polo Wicklow 252
Pommery (team) 221, 222
Port Meadow (grounds) 35, *155*
Portal, Brig. Sir Bertram P. 29, 52, 201
Portales (team) 209
Porteño (pony) 152
Porteous, Maj. John J. 66
Porter, Lt.-Col. Henry 20
Porter-Porter, John 15, 62
Portsmouth, Earl of 71
Post, William H. II (Billy) 132, 137, 142
Potchefstroom Pilgrims (team) 53
Potomac Polo Club 205
Powell, B. 73
Power, Maj. John 166
Preece, Godfrey 142
Prentice, Fergus "Gus" *C5*
Prestbury Park 19
Preston, Thomas E. 79
Preston Park 24
Pretyman, Herbert 79
Pretyman, Walter 79
Price, Aubrey 56
Price, Noel E. 56
Prince of Wales Cup (Beaufort) 253, 271
Prince of Wales Trophy 213, 217, 218, 219, 222, 253, 254, 256, 257, 261, 262, 264, 267, *270*, 274
Prince Philip Trophy *C6*, 222
Prior-Palmer, Maj.-Gen. G. Errol 131, 133, *135*, 136, 137, 139, 141
Prior-Wandesforde, Henry 20
Priory Polo Club 19
Pritchard, Lord 214
Public Schools Cup 54, 98, 112
Puckle, Pelham C. 17, 25
Pulpero (pony) 161
Pyatts Farm 215

Quantock Vale Polo Club 18, 23
Queen Mother Trophy 271
Queen's Bays 21, 133, 138, 166, 167
Queen's Cup *C3*, 163, 189, 186, 187, *195*, 196, *197*, 198, 199, 215–219, 221, 224, 229, 253, 254, 256, 258, 260–262, 264, 268, 270–272, 274
Queen's Dragoon Guards 166, 168
Queen's Own Hussars 168, 177, 201
Queensberry, Marquis of 24
Quidnuncs (team) 43, 103, 104
Quiroga, Lt. Alfredo 37

Raby, Victor 79
Radcliff, James A. 21
R.A.F. Halton Polo Club 100
Rahman, Prince Abdul 221
Rainbows (team) 225

Raleigh Club 49
Ramos Sesma, Capt. Alberto 114
Ramsay, Maj.-Gen. Frank W. 243
Ramsden, Sir John F. 97, 98
Ramsden, Jonathan H. "Jonty" 170
Rand Polo Club 68
Randall, Martin 251
Ranelagh Club 12, 28, 40, 45, 48, 50–54, 61, 66, 74, 97, 98, 101, 127, 129, 152, 159, 172, 174, 225, 226, 231
Ranelagh Invitation Cup 128
Ranelagh Open Cup 42, 53, 55, 67, 87, 97, 101, 130, 131, 136
Rangitikei Polo Club 174
Rangitiki Polo School 214, 230
Ranksboro Polo Club 252, 265
Raoul-Duval, Maurice 108, 109
Rasper (pony) 152
Rasson, J. "Teddy" 138
Ratanada (team) 173, 177
Rathbane Farm 7, 8
Rathbones (team) 265
Rauer, Frank 138
Ravenscroft, John 16, 65, 66
Rawlinson, Sir Alfred "Toby" 50, 57, 108, 153
Read, Clive 272
Read, Robert, Jr. 52
Reading Room Club 69
Readman, Lt.-Col. John J. 46
Real Jam (pony) 181
Recent Form List 57, 280
Redskin (pony) 152, *C1*
Rees-Mogg, Lt.-Col. Graham 126
Reeve, James 251
Reeve, Lady Susan 247
Reid, J. McClymont 20
Reilly, Col. James 60
Reincke, R. Miles 214
Rennie, Capt. George 53
Renton, Lt.-Col. W. Gordon F. 29, 42, 52, 54, 83, 151
Rest of the Commonwealth (team) 192
Resurrection Pie (team) 137
Reynal, Arturo P. 176
Reynal, José C. 176
Reynal, Juan J. 168, 169, 170
Rhimes, Percy 163
Rhine Army Polo Association 252
Rhinefield Polo Club 126, 153, 166, 227, 228, 244
Rhodes, Arthur E.G. 75
Rhodes, Cecil 327
Rhodes, Sir R. Heaton 327
Rhodesia 76, 207
Rhodesian Polo Association 76
Rich, Frank 103
Rich, Henry "Harry" 16, 25, 29, 52, 55, 56, 88, 99
Rich, Herbert T. 29, 110
Richard Mille (team) 272
Richards, Capt. Arthur 52
Richardson, Col. James J. 119, 152
Richardson, Capt. M. Kim Oliver *201*

Richardson, Capt. William H. *157*, 168
Richmond Park 10, 24, 100, 159, 214
Rickett, Brig. John F. 213
Ricketts, Brig. Robert L. 123–125, 243, 244
Ridgeway, Henry 32
Rifle Brigade 166
Rigden, Miss B. 226
Riley, Capt. William 226
Riley-Smith, Jonathan 177, 331
Riley-Smith, W.H. Douglas 176, 202, 203, 219
Riley-Smith, William "Bill" 30, 152, 166, 246
Rimington, Gen. Sir Michael F. 149
Rincón Gallardo, Pablo 209
Rinehart, Owen R. 217, 218, 223, 224, 267
Rio de Janeiro 79, 236
Ritson, John R. 27
Ritson, Col. Ralph Gerald "Jerry" 67, 90, 91, 98, 146, *C2*
Riverside Polo Club 73
Rizzo, Peter J. 205, 247
Roan Mare (pony) 87, 150
Roark, Aidan 63, 122, 123, 128, 130, 131, 133, 144, 226
Roark, Capt. Charles T.I. "Pat" 63, 102, 120–122, *123*, 128, 129, 131, *135*, 136, 137, 140, 142, 146, 152, 279
Roark, Mrs. Charles (Patsy Hostetter Smith) 142
Roark, Edmund C. 148, 164
Roark, Thomas 60, 63
Robbins, S. Howland, Jr. 34
Roberts, Sq. Ldr. A.J. Alan 148, 163, 230, 255
Roberts, Lord Frederick 88
Roberts, Lavinia see Black, L.
Roberts, Michael 242
Roberts, Walter 21
Roberts, William 218
Robertson, Harry 75
Robertson, Miss J. 227
Robinson, Fred 262
Robinson, Sir Hercules 67
Robinson, Maj. John P.B. "Jack" 161, *162*
Robinson, Kelvin 262
Robinson, W.H.B. 68
Robinson, Sir William 67
Roborough, Lord Massey 134
Robuts (team) *102*
Robson, Hugh Noel Scott 16, 28, 128, 129, 131
Robson, Hugh Scott 50, 66
Roche, Walter 154
Rochfort, Horace W.N. 8, 59, 326
Rockaway Club 89
Rocksavage, Earl of see Cholmondeley
Rocky Mountain Polo Championship 72
Roderick Park (grounds) 207
Rodes, Brig. Peter P. 106
Rodríguez, Juan 188
Roe, Frederick 112

Roehampton Club 28, 43, 48, 49, 51, 53, 87, 97, 101, 109, 129, 166, 168, 169, 174
Roehampton Cup 53, 131, 159, 161, 169, 174, 214, 228
Roehampton Freebooters (team) 98
Roehampton Junior Championship 54, 55, 103
Roehampton Open Cup 53, 54, 97, 103, 104, 131, *132*, 133, 135–137, 159, 174
Rogers, John 20
Rogers, T.P. 99
Rojas Lanusse, Eduardo M. 53, 170, 171, 194
Roldán, Nicolás E. 266
Rolt, Miss S.M. 227
Romfh, Jules M. 205
Rookwood Field 99
Roosevelt, Elliott 324
Roper, Capt. Robert 29
Rosamundo (team) 219
Rosario English Race Club 64
Roscommon County 7
Rose, Lt. Bertram T. 325
Rose, Capt. Charles E. 325
Rosebery, Earl of 56
Ross, Colin 21, 74
Ross, D.J. 60, 63
Ross, Juan R. "Buddy" 169, 170
Ross, Rosa 259, 272
Rossmore, Lord Henry 10
Rotheram, Maj. Auston M. 60, 109
Rotheram, Maj. Edward 60
Rotheram, George 60
Rothermere, Jonathan 271
Rothman Trophy **198**
Rothschild, Baron Edouard de 108
Rothschild, Baron Elie de 175, 177, 185, 187, 242
Rothschild, Capt. Evelyn A. de 30, 67
Rothschild, Sir Evelyn R.A. 175, 177, 186–188, 217
Roundwood Park (team) 199
Rous, Hon. W. Keith 129–131, 133, 135, 136
Rousham Cup 100
Routledge, George 183
Routledge, Max 237, 264, 265, 270, 272
Rowan-Hamilton, Hans 227
Rowe, Dick 215
Rowlandson, George D. 154
Roxburghe, Henry, Duke of 142
Royal Academy 137, 148, 152–155
Royal Agricultural Show 1921
Royal Air Force 28, 49, **100**, 127
Royal Air Force Polo Club 252
Royal Artillery Polo Club 28, 102, 129, 131, 133–135, 151, 166
Royal Automobile Club 49, 98
Royal County of Berkshire Polo Club 213, 217, 219, 253, 256, 272
Royal Engineers 166
Royal Horse Guards (The Blues) 10, 11, 28, 39, 47, 97, 177, 186, 203

Royal Lancasters 77
Royal Leamington Spa Polo Club 236, 252, 263
Royal Military Academy (Sandhurst) 15, 93, 201, 255
Royal Naval and Royal Marines Equestrian Association 252
Royal Navy 28, 29, 73–75, 78
Royal Navy (team) 75, 127, 133, 156, 180, 252, 272
Royal Navy Polo Association 20, 28, 79
Royal Navy Saddle Club 243
Royal Pahang (team) 221
Royal Polo Club *see* Lillie Bridge
Royal Scots Greys 46, 52, 60, 120, 131, 133–136, 140, 166, 195, 196, 265 Royal Scots Greys Memorial 46
Royal Welch Fusiliers 77
Royal Wiltshire Yeomanry 177
Royal Windsor Cup 171, 173, 176, 177, 189, 216, 218, 255, 261, 265, 269, 271
Royden, Thomas 16
Rudkin, George R. "Bob" 244
Rufus (pony) 82
Rugby (pony) 152
Rugby Challenge Cup 29, 52, 99
Rugby Polo Club 24, 41–43, 50, 51, 53, 57, 58, 60, 81, 101, 108, 152, 160, 226, 226
Rugby Polo Club (2002) 250
Rugge-Price, Capt. Charles J.N. 99
Rumsey, Charles C. "Pad" 91, 116, 117
Rundle, Maj.-Gen. Sir Leslie 28, 167, 331
Rundle Cup 28, 167, 252
Rupert Thorneloe Memorial Cup 250
Russell, Col. Henry 7
Russell, Lt. Philip L. 325
Russell Allan Cup 170
Russell-Stoneham, Derek 242
Rutherford, Michael J. "Mike" 222
Rutherford, Thomas 236
Rutland Cup 195
Rutland Polo Club 195, 196, 219, 261
Ryan, Percy 163

St. Albans Polo Club 251
St. Clair-Davis, Heather 154
St. Cloud 112
St. John, Capt. Edward 67
St. John, George 180
St. Louis Country Club 70
St. Maur, Lord Percy 59
St. Moritz 234, 235
St. Neot's Polo Club 16
St. Quintin, Henry 67
St. Quintin, John 67
St. Quintin, Col. Thomas A. 9, 10, *36*, 67, 246, 247, 323
St. Stephen's Club 63
Salisbury Plain (team) 27, 46
Salisbury Polo Club 76
Salked (team) 271–273

Samoa 80
Samson, Herbert 74
Samuda, Capt. Cecil 18
San Antonio 69
San Carlos (team) 65, 111
San Cristóbal Club 234
Sanderson, Capt. John F. 129, 131
Sandford, A.P. Wills 18, 73
Sandiway (pony) 153
Sands, Samuel S., Jr. 34
Sands Point Polo Club 122
San Flamingo (team) 198, 199
Sanford, Lt. Gilbert 61
Sanford, John 102
Sanford, Stephen "Laddie" 102, 103, 122, 128, 129, 133, 135, 139, 279
Sanford, William 72
Sanger, Lt.-Col. Percival B. "Tony" 129, 139
San Jorge Polo Club 65
San Mateo 73
San Miguel, Marqués Luis de 112
San Miguel (team) 187
Santa Ana Polo Club 187
Santa Barbara 165, 188, 235
Santa Barbara Polo Club 73, 126, 204, 235
Santa Fe (team) 219, 222
Santa María Polo Club 237
Santamarina, Ricardo S. "Dickie" 138, 142, 177, 242
Santa Monica Polo Club 73
Santiago 234
Santos, Alfredo 80
Sao Silvestre (team) 186, 187
Sartoris, Francis 59
Sassoon, Sir Philip 51
Saunders, Robert 59
Savage, Robin 189
Savile Cup 46, 75
Savill, Sir Eric 173
Savill, Henry 46
Savory, Lt. Albert 325
Sayago Polo Club 138
Schloss Eibreichsdorf Polo Club 269
Schnack, Peter 326
Schools and Universities Polo Association 252
Schreiber, Miss Pamela 227
Schwabe, Alison 214, 251
Schwabe, Clifford 22
Schwartz, A. Charles 122
Schwarzenbach, Guy 260, 265, 271
Schwarzenbach, Urs E. *C6*, 221, 222, 254, 257
Schwind, Harold 37, 66, 80
Scot Fusiliers 166
Scotland 13, 14, 178
Scott, Andrew W. 79
Scott, Camilla "Milly" *C7*, 253, 261
Scott, Lord Charles 180
Scott, Eric 330
Scott, Henry 131
Scott, Jake 178
Scott, Kaiser 330
Scott, Peter 220

Scott, Robin 330
Scott, Maj. Ronald "Ronnie" 203
Scott, William W.B. 28
Scott-Chisholme, John J. 24
Scott-Douglas, Lt. George F.V. 104, 127
Seabrook, Katie 230, 253, 258
Seavill, Andrew J.S. 191, 222
Seavill, Colin 195, 196
Seavill Bowl 196
Seckington, I.M. "Mike" 195
Seddon, Capt. Richard 17
Selby-Lowndes, Col. William 15
Sellschopp, Dirk 53, 171
Selwyn, H. Jasper 29
Sergison-Smith, Capt. Hyde 29
Seven Springs Cup 226
17th Lancers 26, 42, 44, 45, 99, 102, 103, 124, 200
17th/21st Lancers 102, 122, 166, 200
7th Hussars 13, 24, 29, 44, 60, 134, 151, 166, *167*, 168, 201
7th Royal Fusiliers 59
79th Cameron Highlanders 23
Sexsmith, Marton 75
Shah Mizra Beg, Maj. 98
Sharp, James R. "Hap" 196, 200
Shaw, J.F. 24
Shaw Cup 131
Shaw Safe, Thomas *33*
Shearburn, Capt. Egremont E. 69
Shedden, Capt. Lindsey H.C. 53
Sheeran, James 215
Shennan, David A. 180
Sheppard, Edward 54, 147
Sheppard, Col. Richard B. 134
Sherer, Maj.-Gen. Joseph F. 62
Sheridan, Lanto 272
Sheridan Polo Club 70, 71
Sherman, George C., Jr. 187, 188
Sherston, Lt.-Col. John 325
Sherwin, Lt. Malcolm J. 204
Shields, Maj. John Gillies 195
Shirey, Archibald 12
Shirley, Jack 205
Shirley-Ball, Arthur 62
Shongweni (grounds) 207, 208
Shorncliffe Polo Club 27
Shrewsbury, Charles, Earl of 29, 30, 42, 50, 52, 53, 57, 152
Shuttleworth, Capt. Frank 16, 29
Sibley Polo Club 70
Sidebottom, A. 24
Sidney-Humphries, Sydney 51
Silchar Polo Club 62
Silver Jubilee Cup 192
Silver Leys Polo Club 19, 163, 166, 176, 177, 186, 188, 215, 228
Silver Queen (pony) 150
Silver Spring 1870 (team) 272
Silverdale Aquatint (pony) 150
Silvery II (pony) 150
Simmonds, L.V.L. 248
Simmposcourt (team) 104
Simonsen, Wallace "Wally" 186
Simpson, Charles W. 154
Sinclair, Wing-Comdr. Huntly 173
Singapore Sporting Club 77
Singh, Rao Rajah Abhey 131, 136

Singh, Col. Chunga 87
Singh, Risaldar Gaje 163, 186
Singh, Rao Rajah Hanut 103, 128, 131, 136, 140, 142, 155, 161, 171–173, 175, 177, 178, 185, 188, 206, 242, 261
Singh, Hari 173
Singh, Maharajah Jabar 172
Singh, Jagindar 103
Singh, Jaswant 103
Singh, Kisha 188
Singh, Kishen 163
Singh, Col. Prem 163, 164, 172, 186, 188
Singh, Thakur Prithi 103, 131, 136
Singh, Thakur Ram 103
Sinnott, Mark 214
Sioux City Polo Club 70
Sioux Falls Polo Club 70
Sir Patrap Singh Cup 162
Sister Grey (pony) 152
Skene, Charles Robertson "Bob" 129, 130, 142, 144, 164, 165, 242, 250
Skippen, Julia 252
Skippen, Kyron 252
Skipwith, Sir Grey 25
Slacke, Charles 161
Sladmore (team) 216, *218*, 220
Sligo County 61, 62
Sloane, Capt. A.D. 56
Slocock, Benjamin 60
Slocock, Samuel 60
Slocock, Walter 60
Slovakia 260
Smail, Adam 202
Smail, John P. 214
Smail, Mrs. Trevor (Elizabeth) *see* Kelly, Elizabeth
Smart, Capt. Rex 53
Smiley, Col. David 173
Smith, Cecil C. 130, 131, 133, 140, 142–144, 185, 242
Smith, H. Sidney 19
Smith, Lewis A. 188, 279
Smith, Dr. Newman 66
Smith, Thomas G. 29
Smith, William S. 261
Smith-Dorrien, Capt. Thomas A. 9, 10
Smith-Ryland, Sir Charles M.T. 148, 170, 173, 175–177, 204
Smith-Ryland Cup 176
Smith's Lawn (grounds) 150, 151, 154, 190, 194, 229
Smith's Lawn Cup 171, 177
Smithwick, George 62
Smoak, Col. Marion 205
Smyth, Robert McC. "Johnny" 66
Snagge, Sir Harold E. 120
Snell, Geoffrey 154
Snow (pony) 153
Snow, Adam 223, 224, 266, 267
Snowstorm (pony) 153, *C2*
Social Clubs' Cup 37, 48, 49, 66, 98, 171
Sociedade Hípica Paulista 80
Sokoto Polo Club 76
Sola, Facundo 272, 273

Soldati, Alejandro C. 187
Soldati, Francisco P. "Pancho" 187
Solitaire (pony) 87
Songhai (team) 200
Soppe, E. 326
Sosa Basualdo, Luis H.J. 203
Soto Mozanaque, Club de Polo 235
Sotogrande 237
South Africa 22, 29, 68, 206, 282
South Africa (team) 76, 191, 208, 238, 256, 257, 259, 260, 261, 269
South African Polo Association 76
South African Polo Championship 37, 82, 207, 208
South America (team) 190
South Hants Polo Club 20
South Wales 13, 213
South Westmeath 62
Southampton, Lord 40
Southdown (team) 226
Southern Australia (team) 260
Southern Rhodesia 76
Southfields (team) 208, 215–218
Southlands Polo Club 149
Southwell, Tarquin 220, 221, 235
Spain 110–113, 172, 233, 235, 236, 237, 269
Spencer, Earl 11
Spencer, Herbert 242
Spicer, Capt. Julian 15, 43, 44, 46
Spielberger, Francis 170
Spielberger, Pat 170
Spinney (team) 259
sportsmanship 277
Spring Cup 195
Springfield, M.O. 227
Spry, Angela Hume 225
Stacey, Capt. Cyril 152
Staddon House (team) 17
Staff College Polo Club 15
Staffordshire Polo Club 29
Stalbridge, Lord Hugh 22, 98, 99
Stanford, J.K. 154
Stansted Polo Club 19, 21
Stapleford Park Polo Club 189, 251
Startin, Lt. James 180, 181
State, Martin 163
Steeds, Capt. William Hollwey 62
Stephen, St. Leger G. 55
Stephens, Lt. Robert 152
Stephenson, Joseph 26
Stephenson, Maj. Simon *201*
Steta, Billi 271
Stevenson, Malcolm "Mike" 89, 91, 117, 119–121
Stewart, Bobby 178
Stewart, W.T. 59
Stewart Brown, H. 21
Stewart Brown, Milner 21
Stewart-Savile, Robert 46, 75
Stirling, David "Pelón" *197*, 262, 263, 265, *270*
Stobart Polo 272
Stock, Alphons 246
Stock, J. Henry 16
Stock, James Henry 21
Stocks, Henry 21
Stockwell, Capt. G.G. "Pete" 51

Stoddard, Louis E. 87, 89, 91, 116, 117, 119, 144, 152
Stoke D'Abernon Polo Club 56, 127, 138
Stokes, Capt. Antony 53
Stoneleigh Park 214
Stoney, A. 61
Stonyhurst College 7
Storey, Loftus H. 100, 245
Storey, Marion 32
Storey, Adm. William O. 75
Stourbridge Polo Club 25
Stourhead Invitational Cup 189
Stourhead Polo Club 189
Stow, Edward Kenyon 29, 40, 45, 50
Stowe, Rick 220–222, 256
Stowell Park (team) 171, 194, *195*, *197*, 198, 199, *200*, 208, 215
Strakosh, George 164
Strang, D. Walter 76
Strang, J.H.P. "Jack" 76
Strang-Steele, Sir Fiennes M. 201, 205
Stratford-on-Avon Polo Club 25
Strawbridge, Robert E., Jr. 119, 130, 133, 135, 140, 141, 152
Stray Lambs (team) 228
Streeter, Nessie 163
Stuart, Archibald 26
Stubbs, Douglas 330
Suart, Alfred 18
Subalterns' Gold Cup 51, 98, 134, 167, 168, 177, 252
subsidiary goals 282
Suffolk, Earl of 247
Suffolk Polo Club 251
Suffolk Yeomanry 24
Sumaya (team) 264, 268, 272, 273
Summer Lightning (pony) 87
Summer Tournament 52
Summerhays, Reginald 99
Summers, Andrew 53, 171
Summers, C.A. 73
Summit Cup 251
Sunshine (pony) 82
Surrenden Park 30
Sussex County (team) 10, 29, 32, 40, *41*, 42
Sussex Polo Club 250
Sussex Yeomanry 93
Sutherland, Duke of 30, 165, 169
Sutton, Herbert J. 26
Sutton, Thomas 26
Sutton Park 165, 166
Sutton Place 165, 169
Sweeney, Paul 215
Sweethill (grounds) 171
Swetenham, Capt. Foster 14
Swindells, Peter 194
Swindon Polo Club 25
Switzerland 234, 269, 282
Symonds, Mr. (Bowdon player) 16
Szentpály, Capt. Imre 114

Tacker, Col. James 67
Taffy (pony) 152

Tait, Col. Thomas 116
Talandracas 267, 268, 270, 272, 273
Talara Polo Club 79
Talbot Rice, Col. Henry 52
Talbott, Harold E. 132, 137
Tanoira, Gonzalo J. 183, 185–187, 206, 219
Tarapacá Polo Club 79
Targett, Ernest 15
Tari, Louis 218
Tari, Pierre 218
Tasmania 68, 75
Tate, Maj. Alfred L. 22, 103, 132
Tatham-Warter, Miss Kitty 226, 227
Tattersall, Rupert 55
Tattersall Challenge Cup 55
Tattersall Trophy 153
Taucher, H. Edward 174
Taunton Vale Polo Club 17, 18, 149, 166, 225, 228
Taylor, Lt.-Col. Anthony D. 173
Taylor, Charles 20
Taylor, Charles H. 26
Taylor, Gerald W. 20
Taylor, Jeremy 173
Taylor, John 13
Taylor, Lucy 230, 253, 264, 265
Taylor, Oliver J. 222
Taylor, Rodolfo H. "Ralph" 165
Taylor, Simon 265
Tayto (team) 271
Tecamac (team) 209
Tempest, Edward 26
Templeton (team) 130, 133, 135, 154
Tenby Polo Club 12, 13
10th Hussars 7, 8, 9, 10, 11, 43, 44, 63, 134, 168, 194, 246
Terrera, Guillermo 268
Texas Rangers (team) 130, 131, 133, 136, 140, 186
Thame, Robert 258
3rd Hussars 166, 201
Thomas, Graham 216
Thomas, Richard 251, 265
Thorn, William K., Jr. 34, 324
Thornby (team) 97
Thorneloe, Lt.-Col. Rupert S.M. 250
Thornicroft, N. 25
Thorold, William 22
Thynne, Lt. Thomas 73
Thynne, Lt. Ulric 78, 87
Tiarks, Henry 226
Tiarks, Herman 18
Tiarks, Lady Millicent 226
Tidworth Polo Club 27, 116, 151, 167, 177, 244, 252
Tiffany & Co. 35
Tilley, C.H. "Tish" 166
Tilley, Sir John 80
Timins, Rev. Frank 46
Tinsley, F. 16, 21
Tinsley, John M. 195, 219, *266*, 276, 279
Tipperary County 104
Tiverton (team) 17

Toccalino, Ignacio "Cubi" 236, 269, 271
Todd-Naylor, Henry 77
Todd-Naylor Challenge Trophy 77
Todham (team) 187
Tom Tiddler (pony) 152
Tomkin, Col. J.W. Royce 24
Tomkinson, Brig. Henry A. "Mouse" 43, 91, 116, 117, 120, 147, 150
Tomlinson, Claire Lucas *C4*, *C7*, 186, *197*, 198, 229, 236–238, 247, 253, 265, 271
Tomlinson, Emma *C4*, *C7*, *197*, 230, 253, 264, 265, 269, 271
Tomlinson, Capt. G. Simon 229, 230, 271
Tomlinson, Luke *C8*, 192, 193, 236, 238, *239*, 254–257, 260, 261, 264, 266, 268, 269, 271–273
Tomlinson, Mark L. 192, 193, 236, 256, 257, 259, 260, 264, 266, *267*, 268, 269, 271
Tongg, Michael "Tenney" 188
Tongg, Ronald P. "Ronnie" 188, 190, 199
Tongg, Ruddy 188
Torres Zavaleta, José M. "Negro" 185
Tortugas (team) 206
Toulston Polo Club 30, 152, 166, 202, 246
Tower, Lt.-Col. Philip T. 168
Towgood, Aubrey 16
Townsend, F.J. 52
Tracey Cup 17
Traill, Fl.-Lt. James R. "Jimmy" 160
Traill, John A.E. "Johnnie" 54, 65, 66, 91, 102, 116, 118, 122, 129, 131, *132*, 135, 160, 165
Traill, John B. "Jack" 160, 165
Traill, Joseph E. "Joe" 66
Traillers (team) 160
Tramontana 217–219, 221
Transvaal 205
Tredegar, Lord 13
Tredegar Park Polo Club 13, 213
Tredenick, E. 23
Tremayne, Capt. Charles H. 121, 122, 128, 146
Trench, John 60, 104
Trench-Gascoigne, Frederick R.T. 39
Trepplin, Ernest 25
Trinidad 78
Trollope, Clifford C. 56
Trotter, Martin F. 173
Troubridge, Lt. Thomas 180
Troyte-Bullock, Capt. Edward 18
Truter, G. 330
Tucker, Andrew 267
Tucker, Harry 269
Tucker Hill, Lt. William H. 68, 325
Tufton, George R. 43
Tulloch, H. Maurice 154
Tulsa (team) 205
Turnor, Capt. Herbert B. 102, 116

Turquand, Capt. W.M. Glynn 69
Tuthill, Josh 259, 265
Tuthill, Oliver 259, 271
Tweedmouth, Lord 73
12th Lancers 13, 44, 45, 134
20th Hussars 45, 61, 253
Tylden-Wright, Maj. Warrington
    R. 243
Tylor, John 173, 219, *220*
Tylor, Sam 100
Typhoo (team) 265
Tyrer, Alfred 16, 21
Tyro (horse) 153
Tyrone, Earl of *223*
Tyros (team) 12
Tyrrell, H.T. 139
Tyrrell-Martin, Eric H. 130, 131,
    132, 133, 135, 139–142, 144, 150,
    164, 165
Tyrwhitt, Adm. Sir Reginald 327
Tyrwhitt-Drake, Arthur 18

Ubique (team) 129, 131
Ulloa, Hilario 264, 268, 273
Ulster Polo Club 139
Umfreville, Capt. Ralph 20
umpiring 137, 141, 208, 209, 219,
    238, 247, 273, 275–277, 282, 333
Underberg Polo Club 207
U.K. National Arena Tournament
    231
U.K. National Women's Polo Tour-
    nament 214
United Services Cup 166, *201*, 252
United States Polo Association
    122, 144, 204, 233, 240, 266, 267,
    274, 333, 334, 335
Uranga, Carlos D. 103
Uranga, Marcos A. 103, 233, 238,
    240
Urquhart, A. 67
Usandizaga, Gustavo 193

Vachell, Horace 18, 73
Valdés, Luis 233
Vale of the White Horse (team)
    26, 202
Vale of York Polo Club 251
Valent, Martín 193, 268
Valentia, Lord Arthur 8–11
Valenzuela, Hernán H. 187
Valerie Halford Memorial 250
Valintine, Capt. Rudolph 25
Valparaíso 78
Vandamme, Brenda 263
Vandamme, Mark 263
Vandeleur, Lt.-Col. Cecil F.S. 325
Vanderbilt, Cornelius 324
van der Straaten, Clément 110
van Wyk, Sarah 264
Vargas, Víctor 263, 270
Venado Tuerto Athletic & Polo
    Club 65, 176, 187
Verdon, Capt. Timothy O. 255, 266
Verdun Trophy 187
Vere Foster, J. 23
Vere Nicoll, Dr. Douglas 205
Vere Nicoll, Roderick 249, 255
Vernon. Lt.-Col. Hon. Frederick 51

Vestey, Benjamin J. 216, *230*, 254,
    255
Vestey, Carina P. "Nina" 216, *230*,
    237, 238, 255, 256, 264, 265, 269
Vestey, Mrs. Mark (Rose) *197*, 216,
    255
Vestey, Hon. Mark W. 187, 190,
    194, *200*, 216, 217, 219, *220*, 254
Vestey, Lord Samuel G.A. 63, 171,
    187, 194, *195*, *197*, 203, 208, 216
Vestey, Tamara P. 216, *230*, 254,
    261, 264, 269
Vial, Alejandro 192
Vial, Rodrigo 217
Viana, Marqués José de 30
Vickers, Brig. Wilmot G.H. 103,
    243
Vickery, Col. (74th Artillery
    Brigade) 74
Vickery, Maj. Michael J.H. *216*
Victoria, HRH Princess 117
Victoria, HM Queen 9
Victoria Cross 10, 13, 98, 111, 156,
    246, 287
Victoria Cup 176
Victoria Polo Club 73, 74
Vidou, Martín 253
Villar, William 18
Villavieja, Manuel de Escandón,
    Marqués de 54, 101, 246
Villavieja Cup 101
Viña del Mar 78
Vincent, Rev. William 56
Vischer, Peter 121, 140, 141, 244
Visitors Cup 226
Visitors Handicap Tournament 131
Vismara, Francisco 270
Vivian, C.P. 61
von Bulow, Nichola 251
Vulci, Marchese Giacinto G. di 185

Wade, Adrian M. *C5*, 218, 219, 258
Wade, Tristan A. 220, 221
Wagge, Miss 226
Wales 11–13, 213
Wales, Alexandra, Princess of 9,
    10, 39, 47
Wales, Charles, Prince of 183, 184,
    217, 247
Wales, Edward, Prince of (later
    King Edward VII) 9, 11, 39, 47,
    50, 180
Wales, Edward, Prince of (later
    King Edward VIII) 43, 51, 101,
    117, 118, 181, 183, 250
Wales, Prince Harry *184*
Wales, Prince William *184*
Walford, Capt. Hugh C. "Chicken"
    102, 122, 129, 131, 139, 141, 166
Walford, Lt. Simon 166, 167
Walker, Dr. H.J. 79
Walker, Sir Ian P.W.M. 129, 131,
    135, 136, 138
Walker, John 208, 216
Walker, John Reid 29, 46, 152
Walker, Lynda 251
Walker, Munro 21
Walker, Nigel 251
Walker, Sir Peter 21

Walker, Richard 199
Walker, William Hall 16, 21, 46, 148
Walker-Munro, Maj. Ronald 126
Walkinshaw, Christopher 214
Wallace, Harry 255
Wallace, William E. 168
Waller, Sir Francis E. 25
Wallop, Sen. Malcolm 71
Wallop, Oliver 71
Wallop, Oliver Henry 71
Walsh, Mrs. V. 173
Walsh, William F. "Billy" 159, 163,
    164, 214
Walter, Nick 250
Walton, Robert 218, 223
Walton, W. 55
Walton Masters, Cameron S. *C4*
Walton Masters, David 252
Wanamaker, Rodman II 101, 113,
    127
Wanderers (teams) 60, 98
Wankyln, Joan 154
Want, G.P. 67
Warburton-Lee, Capt. Bernard
    A.W. 156, 288
Ward, Cecil 73, 74
Ward, Charles Dudley 93
Ward, Hon. Reginald 16
Ward-Jackson, Maj. Claude 18, 225
Waring, Capt. Holt 61
Warner, Edward 24
Warren, Lt. A.C. 75
Warren, George 21
Warrenton, Lt. George 73
Warrender, Vice-Adm. Sir George
    73
Warwick Parker, Maj. Wilfred 80
Warwickshire Cup 25, 154, *C7*,
    C8, 162, 171, 183, 186, 198, 215–
    219, 221, 222, 229, 230, 253, 254,
    257, 261, 263, 264, 268, 271, 274
Warwickshire Polo Club 24
Wasps (team) 67
Waterbury, James M., Jr. "Monte"
    83–85, 91, 118, 150
Waterbury, Lawrence 83, 85, 91,
    92, 118, 150, *C2*
Waterford, Tyrone Beresford,
    Marquess of 155, 185, 186, 204,
    206, 207, 215, *223*
Waterford Polo Club 253
Waters, Arthur 18, 82
Waters, Miss 226
Watson, Hon. Alastair 126, 163,
    164, 227
Watson, Donald 25
Watson, Lt. Edward 8, 9
Watson, Jack 70
Watson, John Henry *33*, 34, 40,
    45, 46, 59–61, 82, 85, 255
Watson, Maj. John N.P. 147, 155,
    194, 203, 242, 244
Watson, "Kit" 207
Watson, Raymond D. "Jim" 207
Watson, R.F. 227
Watson, Robert 8
Watson, Russell 208, 256, 257
Watson, Stanley 16, 21
Watson, W. Hastings 12

Watt, Col. Alexander 27
Watt, Andrew A. 61
Watt, Maj. Andrew H. 62
Watt, Gen. Sir C. Redmond "Reddy" *201*, 215
Watt, Samuel A. 60–62
Watts, Mrs. "Bobby" 226
Watts, Maj. E.M. 99
Weatherby, Edward 17
Weatherby, Richard 17
Webb, Dr. Gerald 72
Webb, James Watson 116, 117, 119–121, 144
Webb, Peter 222, 260, 261
Webber, Capt. Geoffrey 226
Webley, Mrs. (Ranelagh player) 225
Weekly Cup 131
Welcome, John 244
Weld, Sir Frederick 77
Weldom, Mr. (Cañada de Gómez player) 326
Weldon, Lt. Edric 17
Wellington Club 98
Wellington Hippodrome 110
Wellington Polo Club 15
Wells, Eugene 24
Welman, Maj. Harvey 25
Welsh Guards 93, 176, *201*
Wembley Park Polo Club 55, 56
Wembley Stadium 56
Wentworth, Reeve 24
Wentworth-Fitzwilliam, Hon. William 10
Wernher, Maj. Sir Harold A. 22, 129, 131, 133
Werribee Park 237, 260
Wesendorf 166
West, Capt. Caspar 235, 255
West Country (team) 226
West Essex Polo Club 18
West Germany 234
West Gloucester and Bristol Polo Club 99
West Gloucester Polo Club 20
West India Regiment 78
West of England (team) 226
West Somerset Challenge Cup 23
West Somerset Polo Club 23, 214, 225, 227
West Suffolk Polo Club 24
West Sussex Open Tournament 24
West Sussex Polo Club 24
West Wycombe Polo Club 215, 252
Westbury Cup 188
Westchester Cup: (1886) 32, *33*, 34, 35; (1900) 81–83; (1902) 83, *84*, 85, 154; (1909) 58, 85–88, 148; (1911) 89, 90; (1913) 90, 91, 146, *C2*; (1914) 91, 92; (1921) 116, 117, 150, 152, 242, 245; (1924) 117, 118, 150; (1927) 120, 121; (1930) 121, 122, *123*, 124, 148; (1936) 139–141, 150; (1939) 141–*143*, 144; (1992) 222–224; (1997) 224; (2009) *209*, 266, 267, 274
Westchester Polo Club 35, 69
Western Australia 36, 67
Western Camps (team) 66

Westmeath County 60
Westminster, Duke of 30, 51, 251
Weston, W. Galen, Sr. 199, 203, 215–218, 220, 250
Wexford Challenge Cup 61, 253
Wexford Polo Club 61
Wheeler, Charles W. 66
Wheeley, Capt. William 11, 12
Whitaker, P.A. 15
Whitbread, Col. William H. 176, 196
Whitbread Cup 176, 177, 196
Whitcombe, Susan A.C. 155, 178
White, Hon. Francis W. 66
White, Sir Luke 66
White, Windsor Holden "Mike" 147, *C3*, 161, 179
White Rose Polo Club 251
Whitefoord, Mrs. Marjorie 142
Whitehead, Lt. Ralph 28
Whiteley, Christopher 173
Whiteley, Puff 261
White's Club 49
Whitfield Court 244
Whithworth, Harry 23
Whiting, Miss Noëla 225
Whitney, Cornelius V. "Sonny" 143
Whitney, Harry Payne 49, 85–89, 91, 118, 150
Whitney, John Hay "Jock" 122, 143
Whitney Cup 38, 48, 49, 66, 67, 98, 103, 128, 129, 132, *162*
Wickham, Col. W. 61
Wienholt, Capt. Edward A. 63
Wigan, Capt. John T. 19
Wignall, Frederick E.B. 16
Wild Horse (team) 37, 38, 66, 67
Wildenstein, Guy 184, 199, 217
Wildmoor (team) 256
Wildridge, Fl.-Lt. David 213
Wilkinson, Richard 26
Willans, R. Robin 187
Willett, Capt. Humphrey 22
Williams, Capt. Austin H. "Bill" 103, 116, 120, 121
Williams, Sir Charles 262, 268
Williams, Craig 261
Williams, J. Nicholas "Nick" 194, *197*, 199, 215
Williams, John 262
Williams, John R. "Jack" 53, 160, 171, 177
Williams, Mrs. Marjorie 242
Williams, Roderick B. "Roddy" 192, 253, 255–258, 260, 261
Williamson, Selby 256, 257, 260, 261
Willis, Gen. John 194
Willoughby, Lady Catherine 226
Willoughby, Hon. Ernest 9, 10
Willoughby, Lady Priscilla 226–228
Willoughby Norrie, Lord George 139, 194
Wills, Capt. Arnold S. 62
Wilmot, Capt. Edmund "Teddy" 74
Wilson, A.L. 216
Wilson, Maj. Arthur 105

Wilson, Ben 271
Wilson, Clive 26
Wilson, Craig 264
Wilson, Frank 205
Wilson, Capt. Herbert H. "Bertie" 43, 60, *86*, 87–90, 94, 109
Wilson, Hugh, Jr. 60
Wilson, Sir James G. "Hame" 174
Wilson, Miss Lexia 226
Wilson, Peter R. 207
Wilson, R. Percy 78
Wilson, Robin 206, 07
Wilson, Thomas P. "Tommy" 258, 260, 261, 264
Wilton, H. 21
Wimbledon Park Polo Club 28, 53, 57
Wimborne, Ivor Guest, Lord 51, 91, 103, 116–118, 120
Winans, Julian W. 55
Winans, Paul 55
Winans, Walter 30, 55
Winans Cup 55
Winchester Polo Club 20
Windsor Park 10, 151, 154, 174, 188, 190, 202
Windsor Park (team) 155, 175–177, 183, 185–187, 189, 198, 199, 206, 217
Wingfield, Mrs. David (Mary Ann) 147, 244
Wingfield, Hon. Maurice 16
Wingfield Digby, Frederick J.B. 18
Winser, Capt. Peter 22
Winthrop, Egerton, Jr. 34, 324
Wirral Ladies Cup 17, 265
Wirral Polo Club 13, 16, 17, 21, 26, 126, 170
Wirth, Jerome 267, 272
Wise, Capt. Francis H. 44
Wise, Wing-Comdr. Percival K. 102, 113, 118, 122, 128, 129
Wiseman, Sarah 272
Withers, Gordon 55
Withers, Paul M. 154, 161, 168, 177, 185, 186, 188–190, *196*, *198*, 199, 204, 206–209, 215, 216, *275*
Withycombe, James T.G. "Jim" 56, 155, 164
Withycombe, William M. 56
Wodehouse, Lord John "Jack" 42, 60, 67, 88, 102, 103, 109, 110–112, 116–118, 243
Woldingham Polo Club 20
Wolseley, Sir Charles M. 11, 12, 24, 29, 39, 55
Women's Polo International 261
Women's World Championship *C7*, 253
Wood, C.R. Manners "Roddy" 20
Wood, Roddy 251
Woodchester (team) 221
Woodd, Col. David J.B. *216*, 218, 219, *220*, 266, 276
Woodd, Matilda 265
Woodhouse, William 155
Woodland, E. 21
Woodland Polo Club 205
Woodpeckers (team) 48, 60

Woods, Capt. Hon. Henry J.L. 9, 10
Woodville, Richard C. 155
Woodward, C. 67
Woolcott, Percy 53
Woolmers Park Polo Club 164, 170, 172, 175, 186, 187, 215, 230
Woolwich 21, 28
Worcester Park Polo Club 56
Worcestershire Polo Club 26
Wordsworth, Lt. John 26
World Anti-Doping Agency 277
World Cup (F.I.P.): 1987, Buenos Aires 335; 1989, Berlin 234, 335; 1992, Santiago 234, 335; 1995, St. Moritz 234, 235, 335; 1998, Santa Barbara 235, 335; 2001, Melbourne 235, 236, 335; 2004, Chantilly 236, 237, 335; 2008, Mexico City 237, 238, 335
World Equestrian Games 239
Wormald, Frederick W. "Fritz" 22
Wormald, P.H. 26
Worrall, Lt.-Col. David 166
Worthington, Bailey 21
Wright, George 155

Wright, Gilbert S. 155
Wright, Guillermo H. 108
Wright, Brig. John 202
Wright, Miss Muriel 226, 227
Wright, William 66
Wrightsman, Charles B. 130, 131, 133, 136, 140, 186
Wylde, C.B. 99
Wyndham, Mrs. Ailward 174
Wyndham, Lt.-Col. Hon. Edward 54
Wyndham-Quin, Windham H. 39, 44, 50
Wyoming 70, 71

Yankton Polo Club 70
Yardley, Lt.-Col. John W. 20
Yatman, Capt. Arthur 18
Yeoman, David 208, 216–218
Yeoman, John F. 218
Yerburgh, Harry 18
Yerburgh Cup 22
Yonge, Tony 178
York County Polo Club 26
Yorkshire Open Championship 251

Young, Brig. Henry 168
Young, Maj. H.P. 245
Young, Miss K.S. 225
Young America (team) 151, 184, 190
Young England (team) 151, 184, 190, 253, 272
Young New Zealand (team) 272
Younger, George 13
Younger, John 13
Younger, William J. "Snooks" 13
Younghusband, Maj.-Gen. Sir George J. 241, 243
Ypres Road (grounds) 213

Zacara 264, 265, 273
Zanuck, Darryl F. 133
Zaria Polo Club 76
Zavaleta, Juan Gris 268, 272
Zegers, José 192
Zegers, Julio 172
Zegers, Martín 192
Ziegler, Colin 22
Zimbabwe 76, 233
Zorrilla, Enrique A. 186, 187, 199
Zwartberg Polo Club 207